THE NEW DARE TO DISCIPLINE

From one generation to the next, the challenge of helping children become responsible adults doesn't change. Children need love, trust, affection—and discipline. Dr. Dobson's classic *Dare to Discipline*, a practical, reassuring guide for caring parents, has sold over 3.5 million copies since its release in 1970. What gives a book that kind of staying power? The ability to meet a deep need of families worldwide. Today, a whole new generation of parents is turning to Dr. Dobson's wise counsel in this revised and updated edition of a classic work.

THE NEW STRONG-WILLED CHILD

Is a willful little darling driving you to distraction? Are you wondering where you went wrong as a parent? You may have a strong-willed child! Dr. James Dobson has completely rewritten, updated, and expanded his classic best seller *The Strong-Willed Child* for a new generation of parents and teachers. It offers practical how-to advice on raising difficult-to-handle children and incorporates the latest research with Dr. Dobson's trademark wit and wisdom. This book is a must-read for anyone struggling with children who are convinced they should be able to live by their own rules!

PARENTING ISN'T FOR COWARDS

Does your heart skip a beat when you think of all that could go wrong in the parenting years ahead? Anxiety is normal, but your worst fears don't have to become reality. Speaking both as a therapist and as a father—and drawing on a landmark study of thirty-five thousand parents—Dr. James Dobson helps you prevent child-rearing troubles before they happen, banish your guilt about hard-to-raise children, protect your sanity during a child's adolescence, restore your energy when you're facing burnout, and enhance your relationships with your kids. With more than one million copies sold, this confidence-building classic will help you experience the full joy of parenthood—and what may be the greatest sense of fulfillment you'll ever know.

James C. Dobson

PARENTING
COLLECTION

DR. JAMES
DOBSON

TYNDALE
MOMENTUM

An Imprint of
Tyndale House Publishers, Inc.

Visit Tyndale online at www.tyndale.com.

Visit Tyndale Momentum online at www.tyndalemomentum.com.

TYNDALE, *Tyndale Momentum*, and the Tyndale Momentum logo are registered trademarks of Tyndale House Publishers, Inc. Tyndale Momentum is an imprint of Tyndale House Publishers, Inc.

The Dr. James Dobson Parenting Collection

The New Dare to Discipline (ISBN 978-0-8423-0507-5) copyright © 1970, 1992 by James C. Dobson. All rights reserved.

The New Strong-Willed Child (ISBN 978-0-8423-3622-2) copyright © 1978, 2004 by James Dobson, Inc. All rights reserved.

Parenting Isn't for Cowards (ISBN 978-1-4143-1746-5) copyright © 1987 by James Dobson, Inc. All rights reserved.

Parenting Isn't for Cowards was previously published by Multnomah Publishers, Inc., under ISBN 1-59052-372-5. *Multnomah* is a trademark of Multnomah Publishers, Inc., and is registered in the U.S. Patent and Trademark Office.

The Dr. James Dobson Parenting Collection first published in 2010 by Tyndale House Publishers, Inc.

Cover photo of father and daughter copyright © by Mark Leibowitz/Masterfile. All rights reserved.

Designed by Jennifer Ghionzoli

"Leader of the Band" by Dan Fogelberg. © 1981 April Music, Inc., and Hickory Grove Music. All rights controlled and administered by April Music, Inc. All rights reserved. International copyright secured. Used by permission.

"She's Leaving Home" by John Lennon and Paul McCartney. © 1967 Northern Songs Limited. All rights in the USA, Canada, Mexico, and the Philippines, controlled and administered by Blackwood Music, Inc., under license from ATV Music (MACLEN). All rights reserved. International copyright secured. Used by permission.

ISBN 978-1-4143-3726-5

Printed in the United States of America

21	20	19	18	17	16	15
10	9	8	7	6	5	4

CONTENTS

THE
NEW DARE TO
DISCIPLINE

TO DANAE, RYAN, AND THEIR MOTHER SHIRLEY,

I affectionately dedicate the pages of this book and the remaining years of my life.

(Written initially in 1971, and reconfirmed almost four decades later!)

CONTENTS

The New Dare to Discipline

THE
CHALLENGE

THIS IS A book about children and those who love them. The first edition was written in the early 1970s when I was a professor of pediatrics at the University of Southern California School of Medicine. Our own children were still pre-schoolers, which made it risky to offer advice about parenting techniques. That's like a coach bragging in the first quarter about how he expects to win the game. Nevertheless, I had seen enough academically and professionally to have developed some firm convictions about how children should be raised and what they needed from their parents.

Almost forty years and over 3.5 million copies of *Dare to Discipline* have come and gone since I first sat down to write. That passage of time has broadened my horizon and, hopefully, sharpened my vision. I've worked with thousands of families and I've considered the child-rearing views of many authorities and colleagues. My kids have paddled through adolescence and have established homes of their own. Thus, it is a special privilege for me to roll back the clock now and revisit the themes with which I first grappled so many years ago.

One might expect my views of child development and parenting to have evolved significantly within the intervening years. Such is not the case. Admittedly, the social backdrop for the original *Dare to Discipline* has changed dramatically, which is why this book needed to be revised and expanded. The student revolution that raged through the late sixties and early seventies has subsided. Woodstock and the Viet Nam War are distant memories, and university campuses are again quieter and less rebellious. But children haven't changed, nor will they ever. I'm even more convinced now that the principles of good parenting are eternal, having originated with the Creator of families. The inspired concepts in Scripture have been handed down generation after generation and are just as valid for the twenty-first century as they were for our ancestors. Unfortunately, many of today's parents have never heard those time-honored ideas and have no clue about what they're trying to accomplish at home.

I'll never forget a mother in that predicament who asked for my help in handling her defiant three-year-old daughter, Sandy. She realized that her tiny little girl had hopelessly beaten her in a contest of wills, and the child had become a tyrant and a dictator. On the afternoon prior to our conversation, an incident occurred which was typical of Sandy's way of doing business. The mother (I'll call her Mrs. Nichols) put the youngster down for a nap, but knew it was unlikely she would stay in bed. Sandy was not accustomed to doing anything she didn't fancy, and naptime was not on her list of fun things to do in the afternoon.

On this occasion, however, the child was more interested in antagonizing her mom than in merely having her own way. Sandy began to scream. She yelled loudly enough to upset the whole neighborhood, fraying Mrs. Nichols' jangled nerves. Then she tearfully demanded various things, including a glass of water.

At first Mrs. Nichols refused to comply with the orders, but she surrendered when Sandy's screaming again reached a peak of intensity. As the glass of water was delivered, the mischievous child pushed it aside, refusing to drink because her mother had not brought it soon enough. Mrs. Nichols stood offering the water for a few minutes, then said she would take it back to the kitchen if Sandy did not drink by the time she counted to five.

Sandy set her jaw and waited through the count: "three . . . four . . . five!" As Mrs. Nichols grasped the glass and walked toward the kitchen, the child screamed for the water. Sandy dangled her harassed mom back and forth like a yo-yo until she tired of the sport.

Mrs. Nichols and her little daughter are among the many casualties of an unworkable, illogical philosophy of child management which has long dominated the literature on this subject. This mother had read that a child will eventually respond to reason and forbearance, ruling out the need for firm leadership. She had been told to encourage the child's rebellion because it offered a valuable release of hostility. She attempted to implement the recommendations of the experts who suggested that she verbalize the child's feelings in a moment of conflict: "You want the water but you're angry because I brought it too late" . . . . "You don't want me to take the water back to the kitchen" . . . "You don't like me because I make you take naps." She had also been taught that conflicts between parent and child were to be perceived as misunderstandings or differences in viewpoint.

Unfortunately, Mrs. Nichols and her advisors were wrong! She and her child were involved in no simple difference of opinion: she was being challenged, mocked, and defied by her daughter. No heart-to-heart talk would resolve this nose-to-nose confrontation, because the real issue was totally unrelated to water or the nap or other aspects of the particular circumstances. The actual meaning behind this conflict and a hundred others was simply this: Sandy was brazenly rejecting the authority of her mother. The way Mrs. Nichols handled these confrontations would determine the nature of their future relationship, especially during the adolescent years.

Much has been written about the dangers of harsh, oppressive, unloving discipline; these warnings are valid and should be heeded. However, the consequences of oppressive discipline have been cited as justification for the abdication of leadership. That is foolish. There are times when a strong-willed child will clench his little fists and dare his parents to accept his challenges. He is not motivated by frustration or inner hostility, as it is often supposed. He merely wants to know where the boundaries lie and who's available to enforce them.

Many well-meaning specialists have waved the banner of tolerance, but offered no solution for defiance. They have stressed the importance of parental understanding of the child, and I concur. But we need to teach children that they have a few things to learn about their parents, too!

Mrs. Nichols and all her contemporaries need to know how to set limits, and what to do when defiant behavior occurs. This disciplinary activity must take place within the framework of love and affection, which is often difficult for parents who view these roles as contradictory. *The New Dare to Discipline* is addressed, in part, to this vital aspect of raising healthy, respectful, happy children.

The term "discipline" is not limited to the context of confrontation, and neither is this book. Children also need to be taught *self*-discipline and responsible behavior. They need assistance in learning how to handle the challenges and obligations of living. They must learn the art of self-control. They should be equipped with the personal strength needed to meet the demands imposed on them by their school, peer group, and later adult responsibilities.

There are those who believe these characteristics cannot be taught—that the best we can do is send children down the path of least resistance, sweeping aside the hurdles during their formative years. The advocates of this laissez-faire philosophy would recommend that youngsters be allowed to fail in school if they choose . . . or maintain their bedrooms like proverbial pigpens . . . or let their puppies go hungry.

I reject this notion and have accumulated considerable evidence to refute it. Children thrive best in an atmosphere of genuine love, undergirded by reasonable, consistent discipline. In a day of widespread drug usage, immorality, sexually transmitted diseases, vandalism, and violence, we must not depend on hope and luck to fashion the critical attitudes we value in our children. Permissiveness has not simply failed as an approach to child rearing. It's been a disaster for those who have tried it.

When properly applied, loving discipline works! It stimulates tender affection, made possible by *mutual* respect between a parent and a child. It bridges the gap which otherwise separates family members who should love and trust each other. It allows the God of our ancestors to be introduced to our beloved children. It permits teachers to do the kind of job in classrooms for which they are commissioned. It encourages a child to respect other people and live as a responsible, constructive citizen.

As might be expected, there is a price tag on these benefits: they require courage, consistency, conviction, diligence, and enthusiastic effort. In short, one must *dare to discipline* in an environment of unmitigated love. We'll discuss the methods by which that can be accomplished in subsequent chapters.

TWO

COMMON SENSE
& YOUR CHILD

METHODS AND PHILOSOPHIES of discipline have been the subject of heated debate and disagreement throughout the past seventy years. Psychologists and pediatricians and university professors have all gotten into the act, telling parents how to raise their kids properly. Unfortunately, many of these "experts" have been in direct contradiction with one another, spreading more heat than light about a subject of great importance.

Perhaps that is why the pendulum has swung back and forth regularly between harsh, oppressive control and the unstructured permissiveness we saw in the mid–twentieth century. It is time we realized that *both* extremes leave their characteristic scars on the lives of young victims, and I would be hard pressed to say which is more damaging.

At the oppressive end of the continuum, a child suffers the humiliation of total domination. The atmosphere is icy and rigid, and he lives in constant fear. He is unable to make his own decisions, and his personality is squelched beneath the hobnailed boot of parental authority. Lasting characteristics of dependency; deep, abiding anger; and even psychosis can emerge from this persistent dominance.

Of greater concern are the boys and girls who are being subjected to physical and emotional abuse. There are millions of families out there in which these unthinkable crimes are being committed day after day. It is hard to believe just how cruel some mothers and fathers can be to a defenseless, wide-eyed child who doesn't understand why he or she is hated. The cases I've dealt with over the years—of unloved and abused children—are impossible to forget. I remember the terrible father who regularly wrapped his small son's head in the sheet that the boy had wet the night before. Then he crammed the tot upside down into the toilet bowl for punishment. I also think of the disturbed mother who cut out her child's eyes with a razor blade. That poor little girl will go through life blind, knowing that her own mother deprived her of sight! Horrible acts like these are now occurring every day in cities and towns around us.

We should also recognize that there are many ways to abuse a child without breaking the law. It can be done subtly by ignoring a boy or girl's desperate need for nurturance. It can be accomplished by unjust and unfair punishment, including parental acts that might pass for "corporal punishment"— such as routinely hitting, slapping, kicking, and throwing the child to the ground. Then there is the entire range of humiliating behavior by a mother or father, making a youngster feel stupid and weird and unloved. Within certain limits, these behaviors are not illegal. There is no one to rescue the pitiful child who is being twisted and warped by the big people around him. Let *nothing* in this book ever hint at my approval for such tyranny.

Let me say again with the strongest emphasis that aggressive, hard-nosed, "Mommie Dearest" kinds of discipline are destructive to kids and must not be tolerated. Parents who are cold and stern with their sons and daughters often leave them damaged for life. I could easily be misunderstood at this point, having authored this book in which I recommend (in chapter 4) the judicious use of corporal punishment under specific circumstances and limits. May all doubts be dispelled. *I don't believe in parental harshness.* Period! Children are incredibly vulnerable to rejection, ridicule, criticism, and anger at home, and they deserve to grow up in an environment of safety, acceptance, and warmth.

We must acknowledge, as indicated earlier, that the opposite extreme is also damaging to children. In the absence of adult leadership, the child is his own master from his earliest babyhood. He thinks the world revolves around his heady empire, and he often has utter contempt and disrespect for those closest to him. Anarchy and chaos reign in his home, and his mother is often the most nervous, frustrated woman on her block. When the child is young, the mother is stranded at home because she is too embarrassed to take her little spitfire anywhere. It would be worth the hardships she endures if this condition produced healthy, secure children. It clearly does not.

Many of the writers offering their opinions on the subject of discipline in recent years have confused parents, stripping them of the ability to lead in their own homes. They have failed to acknowledge the desire of most youngsters to rule their own lives and prevail in the contest of wills that typically occurs between generations.

In my book *The Strong-Willed Child* I quoted from a parenting text entitled, *Your Child from Two to Five,* published during the permissive 1950s. In it was a bit of advice paraphrased from the writings of a Dr. Luther Woodward, as follows:

> What do you do when your preschooler calls you a "big stinker" or threatens to flush you down the toilet? Do you scold . . . punish . . . or sensibly take it in your stride? Dr. Woodward recommends a positive policy of understanding as the best and fastest way to help a child outgrow this verbal violence. When parents fully realize that all little tots feel angry and destructive at times, they are better able to minimize these outbursts. Once the preschooler gets rid of his hostility, the desire to destroy is gone and instinctive feelings of love and affection have a chance to sprout and grow. Once the child is six or seven, parents can rightly let the child know that he is expected to be outgrowing sassing his parents.[1]

Having offered that sage advice, with which I disagree strongly, Dr. Woodward then told parents to brace themselves for unjust criticism. He wrote, "But this policy [of letting children engage in defiance] takes a broad perspective and a lot of composure, especially when friends and relatives voice disapproval and warn that you are bringing up a brat."

In this case, your friends and relatives will probably be right. Dr. Woodward's recommendation is typical of the advice given to parents in the mid–twentieth century. It encourages them to stand passively through the formative years when respect for authority can so easily be taught. I responded to that counsel this way in *The Strong-Willed Child.*

> Dr. Woodward's suggestion is based on the simplistic notion that children will develop sweet and loving attitudes if we adults will permit and encourage their temper tantrums during childhood. According to the optimistic Dr. Woodward, the tot who has

been calling his mother a "big stinker" for six or seven years can be expected to embrace her suddenly in love and dignity. That outcome is most improbable. Dr. Woodward's creative "policy of understanding" (which means stand and do nothing) offers a one-way ticket to adolescent rebellion in many cases.[2]

I believe that if it is desirable for children to be kind, appreciative, and pleasant, those qualities should be taught— not hoped for. If we want to see honesty, truthfulness, and unselfishness in our offspring, then these characteristics should be the conscious objectives of our early instructional process. If it is important to produce respectful, responsible young citizens, then we should set out to mold them accordingly. The point is obvious: *heredity does not equip a child with proper attitudes; children learn what they are taught.* We cannot expect the coveted behavior to appear magically if we have not done our early homework.

The kind of advice Dr. Woodward and others have offered to mothers and fathers through the years has led to a type of paralysis in dealing with their kids. In the absence of "permission" to step in and lead, parents were left with only their anger and frustration in response to defiant behavior.

That thought immediately brings to mind a family I knew with four of the most unruly children I had ever met. These youngsters were the terrors of their neighborhood. They were disrespectful, loud, and aggressive. They roamed in and out of other people's garages, helping themselves to tools and equipment. It became necessary for neighbors to remove the handles from outside water faucets, because these children enjoyed leaving the water running when the families were gone.

It was interesting to observe the method of discipline used by their mother, if only because it provided a memorable example of what didn't work. Her system of controlling her brood boiled down to a simple formula. When they became too noisy or cantankerous in the backyard, she would rush out the door about once every hour and scream, "I have had it with you kids! I have just *had* it with you!" Then she would turn and go back into the house. The children never even glanced up at her. If they knew she was there they gave no indication of it. But she apparently felt it was sufficient to burst out the door like a cuckoo clock every so often and remind them she was still on the job. There must be a better way to handle the awesome task of parenting that God has assigned to us.

If both extremes are harmful, how do we find the safety of the middle ground? Surely, there is a logical, reasonable philosophy of child rearing that will guide our day-by-day interactions at home. Can't the social scientists come up with a workable game plan? Perhaps this will sound like heresy coming from a man who spent ten years of his life in behavioral and medical research, but I don't believe the scientific community is the best source of information on proper parenting techniques. There have been some worthwhile studies, to be sure. But the subject of parent-child interactions is incredibly complex and subtle. The only way to investigate it scientifically is to reduce the relationship to its simplest common denominators, so it can be examined. But in so doing, the overall tone is missed. Some things in life are so complicated that they almost defy rigorous scrutiny, and parental discipline (in my view) appears to be one of them.

The best source of guidance for parents can be found in the wisdom of the Judeo-Christian ethic, which originated with the Creator and was then handed down generation by generation from the time of Christ. This is what my mother, my grandmother, and my great-grandmother understood almost intuitively. There was within Western culture a common knowledge about children and their needs. Not everyone applied it, but most people agreed with its tenets. When a new baby was born one hundred years ago, aunts and sisters and grandmothers came over to teach the new mother how to care for her infant. What they were doing was passing along the traditional wisdom . . . the heritage . . . to the next generation, which would later perform the same service for the newcomers on the block. That system worked pretty well until the 1920s and thereafter. Slowly, the culture began to lose confidence in that tradition and shifted its allegiance to the experts. Behaviorist J. B. Watson was one of the first and most influential gurus to come along. He offered what he called a "foolproof" method of child rearing, and mothers bought it hook, line, and sinker. If only they would follow his advice, he said, they could produce any kind of a child they wanted . . . "a doctor, lawyer, artist, merchant-chief, and—yes—even a beggarman and a thief."

Watson advised parents, if they wanted the best results, to show no affection for their offspring. He wrote:

Never hug and kiss them, never let them sit on your lap. If you must, kiss them once on the forehead when they say good night. Shake hands with them in the morning. . . .

Remember when you are tempted to pet your child, that mother love is a dangerous instrument. An instrument which may inflict a never-healing wound, a wound which may make infancy unhappy, adolescence a nightmare, an instrument which may wreck your adult son or daughter's vocational future and their chances for marital happiness.[3]

This advice from Dr. Watson comes across today like pure nonsense, and indeed, that's just what it is. In fact, it's difficult to believe anyone gave credibility to such advice even in 1928. Yet Watson was enormously popular in his day, and his books sold in the millions. Mothers and fathers worked diligently to "condition" their children in the way recommended by this half-baked hot dog.

Then came Dr. Sigmund Freud, and Dr. Benjamin Spock, and Dr. A. S. Neill (see chapter 7), and Dr. Tom Gordon, and Dr. Ruth Westheimer, and Phil Donahue, and Oprah Winfrey, and the *Ladies' Home Journal*, and *Cosmopolitan*, and *Redbook*, and finally, a newspaper for "enquiring minds who want to know." With every new, off-the-wall suggestion that came along, I asked myself: If their new approach to child-rearing is so wonderful, why was it not observed until now? How come 20 billion parents across more than five thousand years failed to notice the concept? Certainly, the accumulated experience of all that mothering and fathering should count for *something*!

My primary purpose in writing this book, both the 1970 version and this recomposition, has been to record for posterity my understanding of the Judeo-Christian concept of parenting that has guided millions of mothers and fathers for centuries. I am convinced that it will prove successful in *your* home, too. Let's move on, then, to examine five underpinnings to commonsense child rearing.

1. *Developing respect for parents is the critical factor in child management.* It is imperative that a child learns to respect his parents—not to satisfy their egos, but because his relationship with them provides the basis for his later attitude toward all other people. His early view of parental authority becomes the cornerstone of his future outlook on school authority, law

enforcement officers, employers, and others with whom he will eventually live and work. The parent-child relationship is the first and most important social interaction a youngster will have, and the flaws and knots experienced there can often be seen later in life.

Respect for parents must be maintained for another equally important reason. If you want your child to accept your values when he reaches his teen years, then you must be worthy of his respect during his younger days. When a child can successfully defy his parents during his first fifteen years, laughing in their faces and stubbornly flouting their authority, he develops a natural contempt for them.

"Stupid old Mom and Dad! I have them wound around my little finger. Sure they love me, but I really think they're afraid of me." A child may not utter these words, but he feels them each time he outsmarts his elders and wins the confrontations and battles. Later he is likely to demonstrate his disrespect in a more blatant manner. Viewing his parents as being unworthy of his respect, he may very well reject every vestige of their philosophy and faith.

This factor is also of vital importance to Christian parents who wish to transmit their love for Jesus Christ to their sons and daughters. Why? Because young children typically identify their parents . . . and especially their fathers . . . with God. Therefore, if Mom and Dad are not worthy of respect, then neither are their morals, their country, their values and beliefs, or even their religious faith.

I was shocked to see this close identification between God and me in the mind of our son when he was two years old. Ryan had watched his mother and me pray before we ate each meal, but he had never been asked to say grace. One day when I was out of town on a business trip, Shirley spontaneously turned to the toddler and asked if he would like to pray before they ate. The invitation startled him, but he folded his little hands, bowed his head, and said, "I love you, Daddy. Amen."

When I returned home and Shirley told me what had happened, the story unsettled me. I hadn't realized the degree to which Ryan linked me with his "Heavenly Father." I wasn't even sure I wanted to stand in those shoes. It was too big a job, and I didn't want the responsibility. But I had no choice, nor do you. God has given us the assignment of representing Him during the formative years of parenting. That's why it is so critically important for us to acquaint our kids with God's two predominant natures . . . His unfathomable love and His justice. If we love our children but permit them to treat us disrespectfully and with disdain, we have distorted their understanding of the Father. On the other hand, if we are rigid disciplinarians who show no love, we have tipped the scales in the other direction. What we teach our children about the Lord is a function, to some degree, of how we model love and discipline in our relationship with them. Scary, huh?

The issue of respect is also useful in guiding parents' interpretation of given behavior. First, they should decide whether an undesirable act represents a direct challenge to their authority . . . to their leadership position as the father or mother. The form of disciplinary action they take should depend on the result of that evaluation.

For example, suppose little Chris is acting silly in the living room and falls into a table, breaking many expensive china cups and other trinkets. Or suppose Wendy loses her bicycle or leaves her mother's coffeepot out in the rain. These are acts of childish irresponsibility and should be handled as such. Perhaps the parent will ignore the event or maybe have the child work to pay for the losses—depending on his age and maturity, of course.

However, these examples do not constitute direct challenges to authority. They do not emanate from willful, haughty disobedience and therefore should not result in serious discipline. In my opinion, spankings (which we will discuss later) should be reserved for the moment a child (between the age of eighteen months to ten years old) expresses to parents a defiant "I will not!" or "You shut up!" When youngsters convey this kind of stiff-necked rebellion, you must be willing to respond to the challenge immediately. When nose-to-nose confrontation occurs between you and your child, it is not the time to discuss the virtues of obedience. It is not the occasion to send him to his room to pout. Nor is it appropriate to postpone disciplinary measures until your tired spouse plods home from work.

You have drawn a line in the dirt, and the child has deliberately flopped his bony little toe across it. Who is going to win? Who has the most courage? Who is in charge here? If you do not conclusively answer these questions for your strong-willed children, they will precipitate other battles designed to ask them again and again. It is the ultimate paradox of childhood that youngsters want to be led, but insist that their parents earn the right to lead them.

When mothers and fathers fail to take charge in moments of challenge, they create for themselves and their families a potential lifetime of heartache. That's what happened in the case of the Holloways, who were the parents of a teen named Becky (not their real names). Mr. Holloway came to see me in desperation one afternoon and related the cause for his concern. Becky had never been required to obey or respect her parents, and her early years were a strain on the entire family. Mrs. Holloway was confident Becky would eventually become more manageable, but that never happened. She held her parents in utter contempt from her youngest childhood and was sullen, disrespectful, selfish, and uncooperative. Mr. and Mrs. Holloway did not feel they had the right to make demands on their daughter, so they smiled politely and pretended not to notice her horrid behavior.

Their magnanimous attitude became more difficult to maintain as Becky steamrolled into puberty and adolescence. She was a perpetual malcontent, sneering at her family in disgust. Mr. and Mrs. Holloway were afraid to antagonize her in any way because she would throw the most violent tantrums imaginable. They were victims of emotional blackmail. They thought they could buy her cooperation, which led them to install a private telephone in her room. She accepted it without gratitude and accumulated a staggering bill during the first month of usage.

They thought a party might make her happy, and Mrs. Holloway worked very hard to decorate the house and prepare refreshments. On the appointed evening, a mob of dirty, profane teens swarmed into the house, breaking and destroying the furnishings. During the course of the evening, Mrs. Holloway said something that angered Becky. The girl struck her mother and left her lying in a pool of blood in the bathroom.

Away from home at the time, Mr. Holloway returned to find his wife helpless on the floor; he located his unconcerned daughter in the backyard, dancing with friends. As he described for me the details of their recent nightmare, he spoke with tears in his eyes. His wife, he said, was still in the hospital contemplating her parental failures as she recovered from her wounds.

Parents like the Holloways often fail to understand how love and discipline interact to influence the attitudes of a child. These two aspects of a relationship are not opposites working against each other. They are two dimensions of the same quality. One demands the other. Disciplinary action is not an assault on parental love; it is a function of it. Appropriate punishment is not something parents do *to* a beloved child; it is something done *for* him or her. That simple understanding when Becky was younger could have spared the Holloways an adolescent nightmare.

Their attitude when Becky rebelled as a preschooler should have been, "I love you too much to let you behave like that." For the small child, word pictures can help convey this message more clearly. The following is a story I used with our very young children when they crossed the line of unacceptable behavior:

> I knew of a little bird who was in his nest with his mommy. The mommy bird went off to find some worms to eat, and she told the little bird not to get out of the nest while she was gone. But the little bird didn't mind her. He jumped out of the nest and fell to the ground where a big cat got him. When I tell you to mind me, it is because I know what is best for you, just as the mommy bird did with her baby bird. When I tell you to stay in the front yard, it's because I don't want you to run in the street and get hit by a car. I love you, and I don't want anything to happen to you. If you don't mind me, I'll have to spank you to help you remember how important it is. Do you understand?

My own mother had an unusually keen understanding of good disciplinary procedures, as I have indicated. She was very tolerant of my childishness, and I found her reasonable on most issues. If I was late coming home from school and I could explain what caused the delay, that was the end of the matter. If I didn't get my work done, we could sit down and reach an agreement for future action. But there was one matter on which she was absolutely rigid: She did not tolerate sassiness. She knew that backtalk and what she called "lip" were a child's most potent weapon to defiance and had to be discouraged.

I learned very early that if I was going to launch a flippant attack on her, I had better be standing at least twelve feet away. This distance was necessary to avoid an instantaneous response—usually aimed at my backside.

The day I learned the importance of staying out of reach shines like a neon light in my mind. I made the costly mistake of sassing her when

I was about four feet away. I knew I had crossed the line and wondered what she would do about it. It didn't take long to find out. Mom wheeled around to grab something with which to express her displeasure, and her hand landed on a girdle. Those were the days when a girdle was lined with rivets and mysterious panels. She drew back and swung that abominable garment in my direction, and I can still hear it whistling through the air. The intended blow caught me across the chest, followed by a multitude of straps and buckles, wrapping themselves around my midsection. She gave me an entire thrashing with one blow! But from that day forward, I measured my words carefully when addressing my mother. I never spoke disrespectfully to her again, even when she was seventy-five years old.

I have shared that story many times through the years, to an interesting response. Most people found it funny and fully understood the innocuous meaning of that moment. A few others, who never met my mother and had no knowledge of her great love for me, quickly condemned her for the abusiveness of that event. One Christian psychologist even wrote a chapter in his book on the viciousness of that spanking. Another man in Wichita, Kansas, was so furious at me for telling the story that he refused to come hear me speak. Later he admitted he had misread the word girdle, thinking my mother had hit me with a *griddle*.

If you're inclined to agree with the critics, please hear me out. I am the only person on earth who can report accurately the impact of my mother's action. I'm the only one who lived it. And I'm here to tell you that the girdle-blow was an act of love! My mother would have laid down her life for me in a heartbeat, and I always knew it. She would not have harmed a hair on my fuzzy head. Yes, she was angry at my insolence, but her sudden reaction was a corrective maneuver. We both knew I richly deserved it. And that is why the momentary pain of that event did not assault my self-worth. Believe it or not, it made me feel loved. Take it or leave it, Dr. Psychologist, but that's the truth.

Now let me say the obvious. I can easily see how the same setting could have represented profound rejection and hostility of the first order. If I had not known I was loved . . . if I had not deserved the punishment . . . if I had been frequently and unjustly struck for minor offenses . . . I would have suffered serious damage from the same whirring girdle. The minor pain was not the critical variable. The *meaning* of the event is what mattered.

This single episode illustrates why it is so difficult to conduct definitive research on child-rearing practices. The critical factors are too subjective to be randomized and analyzed. That complexity also explains why social workers seeking to rescue children from abusive homes often have such problems being fair. Many good parents in loving homes have lost custody of their sons and daughters because of evidence that is misinterpreted. For example, a dime-sized bruise on the buttocks of a fair-skinned child may or may not indicate an abusive situation. It all depends. In an otherwise secure and loving home, that bruise may have had no greater psychological impact than a skinned knee or a stubbed toe. Again, the significant issue is not the small abrasion; it is the *meaning* behind it—the way it occurred and the overall tone of the relationship. Nevertheless, grief-stricken parents have lost their children on the basis of a single piece of evidence of that nature. We call it parent abuse.

Please don't write and accuse me of defending parents who routinely bruise and harm their children even in a minor way. It is wrong. It should not happen. But someone should have the courage to say we must look at the *total* relationship before removing a child from the security of a good home and not base a life-changing decision on a single bit of evidence.

Getting back to our theme of respect, let me emphasize that it will not work properly as a unilateral affair; it must run both ways. Parents cannot require their children to treat them with dignity if they will not do the same in return. Parents should be gentle with their child's ego, never belittling or embarrassing him or her in front of friends. Discipline should usually be administered away from the curious eyes of gloating onlookers. Children should not be laughed at if it makes them uncomfortable. Their strong feelings and requests, even if foolish, should be given an honest appraisal. They should feel that their parents "really *do* care about me." Self-esteem is the most fragile attribute in human nature. It can be damaged by very minor incidents, and its reconstruction is often difficult to engineer.

Thus, a father who is sarcastic and biting in his criticism of children cannot expect to receive genuine respect in return. His offspring might *fear* him enough to conceal their contempt. But revenge will often be sought in adolescence. Children know the wisdom of the old axiom, "Don't mock the alligator until you are across the stream." Thus, a vicious, toothy father may intimidate his household for a time, but if he does not demonstrate respect for its inhabitants, they may return his hostility when they reach the safety of early adulthood.

FULL-BLOWN TODDLERHOOD

Before leaving the topic of respect, let's say a few words about that marvelous time of life known as toddlerhood. It begins with a bang (like the crash of a lamp or a porcelain vase) at about eighteen months of age and runs hot and heavy until about the third birthday. A toddler is the most hard-nosed opponent of law and order, and he honestly believes the universe circles around him. In his cute little way, he is curious and charming and funny and lovable and exciting . . . and selfish and demanding, and rebellious and destructive. Comedian Bill Cosby must have had some personal losses at the hands of toddlers, for he is quoted as saying, "Give me two hundred active two-year-olds and I could conquer the world."

Children between fifteen and thirty-six months of age do not want to be restricted or inhibited in any manner, nor are they inclined to conceal their viewpoint. They resent every nap imposed on them, and bedtime becomes an exhausting, dreaded ordeal each night. They want to play with everything in reach, particularly fragile and expensive ornaments. They prefer using their pants rather than the potty, and insist on eating with their hands. And need I remind you that most of what goes in their mouths is not food. When they break loose in a store, they run as fast as their fat little legs will carry them. They pick up the kitty by its ears and then scream bloody murder when scratched. They want mommy within three feet of them all day, preferably in the role of their full-time playmate. Truly, the toddler is a tiger!

Parents who do everything right in managing these precious babies still are likely to find them hard to control. For this reason, moms and dads should not hope to make their two-year-olds act like more mature children. A controlling but patient hand will eventually succeed in settling the little anarchist, but probably not until he is between three and four. Unfortunately, however, the child's attitude toward authority can be severely damaged during his toddler years. Parents who love their cute little butterball so much that they cannot risk antagonizing him may lose and never regain his control. This is the time to establish themselves, gently but persistently, as the bosses to be reckoned with.

I once dealt with a mother of a rebellious thirteen-year-old boy who snubbed every hint of parental authority. He would not come home until at least two o'clock in the morning, and deliberately disobeyed every request she made of him. Assuming that her lack of control was a long-standing difficulty, I asked if she could tell me the history of this problem. She clearly remembered when it all started: Her son was less than three at the time. She carried him to his room and placed him in his crib, and he spit in her face.

She explained the importance of not spitting in mommy's face, but was interrupted by another moist missile. This mother had been told that all confrontations could be resolved by love, understanding, and discussion. So she wiped her face and began again, at which point she was hit with another well-aimed blast. Growing increasingly frustrated, she shook him . . . but not hard enough to disrupt his aim with the next wad.

What could she do then? Her philosophy offered no honorable solution to this embarrassing challenge. Finally, she rushed from the room in utter exasperation, and her little conqueror spat on the back of the door as it shut. She lost; he won! This exasperated mother told me she never had the upper hand with her child after that night!

When parents lose these early confrontations, the later conflicts become harder to win. Parents who are too weak or tired or busy to win make a costly mistake that will haunt them during their child's adolescence. If you can't make a five-year-old pick up his toys, it is unlikely you will exercise much control during his most defiant time of life.

It is important to understand that adolescence is a condensation or composite of all the training and behavior that have gone before. Any unsettled matter in the first twelve years is likely to fester and erupt during adolescence. The proper time to begin disarming the teenage time-bomb, then, is twelve years before it arrives. As Dr. Bill Slonecker, a Nashville pediatrician and very good friend, said on a "Focus on the Family" radio broadcast, "If discipline begins on the second day of life, you're one day late."

Dr. Slonecker wasn't referring to spanking a baby or any other physical discipline per se. Rather, he was speaking of parents being in charge—loving the child enough to establish control. All too often he saw mothers in his private practice who were afraid to lead their infants. They would call his office and frantically huff, "My six-month-old baby is crying and seems very hot." He would ask the women if the child had a fever, to which they would reply, "I don't know. He won't let me take his temperature."

Those mothers had already yielded some of their authority to their infants. They would live to regret it.

I must point out that some rebellious behavior is distinctly different in origin from the "challenging" defiance I've been describing. A child's antagonism and stiff-lipped negativism may emanate from frustration, disappointment, or rejection, and must be interpreted as a warning signal to be heeded. Perhaps the toughest task in parenthood is recognizing the difference between these two distinct motives.

A child's resistant behavior always contains a message to his parents, which they must decode before responding. That message is often phrased in the form of a question: "Are you in charge or am I?" A distinct reply is appropriate to discourage future attempts to overthrow constituted government in the home. On the other hand, Junior's antagonism may be his way of saying, "I feel unloved now that I'm stuck with a yelling baby brother. Mom used to care for me; now nobody wants me. I hate everybody." When this kind of meaning underlies the rebellion, parents should move quickly to pacify its cause.

The most effective parents are those who have the skill to get behind the eyes of their child, seeing what he sees, thinking what he thinks, feeling what he feels. For example, when a two-year-old screams and cries at bedtime, one must ascertain what he is communicating. If he is genuinely frightened by the blackness of his room, the appropriate response should be quite different than if he is merely protesting about having to go nighty-night. The art of good parenthood revolves around the interpretation of meaning behind behavior.

If parents intuitively *know* their child, they will be able to watch and discern what is going on in his little head. The child will *tell* them what he is thinking if they learn to listen carefully. Unless they can master this ability, however, they will continually fumble in the dark in search of a proper response.

Repeating the first point, the most vital objective of disciplining a child is to gain and maintain his respect. If the parents fail in this task, life becomes uncomfortable indeed. We'll move on now to the other four elements of a traditional approach to child rearing, discussed in the next chapter.

THREE

MORE COMMON SENSE ABOUT CHILDREN

I INDICATED IN THE first chapter that there were certain risks associated with my being a young father and simultaneously choosing to write and speak about the discipline of children. That placed enormous pressure on our imperfect family in those days. But God gave me good kids and we handled the fishbowl experience rather well. There were a few tough moments, however, that proved to be quite embarrassing.

One of those nightmares occurred on a Sunday evening in 1974, when Danae was nine and Ryan nearly five. I was asked to speak on that occasion in a church service near our home. As it turned out, I made two big mistakes that night. First, I decided to speak on the discipline of children, and second, I brought my kids to the church with me. I should have known better.

After I had delivered my thought-provoking, witty, charming, and informative message that evening, I stood at the front of the sanctuary to talk to parents who sought more advice. Perhaps twenty-five mothers and fathers gathered around, each asking specific questions in turn. There I was, dispensing profound child-rearing wisdom like a vending machine, when suddenly we all heard a loud crash in the balcony. I looked up in horror to see Danae chasing Ryan over the seats, giggling and stumbling and running through the upper deck. It was one of the most embarrassing moments of my life. I could hardly go on telling the lady in front of me how to manage her children when mine were going crazy in the balcony; nor could I easily get my hands on them. I finally caught Shirley's eye and motioned for her to launch a seek-and-destroy mission on the second tier. Never again did I speak on that subject with our kids in tow.

I share that story to clarify the goal of proper child rearing. It is not to produce perfect kids. Even if you implement a flawless system of discipline at home, which no one in history has done, your children will be children. At times they will be silly, destructive, lazy, selfish, and—yes—disrespectful. Such is the nature of humanity. We as adults have the same problems. Furthermore, when it comes to kids, that's the way it *should* be. Boys and girls are like clocks; you have to let them run. My point is that the principles in this book are not designed to produce perfect little robots who can sit with their hands folded in the parlor thinking patriotic and noble thoughts! Even if we *could* pull that off, it wouldn't be wise to try.

The objective, as I see it, is to take the raw material with which our babies arrive on this earth, and then gradually mold it into mature, responsible, and God-fearing adults. It is a twenty-year process that will bring progress, setbacks, successes, and failures. When the child turns thirteen, you'll swear for a time that he's missed everything you thought you had taught . . . manners, kindness, grace, and style. But then, maturity begins to take over and the little green shoots from former plantings start to emerge. It is one of the richest experiences in living to watch that progression from infancy to adulthood in the span of two dynamic decades.

Let's move on now to discuss the remaining four principles in the commonsense approach to child rearing.

2. *The best opportunity to communicate often occurs after a disciplinary event.* Nothing brings a parent and child closer together than for the mother or father to win decisively after being defiantly challenged. This is particularly true if the child was "asking for it," knowing full well he deserved what he got. The parents' demonstration of their authority builds respect like no other process, and the child will often reveal his affection after the initial tears have dried.

For this reason, parents should not dread or shrink back from confrontations with their children. These occasions should be anticipated as important events, because they provide the opportunity to convey verbal and nonverbal messages to the boy or girl that cannot be expressed at other times. Let me again stress that I am not suggesting that parents use excessive punishment in these encounters. To the contrary, a small amount of discomfort goes a long way toward softening a child's rebellious spirit. However, the spanking should be of sufficient magnitude to cause genuine tears.

After emotional ventilation, the child will often want to crumple to the breast of his parent, and he should be welcomed with open, warm, loving arms. At that moment you can talk heart to heart. You can tell him how much you love him, and how important he is to you. You can explain why he was disciplined and how he can avoid the difficulty next time. This kind of communication is often impossible with other disciplinary measures . . . such as standing the youngster in the corner or taking away his favorite toy. A resentful child usually does *not* want to talk.

A confrontation my wife once had with our daughter, Danae, can illustrate the point. Back when Danae was but a fifteen-month-old ankle-biter, Shirley wanted to build a fire in the fireplace and needed to go out behind the garage to get some wood. It was raining, so she told Danae, who was barefoot, to wait in the doorway. Having learned to talk quite early, Danae knew the meaning of the command. Nevertheless, she suddenly came skipping across the wet patio. Shirley caught her and took her back, repeating the order more sternly. But as soon as Shirley's back was turned, Danae scooted out again. It was an unmistakable act of disobedience to a clear set of instructions. Then, on the third trip, Shirley stung Danae's little legs a few times with a switch.

After her tears had subsided, the toddler came to Shirley by the fireplace and reached out her arms, saying, "Love, Mommy." Shirley gathered Danae tenderly in her arms and rocked her for fifteen minutes. During those loving moments, she talked softly with her about the importance of obedience.

Parental warmth after such discipline is essential to demonstrate that it is the *behavior*—not the child himself—that the parent rejects. William Glasser, the father of Reality Therapy, made this distinction very clear when he described the difference between discipline and punishment. "Discipline" is directed at the objectional behavior, and the child will accept its consequence without resentment. He defined "punishment" as a response that is directed at the individual. It represents a desire of one person to hurt another; and it is expression of hostility rather than corrective love. As such, it is often deeply resented by the child.

Although I sometimes use these terms interchangeably, I agree with Glasser's basic premise. Unquestionably, there is a wrong way to correct a child that can make him or her feel unloved, unwanted, and insecure. One of the best guarantees against this happening is a loving conclusion to the disciplinary encounter.

3. *Control without nagging (it is possible).* Yelling and nagging at children

can become a habit, and an ineffectual one at that! Have you ever screamed at your child, "This is the last time I'm telling you for the last time!" Parents often use anger to get action instead of using action to get action. It is exhausting and it doesn't work! Trying to control children by screaming is as utterly futile as trying to steer a car by honking the horn.

Let's consider an illustration that could represent any one of a million homes at the end of a long, intense, whirlwind day. Dead-tired, Mom feels her head pounding like a bass drum as she contemplates getting her son to take a bath and go to bed. But eight-year-old Henry does not *want* to go to bed and knows from experience that it will take his harassed mother at least thirty minutes to get him there.

Henry is sitting on the floor, playing with his games. Mom looks at her watch and says, "Henry, it's nearly nine o'clock (a thirty-minute exaggeration), so gather up your toys and go take your bath." Now Henry and Mom both know that she didn't mean for him to *immediately* take a bath. She merely wanted him to start *thinking* about taking his bath. She would have fainted dead away if he had responded to her empty command.

Approximately ten minutes later, Mom speaks again. "Now, Henry, it's getting later and you have school tomorrow; I want those toys picked up and then I want you in that tub!" She still does not intend for Henry to obey, and he knows it. Her *real* message is, "We're getting closer, Hank." Henry shuffles around and stacks a box or two to demonstrate that he heard her. Then he settles down for a few more minutes of play.

Six minutes pass and Mom issues another command, this time with more passion and threat in her voice, "Now listen, young man, I told you to get a move on, and I meant it!" To Henry, this means he must get his toys picked up and m-e-a-n-d-e-r toward the bathroom door. If his mother rapidly pursues him, then he must carry out the assignment posthaste. However, if Mom's mind wanders before she performs the last step of this ritual, or if the phone miraculously rings, Henry is free to enjoy a few minutes' reprieve.

You see, Henry and his mother are involved in a familiar one-act play. They both know the rules and the role being enacted by the opposite actor. The entire scene is preprogrammed, computerized, and scripted. In actuality, it's a virtual replay of a scene that occurs night after night. Whenever Mom wants Henry to do something he dislikes, she progresses through graduated steps of phony anger, beginning with calmness and ending with a red flush and threats. Henry does not have to move until she reaches her flashpoint.

How foolish this game is. Since Mom controls Hank with empty threats, she must stay half-irritated all the time. Her relationship with her children is contaminated, and she ends each day with a pulsing migraine above her left eye. She can never count on instant obedience, because it takes her at least five minutes to work up a believable degree of anger.

How much better it is to use *action* to achieve the desired behavior. There are hundreds of approaches that will bring a desired response, some of which involve slight pain, while others offer the child a reward. The use of rewards or "positive reinforcement" is discussed in the next chapter, and thus will not be presented here. But minor pain or "negative reinforcement" can also provide excellent motivation for the child.

When a parent's calm request for obedience is ignored by a child, Mom or Dad should have some means of making their youngster *want* to cooperate. For those who can think of no such device, I will suggest one: it is the muscle lying snugly against the base of the neck. Anatomy books list it as the trapezius muscle, and when firmly squeezed, it sends little messengers to the brain saying, "This hurts: avoid recurrence at all costs." The pain is only temporary; it can cause no damage. But it is an amazingly effective and practical recourse for parents when their youngster ignores a direct command to move.

Let's return to the bedtime scene with Henry, and let me suggest how it could be replayed more effectively. To begin, his mother should have forewarned him that he had fifteen more minutes to play. No one, child or adult, likes a sudden interruption of his activity. It then would have been wise to set the alarm clock or the stove buzzer. When the fifteen minutes passed and the buzzer sounded, Mom should have quietly told Henry to go take his bath. If he didn't move immediately, his shoulder muscle could have been squeezed. If Henry learns that this procedure or some other unpleasantry is invariably visited upon him, he will move before the consequences ensue.

I know that some of my readers could argue that the deliberate, premeditated application of minor pain to a small child is a harsh and unloving thing to do. To others, it will seem like pure barbarism. I obviously disagree. Given a choice between a harassed, screaming, threatening mother who blows up several times a day versus a mom who has a reasonable, controlled response to disobedience, I would certainly recommend the latter. In the long run, the quieter home is better for Johnny, too, because of the avoidance of strife between generations.

On the other hand, when a youngster discovers there is no threat behind the millions of words he hears, he stops listening to them. The only messages he responds to are those reaching a peak of emotion, which means there is much screaming and yelling going on. The child is pulling in the opposite direction, fraying Mom's nerves and straining the parent-child relationship. But the most important limitation of those verbal reprimands is that their user often has to resort to physical punishment in the end anyway. It is also more likely to be severe, because the adult is irritated and out of control. Thus, instead of the discipline being administered in a calm and judicious manner, the parent has become unnerved and frustrated, swinging wildly at the belligerent child. There was no reason for a fight to have occurred. The situation could have ended very differently if the parental attitude had been one of confident serenity.

Speaking softly, almost pleasantly, Mom says, "Henry, you know what happens when you don't mind me; now I don't see any reason in the world why I should have to make you uncomfortable just to get your cooperation tonight, but if you insist, I'll play the game with you. When the buzzer sounds you let me know what the decision is."

The child then has the choice to make, and the advantages to him of obeying his mother's wishes are clear. She need not scream. She need not threaten to shorten his life. She need not become upset. She is in command. Of course, Mother will have to prove two or three times that she will apply the pain or other punishment, if necessary. Occasionally throughout the coming months, Henry will check to see if she is still at the helm. That question is easily answered.

The shoulder muscle is a surprisingly useful source of minor pain. It can be utilized in those countless situations where face-to-face confrontations occur between adult and child. One such incident happened to me back in the days when my own kids were young. I had come out of a drugstore, and there at its entrance was a stooped, elderly man, approximately seventy-five or eighty years of age. Four boys, probably ninth graders, had cornered him and were running circles around him. As I came through the door, one of the boys had just knocked the man's hat down over his eyes and they were laughing about how silly he looked, leaning on his cane.

I stepped in front of the elderly fellow and suggested that the boys find someone else to torment. They called me names and then sauntered off down the street. I got in my car and was gone about fifteen minutes. I returned to get something I had forgotten, and as I was getting out of my car I saw the same four boys running from a nearby hardware store. The proprietor raced after them, shaking his fist and screaming in protest. I discovered later that they had run down the aisles in his store, raking cans and bottles off the shelves and onto the floor. They also made fun of the fact that he was Jewish and rather overweight.

When the boys saw me coming, I'm sure they thought I viewed myself as Robin Hood II, protector of the innocent and friend of the oppressed. One of the young tormentors ran straight up to my face and stared defiantly in my eyes. He was about half my size, but obviously felt safe because he was a teenager. He said, "You just hit me! I'll sue you for everything you're worth!"

I have rather large hands to go with my six-foot-two, 195-pound frame. It was obviously time to use them. I grasped his shoulder muscles on both sides, squeezing firmly. He immediately dropped to the ground, holding his neck. He rolled away and ran off with his friends, screaming insults back at me.

I reported the incident and later that evening received a phone call from the police. I was told the four young thugs had been harassing merchants and customers along that block for weeks. Their parents refused to cooperate with authorities, and the police felt hamstrung. Without the parents' help, they didn't know what to do. As I reflect now on that incident, I can think of no better way to breed and cultivate juvenile delinquency than for society to allow such early defiance to succeed with impunity. Leonardo da Vinci is quoted as saying, "He who does not punish evil commands it to be done."

Discipline outside the home is not very different from discipline inside. The principles by which children can be controlled are the same in both settings—only the application changes. A teacher, scoutmaster, or recreation leader who tries to control a group of children with anger is due for incredible frustration. The children will discover how far the adult will go before taking any action, and they invariably push him or her right to that line.

It is surprising to observe how often a teacher or group leader will impose disciplinary measures that children do *not* dislike. I knew a teacher, for example, who would scream and threaten and beg her class to cooperate. When they got completely out of hand, she would climb atop her desk and blow a whistle! The kids loved it! She weighed about two hundred and forty pounds, and the children would plot during lunch and recess about how they could get her atop that desk. She was inadvertently offering entertainment—a reward for their unruliness. It was much more fun than studying multiplication tables! Their attitude was much like that of Brer Rabbit, who begged the fox not to throw him in the briar patch. There was nothing they wanted more.

One should never underestimate a child's awareness that he is breaking the rules. I think most children are rather analytical about defying adult authority: they consider the deed in advance and weigh its probable consequences. If the odds are too great that justice will triumph, they'll take a safer course. This observation is verified in millions of homes where a youngster will push one parent to the limit of tolerance, but remain a sweet angel with the other. Mom whimpers, "Rick minds his dad perfectly, but pays no attention to me." Rick is no dummy. He knows Mom is safer than Dad.

To summarize this point, the parent must recognize that the most successful techniques of control are those which manipulate something of importance to the child. Yakkity-yak discussions and empty threats carry little or no motivational power for the child. "Why don't you straighten up and do what's right, Jack? What am I going to do with you, son? Mercy me, it seems like I'm always having to get on you. I just can't see why you don't do what you're told. If one time, just one time, you would act your age." On and on goes the barrage of words.

Jack endures the endless tirades, month in, month out, year after year. Fortunately for him, he is equipped with a mechanism that allows him to hear what he *wants* to hear and screen out everything else. Just as a person living by railroad tracks eventually does not even hear the trains rumbling by, so Jack has learned to ignore meaningless noise in his environment. Jack (and all his contemporaries) would be much more willing to cooperate if it were clearly to his personal advantage.

4. *Don't saturate the child with materialism.* Despite the hardships of the Great Depression, at least one question was then easier to answer than it is today: how can I say no to my child's materialistic desires? It was very simple for parents to tell their children that they couldn't afford to buy them everything they wanted; Dad could barely keep bread on the table. But in more opulent times, the parental task becomes less believable. It takes considerably more courage to say, "No, I *won't* buy you Wanda Wee-Wee and Baby-Blow-Her-Nose," than it did to say, "I'm sorry but you know we can't afford to buy those dolls."

A child's demand for expensive toys is carefully generated through millions of dollars spent on TV advertising by the manufacturers. The commercials are skillfully made so that the toys look like full-sized copies of their real counterparts: jet airplanes, robot monsters, and automatic rifles. The little consumer sits openmouthed in utter fascination. Five minutes later he begins a campaign that will eventually cost his dad $84.95 plus batteries and tax.

The trouble is, Dad often *can* afford to buy the new item, if not with cash, at least with his magic credit card. And when three other children on the block get the coveted toys, Mom and Dad begin to feel the pressure, and even the guilt. They feel selfish because they have indulged themselves for similar luxuries. Suppose the parents are courageous enough to resist the child's urging; he is not blocked—grandparents are notoriously easy to "con." Even if the youngster is unsuccessful in getting his parents or grandparents to buy what he wants, there is an annual, foolproof resource: Santa Claus! When Junior asks Santa to bring him something, his parents are in an inescapable trap. What can they say, "Santa can't afford it"? Is the jolly fat man in the red suit really going to forget and disappoint him? No, the toy will be on Santa's sleigh.

Some would ask, "And why not? Why shouldn't we let our children enjoy the fruits of our good times?" Certainly I would not deny boys and girls a reasonable quantity of the things they crave. But many American children are inundated with excesses that work toward their detriment. It has been said that prosperity offers a greater test of character than does adversity, and I'm inclined to agree.

There are few conditions that inhibit a sense of appreciation more than for a child to feel he is entitled to whatever he wants, whenever he wants it. It is enlightening to watch as a boy or girl tears open stacks of presents at a birthday party or perhaps at Christmas time. One after another, the expensive contents are tossed aside with little more than a glance. The child's mother is made uneasy by his lack of enthusiasm and appreciation, so she says, "Oh Marvin! Look what it is. It's a little tape recorder! What do you say to Grandmother? Give Grandmother a big hug. Did you hear me, Marvin? Go give Grams a big hug and kiss."

Marvin may or may not choose to make the proper noises to Grandmother. His lack of exuberance results from the fact that prizes which are won cheaply are of little value, regardless of the cost to the original purchaser.

There is another reason that the child should be denied some of the things he thinks he wants. Although it sounds paradoxical, you actually cheat him of pleasure when you give him too much. A classic example of this saturation principle is evident in my household each year during the Thanksgiving season. Our family is blessed with several of the greatest cooks who ever ruled a kitchen, and several times a year they do their "thing." The traditional Thanksgiving dinner consists of turkey, dressing, cranberries, mashed potatoes, sweet potatoes, peas, hot rolls, two kinds of salads, and six or eight other dishes.

Prior to my heart attack in 1990, I joined my family in a disgraceful but wonderful gastronomic ritual during the holiday season. We all ate until we were uncomfortable, not saving room for dessert. Then the apple pie, pound cake, and fresh ambrosia were brought to the table. It just didn't seem possible that we could eat another bite, yet somehow we did. Finally, taut family members began to stagger away from their plates, looking for a place to fall.

Later, about three o'clock in the afternoon, the internal pressure began to subside and someone passed the candy around. As the usual time for the evening meal arrived, no one was hungry, yet we had come to expect three meals a day. Turkey and roll sandwiches were constructed and consumed, followed by another helping of pie. By this time, everyone is a bit blank-eyed, absent-mindedly eating what they neither wanted nor enjoyed. This ridiculous ritual continued for two or three days, until the thought of food became rather disgusting. Whereas eating ordinarily offers one of life's greatest pleasures, it loses its thrill when the appetite for food is satisfied.

There is a broader principle to be considered here. Pleasure occurs when an intense need is satisfied. If there is no need, there is no pleasure. A simple glass of water is worth more than gold to a man dying of thirst. The analogy to children should be obvious. If you never allow a child to want something, he never enjoys the pleasure of receiving it. If you buy him a tricycle before he can walk, a bicycle before he can ride, a car before he can drive, and a diamond ring before he knows the value of money, he accepts these gifts with little pleasure and less appreciation. How unfortunate that such a child never had the chance to long for something, dreaming about it at night and plotting for it by day. He might have even gotten desperate enough to work for it. The same possession that brought a yawn could have been a trophy and a treasure. I suggest that you show your child the thrill of temporary deprivation; it's more fun and much less expensive.

Before leaving this thought, let me share a relevant illustration from the closing days of my father's life. He had suffered a massive heart attack, which placed his future in jeopardy. As he contemplated his own passing, he became even more fascinated with life. Everything in God's creation interested him, from science to the arts. He even developed a personal knowledge of and a friendship with the birds that gathered around his house. He named them all and had many eating out of his hand. That is what led to . . . the starling incident.

For some reason, a mother bird abandoned her four baby starlings before they were able to fend for themselves. That precipitated an intense effort in the Dobson household to save the starlings by all means possible. Admittedly, they belonged to a despised, disease-ridden species, but my father was a sucker for *anything* in real need. Thus, a rescue effort was launched. A couple of weeks later, I received the following letter from my mother, describing what had happened to their feathered little friends.

> *Dear Family:*
> *If I could write like you, Jim, I'd make the last eleven days come alive as your dad and I lived them in a bird world. As you know, the four surviving starlings, Eenie, Meenie, Minie and Moe, were evicted from their "under the shingle" nest, and we adopted them. Their feathers were down like fuzz and their bodies seemed to consist of legs, wings, and mouths. They chirped constantly to be fed, after which their cries settled into a lovely lullaby. They outgrew their first cozy nest and your dad transferred them to a larger box from which they could not*

escape. So the only exposure they had to the outside world was the 2' x 3' area above their heads. They seemed to know this opening was where the action was, so they huddled together with their heads turned upward, tweet-tweeting their little tunes. When your dad peered over the top with our dog, Benji, all four birds would open their yellow beaks—chirping—"Worms! Worms!"

As the foursome grew, they sat on a tree limb where your dad placed them. Sometime jumping to the ground, they followed him around the yard, cuddling his shoes and not letting him get more than a few inches away. Their jerky movements made it impossible to keep pace.

From the beginning, we were unsure what we should feed them. Your dad gave them soft bread and milk—dipping it with tweezers into their wide open beaks . . . along with worms, grain, and a few drops of water from an eyedropper. However, on the ninth morning, Jimmy found Moe dead. What to do?! The tenth afternoon Meenie died. The eleventh night he looked down at the two remaining birds. Even while he looked at them, Minie gave a long "Chirp," lay down, stretched out his legs, and died. That left Eenie, the strongest of the birds . . . the one with the most vitality and personality. This morning, however, his vocalizations were desperate and weaker. He only lived until noon. As Jimmy bent over the box nest, Eenie recognized his presence, reached toward him and gave one last "cheep," and was gone.

How sad we both were—that we somehow had failed the helpless creatures who tried so hard to live and fly in the beautiful sky. Your father's love for those insignificant birds and his sadness over their loss reveal the soul of the man I married and have lived with for forty- three years. Does anyone wonder why I love this man?

Your Mother

The man who was so loved by my mother was not long for this world. He died a month later while sitting at the dinner table. His last act before falling into her arms was to express a prayer of blessing on the meal he would not live to eat.

And the starlings? The best explanation for their failure to thrive is that my dad simply overfed them. He was fooled by their constant plea for food. In an effort to satisfy their need, my father actually killed the birds he sought desperately to save.

Does the point come through? We parents too, in our great love for our children, can do irreparable harm by yielding to their pleas for more and more things. There are times when the very best reply we can offer is . . . no.

5. *Establish a balance between love and discipline.* We come now to the foundational understanding on which the entire parent-child relationship rests. It is to be found in a careful balance between love and discipline. The interaction of those two variables is critical and is as close as we can get to a formula for successful parenting.

We've already looked at the first factor, disciplinary control, and what the extremes of oppression and permissiveness do to a child. The other ingredient, parental love, is equally vital. In homes where children are not adored by at least one parent (or a parent-figure), they wither like a plant without water.

It has been known for decades that an infant who is not loved, touched, and caressed will often die of a strange disease initially called marasmus. They simply wither up and die before their first birthday. Evidence of this emotional need was observed in the thirteenth century, when Frederick II conducted an experiment with fifty infants. He wanted to see what language they would speak if they never had the opportunity to hear the spoken word. To carry out this dubious research project, he assigned foster mothers to bathe and suckle the children, but forbade them to fondle, pet, or talk to their charges. The experiment failed dramatically because all fifty infants died. Hundreds of more recent studies indicate that the mother-child relationship during the first year of life is apparently vital to the infant's survival. An unloved child is truly the saddest phenomenon in all of nature.

While the absence of love has a predictable effect on children, it is not so well known that excessive love or "super love" imposes its hazards, too. I believe some children are spoiled by love, or what passes for love. Some Americans are tremendously child-oriented at this stage in their history; they have invested all of their hopes, dreams, desires, and ambitions in their youngsters. The natural culmination of this philosophy is overprotection of the next generation.

I dealt with one anxious parent who stated that her children were the only source of satisfaction in living. During the long summers, she spent most of her time sitting at the front room window, watching her three girls while they played. She feared that they might get hurt or need her assistance, or they might ride their bikes in the street. Her other responsibilities to her family were sacrificed, despite her husband's vigorous complaints. She did not have time to cook or clean her house; guard duty at the window was her only function. She suffered enormous tensions over the known and unknown dangers that could threaten her beloved offspring.

Childhood illness and sudden danger are always difficult for a loving parent to tolerate, but the slightest threat produces unbearable anxiety for the overprotective mom and dad. Unfortunately, the parent is not the only one who suffers; the child is often its victim, too. He or she is not permitted to take reasonable risks—risks which are a necessary prelude to growth and development. Likewise, the materialistic problems described in the previous section are often maximized in a family where the children can be denied nothing. Prolonged emotional immaturity is another frequent consequence of overprotection.

I should mention another unfortunate circumstance, which occurs too often in our society. It is present in homes where the mother and father represent opposing extremes in control. The situation usually follows a familiar pattern: Dad is a very busy man, and he is heavily involved in his work. He is gone from early morning to night, and when he does return, he brings home a briefcase full of work. Perhaps he travels frequently. During the rare times when he is home and not working, he is exhausted. He collapses in front of the TV set to watch a ball game, and he doesn't want to be bothered. Consequently, his approach to child management is harsh and unsympathetic. His temper flares regularly, and the children learn to stay out of his way.

By contrast, Mom is much more supportive. Her home and her children are her sources of joy; in fact, they have replaced the romantic fires which have vanished from her marriage. She worries about Dad's lack of affection and tenderness for the children. She feels that she should compensate for his sternness by leaning in the other direction. When he sends the children to bed without their supper, she slips them some milk and cookies. Since she is the only authority on the scene when Dad is gone, the predominant tone in the home is one of unstructured permissiveness. She needs the children too much to risk trying to control them.

Thus, the two parental symbols of authority act to contradict each other, and the child is caught somewhere between them. The child respects neither parent because each has assassinated the authority of the other. It has been my observation that these self-destructing forms of authority often load a time bomb of rebellion that discharges during adolescence. The most hostile, aggressive teenagers I have known have emerged from this antithetical combination.

Again, the "middle ground" of love and control must be sought if we are to produce healthy, responsible children.

Summary

Lest I be misunderstood, I shall emphasize my message by stating its opposite. I am not recommending that your home be harsh and oppressive. I am not suggesting that you give your children a spanking every morning with their ham and eggs, or that you make your boys sit in the living room with their hands folded and their legs crossed. I am not proposing that you try to make adults out of your kids so you can impress your adult friends with your parental skill, or that you punish your children whimsically, swinging and screaming when they didn't know they were wrong. I am not suggesting that you insulate your dignity and authority by being cold and unapproachable. These parental tactics do not produce healthy, responsible children. By contrast, I am recommending a simple principle: when you are defiantly challenged, win decisively. When the child asks, "Who's in charge?" tell him. When he mutters, "Who loves me?" take him in your arms and surround him with affection. Treat him with respect and dignity, and expect the same from him. Then begin to enjoy the sweet benefits of competent parenthood.

QUESTIONS
& ANSWERS

T HE DISCIPLINE OF children has become such a controversial and
emotional issue, especially in the light of today's plague of child abuse,
that the likelihood of misunderstanding is great in a book of this nature. To
help clarify the philosophy from which I write, I have included the following questions and answers which were drawn from actual interactions with
parents. Perhaps these items will put flesh on the bones of the structure
I have built.

**Q: You spoke of parents having a plan—a conscious goal in their
approach to parenting. Would you apply that to preschoolers? What,
specifically, should we be hoping to accomplish between eighteen
months and five years of age?**
A: There are two messages that you want to convey to preschoolers, and
even those up through elementary school age. They are (1) "I love you,
little one, more than you can possibly understand. You are precious to your
(father) and me, and I thank God that he let me be your (mother)" and
(2) "Because I love you so much, I must teach you to obey me. That is the
only way I can take care of you and protect you from things that might hurt
you."[1] Let's read what the Bible says to us: "Children, obey your parents in
the Lord, for this is right" (Eph. 6:1, NIV). This is an abbreviated answer
to a very important and complex question, but perhaps it will give you a
place to begin formulating your own philosophy of parenting.

**Q: We hear so much about the importance of communication between
a parent and child. If you suppress a child's defiant behavior, how can
he express the hostility and resentment he feels?**

A: The child should be free to say *anything* to his parent, including "I don't like you" or "You weren't fair with me, Mommy." These expressions of true feeling should not be suppressed, provided they are said in a respectful manner. There is a thin line between what is acceptable and unacceptable behavior at this point. The child's expression of strong feeling, even resentment and anger, should be encouraged if it exists. But the parent should prohibit the child from resorting to name-calling and open rebellion. "Daddy, you hurt my feelings in front of my friend, and you were unkind to me" is an acceptable statement. "You stupid idiot, why didn't you shut up when my friends were here?!" is obviously unacceptable. If approached rationally as depicted in the first statement, it would be wise for the father to sit down and try to understand the child's viewpoint. Dad should be big enough to apologize to the child if he feels he was wrong. If he was right, however, he should calmly explain why he reacted as he did and tell the child how they can avoid the collision next time. It is possible to communicate without sacrificing parental respect, and the child should be taught how to express his discontent properly. This will be a very useful communicative tool later in life.

Q: **We have an adopted child who came to us when he was two years old. He lived in fear, however, during those first couple of years, and we feel sorry for him. That's why my husband and I cannot let ourselves punish him, even when he deserves it. We also feel we don't have the right to discipline him, since we are not his biological parents. Are we doing right?**
A: I'm afraid you are making a mistake commonly committed by the parents of older adopted children. They pity their youngsters too much to confront them. They feel that life has already been too hard on the little ones and believe they must not make things worse by disciplining them. As you indicated, there is often the feeling that they do not have the right to make demands on their adopted children.

These guilt-laden attitudes can lead to unfortunate consequences. Transplanted children have the same needs for guidance and discipline as those remaining with their biological parents. One of the surest ways to make a child feel insecure is to treat him as though he is different, unusual, or brittle. If the parents view him as an unfortunate waif to be shielded, he will see himself that way, too.

Parents of sick and deformed children are also likely to find discipline harder to implement. A child with a withered arm or some nonfatal illness can become a little terror, simply because the usual behavioral boundaries are not established by the parents. It must be remembered that the need to be led and governed is almost universal in childhood. This need is not eliminated by other problems and difficulties in life. In some cases, the desire for boundaries is maximized by other troubles, for it is through loving control that parents express personal worth to a child.

Let me make one further comment about adopted children that should be noted. I would have answered the question differently if the adopted child had been physically abused. In cases where beatings and/or other harm occurred before the permanent home was found, it would be unwise to use corporal punishment. The memory of the early horror would likely make it difficult for a child to understand the corrective nature of the punishment. Other forms of discipline and great expressions of love are then in order for an abused child.

Q: Do you think a child should be required to say "thank you" and "please" around the house?
A: I sure do. Requiring those phrases is one method of reminding the child that this is not a "gimme-gimme" world. Even though parents cook for their children, buy for them, and give to them, the youngsters must assume a few attitudinal responsibilities in return. As I have already indicated, appreciation must be taught, and this instructional process begins with fundamental politeness.

Q: My husband and I are divorced, so I have to handle all the discipline of the children myself. How does this change the recommendations you've made?
A: Not at all. The principles of good discipline remain the same, regardless of the family setting. The procedures do become more difficult for one parent, like yourself, to implement, since you have no one to support you when the children become defiant. You have to play the role of the father *and* mother, which is not easily done. Nevertheless, children do not make allowances for your handicap. You must earn their respect, or you will not receive it.

Q: You have discussed the need for establishing boundaries within the home. Do children really want limits set on their behavior?

A: Most certainly! After working with and around children all these years, I could not be more convinced of this fact. They derive security from knowing where the boundaries are and who's available to enforce them. Perhaps an illustration will make this more clear. Imagine yourself driving a car over the Royal Gorge in Colorado. The bridge is suspended hundreds of feet above the canyon floor, and as a first-time traveler you are uneasy as you cross. (I knew one little fellow who was so awed by the view from the bridge that he said, "Wow, Daddy. If you fell off here it'd kill you constantly!") Now suppose there were no guardrails on the side of the bridge; where would you steer the car? Right down the middle of the road! Even though you wouldn't plan to hit the protective rails along the side, you'd feel more secure just knowing they were there.

The analogy to children has been demonstrated empirically. During the early days of the progressive education movement, one enthusiastic theorist removed the chain-link fence surrounding the nursery school yard. He thought children would feel more freedom of movement without the visible barrier surrounding them. When the fence was removed, however, the boys and girls huddled near the center of the playground. Not only did they not wander away, they didn't even venture to the edge of the grounds.

There is security in defined limits. When the home atmosphere is as it should be, children live in utter safety. They never get in trouble unless they deliberately ask for it, and as long as they stay within the limits, there is happiness and freedom and acceptance. If this is what is meant by "democracy" in the home, then I favor it. If it means the absence of boundaries, or that children set their own boundaries in defiance of parents, then I'm unalterably opposed to it.

Q: Permissiveness is a relative term. Please describe its meaning to you.

A: When I use the term permissiveness, I refer to the absence of effective parental authority, resulting in the lack of boundaries for the child. This word represents tolerance of childish disrespect, defiance, and the general confusion that occurs in the absence of adult leadership.

Q: I have never spanked my three-year-old because I am afraid it will teach her to hit others and be a violent person. Do you think I am wrong?

A: You have asked a vitally important question that reflects a common misunderstanding about child management. First, let me emphasize that it *is* possible . . . even easy . . . to create a violent and aggressive child who has observed this behavior at home. If he is routinely beaten by hostile, volatile parents, or if he witnesses physical violence between angry adults, or if he feels unloved and unappreciated within his family, the child will not fail to notice how the game is played. Thus, corporal punishment that is not administered according to very carefully thought-out guidelines is a dangerous thing. Being a parent carries *no* right to slap and intimidate a child because you had a bad day or are in a lousy mood. It is this kind of unjust discipline that causes some well-meaning authorities to reject corporal punishment altogether.

Just because a technique is used wrongly, however, is no reason to reject it altogether. Many children desperately need this resolution to their disobedience. In those situations when the child fully understands what he is being asked to do or not to do but refuses to yield to adult leadership, an appropriate spanking is the shortest and most effective route to an attitude adjustment. When he lowers his head, clenches his fists, and makes it clear he is going for broke, justice must speak swiftly and eloquently. Not only does this response not create aggression in a boy or girl, it helps them control their impulses and live in harmony with various forms of benevolent authority throughout life. Why? Because it is in harmony with nature, itself. Consider the purpose of minor pain in a child's life.

Suppose two-year-old Peter pulls on a tablecloth and a vase of roses on which it rests tips over the edge of the table, cracking him between the eyes. From this pain, he learns that it is dangerous to pull on the tablecloth unless he knows what sits on it. When he touches a hot stove, he quickly learns that heat must be respected. If he lives to be a hundred, he will never again reach out and touch the red-hot coils of a stove. The same lesson is learned when he pulls the doggy's tail and promptly receives a neat row of teeth marks across the back of his hand, or when he climbs out of his high chair when Mom isn't looking and discovers all about gravity.

For three or four years, he accumulates bumps, bruises, scratches, and burns, each one teaching him about life's boundaries. Do these experiences make him a violent person? No! The pain associated with these events teaches him to avoid making the same mistakes again. God created this mechanism as a valuable vehicle for instruction.

Now when a parent administers a reasonable spanking in response to willful disobedience, a similar nonverbal message is being given to the child. He must understand that there are not only dangers in the physical world to be avoided. He should also be wary of dangers in his social world, such as defiance, sassiness, selfishness, temper tantrums, behavior that puts his life in danger, etc. The minor pain that is associated with this deliberate misbehavior tends to inhibit it, just as discomfort works to shape behavior in the physical world. Neither conveys hatred. Neither results in rejection. Neither makes the child more violent.

In fact, children who have experienced corporal punishment from loving parents do not have trouble understanding its meaning. I recall my good friends, Art and Ginger Shingler, who had four beautiful children whom I loved. One of them went through a testy period where he was just "asking for it." The conflict came to a head in a restaurant, when the boy continued doing everything he could to be bratty. Finally, Art took him to the parking lot for an overdue spanking. A woman passerby observed the event and became irate. She chided the father for "abusing" his son and said she intended to call the police. With that, the child stopped crying and said to his father, "What's wrong with that woman, Dad?" *He* understood the discipline even if his rescuer did not. A boy or girl who knows love abounds at home will not resent a well-deserved spanking. One who is unloved or ignored will hate *any* form of discipline!

Q: Do you think you should spank a child for every act of disobedience or defiance?
A: No. Corporal punishment should be a rather infrequent occurrence. There is an appropriate time for a child to sit on a chair to "think" about his misbehavior, or he might be deprived of a privilege, or sent to his room for a "time out," or made to work when he had planned to play. In other words, you should vary your response to misbehavior, always hoping to stay one step ahead of the child. Your goal is to react continually in the way that benefits the child, and in accordance with his "crime." In this regard, there is no substitute for wisdom and tact in the parenting role.

Q: Where would you administer a spanking?
A: It should be confined to the buttocks area, where permanent damage is very unlikely. I do not believe in slapping a child on the face, or in jerking him around by the arms. A common form of injury seen in the emergency room at Children's Hospital when I was there involved children with shoulder separations. Parents had pulled tiny arms angrily and dislocated the shoulder or elbow. If you spank a child only on the "behind" or on the upper part of the legs, I think you will be doing it right.

Q: Is there anyone who should never spank a child?
A: No one who has a history of child abuse should risk getting carried away again. No one who secretly "enjoys" the administration of corporal punishment should be the one to implement them. No one who feels himself or herself out of control should carry through with *any* physical response. And grandparents probably should not spank their grandkids *unless* the parents have given them permission to do so.

Q: Do you think corporal punishment will eventually be outlawed?
A: It is very likely. The tragedy of child abuse has made it difficult for people to understand the difference between viciousness to kids and constructive, positive forms of physical punishment. There are those in the Western world who will not rest until the government interferes with parent-child relationships with all the force of law. It has already happened in Sweden, and the media seems determined to bring that legislation to the United States. It will be a sad day for families. Child abuse will increase, not decrease, as frustrated parents explode after having no appropriate response to defiant behavior.

Q: There is some controversy over whether a parent should spank with his or her hand or with some other object, such as a belt or paddle. What do you recommend?
A: I recommend a neutral object of some type. To those who disagree on this point, I'd encourage them to do what seems right to them. It is not a critical issue to me. The reason I suggest a switch or paddle is because the hand should be seen as an object of love—to hold, hug, pat, and caress. However, if you're used to suddenly disciplining with the hand, your child may not know when he's about to be swatted and can develop a pattern of

flinching when you suddenly scratch your head. This is not a problem if you take the time to get a neutral object.

My mother always used a small switch, which *could not* do any permanent damage. But it stung enough to send a very clear message. One day when I had pushed her to the limit, she actually sent me to the backyard to cut my own instrument of punishment. I brought back a tiny little twig about seven inches long. She could not have generated anything more than a tickle with it. Thereafter, she never sent me on that fool's errand again.

As I conceded above, some people (particularly those who are opposed to spanking in the first place) believe that the use of a neutral object in discipline is tantamount to child abuse. I understand their concern, especially in cases when a parent believes "might makes right" or loses his temper and harms the child. That is why adults must always maintain a balance between love and control, regardless of the method by which they administer disciplinary action.

Q: Is there an age when you begin to spank? And at what age do you stop?

A: There is no excuse for spanking babies or children younger than fifteen to eighteen months of age. Even shaking an infant can cause brain damage and death at this delicate age! But midway through the second year (eighteen months), a boy or girl becomes capable of knowing what you're telling them to do or not do. They can then very gently be held responsible for how they behave. Suppose a child is reaching for an electric socket or something that will hurt him. You say, "No!" but he just looks at you and continues reaching toward it. You can see the smile of challenge on his face as he thinks, "I'm going to do it anyway!" I'd encourage you to thump his fingers just enough to sting. A small amount of pain goes a long way at that age and begins to introduce children to realities of the world and the importance of listening to what you say.

There is no magical time at the end of childhood when spanking becomes ineffective, because children vary so much emotionally and developmentally. But as a general guideline, I would suggest that *most* corporal punishment be finished prior to the first grade (six years old). It should taper off from there and stop when the child is between the ages of ten and twelve.

Q: If it is natural for a toddler to break all the rules, should he be disciplined for his defiance?

A: Many of the spankings and slaps given to toddlers could and should be avoided. They get in trouble most frequently because of their natural desire to touch, bite, taste, smell, and break everything within their grasp. However, this "reaching out" behavior is not aggressive. It is a valuable means for learning and should not be discouraged. I have seen parents slap their two-year-olds throughout the day for simply investigating their world. This squelching of normal curiosity is not fair to the youngster. It seems foolish to leave an expensive trinket where it will tempt him, and then scold him for taking the bait. If little fat-fingers insists on handling the china cups on the lower shelf, it is much wiser to distract him with something else than to discipline him for his persistence. Toddlers cannot resist the offer of a new plaything. They are amazingly easy to interest in less fragile toys, and parents should keep a few alternatives available for use when needed.

When, then, should the toddler be subjected to mild discipline? When he openly defies his parents' spoken commands! If he runs the other way when called, purposely slams his milk glass on the floor, dashes in the street when being told to stop, screams and throws a tantrum at bedtime, hits his friends—these are the forms of unacceptable behavior which should be discouraged. Even in these situations, however, all-out spankings are not often required to eliminate the behavior. A firm rap on the fingers or a few minutes sitting on a chair will convey the same message just as convincingly. Spankings should be reserved for a child's moments of greatest antagonism, usually occurring after the third birthday.

I feel it is important to stress the point made earlier. The toddler years are critical to a child's future attitude toward authority. He should be patiently taught to obey, without being expected to behave like a more mature child.

Without watering down anything I have said earlier, I should also point out that I am a firm believer in the judicious use of grace (and humor) in parent-child relationships. In a world in which children are often pushed to grow up too fast, too soon, their spirits can dry out like prunes beneath the constant gaze of critical eyes. It is refreshing to see parents temper their inclination for harshness with a measure of "unmerited favor." There is always room for more loving forgiveness within our homes.

Likewise, there's nothing that rejuvenates the parched, delicate spirits of children faster than when a lighthearted spirit pervades the home and regular laughter fills its halls. Heard any good jokes lately?

Q: Sometimes my husband and I disagree on our discipline, and we will argue about what is best in front of our children. Do you think this is damaging?
A: Yes, I do. You and your husband should agree to go along with the decision of the other, at least in front of the child. The wisdom of the matter can be discussed later. When the two of you openly contradict each other, right and wrong begin to appear arbitrary to children.

Q: How do you feel about having a family council, where each member of the family has an equal vote on decisions affecting the entire family?
A: It's a good idea to let each member of the family know that the others value his viewpoint and opinion. Most important decisions should be shared within the group because that is an excellent way to build fidelity and family loyalty. However, the equal vote idea is carrying the concept too far. An eight-year-old should not have the same influence that his mother and father have in making decisions. It should be clear to everyone that the parents are the benevolent captains of the ship.

Q: My son obeys me at home, but is difficult to manage whenever I take him to a public place, like a restaurant. Then he embarrasses me in front of other people. Why is he like that? How can I change him?
A: Many parents do not like to punish or correct their children in public places where their disciplinary action is observed by critical onlookers. They'll enforce good behavior at home, but the child is "safe" when unfamiliar adults are around. In this situation, it is easy to see what the child has observed. He has learned that public facilities are a sanctuary where he can act any way he wishes. His parents are in a bind because of their self-imposed restriction. The remedy for this situation is simple: when little Roger decides to disobey in public, respond exactly as you would at home, except that Roger should be removed to a place where there is privacy. Or if he is older, you can promise to take up the matter as soon as you get

home. Roger will quickly learn that the same rules apply everywhere, and that sanctuaries are not so safe after all.

Q: Should a child be disciplined for wetting the bed? How can you deal with this difficult problem?
A: Unless it occurs as an act of defiance after the child is awake, bed-wetting (enuresis) is an involuntary act for which he is not responsible. Disciplinary action under those circumstances is unforgivable and dangerous. He is humiliated by waking up wet, anyway, and the older he gets, the more foolish he feels about it. The bed wetter needs considerable reassurance and patience from parents, and they should try to conceal the problem from those who would laugh at him. Even good-natured humor within the family is painful when it is at the child's expense.

Bed-wetting has been the subject of much research, and there are several different causes in individual cases. In some children, the problem is physiological, resulting from a small bladder or other physical difficulty. A pediatrician or a urologist may be consulted in the diagnosis and treatment of such cases.

For others, the problem is unquestionably emotional in origin. Any change in the psychological environment of the home may produce midnight moisture. During summer camps conducted for young children, the directors often put plastic mattress covers on the beds of all the little visitors. The anxiety associated with being away from home apparently causes a high probability of bed-wetting during the first few nights, and it is particularly risky to be sleeping on the lower level of bunk beds! By the way, mattress covers are widely available and are a worthwhile investment for the home. They don't solve the problem, of course, but they do save in the "mopping up" effort afterward.

There is a third factor that I feel is the most frequent cause of enuresis, other than physical factors. During children's toddler years, they wet the bed because they simply have not mastered nighttime bladder control. Some parents then begin getting their children up at night routinely to go to the potty. There the youngster is still sound asleep, being told to "go tinkle" or whatever. Thus, as the toddler grows older and the need arises to urinate at night, he often dreams he is being told to turn loose. Even when partially awakened or disturbed at night, the child can believe he is being ushered to the bathroom. I would recommend that parents of older bed wetters stop getting them up at night, even if the bed-wetting continues for a while.

There are other remedies which sometimes work, such as electronic devices that ring a bell and awaken the child when the urine completes an electrical circuit. If the problem persists, a pediatrician or child psychologist can guide you in seeking a solution. In the meantime, it is important to help the child maintain self-respect despite his embarrassing trouble. And by all means, conceal your displeasure if it exists.

A sense of humor may help. I received a letter from a mother who wrote down her three-year-old son's bedtime prayer, "Now I lay me down to sleep. I close my eyes, I wet the bed."

Q: How long should a child be allowed to cry after being disciplined or spanked? Is there a limit?
A: Yes, I believe there should be a limit. As long as the tears represent a genuine release of emotion, they should be permitted to fall. But crying can quickly change from inner sobbing to an expression of protest aimed at punishing the enemy. Real crying usually lasts two minutes or less, but may continue for five. After that point, the child is merely complaining, and the change can be recognized in the tone and intensity of his voice. I would require him to stop the protest crying, usually by offering him a little more of whatever caused the original tears. In less antagonistic moments, the crying can easily be stopped by getting the child interested in something else.

Q: I have spanked my children for their disobedience and it didn't seem to help. Does this approach fail with some children?
A: Children are so tremendously variable that it is sometimes hard to believe they are all members of the same human family. Some boys and girls feel crushed from nothing more than a stern look, while others seem to require strong and even painful disciplinary measures to make a vivid impression. This difference usually results from the degree to which a child needs adult approval and acceptance. As I said earlier, the primary parental task is to get behind the eyes of the child, thereby tailoring the discipline to his unique perception.

In a direct answer to the question, it is generally not this individual variation that causes spanking to be ineffectual. When disciplinary measures fail, it is usually because of fundamental errors in their application. It is possible for twice the amount of punishment to yield half the results. I have made a study of situations where parents have told me their child ignores spankings and violates the same rule. There are five basic reasons for the lack of success.

1. *The most recurring problem results from infrequent, whimsical discipline.* Half the time the child is not disciplined for a particular act of defiance; the other half he is. Children need to know the certainty of justice. If there is a *chance* of beating the system, some will repeatedly try it.

2. *The child may be more strong-willed than the parent, and they both know it.* If he can outlast a temporary conflict, he has won a major battle, eliminating discipline as a tool in the parent's repertoire. The strongest of youngsters are tough enough to comprehend, intuitively, that the spanking *must not* be allowed to succeed. Thus, they stiffen their necks and gut it out. The solution is to outlast him and win, even if it takes a few rounds. The experience will be painful for both participants, but the benefits will come tomorrow and tomorrow and tomorrow.

3. *The parent suddenly employs a form of discipline after doing nothing for a year or two prior to that time.* It takes a child a while to respond to a new procedure, and parents might get discouraged during the adjustment period. But take heart in knowing that discipline will be effective over time if consistently applied.

4. *The spanking may be too gentle.* If it doesn't hurt it isn't worth avoiding next time. A slap with the hand on the bottom of a multi-diapered thirty-month-old is not a deterrent to anything. While being careful not to go too far, you should ensure he feels the message.

5. *For a few children, this technique is simply not appropriate.* The neurologically handicapped child who is hyperactive, for example, may be made more wild and unmanageable by corporal punishment. The child who has been abused may identify loving discipline with the hatred of the past. And, the very sensitive child might need a different approach. Once more, there is no substitute for knowledge and understanding of a particular boy or girl.

Q: Should teenage children be spanked for disobedience or rudeness?

A: No! Teens desperately want to be thought of as adults, and they deeply resent being treated like children. Spanking is the ultimate insult at that age, and they are justified in hating it. Besides, it doesn't work. Discipline for adolescents and teens should involve lost privileges, financial deprivation, and related forms of non-physical retribution. Be creative!

My mother, I might note, was a master at trench warfare during my own stubborn adolescent years. My father was a full-time minister and frequently on the road, so Mom had the primary responsibility for raising me. I was giving my teachers a hard time during this era, and on several occasions was sent to the principal's office, where I received stern lectures and a few swats with an infamous rubber hose (which was permissible back then). This discipline did not change my bad attitude, however, and my mother became increasingly frustrated with my irresponsibility and dropping grades. It wasn't long before she reached her limit.

One day after school she sat me down and said firmly, "I know you have been fooling around in school and ignoring your assignments. I also know you've been getting in trouble with your teachers." (She always seemed to have a team of detectives who told her every detail of my private life, although today I think it was little more than a keen mind, good eyes, and an unbelievable intuitive skill.) She continued, "Well, I've thought it over, and I've decided that I'm not going to do anything about what is going on. I'm not going to punish you. I'm not going to take away privileges. I'm not even going to talk about it anymore."

I was about to smile in relief when she said, "I do want you to understand one thing, however. If the principal ever calls *me* about your behavior, I promise you that the next day I'm going to school with you. I'm going to walk two feet behind you all day. I will hold your hand in front of all your friends in the hall and at lunch, and I'm going to enter into all your conversations throughout the whole day. When you sit in your seat, I'm going to pull my chair alongside you, or I'll even climb into the seat with you. For one full day, I will not be away from your side."

That promise absolutely terrified me. It would have been social suicide to have my "mommy" following me around in front of my friends. No punishment would have been worse! I'm sure my teachers wondered why there was such a sudden improvement in my behavior and a remarkable jump in my grades near the end of my freshman year in high school. I simply couldn't run the risk of Mom getting that fatal phone call.

My mother knew that the threat of spanking is not the best source of motivation to a teenager. She had a better idea.

Q: My four-year-old frequently comes running home in tears because she has been hit by one of her little friends. I have taught her that it is not right to hit others, but now they are making life miserable for my little girl. What should I do?

A: I think you were wise to teach your daughter not to hit and hurt others, but self-defense is another matter. Children can be unmerciful to a defenseless child. When youngsters play together, they each want to have the best toys and determine the ground rules to their own advantage. If they find they can predominate by simply flinging a well-aimed fist at the nose of their playmate, someone is likely to get hurt. I'm sure there are those who disagree with me on this issue, but I believe you should teach your child to fight back when attacked.

I recently consulted with a mother who was worried about her small daughter's inability to defend herself. There was one child in their neighborhood who would crack three-year-old Ann in the face at the slightest provocation. This little bully, named Joan, was very small and feminine, but she never felt the sting of retaliation because Ann had been taught not to fight. I recommended that Ann's mother tell her to hit Joan back if she was hit first. Several days later the mother heard a loud altercation outside, followed by a brief scuffle. Then Joan began crying and went home. Ann walked casually into the house with her hands in her pockets, and explained, "Joan socked me so I had to help her remember not to hit me again." Ann had efficiently returned an eye for an eye and a tooth for a tooth. She and Joan have played together much more peacefully since that time.

Generally speaking, a parent should emphasize the stupidity of fighting. But to force a child to stand passively while being clobbered is to leave him at the mercy of his cold-blooded peers.

Q: Look over your forty-plus years of dealing with parents and children. What is the very best disciplinary advice you can offer? What technique or method will help us manage our kids better than any other you've seen attempted?

A: My answer may not be what you expected, but it represents something

I've observed frequently and know to be valid. The *best* way to get children to do what you want is to spend time with them before disciplinary problems occur—having fun together and enjoying mutual laughter and joy. When those moments of love and closeness happen, kids are not as tempted to challenge and test the limits. Many confrontations can be avoided by building friendships with kids and thereby making them *want* to cooperate at home. It sure beats anger as a motivator of little ones!

Q: I see now that I've been doing many things wrong with my children. Can I undo the harm?
A: Once the child reaches adolescence, it is very late to be reversing the trends; before that time, though, you may yet be able to instill the proper attitudes in your child. Fortunately we are permitted to make a few mistakes with our children. No one can expect to do everything right, and it is not the few errors that destroy a child. It is the consistent influence of conditions throughout childhood.

FIVE

THE MIRACLE TOOLS, PART 1

I N THE PRECEDING CHAPTERS, we dealt with the proper parental response to a child's defiant "challenging behavior." Now we turn our attention to the leadership of children where antagonism is not involved. There are countless situations where the parent wishes to increase the child's level of responsibility, but that task is not easy. How can a mother get her child to brush his teeth regularly, or pick up his clothes, or display table manners? How can she teach him to be more responsible with money? What can the parent do to eliminate obnoxious habits, such as whining, sloppiness, or apparent laziness? Is there a solution to perpetual tardiness?

These kinds of behavior do not involve direct confrontations between parent and child, and should not be handled in the same decisive manner described previously. It would be unwise and unfair to punish a youngster for his understandable immaturity and childishness. A much more effective technique is available to use by the knowledgeable parent.

The first educational psychologist, E. L. Thorndike, developed an understanding of behavior in the 1920s that can be very useful for parents. He called it the "law of reinforcement." Later the concept became the basis for a branch of psychology known as behaviorism, which I resoundingly reject. Behaviorism was described by B. F. Skinner and J. B. Watson (mentioned earlier) and includes the unbelievable notion that the mind does not exist. One of my college textbooks referred to behaviorism as "psychology out of its mind." Well said! It perceives the human brain as a simple switchboard, connecting stimuli coming in with responses going out.

Despite my disagreement with the extrapolation of Thorndike's writings, there is no question that the original concept can be helpful to parents. Stated simply, the law of reinforcement reads, "Behavior which achieves desirable consequences will recur." In other words, if an individual likes what happens as a result of his behavior, he will be inclined to repeat that act. If Sally gets favorable attention from the boys on the day she wears a new dress, she will want to wear the dress again and again. If Pancho wins with one tennis racket and loses with another, he will prefer the racket with which he has found success. This principle is disarmingly simple, but it has interesting implications for human learning.

In the first edition of this book, I described the use of these techniques with our little dachshund, Sigmund Freud (Siggy). Old Siggy lived for fifteen years, but has now gone on to wherever feisty dogs go when they die. It was fun training this stubborn animal by the use of reinforcement, which was the *only* thing that got his attention. Most dachshunds will sit up without being taught to do so, for example, because it is a natural response for the long-bodied animals to make. But not Siggy! He was unquestionably the world's most independent animal. During the first year of his life, I thought he was a little bit "slow" between the ears; the second year I began to think he might have been mentally deranged; eventually I came to see him as a recalcitrant, stubborn rascal who just wanted to do things his own way.

In short, it was difficult to entice Siggy to cooperate in any self-improvement programs without offering him an edible incentive. He was particularly fond of cookies, however, and I utilized this passion to good advantage. I propped him in a vertical position where he remained for only a second or two before falling. Then I gave him a piece of an old-fashioned, chocolate chip cookie. He loved it. I sat him up again, and I fed him the goodie as he was falling. Siggy bounced all around the room, trying to take the remaining cookies away from me—but there was only one way to continue the snack. Even Siggy began to get that idea.

In about thirty minutes of this ridiculous exercise, the dachshund received the message loud and clear. Once it hit him, he rarely had four feet on the ground at one time! Throughout the day, he could be found propped up on his haunches, asking for a bite of something—anything. Eventually, I was sorry I started the game, because I felt guilty ignoring him. After all, it was my idea in the first place, and I was compelled to find him something to eat in the kitchen.

This reinforcement technique was also useful in teaching Siggy to go chase a ball (a fantastic demonstration of animal intelligence). I threw the ball about ten feet out in front of us, then dragged Sig by the nape of the neck to where it lay. I opened his mouth, put the ball in place, and dragged him back to the starting place. An oatmeal cookie was waiting at the finish line. It was even easier to get his cooperation this time because he began to grasp the concept of working for a reward. That idea became firmly ingrained and Siggy became rather creative in applying it to his advantage. If the family happened to eat dinner from trays in order to watch the evening news on television, Siggy stationed himself in the exact spot where everyone's line of vision crossed on the way to the tube. There he sat, bobbing and weaving and begging for a bite.

More serious attempts have been made to teach sophisticated behavior to animals by the principles of reinforcement. The results have been remarkable. A pigeon was taught to examine radio parts moving by on a conveyor belt. The bird evaluated each component and knocked the defective ones off the track, for which he received a pellet of grain. He sat there all day long, concentrating on his work. As one might imagine, the labor unions took a dim view of this process; the pigeon did not demand coffee breaks or other fringe benefits, and his wages were disgracefully low. Other animals have been taught to perform virtually human feats by the careful application of rewards.

Let me hasten to acknowledge what some of my readers might be thinking at this point. There is an unbridgeable chasm between children and animals. What do these techniques have to do with kids? Just this: Human beings are also motivated by what pleases them, and that fact can be useful in teaching responsible behavior to boys and girls. However, it is not sufficient to dole out gifts and prizes in an unplanned manner. There are specific principles which must be followed if the law of reinforcement is to achieve its full potential. Let's consider the elements of this technique in detailed application to children.

1. *Rewards must be granted quickly.* If the maximum effectiveness is to be obtained from a reward, it should be offered shortly after the desirable behavior has occurred. Parents often make the mistake of offering long-range rewards to children, but their successes are few. It is usually unfruitful to offer nine-year-old Joey a car when he is sixteen if he'll work hard in school during the next seven years. Second- and third-grade elementary

children are often promised a trip to grandma's house next summer in exchange for good behavior throughout the year. Their obedience is typically unaffected by this lure. It is unsatisfactory to offer Mary Lou a new doll for Christmas if she'll keep her room straight in July. Most children have neither the mental capacity nor the maturity to hold a long-range goal in mind day after day. Time moves slowly for them; consequently, the reinforcement seems impossible to reach and uninteresting to contemplate.

For animals, a reward should be offered approximately two seconds after the behavior has occurred. A mouse will learn the turns in a maze much faster if the cheese is waiting at the end than he will when a five-second delay is imposed. Although children can tolerate longer delays than animals, the power of a reward is weakened with time.

Immediate reinforcement has been utilized successfully in the treatment of childhood autism, a major disorder which resembles childhood schizophrenia. The autistic child does not relate properly to his parents or any other people; he has no spoken language; he usually displays bizarre, uncontrollable behavior. What causes this distressing disorder? The evidence seems to point toward the existence of a biochemical malfunction in the autistic child's neural apparatus. For whatever cause, autism is extremely resistant to treatment.

How can a therapist help a child who can neither talk nor relate to him? All prior forms of treatment have been discouragingly ineffective, which led Dr. Ivar Lovaas and his colleagues to experiment many years ago with the use of rewards. At the University of California at Los Angeles, autistic children were placed on a program designed to encourage speech. At first, a bit of candy was placed into the child's mouth whenever he uttered a sound of any kind; his grunts, groans, and growls were rewarded similarly. The next step was to reward him for more specific vowel sounds. When an "o" sound was to be taught, candy was "paid" for all accidental noises in the proper direction. As the child progressed, he was finally required to pronounce the names of certain objects or people to achieve the reinforcement. Two-word phrases were then sought, followed by more complicated sentence structure. Some language was taught to these unfortunate children by this simple procedure.

The same technique has been employed simultaneously in teaching the autistic child to respond to the people around him. He was placed in a small dark box which had one sliding wooden window. The therapist sat on the outside of the box, facing the child who peered out the window. As long as the child looked at the therapist, the window remained open. However, when his mind wandered and he began gazing around, the panel fell, leaving him in the dark for a few seconds. Although no child with severe autism has been successfully transformed into a normal individual, the use of reinforcement therapy did bring some of these patients to a state of civilized behavior. The key to this success has been the immediate application of a pleasant consequence to desired behavior.

An understanding of how reinforcement works is not only useful in hospitals for autistic children. It also helps explain the way behavior works at home, as we have seen. For example, parents often complain about the irresponsibility of their youngsters, yet they fail to realize that some of this lack of industriousness has been learned. Most human behavior is learned—both the desirable and the undesirable responses. Children learn to laugh, play, run, and jump; they also learn to whine, bully, pout, fight, throw temper tantrums, or be tomboys. The unseen teacher is reinforcement. The child repeats the behavior which he considers to be successful. A youngster may be cooperative and helpful because he enjoys the effect that behavior has on his parents; another will sulk and pout for the same reason. When parents recognize characteristics which they dislike in their children, they should set about teaching more admirable traits by allowing good behavior to succeed and bad behavior to fail.

Described below are the steps of a program devised by Dr. Malcolm Williamson and myself when we were both serving on the attending staff at Children's Hospital of Los Angeles. The system is useful with boys and girls between four and eight years of age; it can be modified in accordance with the age and maturity of the youngster.

    a. The chart on the next page lists some responsibilities and behaviors which the parent may wish to instill. These fourteen items constitute a much greater degree of cooperation and effort than most five-year-old children can display on a daily basis, but the proper use of rewards can make it seem more like fun than work. Immediate reinforcement is the key; each evening, colored dots (preferably red) or stars should be placed by the behaviors that were done satisfactorily. If dots are not available, the squares

"My Jobs"

November	14	15	16	17	18	19	20	21	22	23	24	25	26	27	28	29	30
1. I brushed my teeth without being told.																	
2. I straightened my room before bedtime.																	
3. I picked up my clothes without being told.																	
4. I fed the fish without being told																	
5. I emptied the trash without being told.																	
6. I minded Mommy today																	
7. I minded Daddy today																	
8. I said my prayers tonight																	
9. I was kind to little brother Billy today																	
10. I took my vitamin pill																	
11. I said "thank you" and "please" today																	
12. I went to bed last night without complaining																	
13. I gave clean water to the dog today																	
14. I washed my hands and came to the table when called																	
TOTAL:																	

can be colored with a felt-tip pen; however, the child should be allowed to chalk up his own successes.

b. Two pennies should be granted for every behavior done properly in a given day; if more than three items are missed in one day, no pennies should be given.

c. Since a child can earn a maximum of twenty-eight cents a day, the parent has an excellent opportunity to teach him how to manage his money. It is suggested that he be allowed to spend only sixty to eighty cents per week of these earnings. Special trips to the store or toy shop can be planned. The daily ice cream truck used to provide a handy source of reinforcement, although an increasing number of parents today are trying to limit the fat and sugar their children eat. Of the remaining $1.16 to $1.36 (maximum), the child can be required to give twenty cents in the church offering or to some other charitable recipient; he should then save about thirty cents per week. The balance can be accumulated for a long-range expenditure for something he wants or needs.

d. The list of behaviors to be rewarded does not remain static. Once the child has gotten into the habit of hanging up his clothes, or feeding the puppy, or brushing his teeth, the parent should then substitute new responsibilities. A new chart should be made each month, and Junior can make suggestions for his revised chart.

This system provides several side benefits, in addition to the main objective of teaching responsible behavior. Through its use, for example, the child learns to count. He is taught to give to worthy causes. He begins to understand the concept of saving. He learns to restrict and control his emotional impulses. And finally, he is taught the meaning of money and how to spend it wisely. The advantages to his parents are equally impressive. A father of four young children applied the technique and later told me that the noise level in his household had been reduced noticeably.

Note: This plan is described almost exactly as it appeared in the original *Dare to Discipline*. Since then, I've heard many success stories and a few complaints. The most common negative comments have come from parents who said the task of keeping track of such a complex accounting system is burdensome every night. It takes fifteen or twenty minutes to put up the stars and measure out the pennies. If that is a concern in your family I would suggest that fewer goals be charted. Selecting even five important behaviors and rewarding them with three to five cents each would do the job just as well. *Make the system work for you,* modifying the concept as needed. I assure you, however, it *will* work if properly applied.

If this kind of reinforcement is so successful, why has it not been used more widely? Unfortunately, many adults are reluctant to utilize rewards because they view them as a source of bribery. One of our most successful teaching devices is ignored because of a philosophical misunderstanding. Our entire society is established on a system of reinforcement, yet we don't want to apply it where it is needed most: with young children. As adults, we go to work each day and receive a pay check on Friday. Is that bribery by the employer? Medals are given to brave soldiers; plaques are awarded to successful businessmen; watches are presented to retiring employees. Rewards make responsible effort worthwhile. That's the way the adult world works.

The main reason for the overwhelming success of capitalism is that hard work and personal discipline are rewarded in many ways. The great weakness of socialism is the absence of reinforcement; why should a man struggle to achieve if there is nothing special to be gained? This is, I believe, the primary reason communism failed miserably in the former Soviet Union and Eastern Europe. There was no incentive for creativity and "sweat equity."

I heard of a college chemistry course where the hardest working student in the class, Brains McGuffey, spent many long hours preparing for the first examination. The day of the test, he scored 90 points and earned a solid A. Another student, Ralph Ripoff, rarely ever cracked a book. He took the big exam without any preparation and earned a whopping 50 points for his effort. An F was recorded in the grade book.

However, the professor was a staunch believer in socialistic principles. He was disturbed that Brains had 20 points more than he really needed to pass, and Ralph was 20 points short. This didn't seem fair to the good doctor. Thus the points were redistributed and both students passed with a gentleman's C. But . . . Brains never studied for another chemistry exam. Do you blame him?

Communism and Socialism are *destroyers* of motivation, because they penalize creativity and effort. They reward mediocrity and slovenliness. The law of reinforcement is violated by the very nature of those economic systems. Free enterprise works hand in hand with human nature.

Some parents implement a miniature system of socialism at home. Their children's wants and desires are provided by the "State," and are not linked to diligence or discipline in any way. However, they expect little Juan and René to carry responsibility simply because it is noble for them to do so. They want them to learn and sweat for the sheer joy of personal accomplishment. Most are not going to buy it.

Consider the alternative approach to the "bribery" I've recommended. How are you going to get your five-year-old to perform the behaviors listed on the chart? The most frequently used substitutes are nagging, complaining, begging, screaming, threatening, and punishing. The mother who objects to the use of rewards may also go to bed each evening with a headache, vowing to have no more children. She doesn't like to accentuate materialism in this manner, yet later she may *give* money to her child. Since her youngster never handles his own cash, he doesn't learn how to save it or spend it wisely. The toys she buys him are purchased with her money, and he values them less. But most important, he is not learning the self-discipline and personal responsibility that are possible through the careful reinforcement of that behavior.

Admittedly, there are tasks that a child should do because he is a member of the family. Washing the dishes or carrying out the trash may be expected and not reinforced. I agree that rewards should not be offered for every task done at home. But when you want your children to go above and beyond that base, such as cleaning the garage, or if you want to reinforce a better attitude, there is a more efficient approach than nagging and threatening!

Still, the concept remains controversial. I watched the application of these contrasting viewpoints in two actual home situations. Daren's parents were philosophically opposed to the reinforcement that they called bribes. Consequently, he was not rewarded (paid) for his efforts around the home. Daren hated his work because there was no personal gain involved in the effort; it was something to be tolerated.

When he had to mow the lawn on Saturday, he would drag himself out to the disaster area and gaze with unfocused eyes at the depressing task before him. As might be expected, he did a miserably poor job because he was absolutely devoid of motivation. This sloppiness bought a tongue-lashing from his dad, which hardly made the experience a pleasant one. Daren's parents were not stingy with him. They supplied his needs and even gave him some spending money. When the State Fair came to town, they would provide money for him to spend. Because their gifts were not linked to his responsible efforts, the money provided no source of motivation. Daren grew up hating to work; his parents had inadvertently reinforced his irresponsibility.

Brian's parents took a different view. They felt that he should be paid for the tasks that went beyond his regular household duties. He was not rewarded for carrying out the trash or straightening his room, but he received money for painting the fence on Saturday. This hourly wage was a respectable amount, comparable to what he *could* earn outside the family. Brian loved his work. He'd get up in the morning and attack the weeds in his backyard. He would count his money and work and look at his watch and work and count his money. At times he rushed home from school to get in an hour or two before dark. He opened his own bank account and was very careful about how he surrendered his hard-earned cash. Brian enjoyed great status in his neighborhood because he always had money in his pocket. He didn't spend it very often, but he could have done so at any given moment. That was power! At one point he drew all of his money out of the bank and asked for the total amount in new one dollar bills. He then stacked his twenty-eight bills in his top dresser drawer, and displayed them casually to Daren and his other penniless friends. Work and responsibility were the keys to this status, and he learned a good measure of both.

Brian's parents were careful never to give him a cent. They bought his clothes and necessities, but he purchased his own toys and personal indulgences. From an economic point of view, they spent no more money than did Daren's mom and dad; they merely linked each penny to the behavior they desired. I believe their approach was the more productive of the two.

As implied before, it is very important to know when to use rewards and when to resort to punishment. It is not recommended that rewards be utilized when the child has challenged the authority of the parent. For example, mom may say, "Pick up your toys, Lisa, because friends are coming over," and Lisa refuses to do so. It is a mistake for mom then to offer a piece of candy if Lisa will comply with her request. She would actually be rewarding her defiance.

If there is still confusion about how to respond in this kind of direct conflict, I suggest the reader take another look at chapters 1 to 4 of this book. Rewards should not be used as a substitute for authority; reward and punishment each has its place in child management, and reversals bring unfortunate results.

2. *Rewards need not be material in nature.* When my daughter was three years of age, I began to teach her some pre-reading skills, including the alphabet. In those days, I worried less about nutrition than I do now, and I often used bits of chocolate candy as my reinforcement. Late one afternoon I was sitting on the floor drilling Danae on several new letters when a tremendous crash shook the house. The whole family rushed outside to see what had happened and observed that a teenager had wrecked his car in our quiet residential neighborhood. The boy was not badly hurt, but his automobile was upside-down in the street. We sprayed the smoldering car with water to keep the dripping gas from igniting and made the necessary phone call to the police. It was not until the excitement began to lessen that we realized our daughter had not followed us out of the house.

I returned to the den, where I found her elbow-deep in the two-pound bag of candy I had left behind. She had put at least a quarter-pound of chocolate into her mouth, and most of the remainder was distributed around her chin, nose, and forehead. When she saw me coming, she managed to jam another handful into her chipmunk cheeks. From this experience, I learned one of the limitations of using material, or at least edible, reinforcement.

Anything that is considered desirable to an individual can serve as reinforcement for his behavior. The most obvious rewards for animals are those which satisfy physical needs, although humans are further motivated to resolve their psychological needs. Some children, for example, would rather receive a sincere word of praise than a ten dollar bill, particularly if the adult approval is expressed in front of other children. Children and adults of all ages seek constant satisfaction of their emotional needs, including the desire for love, social acceptance, and self-respect. Additionally, they hope to find excitement, intellectual stimulation, entertainment, and pleasure.

Most children and adults are keenly interested in what their associates think and say. As a result, verbal reinforcement can be the strongest motivator of human behavior. Consider the tremendous impact of the following comments:

"Here comes Phil—the ugliest guy in school."

"Louise is so stupid! She never knows the right answer in class."

"Joe will strike out. He always does."

These unkind words burn like acid to the children they describe, causing them to modify future behavior. Phil may become quiet, withdrawn, and easily embarrassed. Louise will probably display even less interest in her schoolwork than before, appearing lazy to her teachers. Joe may give up baseball and other athletic endeavors.

It happened to me, in fact. I have always thought of myself as a "jock," playing various sports through the years. I lettered in college tennis all four years and captained the team when I was a senior. However, I never had much interest in baseball . . . and for good reason. When I was in the third grade, I stood in right field one day with the bases loaded. The entire third grade class . . . including many girls . . . had turned out to watch the big game, and everything was on the line. The batter slugged a routine fly ball in my direction, which inexplicably went through my fingers and straight to the ground. I picked up the ball in my embarrassment and threw it to the umpire. He stepped aside and let it roll for fifty yards. I can still hear the runner's feet pounding toward home plate. I can still hear the girls laughing. I can still feel my hot face out there in right field. I walked off the field that day and gave up a brilliant baseball career.

We adults are equally sensitive to the idle comments of our peers. It is often humorous to observe how vulnerable we are to the casual remarks of our friends (and even our enemies). "You've gained a few pounds, haven't you, Martha?" Martha may choose to ignore the comment for the moment, but she will spend fifteen minutes before the mirror that evening and start a diet program the next morning.

"Ralph is about your age, Pete; I'd say he is forty-six or forty-eight years old." Pete is only thirty-nine, and the blood drains from his face; the new concern over his appearance may be instrumental in his decision to purchase a hairpiece the following month. Our hearing apparatus is more attuned to this kind of personal evaluation than any other subject, and our sense of self-respect and worthiness emerge largely from these unintentional messages.

Verbal reinforcement should permeate the entire parent-child relationship. Too often our parental instruction consists of a million "don'ts" which are jammed down the child's throat. We should spend more time rewarding him for the behavior we desire, even if our "reward" is nothing more than a sincere compliment. Remembering the child's need for self-esteem and acceptance, the wise parents can satisfy those important longings while using them to teach valued concepts and behavior. A few examples may be helpful:

> Mother to daughter: "You certainly colored nicely within the lines on the picture, René. I like to see that kind of neat art work. I'm going to put this on the refrigerator."

> Mother to husband in son's presence: "Neil, did you notice how Don put his bicycle in the garage tonight? He used to leave it out until we told him to put it away; he is becoming much more responsible, don't you think?"

> Father to son: "I appreciate your being quiet while I was figuring the income tax, Son. You were very thoughtful. Now that I have that job done, I'll have more time. Why don't we plan to go to the zoo next Saturday?"

> Mother to small son: "Kevin, you haven't sucked your thumb all morning. I'm very proud of you. Let's see how long you can go this afternoon."

It is unwise for a parent to compliment the child for behavior she does not admire. If everything the child does earns him a big hug and a pat on the back, Mom's approval gradually becomes meaningless. Specific behavior warranting genuine compliments can be found if it is sought, even in the most mischievous youngster.

Well, let's pause for a few relevant questions and answers, and then return in the next chapter to some additional thoughts about the law of reinforcement.

Questions & Answers

Q: Can rewards be employed in a church or Sunday school program?
A: I have seen reinforcement utilized with great effectiveness in a Christian Sunday school. Instead of earning money, children accumulated "talents" which resemble toy money of various denominations. (The concept of talents was taken from Jesus' parable in Matthew 25:15.) The children earned talents by memorizing Scripture verses, being punctual on Sunday morning, having perfect attendance, bringing a visitor, and so on. This system of currency was then used to obtain new items from those on display in a glass case. Bibles, pens, books, puzzles, and other religious or educational prizes were available for selection.

The children's division blossomed in the church where this system was employed. However, some people may oppose this materialistic program in a church setting, and that is a matter for individual evaluation.

Q: Must I brag on my child all day for every little thing he does? Isn't it possible to create a spoiled brat by telling him his every move is wonderful?
A: Yes, inflationary praise is unwise. As I mentioned in an earlier book, Junior quickly catches on to your verbal game and your words then lose their meaning. It is helpful, therefore, to distinguish between the concepts of *flattery* and *praise*.

Flattery is unearned. It is what Grandma says when she comes for a visit: "Oh, look at my beautiful little girl! You're getting prettier each day. I'll bet you'll have to beat the boys off with a club when you get to be a teenager!" Or, "My, what a smart boy you are." Flattery occurs when you heap compliments upon the child for something he does not achieve.

Praise, on the other hand, is used to reinforce positive, constructive behavior. It should be highly specific rather than general. "You've been a good boy . . . " is unsatisfactory. "I like the way you kept your room clean today," is better. Parents should always watch for opportunities to offer genuine, well-deserved praise to their children, while avoiding empty flattery.[1]

Q: Should a parent try to force a child to eat?
A: No. In fact, the dinner table is one potential battlefield where a parent can easily get ambushed. You can't win there! A strong-willed child is like a good military general who constantly seeks an advantageous place to take on the enemy. He need look no farther. Of all the common points of conflict between generations . . . bedtime, hair, clothes, schoolwork, etc., the advantages at the table are all in the child's favor! Three times a day, a very tiny child can simply refuse to open his mouth. No amount of coercing can make him eat what he doesn't want to eat.

I remember one three-year-old who was determined not to eat his green peas, and a father who had made up his mind the squishy little vegetables were going down. It was a classic confrontation between the irresistible force and an immoveable object. Neither would yield. After an hour of haranguing, threatening, cajoling, and sweating, the father had not achieved his goal. The tearful toddler sat with a forkload of peas pointed ominously at his sealed lips.

Finally, through sheer intimidation, the dad managed to get one bite of peas in place. But the lad wouldn't swallow them. I don't know everything that went on afterwards, but the mother told me they had no choice but to put the child to bed with the peas still in his mouth. They were amazed at the strength of his will.

The next morning, the mother found a little pile of mushy peas where they had been expelled at the foot of the bed! Score one for Junior, none for Dad. Tell me in what other arena a thirty-five-pound child could whip a two-hundred-pound man?

Not every toddler is this tough, of course. But *many* of them will gladly do battle over food. It is their ideal power game. Talk to any experienced parent or grandparent and they will tell you this is true. The sad thing is that these conflicts are unnecessary. Children will eat as much as they need if you keep them from indulging in the wrong stuff. They will not starve. I promise!

The way to deal with a poor eater is to set good food before him. If he claims to not be hungry, wrap the plate, put it in the refrigerator and send him cheerfully on his way. He'll be back in a few hours. God has put a funny little feeling in his tummy that says, "gimme food!" When this occurs, *do not* put sweets, snacks, or confectionery food in front of him. Simply retrieve the earlier meal, warm it up and serve it again. If he protests, send him out to play again. Even if twelve hours or more goes by, continue this procedure until food . . . all food . . . begins to look and smell wonderful. From that time forward, the battle over the dinner table should be history.

Q: You stated earlier that you do not favor spanking teenagers. What would you do to encourage cooperation from my fourteen-year-old who deliberately makes a nuisance of himself? He throws his clothes around, refuses to help with any routine tasks in the house, and pesters his little brother to death. What am I to do about it?

A: The principles of reinforcement are particularly useful with teenagers, because such rewards appeal to youngsters during this typically self-centered time of life. However, laziness is an unavoidable fact of life with many adolescents. Their lack of industriousness and general apathy has a physiological origin. Their energy during early adolescence is being redirected into rapid growth. Also, glandular changes require a physical readjustment. For several years they may want to sleep until noon and drag themselves around until it comes time to do something that suits their fancy. If *any* system will succeed in charging their sluggish batteries, it will probably involve an incentive of some variety. The following three steps can be followed in implementing a system of reinforcement with a teenager:

1. *Decide what is important to the youngster for use as an incentive.* Two hours with the family car on date night is worth the world to most newly licensed drivers. (This could be the most expensive incentive in history if the young driver is a bit shaky behind the wheel.) An allowance is another easily available source of motivation, as described above. Teenagers have a great need for cold cash today. A routine date with Helen Highschool might cost twenty dollars or more—in some cases *far* more. Yet another incentive may involve a fashionable article of clothing which would not ordinarily be within your teen's budget. Offering him or her a means of obtaining such luxuries is a happy alternative to the whining, crying, begging, complaining, and pestering that might occur otherwise. Mom says, "Sure you

can have the ski sweater, but you'll have to earn it." Once an acceptable motivator is agreed upon, the second step can be implemented.

2. *Formalize the agreement.* A contract is an excellent means of settling on a common goal. Once an agreement has been written, it is signed by the parent and teen. The contract may include a point system which enables your teenager to meet the goal in a reasonable time period. If you can't agree on the point values, you could allow for binding arbitration from an outside party. Let's examine a sample agreement in which Marshall wants an MP3 player, but his birthday is ten months away and he's flat broke. The cost of the player is approximately $150. His father agrees to buy the device if Marshall earns 10,000 points over the next six to ten weeks doing various tasks. Many of these opportunities are outlined in advance, but the list can be lengthened as other possibilities become apparent:

a. For making bed and straightening room
each morning . . . . 50 points
b. For each hour of studying. 150 points
c. For each hour of house or yard work done . . . . 300 points
d. For being on time at breakfast and dinner. . . . . 40 points
e. For babysitting siblings per hour. . . . . 150 points
f. For washing car each week . . . . 250 points
g. For arising by 8:00 a.m. Saturday morning. . . . . 100 points

While the principles are almost universally effective, the method of application must be varied. With a little imagination, you can create a list of chores and point values that work in your family. It's important to note that points can be gained for cooperation and lost for resistance. Disagreeable and unreasonable behavior can be penalized 50 points or more. (However, penalties must be imposed fairly and rarely or the entire system will crumble.) Also, bonus points can be awarded for behavior that is particularly commendable.

3. *Establish a method to provide immediate rewards.* Remember that prompt reinforcement achieves the best results. This is necessary to sustain teens' interest as they move toward the ultimate goal. A thermometer-type chart can be constructed, with the point scale listed down the side. At the top is the 10,000-point mark, beside a picture of an MP3 player or other prize. Each evening, the daily points are totalled and the red portion of

the thermometer is extended upward. Steady, short-term progress might earn Marshall a bonus of some sort—perhaps a CD of his favorite musician or a special privilege. If he changes his mind about what he wishes to buy, the points can be diverted to another purchase. For example, 5,000 points is 50 percent of 10,000 and would be worth $75 toward another purchase. However, do not give your child the reward if he does not earn it. That would eliminate future uses of reinforcement. Likewise, do not deny or postpone the goal once it is earned. The system described above is not in concrete. It should be adapted to the age and maturity of the adolescent. One youngster would be insulted by an approach that would thrill another.

SIX

THE MIRACLE TOOLS, PART 2

A S WE HAVE been discussing, increasing a child's level of responsibility and self-discipline is not a simple task. It must be taught by parents with a specific game plan. But the job is made easier by utilizing the Law of Reinforcement. In the previous chapter, we examined two specific principles which maximize the benefits of this technique. These were to (1) grant rewards immediately, and also (2) utilize nonmaterial rewards, such as praise, hugs, and plain old attentiveness, along with financial and material reinforcement.

We'll turn our attention now to the remaining three principles, beginning with this:

3. *Almost any behavior that is learned through reinforcement can be eliminated if the reward is withheld long enough.*

It is an established fact that unreinforced behavior will eventually disappear. This process, called *extinction* by psychologists, can be very useful to parents and teachers who want to alter the behavior of children.

Again, the animal world provides many interesting examples of extinction. For example, the walleyed pike is a large fish with a big appetite for minnows. If placed in a tank of water with its small prey, the pike will soon be in the tank alone. However, an interesting thing occurs when a plate of glass is slipped into the tank, separating the pike from the minnows. The pike cannot see the glass and hits it solidly in pursuit of its dinner. Again and again it will swim into the glass, bumping whatever one calls the front end of a walleyed pike. Clearly, behavior is *not* being reinforced, and, thus, is extinguished gradually.

Eventually, the pike gives up. It has learned that the minnows are not available. The glass can then be taken from the tank, allowing the minnows to swim around their mortal enemy in perfect safety. The pike will not try to eat them. It knows what it knows: They are unreachable. Amazingly, the walleyed pike will actually starve to death while its favorite food casually swims right past its mouth.

Extinction is also utilized to restrain elephants in a circus. When the elephant is young, its foot is chained to a large, immovable cement block. The animal will pull repeatedly against the barrier without success, thereby extinguishing its escape behavior. Later, a small rope attached to a fragile stake from which a dog could break free will be sufficient to restrain the powerful pachyderm. Again, the beast knows what it knows!

Let me say it once more: Children are human and unlike the animal world in most respects. But the principle of extinction is applicable to kids, as well. To eliminate an undesirable behavior in a child, one must identify and then withhold the critical reinforcement. Let's apply this concept to a common childhood problem. Why does a child whine instead of speaking in a normal voice? Because the parent has reinforced whining! When three-year-old Karen speaks in her usual voice, her mom is too busy to listen. Actually, Karen babbles all day long, so her mother tunes out most of her verbiage. But when Karen speaks in a grating, irritating, obnoxious tone, Mom turns to see what's wrong. Karen's whining brings results; her normal voice does not. And so she becomes a whiner.

To extinguish the whining, one must simply reverse the reinforcement. Mom should begin by saying, "I can't hear you because you're whining, Karen. I have funny ears. They just can't hear whining." After this message has been communicated for a day or two, Mom should ignore all moan-tones. On the other hand, she should offer immediate attention to a request made in a normal voice.

If this control of reinforcement is applied properly, it *will* achieve the desired results. Nearly all learning is based on this principle, and the consequences are certain and predictable. Of course, Grandma and Uncle Albert may continue to reinforce the behavior you are trying to extinguish, and thereby keep it alive. So teamwork is a must, especially between parents.

Extinction is not only a tool for use in a deliberate training program. It also happens accidentally at times. Consider the case of four-year-old Mark. His mother and father were concerned about his temper tantrums, especially since he habitually threw them when his parents least wanted him to misbehave. For example, when guests were visiting in their home, he would explode just before bedtime. The same outbursts occurred in restaurants, church services, and other public places.

Mark's parents were no strangers to discipline, and they tried every approach on their little rebel. They spanked him, stood him in the corner, sent him to bed early, and shamed and scolded him. Nothing worked. The temper tantrums continued regularly.

Then one evening Mark's parents were both reading a newspaper in their living room. They had said something that angered their son, and he fell on the floor in a rage. He screamed and whacked his head on the carpet, kicking and flailing his small arms. They were totally exasperated at that point and didn't know what to do, so they did nothing. They continued reading the paper in stony silence, which was the last thing the little tornado expected. He got up, looked at his father, and fell down for Act Two. Again his parents made no response. By this time they were glancing at one another knowingly and watching junior with curiosity. Again, Mark's tantrum stopped abruptly. He approached his mother, shook her arm, then collapsed for Act Three. They continued ignoring him. His response? This child felt so silly flapping and crying on the floor that he never threw another tantrum.

Now it can be told: The illustration cited above was included in the first edition of *Dare to Discipline*, back in 1970. It is time now to reveal that Mark was not the real name of that child. It was Jim. Alas, *I* was the brat in the story. And I can tell you, it's no fun staging a performance if the crowd won't come!

It is clear that the reinforcement for my tantrums was parental manipulation. Through violent behavior, I had gotten those big, powerful adults upset and distraught. I must have loved it. With most children, tantrums are a form of challenging behavior that can be eliminated by one or more appropriate spankings. For a few like me, however, something else was going on. Like a pyromaniac, I enjoyed seeing how much commotion I could precipitate. That, in itself, was my reward.

Although my parents extinguished this negative behavior in one episode, it usually takes much longer. It is important to understand the typical rate at which a characteristic will disappear without reinforcement.

Consider again the example of the pigeon checking radio parts, mentioned in the previous chapter. Initially, the bird missed all the defective components, and only gradually recognized a higher percentage. As illustrated in Figure A, the pigeon eventually identified 100 percent of the parts, and continued with perfect accuracy while the reinforcement (grain) was paid for each success.

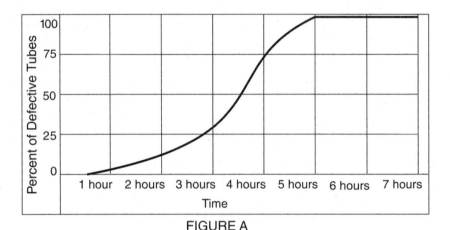

FIGURE A

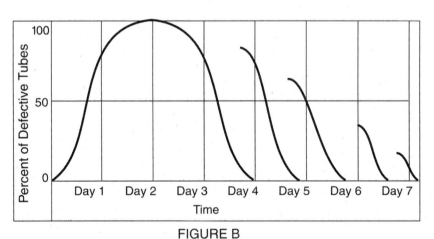

FIGURE B

Suppose the reinforcement was then withheld. The pigeon would continue to intercept the broken parts with perfect accuracy, but not for long. Soon he would begin to miss a few bad components. If he continued to work for nothing, he would become more and more distracted and disinterested in his task. By the end of the day, he would miss all or most of the defective parts.

However, the following day, he would again go to work as before. *Even though the behavior is extinguished one day, it will likely return the next.* This reawakening is called "spontaneous recovery." Each day, the behavior returns as illustrated in Figure B. But the accuracy is less and the daily extinction occurs more quickly than the day before.

This principle is important in extinguishing undesirable behavior in children. A parent or teacher should not become discouraged if an extinguished behavior reappears. Its complete elimination may require considerable time.

The principle of extinction has helped many people break bad habits. One such system is designed for those who want to quit smoking. It is based on eliminating the pleasantness (reinforcement) usually produced by inhaling cigarette smoke. To do this, a tube filled with very stale, concentrated tobacco smoke is aimed at the smoker's face. Whenever the individual takes a puff from his cigarette, he is shot in the face with the putrid smoke from the tube. The smoker begins to associate cigarettes with the foul blast in his face, and by this means sometimes develops a strong dislike for smoking. Unfortunately, nicotine is one of the most addictive narcotics known, and the chemical impact is extremely difficult to overcome.

Extinction can also help children overcome some of their unnecessary fears. I once consulted with a mother who was very concerned about her three-year-old daughter's fear of the dark. Despite the use of a night light and leaving the bedroom door open, little Marla was afraid to stay in her room alone. She insisted that her mother sit with her until she went to sleep each evening, which was extremely time-consuming and inconvenient. If Marla happened to awaken in the night, she would call for help. It was apparent that she was genuinely frightened.

Fears such as these are not innate: they have been learned. If parents truly realized this, they would be more careful about what they say and how they act. The fact is, youngsters are amazingly perceptive and often adopt the behaviors and concerns they see in adults. Even good-natured teasing can produce problems for a child. If a youngster walks into a dark room and is pounced upon from behind the door, he quickly learns that the dark is not always empty!

In Marla's case, it was unclear where she learned to fear the dark, but I believe her mother inadvertently magnified the problem. In her concern for her daughter, she conveyed anxiety, and Marla began to think her own fears must be justified. "Even mother is worried about it," she undoubtedly reasoned. Marla became so frightened that she could not walk through a dimly lit room without an escort. It was at this point that she was referred to me.

Since it is usually unfruitful to try to talk children out of their fears, I suggested that the mother *show* Marla there was nothing to be afraid of. That would help the child perceive her mother as being confident and unthreatened. So she bought a bag of candy (okay, okay . . . I would use pieces of the popular rolled-up fruit today) and placed her chair just outside Marla's bedroom door. Marla was then offered a piece of candy if she spent a few seconds in her bedroom with the light on and door shut. This first step was not very threatening, and Marla enjoyed the game. It was repeated several times, and then she was asked to walk several feet into the darkened room while her mother, clearly visible in the hall, counted to ten. This was also easy, and Marla continued playing along for the bits of candy.

On subsequent trips, the door was shut a few inches more and the lights were lowered. Finally, Marla had the courage to enter the dark room and shut the door while her mother counted to three—then five—then eight. The time in the dark was gradually lengthened, and instead of producing fear it produced candy: ultimate pleasure to a small child. She also heard her mother talking confidently and quietly, and knew she could come out whenever she wished. Through these means, courage was reinforced and fear extinguished.

Like the kind of reward you choose, the uses of extinction are limited only by the imagination and creativity of the parent or teacher. Try it in various settings. With a little practice and patience, you will see for yourself that one of the best methods of changing a behavior is to withhold reinforcement while rewarding its replacement.

Moving ahead, the fourth principle of getting the most from the miracle tool is:

4. *Parents and teachers are also vulnerable to reinforcement.* Reinforcement is not only the mechanism by which *children* and *animals* learn new behavior. Adults also modify their behavior according to the positive and negative feedback they receive. Inevitably children sometimes train their parents, rather than the reverse, by reinforcing certain behaviors and extinguishing others.

For example, when Mom and Dad take their children to some exciting place, such as Disneyland, the youngsters put on their best behavior. They may be sweet and cooperative—an unsubtle attempt to reinforce or reward their parents' action. In extreme cases, I have seen children adeptly manipulate their parents to get what they want or the behavior they prefer.

A case in point is when Mom disciplines her eight-year-old daughter, only to hear, "You don't love me anymore." Most children know their parents are anxious to convey their love, so they use this delicate issue to extinguish punishment. It often succeeds.

Another example is when the teacher announces, "It is time to study health, so get out your textbooks," and the entire class groans. For some instructors, this lack of reinforcement is difficult to tolerate, and they'll either eliminate a boring subject from their future curriculum or teach it in the most perfunctory way.

Similar phenomena occur in higher education, too. I knew of a graduate school psychology class in which the students experimented with reinforcement on their professor. This instructor utilized two distinct teaching methods. He either lectured from his notes, which was a dry, dismal experience for students, or he spoke extemporaneously, resulting in lively and interesting discussions. One day the students agreed before class to reward his conversational style and extinguish his formal behavior. Whenever he used notes, they shuffled their feet, looked out the window, yawned, and whispered to each other. On the other hand, they exhibited fascination with his unstructured lessons. The professor responded in classic fashion. He adopted the informal approach almost exclusively, although he didn't know he was being manipulated until nearly the end of the semester.

A final example is the dad who has a very low frustration tolerance with his children. He screams at them whenever they fall short of his expectations, which seems to make them obey. He has been reinforced for his screaming and becomes a loud, aggressive parent.

The point is simple: Parents should be aware of their own reactions to reinforcement and make certain they are in control of the learning situation.

The fifth and final key of the Law of Reinforcement is:

5. *Parents often reinforce undesirable behavior and weaken behavior they value.*

Perhaps the most important aspect of the past two chapters relates to accidental reinforcement. It is remarkably easy to reward undesirable behavior in children by allowing it to succeed. Suppose, for example, that Mr. and Mrs. Weakknee are having dinner guests, and they put three-year-old Ricky to bed at seven o'clock. They know Ricky will cry, as he always does, but what else can they do? Indeed, Ricky cries. He begins at a low pitch and gradually builds to the decibel level of a jet at takeoff.

Finally, Mrs. Weakknee becomes so embarrassed by the display that she lets Ricky get up. What has the child learned? That he must cry *loudly* if he doesn't want to go to bed. Quiet protests don't work. Mr. and Mrs. Weakknee had better be prepared for a tearful battle the following night, too, because the response eventually succeeded. And if they forget, Ricky will undoubtedly remind them.

To explain this principle further, let's consider another scenario. An argumentative teenager, Laura Beth, never takes "no" for an answer. She is so cantankerous that she's only homesick when she's home. Whenever her mother is unsure whether she should allow Laura Beth to go out at night, she first tells her she *can't* go. By saying "no" initially, Laura Beth's mom buys some extra time to think the request over. She can always change her mind, but she knows it's easier to go from "no" to "yes" than the other way. However, what all of this tells Laura Beth is that "no" really means "maybe" . . . and that "yes" is possible if she argues and complains enough.

Many parents make the same mistake as Laura Beth's mother. They allow arguing, sulking, pouting, door slamming, and bargaining to succeed. Parents should not take a definitive position on an issue until they have thought it over thoroughly and listened to the child's argument. Then they should stick tenaciously to their decision. If the teenager learns that "no" means "absolutely not," she is less likely to waste her effort appealing her case.

Or suppose it is Mr. and Mrs. Smith's tenth wedding anniversary and they are going out for dinner. As they prepare to leave, their five- and six-year-old children begin howling about being left behind. Mr. Smith is vaguely familiar with the principles of reinforcement, so he offers a pack of gum to the children if they'll stop crying. Unfortunately, Mr. Smith has not reinforced the silence; he has rewarded the tears. The next time he and Mrs. Smith leave it will be to the children's advantage to cry again. A small alternative would have changed the setting entirely. Mr. Smith should have offered the gum for their cooperation before the tears began to fall.

Let's apply the principle to babies and their tears. Crying is an important form of communication for infants. Through their wails we learn of their hunger, fatigue, discomfort, or diaper disaster. Although we don't want to eliminate crying in babies, it is possible to make them less fussy by minimizing the reinforcement of their tears. If an infant is immediately picked up or rocked each time he cries, he may quickly observe the relationship between tears and adults' attention. How well I remember standing at the doorway of my infant daughter's nursery for several minutes, awaiting a momentary lull in the crying before going to her crib. By doing so, I reinforced the pauses rather than the howls.

Obviously, parents must be careful about the behaviors they allow to succeed. They must exercise self-discipline and patience to ensure that the tools of reinforcement and extinction are being used to encourage responsible and mature behavior.

QUESTIONS & ANSWERS

Q: How can I acquaint my junior higher with the need for responsible behavior throughout his life? He is desperately in need of this understanding.
A: Rather than reinvent the wheel, let me again quote from one of my other books which addresses this very issue. There, I said the overall objective during preadolescence is teaching the child that actions have inevitable consequences. One of the most serious casualties in a permissive society is the failure to connect those two factors: behavior and consequences.

Too often, a three-year-old child screams insults at his mother, but Mom stands blinking her eyes in confusion. A first grader launches an attack on his teacher, but the school makes allowances for his age and takes no action. A ten-year-old is caught stealing CDs in a store, but is released to the recognizance of his parents. A fifteen-year-old sneaks the keys to the family car, but his father pays the fine when he is arrested. A seventeen-year-old drives his Chevy like a maniac and his parents pay for the repairs when he tears off the front fender. You see, all through childhood, loving parents seem determined to intervene between behavior and consequences, breaking the connection and preventing the valuable learning that could have occurred.

Thus, it is possible for a young man or woman to enter adulthood without knowing that life bites—that every move we make directly affects our future, and that irresponsible behavior eventually produces sorrow and pain. Such a person applies for his first job and arrives late for work three times during the first week. Later, when fired in a flurry of hot words, he becomes bitter and frustrated. It was the first time in his life that Mom and Dad couldn't come running to rescue him from the unpleasant consequences. Unfortunately, many North American parents still "bail out" their children long after they are grown and living away from home. What is the result? This overprotection produces emotional cripples who often develop lasting characteristics of dependency and a kind of perpetual adolescence.

How does one connect behavior with consequences? By being willing to let the child experience a reasonable amount of pain or inconvenience when he behaves irresponsibly. When Barbara misses the school bus through her own dawdling, let her walk a mile or two and enter school in midmorning (unless safety factors prevent this). If Janie carelessly loses her lunch money, let her skip a meal. Obviously, it is possible to carry this principle too far and become harsh and inflexible with an immature child. The best approach is to expect boys and girls to carry the responsibility that is appropriate for their age and occasionally to taste the bitter fruit that irresponsibility bears.

Q: You have referred to children who manipulate their mothers and fathers. On the other hand, isn't the parent manipulating the child by the use of rewards and punishment?

A: No more than a factory supervisor is manipulating his employees by insisting that they arrive at work by 9:00 a.m. No more than a policeman manipulates the speeding driver by giving him a traffic ticket. No more than an insurance company manipulates that same driver by increasing his premium. No more than the IRS manipulates a taxpayer who files his return one day late and pays a penalty for his tardiness. The word "manipulation" implies a sinister or selfish motive. I prefer the term "leadership," which is in the best interest of everyone—even when it involves unpleasant consequences.[1]

Q: I am a teacher in junior high school, and there are five separate classes that come to my room to be taught science each day. My biggest problem is getting those students to bring books, paper, and pencils to class with them. I can lend them the equipment they need, but I never get it back. What do you suggest?

A: I faced an identical problem the year I taught junior high school. My students were not malicious; they just had too many other things on their minds to remember to bring their school materials. I tried various motivational techniques, but without success. I appealed to the students' desire for responsibility, but generated only yawns. I launched an emotional tirade, but that seemed like a great waste of energy for such a small issue. There had to be a better way!

I finally reached a solution based on the certainty that young people will cooperate if it's to their advantage. I announced one morning that I no longer cared whether they brought their pencils and books to class. I had twenty extra books and several boxes of sharpened pencils which they could borrow. If they forgot to bring these materials, all they had to do was ask for a loan. I would not gnash my teeth or get red in the face; they would find me very willing to share my resources.

However, there was one catch. The borrowing student had to stand beside his desk (or lean over if written work was required) for that one-hour period. I smiled to myself in subsequent days as the kids raced around before class, trying to scrounge up books or pencils from friends. Two hundred and twenty students came to my classroom every day, and yet I only had to enforce the "standing" rule about once a week. The pupils watched out for their own best interests. One lapse in their memory was all it took; they didn't blunder into the same situation twice.

At the risk of being redundant, I will repeat the valuable formula for managing children and teenagers: give them maximum reason to comply with your wishes. Your anger is the *least* effective motivation I can imagine.

Q: If rewards and punishment should be given very quickly, why does God not interact that way with us, His children? People seem to "get away" with bad behavior for years, and the ultimate reward for those who live a Christian life will come only after death. Surely the Lord knows about "immediate reinforcement."

A: He certainly does. He created the characteristics we only observe and try to understand. So why does He not reinforce the behavior He desires more quickly? I don't know, although that fact is acknowledged in Scripture: "When the sentence for a crime is not quickly carried out, the hearts of the people are filled with schemes to do wrong. Although a wicked man commits a hundred crimes and still lives a long time, I know that it will go better with God-fearing men, who are reverent before God" (Ecclesiastes 8:11-12, NIV).

Whether they arrive on time or not, the warnings and promises in Scripture are more reliable than anything else in the universe. He *will* have the last word!

Q: What is your opinion of the juvenile courts? Do they reward good behavior and extinguish bad? Are they efficient in discouraging delinquency?

A: Not generally, but the blame is difficult to locate. I served for three years on President Ronald Reagan's National Advisory Commission to the Office of Juvenile Justice and Delinquency Prevention. It was a fascinating although occasionally discouraging assignment. I observed that the courts build delinquents in some cases as systematically as if they were placing stone on stone.

This happened with a ninth grader I knew who had broken every rule he could violate, just to demonstrate the toothlessness of the law. Craig would brag to his friends before committing an illegal act, and then laugh when he was not punished. In a matter of two years' time, he had stolen two cars and one motorcycle, had run away from home twice, was suspended from school three times, and was arrested once as a peeping Tom. I watched him march off to court repeatedly where he was released after receiving another worn-out lecture from the judge.

Finally, Craig was sent to a camp for delinquent boys where he wrote me a letter saying how he regretted the mess he'd made of his life. He was anxious to get home and take advantage of his educational opportunity. I think Craig wanted to know how far he could push "John Law." As soon as he got the answer, he no longer wanted to fight. He should have been punished the first time he was arrested.

Shortly after hearing from Craig, I talked to a well-known judge about the obvious leniency of the courts. I asked him why juvenile authorities are so reluctant to take action against a defiant teenager, even though he may be begging for punishment. The judge cited two reasons for the attitudes of his colleagues:

(1) There aren't enough correctional facilities available for boys like Craig. The work camps must be reserved for the greatest troublemakers.

(2) It is difficult for judges to get excited about milder forms of delinquency when they have been dealing with more serious cases involving murder, rape, and robbery. It is unfortunate that the judges are limited in this fashion. A teenager's first encounter with the law should be so painful that he would not want to make the same mistake again, but our legal apparatus is not designed to accomplish that objective.

The juvenile courts occasionally commit the opposite error of dealing too harshly with a teenager. Such had been the case with Linda, a girl I met late one rainy afternoon. I was working on a report at my desk when I suddenly realized I was not alone. I looked up to see a barefoot, rain-soaked girl in my doorway. She was a pretty adolescent of about fifteen years.

"You can call the police now," she instructed me.

"Why would I want to call the police?" I asked.

"Because I have run away from ———." (She named a nearby detention home for delinquent girls.) She said she'd spent the day hiding from the authorities.

She told me her name was Linda, and I asked her to sit down and tell me why she had run away. She started at the beginning, and I later verified the facts to be true. Her mother had been a prostitute who gave no supervision or guidance to her daughter. Linda was even allowed to remain in the bedroom while her mother entertained men. The child was eventually taken away from her mother and made a ward of the court. She was placed in a home for young victims where there was not enough love to go around. Her mother came to see her for a few years, but then ignored her completely.

Linda was so starved for love that she ran away to find her mother. She was immediately returned to the home. A year later she tried to escape again, with the same result. Linda continued to run away, each time becoming more sophisticated in evading the police. The year before my introduction to this girl, she had vanished again, this time being picked up by several boys. They lived together for two weeks and were involved in several misdemeanors and various sexual escapades during that period.

Linda was subsequently arrested and brought before the juvenile court as a delinquent. She was sentenced to the detention center for delinquent girls, surrounded by ten-foot chain link fences. The court considered her to be an unmanageable, incorrigible adolescent, yet this was wrong. Linda was a lonely, love-starved girl who had been cheated by the circumstances of life. She needed someone to care—not someone to punish. Perhaps the judge was too busy to study her background; perhaps he had no alternative facility for Linda. Either way, the needs of this wispy girl remained unmet at this critical time of her life.

Juvenile justice must be designed to be lenient with the child who has been hurt, like Linda, and to sting the child who has challenged authority, like Craig. It is sometimes difficult to recognize the difference.

SEVEN

DISCIPLINE IN LEARNING

WHEN I WAS in college, there was a malicious little rumor going around that an amazing discovery had been made about human learning. A new technique called "sleep teaching" made it possible to cram one's head full of facts while sawing the logs. I have to tell you that idea was very appealing to me. It would have fit into my program perfectly to do the big-man-on-campus thing during the day and accomplish my studying while dreaming. Also being a psychology major, I was interested in brain function and promptly set out to test the hypothesis.

I selected a class in which three tests were given during the semester with the lowest score being dropped by the professor. I studied hard on the first two exams and earned respectable grades, which permitted me to experiment with the third. When the exam was scheduled, I recorded all the necessary factual information on my tape machine, being careful not to learn the detail as I spoke into the microphone. In all, about sixty minutes of data were packed on one side of an old reel to reel tape. Then I went out and enjoyed myself the night before the test. While my brighter friends were grinding away in the library, I was shooting the breeze in a restaurant with some guys who never studied much anyway. It felt wonderful.

At bedtime that night, I plugged the tape recorder into my clock radio so that my own voice would begin speaking to my unconscious mind at two o'clock in the morning. One hour later, I was awakened by the flopping of the tape at the end of the reel, and I reset the timer for four o'clock. The tape played for another hour and awakened me again at five. The final "hearing" occurred between six and seven. So passed the restless night.

The examination was scheduled for eight o'clock and I was there, yawning and bleary-eyed. The first thing I noted was that the questions on the printed test were not even vaguely familiar to me (always a bad sign). But I was still confident that the information was stored down deep in my brain, somewhere. I turned in the test and stood waiting for a proctor to calculate my score. It only took a few minutes.

There were seventy-three people in the class, and I got the seventy-second-lowest score. I managed to beat the class dummy by one point, but he appealed to the professor over a disputed answer and was granted two additional points. I came in dead last! The only thing I got from that experiment was a terrible night's sleep and the wrath of a roommate who had lain there in the moonlight learning junk he didn't want to know.

Many years have passed since those days of my callow youth when I still thought getting something for nothing was possible. I was dead wrong. Everything worth having comes with a price. The natural progression of the universe is movement from order to chaos, not the other way around. The only way to beat that curse is to invest energy into a project or objective. If improvement is to be made in anything, *especially* in the development of mental skills and knowledge, it will be accomplished through blood, sweat, and a few tears. There's no way around it.

It is my belief that some, but by no means all, professional educators began to lose sight of that need for discipline in learning as we came through the turbulent sixties. They enthusiastically searched for an easier way to teach kids than putting them through the rigors of structured classrooms, examinations, grades, rules, and requirements. Society was changing, authority went out of style, and all the traditional values began to look suspect. Why not throw out convention and try something new? How about—an "open" classroom?

One of the most foolish ideas in the history of education was born. Let me cite excerpts from an article appearing in the *Seattle News Journal,* May 27, 1971, describing an open classroom in its full glory. Before doing so, however, let me emphasize that the excesses of the past are no longer evident in today's public schools. I'm hearing good things about the Seattle School District, for example, that experimented back in 1971 with the unstructured program described below. If those days have passed, then why do we focus on a time when schools went off the deep end? Because we can't fully understand who we are today without examining where we've been. And because we can learn from the excesses of yesterday, when authority and discipline were distrusted. And because the remnants of this free-wheeling philosophy still lurk within our permissive society and the halls of academia.

The article referred to above was called "The School Nobody Talks About," and was written by James and John Flaherty. As you read the following excerpts, imagine your own child enrolled in a program of this nature.

Picture if you can, five- to twelve-year-olds riding tricycles down the school hall, painting on the walls, as they wish and what they wish, doing what they want to and when they want, communicating openly with their teachers in three- and four-letter words, dictating school policy, teaching, and curriculum as they wish. And all of this in a public school in Seattle! Far out or impossible? No! It's happening right now in conservative old Seward Park. And the Seattle School District is picking up the tab.

The Elementary Alternative School is an experimental project of the school district. It began in November 1970 and was founded on the premise that regular elementary schools are too restrictive. It was cited that a school should teach the child to learn in a more natural environment and that his motivations to learn should arise from within himself. Also, that a child of any age is capable of making his own decisions and should be allowed to do so.

It's a kid's paradise. There is no formal curriculum, no age barriers, no classroom structure, no overall program. In fact, if the child doesn't want to learn the three Rs he doesn't have to.

On our tour, no formal classwork was being conducted. The children seemed to mill aimlessly in the three unkept classrooms. Apparently no class was in session. Then we entered the basement of the building next door . . . to consult with Mr. Bernstein (who directs the school). Bernstein . . . pointed out that this was a "fully new concept in learning, as exemplified by A. S. Neill at Springhill, a progressive school in eastern U.S." Bernstein said that four-letter words are often used to get attention or hammer home a point in his college classes, and he didn't see that it would harm any of the children in the Alternative School. "You have to communicate with children in the language they understand," he said.

Bernstein [was] queried on the fact that no formal classes were kept, no grades given, and therefore, how could a pupil finishing the sixth grade enter a regular school. "In six years," Bernstein replied, "perhaps all our schools will be like this one, and there'll be no problem."

Not many school districts experimented with programs as extreme as this one, fortunately, but the tenor of the times held authority and discipline in contempt. A depressing example of that changing philosophy was spelled out in a widely published book entitled *Summerhill,* by A. S. Neill, to whom Mr. Bernstein referred. I was required to read this ridiculous book while in graduate school. It contradicted everything I believed about children, and indeed, about life itself. But Neill's writings and work were given great credibility in educational circles, and many teachers and principals (like Bernstein) were influenced by his laissez-faire philosophy.

Summerhill in England and Springhill in the U.S. were permissive institutions that conformed to the easy-come, easy-go philosophy of their superintendent, A. S. Neill. Resident students were not required to get out of bed in the morning, attend classes, complete assignments, take baths, or even wear clothes. Rarely in human history have children been given wider latitude.

Let me list the elements of Neill's philosophy that governed his much-vaunted program and which he recommended with great passion to parents the world over:

1. Adults have no right to insist on obedience from their children. Attempts to make the youngsters obey are merely designed to satisfy the adult's desire for power. There is no excuse for imposing parental wishes on children. They must be free. The best home situation is one where parents and children are perfect equals. A child should be required to do nothing until he *chooses* to do so. Neill went to great lengths to show the students that he was one of them—not their superior.

2. Children must not be asked to work at all until they reach eighteen years of age. Parents should not even require them to help with small errands or assist with the chores. We insult them by making them do our menial tasks. Neill actually stressed the importance of withholding responsibility from the child.

3. Religion should not be taught to children. The only reason religion exists in society is to release the false guilt it has generated over sexual matters. Our concepts of God, heaven, hell, and sin are based on myths. Enlightened generations of the future will reject traditional religion.

4. Punishment of any kind is strictly forbidden, according to Neill's philosophy. A parent who spanks his child actually hates him, and his desire to hurt the child results from his own unsatisfied sex life. At Summerhill, one young student broke seventeen windows without receiving so much as a verbal reprimand.

5. Adolescents should be told sexual promiscuity is not a moral issue at all. At Summerhill, premarital intercourse was not sanctioned only because Neill feared the consequences of public indignation. He and members of his staff sometimes went nude to eliminate sexual curiosity. He predicted that the adolescents of tomorrow would find a more healthy existence through an unrestricted sex life. (What they found was a disease called AIDS and a firsthand knowledge of other sexually transmitted diseases.)

6. No pornographic books or materials should be withheld from the child. Neill indicated that he would buy filthy literature for any of his students who wished to have it. This, he felt, would cure their prurient interests—without harming the child.

7. Children should not be required to say "thank you" or "please" to their parents. Further, they should not even be encouraged to do so.

8. Rewarding a child for good behavior is a degrading and demoralizing practice. It is an unfair form of coercion.

9. Neill considered books to be insignificant in a school. Education should consist largely of work with clay, paint, tools, and various forms of drama. Learning is not without value, but it should come after play.

10. Even if a child fails in school, the matter should never be

mentioned by his parents. The child's activities are strictly his business.

11. Neill's philosophy, in brief, was as follows: Eliminate all authority; let the child grow without outside interference; don't instruct him; don't force anything on him.

If A. S. Neill had been the only lonely proponent of this assault on authority, he would not have been worthy of concern. To the contrary, he represented an extreme example of a view that became very widely accepted in educational circles. Herbert R. Kohl authored *The Open Classroom* and helped give respectability to a somewhat more sane version of the concept in public schools. Believe it or not, this was "cutting edge" stuff for more than a decade. We've now had twenty-five years to evaluate the fallout from the lessening of discipline and authority in the classroom. Look at what happened to the generation that was influenced most by it.

They concluded in the late sixties that God was dead, that immorality was the new morality, that disrespect and irreverence were proper, that unpopular laws were to be disobeyed, that violence was an acceptable vehicle for bringing change (as were their childhood tantrums), that authority was evil, that pleasure was paramount, that older people were not to be trusted, that diligence was distasteful, and that their country was unworthy of allegiance or respect. Every one of those components can be linked to the philosophy taught by A. S. Neill, but also believed by many of his contemporaries. It cost us a generation of our best and brightest, many of whom still suffer from the folly of their youth!

Not only did the misguided philosophy set up the student revolution of the late sixties. It also caused serious damage to our school system and the kids who became the victims of it. I was a young teacher at the time and was shocked to see the lack of order and control in some of my colleagues' classrooms. The confusion was evident at every grade level. Tiny first graders cowed their harassed teachers as systematically as did the boisterous high school students. In some situations, entire classes became so proficient at disrupting order that they were dreaded and feared by their future teachers. It seemed ridiculous for school officials to tolerate such disobedience when it could have been easily avoided. However, in instances when the educators did exercise firmness, many parents protested and demanded leniency for their children.

I have lived long enough, now, to have followed some of those kids into adult life. I've talked to them personally. I've read their testimonials. I've felt their anger. One of the most poignant statements I've seen was written in the "My Turn" section of *Newsweek* magazine, August 30, 1976. The author, Mara Wolynski, was a product of the philosophy I have been describing. Her story, "Confessions of a Misspent Youth," tells it all.

The idea of permissive education appealed to my mother in 1956 when she was a Bohemian and I was four. In Greenwich Village, she found a small private school whose beliefs were hers and happily enrolled me. I know it was an act of motherly love but it might have been the worst thing she ever did to me. This school—I'll call it Sand and Sea—attracted other such parents, upper-middle-class professionals who were determined not to have their children pressured the way they had been. Sand and Sea was the school without pain. And it was the kind of school that the back-to-basics people rightly fear most. At Sand and Sea, I soon became an exemplar of educational freedom—the freedom not to learn.

Sand and Sea was run by fifteen women and one man who taught "science." They were decent people, some old, some young, and all devoted to cultivating the innate creativity they were convinced we had. There was a tremendous emphasis on the arts. We weren't taught techniques, however, because any kind of organization stunted creativity.

Happiness and Hieroglyphics. We had certain hours allotted to various subjects but we were free to dismiss anything that bored us. In fact, it was school policy that we were forbidden to be bored or miserable or made to compete with one another. There were no tests and no hard times. When I was bored with math, I was excused and allowed to write short stories in the library. The way we learned history was by trying to re-create its least important elements. One year, we pounded corn, made tepees, ate buffalo meat, and learned two Indian words. That was early American history. Another year we made elaborate costumes, clay pots, and papier-mâché gods. That was Greek culture. Another year we were all maidens and knights in armor because it was time to learn about the Middle Ages. We drank our orange juice from tin-foil goblets but never found out what the Middle Ages were. They were just "The Middle Ages."

I knew that the Huns pegged their horses and drank a quart of blood before going to war, but no one ever told us who the Huns were or why we should know who they were. And one year, the year of ancient Egypt, when we were building our pyramids, I did a thirty-foot-long mural for which I laboriously copied hieroglyphics onto the sheet of brown paper. But no one ever told me what they stood for. They were just there and beautiful.

Ignorance Is Not Bliss. We spent great amounts of time being creative because we had been told by our incurably optimistic mentors that the way to be happy in life was to create. Thus, we didn't learn to read until we were in the third grade, because early reading was thought to discourage creative spontaneity. The one thing they taught us very well was to hate intellectuality and anything connected with it. Accordingly, we were forced to be creative for nine years. And yet Sand and Sea has failed to turn out a good artist. What we did do was to continually form and re-form interpersonal relationships, and that's what we thought learning was all about, and we were happy. At ten, for example, most of us were functionally illiterate, but we could tell that Raymond was "acting out" when, in the middle of what passed for English, he did the twist on top of his desk. Or that Nina was "introverted" because she always cowered in the corner.

When we finally were graduated, however, all the happy little children fell down the hill. We felt a profound sense of abandonment. So did our parents. After all that tuition money, let alone the loving freedom, their children faced high school with all the glorious prospects of the poorest slum-school kids. And so it came to be. No matter what school we went to, we were the underachievers and the culturally disadvantaged.

For some of us, real life was too much—one of my oldest friends from Sand and Sea killed himself two years ago after flunking out of the worst high school in New York at twenty. Various others have put in time in mental institutions where they were free, once again, to create during occupational therapy.

During my own high-school years, the school psychologist was baffled by my lack of substantive knowledge. He suggested to my mother that I be given a battery of psychological tests to find out why I was blocking out information. The thing was, I wasn't blocking because I had no information to block. Most of my Sand and Sea classmates were also enduring the same kinds of hardships that accompany severe handicaps. My own reading comprehension was in the lowest eighth percentile, not surprisingly. I was often asked by teachers how I had gotten into high school. However, I did manage to stumble *not* only through high school but also through college (first junior college—rejected by all four-year colleges, and then New York University), hating it all the way as I had been taught to. I am still amazed that I have a B.A., but think of it as a B.S.

The Lure of Learning. The parents of my former classmates can't figure out what went wrong. They had sent in bright, curious children and gotten back, nine years later, helpless adolescents. Some might say that those of us who freaked out would have freaked out anywhere, but when you see the same bizarre behavior pattern in succeeding graduating classes, you can draw certain terrifying conclusions.

Now I see my twelve-year-old brother (who is in a traditional school) doing college-level math and I know that he knows more about many other things besides math than I do. And I also see traditional education working in the case of my fifteen-year-old brother (who was summarily yanked from Sand and Sea, by my reformed mother, when he was eight so that he wouldn't become like me). Now, after seven years of real education, he is making impressive film documentaries for a project on the Bicentennial. A better learning experience than playing Pilgrim for four and a half months, and Indian for four and a half months, which is how I imagine they spent this year at Sand and Sea.

And now I've come to see that the real job of school is to entice the student into the web of knowledge and then, if he's not enticed, to drag him in. I wish I had been.

It was noble of the *Newsweek* publishers to print this emotional "confession" by Myra Wolynski. After all, the popular press has been a significant part of the problem, extolling the virtues of avant-garde trends in the classroom. *Newsweek* magazine, for example, devoted its May 3, 1971, cover story to the topic, "Learning Can Be Fun." On the cover was an elementary school girl making something with papier-mâché. Four years later, *Newsweek's* cover story considered "Why Johnny Can't Write." I wrote the senior editor of *Newsweek* after the second article appeared, December 8, 1975, and suggested that maybe there was a link between the two stories. Perhaps Johnny couldn't write because he spent too much time having fun in the classroom. I received no reply.

Please understand, I am a supporter of the arts in the curriculum, and I certainly want the educational process to be as exciting and as much fun as possible. But children will not learn reading, writing, and math by doing papier-mâché. And many of them will not pay the price to learn anything unless they are required to do so! Some educators have disagreed with this understanding and postulated that kids will sweat and study because they have an inner thirst for knowledge.

A former superintendent of public instruction in the state of California is quoted as saying, "To say that children have an innate love of learning is as muddle-headed as to say that children have an innate love of baseball. Some do. Some don't. Left to themselves, a large percentage of the small fry will go fishing, pick a fight, tease the girls, or watch Superman on the boob tube. Even as you and I!"

It is a valid observation. Most of the time students will not invest one more ounce of effort in their studies than is required, and that fact has frustrated teachers for hundreds of years. Our schools, therefore, must have enough structure and discipline to *require* certain behavior from their students. This is advantageous not only for academic reasons, but because one of the purposes of education is to prepare the young for later life.

To survive as an adult in this society, one needs to know how to work, how to get there on time, how to get along with others, how to stay with a task until completed, and, yes, how to submit to authority. In short, it takes a good measure of self-discipline and control to cope with the demands of modern living. Maybe one of the greatest gifts a loving teacher can contribute to an immature child, therefore, is to help him learn to sit when he feels like running, to raise his hand when he feels like talking, to be polite to his neighbor, to stand in line without smacking the kid in front, and to do language arts when he feels like doing football.

Likewise, I would hope to see our schools readopt reasonable dress codes, eliminating suggestive clothing, T-shirts with profanity or those promoting heavy metal bands, etc. Guidelines concerning good grooming and cleanliness should also be enforced.

I know! I know! These notions are so alien to us now that we can hardly imagine such a thing. But the benefits would be apparent immediately. Admittedly, hair styles and matters of momentary fashion are of no particular significance, but adherence to a standard is an important element of discipline. The military has understood that for five thousand years! If one examines the secret behind a championship football team, a magnificent orchestra, or a successful business, the principal ingredient is invariably discipline. Thus, it is a great mistake to require nothing of children—to place no demands on their behavior. We all need to adhere to some reasonable rules.

How inaccurate is the belief that self-control is maximized in an environment which places no obligations on its children. How foolish is the assumption that self-discipline is a product of self-indulgence. How unfortunate has been the systematic undermining of educational rules, engineered by a minority of parents through the legal assistance of the American Civil Liberties Union and the tired old judges to whom they have appealed. Despite the will of the majority, the antidisciplinarians have had their way. The rules governing student conduct have been cut down, and in their place have come a myriad of restrictions on educators. School prayers are illegal even if addressed to an unidentified God. The Bible can be read only as uninspired literature. Allegiance to the flag of our country cannot be required. Educators find it very difficult to punish or expel a student. Teachers are so conscious of parental militancy that they often withdraw from the defiant challenges of their students. As a result, academic discipline lies at the point of death in some of the nation's schools.

The proposal to put standards and reasonable rules back in those schools which have abandoned them (many *haven't*) may sound horribly oppressive to the ears of some Western educators or parents. But it need not be so. Class work *can* be fun and structured at the same time. Indeed, that *is* what happens in Japanese schools, and Russian schools, and English schools. And that's one reason we get whipped when our kids compete against other nations on tests of academic achievement.

You've heard about international achievement tests, of course. You know that our students do poorly when compared to young people from other countries. American high school seniors ranked fourteenth out of fifteen countries on a test of advanced algebra skills.[1] Their science scores were lower than those from students in almost every industrialized nation.[2] According to the U.S. Department of Education, only one in five eighth graders has achieved competence for his or her age level.[3] The United States ranks only 49th among 158 member nations of the U.N. in its literacy levels.[4] And SAT scores have been dropping for years.[5]

Before we leap to blame the educators for everything that has gone wrong, however, we need to take another look at the culture. The teachers and school administrators who guide our children have been among the most maligned and under-appreciated people in our society. They are an easy target for abuse. They are asked to do a terribly difficult job, and yet they are criticized almost daily for circumstances beyond their control. Some of their critics act as though educators are deliberately failing our kids. I strongly disagree. We would still be having serious difficulties in our schools if the professionals did everything right. Why? Because what goes on in the classroom cannot be separated from the problems occurring in society at large.

Educators certainly can't be blamed for the condition our kids are in when they arrive at school each day. It's not the teachers' fault that families are unraveling and that large numbers of their students have been sexually and/or physically abused, neglected, and undernourished. They can't keep kids from watching mindless television or R-rated videos until midnight, or from using illegal substances or alcohol. In essence, when the culture begins to crumble from massive social problems that defy solutions, the schools will also look bad. That's why even though I disagree with many of the trends in modern education, I sympathize with the dedicated teachers and principals out there who are trying to do the impossible on behalf of our youngsters. They are discouraged today, and they need our support.

Still, there are steps that could be taken to reverse the errors of the past and create a more conducive climate for learning. At the secondary level, we can and *must* make schools a safer place for students *and* teachers. Guns, drugs, and adolescence make a deadly cocktail. It is unbelievable what we have permitted to happen on our campuses. No wonder some kids can't think about their studies. Their *lives* are in danger! Yes, we can reduce the violence if we're committed to the task. Armed guards? Maybe. Metal detectors? If necessary. More expulsions? Probably. No-nonsense administrators? Definitely. Schools with strong leadership, like Joe Clark at Eastside High School in Paterson, New Jersey, have made dramatic progress in improving the academic environment. Above all, we must do what is required to pacify the combat zones in junior and senior high schools.

We will not solve our pervasive problems, however, with the present generation of secondary school students. Our best hope long-term is to start over with the youngsters just coming into elementary school. We can rewrite the rules with these wide-eyed kids. Let's redesign the primary grades to include a greater measure of discipline. I'm not talking merely about more difficult assignments and additional homework. I'm recommending more structure and control in the classroom.

As the first official voice of the school, the primary teacher is in a position to construct positive attitudinal foundations on which future educators can build, or conversely, she can fill her young pupils with contempt and disrespect. A child's teachers during the first six years will largely determine the nature of his attitude toward authority and the educational climate in junior and senior high school (and beyond).

As indicated earlier, I taught school for several years before completing my graduate training and learned more about how children think from that daily exposure than could ever have been assimilated from a textbook. It was also enlightening to observe the disciplinary techniques utilized by other teachers. Some of them exercised perfect classroom control with little effort, while others faced the perpetual humiliation of student defiance. I observed that there was a fundamental difference in the way they approached their classes.

The unskilled teacher would stand in front of the boys and girls and immediately seek their affection. Although most good teachers want to be liked by their classes, some are very dependent on the acceptance of the children. On the first day of school in September, the new teacher, Miss Peach, gives the class a little talk which conveys this message: "I'm so glad we had a chance to get together. This is going to be such a fun year for you; we're going to make soap, and soup, and we're going to paint a mural that will cover that entire wall. We'll take field trips and play games . . . this is going to be a great year. You're going to love me and I'm going to love you, and we'll just have a ball."

Her curriculum is well saturated with fun, fun, fun activities, which are her tokens of affection to the class. All goes well the first day of school, because the students are a little intimidated by the start of a new academic year. But about three days later, little Butch is sitting over at the left and he wants to know what everyone else is questioning too: How far can we push Miss Peach? He is anxious to make a name for himself as a brave toughie, and he might be able to build his reputation at Miss Peach's expense.

At a well-calculated moment, he challenges her with a small act of defiance. Now the last thing Miss Peach wants is conflict, because she had hoped to avoid that sort of thing this year. She does not accept Butch's challenge; she pretends not to notice that he didn't do what she told him to do. He wins this first minor confrontation. Everyone in the class saw what happened: it wasn't a big deal, but Butch survived unscathed.

The next day, Matthew has been greatly encouraged by Butch's success. Shortly after the morning flag salute, he defies her a little more openly than Butch did, and Miss Peach again ignores the challenge. From that moment forward, chaos begins to grow and intensify. Two weeks later Miss Peach is beginning to notice that things are not going very well. She's doing a lot of screaming each day and doesn't know how it got started; she certainly didn't intend to be an angry teacher. By February, life has become intolerable in her classroom; every new project she initiates is sabotaged by her lack of control. And then the thing she wanted least begins to happen: the students openly reveal their contempt for her. They call her names; they laugh at her weaknesses. If she has a physical flaw, such as a large nose or poor eyesight, they point this out to her regularly. Miss Peach cries quietly at recess time, and her head throbs and pounds late into the night. The principal comes in and witnesses the anarchy, and he says, "Miss Peach, you must get control of this class!" But Miss Peach doesn't know how to get control because she doesn't know how she lost it.

It has been estimated that 80 percent of the teachers who quit their jobs after the first year do so because of an inability to maintain discipline in their classroom. Some colleges and teacher training programs respond to this need by offering specific courses in methods of control. Others do not! Some state legislatures require formal coursework to help teachers handle this first prerequisite to teaching. Others do not, despite the fact that learning is impossible in a chaotic classroom!

Consider the contrasting approach of the skillful teacher, Mrs. Justice. She wants the love of the class too, but she is more keenly aware of her responsibility to the students. On the first day of school she delivers her inaugural address, but it is very different from the one being spoken by Miss Peach. She says, in effect, "This is going to be a good year, and I'm glad you are my students. I want you to know that each one of you is important to me. I hope you will feel free to ask your questions, and enjoy learning in this class; I will not allow anyone to laugh at you, because it hurts to be laughed at. I will never embarrass you intentionally, and I want to be your friend. Well, we have some work to do so let's get started. Would you take out your math books and turn to page 4."

Mrs. Justice just sounds like she knows what she's doing. Nevertheless, Butch's counterpart makes himself known about three days later. (There's at least one Butch in every classroom. If the troublemaker leaves during the year, a new demagogue will rise to take his place.) He challenges Mrs. Justice in a small way, but she was not caught unprepared. She's been expecting him, and she socks it to him. He loses big! Everyone in the class gets the message: It doesn't pay to attack Mrs. J. Wow! Poor Butch didn't do so well, did he?

Mrs. Justice then delivers a little speech she has been saving for this moment. She says, "There's something each of you should know. Your parents have given me the responsibility of teaching you some very important things this year, and I intend not to disappoint them. I have to get you ready for the things you will need to know next year. That's why I can't let one or two show-offs keep me from doing my job. Now, if you want to try to interfere with that purpose and disrupt what we're here to do, I can tell you it will be a miserable year for you. I have many ways to make you uncomfortable, and I will not hesitate to use them. Any questions? Good, let's get back to work."

Mrs. Justice then proceeds to follow a little formula that I favor tongue in cheek: don't smile till Thanksgiving. By November, this competent teacher has made her point. The class knows she's tougher, wiser, and braver than they are. Here comes the good news: Then they can begin to enjoy the pleasure of this foundation. She can loosen her control; the class can laugh together, talk together, and play together. But when she says, "It is time to get back to work," they do it because they know she is capable of enforcing her leadership. She does not scream. She does not hit. In fact, she can pour out the individual affection that most children need so badly. The class responds with deep love that will never be forgotten in those thirty-two lives. Mrs. Justice has harvested the greatest source of satisfaction available in the teaching profession: awareness of profound influence on human lives.

Let me add, in conclusion, that there are tens of thousands of "Mrs. Justices" out there in public and private education today, who have put their lives on the line for their students. They should be among the most highly respected members of society because of their contribution to the development of human potential. Each of us can think back to teachers like Mrs. J. in our earlier years who inspired us with a love of learning and helped make us who we are.

There are many men and women who hold this place of honor for me. I think of Mrs. McAnally, my high school English teacher. She was tough as nails, but I loved her. I thought she was going to work me to death, but she taught me the fundamentals of grammar. She also taught me to keep my big mouth shut and listen to what I was told. In college and graduate school there were other strong professors who shaped and molded my thinking: Dr. Eddie Harwood, Dr. Paul Culbertson, Dr. C. E. Meyers, and Dr. Ken Hopkins. All of these men became my good friends. I owe them an unpayable debt.

In each case, however, their contributions to my life came through the avenue of *discipline*. Formal learning is impossible without it. The boring professors who asked and received nothing from me have been forgotten. The ones I remember today are those who invested themselves in me, and wouldn't take anything less than my best in return.

Does your local school district understand this necessity for structure, respect, commitment, and discipline in the classroom? If so, why don't you call your child's teacher or the principal and express your appreciation. They could use a pat on the back. Tell them you stand ready to assist in carrying out their important mission. If your school system is not so oriented, get involved to help turn the tide. Meet with parent groups. Join the PTA. Review the textbooks. Work for the election of school board members who believe in traditional values and academic excellence. Schools function best when the time-honored principles of local control—by parents—prevails. I believe it is making a comeback!

We'll pause now for a few more questions related to these unbiased and absolutely objective thoughts, and then look at a correlated aspect of discipline in learning.

QUESTIONS & ANSWERS

Q: When Mrs. Justice told her class that she had many ways to make her rebellious students uncomfortable, I would like to know what those things are. I feel handicapped in my district. What alternatives are there, given the limitations that are now on teachers?
A: If a school district is committed to discipline and structure in the classroom, there are many things that Mrs. Justice can do when challenged. Before I suggest a couple, let me say that the strong teacher rarely has to deliver on a threat, just as a father who may be the stronger disciplinarian at home usually punishes less than the mother. There is something in the manner of a confident leader that says, "Don't push me too far." Some of it is convincing bluff. Some is in the way the first challenge is handled, as with Mrs. Justice. And some is in the teacher's ability to express love to the child. Unfortunately, these are not skills that can be easily taught or reduced to a formula in a textbook. They *can* be learned somewhat from experience and from working with a good role model.

My wife, who was a wonderful teacher and a skilled manager of children, learned a new technique from another teacher who also taught second grade in her school. This woman used an approach that was highly effective with her seven-year-olds. She spoke in very soft tones that forced them to listen very carefully in order to hear her. Somehow, she managed to infuse those thirty children with a quiet, orderly manner just by the way she led the class. Throughout the year, her room was rather like a public library where people whispered and moved quietly around the stacks. It was an impressive, God-given skill. Some have it. Some must work hard to acquire it.

Let me address the question more specifically, now, considering those situations where disruptive students are tough and determined to force a showdown. What then? Everything depends on the age of the class, of course, but let me direct my answer at, say, sixth graders. First, one must decide what is motivating the rebellious behavior. Typically, the noisy kid seeks the attention of the group. Some children had much rather be thought of as obnoxious than to be unthought of at all. For them, anonymity is unacceptable. The ideal prescription is to extinguish their attention-getting behavior and then meet their need for acceptance by less disruptive behavior. An example may help.

I worked with a giddy little sixth grader named Larry whose mouth never shut. He perpetually disrupted the tranquility of his class, setting up a constant barrage of silliness, wise remarks, and horseplay. His teacher and I constructed an isolation area in a remote corner of the schoolroom; from that spot he could see nothing but the front of the room. Thereafter, Larry was sentenced to a week in the isolation booth whenever he chose to be disruptive, which effectively eliminated the supporting reinforcement. Certainly, he could still act silly behind the screen, but he could not see the effect he was having on his peers, and they could not see him. Besides this limitation, each outburst lengthened his lonely isolation.

Larry spent one entire month in relative solitude before the extinction was finalized. When he rejoined society, his teacher immediately began to reward his cooperation. He was given the high status jobs (messengers, sergeant-at-arms, etc.) and praised for the improvement he had made. The results were remarkable.

Sometimes these kinds of in-class responses to defiance do not work. Let's admit it. *Nothing* works for every child. In those cases, I have recommended an approach called "Systematic Exclusion." The parents are asked to come for a conference and are made aware of the extreme behavioral problems that have developed. They are then informed that the only way for their child to remain in a public school is for the student, the school, and the parents to enter into a three-party contract. It must be agreed that the mother or father will come to school and pick up the child if they are called during the school day. The child is told that he can come to school each morning, but the moment he breaks one of the well-defined rules, he will be sent home. No protests will be successful. He might be ejected for pushing other pupils in the line at 9:01 a.m. Or he may make it until 1:15 or later before dismissal occurs. There are no second chances, although the child is free to return at the start of school the following morning.

Despite the common belief that children hate school, most of them hate staying home even more. Daytime television gets pretty monotonous, particularly under the hostile eye of a mom who had to interrupt her activities to come get her wayward son. Disruptive behavior is sometimes quickly extinguished under this controlled setting. It just isn't profitable for the student to challenge the system. Positive reinforcement in the form of rewards is then generously applied for the child's attempts to learn and study.

I worked with another child in a behavior modification classroom who was termed the most disruptive youngster ever seen at a major Los Angeles neuropsychiatric hospital. After four months in this controlled setting, he was able to attend a regular class in the public schools. *If you can control the variables, you can usually influence behavior.*

Finally, let me return to the first comment I made in response to your question. Everything depends on the policy of a local school district. If the board and administration are committed to discipline and structure, control *can* be achieved. The teacher is not left to do battle with a room full of energetic, giggling, blabbing troops who outnumber him or her thirty-five to one. That classroom teacher is like a policeman in a squad car. He can call for backup any time he needs it, and no one blames him if that support is required.

Every teacher needs to know the principal backs her in this way. Having been in the classroom myself, I can tell you I would not work in a district that didn't believe in discipline.

Q: You didn't mention corporal punishment as a deterrent to school misbehavior. Do you believe in spanking our students?
A: Corporal punishment is not effective at the junior and senior high school levels, and I do not recommend its application. It can be useful for elementary students, especially with amateur clowns (as opposed to hard-

core professionals). I am also opposed to abolishing spanking in schools because we have systematically eliminated the tools with which teachers have traditionally backed up their word. We're down now to a precious few. Let's not go any farther in that direction.

Q: Would you provide one more example of discipline in the classroom? Teachers need every technique they can get to reinforce their leadership these days. Describe a system that has worked.

A: Here's an idea that you might try. My wife, Shirley, taught school for five years before resigning to have a baby. Several years after Danae was born, Shirley decided to substitute a few days per week to help us support my expenses in U.S.C. graduate school. The first thing she noticed when she went back to teaching was that it was much harder to control a class as a substitute than as a full-time teacher.

"Oh boy!" shouted the kids when they saw her coming. "We'll have fun today!"

Shirley and I sat down and discussed the struggles she was having with the children (grades 2–5) she encountered each day. "Loving them isn't enough," she said. "I need some leverage to keep them in order."

We put our heads together and came up with a concept we called "Magic Chalk." This is how it worked. Shirley would get to the classroom early and draw a simple skull and crossbones on the left side of the chalk board. Underneath were the words *POISON LIST*.

Beside the scary drawing she taped a single piece of paper. Then Shirley opened the doors and invited the students to come in. She did not, however, mention the skull as she pleasantly greeted her wide-eyed students. Within minutes, someone raised a hand to ask what everyone wanted to know: "What's that picture there on the board?"

"Oh yes," said Mrs. Dobson. "I meant to tell you about the Poison List."

"First," she said, "let me describe our class rules, today." She told them they would need to raise their hands before talking; to stay in their seats until given permission to leave, and to ask for help if they needed paper or to sharpen a pencil, etc.

"Now, if you forget and break one of the rules, you will be asked to write your name on the board to the left of the poison symbol. Nothing will happen if you do. *But*, if you get your name on the board and then get two more marks by it—then—(she said with ominous overtones) . . . *then!* your name goes on the Poison List. All I have to say to you is . . . *Don't!* get your name on the Poison List." Shirley never quite told them what would happen to those unfortunate troops who made the big, bad list, but it *sounded* terrible. She hinted that it involved the principal, but she never explained how.

Then Shirley quickly walked over to her desk where a brand-new piece of chalk sat in a cup on the edge of her desk.

"Does anyone know what this is?" she asked cheerfully.

"That's a piece of chalk," several said at once.

"Not so!" replied Mrs. Dobson. "It may look like ordinary chalk, but it is much more important than that. This is *Magic Chalk*. Believe it or not, this little white stick has the ability to hear. It has tiny little ears right there on the side. It can also see you. Tiny eyes appear right there on the end." (She had drawn them in.) "The Magic Chalk is going to sit here on the edge of my desk, watching you and listening to what you say. It is looking for someone in particular. The Magic Chalk is hoping to see a boy or girl who is working very hard and being very quiet. And if it finds a student like that, it will suddenly appear on that person's desk.

"If you are the one chosen by the Magic Chalk, you do not have to ask what to do. Just pick it up, walk to the board and write your name over at the right side. Then for everyone chosen by the last class in the afternoon, you get a special treat." (Are you ready for this?) "You will be permitted to leave school three minutes early at the end of the day!"

Big deal? You bet it was. The three-minute factor was not so important in itself, but enjoying the status of being chosen by the Chalk—writing your name on the board for all the world to see—and then walking out of class when others had to stay—it was a treasure. There was also the thrill of having the chalk show up on one's desk, while others were working for the same goal.

The system worked like a charm because the kids loved it. In nearly two years of application every time Shirley was in the classroom, she usually managed to include most boys' and girls' names on the Magic Chalk list. But in all that time, she never once got a child's name on the Poison List.

I consider this approach to have had all ingredients of a well-designed system of discipline. First, it was fun for the kids. Second, it offered something to gain for doing things right and something to lose for misbehaving. Third, it required no anger on the part of the teacher. And fourth, it was easy to implement.

Use your creativity to design a program for yourself. Elementary school students are suckers for games, fantasies, and contrived symbols or status. Junior and senior high students are remarkably tougher to entice.

Q: Did any parent or administrator complain about Shirley's use of the symbol for death, or about having the children unsupervised in the hall three minutes early? And what about associating a child with poison—a deadly substance.

A: No one ever criticized the system, to my knowledge, although they certainly *could* have. *Any* system of discipline will be opposed by some people today. Whether misbehaving children are kept after school ("The day is long enough already") or made to write sentences one hundred times ("What a waste of effort—there's no learning in it"), or if really troubled kids are suspended from school ("Philosophically we're opposed to it"), or if corporal punishment is used ("It doesn't work and is cruel"), there is no method of controlling children that won't draw fire from *someone*. I think, however, that teachers should be given a little latitude for the common good. Otherwise, chaos will reign in the classroom.

Q: Myra Wolynski said in her "Confessions" article that Sand and Sea would not allow classroom organization or structure because it damaged creativity. I have heard that view expressed many times. Can it be supported?

A: We've all heard the warning that firm discipline destroys creativity, and there have been some studies to validate that assumption. However, it seems to me that creativity can flourish only when there's enough order to allow for concentrated thought. Chaos and creativity don't mix. On the other hand, an extremely oppressive atmosphere also stifles learning, which is what the research demonstrates. Everything seems to circle back to that word *balance,* which certainly has its place in the classroom.

Q: What would you do if you had an elementary school child in a chaotic classroom with a disorganized teacher?

A: I would do everything I could to reassign my child with another teacher. Some very bad habits and attitudes can develop in ten months with an incompetent role model. Home schooling or private education might be considered, if resources permitted.

Q: How do you feel about year-round schools in areas where over-crowding makes them advantageous?

A: Year-round schools are very hard on families. Siblings attending differ-ent schools may have their vacations at different times, making it impos-sible for families to take trips together. It is also more difficult to coordinate children's time off with parent's schedules. In short, year-round schools represent just one more hardship on families seeking to do fun and recre-ational things together each year.

Q: You indicated the Alternative School in Seattle had no formal cur-riculum, no grades, no overall program, etc. I assume, by contrast, that you favor a curriculum that emphasizes the memorization of spe-cific facts, which I consider to be a very low level of learning. We need to teach concepts to our kids and help them learn how to think—not just fill their heads with a bunch of details.

A: I agree that we want to teach concepts to students, but that does not occur in a vacuum. For example, we would like them to understand the concept of the solar system and how the planets are positioned in rotation around the sun. How is that done? One way is for them to learn the dis-tances between the heavenly bodies, i.e., the sun is 93 million miles from earth, but the moon is only 240,000. The concept of relative positions is then understood from the factual information. What I'm saying is that an understanding of the right factual information can and should lead to conceptual learning.

Q: But again, you're putting too much emphasis on the memorization process, which is a low academic goal.

A: The human brain is capable of storing some two billion bits of informa-tion in the course of a lifetime. There are many avenues through which that programming can occur, and memorization is one of them. Let me put it this way. If you ever have to go under a surgeon's knife, you'd better hope that physician has memorized—I said memorized—every muscle, every bone, every blood vessel, and every Boy Scout knot in the book. Your life will depend on his accessibility to factual information during the operation. Obviously, I strongly oppose the perspective held in some academic circles that says, "There's nothing we know for certain so why learn anything?" Those who feel that way have no business teaching. They are salesmen with nothing to sell!

Q: Like you, I have observed that elementary and junior high school students—even high schoolers—tend to admire the more strict teachers. Why is this true?
A: Teachers who maintain order are often the most respected members of the faculty, provided they aren't mean and grouchy. One who can control a class without being oppressive is almost always loved by her students. That is true because there is safety in order. When a class is out of control, particularly at the elementary school level, the children are afraid of each other. If the teacher can't make the class behave, how can she prevent a bully from doing his thing? How can she keep the students from laughing at one of its less able members? Children are not very fair and reasonable with each other, and they feel good about having a strong teacher who is.

Second, children love justice. When someone has violated a rule, they want immediate retribution. They admire the teacher who can enforce an equitable legal system, and they find great comfort in reasonable social expectations. By contrast, the teacher who does not control her class inevitably allows crime to pay, violating something basic in the value system of children.

Third, children admire strict teachers because chaos is nerve-wracking. Screaming and hitting and wiggling are fun for about ten minutes; then the confusion begins to get tiresome and irritating.

I have smiled in amusement many times as second- and third-grade children astutely evaluated the relative disciplinary skills of their teachers. They know how a class should be conducted. I only wish all of their teachers were equally aware of this important attribute.

Q: Can you give us a guideline for how much work children should be given to do?
A: There should be a healthy balance between work and play. Many farm

children of the past had daily chores that made life pretty difficult. Early in the morning and again after school they would feed the pigs, gather the eggs, milk the cows, and bring in the wood. Little time was reserved for fun, and childhood became a pretty drab experience. That was an extreme position, and I certainly don't favor its return.

However, contrast that level of responsibility with its opposite, recommended by Neill, where we shouldn't even ask our children to water the lawn or let out the cat. According to this recommendation, Junior should be allowed to lie on his overfed stomach watching six or eight hours of worthless television while his schoolwork gathers dust in the corner. Both extremes, as usual, are harmful to the child. The logical middle ground can be found by giving the child an exposure to responsibility and work, but preserving time for his play and fun. The amount of time devoted to each activity should vary with the age of the child, gradually requiring more work as he grows older.

A FINAL THOUGHT

As we conclude this discussion of discipline in learning, I would like to return to an interview published in the first edition of *Dare to Discipline*. It was originally printed in *U.S. News & World Report,* April, 1965, and featured world renowned criminologists, Professor and Mrs. Sheldon Glueck.[6] The Gluecks are most noted for their longitudinal study of juvenile delinquency and its causes. Note how prophetic their words were as they described the teens of their day and where society appeared to be moving.

U.S. News: What seems to be causing delinquency to grow so fast nowadays?

Glueck: There are many causes for this. For the most part, however, what we are seeing now is a process that has been going on since the second World War.

First, you have more and more mothers going to work. Many have left their children more or less unattended, at home or on the streets. This has deprived children of the constant guidance and sense of security they need from their mothers in their early years.

Along with that change, parental attitudes toward disciplining their young have changed quite rapidly. In the home and outside, the trend has been steadily toward more permissiveness—that is, placing fewer restraints and limits on behavior.

U.S. News: *How has that philosophy worked out in practice?*

Glueck: Not very well, it seems, Life requires a certain amount of discipline. You need it in the classroom, you need it in the home, you need it in society at large. After all, the Ten Commandments impose a discipline. *Unless general restraints are built into the character of children, you can arrive eventually at social chaos.*

U.S. News: *Are you saying that moral values are crumbling? (Author's note: This question preceded the so-called "new morality" by several years.)*

Glueck: This is part of the picture. Not only parents, but others are uncertain in many cases as to what is morally right or wrong, and that makes discipline harder to enforce.

For instance, children today are being exposed to all kinds of moving pictures and books. It is difficult to decide what moving pictures and books should be censored.

In a broad sense, actually, you might feel that censorship in general is undesirable. Yet you also know that restraint must be imposed at some point—especially where children are involved. But in trying to decide at what point restraint should be imposed, it very often turns out that no restraint at all results. And it is this lack of restraint in the home and on the outside that is back of so much of our delinquency.

U.S. News: *Do juvenile courts tend to be too soft on youngsters?*

Glueck: Sometimes, yes, but more often there is inconsistency because judges have wide discretion; and they may rely on intuition and hunches rather than the use of predictive data which their staff could gather for them on each case.

U.S. News: *Then is stern punishment a deterrent to further crime?*

Glueck: Certainty of punishment is definitely a deterrent. After all, fear is a primary emotion in man. It plays an important part in his training. We have gone rather far in the other direction, in letting the child feel that he isn't going to be punished for his misdeeds.

   Of course, it is wrong to rely exclusively on fear of punishment, but it is equally wrong to do away with this deterrent.

U.S. News: *Can schools help in keeping children from developing into troublemakers?*

Glueck: They certainly can. As we have said, there are children whose energies are not suited to long periods of sitting still and whose adventuresomeness has to be satisfied in some acceptable way.

   We also think that one of the basic needs of schools, along with other elements of society, is a general recognition that rules must be observed— that, without rules, you drift into chaos and tyranny and into taking the law into your own hands. You see it not only among delinquents, but among young college students, in their demand for more and more freedom from restraints and from higher authority.

U.S. News: *Do you look for crime and delinquency to grow?*

Glueck: *Probably. Our own feeling is that, unless much is done to check the vicious cycles involved, we are in for a period of violence beyond anything we have yet seen.*

All you have to do is to read about the murders and assaults taking place in New York subways. Only a few years ago nobody thought of public conveyances as being unsafe. *We foresee no letup in this trend.* A delinquent child often grows up to produce delinquent children—not as a matter of heredity, but of his own unresolved conflicts which make him an ineffective parent.

Professor and Mrs. Glueck clearly anticipated the anarchy that is now rumbling through the midsection of democracy. Even they, however, might not have expected drive-by shootings, random killings, and murders over minor arguments in traffic. Isn't it time for us to address the root causes which the Gluecks recognized over four decades ago?

EIGHT

THE BARRIERS TO LEARNING, PART 1

W E HAVE BEEN discussing the importance of discipline in the parent-child relationship, particularly as concerned with obedience, respect, and responsibility. We have also examined the importance of authority in the classroom. Now it is appropriate to examine another aspect of discipline: that dealing with the training of a child's mental faculties and moral character.

The primary concern will be with the millions of children who do not succeed in school—the "academic casualties" who cannot, or will not, carry the intellectual responsibility expected of them. Their parents cry and beg and threaten; their teachers push and shove and warn. Nevertheless, they sit year after year in passive resistance to the adult coercion. Who are these youngsters for whom academic discipline seems so difficult? Are they lazy? Are they unintelligent? Do they care? Are our teaching methods ineffective? How can we help them avoid the sting of failure in these early experiences?

During my years of service as a school psychologist, I was impressed by the similarities in the students who were referred to me with learning problems. Although each child was an individual with unique characteristics, the majority of failing youngsters shared certain kinds of problems. There were several sets of circumstances which repeatedly interfered with disciplined learning in the classroom. In this chapter and the next, I will describe the three major categories of children who do poorly in school. Parents should look closely for the footprints of their own children.

THE LATE BLOOMER
Donald is five years old and will soon go to kindergarten. He is an immature little fellow who is still his mama's baby in many ways. Compared to

his friends, Donald's language is childish and he lacks physical coordination. He cries three or four times a day, and other children take advantage
of his innocence. A developmental psychologist or a pediatrician would
verify that Donald is neither physically ill nor mentally retarded; he is
merely progressing on a slower physiological timetable than most children
his age.

Nevertheless, Donald's fifth birthday has arrived, and everyone knows
that five-year-olds go to kindergarten. He is looking forward to school, but
deep inside he is rather tense about this new challenge. He knows his
mother is anxious for him to do well in school, although he doesn't really
know why. His father has told him he will be a "failure" if he doesn't get a
good education.

He's not certain what a failure is, but he sure doesn't want to be one.
Mom and Dad are expecting something outstanding from him and he
hopes he won't disappoint them. His sister Pamela is in the second grade
now; she is doing well. She can read and print her letters and she knows
the names of every day in the week. Donald hopes he will learn those
things too.

Kindergarten proves to be tranquil for Donald. He rides the tricycle
and pulls the wagon and plays with the toy clock. He prefers to play alone
for long periods of time, provided his teacher, Miss Moss, is nearby. It
is clear to Miss Moss that Donald is immature and unready for the first
grade, and she talks to his parents about the possibility of delaying him
for a year.

"Flunk kindergarten?!" says his father. "How can the kid flunk kindergarten? How can anybody flunk kindergarten?"

Miss Moss tries to explain that Donald has not failed kindergarten; he
merely needs another year to develop before entering the first grade. The
suggestion sends his father into a glandular upheaval.

"The kid is six years old; he should be learning to read and write.
What good is it doing him to drag around that dumb wagon and ride on
a stupid tricycle? Get the kid in the first grade!"

Miss Moss and her principal reluctantly comply. The following
September Donald clutches his Mickey Mouse lunch pail and walks on
wobbly legs to the first grade. From day one he has academic trouble, and
reading seems to be his biggest source of difficulty. His new teacher, Miss
Fudge, introduces the alphabet to her class, and Donald realizes that most

of his friends have already learned it. He has a little catching up to do. But too quickly Miss Fudge begins teaching something new. She wants the class to learn the sounds each letter represents, and soon he is even further behind.

Before long, the class begins to read stories about interesting things. Some children can zing right along, but Donald is still working on the alphabet. Miss Fudge divides the class into three reading groups according to their initial skill. She wants to conceal the fact that one group is doing more poorly than the others, so she gives them the camouflage names of "Lions," "Tigers," and "Giraffes." Miss Fudge's motive is noble, but she fools no one. It takes students about two minutes to realize that the Giraffes are all stupid! Donald begins to worry about his lack of progress, and the gnawing thought looms that there may be something drastically wrong with him.

During the first parent-teacher conference in October, Miss Fudge tells Donald's parents about his problems in school. She describes his immaturity and his inability to concentrate or sit still in the classroom. He's out of his seat most of the day.

"Nonsense," says his father. "What the kid needs is a little drill." He insists that Donald bring home his books, allowing father and son to sit down for an extended academic exercise. But everything Donald does irritates his father. His childish mind wanders and he forgets the things he was told five minutes before. As his father's tension mounts, Donald's productivity descends. At one point, Donald's father crashes his hand down on the table and bellows, "Would you just pay attention and quit being so STUPID!" The child will never forget that knifing assessment.

Whereas Donald struggled vainly to learn during his early days in school, by November he has become disinterested and unmotivated. He looks out the window. He draws and doodles with his pencil. He whispers and plays. Since he can't read, he can neither spell, write, or do his social studies. He is uninvolved and bored, not knowing what is going on most of the time. He feels weird and inadequate.

"Please stand, Donald, and read the next paragraph," says his teacher. He stands and shifts his weight from foot to foot as he struggles to identify the first word. The girls snicker and he hears one of the boys say, "What a dummy!" The problem began as a developmental lag, but has now become an emotional time bomb and a growing hatred for school.

The tragedy is that Donald need not have suffered the humiliation of academic failure. One more year of growing and maturing would have prepared him to cope with the educational responsibilities which are now destroying him. A child's age is the *worst* possible criterion on which to determine the beginning of his school career. Six-year-old children vary tremendously in their degree of maturity. Some are precocious and wise, while others are mere babies like Donald. Furthermore, the development of boys tends to be about six months behind girls at this age. As can be seen, a slow-maturing boy who turns six right before school starts is miles behind most of his peers. This immaturity has profound social and intellectual implications.

One reason an immature child does poorly in school may be related to the absence of an organic substance called myelin. At birth, the nervous system of a body is not insulated. An infant is unable to reach out and grasp an object because the electrical command or impulse is lost on its journey from the brain to the hand. Gradually, a whitish substance (myelin) begins to coat the nerve fibers, allowing controlled muscular action to occur.

Myelinization proceeds from the head downward (cephalocaudal) and from the center of the body outward (proximodistal). In other words, a child can control the movement of his head and neck before the rest of his body. Control of the shoulder precedes the elbow, which precedes the wrist, which precedes the large muscles in the hands, which precedes small muscle coordination of the fingers.

Elementary school children are taught block letter printing before they learn cursive writing because of the delayed development of minute finger control. This development pattern is critically important to the late bloomer. Since the visual apparatus in humans is usually among the last neural mechanisms to be myelinated, the immature child may not have undergone this necessary development process by the time he is six.

A child who is extremely immature and uncoordinated may be neurologically unprepared for the intellectual tasks of reading and writing. Reading, particularly, is a highly complex neurological process. The visual stimulus must be relayed to the brain without distortion where it should be interpreted and retained in the memory. Not all six-year-olds are equipped to perform this task. Unfortunately, however, our culture permits few exceptions or deviations from the established timetable. A six-year-old must learn to read or else face the emotional consequences of failure.

The question may be asked, "Why doesn't the late bloomer catch up with his class when he matures in subsequent years?" If the problem were simply a physical phenomenon, the slow maturing child could be expected to gain on his early developing friends. However, emotional factors are invariably tangled in this difficulty.

The self-image is amazingly simple to damage but exceedingly difficult to reconstruct. Once a child begins to think he's stupid, incapable, ignorant, or foolish, the concept is not easily eliminated. If he falters in the early academic setting, he is squeezed by the viselike demands at school and expectations at home. The emotional pressure is often unresolvable. There is no rationalization he can give parents and teachers to explain his perceived failure. Nor is there a balm they can offer which will help soothe his damaged psyche. His self-concept is often wounded by this tension, and his personality will probably reflect the experience well into adult life.

The solution for late bloomers is relatively simple: instead of scheduling the child's entrance into the first grade according to his age, the optimal timetable should be determined by neurological, psychological, social, and pediatric variables. A simple screening test could identify extreme cases, such as Donald. The majority of children could begin school at six, although more flexibility would be reserved for the exceptional child.

Regardless of the school's adoption or rejection of this recommendation, I would suggest that parents of an immature kindergarten youngster have him examined for educational readiness by a child development specialist (child psychologist, pediatrician, neurologist, etc.). This procedure should be a "must" for slow-maturing boys for whom birthdays occur late in the academic year. The consequences of doing this cannot be underestimated. This simple procedure may spare your child many years of grief.

If it is determined that the child is a late bloomer, he can either repeat kindergarten or stay at home for another year or two. Despite common wisdom on this issue, kids who are home-schooled in the first few years of elementary school do not tend to be maladjusted or handicapped when they reenter formal education. Nor are they "unsocialized." If parents are willing to bring the at-home child into their world, talking to them and allowing them to go to the store, take field trips, help cook and work in the garage with dad, they do not need hour upon hour of formal desk work.[1] Research on this issue has been specific and most encouraging.[2]

What happens, then, when the time for re-entry occurs? In most cases, those home-schooled kids catch up and pass their classmates in a matter of months. They're also inclined to be leaders in years to come[3] because they haven't been bludgeoned in the early days of vulnerability. In other words, they are less peer-dependent.[4]

If that seems strange, remember that Jesus didn't go to school until He was twelve years old. That was the custom in Israel in those days. Formal classwork for the immature child, and indeed, even for the go-getter, is simply not necessary at the very young ages. I know this fact contradicts what the National Education Association would like us to believe; they recommend mandatory education for all four year olds. It is also unpopular among parents who have two-career families and need some safe, wholesome place for their children. But that effort to take children out of the home at an earlier age simply will not conform to the realities of child development.

This is why the home-schooling movement is growing by leaps and bounds. Our organization, Focus on the Family, polled a random sample of four thousand constituents to see what trends and opinions were evident among them. To our surprise, 13 percent were involved in home schooling. Though challenging for mothers (and fathers), this approach to the education of the next generation has been highly successful. It is especially appropriate for kids like Donald, who need some time to grow up before formal classwork begins.

At the time I first authored *Dare to Discipline,* I had never heard of home schooling. I had been taught in graduate school to believe in the value of earlier and earlier formal classroom experience. Now, I am an enthusiastic supporter of keeping kids with their parents for a longer time. Dr. Raymond Moore, author of *School Can Wait* and an early leader of the home-schooling movement, had a great influence on me in the early eighties. Admittedly, home schooling is not for everyone, but it has been highly successful for most who have tried it. I will say this: If Shirley and I had to do it over, we would have home-schooled our two children, at least for the first few years!

Whether you home-school your little "Donald" or simply allow him to repeat kindergarten, I strongly recommend that he be spared academic pressure until he can get his spindly legs stabilized beneath his body.

THE SLOW LEARNER

The "slow learner" is another youngster likely to have great trouble with academic discipline, resulting from his inability to learn as quickly as his peers. Before going further, I must ask the reader to endure a brief technical explanation at this point. To understand slow learners, we must refer to the normal distribution of intelligence quotients representing the general population.

The lightly shaded area in the center of the distribution represents the "normal range" of IQ scores, which fall between 90 and 110. The precise IQ points for each category will vary according to the standard

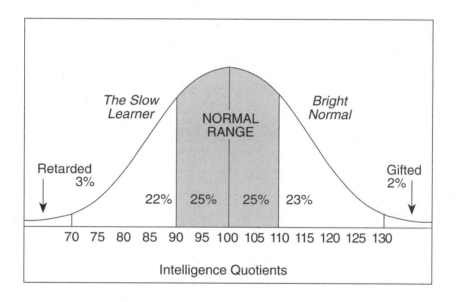

deviation of the intelligence test utilized. Fifty percent of all individuals score within this middle area on most tests of intelligence. It is interesting to note that virtually everyone thinks his IQ is above 100. If we asked ten thousand people to estimate their expected level of ability, very few would guess an IQ score below average. The fact is, half the total population would actually score below 100.

Likewise, parents will often ascribe fantastic intelligence quotients to their children. A familiar but comical remark is "Herbert has an IQ of 214, according to a test he took in the Sunday Supplement." *Very* few individuals score above 150, and Herbert is not likely to be one of them.

The "gifted" individuals are represented at the far right of the distribution. Approximately 2 percent of all children and adults have this exceptionally bright level of ability. By contrast, nearly 3 percent of the population appears at the other end of the intellectual continuum, and are referred to as "retarded." Most states provide special education for the children with intellectual deficits, and some offer an enriched program to the gifted.

As indicated, the purpose of presenting these facts is to highlight the problems of the slow learners—those children having IQs between 70 and 90. These students comprise nearly one-fourth of the children in a typical school. In many ways, they are the saddest youngsters with whom child development specialists deal. Of particular concern are the individuals with IQs in the lower range of the slow learner classification (70 to 80) who are virtually destined to have difficulties in school. No special education is available for them, *although they are not appreciably different from the borderline retarded students.*

A retarded child with an IQ of 70 would probably qualify for highly specialized and expensive educational programs, including a smaller class, specially trained teacher, audio-visual aids, and a "no fail" policy. By contrast, a slow learning child with an IQ of 80 would usually receive no such advantages. He must compete in regular classes against the full range of more capable students. Such competition implies winners and losers, and it is the slow learner who invariably "loses."

Let's consider the plight of the unintelligent young student in the classroom. Here is the child who "would if he could—but can't." He rarely, if ever, gets the thrill of earning a "hundred" on his spelling test. He is the last child chosen in any academic game or contest. He often has the *least* sympathy from his teachers. He is no more successful in social activities than academic pursuits, and the other children reject him openly.

Like the late bloomer, the slow learner gradually develops a crushing image of failure that distorts his self-concept and damages his ego. This was exemplified by a conversation overheard by a colleague of mine between two intellectually handicapped students. Discussing their prospects with girls, one of them said, "I do okay until they find out I'm a retard." Obviously, this child was keenly aware of his inadequacy.

There is no better way to assassinate self-confidence in our children than to place 25 percent of them in a situation where excellence is impossible to achieve, where inadequacy is the daily routine, and where inferiority is a living reality. It is not surprising that such a child is often a mischievous tormentor in the third grade, a bully in the sixth grade, a loudmouth in junior high, and a drop-out/delinquent in high school.

The slow learner is unlike the late bloomer in one major respect: time will not resolve his deficiency. He will not do better next year. In fact, he tends to get further behind as he grows older. Traditionally, the schools have retained the incapable child in the same grade level for an extra year or two, which proves to be most unworkable, unscientific, and unfortunate.

Retention accomplishes absolutely nothing but to ice the cake of failure. The accumulated scientific evidence on this issue is indisputable. Many follow-up studies have shown that children who were retained continued to fail the following year, and their academic problems were then compounded by emotional difficulties. The retained child is held back with the "little kids" while his contemporaries move on to a new grade level and a new teacher. He feels overgrown, foolish, and dumb. His relatives all know that he failed. Throughout his school life, people will ask revealing questions, such as "How come you're thirteen and only in the fifth grade?" He will reply, "Aw, I flunked third grade." It is a painful confession.

A further problem can be anticipated; the child who is retained once or twice will probably undergo sexual development (puberty) before his classmates, which can produce many unfortunate circumstances. When the slow learner finally reaches high school a year or more late, he usually finds even less tolerance for his difficulty.

One mature tenth grader was once referred to me because he announced he was dropping out of school. I asked why he was quitting, and he said, "I've been miserable since first grade. I've felt embarrassed and stupid every year. I've had to stand up and read, but I can't even understand a second grade book. You people have had your last laugh at me. I'm getting out." I told him I didn't blame him for the way he felt; his suffering was our responsibility.

Surprisingly, some unsuccessful students are still willing to struggle even after years of failure. As a psychologist, I was always encouraged when the toughest, roughest boys in high school got excited about a remedial reading program. They wanted desperately to learn this skill, but were convinced they were too dumb. This all changed when the remedial reading teacher showed them they *could* learn.

One brawny lad named Jeff was awed by his own progress. He looked up at his teacher with tears in his eyes, and said, "When I was in second grade I brought home a report card with an F in reading. I was sitting on the couch while my old man read it. He came over with a strap and beat the ——— out of me. Since then, this is the first time I've done anything right in school."

I was once asked to evaluate a high school boy named Willie who failed history three times. He was unable to graduate because he couldn't earn a D or better in this required course. I tested Willie and learned that he was a slow learner. His teacher, who had previously required Willie to compete equally with other students, was surprised by the results. His lack of awareness of the child's limited ability seemed unfair to me, so I devised the following form letter to notify teachers of others like Willie:

Strictly Confidential

Name of Student _____

The above-named student apparently has some limitations which may be important to understanding his academic perfor-mance and class-room behavior. Although he does not qualify for Special Education, according to a strict interpretation of the Education Code, his intel-lectual ability seemingly falls into a "borderline" category. There is no legal basis for his removal from the regular classroom, but he should not be expected to compete with more capable students.

If he is required to meet an arbitrary percentage of correct examination answers, as are students with average capabilities, he must be expected to fail consistently. On the other hand, he should not be allowed to coast along without using his potential.

It seems appropriate that his grade be based on his efforts and progress, based on his individual learning capacity. To fail him in spite of his efforts is to deny him the opportunity to graduate.

I would be glad to discuss the matter with you if further infor-mation is desired.

NOTE: Please destroy this note to minimize potential embarrass-ment to the student.

Some teachers had never considered giving a slow learner an easier academic target until receiving this note. A few did not consider it *after* reading this note, either.

When I think of slow learners, the case of fourteen-year-old Robert sticks in my mind. He was five inches taller and twenty pounds heavier than the next largest student in his sixth grade class. Though retained in the second and fourth grades, Robert still had not learned to read or write. His teacher tried to motivate him every way she knew how, but Robert withstood all challenges and gimmicks. He simply quit trying.

When his teacher threatened to fail him a third time, Robert responded with horror. He could visualize himself as a seventy-three-year-old student, still sitting in a sixth grade class. That nightmarish thought motivated him to do his best in class, but his deficient academic skills prevented much progress. Robert remained in a state of anxiety until the final report cards were issued. On that morning, he was literally white around the mouth and shaking with tension until he read the pronouncement, "Promoted to the Seventh Grade."

Robert's teacher had not meant to be unkind earlier; he only wanted to obtain the best effort from this lad. Nevertheless, it was a mistake to threaten him with social disaster. A slow learner or retarded individual has the *same* emotional needs for adequacy and acceptance as a gifted or bright child, and emotional stability should not be sacrificed on the altar of education.

Despite the effects of failing a slow learner, I believe some children *do* profit from a second year in the same grade level. The best guideline for retention is this: hold back the child for whom something will be *different* next year. For example, a child who was sick for seven months in one academic year might profit from another run-through when he is well. And again, the late bloomer should be held back in kindergarten (or the first grade at the latest) to place him with youngsters of comparable development.

For the slow learner, however, nothing will be changed. If he was failing fourth grade in June, he will continue failing fourth grade in September. That's because the curricular content of each grade level is similar to the year before and the year after. The same concepts are taught year after year; the students in each grade are taken a little farther, but much of the time is spent in review.

For example, addition and subtraction are taught in the primary years, but considerable work is done on these tasks in sixth grade, too. Nouns and verbs are taught repeatedly for several years. The overlap in curricular material from grade to grade is represented more accurately in Figure A, below, than by Figure B.

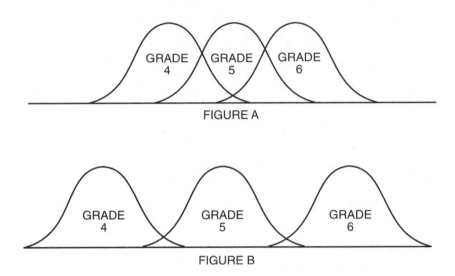

FIGURE A

FIGURE B

Thus, the most unjustifiable reason for retention is to expose the slow learner to another year with easier concepts. He will not do better the second time around! Nor is there much magic in summer school. Some parents hope that a six-week program in July and August will accomplish what was impossible in the ten months between September and June. They are often disappointed.

Since retention and summer school do not solve the problem of the slow learner, we are faced with the obvious question: What can be done for these children? Listed below are the steps that could tip the scales in favor of this vast number of youngsters:

1. *Teach them to read, even if a one-to-one teacher-student ratio is required (and it probably will be).* Nearly every child can learn to read, but *many* children have difficulty if taught only in large groups. Their minds wander and they do not ask questions as readily. It would be expensive for the school to support additional remedial reading teachers, but no expenditure would be more helpful. Special techniques, teaching machines, and individual reinforcement can be successful in teaching this most basic skill to children

who are least likely to learn without individual attention. This assistance should *not* be delayed until the fourth or fifth grades or in junior high. By then the slow learner has already endured the indignities of failure.

Many school districts have implemented creative programs to focus on reading problems. One such program, the "ungraded primary," eliminates distinctions between students in the first three grades. Instead of grouping children by age, they are combined according to reading skill. Good readers in the first, second, and third grades may occupy the same classes. Poor readers are also grouped together. This procedure takes the sting out of retention and allows slow learners to benefit from homogeneous grouping.

Another popular system is called the "split reading" program. In this method, the better half of readers in a class arrive at school thirty minutes early for specialized instructions. The slower half remains a half an hour later each day for the same purpose.

There are many such programs to teach reading more effectively. Parents who are concerned about their child's basic academic skills may wish to seek tutorial assistance to supplement these school programs.

2. *The slow learner should be shielded from the devastation of failure.* Scholastic goals which the slow learner can't attain should be de-emphasized. He should be required to do only things that are within his reach. He should be praised when he does his best, even if his work isn't on par with his peers. The slow learner is entitled to self-acceptance too, even in this fast-paced technological world.

3. *Remember that success breeds success.* The best motivation for a slow learner is to know he is succeeding. If adults in his life show confidence in him, he will more likely have confidence in himself. In fact, most humans share this characteristic. We tend to act the way we think other people "see" us.

I learned this when I joined the National Guard at twenty-two years of age. I had recently graduated from college and had already been accepted into graduate school. Thus, I enlisted for extended reserve duty in the military rather than serve two years active duty. I was immediately packed on a bus for Fort Ord, California, to undergo a six-month basic training and Army administrative course. Contrary to the recruiting posters, this exciting new career opportunity was not a matter of personal choice; it was selected for me. Nevertheless, I spent the next half year learning the fascinating world of military forms, typing, and filing. It bored me nearly out of my mind.

One hundred and eighty-three days later I returned to the local National Guard unit with this newly acquired knowledge available for usage. Surprisingly, I was not welcomed back with much enthusiasm. That's because I was a private and everyone knows privates are stupid. I was outranked by practically the whole world—so it stood to reason there was thickness between my ears. Everybody from the privates-first-class to the colonel anticipated ignorant behavior from me. To my amazement, their expectation proved accurate.

My first assignment after those months of office training was to type a simple letter in two copies. After twenty-five minutes of concentrated effort, I realized the carbon paper, used in those days, was upside down. Reverse lettering was smudged all over the back of the main copy, which did not ingratiate me with the sergeant. Similar complex procedures, like remembering regulations and procedures, were strangely difficult to perform. Looking back, it is clear that *my performance was consistent with my image.*

I then went into a tough graduate school program and earned a Ph.D. with a 3.91 grade average. Self-image was the difference.

Likewise, many children who fail in school are merely doing what they think others expect of them. Our reputation with our peers is a very influential force in our lives. This is especially true of slow learners, who represent one-quarter of all students. Perhaps your child is one of them.

In the next chapter, we'll follow the footprints of the third type of child for whom academic discipline seems so difficult. Stay tuned.

QUESTIONS & ANSWERS

Q: If age is such a poor factor to use in determining the start of the first grade, why is it applied so universally in our country?
A: Because it is so convenient. Parents can plan for the definite beginning of school when their child turns six. School officials can survey their districts and know how many first-graders they will have the following year.

If an eight-year-old moves into the district in October, the administrator knows the child belongs in second grade, and so on. The use of chronological age as a criterion for school entrance is great for everybody—except the late bloomer.

Q: What causes a child to be a slow learner?
A: There are many hereditary, environmental, and physical factors which contribute to one's intellect, and it is difficult to isolate the particular influences. Accumulating evidence seems to indicate that some slow learning and even borderline retardation are caused by a lack of intellectual stimulation in the child's very early years. There appears to be a critical period during the first three to four years when the potential for intellectual growth must be seized. There are enzyme systems in the brain that must be activated during this brief window. If the opportunity is missed, the child may never reach his capacity.

Children who grow up in deprived circumstances are more likely to be slow learners. They may not have heard adult language regularly. They have not been provided with interesting books and puzzles to occupy their sensory apparatus. They have not been taken to the zoo, the airport, or other exciting places. They have not received daily training and guidance from adults. This lack of stimulation may inhibit the brain from developing properly.

The effect of early stimulation on living brains has been studied in several fascinating animal experiments. In one, researchers divided littermate rats into two identical groups. The first group was given maximum stimulation during the first few months of life. These rats were kept in well-lighted cages, surrounded by interesting paddle wheels and other toys. They were handled regularly and allowed to explore outside their cages. They were subjected to learning experiences and then rewarded for remembering. The second group lived the opposite kind of existence. These rats crouched in dimly lit, drab, uninteresting cages. They were not handled or stimulated in any way, and were not permitted outside their cages. Both groups were fed identical food.

At 105 days of age, all the rats were sacrificed to permit examination of their neurological apparatus. The researchers were surprised to find that the high stimulation rats had brains that differed in several important ways: (1) the cortex (the thinking part of the brain) was thicker and wider;

(2) the blood supply was much more abundant; (3) the enzymes necessary for learning were more sophisticated. The researchers concluded that high stimulation experienced during the first group's early lives had resulted in more advanced and complex brains.

It is always risky to apply conclusions from animal research directly to humans, but the same kinds of changes probably occur in the brains of highly stimulated children. If parents want their children to be capable, they should begin by talking to them at length while they are still babies. Interesting mobiles and winking-blinking toys should be arranged around the crib. From then on through the toddler years, learning activities should be programmed regularly.

Of course, parents must understand the difference between stimulation and pressure. Providing books for a three-year-old is stimulating. Ridiculing and threatening him because he can't read them is pressuring. Imposing unreachable expectations can have a damaging effect on children.

If early stimulation is as important as it now appears, then the lack thereof may be a leading cause of slow learning and even mild retardation. It is imperative that parents take the time and invest their resources in their children. The necessity for providing rich, edifying experiences for young children has never been so obvious as it is today.

Q: I've read that it's possible to teach four-year-olds to read. Should I be working on this with my child?
A: If a youngster is particularly sharp and can learn to read without feeling undue adult pressure, it might be advantageous to teach him this skill. But that's a much bigger "if" than most people realize. Few parents can work with their own children without showing frustration over natural failures. It's like teaching your wife to drive: risky at best, disastrous at worst.

Besides this limitation, learning should be programmed at the age when it is most needed. Why invest unending effort in teaching a child to read when he has not yet learned to cross the street, tie his shoes, count to ten, or answer the telephone? It seems foolish to get panicky over pre-school reading, as such.

The best policy is to provide your children with many interesting books and materials, read to them and answer their questions. Then let nature take its unobstructed course.

Q: Should school children be required to wear clothes which they dislike?

A: Generally not. Children are very concerned about the threat of being laughed at by their friends and will sometimes go to great lengths to avoid that possibility. Conformity is fueled by the fear of ridicule. Teens, particularly, seem to feel, "The group can't laugh at me if I am identical to them." From this perspective, it's unwise to make a child endure unnecessary social humiliation. Children should be allowed to select their own clothes, within certain limits of the budget and good taste.

Q: Do slow learners and mentally retarded children have the same needs for esteem that others have?

A: As I have explained elsewhere, I sometimes wish they didn't, but their needs are no different. During a portion of my early psychology training at Lanternman State Hospital in Pomona, California, I was impressed by the vast need for love shown by some of the most retarded patients. There were times when I would step into the door of a children's ward and forty or more severely retarded youngsters would rush toward me screaming, "Daddy! Daddy! Daddy!" They would push and shove around my legs with their arms held up, making it difficult to avoid falling. Their deep longing to be loved simply couldn't be satisfied in the group experiences of hospital life, despite the exceptionally high quality of care at Lanternman.[5]

The need for esteem has led me to favor a current trend in education, whereby borderline mentally retarded children are given special assistance *in* their regular classrooms without segregating them in special classes. The stigma of being a "retard," as they call themselves, is no less insulting for a ten-year-old than it would be for you or me.

NINE

THE BARRIERS TO LEARNING, PART 2

A S WE SAW in the previous chapter, millions of children fall short of the standards expected of them in school, and thereby wind up as "academic casualties." These youngsters can be grouped into three general categories, including late bloomers and slow learners. In this chapter I will describe the unique characteristics of the third group:

THE UNDERACHIEVER

The underachiever is a student who is unsuccessful in school *despite* his ability to do the work. He may have an IQ of 120 or better, yet earn D's and F's on his report card. In recent years, underachievers have attained a rather high profile, thanks to Bart Simpson's self-proclaimed "UNDERACHIEVER, AND PROUD OF IT!" Despite this dubious publicity, underachievers are less understood (and more numerous) than either slow learners or late bloomers.

The apparent confusion about this group is related to the fact that *two* specific qualities are necessary to produce academic excellence, the second of which is often overlooked. First, *intellectual ability* must be there. But mental capacity is insufficient by itself. *Self-discipline* is also required. An able child may or may not have the self-control necessary to bear down day after day on something he considers painful and difficult.

Intelligence and self-discipline are frequently *not* correlated. A child often has one without the other. Occasionally, an untalented child will struggle to achieve above his expected level. This phenomenon is called overachievement. The opposite combination, known as underachievement, is much more common. It is typified by the child who has considerable intellectual potential but insists on wasting it.

It is apparent that underachievers are handled in a way that compounds their problem. This is because, as indicated in chapter 7, we often fail to acknowledge that learning requires the hardest kind of effort. Examine for a moment what is required of a high school student in a daily homework assignment. He must understand what the teacher wants, including page numbers and other details. He must remember to bring home the right book. He must turn off the television set and ignore the phone in the evening. He must concentrate on the task long enough to do it correctly. He must take the finished product back to class the following day and turn it in. He must remember what he learned until the next test. Lastly, he must complete these homework assignments more than once or twice; they must be done repeatedly throughout the year.

This kind of performance requires more than intelligence. The fact that a child has a good vocabulary and can piece together various manipulative puzzles does not mean he can push himself week after week, year after year. Some children succeed through the elementary school years, but give up later. In fact, it has been estimated that 75 percent of all students experience an academic slump sometime between the seventh and the tenth grades. Despite this common occurrence, neither the school nor the home is usually prepared to deal with it.

The typical parent reacts one of three ways to their underachieving child:

The first reaction is treating the problem as though it resulted from sheer stubbornness. Thus, parents may take away the bicycle for six months, ground the youngster until spring, or tear into his personhood and position in the family. Assuming the accuracy of my premise (that the behavior results from an understandable, childish lack of self-control), this reaction will not make consistent bookwork any likelier. Under these conditions, school takes on the blue hue of threat, which hardly makes the youngster more diligent.

Parents who become angry about underachievement in their child might also find studying difficult if they were suddenly thrust back in school. Resistance to mental exercise is considered natural in a mature adult but in an immature child it is assumed to reflect stubbornness.

The second approach is to offer the child a long-range bribe: a new bicycle in a couple of years or a hunting trip next fall. These delayed offers are also ineffective for reasons outlined in a previous chapter. Postponed reinforcement is tantamount to no reinforcement.

The third parental reaction is to say, "He's got to learn responsibility sometime! I can't always be there to help—so it's his problem."

If parents seem unrealistic in handling the difficulty, some schools may not be any more helpful. Teachers and counselors sometimes tell parents, "Don't worry about it. Johnny will outgrow the problem." That's the biggest falsehood of the year. Johnny usually doesn't outgrow the problem—gross underachievement in the elementary years tends to be rather persistent. Furthermore, I've observed that most underachievers are lifelong "messies." They are often sloppy and disorganized in everything they do. It is a persistent trait that goes cross-grain to what is needed in the classroom.

Over the years I have dealt with more than five hundred under-achievers and have concluded that there are only two functional solutions to this syndrome. The first is certainly no panacea: Parents can become so involved in the schoolwork that the child has no choice but to do the job. This is possible only if the school takes the time to communicate assignments and progress to the parents, because Junior certainly won't carry the message! Adolescents, particularly, will confound the communication between school and home as much as possible.

In one of the high schools where I served, for example, the students had a twenty-minute homeroom experience each day. This period was used for council meetings, announcements, and related matters. Very little opportunity for studying occurred there, yet each day hundreds of parents were told that all the homework was finished during that session. The naive parents were led to believe that homeroom was a lengthy block of concentrated effort. Parents must know what goes on in school if they want to influence their child's academic responsibilities.

Also, the parents should provide *support* in areas where pure self-discipline is needed. The evening study period should be highly structured—routine hours and a minimum of interferences. The parent must know what was assigned and how the finished product should look. Ongoing research by the Center for the Study of the Family, Children, and Youth at Stanford University is finding that one method of helping the underachiever that results in a sustained improvement in grades is parental involvement. When Mom and Dad offer regular encouragement, praise for a job well done, and meaningful assistance, grades tend to go up.[1]

I must hasten to say that this can be quite difficult. Intense parental involvement can rarely be sustained for more than a week or two, because many moms and dads don't have the required self-discipline themselves. There must be a way to supplement their effort, and I believe there is.

The underachiever often thrives under a system of immediate reinforcement, as described previously. If the child is not challenged by the rewards and motivators given at school, he'll need additional incentives. These positive reinforcements should be based on definite, reachable goals. Further, the payoff should be applied to small units of behavior. Instead of rewarding the child for earning an A in English at the end of the semester, he should be given a dime or quarter for each math problem accurately computed.

"Bribery!" some readers will charge.

"Who cares?" is my reply, if it puts the child to work.

The use of immediate reinforcement serves the same function as a starter on a car. You can't drive very far with it, but it gets the engine going much easier than pushing. For the idealist who objects to using this extrinsic motivation, I would ask: "What alternative do we have, other than to 'let the child grow out of his problem'?"

Several examples may illustrate the specific application of reinforcement within the school setting. One of the most successful uses of this technique occurred with a classic underachiever named Billy, who was repeating second grade. His motivation had been assassinated by early failures, and he did nothing in school. Furthermore, his younger sister was also in second grade, having been promoted the same year Billy was held back. And wouldn't you know, she was an academic whiz while Billy was mired in intellectual despair.

After talking with his mother, we agreed upon a motivation system to be implemented at home. On the basis of our conference, Billy's mother quickly constructed the following chart:

For each five minutes Billy spent working on his weekly spelling words with a parent, he got to color in a bar on the chart. When all bars were colored, he would receive a new bicycle seat. He also colored a bar for each ten minutes spent working on arithmetic flash cards. Fifty bars would earn him a bowling trip with his father. Billy's mother considered

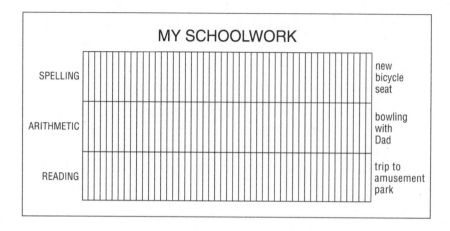

reading to be his greatest problem. Thus, reading provided the pathway to a day at the amusement park (in this case, Disneyland). As the biggest prize, it naturally took longer to earn (one bar was colored for each fifteen minutes of reading).

By staggering the reinforcement, one pleasant reward could be earned quickly, another soon after, and a grand prize waited at the end. Billy quickly caught the excitement of the game. He rushed home after school and went to work with his mother. Whereas she was previously unable to make him open a book, he suddenly wanted to "study" throughout the evening. The reinforcement system worked so well that it had an unexpected consequence. Billy's mother called me the following week to complain about not being able to get her work done when Billy was at home!

After a while, a strange thing began to happen. Billy began to learn, though that was not his intent. He spelled all his words correctly on the weekly test for the first time, and enjoyed the feeling of success that followed. When the class was discussing arithmetic he knew the answers, and waved his hand for a chance to prove his knowledge. His reading improved noticeably, and his teacher moved him out of the slow reading group. Without meaning to do so, Billy discovered the joy of learning. The vicious cycle of failure had been broken.

It would be wrong to imply that all learning problems can be eliminated as easily and successfully as Billy's. Some underachievers are "hardcore" and *nothing* will shake them loose. Yet reinforcement offers the best possibility for improvement. This system has been employed throughout the world, often with remarkable results.

In New York City, for example, it was used to help many delinquent youth who couldn't read. The young rebels, who would have laughed off a direct offer to teach them to read, had to be enticed via the back door. That's exactly what happened. Researchers told them, "Look, we've got some machines that *might* be able to teach reading, but we need your help to determine if they work. There's money involved: we'll actually pay you for each right answer." The amount of money was decent for the summer program, and most of the adolescents who accepted the offer learned to read. This, in turn, helped steer them off the street and into the classroom, thereby opening new academic challenges to them.

A similar system was applied in the Alabama prisons, whereby inmates could earn money by learning new skills and completing instructional courses. The future will bring even wider application of these principles to difficult behavioral problems, including the one of academic underachievement.

Children and adolescents, like people of all ages, want to be responsible. They want to feel the self-respect and dignity of doing what is right. The ones who fail in school are often the most miserable, but they lack the self-discipline to overcome their own inertia.

Summary

In these past two chapters, I have described three great barriers to discipline in the classroom. Of course, there are additional problems which I have not presented in detail. Anything that worries or troubles a child can result in school failure. For example, deep feelings of inadequacy and inferiority can prevent academic concentration. The child who must cope with such emotions has little time for less important matters. Adults who have tried to work or think while awaiting a threatening medical report, such as a lab test for cancer, may understand this mechanism of mental interference.

Parents and teachers must never underestimate the threats a child associates with school. Regardless of whether or not he verbalizes his fears, he is often aware of many "dangers" which lurk just inside the school gate. That is, other students might laugh at him. He may be ridiculed or criticized by teachers. He could be rejected by members of the opposite sex. He may fail despite his best efforts. These and similar fears can permeate the entire world of a bewildered young student, causing him to act in ways which appear lazy. Thus, the solution to school failure often requires dealing with problems which seem unrelated to classroom work.

One further thought strikes me as very important at this point. We have discussed three categories of children, those who are late bloomers, slow learners, or underachievers. But how can a parent or teacher know if a child has one of these problems or some other intellectual deficit? The answer in a particular case can only be determined from a complete educational assessment conducted by a person trained, certified, or licensed to evaluate children. In each of the three categories I have described, a test of intelligence (IQ) is necessary to identify a child's problem. How can we know the underachiever is not a slow learner unless we measure basic intellectual skills? How can we separate the late bloomer from a child with a severe learning deficit without assessing fundamental abilities? The IQ test is an extremely valuable tool in this differentiation.

Unfortunately, IQ testing has all but disappeared in many school districts. Because these instruments (such as the WISC-R or Stanford Binet) were perceived to be unfair to minorities, their use has come under increasing criticism in recent years. Thus, it is no longer "politically correct" to use them. As a result, parents who desperately need the information previously available from testing in public school settings now have to seek out a psychologist or counselor in private practice who can conduct the evaluation. Those who lack the funds to obtain this expensive assistance, including many minorities, are deprived of the help their children need. I regret the political situation that prevents school districts from evaluating their students with the best tests available.

But what about minorities? Are standardized IQ tests unfair to African-Americans, Hispanics, and Native Americans? I do not think so. It is true that minorities sometimes do more poorly on these tests because their cultures do not prepare them for that kind of exam. But read carefully, now: The same cultural factors that affect the test results also affect school performance. Performance on test questions is correlated with classroom work. If we seek a test that does not reflect the impact of an inner-city culture, then it will be useless because it will no longer *predict* classroom performance.

Let me say it once more. The purpose of testing is to estimate how well a given child is likely to do in an academic setting. To create an instrument that will not reflect the handicap his culture will place on him, when that culture will definitely handicap him in the classroom, is to play games with "political correctness."

If you didn't understand what I just wrote, please remember this. All children with learning problems, including some minorities, need to be evaluated with standardized tests of intelligence. Until that occurs, we don't know what the difficulty is and how it should be treated. I say, bring back the IQ test.

QUESTIONS & ANSWERS

Q: It is my understanding that we forget 80 percent of everything we learn in three months' time and a higher percentage is forgotten as time passes. Why, then, should we put children through the agony of learning? Why is mental exercise needed if the effort is so inefficient?

A: Your question reflects the viewpoint of the old progressive education theorists. They wanted the school curriculum to be nothing more than "life adjustment." They placed a low priority on intellectual discipline for the reasons you mentioned. Even some college professors have adopted this "no content" philosophy, as I mentioned in a previous chapter. They reason that the material we learn today may be obsolete tomorrow, so why learn it? I strongly disagree with this approach to education. There are at least five reasons why learning is important, even if we forget much of what we're taught:

(1) As indicated earlier, teaching self-discipline is a very important component of the academic experience. Good students learn to sit for long hours, follow directions, complete assignments, and use their mental faculties. Accordingly, homework is relatively unimportant as an educational tool; it *is* a valuable instrument of discipline. Since adult life often requires self-sacrifice, sweat, and devotion to causes, school should help shape a child's capacity to handle this future responsibility. Certainly, play is important in a child's life, too. Youngsters should not work all the time. The home and school should provide a healthy balance between discipline and play.

(2) Learning is important because we are *changed* by what we learn, even if the facts are later forgotten. No college graduate could remember everything he learned in school, yet he is a very different person for having gone to college. Learning changes values, attitudes, and concepts which don't fade in time.

(3) Even if the learned material cannot be recalled, the individual knows the facts exist and where to find them. If we asked a complicated question of an uneducated man, he would likely give a definite, unqualified response. The same question would probably be answered more cautiously by a person with an advanced degree. The latter individual would say, "Well, there are several ways to look at it. . . ." He knows the matter is more complex than it appears, even if he doesn't have the complete answer.

(4) We don't forget 100 percent of what we learn. The most important facts lodge in our permanent memory for future use. The human brain is capable of storing two billion bits of data in a lifetime; education is the process of filling that memory bank with useful information.

(5) Old learning makes new learning easier. Each mental exercise gives us more associative cues with which to link future ideas and concepts.

I wish there were an easier, more efficient process for shaping human minds than the slow, painful experience of education. But I'm afraid we must depend on this old-fashioned approach until a "learning pill" is developed.

Q: Some educators have said we should eliminate report cards and academic marks. Do you think this is a good idea?
A: No, academic marks are valuable for students in the third grade or higher. They reinforce and reward the child who has achieved in school and nudge the youngster who hasn't. It is important, though, that marks be used properly. They have the power to create or destroy motivation.

Through the elementary years and in required courses of high school, a child's grades should be based on what he does with what he has. In other words, I think we should grade according to ability. A slow child should be able to succeed in school just as certainly as a gifted youngster. If he struggles and sweats to achieve, he should somehow be rewarded—even if his work falls short of an absolute standard. By the same token, gifted children should not be given A's just because they are smart enough to excel without working.

The primary purpose in grading should be to reward academic effort. Those who disagree should consider the alternative reflected in the following illustration: Joe is less than brilliant and knows it. In second grade, he quit trying to do well in school. However, when he reached sixth grade he was taught by a man who challenged him to do his best. He worked very hard to please this teacher, despite his problems with reading, writing, and arithmetic.

At the end of the term, Joe was still hard at work, although his writing had improved little and he was struggling with a third grade reader. What was his teacher to do with Joe's report card? If he graded the youngster in relation to his peers, he would have to fail him. If he failed him, Joe would never work again.

Since Joe had done his best, should he receive the same grade he got last year when he sat with unfocused eyes day after day? I think not. Joe should be praised for his diligence in the most obvious manner, and given at least C's on his report card. The teacher should quietly inform his parents of the bigger picture, and enlist their support in encouraging Joe's continued effort.

Any other system of grading will result in discouragement to children of lesser ability. Even sharper students usually work better when they must stretch for excellence.

One exception to the "grade on ability" policy should be implemented: college preparation courses in high school must be graded on an absolute standard. An A in chemistry or calculus is accepted by college admission boards as a symbol of excellence, and high school teachers must preserve that meaning. But then, Joe and his friends need not take those difficult courses.

To repeat, marks can be the teacher's most important motivational tool—provided they are used correctly. Therefore, the recommendation that schools eliminate grading is a move away from discipline in the classroom.

Q: My child has what has been called an attention deficit disorder (ADD) that makes it hard for him to do well in school. I understand his difficulty. But he brings home D's and F's in most of his classes,

and I know that will limit his opportunities in life. What should be the attitude of a parent toward a child who fails year after year?
A: Obviously, tutorial assistance and special instruction should be provided, if possible. Beyond that, however, I would strongly suggest that academic achievement be de-emphasized at home for the youngster who has a demonstrated learning deficiency.

Requiring a child with ADD or dyslexia (an inability to read) to compete academically is like forcing a child with cerebral palsy to run the hundred yard dash. Imagine a mother and father standing disapprovingly at the end of the track, berating their handicapped child as he hobbles across the finish line in last place.

"Why don't you run faster, son?" his mother asks with obvious displeasure.

"I don't think you really care whether you win or lose," says his embarrassed father.

How can this lad explain that his legs will not carry him as fast as those of his peers? All he knows is that the other sprinters run past him to the cheering of the crowd. But who would expect a disabled child to win a race against healthy peers? No one, simply because his handicap is obvious. Everyone can see it.

Unfortunately, the child with a learning deficit is not so well understood. His academic failure is more difficult to understand and may be attributed to laziness, mischievousness, or deliberate defiance. Consequently, he experiences pressures to do the impossible. And one of the most serious threats to emotional health occurs when a child faces demands that he cannot satisfy.

Let me restate the preceding viewpoint in its most concise terms. I believe in academic excellence. I want to maximize every ounce of intellectual potential which a child possesses. I don't believe in letting him behave irresponsibly simply because he doesn't choose to work. Without question, there is a lasting benefit to be derived from educational discipline.

On the other hand, some things in life are more important than academic excellence, and self-esteem is one of them. A child can survive, if he must, without knowing a noun from a verb. But if he doesn't have some measure of self-confidence and personal respect, he won't have a chance in life.

I want to assert my conviction that the child who is unequipped to prosper in the traditional educational setting is not inferior to his peers. He possesses the same degree of human worth and dignity as the intellectual young superstar. It is a foolish cultural distortion that causes us to evaluate the worth of children according to the abilities and physical features they may (or may not) possess.

Every child is of equal worth in the sight of God, and that is good enough for me. Thus, if my little boy or girl can't be successful in one environment, we'll just look for another. Any loving parent would do the same.[2]

DISCIPLINE
IN MORALITY

M Y FRIEND AND COLLEAGUE, attorney Gary Bauer, served for
eight years in the Reagan administration, ultimately being appointed
Senior Domestic Policy Advisor to the President. During his latter years in
the White House, Bauer also headed an historic Commission on the Family
that revealed surprising findings about the nation's adolescents.

After two years of investigation, Bauer's commission learned that
Americans in every age category were better-off at the time of the study
than they had been ten years earlier. Both adults and younger children
were found to be more healthy, better fed, and better educated than before.
More tax money was being spent on children and more programs and
bureaucrats were in place to address their needs. There was, however, a
striking exception to this conclusion.

Teenagers were found to be considerably *worse* off than in the prior
decade. Their many problems could not be blamed on government, on
educators, or on the medical community. Rather, Bauer and his co-workers
found that young people were busily killing *themselves* at an alarming rate.
It is shocking to see just how hostile the world of the young has become
and how poorly they are coping with their difficulties.

Suppose the parents of yesterday could visit our time to observe the
conditions that prevail among our children. They would be appalled by
the problems which have become widespread (and are spreading wider)
in our homes, schools, and neighborhoods.

Gang violence and one-on-one crime among the young is an indescribable shame. Wandering droves of children and teens are shooting,
knifing, and bludgeoning each other at an unprecedented rate. Commonly,

now, innocent bystanders and little children are caught in the crossfire, as bullets from automatic weapons spray once peaceful neighborhoods. It is not unusual in the large cities for ten or fifteen young people to die in a single violent weekend. Emergency units of virtually every inner city hospital are taxed to the limit trying to deal with the casualties of gang warfare now being waged. They call it "battlefield medicine." The killings are so common that many don't even get reported in the news. Only when the body count reaches record proportions do people seem alarmed by what is happening. Who would have believed in 1970 when *Dare to Discipline* was first written that this would have occurred?

Isaac Fulwood, Chief of Police in Washington, D.C., blamed the city's "love of drugs," when the homicide rate there set another record for the third straight year.[1] He could have just as easily pointed his finger at City Hall. At that same time, Mayor Marion Barry was making headlines around the country (and a mockery of law enforcement) for his conviction of cocaine possession.

"The United States is breeding a lost generation of children," proclaimed one authority, citing teen violence statistics compiled by the U.S. Justice Department. These figures showed that since 1983, robberies committed by juveniles under eighteen have increased five times, murders have tripled, and rapes have doubled. The leading killer of black males aged fifteen to twenty-four is now homocide; only car accidents kill more white youths.[2]

"During every one hundred hours on our streets we lose more young men than were killed in one hundred hours of ground war in the Persian Gulf," lamented Dr. Louis Sullivan, secretary of the Department of Health and Human Services during the first Bush administration. "Where are the yellow ribbons of hope and remembrance for our youth dying in the streets?"[3]

No longer is extreme violence something that happens only on television. It is a reality of daily life for many of our youth. In 1987, gifted students in a Washington, D.C., public school science class were asked how many knew somebody who'd been killed. Of the nineteen students, fourteen raised their hands. How were they killed? "Shot," said one student. "Stabbed," said another. "Shot." "Shot." "Drugs." "Shot." All of this from thirteen-year-old children.[4]

Similar findings were compiled in a study of 168 teenagers by researchers at the University of Maryland School of Medicine. When asked about their exposure to violent crime, an amazing 24 percent of these Baltimore teens had witnessed a murder; 72 percent knew someone who had been shot.[5]

Wherever one chooses to look within adolescent society, trouble is evident. A root cause for much of the unrest, of course, is the continued prevalence of alcohol and substance abuse by the young. A recent Gallup Report indicated that before graduating from high school, a staggering percentage of teenagers are hooked on mind-altering drugs of some type. Eighty-five percent experiment with alcohol. Fifty-seven percent try an illicit drug, and 35 percent get drunk at least once a month.[6] And lest those of us with Christian homes get complacent, there is not much difference between churched and unchurched families in the evidence of teen substance abuse.[7] It's enough to make a grown man or woman sick!

Indeed, there is an ache deep within my spirit over what we have allowed to happen to our kids. What is it going to take to alarm the mass of humanity that sits on the sidelines watching our kids struggle for survival? It is time for every God-fearing adult to get on our faces in repentance before the Almighty. We have permitted this mess to occur! We allowed immoral television and movie producers to make their fortunes by exploiting our kids. We allowed their filth and their horribly violent productions to come into our homes via cable, video, CDs, and network trash. We stood by passively while Planned Parenthood taught our teenagers to be sexually promiscuous. We allowed them to invade our schools and promote an alien value system that contradicted everything we believed and loved. We granted profit-motivated abortionists unsupervised and unreported access to our minor daughters, while we were thinking about something else. We, as parents, are guilty of abandoning our children to those who would use them for their own purposes. Where in God's name have we been? How bad does it have to get before we say, enough is enough?!

At the core of these individual tragedies is a moral catastrophe that has rocked our families to their foundation. We have forgotten God and disregarded His holy ordinances. But it is our children who have suffered and will continue to pay for our lack of stewardship and diligence.

Of all the dimensions wherein we have mishandled this younger generation, none is more disgraceful than the sexual immorality that has permeated the world in which they live. There is no more effective way to destroy the institution of the family than to undermine the sexual exclusivity on which it is based. Yet that has been accomplished, deliberately and thoughtfully by those who despised the Christian system of values. Today's "safe-sex" advocates are advancing that campaign with devastating effectiveness.

In 1991, the humanistic organization known as the Sex Information and Education Council of the United States (SIECUS) assembled a task force of twenty educators, social workers, and health personnel who were asked to draw up a comprehensive sex education program for children and young people. They prepared a forty-page report for local officials preparing sex education curriculum, entitled *Guidelines for Comprehensive Sexuality Education*. The individual members of the task force are among the foremost molders of opinion and sexual behavior among the young. Take a look at what they advocate for those in their teen years.

- People do not choose their sexual orientation.
- The traditional gender roles about sexuality in our society are becoming more flexible.
- The telephone number of the gay and lesbian switchboard is _____.
- There do not have to be prescribed gender roles for dating partners.
- Masturbation either alone or with a partner is one way a person can enjoy and express their [sic] sexuality without risking pregnancy or an STD/HIV.
- Some people use erotic photographs, movies, or literature to enhance their sexual fantasies when alone or with a partner.
- The right of a woman to have an abortion is guaranteed by the Supreme Court, although there are restrictions in some states.
- Gender role stereotypes can lead to such problems as low aspirations, low paying jobs, date rape, and stress-related illnesses.
- There is no evidence that erotic images in the arts cause inappropriate sexual behavior.
- Teenagers can get confidential testing and treatment for STD/HIV without parental consent.
- Many religions today acknowledge that human beings were created to be sexual beings, and that their sexuality is good.[8]

The task force that prepared these guidelines clearly has an agenda, including the promotion of homosexuality, abortion on demand, sexual relations among unmarried people, unrestricted access to pornography by the young, etc. How about it, parents? Is this what you want taught to *your* teenagers? I don't believe the majority of today's mothers and fathers agree with these objectives, but most don't care enough to oppose it, apparently.

Well, the organization I represent *is* concerned enough to speak out. We will do everything we can to save this generation of kids, who now face the threat of death from the dreaded HIV. We are passive no longer.

In 1992, Focus on the Family placed a full-page ad in *USA Today* to explain the *health* risks associated with the myth of safe sex. Its contents are so vital that I am including the entire statement, along with appropriate references, on the pages that follow. Please note as you read that even if morality were of no consequence, the sex liberators are creating enormous medical problems for us. Sooner or later, the epidemic of sexually transmitted diseases will expose the lies our kids have been told.

IN DEFENSE OF A LITTLE VIRGINITY
A message from Focus on the Family

The federal government has spent almost $3 billion of our taxes since 1970 to promote contraceptives and safe sex among our teenagers. Isn't it time we asked, What have we gotten for our money? These are the facts:

- The federal Centers for Disease Control estimate that there are now one million cases of HIV infection nationwide.[9]
- 1 in 100 students coming to the University of Texas health center now carries the deadly virus.[10]
- The rate of heterosexual HIV transmission has increased 44 percent since September 1989.[11]
- Sexually transmitted diseases (STDs) infect 3 million teenagers annually.[12]
- 63 percent of all STD cases occur among persons less than twenty-five years of age.[13]
- 1 million new cases of pelvic inflammatory disease occur annually.[14]
- 1.3 million new cases of gonorrhea occur annually;[15] strains of gonorrhea have developed that are resistant to penicillin.
- Syphilis is at a forty-year high, with 134,000 new infections per year.[16]

- 500,000 new cases of herpes occur annually;[17] it is estimated that 16.4 percent of the U.S. population ages fifteen to seventy-four is infected, totaling more than 25 million Americans—among certain groups, the infection rate is as high as 60 percent.[18]
- 4 million cases of chlamydia occur annually;[19] 10 to 30 percent of fifteen- to nineteen-year-olds are infected.[20]
- There are now 24 million cases of human papilloma virus (HPV), with a higher prevalence among teens.[21]

To date, over twenty different and dangerous sexually transmitted diseases are rampant among the young. Add to that the problems associated with promiscuous behavior: infertility, abortions, and infected newborns. The cost of this epidemic is staggering, both in human suffering and in expense to society; yet epidemiologists tell us we've only seen the beginning.

Incredibly, the safe-sex gurus and condom promoters who got us into this mess are still determining our policy regarding adolescent sexuality. Their ideas have failed, and it is time to rethink their bankrupt policies.

How long has it been since you've heard anyone tell teenagers why it is to their advantage to remain virgins until married? The facts are being withheld from them, with tragic consequences. Unless we come to terms with the sickness that stalks a generation of Americans, teen promiscuity will continue, and millions of kids . . . thinking they are protected . . . will suffer for the rest of their lives. Many will die of AIDS.

There is only one safe way to remain healthy in the midst of a sexual revolution. It is to abstain from intercourse until marriage, and then wed and be faithful to an uninfected partner. It is a concept that was widely endorsed in society until the 1960s. Since then, a better idea has come along . . . one that now threatens the entire human family.

Inevitable questions are raised whenever abstinence is proposed. It's time we gave some clear answers:

Why, apart from moral considerations, do you think teenagers should be taught to abstain from sex until marriage?

No other approach to the epidemic of sexually transmitted diseases will work. The so-called safe-sex solution is a disaster in the making. Condoms can fail at least 15.7 percent of the time annually in preventing pregnancy.[22] They fail 36.3 percent of the time annually in preventing pregnancy among young, unmarried minority women.[23] In a study of homosexual men, the British Medical Journal reported the failure rate due to slippage and breakage to be 26 percent.[24] Given these findings, it is obvious why we have a word for people who rely on condoms as a means of birth control. We call them . . . parents.

Remembering that a woman can conceive only one or two days per month, we can only guess how high the failure rate for condoms must be in preventing disease, which can be transmitted 365 days per year! If the devices are not used properly, or if they slip just once, viruses and bacteria are exchanged and the disease process begins. One mistake after five hundred protected episodes is all it takes to contract a sexually transmitted disease. The damage is done in a single moment when rational thought is overridden by passion.

Those who would depend on so insecure a method must use it properly on every occasion, and even then a high failure rate is brought about by factors beyond their control. The young victim who is told by his elders that this little latex device is safe may not know he is risking lifelong pain and even death for so brief a window of pleasure. What a burden to place on an immature mind and body!

Then we must recognize that there are other differences between pregnancy prevention and disease prevention. HIV is one twenty-fifth the width of sperm,[25] and can pass easily through even the smallest gaps in condoms. Researchers studying surgical gloves made out of latex, the same material in condoms, found channels of 5 microns that penetrated the entire thickness of the glove.[26] HIV measures .1 microns.[27] Given these findings, what rational, informed person would trust his or her very life to such flimsy armor?

This surely explains why not one of eight hundred sexologists at a conference a few years ago raised a hand when asked if they would trust a thin rubber sheath to protect them during intercourse with a known HIV-infected person.[28] Who could blame them? They're not crazy, after all. And yet they're perfectly willing to tell our kids that safe sex is within reach and that they can sleep around with impunity.

There is only one way to protect ourselves from the deadly diseases that lie in wait. It is abstinence before marriage, then marriage and mutual fidelity for life to an uninfected partner. Anything less is potentially suicidal.

That position is simply NOT realistic today. It's an unworkable solution: Kids will NOT implement it.

Some will. Some won't. It's still the only answer. But let's talk about an unworkable solution of the first order. Since 1970, the federal government has spent nearly $3 billion to promote contraception and safe sex. This year alone, 450 million of your tax dollars will go down that drain![29] (Compared with less than $8 million for abstinence programs, which Sen. Teddy Kennedy and company have sought repeatedly to eliminate altogether.) Isn't it time we ask what we've gotten for our money? After twenty-two years and nearly $3 billion, some 58 percent of teenage girls under eighteen still did not use contraception during their first intercourse.[30] Furthermore, teenagers tend to keep having unprotected intercourse for a full year, on average, before starting any kind of contraception.[31] That is the success ratio of the experts who call abstinence unrealistic and unworkable.

Even if we spent another $50 billion to promote condom usage, most teenagers would still not use them consistently and properly. The nature of human beings and the passion of the act simply do not lend themselves to a disciplined response in young romantics.

But if you knew a teenager was going to have intercourse, wouldn't you teach him or her about proper condom usage?

No, because that approach has an unintended consequence. The process of recommending condom usage to teenagers inevitably conveys five dangerous ideas: (1) that safe sex is achievable; (2) that everybody is doing it; (3) that responsible adults expect them to do it; (4) that it's a good thing; and (5) that their peers know they know these things, breeding promiscuity. Those are very destructive messages to give our kids.

Furthermore, Planned Parenthood's own data show that the number one reason teenagers engage in intercourse is peer pressure![32] Therefore, anything we do to imply that everybody is doing it results in more . . . not fewer . . . people who give the game a try. Condom distribution programs do not reduce the number of kids exposed to disease . . . they radically increase it!

Want proof of that fact? Since the federal government began its major contraception program in 1970, unwed pregnancies have increased 87 percent among fifteen- to nineteen-year-olds.[33] Likewise, abortions among teens rose 67 percent;[34] unwed births went up 61 percent.[35] And venereal disease has infected a generation of young people. Nice job, sex counselors. Good thinking, senators and congressmen. Nice nap, America.

Having made a blunder that now threatens the human family, one would think the designers would be backtracking and apologizing for their miscalculations. Instead, they continue to lobby Congress and corporate America for more money. Given the misinformation extant on this subject, they'll probably get it.

But if you were a parent and knew that your son or daughter was having sex, wouldn't you rather he or she used a condom?

How much risk is acceptable when you're talking about your teenager's life? One study of married couples in which one partner was infected with HIV found that 17 percent of the partners using condoms for protection still caught the virus within a year and a half.[36] Telling our teens to reduce their risk to one in six (17 percent) is not much better than advocating Russian roulette. Both are fatal, eventually. The difference is that with a gun, death is quicker. Suppose your son or daughter were joining an eighteen-month skydiving club of six members. If you knew that one of their parachutes would definitely fail, would you recommend that they simply buckle the chutes tighter? Certainly not. You would say, "Please don't jump! Your life is at stake!" How could a loving parent do less?

Kids won't listen to the abstinence message. You're just wasting your breath to try to sell them a notion like that.

It is a popular myth that teenagers are incapable of understanding that it is in their best interest to save themselves until marriage. Almost 65 percent of all high school females under eighteen are virgins.[37]

A few years ago in Lexington, Ky., a youth event was held that featured no sports contest, no rock groups—just an ex-convict named Harold Morris talking about abstinence, among other subjects. The coliseum seated 18,000 people, but 26,000 teenagers showed up! Eventually, more than 2,000 stood outside the packed auditorium and listened over a hastily prepared public address system. Who says kids won't listen to this time-honored message?

Even teens who have been sexually active can choose to stop. This is often called secondary virginity, a good concept that conveys the idea that kids can start over. One young girl recently wrote Ann Landers to say she wished she had kept her virginity, signing the letter, "Sorry I didn't and wish I could take it back." As responsible adults we need to tell her that even though she can't go back, she can go forward. She can regain her self-respect and protect her health, because it's never too late to start saying no to premarital sex.

Even though the safe-sex advocates predominate in educational circles, are there no positive examples of abstinence-based programs for kids?

Thankfully, some excellent programs have been developed. Spokane-based Teen-Aid and Chicago's Southwest Parents Committee are good examples. So are Next Generation in Maryland, Choices in California, and Respect Inc. in Illinois. Other curricula such as Facing Reality; Sex Respect; Me, My World, My Future; Reasonable Reasons to Wait; Sex, Love & Choices; and F.A.C.T.S. etc. are all abstinence-themed programs to help kids make good sexual decisions.

A good curriculum for inner-city youth is Elayne Bennett's Best Friends program. This successful mentoring project helps adolescents in Washington, D.C. graduate from high school and remain abstinent. In five years, not one female has become pregnant while in the Best Friends program!

Establishing and nurturing abstinence ideas with kids, however, can be like spitting into the wind. Not because they won't listen, because most will. But pro-abstinence messages are drowned out in a sea of toxic teen-sex-is-inevitable-use-a-condom propaganda from safe-sex professionals.

You place major responsibility on those who have told adolescents that sexual expression is their right as long as they do it "properly." Who else has contributed to the epidemic?

The entertainment industry must certainly share the blame, including television producers. It is interesting in this context that all four networks and the cable television entities are wringing their hands about this terrible epidemic of AIDS. They profess to be very concerned about those who are infected with sexually transmitted diseases, and perhaps they are sincere. However, TV executives and movie moguls have contributed mightily to the existence of this plague. For decades, they have depicted teens and young adults climbing in and out of each other's beds like so many sexual robots. Only the nerds were shown to be chaste, and they were too stupid or ugly to find partners.

Of course, the beautiful young actors in those steamy dramas never faced any consequences for their sexual indulgence. No one ever came down with herpes, or syphilis, or chlamydia, or pelvic inflammatory disease, or infertility, or AIDS, or genital warts, or cervical cancer. No patients were ever told by a physician that there was no cure for their disease or that they would have to deal with the pain for the rest of their lives. No one ever heard that genital cancers associated with the human papilloma virus (HPV) kill more women than AIDS,[38] or that strains of gonorrhea are now resistant to penicillin.[39]

No, there was no downside. It all looked like so much fun. But what a price we are paying now for the lies we have been told.

The government has also contributed to this crisis and continues to exacerbate the problem. For example, a current brochure from the federal Centers for Disease Control and the city of New York is entitled "Teens Have the Right" and is apparently intended to free adolescents from adult authority. Inside are the six declarations that make up a Teenagers Bill of Rights, as follows:

- I have the right to think for myself.
- I have the right to decide whether to have sex and who[m] to have it with.
- I have the right to use protection when I have sex.
- I have the right to buy and use condoms.
- I have the right to express myself.
- I have the right to ask for help if I need it.

Under this final item (the right to ask for help) is a list of organizations and phone numbers that readers are encouraged to call. The philosophy that governs several of the organizations reflects the homosexual agenda, which includes recruitment of the young and vigorous promotion of a teen's right to sexual expression.

Your tax dollars at work!

Surely there are other Americans who recognize the danger now threatening a generation of our best and brightest. It is time to speak up for an old-fashioned value called virginity. Now, more than ever, virtue is a necessity.

The response was overwhelming to this advertisement and to our continued distribution of its message. More than fifty thousand letters came to our offices from enthusiastic parents, teachers, health workers, and church leaders who applauded our efforts. Many have felt exactly as we, but perceived themselves to be powerless against the media and the government sponsored purveyors of propaganda. But the time has come for action. It's time to tell Congress to quit funding suicidal safe-sex programs . . . or else. It's time to teach old fashioned principles of morality to our children . . . not just because it's the only safe approach, but because it's *right*. It's in harmony with the prescription of Him who said,

> *Woe to those who call evil good and good evil, who put darkness for light and light for darkness, who put bitter for sweet and sweet for bitter. . . . Therefore, as tongues of fire lick up straw and as dry grass sinks down in the flames, so their roots will decay and their flowers blow away like dust; for they have rejected the law of the* LORD *Almighty and spurned the word of the Holy One of Israel.* (Isaiah 5:20, 24, NIV)

A FEW WORDS ABOUT SEX EDUCATION

I have devoted the remainder of this chapter to parents and teachers who believe in moral decency and want to instill responsible sexual attitudes in their children. Their task is not an easy one. The sexual urge is stronger during adolescence than in any other period of life, and there is no way to guarantee that an independent teen will choose to control it. It is impossible to shield these youth from the permissive attitudes which are prevalent today. Television brings every aspect of sexual gratification into the sanctuary of one's living room, and the details of immorality and perversion are readily available in the theater, from the neighborhood video store, or on the Internet. Obviously, solitary confinement for a child is not the answer.

Furthermore, there is a danger that parents will make one mistake in their efforts to avoid another. While attempting to teach discipline in matters of morality, they must be careful not to inculcate unhealthy attitudes that will interfere with sexual fulfillment in future marital relations. Those who would teach this subject have the difficult responsibility of saying "sex can be wonderful" and "sex can be dangerous" in the same breath, which takes some doing.

How then can conscientious adults instill self-control in their children without generating deep emotional hang-ups or negative attitudes? Discussed below are the aspects of sex education which are critical to the achievement of this delicate assignment.

WHO SHOULD TEACH THE CHILD ABOUT SEX?

The task of forming healthy sexual attitudes and understandings in children requires considerable skill and tact, and parents are often keenly aware of their lack of preparation to do the job. However, for those parents who *are* able to handle the instructional process correctly, the responsibility should be retained in the home. There is a growing trend for all aspects of education to be taken from the hands of parents (or the role is deliberately forfeited by them). This is a mistake.

Particularly in the matter of sex education, the best approach is one that begins in early childhood and extends through the years, according to a policy of openness, frankness, and honesty. Only parents can provide this lifetime training.

The child's need for information and guidance is rarely met in one massive conversation provided by dry-mouthed, sweaty-palmed parents as their child approaches adolescence. Nor is a concentrated formal educational program outside the home the best alternative. The ideal approach is a gradual enlightenment that begins during the third or fourth year of life and culminates shortly before puberty.

Despite the desirability of sex education being handled by highly skilled parents, one must admit this is an unrealistic objective in many homes (perhaps the majority of them). Parents are often too sexually inhibited to present the subject with poise, or they may lack the necessary technical knowledge of the human body. For such families which cannot, or will not, teach their children the details of human reproduction, assistance must be sought from outside the home.

It is my strong conviction that churches believing in abstinence before marriage and in lifelong marital fidelity should step in and offer their help to families sharing that commitment. Where else will moms and dads find proponents of traditional morality in this permissive day? There is no other agency or institution likely to represent the theology of the church better than representatives of the church, itself. It is puzzling to me why so few have accepted this challenge, given the attack on biblical concepts of morality today.

A few parents who have their children in Christian schools are able to get the help they need with sex education. Even there, however, the subject is often ignored or handled inadequately. What has developed, quite obviously, is an informational vacuum that sets the stage for far-reaching programs in the public schools, beginning in some cases with kindergarten children.

One of the problems with sex education as it is currently taught in public schools is that it breaks down the natural barriers between the sexes and makes familiarity and casual sexual experimentation much more likely to occur. It also strips kids—especially girls—of their modesty to have every detail of anatomy, physiology, and condom usage made explicit in co-ed situations. Then, the following Friday night when the kids are on a date and attend a sexually explicit movie or watch a hot TV program showing teenagers in bed with one another, it is just a tiny step to intercourse—whereas a hundred years ago it was an enormous decision to give up one's virginity. This familiarity also contributes to the terrible incidence of "date rape" in North America. In short, the way sex education is handled today is worse than no program at all. Look at what has happened to the incidence of teen pregnancy and abortion since it was instituted!

For those moms and dads whose kids are in public schools today, it is imperative that they investigate what is being taught in the name of sex education. You have a *right* to examine curricular materials and textbooks. You can and must talk to the teachers and principal about what they hope to communicate. Look carefully for the hidden agenda listed earlier in the SIECUS guidelines, such as pro-homosexual and lesbian behavior, the safe-sex distortion, the belief that premarital intercourse is a "right," and any suggestion that pits teenagers against their parents. Find out if a pro-abortion stance is taken, and if Planned Parenthood or similar organizations are invited into the classroom.

If these elements are there, I strongly suggest that you keep your kids out of the program. What better way is there to undermine the value system we have taught than to invest authority and leadership in a teacher who ridicules and undermines it. Not only would I not allow my youngster to participate in such a program, but I would help organize parent groups to institute an abstinence-based curriculum in the school. And if that didn't work, I'd begin campaigning for new school board members. I might even campaign for that office, myself.

WHY IS THERE SO MUCH RESISTANCE TO ABSTINENCE-BASED PROGRAMS?

Well, some educators honestly believe that "kids will be kids," so we should show them how to play the game right. I don't agree with them, but I can respect their honest difference of opinion. There are others, however, particularly those Planned Parenthood and SIECUS types who are in the business of promoting promiscuity and abortion, whom I believe have other motives. For them, something else is going on. The subject is not merely an intellectual debate about children and what is in their best interest. No, the topic is highly inflammatory. They become incensed when the word *abstinence* is even mentioned. Have you ever wondered why?

I served on Secretary Otis Bowen's Teen Pregnancy Prevention Panel during the Reagan era. I accepted that responsibility because I thought our purpose was to prevent teen pregnancies. During our first meeting in Washington, D.C., however, I learned that fifteen of the eighteen panel members had other ideas. They were all "safe-sex" gurus, who wanted to spend millions of federal dollars distributing condoms and immoral advice to the nation's teens. I can't describe how emotional they were about this objective. In time, I began to understand a little more of the motivation propelling the community that makes a living from teen sexual irresponsibility.

I described them this way in the book I co-authored with Gary Bauer, entitled *Children at Risk*:

Let's deal with the obvious question head on: Why do bureaucrats and researchers and Planned Parenthood types fight so hard to preserve adolescent promiscuity? Why do they balk at the thought of intercourse occurring only in the context of marriage? Why have they completely *removed* the door marked "Premarital Sex" for a generation of vulnerable teenagers?

Their motivation is not difficult to understand. Multiplied millions of dollars are generated each year in direct response to teenage sexual irresponsibility. Kids jumping into bed with each other is supporting entire industries of grateful adults. The abortion business alone brings in an estimated $600 million annually. Do you really believe the physicians, nurses, medical suppliers and bureaucrats who owe their livelihood to the killing of unborn babies would prefer that adolescents abstain until marriage?!

How about condom manufacturers or the producers of spermicide, "the pill," IUD's, or diaphragms? Would they want their business decimated by a sweeping wave of morality among the young? I doubt it. Then there are the producers of antibiotics and other drugs for use in treating sexually transmitted diseases. They have a financial stake in continued promiscuity, as well.

At the top of the list of those who profit from adolescent irresponsibility, however, are those who are purportedly working to fight it! Planned Parenthood and similar organizations would simply fade away if they were ever fully successful in eliminating teen pregnancies. They currently receive an estimated $106 million in federal subsidies to carry out their mission, plus approximately $200 million in contributions from private sources. Do you *really* believe they want to kill the goose that lays those golden eggs?

Imagine how many jobs would be lost if kids quit playing musical beds with one another! This is why professionals who advise young people about sex are so emotional about the word *abstinence*. If that idea ever caught on, who would need the services of Planned Parenthood and their ilk? It's a matter of self-preservation.

To fully comprehend the danger posed by Planned Parenthood and related organizations, it is important to examine their philosophy and intent. What is their program? What do their leaders want? What would they do if given free rein? As I understand their agenda, it can be summarized in the following four-point plan:

1. *Provide "value free" guidance on sexuality to teenagers.* Heaven forbid any preference for morality or sexual responsibility being expressed.

2. *Provide unlimited quantities of contraceptives to adolescents,* dispensed aggressively from clinics located on junior and senior high campuses. In so doing, a powerful statement is made to teenagers about adult approval of premarital sexual activity.

3. *Keep parents out of the picture by every means possible.* Staff members for Planned Parenthood can then assume the parental role and communicate libertarian philosophy to teens.

4. *Provide unlimited access to free abortions for young women who become pregnant;* again, without parental involvement or permission.

Incredibly, the American and Canadian public seems to "buy" this outrageous plan, which would have brought a storm of protest from yesterday's parents. Imagine how your father or grandfather would have reacted if a school official had secretly given contraceptives to you or arranged a quiet abortion when you were a teenager. The entire community would have been incensed. Someone may well have been shot! Yet today's parents have tolerated this intrusion without so much as a peep of protest. Why? What has happened to that spirit of protection for our families—that fierce independence that bonded us together against the outside world? I wish I knew.[40]

WHEN TO SAY WHAT

Let me offer some counsel now, to mothers and fathers who want to handle the instruction of their own children and are looking for a few helpful "how-tos." My hat is tipped to them. Even in this enlightened day, the subject of sex is charged with emotion. There are few thoughts which disturb Mom and Dad's tranquility more than the vision of answering all of their children's probing questions—particularly the ones which become uncomfortably personal.

This tension was apparent in the mother of nine-year-old Davie, after his family had recently moved into a new school district. Davie came home from school on the first afternoon and asked his mother point-blank: "Mom, what's sex?"

The question smacked her hard. She thought she had two or three years before dealing with that issue and was totally unprepared to field it now. Her racing mind concluded that Davie's new school must be engaged in a liberal sex education program, and she had no choice but to fill in the details. So, she sat down with her wide-eyed son, and for forty-five minutes gave him a tension-filled harangue about the birds and the bees and the coconut trees.

When she finished, Davie held up his enrollment card and said, "Gee, Mom, how am I going to get all that in this little bitty square?"

As Davie's mother discovered, there is a delicate art in knowing when to provide the younger generation with additional information about sex.

One of the most common mistakes committed by some parents and many overzealous educators is the trend toward teaching too much too soon. One parent wrote to me, for example, and said the kindergarten children in her local district were shown films of animals in the act of copulation. That is unwise and dangerous! Available evidence indicates that there are numerous hazards involved in moving too rapidly. Children can sustain a severe emotional jolt by being exposed to realities for which they are not prepared.

Furthermore, it is unwise to place the youngster on an informational timetable that will result in full sophistication too early in life. If eight-year-old children are given an advanced understanding of mature sexual behavior, it is less likely that they will wait ten or twelve years to apply this knowledge within the confines of marriage.

Another danger resulting from premature instruction involves the threat of overstimulation. Young people can be tantalized by what is taught about the exciting world of grown-up sexual experience. Childhood education should be focused on childish interests, not adult pleasures and desires. I am not implying that sex education should be delayed until childhood has passed. Rather, it seems appropriate that the amount of information youngsters are given should coincide with their social and physical requirement for that awareness.

The child's requests for information provide the best guide to readiness for sex education. Their comments reveal what the youngster thinks about and wants to know. Such questions also offer a natural vehicle for instruction. It is far better for parents to answer these questions at the moment of curiosity than to ignore or evade them, hoping to explain later. Premeditated training sessions often become lengthy, one-way conversations which make both participants uncomfortable.

Although the question-answering approach to sex education is usually superior, the technique is obviously inadequate with children who never ask for information. Some boys and girls are fascinated by sexual reproduction while others never give it a second thought. If a child is uninterested in or doesn't ask about sex, the parent is not relieved of responsibility.

Our two children were opposites at this point. Danae asked all the right (or wrong?) questions one night when she was seven years old. Her shocked mother hadn't expected to have to deal with that subject for a few more years. Shirley stalled for time and came to share the situation with me as I sat at my desk. We promptly invited Danae to sit down for a conversation. Shirley made some hot chocolate and we talked for an hour or so. It all went very smoothly.

Ryan, on the other hand, never asked questions about sex at all. We volunteered bits and pieces of the story as it seemed appropriate and comfortable, but the specific facts were more difficult to convey. Finally, I took my son on a fishing trip . . . just the two of us. Then as we sat there on the bank waiting for the trout to bite, I said, "It occurs to me, Ryan, that we have never talked much about sex . . . you know, how babies are made and all that. Maybe this would be a good time to discuss it."

Ryan sat thoughtfully for several minutes without saying anything. I wondered what he was thinking. Then he said, "What if I don't wanna know?"

I dragged my kid into the world of reproduction and sexuality, kicking and screaming, but I got him there nonetheless. That is a parental responsibility. Even when it is not easy, the job must be done. If you won't accept the assignment, someone else will . . . someone who may not share your values.

One final comment is important regarding the timing of sex education in the home. Parents should plan to end their formal instructional program about the time their child enters puberty (the time of rapid sexual development in early adolescence). Puberty usually begins between ten and thirteen for girls and between eleven and fourteen for boys. Once they enter this developmental period, they are typically embarrassed by discussions of sex with their parents. Adolescents usually resent adult intrusion during this time . . . *unless* they raise the topic themselves. In other words, this is an area where teens should invite parents into their lives.

I feel that we should respect their wish. We are given ten or twelve years to provide the proper understanding of human sexuality. After that foundation has been constructed, we largely serve as resources to whom our children can turn when the need exists.

That is *not* to say parents should abdicate their responsibility to provide guidance about issues related to sexuality, dating, marriage, etc., as opportunities present themselves. Again, sensitivity to the feelings of the teen is paramount. If he or she wishes to talk, by all means, welcome the conversation. In other cases, parental guidance may be most effective if offered *indirectly*. Trusted youth workers at church or in a club program such as Campus Life or Young Life can often break the ice when parents can't.

I'd also suggest that you direct your kids to online resources that provide solid Christian advice—from the perspective of a friend, rather than an authority figure. Examples include *Brio* (www.briomag.com), and *Breakaway* (www.breakaway.com).

ASSISTANCE FROM MOTHER NATURE?

One of the areas where I have changed my perspective radically since 1970 is in recommending the use of animals, especially dogs and cats, to help explain the reproductive process to children. I *still* think a demonstration of birth is enlightening and helpful, but I am now more familiar with and concerned about the overpopulation of pets and what happens to these poor creatures when they don't have homes. In Los Angeles County alone, more than 100,000 dogs are killed every year in pounds and humane societies. Other homeless animals go hungry or are crushed on our streets and highways. Their suffering is our responsibility!

Our family has adopted our last two dogs from this population of strays, and they have made wonderful pets. Little Mitzi, our last dog, was just hours away from death when we selected her at the pound. But as a life-long dog lover, I have to tell you the selection process was a difficult experience for us. There in the plastic cages were hundreds of pitiful dogs and cats in need of adoption. Most were traumatized by their circumstances, having been lost or dumped by their owners.

As we strolled down the walkway, dogs barked and thrust their paws through the wire to get our attention. Danae put her hand in one cage to pet a lonely pup, who immediately pressed his head into her palm and closed his eyes. I'm sure he did not survive the week. I'll never forget a big brown dog with a hoarse voice who was staring at the doorway when we arrived. He was looking intently at us and yet did not seem to see. Even when we stood in front of his cage, he never took his eyes off the door. Every now and then he would emit a throaty bark that seemed to end in a question mark. Danae then read the identifying card above the cage indicating how he came to be picked up. This dog had also been brought in by his owners, and he was intently watching for their return. Obviously, we were not the folks he had in mind.

Perhaps you can understand why Danae and I were looking for the most needy animal we could find. The cute, healthy puppies and kittens had a chance of being adopted, at least. We wanted to give a home to a dog that was certain to be put down. Danae finally called me on a Saturday afternoon to tell me that she had found a good candidate.

I drove to the shelter and quickly agreed with her selection. There, huddled at the back of a cage was a twelve-week-old pup in terrible condition. She was in a state of semi-starvation, having been picked up on the street a few days earlier. Her jaw had been broken, perhaps by a fierce kick, and someone had put three stitches in her lip. We learned later she had pneumonia, round worms, tape worms, and who knows what other problems. She trembled as we approached her cage, but did not rise.

I asked the attendant to let the dog out, and he handed her to me. It was an instant friendship. She nuzzled my hand and looked up as if to say, "I'm really in a mess, aren't I?" We were hooked.

We left to talk over the matter, but couldn't forget that gentle nuzzle from so helpless a creature. Danae went back and got the dog.

I wish you could have seen Mitzi in her prime. She was fat, healthy, and deliriously happy. When I got home at night, she romped to the front door like a buffalo in stampede. It was as though she knew we had rescued her from a living death. And surprisingly, except for a crooked mouth, she looked very much like our previous dog. So Shirley and I no longer had an empty nest at home.

Forgive this diversion from our theme, but it does relate to my earlier recommendation that animals be used to teach the miracle of reproduction and birth. Now I advise parents to have their pets spayed or neutered to prevent the continued problem with overpopulation. If puppies or kittens are desired, be sure you have good homes for them before bringing them into the world.

And if you want to befriend a lonely animal who sits today in a cage just hoping you'll give him a home, head on down to the animal shelter in your area. Neither you nor your kids will ever forget it.

(To all the animal lovers out there who've been mad at me for several decades for what I wrote about pet reproduction in *Dare to Discipline,* is all forgiven?)

CONCLUSION

In the first chapters of this book I discussed the importance of the child's respect for his parents. His attitude toward their leadership is critical to his acceptance of their values and philosophy, including their concept of premarital sexual behavior. Likewise, the most fundamental element in teaching morality can be achieved through a healthy parent-child relationship during the early years. The obvious hope is that the adolescent will respect and appreciate his parents enough to believe what they say and accept what they recommend.

Unfortunately, however, this loyalty to parents is often an insufficient source of motivation. It is my firm conviction that children should also be taught ultimate loyalty to God. We should make it clear that the merciful God of love whom we serve is also a God of justice. If we choose to defy His moral laws we will suffer certain consequences. God's spiritual imperatives are as inflexible as His physical laws. Those who defy those physical laws will not long survive. Likewise, the willful violation of God's commandments is equally disastrous, for "the wages of sin is death." An adolescent who understands this truth is more likely to live a moral life in the midst of an immoral society.

One further comment may be relevant. Many years ago on my daughter's tenth birthday, Shirley and I gave her a small, gold key. It was attached to a chain worn around her neck, and represented the key to her heart. Through the years, she has kept her vow to give that key to one man only—the one who will share her love through the remainder of her life. You might consider a similar gift for your daughter, or a special ring for your son. These go with them when you're not there and provide a tangible

reminder of the lasting, precious gift of sexual fulfillment that God intends
for His children. (They can also be ordered from Focus on the Family.)

QUESTIONS & ANSWERS

**Q: Your comments about sexually transmitted disease are very unset-
tling to me. I have three teenagers and am afraid they don't understand how diseases are transmitted and what they can do to the body.
That is a very scary subject.**
A: Like you, I wonder what it will take to awaken our young people. I
interviewed Dr. C. Everett Koop while he was Surgeon General of the
United States in the mid-eighties. He said then, "The AIDS epidemic will
soon change the behavior of everyone. When infected young people begin
dying around us, others will be afraid to even kiss anyone."

That has not occurred as of this writing, even though young people
are indeed dying as Dr. Koop predicted. The following article, written by
reporter Kim Painter, appeared in *USA Today*, April 13, 1992:

AIDS SURGING AMONG TEENS

AIDS cases among teens and young adults grew 77 percent in the past two
years.

And the 9,000 cases among 13- to 24-year-olds form just the tip of an
iceberg: Thousands more are likely HIV-infected; millions more are at risk,
says a report by a House committee on children and families.

The report says federal prevention efforts have been inadequate. It cites
evidence that teens are risking infection through sex and drug abuse:

- 68 percent of girls, 86 percent of boys have sex before age 20; fewer
  than half report condom use.
- 3 million teens get a sexually transmitted disease yearly.
- Nearly 3 percent of high school seniors have used steroids; 1.3 percent,
  heroin. Shared needles can spread HIV.[41]

So why have teenagers not become "afraid to even kiss anyone," as
Dr. Koop predicted? Because the natural fear of the deadly HIV has been

pacified by the safe-sex nonsense. We have seemingly come up with a way to have our cake and eat it, too. It'll be the first time.

Thank goodness for a few physicians who are sounding the alarm and trying to get the uncensored facts to our kids. They don't get much press, but someday they will be vindicated. One of the most vocal of these concerned doctors is my good friend, Dr. Joe McIlhaney, an obstetrician-gynecologist in private practice in Austin, Texas. His book, *Sexuality and Sexually Transmitted Diseases*, should be read by every parent and every teenager. A frequent "Focus on the Family" broadcast guest, he talked about the fallacy of "safe sex" on a recent program:

"What you hear mostly from the press is what science is going to do for people who have a sexually transmitted disease (STD), how science is going to come up with a vaccine or treatment for AIDS, how antibiotics will kill gonorrhea and chlamydia. What is not discussed is how these STDs leave women's pelvic structures scarred for life, and they end up infertile or having to do expensive procedures to get pregnant later on.

"I could name patient after patient in the twenty-two years I've been in practice where I've had to perform a hysterectomy before a woman had the children she wanted because of Pelvic Inflammatory Disease, which is caused by chlamydia and gonorrhea," he continued.

"The public announcements about 'safe sex' infuriate me, because what they're saying is that you can safely have sex outside of marriage if you use condoms, and you don't have to worry about getting an STD. The message is a lie. The failure rate of condoms is extremely high, and that's why married people don't use them."

He went on to say, "I see the victims of these failures in my office every day. These include victims of chlamydia, probably the most prevalent STD, and of human papilloma virus (HPV), which can cause a lasting irritation of the female organs, as well as cancer of the vulva, vagina, and cervix. It is one of the most difficult diseases to treat, and kills more than 4800 women a year. I also see victims of herpes, which some studies indicate is present in up to 30-40 percent of single, sexually active people, as well as victims of syphilis, which is at a forty-year high."

Rather than expecting science to solve our problems, Dr. McIlhaney said a better solution involves a return to spiritual and moral guidelines that have been with us for thousands of years:

Dr. McIlhaney concluded, "The people who made my automobile

know how it works best and what I need to do to avoid car problems. They tell me that in my Ford manual. Likewise, God knows how we work best, and gave us an 'owner's manual' for the human race: the Bible. In it, He tells us not to have sex until we are married; not to have sex with anybody other than the one man/one woman to whom we are married; and to stay married the rest of our lives. That's the one and only prescription for safe sex."[42]

Q: Should a child be allowed to "decide for himself" on matters related to God? Aren't we forcing our religion down children's throats when we tell them what to believe?

A: Let me answer with an illustration from nature. A little gosling (baby goose) has a peculiar characteristic that is relevant at this point. Shortly after it hatches from its shell it becomes attached, or "imprinted," to the first thing seen moving nearby. From that time forward, the gosling follows that particular object when it moves in the vicinity. Ordinarily, it becomes imprinted to the mother goose which hatched the new generation.

If she is removed, however, the gosling settles for any mobile substitute, whether alive or not. In fact, a gosling becomes imprinted most easily to a blue football bladder, dragged by on a string. A week later, the baby falls in line behind the bladder as it scoots by.

Time is the critical factor in this process. The gosling is vulnerable to imprinting for only a few seconds after hatching from the shell. If that opportunity is lost, it cannot be regained. In other words, there is a critical, brief period in the gosling's life when this instinctual learning is possible.

There is also a critical period when certain kinds of instruction are easier in the life of children. Although humans have no instincts (only drives, reflexes, urges, etc.), there is a brief period during childhood when youngsters are vulnerable to religious training. Their concepts of right and wrong are formulated during this time, and their view of God begins to solidify.

As in the case of the gosling, the opportunity of that period must be seized when it is available. Leaders of the Catholic Church have been widely quoted as saying, "Give us the child until he is seven years old and we'll have him for life." They are usually correct, because permanent attitudes can be instilled during these seven vulnerable years.

Unfortunately, however, the opposite is also true. The absence or misapplication of instruction through that prime-time period may place a severe limitation on the depth of a child's later devotion to God. When parents withhold indoctrination from their small children, allowing them to "decide for themselves," the adults are almost guaranteeing that their youngsters will "decide" in the negative. If parents want their children to have a meaningful faith, they must give up any misguided attempts at objectivity. Children listen closely to discover just how much their parents believe what they preach. Any indecision or ethical confusion from the parent is likely to be magnified in the child.

After the middle adolescent age (ending at about fifteen years), children resent being told exactly what to believe. They don't want religion "forced down their throats," and should be given more autonomy in what they believe. If the early exposure has been properly conducted, children will have an inner mainstay to steady them. Their early indoctrination, then, is the key to the spiritual attitudes they carry into adulthood.

Q: My young daughter recently told me that she is two months pregnant. What should be my attitude to her now?
A: You cannot reverse the circumstances by being harsh or unloving at this point. Your daughter needs more understanding now than ever before, and you should give it to her if possible. Help her grope through this difficulty and avoid "I told you so" comments. Many important decisions will face her in the next few months and she will need cool, rational parents to assist in determining the best path to take. Remember, lasting love and affection often develop between people who have survived a crisis together.

Q: When do children begin to develop a sexual nature? Does this occur suddenly during puberty?
A: No, it occurs long before puberty. Perhaps the most important understanding suggested by Freud was his observation that children are not asexual. He stated that sexual gratification begins in the cradle and is first associated with feeding. Behavior during childhood is influenced considerably by sexual curiosity and interest, although the happy hormones do not take full charge until early adolescence. Thus, it is not uncommon for a four-year-old to be interested in nudity and the sexual apparatus of boys versus girls.

This is an important time in the forming of sexual attitudes. Parents should be careful not to express shock and extreme disapproval of this kind of curiosity. It is believed that many sexual problems begin as a result of inappropriate training during early childhood.

Q: Most colleges and universities permit men and women to live in coeducational dormitories, often rooming side by side. Others allow unrestricted visiting hours by members of the opposite sex. Do you think this promotes more healthy attitudes toward sex?
A: It certainly promotes more sex, and some people think that's healthy. The advocates of cohabitation try to tell us that young men and women can live together without doing what comes naturally. That is nonsense. The sex drive is one of the strongest forces in human nature, and Joe College is notoriously weak in suppressing it. I would prefer that supporters of coeducational dormitories admit that morality is not very important to them. If abstinence is something we value, then we should at least give it a wobbly-legged chance to survive. The sharing of collegiate bedrooms (*and* bathrooms!) hardly takes us in that direction.

Q: You have said on several occasions that a society can be no more stable than the strengths of its individual family units. More specifically, you said sexual behavior is directly linked to survival of nations. Explain how.
A: A book could be written on that topic, but let me give you a short answer to it. This linkage you referred to was first illuminated by J. D. Unwin, a British social anthropologist who spent seven years studying the births and deaths of eighty civilizations. He reported from his exhaustive research that every known culture in the world's history has followed the same sexual pattern: during its early days of existence, premarital and extramarital sexual relationships were strictly prohibited. Great creative energy was associated with this inhibition of sexual expression, causing the culture to prosper. Much later in the life of the society, its people began to rebel against the strict prohibitions, demanding the freedom to release their internal passions. As the mores weakened, the social energy abated, eventually resulting in the decay or destruction of the civilization.

Dr. Unwin stated that the energy which holds a society together is sexual in nature. When a man is devoted to one woman and one family, he is motivated to build, save, protect, plan, and prosper on their behalf. However, when his sexual interests are dispersed and generalized, his effort is invested in the gratification of sensual desires. Dr. Unwin concluded: "Any human society is free either to display great energy, or to enjoy sexual freedom; the evidence is that they cannot do both for more than one generation."

It is my belief that the weakening of America's financial position in the world and the difficulties its families and children are experiencing can be traced to our departure from traditional values and Biblical concepts of morality.

Q: Do you think religion should be taught in public schools?
A: Not as a particular doctrine or dogma. The right of parents to select their child's religious orientation must be protected and no teacher or administrator should be allowed to contradict what the child has been taught at home. On the other hand, the vast majority of Americans do profess a belief in God. I would like to see this unnamed God acknowledged in the classroom. The Supreme Court decision banning nonspecific school prayer (or even silent prayer) is an extreme measure, and I regret it. The tiny minority of children from atheistic homes could easily be protected by the school during prayerful moments.

Q: You spoke of kindness to animals. That reminds me to ask you about my seven-year-old son who is cruel to animals. We've caught him doing some pretty awful things to neighborhood dogs and cats. Of course, we punished him, but I wonder if there is anything to be more concerned about here?
A: I would consider cruelty to animals as a serious symptom to be evaluated by a professional. Children who do such things are not typically just going through a phase. It should be seen as a warning sign of a possible psychological problem that could be rather persistent. It also appears to be associated with sexual abuse in childhood. I don't want to alarm you or over-state the case, but adults committed to a life of violent crime were often cruel to animals in their childhood. This fact has been verified in a study by the American Humane Association.[43,44] I suggest that you take your son to a psychologist or other behavioral specialist who can evaluate his mental health. And by all means, do not tolerate unkindness to animals.

Q: Is AIDS God's plague sent to punish homosexuals, lesbians, and other promiscuous people?

A: I would think not, because little babies and others who bear no responsibility are suffering. But consider this: If I choose to leap off a ten-story building, I will die when my body hits the ground below. It's inevitable. But gravity was not designed by God to punish my folly. He established physical laws that can be violated only at great peril. So it is with his moral laws. They are as real and predictable as the principles that govern the physical universe. Thus, we knew (and He *certainly* knew) with the onset of the sexual revolution back in 1968 that this day of disease and promiscuity would come. It is here, and what we do with our situation will determine how much we and our children will suffer in the future.

By the way, did you know that God created the moral basis for the universe *before* he made the heavens and the earth? His concept of right and wrong were not afterthoughts that came along with the Ten Commandments. No, it was an expression of God's divine nature and was in force before "the beginning."

That's what we read in Proverbs 8:22-36 (NIV), referring to the universal moral law in first person:

> *The LORD brought me forth as the first of his works, before his deeds of old; I was appointed from eternity, from the beginning, before the world began. When there were no oceans, I was given birth, when there were no springs abounding with water; before the mountains were settled in place, before the hills, I was given birth, before he made the earth or its fields or any of the dust of the world. I was there when he set the heavens in place, when he marked out the horizon on the face of the deep, when he established the clouds above and fixed securely the fountains of the deep, when he gave the sea its boundary so the waters would not overstep his command, and when he marked out the foundations of the earth. Then I was the craftsman at his side. I was filled with delight day after day, rejoicing always in his presence, rejoicing in his whole world and delighting in mankind. Now then, my sons, listen to me; blessed are those who keep my ways. Listen to my instruction and be wise; do not ignore it. Blessed is the man who listens to me, watching daily at my doors, waiting at my doorway. For whoever finds me finds life and receives*

favor from the LORD. *But whoever fails to find me harms himself; all who hate me love death.*

These last two verses say it all. If we conform our behavior to God's ancient moral prescription, we are entitled to the sweet benefits of life, itself. But if we defy its clear imperatives, then death is the inevitable consequence. AIDS is only one avenue by which sickness and death befall those who play Russian roulette with God's moral law.

ELEVEN

A MOMENT FOR MOM

A S THE PREVIOUS chapters have indicated, the responsibilities of effective parenthood are staggeringly heavy at times. Children place great demands on their guardians, as a colleague of mine discovered one morning when he told his three-year-old daughter good-bye.

"I have to go to work, now," he said.

"That's all right, Daddy, I'll forgive you," she tearfully replied. She was willing to overlook his insult just once, but she didn't want him to let it happen again. As this little girl demonstrated, children are terribly dependent on their parents and the task of meeting their needs is a full-time job.

Some of them are much more aware of the power struggle with their parents than Mom and Dad appear to be. That fact was illustrated numerous times after the original publication of *Dare to Discipline*. Some kids who couldn't even read knew there was stuff in that green book that helped their parents control them. One youngster went to a bookshelf, pulled this publication from among hundreds, and proceeded to throw it in the fire. Others were even more explicit about how they felt.

The mother of a very strong-willed three-year-old shared a story with me that made me smile. This youngster named Laura had managed to wind the entire family around her little finger. She was out of control and seemed to be enjoying it. Both the mother and father were exasperated in trying to deal with their little spitfire—until, that is, Mom happened to be in a bookstore and stumbled across *Dare to Discipline*. She bought a copy and soon learned, at least according to the opinion of its author, that it is appropriate under certain circumstances to spank a child. Thus, the next time Laura played her defiant games, she got a shocking surprise on her little fanny.

Laura was a very bright child and she was able to figure out where mama got that idea. Believe it or not, the mother came in the next morning and found her copy of *Dare to Discipline* floating in the toilet.

That may be the most graphic editorial comment anyone has made about my writings. I'm told Dr. Benjamin Spock is loved by millions of kids who are being raised according to his philosophy. I have an entire generation that would like to catch me in a blind alley. But I'm also convinced that some young adults who have grown up on love and discipline in balance are now raising *their* children that way. It is still true today, as it was when they were tots, that a child will be ruled by the rudder or the rock. Some things never change.

Even with a clear game plan in mind, however, raising kids properly is one of life's richest challenges. It is not uncommon for a mother, particularly, to feel overwhelmed by the complexity of her parental assignment. In many homes, she is the primary protector for each child's health, education, intellect, personality, character, and emotional stability. As such, she must serve as physician, nurse, psychologist, teacher, minister, cook, and policeman. Since in many cases she is with the children longer each day than her husband, she is the chief disciplinarian and main giver of security and love.

The reality is that she and her husband will not know whether or not she is handling these matters properly until it is too late to change her methodology. Furthermore, Mom's responsibilities extend far beyond her children. She must also meet her obligations to her husband, her church, her relatives, her friends, and often times, her employer. Each of these areas demands her best effort, and the conscientious mother often finds herself racing through the day in a breathless attempt to be all things to all people.

Most healthy individuals can tolerate encircling pressures as long as each responsibility can be kept under relative control. Hard work and diligence are personally rewarding, provided anxiety and frustration are kept at a minimum. However, much greater self-control is needed when a threatening problem develops in one of the critical areas.

That is, if a child becomes very ill, marital problems erupt, or Mom is unjustly criticized in the neighborhood, then the other routine tasks become more difficult to accomplish. Certainly, there are occasions in the life of every mother when she looks in the mirror and asks, "How can I make it through this day?" The simple suggestions in the remaining portion of this book are designed to help her answer that exasperated question.

1. *Reserve some time for yourself.* It is important for a mother to put herself on the priority list, too. At least once a week she should play tennis, go bowling or shopping, stop by the gym, or simply "waste" an occasional afternoon. It is unhealthy for anyone to work all the time, and the entire family will profit from her periodic recreation.

Even more important is the protection and maintenance of romance in her marriage. A husband and wife should have a date every week or two, leaving the children at home and forgetting the day's problems for an evening. If the family's finances seemingly prohibit such activities, I suggest that other expenditures be re-examined. I believe that money spent on togetherness will yield many more benefits than an additional piece of furniture or a newer automobile. A woman finds life much more enjoyable if she knows she is the sweetheart, and not just the wife, of her husband.

2. *Don't struggle with things you can't change.* The first principle of mental health is to learn to accept the inevitable. To do otherwise is to run with the brakes on. Too many people make themselves unhappy over insignificant irritants which should be ignored. In these cases, contentment is no more stable than the weakest link in the chain of circumstances surrounding their lives. All but one of the conditions in a particular woman's life might be perfect: she has good health, a devoted husband, happy children, plenty of food, warmth and shelter, and a personal challenge. Nevertheless, she might be miserable because she doesn't like her mother-in-law. This one negative element can be allowed to overshadow all the good fortune surrounding her.

Life has enough crises in it without magnifying our troubles during good times, yet peace of mind is often surrendered for such insignificant causes. I wonder how many women are discontented today because they don't have something which either wasn't invented or wasn't fashionable just fifty years ago. Men and women should recognize that dissatisfaction with life can become nothing more than a bad habit—a costly attitude that can rob them of life's pleasures.

3. *Don't deal with big problems late at night.* Fatigue does strange things to human perception. After a hard day, the most simple tasks may appear

insurmountable. All problems seem more unsolvable at night, and the decisions that are reached then may be more emotional than rational. When couples discuss finances or other family problems in the wee hours, they are asking for trouble. Their tolerance to frustration is low, often leading to fights which should never have occurred. Tension and hostility can be avoided by simply delaying important topics until morning. A good night's sleep and a rich cup of coffee can go a long way toward defusing the problem.

4. *Try making a list.* When the work load gets particularly heavy there is comfort to be found in making a list of the duties to be performed. The advantages of writing down one's responsibilities are threefold: (1) You know you won't forget anything. (2) You guarantee that the most important jobs will get done first. Thus, if you don't get finished by the end of the day, you will have at least done the items that were most critical. (3) You leave a record of accomplishments by crossing tasks off the list as they are completed.

5. *Seek divine assistance.* The concepts of marriage and parenthood were not human inventions. God, in his infinite wisdom, created and ordained the family as the basic unit of procreation and companionship. The solutions to the problems of modern parenthood can be found through the power of prayer and personal appeal to the Creator. Indeed, I believe parents should commit themselves to *daily* prayer and supplication on behalf of their children. The task is too scary on our own, and there is not enough knowledge on the books (including this one) to guarantee the outcome of our parenting duties. We desperately need divine help with the job!

The principles of discipline which I have summarized in this book can hardly be considered new ideas. Most of these recommendations were first written in the Scripture, dating back at least two thousand years to biblical times. Consider the clarity with which the following verses outline a healthy parental attitude toward children and vice versa.

> *He [the father] must have proper authority in his own household, and be able to control and command the respect of his children. (For if a man cannot rule in his own house how can he look after a church of God?)* (1 Timothy 3:4-5, PHILLIPS)

This verse acknowledges the fact that respect must be "commanded." It is not a by-product of human nature, but it is inherently related to control and discipline.

> *My son, do not regard lightly the discipline of the Lord, nor lose courage when you are punished by him. For the Lord disciplines him whom he loves* [Note: Discipline and love work hand and hand; one is a function of the other.]*, and chastises every son whom he receives. It is for discipline that you have to endure. God is treating you as sons; for what son is there whom the father does not discipline? If you are left without discipline, in which all have participated, then you are illegitimate children and not sons. Besides this, we have had earthly fathers to discipline us and we respected them.* [Note: The relationship between discipline and respect was recognized more than two thousand years ago.] . . . *For the moment all discipline seems painful rather than pleasant; later it yields the peaceful fruit of righteousness to those who have been trained by it.* (Hebrews 12:5-9, 11, RSV)

The purpose of this Scripture is to demonstrate that the parent's relationship with his child should be modeled after God's relationship with man. In its ultimate beauty, that interaction is characterized by abundant love—a love unparalleled in tenderness and mercy. This same love leads the benevolent father to guide, correct, and even bring some pain to the child when it is necessary for his eventual good. I find it difficult to comprehend how this message has been so thoroughly misunderstood.

> *Children, the right thing for you to do is to obey your parents as those whom God has set over you. The first commandment to contain a promise was: "Honor thy father and thy mother that it may be well with thee, and that thou mayest live long on the earth." Fathers, don't over-correct your children or make it difficult for them to obey the commandment. Bring them up with Christian teaching in Christian discipline.* (Ephesians 6:1-4, PHILLIPS)

> *Foolishness is bound in the heart of a child; but the rod of correction shall drive it far from him.* (Proverbs 22:15, KJV)

This recommendation has troubled some people, leading them to claim that the "rod" was not a paddle, but a measuring stick with which to evaluate the child. The following passage was included expressly for those who were confused on that point.

> Withhold not correction from the child: for if thou beatest him with the rod, he shall not die. Thou shalt beat him with the rod, and shalt deliver his soul from hell. (Proverbs 23:13-14, KJV)

Certainly, if the "rod" is a measuring stick, you now know what to do with it? (Note: Please don't grill me on this. I would ask that you heed all of my disclaimers related to child abuse, which I expressed in earlier chapters—especially on pages 9-10.)

> He that spareth his rod hateth his son: but he that loveth him chasteneth him betimes. (Proverbs 13:24, KJV)

> The rod and reproof give wisdom: but a child left to himself bringeth his mother to shame. (Proverbs 29:15, KJV)

> Correct thy son, and he shall give thee rest; yea, he shall give delight unto thy soul. (Proverbs 29:17, KJV)

From Genesis to Revelation, there is consistent foundation on which to build an effective philosophy of parent-child relationships. It is my belief that we have departed from the standard which was clearly outlined in both the Old and New Testaments, and that deviation is costing us a heavy toll in the form of social turmoil. Self-control, human kindness, respect, and peacefulness can again be manifest in America if we will *dare to discipline* in our homes and schools.

Let me leave you, now, with a wonderful old poem written by Alice Pearson. It focuses on *the* most vital responsibility in parenting—that of introducing our children to Jesus Christ and getting them safely through this dangerous and turbulent world. That should be, after all, the ultimate goal for every believing parent the world over.

ARE ALL THE CHILDREN IN?

I think oftimes as night draws nigh,
Of an old house on the hill,
And of a yard all wide
And blossom-starred
Where the children played at will.
And when the night at last came down
Hushing the merry din,
Mother would look around and ask,
"Are all the children in?"

Oh, it's many and many a year since then,
And the old house on the hill
No longer echoes to childish feet,
And the yard is still, so still.
But I see it all as the shadows creep,
And though many the years have been since then,
I can hear mother ask,
"Are all the children in?"

I wonder if when the shadows fall
On the last short earthly day;
When we say goodbye to the world outside
All tired with our childish play;
When we step out into the other land
Where mother so long has been,
Will we hear her ask,
Just as of old,
"Are all the children in?"[1]

A Quick Survey of Drugs & Substance Abuse for Parents

THERE IS NO more certain destroyer of self-discipline and self-control than the abusive use of drugs. Teens who have begun taking drugs, in whatever form, often show a sudden disinterest in everything that formerly challenged them. Their school work is ignored and hobbies are forgotten. Their personal appearance often becomes sloppy. They refuse to carry responsibility and avoid activities that require effort. Their relationship with parents deteriorates rapidly, and they suddenly terminate many of their lifelong friendships. Young drug users are clearly marching to a new set of drums—and disaster often awaits them at the end of the trail.

To help parents recognize and understand a possible drug problem in their sons and daughters, we have provided the following overview of the basics. I pray that neither you, nor they, will ever need it. Though some of the facts are technical, I recommend that you carefully study and even memorize the important details from this summary, and review the glossary of drug-world slang later in this chapter. I am indebted to several law enforcement agencies and other sources for their help in compiling this information.[1]

WHAT ARE THE SYMPTOMS OF DRUG ABUSE?

At the beginning of this appendix I mentioned several of the attitudinal and behavioral characteristics of individuals who use harmful drugs. Listed below are eight related physical and emotional symptoms that may indicate drug abuse by your child.

1. Inflammation of the eyelids and nose is common. The pupils of the eyes are either very wide or very small, depending on the kind of drugs used.
2. Extremes of energy may be represented. The individual may be sluggish, gloomy, and withdrawn . . . or loud, hysterical, and jumpy.
3. The appetite is extreme—either very great or very poor. Weight loss may occur.
4. The personality suddenly changes. The individual may become irritable, inattentive, and confused . . . or aggressive, suspicious, and explosive.
5. Body and breath odor is often bad. Cleanliness may be ignored.
6. The digestive system may be upset—diarrhea, nausea, and vomiting may occur. Headaches and double vision are also common. Other signs of physical deterioration may include change in skin tone and body stance.
7. With intravenous drug users, needle marks on the body, usually appearing on the arms, are an important symptom. These punctures sometimes get infected and appear as sores and boils.
8. Moral values often crumble and are replaced by new, outlandish ideas and values. Each drug produces its own unique symptoms. Thus, the above list is not specific to a particular substance. Parents who suspect their child is using dangerous drugs (including alcohol and tobacco) should contact their family physician immediately.

WHERE ARE THE DRUGS OBTAINED?

Illicit drugs are surprisingly easy to obtain by adolescents. The family medicine cabinet usually offers a handy stockpile of prescription drugs, cough medicines, tranquilizers, sleeping pills, reducing aids, and pain killers. Paint thinner, glue, and other toxic materials in the garage are also liable to be used as a means of getting high. Furthermore, a physician can be tricked into prescribing the desired drugs. A reasonably intelligent person can learn from a medical text the symptoms of diseases which are usually treated with the drug he wants.

Prescriptions can also be forged and passed at local pharmacies. Some drugs reach the street market after having been stolen from pharmacies, doctor's offices, or manufacturer's warehouses. However, the vast majority of drugs are smuggled into this country. Surprisingly, many of them are first manufactured here and sold abroad before finding their way back as contraband.

HOW MUCH DO DRUGS COST?

Though the prices of various illicit drugs vary a great deal from area to area and dealer to dealer, depending on quantity and quality, the following figures represent the approximate black market values for the substances indicated at the present time:

1. Amphetamines: $1 and up per pill.
2. Methamphetamine: $10 per injection or snort. It is widely available in both powder and "ice" formulations, and typically sold in small plastic bags containing about a quarter-gram of the drug. Many people call it the "poor man's cocaine."
3. Barbiturates: $1 and up per pill.
4. Marijuana cigarettes: $2.50 and up for each. Marijuana is commonly sold in small plastic bags for $10 (enough for three to four cigarettes). Due to advanced growing techniques, today's marijuana is about three times as strong as what was available to the Woodstock generation during the '60s and '70s. By the pound, cheap homegrown marijuana sells for approximately $250. The same amount of a more potent, better grade marijuana can sell for anywhere between $1,300 and $3,000.
5. Heroin: $10 to $25 per injection. It is often packaged for sale in small kiddy balloons for $30 and up (enough for three "hits"). A pound, with an average street purity of 10%, costs $20,000 to $25,000. Heroin is still as popular today as it ever has been, though cocaine and marijuana currently seem to attract more attention in the media.

6. Cocaine: $5 to $20 per usage, whether in powder (for snorting) or hardened "rock"/"crack" format (for smoking). Commonly sold on the street in plastic bags for about $25 and up per quarter-gram (enough for two to four "hits"). A kilo of cocaine (about 2.2 pounds) typically sells for between $17,500 to $28,000, but can soar as high as $40,000 depending on supply. A pound, with a typical street purity of 55%-65%, costs between $12,000 to $16,000. The sale of this drug is truly big business.

7. Hallucinogens: $1 to $10 per usage, though prices vary considerably depending on the quality and type. These days, LSD (acid) typically sells on blotter paper imprinted with colorful decals of cartoon characters, cars, etc., and is frequently referred to by the decal. Thus, if the picture on the blotter paper were of Mickey Mouse, it would be called "Mickey Mouse Acid." LSD also comes as a liquid and as a gelatin substance. Figure $100 to $300 for a hundred hits. Another common hallucinogen, Phencyclidine (PCP), is widely available in liquid form at about $150 to $250 per ounce, but costs about $1,000 per ounce in powder or crystal formulations. PCP is often used to lace other drugs, especially marijuana and cocaine.

WHAT ARE THE MOST COMMON ILLICIT DRUGS?

Dangerous drugs can be categorized into the five major divisions appearing below. Fundamental details are also presented to allow parents to learn what their teen probably knows already.

1. **Stimulants:** (Uppers) These drugs excite the user, inducing talkativeness, restlessness, and overstimulation. They are commonly called pep pills.
   a. Specific drugs
      (1) Benzedrine (Bennies, whites, etc.)
      (2) Dexedrine (dexies, hearts, etc.)
      (3) Methamphetamine (speed, meth run, crystal meth, etc.)
   b. Psychological and physiological effects of abusive use
      (1) Insomnia
      (2) Loss of appetite
      (3) Dry mouth
      (4) Vomiting

    (5) Diarrhea

    (6) Nausea

    (7) Inhibitions released

    (8) Blurred vision

    (9) Aggressiveness

  (10) Hallucinations and confusion

2. **Depressants:** (Barbiturates, Downers) These drugs are used in medicine to relax and induce sleep in the patient. They are commonly called sleeping pills.

  a. Specific drugs

    (1) Seconal (red, red devils, pinkies, pink ladies, etc.)

    (2) Nembutal (yellows, yellow jackets, etc.)

    (3) Tuinal (rainbows, double trouble, etc.)

    (4) Amytal (blues, blue heavens, etc.)

  b. Psychological and physiological effects of abusive use

    (1) Drowsy confusion and an inability to think clearly

    (2) Lack of coordination

    (3) Lethargic speech

    (4) Defective judgment

    (5) Tremors

    (6) Involuntary movement of the eyes

    (7) Hostility

    (8) More deaths are caused by overdoses of barbiturates than any other drug—often occurring accidentally.

3. **Hallucinogens:** These drugs are capable of provoking changes in sensation, thinking, self-awareness, and emotion.

  a. Specific drug

    (1) Lysergic acid diethylamide tartrate (LSD-25, LSD, acid, Vitamin A, etc.)

    (2) Psilocybin/Psilocyn (Magic mushrooms, shrooms, etc.)

    (3) Peyote (Mescaline)

    (4) Phencyclidine (PCP, Sherms, Lovely, Dusters, etc.)

  b. Psychological and physiological effects

    (1) Bizarre psychic experiences with heightened sensitivity to color and other stimuli.

    (2) Psychotic illness occasionally occurs.

(3) Chromosomal breakage may develop.

(4) The psychic phenomena occasionally recur weeks after the last dosage is taken.

(5) Alterations in time and space perception occur.

(6) Illusions and hallucinations are experienced.

4. *Marijuana:* (Grass, pot, joint, weed, etc.) Marijuana is usually rolled into cigarettes. When smoked, the initial effect is that of a stimulant. However, continued usage will produce drowsiness and unconsciousness. Thus, marijuana is technically classified as a sedative.

  a. Psychological and physiological effects

    (1) Pupils of the eyes become dilated; the white part becomes bloodshot.

    (2) A loss of time and space orientation

    (3) Muscle tremors

    (4) Accelerated pulse and heartbeat

    (5) Apparent dizziness

    (6) Odd behavior

    (7) Loss of inhibitions

    (8) Delusions

    (9) User becomes "psychologically dependent" on marijuana.

5. *Narcotics:* These drugs relieve pain and induce sleep.

  a. Specific drug

    (1) Heroin (horse, H, Harry, smack, brown, etc.) Heroin is an opiate. It is processed from morphine but it is much stronger. The tolerance for this drug builds up faster than any other opiate and it is therefore more dangerous. Heroin is the most devastating and enslaving drug in existence. It is not even used medically in America.

  b. Psychological and physiological effects

    (1) Heroin is a cerebral, spinal, and respiratory depressant.

    (2) The initial reaction is one of euphoria and comfort. This feeling disappears quickly, requiring a larger dose on the next occasion.

    (3) Immediately after injecting heroin, the user becomes drowsy. This is called "going on the nod" or "nodding."

    (4) Pupils of the eyes contract tightly.

GLOSSARY OF DRUG-WORLD SLANG

The following list will help you identify today's common drug-world slang, but keep in mind that the terminology varies in different parts of the country and changes extremely rapidly. Also, with the prevalence of wire taps and electronic surveillance techniques used in drug enforcement, users often call drugs by anything but what you see on the list. For example, an individual who wants to buy, say, a couple of pounds of marijuana from his usual source might use the word taco, banana, radio, shirt, telephone, or some other nonsense word instead of the more usual grass, pot, weed, etc. Thus, if you were to hear their conversation, it might go something like this:

"I'm looking to cop a couple bananas."

"I've got one banana now, and can clean another banana and a half by Saturday."

As it is said, a rose by any other name smells just as sweet. Likewise, drugs by any other name are just as dangerous. Don't be fooled.

Having said that, let's open the dictionary to the drug world:

Acid	Lysergic Acid Diethylamide (LSD-25) (Also: LSD, Paper Acid, Blotter, Blots, Tabs, Window Pane, Green Star, Sugar Cube, Blotter, White Lightning, Microdot, Acid Green, Red Green, Blue Heaven, Vitamin A, AC, Cid, Fry)
Acid Heads	Users of LSD
Bindle	Small packet of narcotics (Also: Nickel Bag, Dime Bag, Quarter Bag)
Blue-Velvet	Combination of a paregoric (upper) with an antihistamine
Booze	Alcohol (Also: Brew, Juice, Suds, Liquid Gold, Sauce)
Bunk	Poor quality narcotics
Caviar and Champagne	Combination of rock or crack cocaine with marijuana
Clean	To prepare marijuana for street sale (Also: Cut, Manicure)
Coke	Cocaine (Also: Blow, Flake, Crack, Rock, Kibble Bits, Lines, Snow, Cola, Powder, Dove, C, Lady, Freebase, Toot, Baseball, Base, Girl, Doing A Line, Snorting, Dynamite, 8-Ball, White)
Dime Bag	$10 purchase of drugs
Dope	Drugs (Also: Junk, Stuff)
Downers	A Sedative-hypnotic (Barbiturates, tranquilizers, methaqualone, depressants) (Also: Barbs, Valium,

Candy, Amytal, Blue Devils, Blue Heaven, Blues,
Double Trouble, Tuinal, Rainbows, Pinks, Red
Devils, Reds, Seconal, Yellows, Yellow Jacket,
Nembutal, Qs, Roaches, Ludes, Tooies, On Downs,
Doriden, Quaaludes, Librium, Equanil, Miltown,
Serax, Tranxene, Zanax, Pentobarbital, Librium,
Methaqualone, Special K (animal tranquilizer)

Drying Out............................ Abandon drug habit (Also: Kick, Cleaning Up
Act, Cold Turkey—when a user quits without
help or other drugs)

Ecstasy .... Designer Drugs (Ecstasy, analogs) (Also: XTC,
Eve, STP, DOB, MDA, MDMA, MMDA, MDEA,
MPTP, MPPP, PEPAP, TMA, PMA)

Feds .... Federal narcotics agents (Also: Wally Narc, Sam)

Five-o.................................... $50 purchase of drugs, typically rock cocaine
(Also: Two-o, etc.)

Fix.. Injection of narcotics

Grass .... Marijuana (Also: Pot, Reefer, Weed, Joint, J, Mary
Jane, Bag, Herb, Hay, Tea, Dope, Bud, Sinsemilla,
Thai Sticks, Hash, Hashish, Dime, Nickel,
Quarter, Smoke, Green, Skunk-Weed, Rope,
Acapulco Gold, Panama Red, Mexican Red Hair,
Kona Gold, Maui Wowi)

Green .... Money (Also: Bread, Coins, Dead Presidents)

Hashish .... More potent form of marijuana made from a
concentration of marijuana flower tops. (Also:
Hash, Kif, Shish, Ganja, Rope, Leb, Black Russian,
Blond Lebanese, Black Afghani)

The Heat .... Police (Also: Pigs, The Man, Big John, Cops,
Narcs, Fuzz)

Hit.. Single drug dosage; Drag on marijuana cigarette;
Purchase drugs in arrest

Hooked .... Addicted

Hooker.................................. Prostitute (Also: Working Girl, Strawberry, Hos,
Whore, Street Walker, Lady of the Night, Turning
Tricks)

Hot....................................... Wanted by police

Hot shot .... Fatal or potentially fatal drug dosage (Also:
Overdose, OD)

I'm holding/serving .... I have drugs; can make a deal

I'm looking to cop .... I wish to buy

Jim Jones.............................. Marijuana cigarette laced with cocaine and
dipped in PCP

Junkie................................... Drug addict (Also: Hype)

Loaded .... Intoxicated by drugs, including alcohol
(Also: High, Wasted, Stoned, Cranked, Slammed,
Nodding, On the Nod, Smashed, Down, Spacing,
Wired, Hammered, Blitzed, Speeding, Flying,
Messed Up, Bombed, Banged Up, Shot Up,
Jacked Up, Tore Up, Wired, Tweeked, Amped
Out, Fried, Right, Straight)

Locked Up .... To be in jail (Also: Boxed, Canned, Jailed)

Mainlining .... Injecting drugs directly into vein (Also: Shooting,
Banging, Geezing, Hitting Home, Registering,
Hyping)

Mouth Holding .... Drugs packaged in balloons and hidden in mouth
from police

Mule .... One who sells or transports for a regular peddler
(Also: Runner, Carrier, Pigeon)

Nickel Bag .... $5 purchase of drugs

Outfit .... Equipment for narcotics injection (Also: Fit, Kit,
Gizmo, Dropper, Works, Toys, Cooker, Point,
Spike, Tie-Off/Tie-Rag)

Pass Out .... Lose consciousness from drugs (Also: Black Out,
Tube)

PCP .... Phencyclidine (Also: Angel Dust, Hog, Lovely,
Love Boat, Sherms, Wac, Crystal, Ozone, Dusters,
Water, Stick, Wet One, Seems, Super Kool, Killer
Weed)

Poly-User .... Users who combine two or more drugs to counteract or heighten the effects of the first drug.
(For example, see: Blue-Velvet, Caviar and
Champagne, Space Basing, Speed Ball, T's and B's,
and Jim Jones.)

Quarter bag .... $25 purchase of drugs

Rush .... Physical sensations after taking drugs (Also:
Flash, High, Bang, Hit Home, Register)

Script .... Prescription

Smack .... Heroin (including narcotics and prescription
drugs). (Also: H, Harry, Horse, Junk, Powder,
Snow, Stuff, Boy, China White, C-and-W, Balloon,
Dope, White, Brown, Mud, Gum, Chiva, Black
Tar, Spoons, Papers, Tar;— other narcotics and
prescription drugs used in place of heroine:
Dolophine, Methadone, Amidone, Codeine,
Pectoral Syrup, Percocet, Pethidine, Talwin,
Mepergan, Percodan, Lomitil, Paregoric, Darvon,
Parepectolin, Fentanyl)

Smokes.................................. Tobacco (nicotine) (Also: Cigarettes, Chew, Cigars, Puffs, Snuff)

Snitch.................................... Informer (Also: Rat, Gonner, Dead Man)

Source .... Drug Supplier (Also: Dealer, Pusher, Dope Man, Dope Lady)

Spacebasing.......................... Combination of rock or crack cocaine with PCP (Also: Whacking)

Speed Ball............................. Combination of heroin and cocaine or other amphetamines (Also: Goof Ball)

STP .... An hallucinogen (mescaline, peyote, psilocybin, etc.) (Also: Mesc, Buttons, Cactus, Magic Mushrooms, Mushrooms, Shrooms, Boomers, DMT)

Strawberry............................. Prostitute (see Hooker) who works for cocaine

THC...................................... Active ingredient in marijuana and hashish

T's and B's............................. Combination of Pentazocine and Tripelennamine (Also: T's and Blues)

Uppers .... A stimulant (amphetamines, methamphetamines, dextroamphetamines, and Ritalin) (Also: Crystal, Crank, Speed, Fast, Go-Fast, Peanut Butter Crystal, Yellow, Cross Tops, White Tops, Hearts, Benzedrine, Bennies, Co-Pilots, Dexedrine, Dexies, Peaches, Whites, Whities, LA Turnabouts, Black Beauties, Crystal Meth, Mother's Little Helpers, Preludin, Bumble Bees, Footballs, Biphetamine, Lid Poppers, Wake Ups, Popping Uppers, Speeding, Being Wired, Flying, Pre-state, Didrex, Voranil, Tenuate, Tepanil, Pondimin, Sanorex, Plegine, Ionamin)

Vapors .... Inhalants (solvents, glue, gases, nitrous oxide, amyl and butyl nitrite, hydrocarbons, chlorogydrocarbons) (Also: Honk, Laughing Gas, Glue, Aerosol, Gunk, Locker Room, Buzz Bombs, Bolt, Whippets, Rush, Poppers, Snappers, Whip Cream, Climax)

Zig Zag .... Brand of cigarette paper used to roll marijuana smokes

CHAPTER 2. COMMON SENSE & YOUR CHILD

1. Dr. Luther Woodward, with Morton Edwards, editor, *Your Child from Two to Five* (New York: Permabooks, 1955).

2. Dr. James Dobson, *The Strong-Willed Child* (Carol Stream: Tyndale House Publishers, Inc., 1978), p. 55.

3. John B. Watson & R. R. Watson, *Psychological Care of Infant and Child* (Norton & Company, 1928), pp. 81–82, 87.

CHAPTER 4. QUESTIONS & ANSWERS

1. Dr. James Dobson, *The Strong-Willed Child* (Carol Stream: Tyndale House Publishers, Inc., 1978), p. 52.

CHAPTER 5. THE MIRACLE TOOLS, PART 1

1. Dr. James Dobson, *Hide or Seek* (Old Tappan, NJ: Fleming H. Revell Company, 1974), p. 69.

CHAPTER 6. THE MIRACLE TOOLS, PART 2

1. Dr. James Dobson, *The Strong-Willed Child* (Carol Stream: Tyndale House Publishers, Inc., 1978), p. 136.

CHAPTER 7. DISCIPLINE IN LEARNING

1. Jerry Adler, "Creating Problems," *Newsweek* (Fall/Winter 1990) Special Issue, p. 16.

2. Tom Morganthau, "The Future Is Now," *Newsweek* (Fall/Winter 1990) Special Issue, p. 72.

3. *Newsweek,* October 14, 1991, p. 14.

4. Jonathan Kozol, *Illiterate America* (New York: Anchor Press/Doubleday, 1985).

5. *The World Almanac and Book of Facts: 1991* (New York: Pharos Books, 1990).

6. Dr. Sheldon Glueck & Eleanor T. Glueck, *Unraveling Juvenile Delinquency* (Commonwealth Fund, 1950).

CHAPTER 8. THE BARRIERS TO LEARNING, PART 1

1. Sources include the following:

    Ray, Brian D. "A nationwide study of home education: Family character-
istics, legal matters, and student achievement." (1990, available from the
National Home Education Research Institute, P.O. Box 13939, Salem, OR
97309)

    Ray, Brian D. "Home education in North Dakota: Family characteristics
and student achievement." (1991, available from the National Home
Education Research Institute.)

    Ray, Brian D. "Home education in Oklahoma: Family characteristics, stu-
dent achievement, and policy matters." (1991, available from the National
Home Education Research Institute).

2. Sources include the following:

    Ray, Brian D. "A nationwide study of home education; family character-
istics, legal matters, and student achievement." (1990, available from the
National Home Education Research Institute, P.O. Box 13939, Salem, OR
97309)

    Greene, Sue S. "Home study in Alaska: A profile of K–12 students in
the Alaska Centralized Correspondence Study Program." ERIC Document
Reproduction Service No. ED 255 494

    Ray, Brian D. and Jon Wartes. "The academic achievement and affec-
tive development of home-schooled children." *Home Schooling: Political,
Historical, and Pedagogical Perspectives.* (Norwood, N.J.: Ablex Publishing
Corporation, 1991).

    Rakestraw, Jennie F. "Home Schooling in Alabama." *Home School
Researcher.* 4(4), 1988, 1–6.

    Wartes, Jon. "Five years of home-school testing within Washington
state." (December 1991, available from the Washington Home-School
Research Project at 15109 N.E. 169 Pl., Woodinville, WA, 98072).

3. Montgomery, Linda R. "The effect of home schooling on the leadership
skills of home-schooled students." *Home School Researcher.* 5(1), 1–10.

4. Sources include the following:

    Aikin, Wilfred. *The Story of the Eight Year Study.* 4 vols. (New York:
Harper, 1942).

    Delahooke, Mona Maarse. "Home educated children's social/emotional
adjustment and academic achievement: A comparative study." Unpublished
doctoral dissertation, California School of Professional Psychology, Los
Angeles, CA.

    Montgomery, Linda R. "The effect of home schooling on the leadership
skills of home-schooled students." *Home School Researcher.* 5(1), 1–10.

5. Dr. James Dobson, *The Strong-Willed Child* (Carol Stream: Tyndale House
Publishers, Inc., 1978), p. 158–160.

CHAPTER 9. THE BARRIERS TO LEARNING, PART 2

1. Mona Behan, "What Do You Say to a C?" *Parenting Magazine,* April 1992, p. 47.

2. Dr. James Dobson, *The Strong-Willed Child* (Carol Stream: Tyndale House Publishers, Inc., 1978), p. 158–160.

CHAPTER 10. DISCIPLINE IN MORALITY

1. Gabriel Escobar, "Slayings in Washington Hit New High, 436, for 3rd Year," *Washington Post,* November 24, 1990.

2. Steven Manning, "A National Emergency," *Scholastic Update,* April 5, 1991, p. 2.

3. Gordon Witkin, "Kids Who Kill," *U.S. News & World Report,* April 8, 1991, p. 27.

4. Karl Zinsmeister, "Growing Up Scared," *Atlantic Monthly,* June 1990, p. 50.

5. Zinsmeister, "Growing Up Scared," p. 50

6. "Alcohol Use and Abuse in America," *Gallup Report,* No. 265, October 1987, p. 3.

7. Barbara R. Lorch and Robert H. Hughes, "Church Youth, Alcohol and Drug Education Programs, and Youth Substance Use," *Journal of Alcohol and Drug Education*, Vol. 33, No. 2, Winter 1988, p. 15.

8. *Guidelines for Comprehensive Sexuality Education,* National Guidelines Task Force, Sex Information and Education Council of the U.S., 1991.

9. Pamela McDonnell, Sexually Transmitted Diseases Division, Centers for Disease Control, U.S. Dept. of Health & Human Services, t.i., March 16, 1992.

10. Scott W. Wright, "1 in 100 tested at UT has AIDS virus," *Austin American Statesman,* July 14, 1991, p. A14. The federally funded study was based on a nonrandom sample.

11. "Heterosexual HIV Transmission Up in the United States," *American Medical News* (Feb. 3, 1992): 35.

12. U.S. Dept. of Health & Human Services, Public Health Service, Centers for Disease Control, 1991 Division of STD/HIV Prevention *Annual Report,* p.13.

13. Health & Human Services *Annual Report,* p.13.

14. McDonnell, Centers for Disease Control.

15. Health & Human Services *Annual Report,* p.13.

16. Health & Human Services *Annual Report,* p.13.

17. Health & Human Services *Annual Report,* p.13.

18. Robert E. Johnson, et al., "A Seroepidemiologic Survey of the Prevalence of Herpes Simplex Virus Type 2 Infection in the United States," *New England Journal of Medicine,* 321 (July 6, 1989): 7–12.

19. Health & Human Services *Annual Report,* p.13.

20. C. Kuehn and F. Judson, "How common are sexually transmitted infections in adolescents?" *Clinical Practice Sexuality* 5 (1989): 19–25; as cited by Sandra D. Gottwald, et al., Profile: Adolescent Ob/Gyn Patients at the University of Michigan, 1989, *The American Journal of Gynecologic Health* 5 (May/June 1991), 23.

21. Kay Stone, Sexually Transmitted Diseases Division, Centers for Disease Control, U.S. Dept. of Health & Human Services, t.i., March 20, 1992.

22. Elise F. Jones and Jacqueline Darroch Forrest, "Contraceptive Failure in the United States: Revised Estimates from the 1982 National Survey of Family Growth," *Family Planning Perspectives* 21 (May/June 1989): 103.

23. Jones and Forrest, "Contraceptive Failure," p. 105.

24. Lode Wigersma and Ron Oud, "Safety and Acceptability of Condoms for Use by Homosexual Men as a Prophylactic Against Transmission of HIV during Anogenital Sexual Intercourse," *British Medical Journal* 295 (July 11, 1987): 94.

25. Marcia F. Goldsmith, "Sex in the Age of AIDS Calls for Common Sense and Condom Sense," *Journal of the American Medical Association* 257 (May 1, 1987): 2262.

26. Susan G. Arnold, et al., "Latex Gloves Not Enough to Exclude Viruses," *Nature* 335 (Sept. 1, 1988): 19.

27. Nancy E. Dirubbo, "The Condom Barrier," *American Journal of Nursing,* Oct. 1987, p. 1306.

28. Theresa Crenshaw, from remarks made at the National Conference on HIV, Washington, D.C., Nov. 15–18, 1991.

29. "Condom Roulette," *Washington Watch* 3 (Washington: Family Research Council, Jan. 1992), p. 1.

30. William D. Mosher and James W. McNally, "Contraceptive Use at First Premarital Intercourse: United States, 1965–1988." *Family Planning Perspectives* 23 (May/June 1991): 111.

31. Cheryl D. Hayes, ed., *Risking the Future: Adolescent Sexuality, Pregnancy and Childbearing* (Washington: National Academy Press, 1987), pp. 46–49.

32. Planned Parenthood poll, "American Teens Speak: Sex, Myths, TV and Birth Control" (New York: Louis Harris & Associates, Inc., 1986), p. 24.

33. "Condom Roulette," *In Focus* 25 (Washington: Family Research Council, Feb. 1992), p. 2.

34. Gilbert L. Crouse, Office of Planning and Evaluation, U.S. Dept. of Health & Human Services, t.i., March 12, 1992, based on data from Planned Parenthood's Alan Guttmacher Institute. Increase calculated from 1973, first year of legal abortion.

35. U.S. Congress, House Committee on Energy and Commerce, Subcommittee on Health and the Environment, "The Reauthorization of Title X of the Public Health Service Act" (testimony submitted by Charmaine Yoest), 102nd Congress, 2nd session, March 19, 1991, p. 2.

36. Margaret A. Fischl et al., "Heterosexual Transmission of Human Immunodeficiency Virus (HIV): Relationship of Sexual Practices to Seroconversion," III International Conference on AIDS, June 1–5, 1987, Abstracts Volume, p. 178.

37. U.S. Dept. of Health & Human Services, National Centers for Health Statistics, Centers for Disease Control, "Percent of Women 15–19 Years of Age Who Are Sexually Experienced, by Race, Age and Marital Status: United States, 1988," National Survey of Family Growth.

38. Joseph S. McIlhaney, Jr., M.D., *Sexuality and Sexually Transmitted Diseases* (Grand Rapids: Baker Book House, 1990), p. 137.

39. A.M.B. Goldstein and Susan M. Garabedian-Ruffalo, "A Treatment Update to Resistant Gonorrhea," *Medical Aspects of Human Sexuality,* (August 1991): 39.

40. Reprinted with permission by Word Publishing. Dr. James C. Dobson and Gary L. Bauer, *Children at Risk* (Dallas: Word Publishing, 1990), pp. 11–13.

41. Reprinted with permission by *USA Today.* Kim Painter, "AIDS Surging Among Teens," *USA Today,* April 13, 1992.

42. Dr. Joe McIlhaney, "A Doctor Speaks Out on Sexually Transmitted Diseases" (Colorado Springs: Focus on the Family).

43. S. R. Kellert and A. R. Felthouse. "Childhood cruelty toward animals among criminals and noncriminals." *Human Relations* 38 (1985): 1113–1129.

44. A. R. Felthous and S. R. Kellert, "Childhood cruelty to animals and later aggression against people: A review," *American Journal of Psychiatry,* (1987), pp. 144, 710–717.

CHAPTER 11. A MOMENT FOR MOM

1. Reprinted with permission by Randall Pearson. Mrs. Alice Pearson, "Are All the Children In?" *Heartspun and Homespun Poems* (Adventure Publications, 1982).

APPENDIX
1. Sources include the following:
  Pomona, California, Police Department
  Los Angeles, California, Police Department
  Denver, Colorado, Police Department
  Colorado Springs, Colorado, Police Department
  Drug & Alcohol Treatment Program, El Paso County, Colorado, Health Department
  U.S. Department of Justice, Drug Enforcement Administration, San Diego, California, Field Division
  Stephen Arterburn & Jim Burns, *Drug Proof Your Kids* (Focus on the Family Publishing, 1989).
  Growing Up Drug-Free: A Parent's Guide to Prevention, U.S. Dept of Education, Washington, D.C., 1990.

THE NEW
STRONG-WILLED
CHILD

THIS BOOK IS AFFECTIONATELY DEDICATED TO MY OWN LATE MOTHER, *who was blessed with a brilliant understanding of children. She intuitively grasped the meaning of discipline and taught me many of the principles I've described on the following pages. And, of course, she did an incredible job raising me, as everyone can plainly see today. But I've always been puzzled by one troubling question: Why did my fearless mother become such a permissive pushover the moment we made her a grandmother?*

CONTENTS

The New Strong-Willed Child

I N 1978, when the first edition of *The Strong-Willed Child* was published, I had recently made a dramatic career move. I had resigned from the faculty of the University of Southern California School of Medicine where I had been an associate clinical professor of pediatrics for a number of years. My decision to leave this rewarding position resulted from an increasing awareness that the institution of the family was rapidly deteriorating—and that I needed to do what I could to help. Thus, I left my secure nest to create a humble little nonprofit outfit called Focus on the Family and began a radio program heard initially on thirty-four stations. Frankly, I wondered if the phone would ever ring.

More than 30 years later, the radio program and its derivatives are heard by 220 million people each day on 7,300 radio stations located in 160 countries around the world. The staff consists of 850 members, who are also committed to the preservation of the family. Upwards of 200,000 listeners and readers call or write to us each month, many of whom are asking questions about how to raise healthy, well-adjusted kids. Today, when I meet these moms and dads whose lives we have touched through the years, some of them smile and tell me stories about their children, some hug me, and some get teary eyed. Many will say, "Thank you for helping me raise my kids." Being able to assist these special folks through the child-rearing years has provided one of the greatest satisfactions of my life, both personally and professionally.

One of the first writing projects I tackled after leaving academia in 1977 was the original version of the book you hold. As the title indicates, it focused on the basic temperaments of boys and girls and what influences them to do what they do. Of particular interest to me is a characteristic I call "the strength of the will." Some kids seem to be born with an easygoing, compliant nature that makes them a joy to raise. As infants they don't cry very often; they sleep through the night from the second week; they goo at their grandparents; they smile while being diapered; and they are very patient when dinner is overdue. And, of course, they never spit up on the way to church. During later childhood, they love to keep their room clean and they especially like doing their homework. There aren't many of these supercompliant children, I'm afraid, but they are known to exist in some households (though they didn't in ours).

Just as surely as some children are naturally compliant, others seem to be defiant upon exit from the womb. They come into the world smoking a cigar and yelling about the temperature in the delivery room and the incompetence of the nursing staff and the way the doctors are running things. Long before their children are born, mothers of strong-willed children know there is something different going on inside, because their babies have been trying to carve their initials on the walls. In infancy, these children fairly bristle when their bottle is late and demand to be held throughout the day. Three o'clock in the morning is their favorite "playtime." Later, during toddlerhood, they resist all forms of authority and their greatest delights include "painting" the carpet with Mom's makeup or trying to flush the family cat down the toilet. Their frustrated parents wonder where they went wrong and why their child-rearing experience is so different from what they had expected. They desperately need a little coaching about what to do next.

That was the basic premise of my book back in 1978. But the years since then have passed very quickly, and the tough-as-nails kids about whom I was writing are now grown, having made the breathless journey from babyhood to adolescence and on into adulthood. Most of them now have strong-willed children of their own, which is rather humorous to contemplate. As kids, they gave their parents fits, but now the chickens have come home to roost. These new moms and dads are getting their just desserts, and they deserve everything their kids are doing to rattle their nerves. Their parents, to whom I addressed the original book, are likely to be grandparents now who have probably evolved into permissive pushovers just as my marvelous mom did when we made her a grandmother. And so the cycle of life continues, generation by generation, with each family member playing a prearranged part that feels entirely new, but which is actually rooted in antiquity.

It is with relish, therefore, that I return to this subject, which has been a lifelong fascination. Nearly 3 million copies of *The Strong-Willed Child* have sold in dozens of languages, but it became clear to me recently that the time had come to revise the manuscript. A wealth of new information has come to light since I first put my thoughts on paper (yes, on paper—I wrote the original manuscript with pencils on yellow pads, resulting in sheets that were taped together to produce a scroll that sometimes exceeded fifty feet. Inexplicably, I didn't get into the computer thing until the twentieth century was almost over).

But why did this book need to be retooled more than twenty-five years downstream? It is certainly not because the nature of children has changed since the seventies. Kids are kids and always will be. It is rather because the scientific understanding of inborn temperaments in little people is far greater now than it was two or three decades ago. Some of the more recent insights have come from careful research in the field of child development, and I will share those conclusions with you presently. For example, research on attention deficit/hyperactivity disorder (ADHD), or "hyperactivity," as it was previously called, was in its infancy when I first sat down to write. Little was known about the disorder in those days, much less how to deal with it. Given this and other newer developments, it is time to reconsider the strong-willed child and how best to raise him or her. Far from contradicting my basic thesis, however, the intervening years have only served to validate the principles I described as a young psychologist and professor.

The other reason I set about revising *The Strong-Willed Child* is because I've now had many more years to work with families and to compare the approaches that succeed with those that clearly do not. Those experiences have been interwoven into the fabric of this edition, in hopes that they will be of help and encouragement to today's parents and for generations to come. Who knows? Maybe the testy boys and girls who are challenging their parents today will grow up to read these words in the distant future, searching desperately for advice about handling their own bratty little kids. I hope so.

Let's begin by acknowledging that rearing boys and girls can be a difficult assignment, especially today when the culture is battling mightily with parents for the hearts and minds of their kids. To bring them up properly requires the wisdom of Solomon and the determination of an Olympic champion. Admittedly, the job looks much easier than it is in reality. Overconfident parents, particularly those who are new to the responsibility, remind me of a man watching the game of golf for the first time. He thinks, *This is going to be simple. All you have to do is hit that little white ball out there in the direction of the flag.* He then steps up to the tee, draws back his club, and dribbles the "little white ball" about nine feet to the left. *Maybe,* he says to himself, *I ought to swing harder. That's what a pro golfer does.* But the more he hacks at the ball, the farther into the rough he goes. So it is with child rearing. There are sand traps and obstacles everywhere for parents who are blessed with strong-willed kids. What those moms and dads need is a well-designed "game plan" for the inevitable challenges they will face at home. Without such a plan, they will find themselves muddling through by trial and error.

Consider the experience of a friend of mine, who was a recreational pilot when he was younger. On one occasion, he flew his single-engine plane toward his home base at a small country airport. Unfortunately, he waited too long to start back and arrived in the vicinity of the field as the sun dropped behind a mountain. By the time he maneuvered his plane into position to land, he could not see the hazy runway below. There were no lights to guide him and no one on duty at the airport. He circled the field for another attempt to land, but by then the darkness had become even more impenetrable. For two desperate hours, he flew his plane around and around in the blackness of the night, knowing that probable death awaited him when he ran out of fuel. Then as greater panic gripped him, a miracle occurred. Someone on the ground heard the continuing drone of his engine and realized his predicament. That merciful man drove his car back and forth on the runway to show my friend the location of the airstrip. Then he let his lights cast their beam from the far end while the plane landed.

I think of that story now when I am descending at night in a commercial airliner. As l look ahead, I can see the green lights bordering the runway that tell the captain where to direct the plane. If he stays between those lighted boundaries, all will be well. But disaster lies to the left and to the right.

So it is with this challenging task of child rearing. What parents need are some runway lights—some reliable markers—that will illuminate the safe region between extremes. Two of those guiding principles are, quite simply, *love* and *control*. If they are understood and implemented properly by moms and dads, the relationship with their children is likely to be healthy—despite inevitable mistakes and shortcomings. But beware! It is often very difficult to balance love and control when dealing with a strong-willed child. The temptation is to tilt beyond one of the two boundaries—toward white-hot anger and oppressiveness, or toward permissiveness and disengagement. Why? Because the constant battles that these tougher kids precipitate can cause a parent to become a screamer and a tyrant or one who lets the child rule pathetically. There is danger for a youngster on either side of the "runway." If the parental plane comes down wide or short, it will bump through the cornfield with unpredictable consequences. We'll talk more about that presently.

The purpose of this book, then—both the original version and this revision—is to provide these and other understandings that will contribute to competent parenthood. We will deal specifically with the subject of discipline as it relates to the independent youngsters who are more challenging to raise.

Suffice it to say at this point that the rewards for doing a good job of parenting are worth all the blood, sweat, and tears that are invested in it. Although my children are now grown, the way they have turned out is the most satisfying accomplishment of my life. You can be sure I'll say more about that in pages to come.

Well, let's get started. It is my hope that this discourse will help illuminate the runway for those parents trying to pilot their children through the darkness.

James C. Dobson, Ph.D.

ONE

THE WILD & WOOLLY WILL

AT ONE TIME, the Dobson household consisted of a mother and a father, a boy and a girl, one hamster, one parakeet, one lonely gold-fish, and two hopelessly neurotic cats. We all lived together in relative harmony with a minimum of conflict and strife. But there was another member of our family who was less congenial and cooperative. He was a stubborn, twelve-pound dachshund named Sigmund Freud (Siggie), who honestly believed that he owned the place. All dachshunds tend to be independent, I'm told, but Siggie was a confirmed revolutionary. He was not vicious or mean; he just wanted to run things—and the two of us engaged in a power struggle throughout his lifetime.

Siggie was not only stubborn, but he wouldn't pull his own weight in the family. He wouldn't bring in the newspaper on cold mornings; he refused to chase a ball for the children; he didn't keep the gophers out of the garden; and he didn't do any of the usual tricks that most cultured dogs perform. Alas, Siggie refused to engage in any of the self-improvement programs that I initiated on his behalf. He was content just to trot through life, watering and sniffing and barking at everything that moved.

Sigmund was not even a good watchdog. This fact was confirmed the night we were visited by a prowler who entered our backyard at three o'clock in the morning. I suddenly awoke from a deep sleep, got out of bed, and felt my way through the house without turning on the lights. I knew someone was on the patio and Siggie knew it too, because the coward was crouched behind me! After listening to the thumping of my heart for a few minutes, I reached out to take hold of the rear doorknob.

At that moment, the backyard gate quietly opened and closed. Someone had been standing three feet from me and that someone was now tinkering in my garage. Siggie and I held a little conversation in the darkness and decided that he should be the one to investigate the disturbance. I opened the back door and ordered my dog to "Attack!" But Siggie had just had one! He stood there throbbing and shaking so badly that I couldn't even push him out the back door. In the noise and confusion that ensued, the intruder escaped (which pleased both dog and man).

Please don't misunderstand me: Siggie was a member of our family and we loved him dearly. And despite his anarchistic nature, I did finally teach him to obey a few simple commands. However, we had some classic battles before he reluctantly yielded to my authority. The greatest confrontation occurred when I had been in Miami for a three-day conference. I returned to observe that Siggie had become boss of the house while I was gone. But I didn't realize until later that evening just how strongly he felt about his new position as captain.

At eleven o'clock that night, I told Siggie to go get into his bed, which was a permanent enclosure in the family room. For six years, I

had given him that order at the end of each day, and for six years Siggie had obeyed. On that occasion, however, he refused to budge. He was in the bathroom, seated comfortably on the furry lid of the toilet seat. That was his favorite spot in the house, because it allowed him to bask in the warmth of a nearby electric heater. Incidentally, Siggie had to learn the hard way that it was extremely important that the *lid be down* before he left the ground. I'll never forget the night he learned that lesson. He came thundering in from the cold and sailed through the air—and nearly drowned before I could get him out.

On the night of our great battle, I told Sigmund to leave his warm seat and go to bed. Instead, he flattened his ears and slowly turned his head toward me. He braced himself by placing one paw on the edge of the furry lid, then hunched his shoulders, raised his lips to reveal the molars on both sides, and uttered his most threatening growl. That was Siggie's way of saying, "Get lost!"

I had seen this defiant mood before and knew that I had to deal with it. The only way to make Siggie obey was to threaten him with destruction. Nothing else worked. I turned and went to my closet and got a small belt to help me "reason" with 'ol Sig. My wife, who was watching this drama unfold, told me that as soon as I left the room, Siggie jumped from his perch and looked down the hall to see where I had gone. Then he got behind her and growled.

When I returned, I held up the belt and again told the angry dog to get into his bed. He stood his ground so I gave him a firm swat across the rear end, and he tried to bite the belt. I popped him again and he tried to bite me. What developed next is impossible to describe. That tiny dog and I had the most vicious fight ever staged between man and beast. I fought him up one wall and down the other, with both of us scratching and clawing and growling. I am still embarrassed by the memory of the entire scene. Inch by inch I moved him toward the family room and his bed. As a final desperate maneuver, Siggie jumped on the couch and backed into the corner for one last snarling stand. I eventually got him into his bed, but only because I outweighed him two hundred to twelve!

The following night I expected another siege of combat at Siggie's bedtime. To my surprise, however, he accepted my command without debate or complaint and simply trotted toward the family room in perfect submission. In fact, Siggie and I never had another "go for broke" stand.

It is clear to me now that Siggie was saying on the first night, in his canine way, "I don't think you're tough enough to make me obey." Perhaps I seem to be humanizing the behavior of a dog, but I think not. Veterinarians will confirm that some breeds of dogs, notably dachshunds and shepherds, will not accept the leadership of their masters until human authority has stood the test of fire and proved itself worthy. I got that message across to Siggie in one decisive encounter, and we were good friends for the rest of his life.

This is not a book about the discipline of dogs. But there is an important aspect of my story that is highly relevant to the world of children. Just as surely as a dog will occasionally challenge the authority of his leaders, a child is inclined to do the same thing, only more so. This is no minor observation, for it represents a characteristic of human nature that has escaped the awareness of many experts who write books on the subject of discipline. When I wrote twenty-five years ago, there was hardly a text for parents or teachers that adequately acknowledged the struggle—the confrontation of wills—that strong-willed children seem to love. For them, adult leadership is rarely accepted unchallenged; it must be tested and found worthy before it is respected. It is one of the frustrating aspects of child rearing that most parents have to discover for themselves.

THE HIERARCHY OF STRENGTH AND COURAGE

But why do some children, particularly those who are strong-willed, have such a pugnacious temperament? One of the simplistic answers (there is a more complete explanation in chapter 3) is that it reflects the admiration boys and girls have for strength and courage. They will occasionally disobey parental instructions for the precise purpose of testing the determination of those in charge. Why? Because they care deeply about the issue of "who's toughest." This helps explain the popularity of superheroes—Robin Hood and Tarzan and Spider-Man and Superman—in the folklore of children. It also explains why they often brag, "My dad can beat up your dad!" (One child said in response, "That's nothing, my mom can beat up my dad too!")

Whenever a youngster moves into a new neighborhood or a new school district, he usually has to fight (either verbally or physically) to establish himself in the hierarchy of strength. This respect for power and courage also makes children want to know how tough their leaders are. Thus, whether you are a parent, a grandparent, a Scout leader, a bus driver, or a schoolteacher, I can guarantee that sooner or later, one of the children under your authority will clench his little fist and take you on. Like Siggie at bedtime, he will say with his manner: "I don't think you are tough enough to make me obey." You had better be prepared to prove him wrong in that moment, or the challenge will happen again and again.

This defiant game, which I call Challenge the Chief, can be played with surprising skill by very young children. A father told me of taking his three-year-old daughter to a basketball game. The child was, of course, interested in everything in the gym except the athletic contest. Dad permitted her to roam free and climb on the bleachers, but he set definite limits regarding how far she could stray. He took her by the hand and walked with her to a stripe painted on the gym floor. "You can play all around the building, Janie, but don't go past this line," he instructed her. He had no sooner returned to his seat than the toddler scurried in the direction of the forbidden territory. She stopped at the border for a moment, then flashed a grin over her shoulder to her father, and deliberately placed one foot over the line as if to say, "Whatcha gonna do about it?" Virtually every parent the world over has been asked the same question at one time or another.

The entire human race is afflicted with the same tendency toward willful defiance that this three-year-old exhibited. Her behavior in the gym is not so different from the folly of Adam and Eve in the Garden of Eden. God had told them they could eat anything in the Garden except the forbidden fruit ("do not go past this line"). Yet they challenged the authority of the Almighty by deliberately disobeying His commandment. Perhaps this tendency toward self-will is the essence of original sin that has infiltrated the human family. It certainly explains why I place such stress on the proper response to willful defiance during childhood, for that rebellion can plant the seeds of personal disaster. The weed that grows from it may become a tangled briar patch during the troubled days of adolescence.

When a parent refuses to accept his child's defiant challenge, something changes in their relationship. The youngster begins to look at his mother and father with disrespect; they are unworthy of her allegiance. More important, she wonders why they would let her do such harmful things if they really loved her. The ultimate paradox of childhood is that boys and girls want to be led by their parents but insist that their mothers and fathers earn the right to lead them.

On behalf of those readers who have never experienced such a confrontation, let me describe how a determined kid is typically constructed. At birth he looks deceptively like his more compliant sibling. He weighs seven pounds and is totally dependent on those who care for him. Indeed, he would not survive for more than a day or two without their attention.

Ineffectual little arms and legs dangle aimlessly in four directions, appearing to be God's afterthoughts. What a picture of vulnerability and innocence he is!

Isn't it amazing, given this beginning, what happens in twenty short months? Junior then weighs twenty-five pounds and he's itching for action. This kid who couldn't even hold his own bottle less than two years earlier now has the gall to look his two-hundred-pound father straight in the kisser and tell him where to get off? What audacity! Obviously, there is something deep within his soul that longs for control. He will work at achieving it for the rest of his life.

When our children were young, we lived near one of these little spitfires. He was thirty-six months old at the time and had already bewildered and overwhelmed his mother. The contest of wills was over. He had won it. His sassy talk, to his mother and anyone else who got in his way, was legendary in the neighborhood. Then one day my wife watched him ride his tricycle down the driveway and into the street, which panicked his mother. We lived on a curve and the cars came around that bend at high speed. The woman rushed out of the house and caught up with her son as he pedaled down the street. She took hold of his handlebars to redirect him, and he came unglued.

"Get your dirty hands off my tricycle!" he screamed. His eyes were squinted in fury. As Shirley watched in disbelief, this woman did as she was told. The life of her child was in danger, yet this mother did not have the courage to make him obey her. He continued to ride down the street while she trailed along behind, hoping for the best.

How could it be that a tiny little boy at three years of age was able to buffalo his thirty-year-old mother in this way? Clearly, she had no idea how to manage him. He was simply tougher than she—and they both knew it. This mild-mannered woman had produced an iron-willed youngster who was willing to fight with anyone who tried to run him in, and you can be sure that his mom's physical and emotional resources were continually drained by his antics. We lost track of this family, but I'm sure this kid's adolescent years were something to behold.

A LESSON IN A SUPERMARKET

In thinking about the characteristics of compliant and defiant children, I sought an illustration to explain the vastly differing thrusts of human temperaments. I found an appropriate analogy in a supermarket. Imagine yourself in a grocery store, pushing a cart up the aisle. You give the basket a small shove, and it glides at least nine feet out in front and then comes to a gradual stop. You walk along happily tossing in the soup and ketchup and loaves of bread. Grocery shopping is such an easy task, for even when the cart is burdened with goods, it can be directed with one finger.

But buying groceries is not always so blissful. On other occasions, you select a cart that ominously awaits your arrival at the front of the market. When you push the stupid thing forward, it tears off to the left and knocks over a stack of bottles. Refusing to be outmuscled by an empty cart, you throw all your weight behind the handle, fighting desperately to keep the ship on course. It seems to have a mind of its own as it darts toward the eggs and careens back in the direction of a terrified grandmother in green tennis shoes. You are trying to do the same shopping assignment that you accomplished with ease the week before, but the job feels more like combat duty today. You are exhausted by the time you herd the contumacious cart toward the checkout counter.

What is the difference between the two shopping baskets? Obviously, one has straight, well-oiled wheels that go where they are guided. The other has crooked, bent wheels that refuse to yield.

Do you get the point? We might as well face it; some kids have crooked wheels! They do not want to go where they are led, because their own inclinations take them in other directions. Furthermore, the parent who is pushing the cart must expend seven times the energy to make it move, compared with the parent of a child with straight wheels. (Only mothers and fathers of strong-willed children will fully comprehend the meaning of this illustration.)

But how is the strength of the will distributed among children? My original assumption was that this aspect of human temperament is represented by a typical bell-shaped curve. In other words, I presumed that a relatively small number of very compliant kids appeared at one end of the continuum and an equally small number of defiant youngsters were represented at the other. The rest, comprising the majority, were likely to fall somewhere near the middle of the distribution, like this:

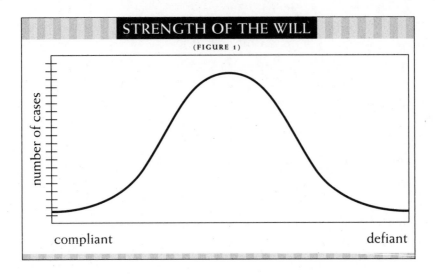

However, having talked to at least 100,000 harried parents, I'm convinced that my supposition was wrong. The true distribution probably looks more like this:

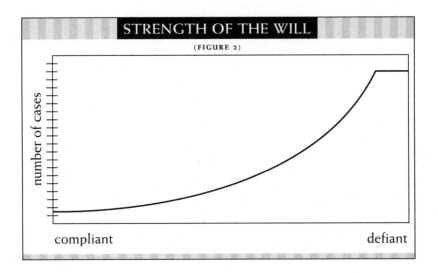

Don't take this observation too literally. Maybe it only *seems* that the majority of toddlers are confirmed anarchists. Furthermore, there is a related phenomenon regarding sibling relationships that I have never been able to explain. When there are two children in the family, one is likely to be compliant and the other defiant. Who knows why it works out that way.

There they are, born to the same parents, but as different as though they came from different planets. One cuddles to your embrace and the other kicks you in the navel. One is a natural sweetheart and the other goes through life like hot lava. One follows orders and the other gives them. Quite obviously, they are marching to a different set of drums.

Former U.S. president Franklin Roosevelt was clearly a strong-willed child and grew up to be a very strong-willed man. When he was a boy, he once strung a string across the top of the stairs where it could not be seen. Predictably, his nurse came along carrying a supper tray and tripped, making what must have been a spectacular plunge downward. The record does not reveal what punishment he received for this wicked trick. We are told, however, that Franklin was very bossy with his peers and that he liked to win at everything. When he was once scolded for the way he treated other children, he said, "Mummie, if I didn't give the orders, nothing would happen."[1] *That* is a strong-willed child.

Temperamental differences often create serious relational problems within the family. The strong-willed child faces constant discipline and is subjected to many threats and finger-wagging lectures, while his angelic brother, little Goody Two-shoes, polishes his halo and soaks up the warmth of parental approval. They are pitted against each other by the nature of their divergent personalities and may spend a lifetime scratching and clawing one another. (Chapter 9 offers specific suggestions regarding the problem of sibling rivalry and conflict.)

I have described the approach to life taken by the tougher kids. Let's look quickly at the easygoing child, who spends most of his time trying to make his parents happy. In reality, he needs their praise and approval; thus his personality is greatly influenced by this desire to gain their affection and recognition. A word of displeasure or even the slightest frown from his parents can disturb him. He is a lover, not a fighter.

A few years ago I talked with the mother of one of these pleasant kids. She was concerned about the difficulties her son was having in nursery school. He was being bullied every day by the more aggressive children, but it was not within him to defend himself. Thus, each afternoon when his mother came to get him, he had been whacked and harassed again by these other boys. Even the girls were joining in the fun.

"You must defend yourself!" his mother said again and again. "Those other children will keep hitting you until you make them stop!"

Each day she urged her little lover to be more assertive, but it contradicted his nature to do so. Finally, his frustration became so great that he began reaching for the courage to follow his mother's advice. As they rode to school one morning he said, "Mom! If those kids pick on me again today, I'm—I'm—I'm going to beat them up! Slightly."

How does one beat up someone else "slightly"? I don't know, but it made perfect sense to this compliant child. He didn't want to use any more force than was absolutely necessary to survive. Why? Because he had a peace-loving nature. His parents didn't teach it to him. It was rooted deep within his psyche.

I must make it clear that the compliant child is not necessarily wimpy or spineless. That fact is very important to our understanding of his nature and how he differs from his strong-willed sibling. The distinction between them is not a matter of confidence, willingness to take risks, sparkling personalities, or other desirable characteristics. Rather, the issue under consideration here is focused on the strength of the will—on the inclination of some children to resist authority and determine their own course, as compared with those who are willing to be led. It is my supposition that these temperaments are prepackaged before birth and do not have to be cultivated or encouraged. They will make themselves known soon enough.

By the way, there is another category of temperaments in children that some parents will recognize instantly. These kids are not really strong-willed—at least, their assertiveness is not expressed in the same way. The distinction here is not one of independence and aggressiveness. It is a matter of tactics. They rarely challenge the authority of their parents or teachers in a stiff-necked manner, but they are willful nonetheless. I call them "sneaky." Adults think these youngsters are going along with the program, but inside, there's subversion afoot. When no one is looking, they break the rules and push the limits. When caught, as inevitably they are, they may lie or rationalize or seek to hide the evidence. The appropriate approach to these sneaky kids is not appreciably different from handling the strong-willed child. Sooner or later, his or her self-will can be expected to break into the open, usually during early adolescence. Then it's "Katie, bar the door."

I'll close this introductory chapter by offering two more observations for parents who are raising strong-willed children. First, it is very common for these moms and dads to feel great guilt and self-condemnation. They are trying so hard to be good parents, but the struggle for control that goes on at home day after day leaves them frustrated and fatigued. No one told them that parenthood would be this difficult, and they blame themselves for the tension that arises. They had planned to be such loving and effective parents, reading fairy tales by the fireplace to their pajama-clad angels, who would then toddle happily off to bed. The difference between life as it is and life as it ought to be is distressing. We'll talk more about that presently.

Second, I have found that the parents of compliant children don't understand their friends with defiant youngsters. They intensify guilt and embarrassment by implying, "If you would raise your kids the way I do mine, you wouldn't be having those awful problems." May I say to both groups that willful children can be difficult to manage even when parents handle their responsibilities with great skill and dedication. It may take several years to bring such a youngster to a point of relative obedience and cooperation within the family unit, and indeed a strong-willed child will be a strong-willed individual all her life. While she can and must be taught to respect authority and live harmoniously with her neighbors, she will always have an assertive temperament. That is not a bad thing. It simply "is." During the childhood years, it is important for parents not to panic. Don't try to "fix" your tougher boy or girl overnight. Treat that child with sincere love and dignity, but require him or her to follow your leadership. Choose carefully the matters that are worthy of confrontation, then accept her challenge on those issues and win decisively. Reward every positive, cooperative gesture she makes by offering your attention, affection, and verbal praise. Then take two aspirin and call me in the morning.

Well, that is the subject of our discussion. In the chapters to come, we will explore ways of leading the toughie, approaches to discipline at each age level, reasons why he is the way he is, and many other aspects of child rearing. There's so much to share.

Before pressing on, however, let me give you an update on our little dachshund, Siggie, whom people still ask me about. This delightful dog lived for seventeen years and gave our family so much pleasure, despite his revolutionary tendencies. Shortly before he died, some teenagers drove through our neighborhood at three o'clock in the morning and tossed a hapless pup out of their car. She showed up at our front door the next morning, scared, hungry, and lost. We didn't want another dog at the time, even though Siggie had seen his better days. We were especially disinterested in owning a cur whose daddy had been a traveling man. Nevertheless, we couldn't bring ourselves to take her to the pound. While we were trying to find her another home, we fell head over heels in love with this gentle, vulnerable animal that our daughter named Mindy.

Mindy grew to become the most beautiful, noble dog I've ever owned. She simply had no will of her own, except to do the bidding of her masters. Probably because of the unknown horrors of her puppyhood, she could not stand any expression of displeasure on my part. If scolded, she would jump in my lap and hide her eyes in the crook of my arm. Her only wish was to be with her human companions. Many times as I sat reading or studying at my desk, Mindy would quietly slip in beside me and rest her head on my knee. I'll tell you, I'm a sucker for any living thing with that

kind of need. When forced to stay outside, Mindy would sit and stare at us through the family-room window. My wife would get uncomfortable with the dog's pleading brown eyes focused on her every move, so she actually pulled down the shades. Then Shirley would mutter in exasperation, "Mindy, get a life!"

An incident occurred several years later that illustrated Mindy's sweet nature. Our family had gone on a two-week vacation and left her alone in the backyard. A neighbor boy came by once each day to feed her and give her fresh water. Thus, her physical needs were met, but we underestimated the loneliness she must have experienced throughout those fourteen days. Why else would this forty-pound dog have gone into our garage and dug through the boxes of toys that our children, Danae and Ryan, had outgrown? She found the stuffed animals that had long since been discarded and brought them one at a time to her bed near the house. When we arrived home, Mindy was lying on her blanket with eight of these furry friends arranged in front of her.

I know! I know! No dog deserves the affection our family bestowed on this ol' hound, and some of my readers will think it foolish. For my part, however, I believe God designed this species specifically for companionship and devotion to man. (Who knows why the Lord made cats?) Surprisingly, it is believed that the death rate for people who have lost a spouse is 500 percent lower the first year for those who own a dog. Take my advice: If you need something to love, go to the nearest pound and look for a furry little pup who'll think you're the neatest boss in the world! That's what Mindy thought about the Dobsons.

But, alas, this beautiful animal is also gone. My wife, Shirley, called her one day and she failed to come. That had never happened before. We found her lying by the side of the house where she had fallen. Mindy died of lymphoma that had spread throughout her body. And so ended a twelve-year love affair between a devoted dog and her affectionate masters. Good-bye, gentle friend.

I have shared these two dog stories, describing Siggie and Mindy, to illustrate the difference in temperaments between the two animals we have loved. One of them was determined to run the world and the other was deliriously happy just to be part of the family. They represented opposite ends of the canine universe.

Well, I hope the analogy is clear. In this book, we're focusing not on dogs but on the varied and infinitely complex personalities of children. We'll talk in subsequent chapters about what those temperaments mean for parents and how that understanding helps us raise our children properly.

(By the way, I was only kidding when I asked why God created cats. It was a joke. Honest. I didn't mean it. Please don't write and say hateful things to me. Like Mindy, I can't stand to be criticized.)

TWO

MOTHERS SHARE THEIR STORIES

There was a little girl,
Who had a little curl,
Right in the middle of her forehead.
When she was good,
She was very good indeed,
But when she was bad, she was horrid.[1]

T O BETTER UNDERSTAND the nature of strong-willed children (and I am referring now to those who are *very* strong-willed), I invited several parents into the Focus on the Family radio studio a few years ago to discuss their experiences in child rearing. What resulted was an enlightening, and sometimes tearful, discussion of these tough-as-nails kids and what it was like dealing with them on a daily basis. If you are not yet convinced that such youngsters exist or that leading them successfully can be one of life's great challenges, then read on. I think the recollections of the moms you're about to meet will be insightful and helpful. What follows is a transcript of the interchange that occurred in our studio during a two-hour dialogue.

JCD: First, we are pleased to welcome Debra Merritt, mother of four children. She brought her seventeen-year-old strong-willed daughter, Lizz, with her today, and I'm anxious to get her perspective. Also

NOTE: *This transcript was edited somewhat to transform the imprecise "spoken language" into the more readable "written language," while being faithful to the context.*

with us is Kristen Walker, who has four children. And, finally, Joy Solomon is here, who is a homemaker with two grown kids. These three moms have raised ten children between them, and they learned some valuable lessons along the way.

Let me begin by providing the background for this program. Shirley and I went to Alabama for a visit several years ago, and while there, we were invited to have lunch with about twenty people. We happened to be seated across from Joy and her husband, Davey, whom we had never met. Immediately, the four of us found common ground. Joy, what do you remember about that lunch?

Joy: Well, our conversation started when you said, "Hi, I'm Jim," as if we wouldn't recognize that voice immediately. I said, "Well, I'm Joy, but I'm surprised you don't remember me because you lived with us for a while." You said, "I did?" I said, "Yes, for about three years when we were really struggling with our strong-willed child." Then you said, "Oh, you have one of those." I said, "Yes," and you asked how old he was. I said, "Well, it's a she and she is now nineteen and doing very well, but we had some dark days along the way—no, we had some very, very dark days back then.

JCD: That is the reason I asked you to be here today, Joy, because you are the quintessential mother of a strong-willed child. You experienced many of the frustrations that I have written about through the years, including guilt, self-condemnation, and self-doubt.

Joy: All of them.

JCD: How soon after your daughter was born did you know that she was going to be hard to handle?

Joy: I think she slept through the night at maybe fifteen months old. At eighteen months old, you could tell her no and she would fall on the floor, throw a fit, and roll around. We would sit and watch her for a while because we weren't going to give in. We were going to be strong. She would stand up, and she would have that beautiful angelic face, and she would say, "I'm sorry." She would come over and lay her head in my lap, and then she would bite me. That was the first clue because it was a manipulation. She made sure that you weren't worried about what she was going to do, and then she would bite. She was very, very tough.

JCD: Does she know that you're here today?

Joy: Yes, she does. She has given her permission for me to tell this story. We've been on a difficult journey. When you combine a keen intelligence with our daughter's strong will, and especially when her spirit turned more defiant at sixteen, we were in a world of hurt.

JCD: Now, Joy, I really want you to help folks who have never dealt with a very strong-willed child begin to understand. There are some families with four or six kids, and none of them have a defiant temperament like we are describing. Their children are generally happy, cooperative, and obedient. Such moms and dads are inclined to assume that parents who struggle to maintain control at home are just weak or ineffective. Sometimes that is an accurate assessment, but in other cases, the difficulties result from the nature of a particular child. You need to help people grasp how difficult it can be to raise a defiant youngster. Your daughter didn't simply disobey occasionally. Every child does that. You were in a war of wills with Dana almost from the very earliest moments of life.

Joy: Yes. I remember a key time for us was when she was five years old and she was a physically strong child. There was an episode where she had been out throwing rocks at cars. I called her in and I said, "Dana, why were you throwing rocks at cars?" She said, "Well, I did warn them. I told them they didn't belong on my street. As they went down the road I told them if they came back by, that I'd have to throw a rock at their car. So I threw rocks at them."

I said, "We live on a cul-de-sac. Where were they going?" She had that look that she would give you when you just really weren't understanding what she was saying, and she said, "That's not my fault." What she did was entirely understandable to her. It wasn't her fault that someone had built the street that way. I took her in to spank her and she said, "You're not going to spank me. I'm going to wait until my daddy gets home." Well, you've met Davey. He is a large man.

She knew the longer she could put off a spanking, the longer she had to work up her defense. I said, "No, I'm going to spank you now." She said, "No, you're not. You will not spank me." I said, "Yes, I will." That day, I think, was a terrifying day because I physically could not control her. She threw every ounce of strength and determination into fighting me. It was a battle that probably lasted an hour and a half—and this child was five years old.

JCD: How did it end?

Joy: It ended with me putting her out in the garage. She was walking around screaming. Then she rang the doorbell, and she said, "I'll take my spanking now." I did spank her, because I knew if I ever let her win one of those battles, I would never have control of her again. But it was a constant struggle.

I went to see a good friend of ours, a pastor in Columbus, and said to him, "I'm at my wit's end. I don't know how to control this child." He said, "Every night when you put her to bed, I want you and Davey to go in and lay your hands on her while she's asleep. What you're going to pray is for the Holy Spirit to conquer the strong will while not destroying her spirit, because that's what makes Dana who she is."

We did that every night. We would go in and pray over her and lay hands on her. It was about six months later she got up one morning and she said, "You know, I'm bad sometimes." I said, "I know." She said, "I don't mean the things I say. I'm not going to do that anymore." For about the next ten years, she was able to control it. Then she hit adolescence.

JCD: When we were having lunch together in Alabama, you told me a story that I want you to share. It involved your son, who decided to run away from home.

Joy: We called it lovingly "the Dr. Dobson spiel," where I would say, "Oh, Mother loves you so much, and you have to be my big boy." I would go through that every time he would say, "I'm going to run away from home." Well, one night it just struck me, "Okay, this is it." So he was in his little pajamas and he said, "If you make me go to bed, I'm going to run away from home." So I said, "Well, we'll see you later, buddy. Have a nice trip." So he walked out the door but quickly rang the doorbell, and he said, "I didn't mean tonight." I said, "Well, I do. I am really tired of this. It's time for you to go, but let me pack you a bag. You'll need pajamas and things."

He said, "Well, I might need to think about this." I said, "Well, you've got about three minutes while I go pack your bag. It's important to me that you stay here and be our son, but this is your decision. Either you run away, or I never want to hear you threaten to leave again. If you decide to live here, I don't want you to threaten to leave again." So I went and packed the suitcase. I don't think I put anything in it. I went back, and I opened the door, and he said, "Well, I've been thinking about it and I guess I'm gonna stay." I said, "But never say that to me again, do you understand?" He said, "Yes, ma'am." From then on, he would say, "If you make me do that, I . . . I . . . I'm not going to be your best friend." I'd say, "Well, that's sad."

What works for one has to work for the other, right? I was a stay-at-home mom and Dana was going through her own "I'm going to run away from home" routine. So one night I had had it, and I said, "Well, I'll see you later." It's funny the pictures that stay in your mind. She had on a Strawberry Shortcake robe and Strawberry Shortcake slippers, and her little blonde hair. Then she walked out the door. I went and sat down and Davey looked at me and he said, "Well, she's been out there about five minutes. Do you think—you know—maybe she should have rung the doorbell by now?" I said, "No, she's got that defiant spirit. We're going to give her about ten minutes." Then I went to the front door. There was nobody there. She was gone. By the grace of God, we lived on a cul-de-sac, because there was a street lamp and she was underneath it with her thumb out. She was hitching a ride! *(laughter and surprise from the panel)*

JCD: How old was she then?

Joy: She was six at the time and she had no fear whatsoever. There she was in her robe and slippers and nothing else. She was going to leave with no other clothes. I had to drag her into the house kicking and screaming because she was running away. "You told me I could run away." I thought, *This isn't what I'm supposed to be dealing with!*

JCD *(to the listening audience)*: Can you see why I wanted Joy here? I wanted people to understand that children who have Dana's brand of fortitude and determination are tough to handle, even if the parents use great wisdom and tact in raising them. A compliant child would never pull a stunt like that, but for the strong-willed youngster, it was just another challenge—just another opportunity to do battle—because they just love to go toe-to-toe with their parents. They get their kicks by playing power games. That is what was happening in this instance.

I want to hear about Dana's adolescent years, Joy, but first, let me ask Kristen to tell us her story.

Kristen: Well, in hindsight, I think we knew shortly after birth that our daughter, Lizz, was strong-willed. At ten days old she was taken to the hospital with a case of spinal meningitis. As they were trying to get a spinal tap from her, she would arch her back instead of compliantly lying in a fetal position. They had to hold her down at ten days of age. The technicians ended up trying ten or twelve times before they could get untainted spinal fluid to culture so they could verify that she really had spinal meningitis. In fact, it was so bad they ended up going through a vein in her skull to get a sample. Then at eighteen months of age, we were visiting some friends for dinner. My two older kids were there, and our hostess had cut-glass candy dishes at each end of her couch. They didn't have any children yet so they could risk having something that fragile sitting out.

I told my two oldest children, "These are glass. They'll break. Don't touch them. Don't play rough around here." I didn't even mention them to Lizz. I thought, *I'll deal with that when the time comes.* When she finally saw the candy dishes after dinner, we told her emphatically, "No, you're not going to touch that." And again I said with conviction, "No, we're not going to touch it." After the battle was over, my friend said, "Do you realize, you slapped her hand nine times before she yielded?"

JCD: Did she eventually obey you?

Kristen: Yes, for that moment.

JCD: But she was saying emphatically, "I think I can outlast you."

Kristen: Oh yes. But the biggest fight we fought happened when she was five. I had been homeschooling the kids. Lizz decided she wasn't getting enough attention one day. So I pulled her up on my lap. While she was sitting on my lap and I was still trying to teach, she started kicking me with one of her legs. Well, I put her leg between my legs so she couldn't kick me anymore. Then she started kicking me with the other leg. I put both legs between mine, and she started pinching and scratching.

We ended up on the floor. She was actually spread-eagle on

the floor. I was holding her down so that she could not hurt me or try to do damage to me. She was screaming, "Let go of me, let go of me," and I was saying, "We're here until you calm down." She'd quit crying and I'd start to pray, and she'd immediately start to scream again, "Don't you pray for me." So we'd start again. It turned out to be a forty-five-minute battle.

JCD: Lizz, do you remember that?

Lizz: I remember several times when I would just argue and end up on the floor with Mother on top of me. I was thinking, *Who's going to win?!* So it went on and on—I mean, it seemed like hours, sometimes.

JCD: Do you remember how you felt during those battles?

Lizz: I was just determined to win. My pride got in there too, you know? I believed I was stronger than Mom, and it was all about being rebellious and getting my own way.

JCD (*to the radio audience*): We're hearing some classic examples today of the battle of wills between parents and children. I have been witnessing conflicts of this sort within families for the past thirty years. What Lizz said about her determination to win over her mother goes right to the heart of what these little revolutionaries are after. Standing up to a big, powerful adult who is supposed to be in charge is fun for them. The winner of the "game," as every strong-willed child knows intuitively, is the one who either comes out on top or who reduces the other to tears. Quiet conversations and gentle explanations simply don't work.

Some authors contend that a child only acts naughty when she is frustrated over her circumstances. That certainly happens. But what we are dealing with in the illustrations we're hearing about today were not incidents motivated by frustration; they were driven by willful defiance.

[We'll talk more about that behavior and the proper parental response to it in subsequent chapters.]

Debra, let's hear your stories. Tell us about your strong-willed child.

Debra: Well, I had two of them, but one was really tough: I knew she was a strong-willed child before she was born. She was part of a twin set. I wanted her twin brother to be the football player and my daughter to be the nice, sweet, little cheerleader. As it turned out, she is the one being recruited by the football team, and my son is a wonderful child who writes tender poetry. He'll be the best pediatrician in the whole world. So my kids kind of flip-flopped.

The night before they were born, I was scheduled for a C-section because I don't dilate. I was playing table games with some friends next door, and I had this eruption, like a volcano or an earthquake, in my stomach. I know that it's probably not possible, but I swear my daughter switched places with my son. He was the lower child so he was expected to come out first, and she just went "shoo." I had this horrible experience the next morning. I woke up in a pool of blood. My baby girl was going to come out of that cervix whether it dilated or not. I was raced to the hospital and taken into emergency surgery. My daughter was going to come out no matter what the obstacles. So talk about being born smoking a cigar, yelling orders at the nursing staff, complaining about the temperature—that was my baby girl.

JCD: What was her babyhood like?

Debra: She was a challenge from the very first day! I had a five-year-old and a three-year-old, and then the twins were born. No grandparents lived close by. They would come and visit and help us, but I was a very busy young mother.

Christina would scream and scream and scream. I thought, *Well, she's sick. She must have medical problems, such as colic or whatever.* But then her dad would walk in the room and she would start baby flirting and cooing. You know, that sweet little thing. All she wanted was her dad. So I thought, *You can raise this child. I'll raise the other three.* Because she's stronger willed than I am by a long shot.

JCD: How difficult was that for you emotionally?

Debra: It was very difficult because I was a mother at heart. I'd always wanted to be a mom. I had good relationships with my other children. My second is precious. She does what she can to help me and to serve. She's just a wonderful child. Then I get this child who's like . . . well, my in-laws and others call her "the kid and a half."

JCD: There are very few experiences in life, I believe, that are more stressful than bringing a child into the world with one major goal—and that's to be a good mom or dad. You pour every effort and every resource into that assignment, only to have your beloved child reject your leadership almost from birth and engage in a never-ending battle of wills. That is terribly painful. It produces great guilt and self-condemnation, especially for the parents who care the most.

Debra: You're right. I believe firmly that strong-willed children love conflict. They just love the battle, and I don't love the battle. It was a very difficult experience for me because I'm not strong-willed.

JCD: I conducted an extensive survey on this subject some years ago that involved thirty-five thousand parents. One of the things we observed was the enormous agitation that occurs when a compliant, loving mother, who would never have dreamed of disobeying her parents, gives birth to a kid who gets his greatest thrill out of fighting with his mother. Debra, you have tears in your eyes, don't you?

Debra: I do have tears in my eyes. But let me tell you a funny story. My husband and I used to count to three, and if the kids had not minded by then, they would have to face the wooden spoon. But, unfortunately, my kids are all very strong-willed. One morning I put Elizabeth in her high chair so I could feed her. I was giving her Cheerios and fun things to eat. I was working around the house and I just wanted to keep her busy. Well, at some point during that time she became impatient, so she said, "Mother, I want to eat now. One, two, three . . . "

JCD: She was counting you down.

Debra: Right. And by the time she hit two, I had her dinner ready and my husband walked in the door. And I said, "John, it works. I had done everything that she wanted me to do before she got to three." *(laughter)*

Debra: And he said, "Yeah, that's all we need—a compliant mother and a strong-willed child." *(laughter)*

JCD: Joy, you saw the tears in Debra's eyes a minute ago.

Joy: Yes.

JCD: Did you ever cry when your daughter took you on?

Joy: I cried a lot when she was young. I cried even more during the teenage years. I was so shy as a child. And to please my parents was my greatest accomplishment in life—to make them proud of me and to please them. But Dana didn't feel that way about me. She could turn her back on me in a heartbeat. She was so tough. One day at preschool, there was a young handicapped boy whom the teachers were mainstreaming. Dana immediately befriended this child. More than anyone else in the class, she was drawn to that child. Another boy was making fun of this child, and Dana said, "I'm only going to warn you once. Don't make fun of him again, or I'm going to have to beat you up." Well, he came back and made fun of him again, and Dana said, "This was your last warning; I only give two warnings. Don't make fun of him again." Well, he came back, and before she was through with him, she had dragged him up one side of the playground and down the other. She had torn his shirt. She had torn his shorts, and he was screaming for Dana to let him go. And the teachers finally got ahold of her and said, "Dana, did you not hear him asking you to let him go?" And she said something I had said to her repeatedly, "I refuse to negotiate with a four-year-old." It came right back to me.

JCD: It is interesting that the same strong will that parents have to deal with is often expressed with peers. That temperament can be advantageous as the years unfold, because these youngsters are tough enough to withstand peer pressure and chart their own course.

This gets really personal, but tell me, Lizz, have you ever seen your mom cry in a moment of conflict?

Lizz: Hardly ever.

JCD: Kristen, you're obviously not a crier. But can you understand why the other two ladies here were so emotional?

Kristen: Oh yes, oh yes.

JCD: You just didn't express it the same way.

Kristen: I didn't express it in tears. I think I became more strong-willed . . .

JCD: In order to cope with it?

Kristen: Yes—in order to cope with it. I've always wanted to please people. I still do but I was bound and determined that my children were not going to defeat me in anything. Yet there were days and weeks when all I did was defend my right to lead. My entire days were consumed with disciplining Lizz and trying to get her to follow the rules the way we had laid them out.

JCD: And the other children were not behaving quite that way.

Kristen: Oh no, no, not at all. You'd tell my oldest and my youngest not to do something, and they'd look up at you with their big blue eyes, and they'd say, "Oh, Mommy, I'm sorry." And they'd never do it again. Lizz would say, "Let's go for it."

JCD: There are millions of kids like you, Lizz, which raises an interesting question. Many parents have asked me whether their children's rebellious behavior is the result of parental mistakes and poor judgment, or whether there is something else responsible for it. Well, clearly, some moms and dads are more effective at handling kids than others are, and some of them regularly make a mess of things. Their children sometimes respond with increasingly testy behavior. Parenting is just like any other skill. It's given in greater portions to some than to others. Men, for example, just by their masculine presence, are typically better at handling tough kids than women are. If I may be candid, the three of you here today have described moments when you lost control of your children and were literally fighting physically to deal with your very difficult kids. It would appear that you were making some tactical errors at that point.

Nevertheless, a strong-willed child is a strong-willed child. The kids we are talking about here are born that way, and some of them are so tough that Hulk Hogan couldn't handle them without a struggle. As I indicated, these particularly contentious kids just love to reduce big powerful adults to tears and leave them shaken and discouraged. Their personalities are rooted in their genetic makeup.

I know I'm not giving Lizz much hope about the children she will bear. (laughter)

Kristen: Sorry, Lizz, you may have the mother's curse. You may produce a child just like you were.

JCD: Wait 'til you get your own.

Kristen: I've taken it further. I said to Lizz, "I hope all of yours are just like you."

Joy: I disagree. I have told Dana that I hope she never experiences what I went through because that would give me a strong-willed grandchild. (laughter)

JCD: It would, at that.

Joy: So, I'm looking for easier grandchildren.

JCD: Debra, do you have only one tough child?

Debra: Well, I have several who are strong-willed, plus I have one who trained another one to have a strong will. When you have twins and one of them is tough, you have double trouble. When they were little, we had difficulty keeping them in their cribs because Christina did not need to sleep. She was very strong physically. She could climb. She could walk. All my kids walked and ran at ten months old, and she would help her brother get out of the crib in the middle of the night. They were in the house running around unsupervised. And this is where our battles took place.

JCD: How did Christina spring her brother from the crib?

Debra: She would jump out of bed, and then she would collect whatever was in the room and put it in his crib, so he would step up on stuffed animals, or whatever she collected. And then, the two of them would be running loose while we slept.

Now, I was used to my other kids getting out of their crib, and it was no big deal; they would come and cuddle with us. But the twins had each other. They did not want me. We would, literally, find them in the kitchen, in the sink, playing with knives, opening the refrigerator, and throwing things around. It got to the point where keeping them alive was all I could do. I slept outside their door with a pillow and a blanket for a time because they would have to cross over me before they would leave the room. It was the only way I could protect them, and I just prayed for them. Like you, Joy, we laid hands on the kids and said, "Oh, Lord." I just prayed that they wouldn't kill themselves when they were little. And that sounds extreme, but it's true.

JCD: Debra, have you found yourself in moments like that with your face in your hands, saying, "I am a total failure as a mom"?

Debra: I did. I had four children, and a set of twins, and I was tired.

JCD: You just couldn't fight all the time.

Debra: I couldn't fight it. I just trusted in the power of prayer. The Lord is good. When my kids became saved and they were baptized by their own choice, they all changed. They all became new people in Christ.

JCD: Isn't that wonderful?

Debra: And their personalities changed, and that happened at about fourteen or fifteen for each one of them. And, truly, the Lord has done an incredible work, but I can't take any responsibility for it. I wish

I'd been stricter. I wish I'd been firmer, but I did what I could in the midst of very difficult circumstances.

JCD: See, Debra, every one of us is inadequate as a parent. We all have to depend on the Lord. That reality hit me when my daughter was three. I saw that she would eventually make her own choices in life. My Ph.D. in child development was helpful to me, but it would not guarantee the eventual outcome. There are no certainties in raising a child. It is true for all parents. We come to the point where, even in our greatest strength, we have to say, "Lord, I need your help here." That's what being a parent is all about.

Did you depend on the Lord that way, Joy?

Joy: Oh, boy, did I ever.

JCD: So, it was a constant battle . . .

Joy: All day long, from the time she woke up until the time she went to bed. And there were times that she would be such an angel. She would be so caring and loving, and I would think, *Okay, okay, we're making progress. We're making progress.* And then, thirty seconds later, one thing would trigger that defiant will, and she would be off and running. There were times, especially for me as a stay-at-home mom, when I felt like such a failure. I felt like, *This is a career I chose?* It's like starting a small business and watching it go under. Here I was looking at this child whom God had entrusted to me, and I couldn't even control her.

JCD: You said that after a period of time you and your husband, Davey, began praying for Dana—laying hands on her at night when she was asleep, and asking the Lord to help you bring that rebellious spirit under subjection. You said God answered those prayers and that Dana was able to control her behavior for four or five years. But you said she later went into adolescence and the rebelliousness resurfaced.

Joy: That is what we refer to as the dark period. She became very unhappy with herself. She didn't like her personal appearance because she was a heavy child. She had very curly hair, which no one else in our family has. Yet she was very intelligent. So, with the combination of her personality and intelligence, and being unhappy with her looks, she decided she was going to change everything. She began running around with kids who said, "Your parents are still trying to control you. Your parents don't really want you to be happy. Your parents want to live your life for you. They don't want you to leave home." She found a boyfriend who told her this and everything she wanted to hear. He said, "You're wonderful, but your parents don't understand you." And because she was so needy at that time, she became totally addicted to that relationship.

When I think back on our conversation in Alabama, I remember that you asked me if Dana had gotten into drugs and alcohol, and I said I didn't think so. And you said, "Well, we need to thank God for that." And I said, "We do, but when your child is addicted to a relationship, there is no help available." There was really nothing we could do about Dana's dependence on this guy, but it was as destructive as anything she could have been involved in.

JCD: How long did it go on?

Joy: Two and a half years.

JCD: And during that time, what were you doing?

Joy: I was crying every day. School didn't matter. (*crying*) I'm sorry.

JCD: That's all right.

Joy: She lost her relationship with her family and with God. School didn't matter. Soccer didn't matter, which had been a tremendous part of her life. The only thing that she could see in her future was that young man, and she totally built her life—her future life—around him. Her total existence depended on him.

JCD: Were you fasting and praying during that time?

Joy: We fasted. We prayed. We went for counseling. I was working at a Christian outlet store and people would come in—wonderful people—and they would say, "How are you doing today?" And I would say, "Fine, thanks, how are you?" One of the problems we had with Dana at that time was [that she was] lying constantly about everything. But I was lying too. I thought, *I lie every day. Every time I tell somebody that we're doing wonderful, thanks, I'm lying too.* Finally, I turned to someone who had asked that question and I said, "I'm sorry. I'm not trying to burden you with my problems, but I need to tell you I'm not okay. I'm losing a child." (*weeping*)

JCD: There are so many parents out there who have been through something like this, and others that are there right now. Some good, solid Christian families are crying with us today because they're

experiencing the same thing. Most would give their lives for their
children in a heartbeat. They've done everything they know to do,
and they can't fix it. But the Lord still hears and answers prayer, and,
Joy, He was hearing you all that time, wasn't He?

Joy: He heard all of my prayers, every one of them. The people who
carried my child to the mercy seat, I can never thank them enough.
There are no words to describe my gratitude, because the relationship we have with her now is so much better than I ever imagined
when she was a child.

JCD: I want to hear more about that in a moment, but, Kristen, what was
the low point for you and your husband?

Kristen: We finally had to go to the elders of our church at one point
because our daughter would steal. She would take whatever she
wanted, and we'd ask, "Lizz, why are you taking something that
doesn't belong to you?" And she'd say, " 'Cause I want it." It was
just amazing to me that a four- or a five-year-old could articulate
the bottom line like that: "I wanted it. I took it." She'd steal money
from the church or from the offering plate to buy a Coke from the
Coke machine, and she stole some of the decorations out of the
bathroom—just a little cinnamon stick, but she wanted it; therefore,
she took it.

It got to the point where we took her back to the Scripture.
My husband sat down with her and said, "This is what the Bible says.
You've got to obey the leaders in your life, and if you don't, we've got
to take you to a higher authority." And he went to the elders of our
church and asked a couple of them who had children if they would
be willing to sit down with Lizz. At that time, she was probably in
kindergarten, maybe first grade. And these two godly men sat down
with her and made her accountable—made her memorize Scripture.
She had gotten to the point where she needed to know that there was
a higher authority. That's why we went to the elders.

JCD: Lizz, that had a big impact on you, didn't it?

Lizz: Extremely, yes.

JCD: What do you remember about that time?

Lizz: I remember just being thoroughly embarrassed and having to be
responsible for what I did to someone else and having to " 'fess up" to
that responsibility. Until probably second grade, I would take things

from my teachers. I would get into their desks. If they had food in there, I would take their food. And I stole my kindergarten teacher's earrings. And eventually . . . you know, I was thinking, *Who cares? I'll be disciplined, but who cares?* And the discipline didn't bother me. It was when they said, "Okay, you have to go to your teacher. You have to go to the elders, and you have to apologize for doing that." And that's when I thought, *Oh no!* It was embarrassing and humbling, and I realized what I had done.

JCD: Punishment was not something that deterred you in any way.

Lizz: Didn't faze me, not a bit.

JCD: You just figured out a way to get around it.

Lizz: Uh-huh.

JCD: It was a challenge for you.

Lizz: Yeah. If I got grounded from the phone, I'd try to get on the phone. If I got grounded from the computer, I'd try to get on the computer. So, it was just something else to be defiant about.

JCD: To the parents who are raising such a child, it is important for you to figure out what the kid is thinking. You have to get behind the eyes of that child and see it the way that he or she sees it. Only then will you have a better idea of how to respond.

You know, Lizz, my mother was able to do that. She knew that I was messing around in school when I was in the ninth grade. I was a big disciplinary problem at that time, but my mother figured out how to get to me. She said one day, "You can behave any way you want to at school, and I'm not going to do anything about it. Nothing, that is, unless the school calls to tell me about it. If they do, I'm going to school with you the next day. I will sit beside you in class, and I will be in the hall when you are standing with your friends. I'm going to be right there all day, and you will not be able to get rid of me." Man, that shaped me up in a big hurry. That would have been social suicide to have my mom trailing along behind me; I absolutely could not run the risk of her standing around with my friends. It shaped me up in one day.

Joy: A parent has to get very creative in response to the challenges that come his or her way. When we were riding in the family car and Dana was in trouble and knew what was waiting for her at home, she would put both hands on the window and scream at people when we stopped at red lights. She would shout, "Save me! Save me!"

JCD: You are kidding, Joy.

Joy: No, no. I'm not kidding. I was thinking, *If the police pull me over, I'm going to have to show them that this really is my child.*

JCD: Well, we've heard some pretty scary things here today about several very tough kids. But our purpose is not to depress everyone. In fact, there is good news for us to share about each of the children we have discussed. That's why we're here, because there is reason for hope. And, Joy, the update on your story that you shared with me when we met in Alabama is very inspirational. As we sat at the table, you took a crumpled piece of paper out of your purse that day and read something to me.

Joy: I did.

JCD: I don't think you intended to share that note with me on that day.

Joy: No, I had no idea.

JCD: You just happened to have it with you.

Joy: Well, it didn't just happen. I take it everywhere I go. I keep this with me. It is such a reminder.

JCD: Tell everyone what the note says.

Joy: Well, Dana was in her first year in college, and she wrote me this note in midyear:

Dear Mom,

Hey there. This is going to be a weird letter. I've been doing a lot of lifelong thinking. Mom, sometimes I wonder where I would be and what life would be like if I hadn't come back from the dark side. You know, I never thought that I would consider my mother to be my best friend, but you are. I would never trade this closeness I've gained with you for anything in the world. You and Dad used to say that if I would just wait until it was time for me to move out, that you would be behind me 100 percent. Now I understand. I know that you and I were growing, even when I was at home, but I don't think that I ever truly appreciated you until now. At least, not as much as you deserve to be appreciated. I miss you every day. I mean, I thought that when I went to school that I would never want to go home or even call. But I don't like to go through the day without talking to you. You know, I hope that one day I will be as successful as Daddy. I want to be as keen and respected in my field as he is in his. But you, above all, had the hardest profession of all. You had to raise me. Mom, I hope that you understand what a gift God gave you. He gave you the will and the power to raise me. You showed me the kinds of things that no college or professional school could ever teach me. I can only pray that one day God will make me the kind of mother you have been and will always be to me. I just wanted to take a minute to say, "Thank you" and "I love you."

Your baby girl,
Dana

(Joy was crying as she read.)

JCD: Oh, Joy. That was worth a million dollars, wasn't it? Would you have ever believed that Dana would send you a loving letter like that when you were going through your struggles with her?

Joy: Never.

JCD: Lizz, do you sense a mother's heart here?

Lizz: Yes, very much.

JCD: That's what you've heard today.

Lizz: Um-hmm.

JCD: Do you want to be a mother someday?

Lizz: Absolutely.

JCD: And can you imagine bringing a child into the world as dedicated to your baby as you hope to be, and then having this kind of conflict take place?

Lizz: I'm sure it'll happen. I do want to say one thing about strong-willed children like me. God has this amazing, amazing way of saying, "I want you, and I want you to be strong-willed for Me." And instead of being rebellious and disobedient, He wants us to be strong-willed for Him.

JCD: Do you remember actually having those thoughts?

Lizz: Oh, absolutely. I went out with a bunch of my friends, and I was being stupid. And I had come home, and then I just sat down, and I just felt the presence of God. I looked at myself, and I was thinking, "My life has been pointless. I've spent all of my life being strong-willed and wanting to win every battle." And then, God just grabbed me. It was as though He said, "Leave it behind, Lizz," you know?

JCD: Kristen, you were praying for Lizz at that time, weren't you?

Kristen: Oh, I am a lot like Joy. We had all prayed as a family. Her grandparents have been faithful prayer partners. Rich and I pray continually for her. Everybody we know . . . we have not hidden from her the fact that she has been a strong-willed child, so, it is not necessarily an uncommon topic of conversation among people whom we have dealt with this. So, yes, we've had many people praying as well. I am really blessed by the fact that I have seen what God can do and still have time with my daughter to build a relationship that every parent wants. So, I do cry when I think about that.

JCD: Debra, you were praying during your difficulties too, weren't you?

Debra: Oh yes, and my oldest daughter, who's getting married in a month, has become the mentor for my second strong-willed child, and that has been an answer to prayer because their relationship was tainted. When you're an only child or a firstborn child and then your position is usurped by a younger sister, that's a big deal. And so, they were not friends when my oldest daughter was in high school. But now they have become close friends. Elizabeth has mentored Christina to where she is today. And she helped her understand herself and her place in the family.

We had a similar experience last summer. Christina had just gone crazy. I listened to her scream at me until about two in the morning for no reason. And, all of a sudden, it was like the Holy Spirit came over her, and she started repeating things that I would have said to her if I had been talking. And she said, "Mom, I will fight a battle all the way because I want to win." But, she said, "Don't ever be scared to put boundaries in my way because I need rules. I need boundaries. And I respect everything you've done—"

And then she said something else. She said, "I know who I am in God. And I know that I will make right choices." She said, "I've had a bad year. I'm going to change this next year," and she has. She's a different person this year. She said, "You have trained me well. You have given me the stability of a Christian school and a church and a Christian family." She said, "I will choose wisely, and I want to live my life because you've modeled it for me with Jesus."

JCD: Let me say it again: I'm telling our listeners and readers that there is hope here. That is the reason I wanted to address this topic on our program. On their behalf, I want to ask you, the three mothers here, a very important question. The Scripture says that children are a blessing from the Lord. Do you still feel that way, even though raising your kids was a struggle for you? Was it worth it?

Joy: Children are a treasure. That is what I told my children when they were young. . . . But, for a while, Dana forgot that, or she didn't seem to believe it. Now, I think she is to the point where she understands that she truly is a treasure to us. The strong will that she has will be an asset to her in life. She wants to be an attorney. That will be wonderful, because she'll argue with a rock. *(laughter)*

JCD: And the Lord's going to use that temperament.

Joy: I believe He will. I am so blessed.

JCD: How about the other two?

Kristen: Worth every minute, every battle, every ounce of energy that I put into it. I would never, never trade anything.

JCD: Debra?

Debra: One of my children's names means "house of God," another means "great woman of God," and the third means "precious gift of God." So, I did tell each of them that they were gifts. I didn't know if I could have children. They were all tremendous miracles and blessings. Absolutely, every minute was worth it, even the conflicts we had, because I know that God is sufficient, I know He's able, and I know He's going to use them mightily.

JCD: You know, anyone can raise the easy kids. I'm reminded of a very difficult time when I was asked to interview convicted serial murderer Ted Bundy at the Florida State Prison. We had more than nine hundred requests for media appearances in three days, and there was tremendous pressure on me. Added to that was the emotion of dealing with a man who had killed at least twenty-eight women and girls in cold blood. I remember the morning before I went to talk to Bundy that I didn't want to do it. At that point the Lord seemed to speak to me, and He said, *I sent you to do this job because I knew you could handle it. I selected you for this difficult assignment.*

This is my point. When parents bring one of these tough youngsters into the world, they need to recognize that while raising that child may be difficult for a time, it is worth their effort to do the job right. Their attitude should be, "The Lord gave me this challenging child for a purpose. He wants me to mold and shape this youngster and prepare him or her for a life of service to Him. And I'm up to the task. I'm going to make it with the Lord's help." That's the healthy way of looking at parenting when the pressure is on. There is a tendency, I think, for parents of strong-willed children to feel cheated and oppressed because other moms and dads seem to have smooth sailing with their children, whereas they are at war every day of the week. But if they can perceive their task as a God-given assignment and believe that He's going to help them to fulfill it, then the frustrations become more manageable.

Let me give you one other word of encouragement. Just as the three mothers have now experienced, most strong-willed children tend to come around when they get through adolescence. Don't be too quick as a parent to brand yourself as a failure. Kids do grow up, and you will find out later that the values and principles that you tried so hard to instill were actually going inside and sticking. It may be that your difficult children will become your best friends, as it is now for Joy and Dana, if . . . if you persevere. So, when your child's behavior is saying "I hate you" in every way possible, hang in there. Keep your courage. Don't panic. Better days are coming.

Joy: We were at home one day recently and Dana was home. She said, "Why did you never give up on me?" And I said, "Because you're a treasure. God gave you to us. I could never have given up on you." She said, "A lot of people would." And I said, "Not if they believed in the power of God and the power of prayer, because I wasn't sure how soon it was going to be, but I always believed that you would come back." I had tremendous hope and faith.

Another thing happened when Dana was at home. She said, "You know, I remember one night when it was really, really bad, and there was a big fight. You were crying. I got used to you crying because you did it all the time." But then Dana said what really got to her that night was that she made her daddy cry. Her father's tears touched her heart. (*There were tears around the table at that point.*)

JCD: Debra, what advice do you have for the mother out there today who is experiencing what you were feeling when your kids were small?

Debra: Well, I think what I'm going to do is quote your book. I think it's page 24 of *The Strong-Willed Child*. You said, in effect, "Pick your battles. Win decisively. Take two aspirin and call me in the morning." *(laughter)*

JCD: Well, do all that, but don't call me. *(laughter)*

Debra: I think I lived on your broadcasts when my children were little. I used to wash my floors and pick up the food that had been thrown on the floor while they were eating, and I would sob through the broadcasts. But it helped me because I knew that other people were also struggling. I knew that God was in control, and I knew there were people out there who understood.

Now I go to people like Kristen, because we share an office together, and we talk about our strong-willed daughters, and we pray for you very regularly, and we watch you, and we love you, and we nurture you together.

JCD: The folks here at Focus on the Family get the credit for that, but this is why we're here. A reporter came to my office yesterday for an interview about the ministry. As far as I know, she is not a Christian. After we talked for almost an hour, she asked, "Why do you do this? You've said that you care about all those people who reach out for help. Why have you invited hundreds of thousands of them every month to bring their troubles here? Why do you put yourself and your staff through this?" I tried to explain that this is the essence of my Christian faith. Jesus said, "Inasmuch as ye have done it unto one of the least of these my brethren, ye have done it unto me" (Matthew 25:40, KJV). It gives me a great deal of satisfaction to put an arm around a mom who's depressed or discouraged or hopeless and to offer support and encouragement to her. As I talked, I noticed that this tough reporter got big tears in her eyes. So I'm just thankful that we have this opportunity to express care and concern for those who are hurting. And, Debra, I'm pleased that you were one of them.

Let me say one last thing to you, Lizz. I think you're going to make a great mom. I can just see it. You're very bright, and you're very dedicated, and the fact that you've landed on your feet this early is a very good sign. I trust that you will have a good year in school next year, and then go on into college. Then I want you to write your mom an e-mail that will make her cry. She's not a crier, but I'll bet you could bring "happy tears" to her eyes.

      Joy, you brought a Bible with you today. That's been your main-stay, hasn't it?

Joy: It has.

JCD: Well, come back and see us when you've got grandkids who are strong-willed children, will you? *(laughter)*

JCD: Thanks for being with us.

Panel: Thank you.

Final post-interview comments: I'm sure this interchange has been unsettling to some readers, particularly those who have young children and envision a future of all-out warfare with their irritable kids, much like that described by our panel. Let me hasten to say that the children whom we have read about in this chapter are at the far end of the continuum with regard to the strength of the will. Most boys and girls, even those who qualify for the title *strong-willed,* are less determined and more easily led. My purpose in providing what might be called a worst-case scenario, therefore, is to illustrate the varying ways children respond to authority, and to give hope and direction to those who are, in fact, raising one or more little revolutionaries. The good news, as we saw, is that the outcome even for those youngsters can be positive and deeply satisfying in the long run.

WHAT MAKES THEM THE WAY THEY ARE?

HAVING HEARD FROM the mothers on our panel, who no doubt represent millions of other moms who have struggled to control their children, one has to wonder why so many "experts" on parenting have failed to notice that some children are tougher to raise than others. One would never get that impression from reading the advice offered by this army of permissive psychologists, counselors, pediatricians, psychiatrists, and columnists for women's magazines, who are convinced that raising kids is as simple as falling off a log. All parents need to do, they have been saying for decades, is give them a lot of space, treat them like adults, and if absolutely necessary, explain every now and then why they might want to consider behaving better. How nice it would be if that were true. Unfortunately, this rosy view is cruel nonsense. It leaves Mom and Dad with the impression that every other parent in the world finds it easy to lead children, and those who are having trouble with it are miserable failures. In most cases, it is not fair and it is not true.

Misguided advice on child rearing has been prominent in the literature for at least seventy-five years. For example, best-selling author of books for parents John Caldwell Holt wrote a terrible text in 1974 entitled *Escape from Childhood*.[1] It was straight out of left field. Jim Stingley reviewed the book for the *Los Angeles Times*:

> In the latest one, [Holt] plainly advocates the overthrow of parental authority in just about every area. He sets forth that children, age whatever, should have the right to: experience sex, drink and use drugs, drive, vote, work, own property, travel,

have a guaranteed income, choose their guardians, control their learning, and have legal and financial responsibility. In short, Holt is proposing that parents discard the protectorate position they have held over their children in this and other countries over the past several hundred years, and thrust them, or rather let them thrust themselves—when they feel like they want to—into the real-life world.[2]

Doesn't that sound utterly foolish? Even the *Los Angeles Times* reviewer, a supposedly unbiased journalist, implies that Holt's ideas are ludicrous. Can you imagine a six-year-old girl driving her own car to an escrow office, where she and her preschool male friend will discuss the purchase of a new home over a martini or two? Can you visualize a teary-eyed mother and father standing in the doorway, saying good-bye to their five-year-old son who has decided to pack his teddy bear and go live with someone else? Have we gone completely mad? Discard the protectorate position, indeed! The surprising thing is that this man and his cockamamy theories were taken seriously by many people during the revolutionary days of the late sixties and seventies. In fact, Holt was quoted in the *Times* article as saying:

> "Oddly enough, the chapter on the matter of drinking and drugs, letting young people do whatever older people do, as well as manage their own sex lives, hasn't brought as much flak as I would have expected. . . . The understanding, sympathetic responses [from readers] have clearly outweighed the negative or hostile ones," he said.

About the time the Holt book came along, an article appeared in *Family Circle* that also revealed the permissiveness of the day. Its title, "A Marvelous New Way to Make Your Child Behave," should have been the first clue as to the nature of its content.[3] (If its recommendations were so fantastic, why hadn't they been observed in more than five thousand years of parenting?) The subtitle was even more revealing: "Rewards and Punishment Don't Work." Those two Pollyannaish headlines revealed the primrose path down which the authors were leading its readers. Never once did they admit that a child is capable of the kind of rebellion described by the three mothers we just met. Instead, the examples given in the article focused on relatively minor incidents of childish irresponsibility, such as a child not washing his hands before dinner or wearing improper clothing or not taking out the garbage. Responsible behavior is a noble objective for our children, but let's admit that the more difficult task is shaping the child's will in moments of rebellion.

A more current example of permissive approaches to child rearing is referred to as "positive discipline," or the "positive parenting" movement. It sounds good, but it is little more than repackaged permissive claptrap. Consider the following advice, featured on the Oklahoma State Department of Health's "Positive Discipline" Web page. It reads, "The goal of discipline is not to control children and make them obey but to give them skills for making decisions, gradually gaining self-control, and being responsible for their own behavior." Instead of telling a child, "Don't hit the kitty" or "Stop kicking the table," they suggest that parents say, "Touch the kitty gently" or "Keep your feet on the floor." The Web site goes on to assert that "Giving a child choices allows him some appropriate power over his life and encourages decision making." Parents are advised to "redirect" childish behavior. For example, if a child is throwing a truck around the house, instead of telling him to stop, they suggest you say to him, "I can't let you throw your truck, but you may throw the ball outside." Or if the child is kicking a door, you are to tell him, "You may not kick the door, but you may kick this ball or plastic milk jug." Their suggestion for dealing with willful defiance is to ignore it or to allow the child to engage in "something pleasant" until he cools off.[4]

What ridiculous advice that is. Notice how hard the parent is supposed to work to avoid being the leader at home. What's wrong with explaining to a child exactly what you want him or her to do and expecting obedience in return? Why is it unacceptable for a parent to insist that a child engaging in destructive or irritating behavior immediately cease and desist? Why not tell the child, "Kitties have feelings just like you do. You will not hit the kitty"? A youngster whose parent has never taken charge firmly is being deprived of a proper understanding of his mom's or dad's authority. It also keeps him from comprehending other forms of authority that will be encountered when he leaves the safety of his permissive cocoon. Sooner or later, that boy or girl is going to bump into a teacher, a police officer, a Marine Corps drill sergeant, or an employer who never heard of positive discipline and who will expect orders to be carried out as specified. The child who has only heard "suggestions" for alternative behavior through the years, which he may choose to accept or reject, is not prepared for the real world.

Here's yet another example of bad parental advice, also reflecting the positive discipline philosophy. Lini Kabada, writing for the Knight-Ridder newspaper chain, relayed this advice:

> [Karen] Gatewood once spanked and called "time-out." Now she talks about her children's feelings. When the girls act up, she sweetly and calmly suggests alternative activities and offers support ("I know you're sad") in the midst of tantrums, a touchy-feely technique called "time-in."
>
> Ms. Gatewood . . . allows what positive-parenting attitudes call "natural and logical consequences" of behavior to flow. For example, [her daughter] Amanda recently wanted to take a favorite piece of string on an outing. Ms. Gatewood warned that she might lose it, but didn't argue with the child. She allowed the natural and logical consequence to unfold. Sure enough, Amanda lost the string and she cried.
>
> Ms. Gatewood didn't ignore Amanda's feelings, as pediatricians suggest in the face of a tantrum. "I said, 'That is sad. It's horrible,' because to her it was horrible. She said, 'I won't bring my toys next time.'"[5]

How utterly simplistic and unworkable! Ms. Gatewood doesn't know much about children apparently, and she is certainly confused about how to manage them. What if little Amanda had wanted to take Mom's wedding ring on the outing instead of a piece of worthless string? What if she refused to go to bed until she collapsed in exhaustion night after night? What if she began regularly pouring her Cream of Wheat and orange juice into the television set? What if she refused to take necessary medication? Somewhere along the way, parental leadership has to make a showing. Boys and girls must be taught what is and is not acceptable behavior; the responsibility to establish those boundaries is an assignment given to moms and dads by the creator of families. Parents can't always just wait around for logical consequences to do a job they should be doing themselves.

Of course, logical consequences have a place in child rearing. But one very logical consequence of misbehavior might be sitting his wiggly bottom on a chair with instructions to think about why he must never spit in Mommy's face or run down a busy street or drive nails in the furniture or try to flush baby sister down the toilet. The "positive-parenting" books don't admit that these misbehaviors and a thousand others do happen— regularly in some families. They won't acknowledge that some mothers and fathers go to bed at night with pounding, throbbing headaches, wondering how raising kids became such an exhausting and nerve-racking experience. Instead, the Karen Gatewoods of the world offer squishy advice and touchy-feely explanations, such as "time-in," that leave parents confused, misinformed, and guilt ridden. My colleague, John Rosemond, with whom I am usually in strong agreement, gave the best assessment of the positive-parenting concept: "That's horse manure," he said, "and that's my most polite term. It's wimp parenting."

Let's examine now a more thorough answer to the fundamental question about willful defiance: Why is it that most children seem to have a need to take on those in authority over them? Why can't they just be satisfied with quiet discussions and patient explanations and gentle pats on the head? Why won't they follow reasonable instructions and leave it at that? Good questions.

I hope I have made the case by now that willfulness is built into the nature of some kids. It is simply part of their emotional and intellectual package brought with them into the world. This aspect of inborn temperament is not something boys and girls *learn*. It is something they *are*. Mothers know this instinctively. Virtually every mom with two or more children will affirm that she noticed differences in their personality—a different "feel"—the first time she held them. They'll tell you that some of them were tough and some were easy. But each was unique.

The early authorities in the field of child development denied what their eyes told them. They thought they had a better idea, concluding that babies come into the world devoid of individuality. Children, they said, are blank slates upon which the environment and experience will be written. John Locke and Jean-Jacques Rousseau, among others, promoted this notion and thereby confused the scientific understanding of children for decades. Most of the best-known psychologists in the world ascribed to this theory at one time or another, and many are still influenced by it. The more accurate view, however, based on careful research, recognizes that while experience is very important in shaping the human personality, the "blank slate" hypothesis is a myth. Children don't start life at the same place. They bring with them an individuality that is uniquely their own, different from that of every other individual who has ever lived. Let me say again that one of their innate characteristics is what I have termed "the strength of the will," which varies from child to child. If you have regular contact with children, you will be able to see this aspect of temperament, more or less, in living color.

A classic study of inborn temperaments was conducted more than twenty-five years ago by psychiatrists Stella Chess and Alexander Thomas and outlined in their excellent book, *Know Your Child*.[6] The authors reported that not only do babies differ significantly from one another at the moment of birth, but those differences tend to be rather persistent throughout childhood. Even more interestingly, they observed three broad categories or patterns of temperaments into which the majority of children can be classified. First, they referred to the "difficult child," who is characterized by negative reactions to people, intense mood swings, irregular sleep patterns and feeding schedules, frequent periods of crying, and violent tantrums when frustrated.[7] This is the youngster I have designated the "strong-willed child." Chess and Thomas described the second category as the "easy child," who exhibits a positive approach to people, quiet adaptability to new situations, regular sleep patterns and feeding schedules, and a willingness to accept the rules of the game.[8] The authors concluded, "Such a youngster is usually a joy to his or her parents, pediatrician, or teachers."[9] Amen. My term for the easy child is "compliant."

Chess and Thomas called the third personality pattern "slow to warm up" or "shy."[10] Youngsters in this category respond negatively to new situations and adapt slowly. However, they are less intense than difficult children, and they tend to have regular sleeping and feeding schedules. When they are upset or frustrated, they typically withdraw from the situation and react mildly rather than explode with anger and rebellion.

Not every child fits into one of these categories, of course, but according to Drs. Chess and Thomas, approximately 65 percent do.[11] The researchers also emphasized that babies are fully human at birth, being able immediately to relate to their parents and learn from their environment.[12] Blank slates at birth? Hardly!

We know now that heredity plays a much larger role in the development of human temperament than was previously understood. This is the conclusion of meticulous research conducted over many years at institutions like the University of Minnesota. The researchers there identified more than one hundred sets of identical twins that had been separated near the time of birth. They were raised in varying cultures, religions, and locations. They did not know each other, however, until they were grown. Because each set of twins shared the same DNA, or genetic material, and the same architectural design, it became possible for the researchers to examine the impact of inheritance by comparing their similarities and their differences on many variables. From these and other studies, it became clear that much of the personality, perhaps 70 percent or more, is inherited.[13] Our genes influence such qualities as creativity, wisdom, loving-kindness, vigor, longevity, intelligence, and even the joy of living.

Consider the brothers known in the Minnesota study as the "Jim twins," who were separated until they were thirty-nine years old. Their similarities were astonishing. Both married a woman named Linda. Both had a dog named Toy. Both suffered from migraine headaches. Both chain-smoked. Both liked the same brand of beer. Both drove Chevys, and both served as sheriff's deputies. Their personalities and attitudes were virtual carbon copies.[14] Though this degree of symmetry is exceptional, it illustrates the finding that most identical twins reveal surprising similarities in personality that are linked to heredity.

A person's genetic structure is thought to even influence the stability of his or her marriage. If an identical twin gets a divorce, the risk of the other also divorcing is 45 percent.[15] However, if a fraternal twin, who shares only half as many genes, divorces, the risk to the other twin is only 30 percent.[16]

What do these findings mean? Are we mere puppets on a string, playing out a predetermined course without free will or personal choices? Of course not. Unlike birds and mammals that act according to instinct, humans are capable of rational thought and independent action. We don't act on every sexual urge, for example, despite our genetic underpinnings. What is clear is that heredity provides a nudge in a particular direction—a definite impulse or inclination—but one that can be brought under the control of our rational processes. In fact, we must learn early in life to do just that.

What do we know specifically about children with particularly strong wills? That question has intrigued me for years. There has been very little written about these youngsters and almost no research on which to base an understanding. That dearth of information left parents of difficult children to muddle through on their own. In response, I conducted a survey of thirty-five thousand parents, mentioned earlier, to learn what their experiences have been. It was not a "scientific" investigation, since there was no randomized design or availability of a control group.[17] Nevertheless, what I learned was fascinating to me and, I hope, will be useful to you. Here is a summary of a huge volume of information that was provided by the people who have the most knowledge of kids who are as hardheaded as mules—the parents who live with them every day.

- We found that there are nearly three times as many strong-willed kids as those who are compliant. Nearly every family with multiple children has at least one who wants to run things. Male strong-willed children outnumber females by about 5 percent, and female compliant children outnumber males by about 6 percent. Thus, there is a slight tendency for males to have tougher temperaments and for females to be more compliant, but it can be, and often is, reversed.
- Birth order has nothing to do with being strong-willed or compliant. These elements of temperament are basically inherited and can occur in the eldest child or in the baby of the family.
- Most parents know they have a strong-willed child very early. One-third can tell at birth. Two-thirds know by the youngster's first birthday, and 92 percent are certain by the third birthday. Parents of compliant children know it even earlier.
- The temperaments of children tend to reflect those of their parents. Although there are many exceptions, two strong-willed parents are more likely to produce tough-minded kids and vice versa.
- Parents of strong-willed children can expect a battle during the teen years, even if they have raised them properly. Fully 74 percent of strong-willed children rebel significantly during adolescence. The weaker the authority of the parents when the kids are young, the greater the conflict is in later years.
- Incredibly, only 3 percent of compliant children experience severe rebellion in adolescence, and just 14 percent go into even mild rebellion. They start out life with a smile on their face and keep it there into young adulthood.

- The best news for parents of strong-willed children is the rapid decrease in their rebellion in young adulthood. It drops almost immediately in the early twenties and then trails off even more from there. Some are still angry into their twenties and early thirties, but by then the fire is gone for the majority. They peacefully rejoin the human community.
- The compliant child is much more likely to be a good student than the strong-willed child. Nearly three times as many strong-willed children made D's and F's during the last two years of high school as did compliant children. Approximately 80 percent of compliant children were A and B students.
- The compliant child is considerably better adjusted socially than the strong-willed child. It would appear that youngsters who are inclined to challenge the authority of their parents are also more likely to behave offensively with their peers.
- The compliant child typically enjoys higher self-esteem than the strong-willed child. It is difficult to overestimate the importance of this finding. Only 19 percent of compliant teenagers either disliked themselves (17 percent) or felt extreme self-hatred (2 percent). Of the very strong-willed teenagers, 35 percent disliked themselves and 8 percent experienced extreme self-hatred. The strong-willed child seems compelled from within to fuss, fight, test, question, resist, and challenge.

Obviously, the findings I have shared in this chapter are of enormous significance to our understanding of children. They and related concepts are described in greater detail in my book *Parenting Isn't for Cowards*.[18]

QUESTIONS & ANSWERS

Q: Tell me why some kids with every advantage and opportunity seem to turn out bad, while others raised in terrible homes become pillars in the community. I know one young man who grew up in squalid circumstances, yet he is such a fine person today. How did his parents

manage to raise such a responsible son when they didn't even seem to care?

A: That illustrates just the point I have been trying to make. Neither heredity nor environment will account for all human behavior. There is something else there—something from within—that also operates to make us who we are. Some behavior is caused, and some plainly isn't.

Several years ago, for example, I had dinner with two parents who had unofficially "adopted" a thirteen-year-old boy. This youngster followed their son home one afternoon and asked if he could spend the night. As it turned out, he stayed with them for almost a week without receiving so much as a phone call from his mother. It was later learned that she worked sixteen hours a day and had no interest in her son. Her alcoholic husband had divorced her several years earlier and left town without a trace. The boy had been abused, unloved, and ignored through much of his life.

Given this background, what kind of kid do you think he is today—a druggie? a foul-mouthed delinquent? a lazy, insolent bum? No. He is polite to adults; he is a hard worker; he makes good grades in school; and he enjoys helping around the house. This boy is like a lost puppy who desperately wants a good home. He begged the family to adopt him officially so he could have a real father and a loving mother. His own mom couldn't care less.

How could this teenager be so well-disciplined and polished despite his lack of training? I don't know. It is simply within him. He reminds me of my wonderful friend David Hernandez. David and his parents came to the United States illegally from Mexico more than fifty years ago and nearly starved to death before they found work. They eventually survived by helping to harvest the potato crop throughout the state of California. During this era, David lived under trees or in the open fields. His father made a stove out of an oil drum half-filled with dirt. The open campfire was the centerpiece of their home.

David never had a roof over his head until his family finally moved into an abandoned chicken coop. His mother covered the boarded walls with cheap wallpaper, and David thought they were living in luxury. Then the city of San Jose condemned the area, and David's "house" was torn down. He couldn't understand why the community would destroy so fine a place.

Given this beginning, how can we explain the man that David Hernandez became? He graduated near the top of his class in high school and was granted a scholarship to college. Again, he earned high marks and four years later entered Loma Linda University School of Medicine. Once more, he scored in the top 10 percent of his class and continued in a residency in obstetrics and gynecology. Eventually, he served as a professor of obstetrics and gynecology at both Loma Linda University and the University of Southern California medical schools. Then, at the peak of his career, his life began to unravel.

I'll never forget the day Dr. Hernandez called me after he'd been released from the hospital following a battery of laboratory tests. The diagnosis? Sclerosing cholangitis, a liver disorder that was invariably fatal at that time. The world lost a fine husband, father, and friend six years later when he was only forty-three. I loved him like a brother, and I still miss him today.

Again, I ask how such discipline and genius could come from these infertile circumstances. Who would have thought that this deprived boy sitting in the dirt would someday become one of the most loved and respected surgeons of his era? Where did the motivation originate? From what bubbling spring did his ambition and thirst for knowledge flow? He had no books, took no educational trips, knew no scholars. Yet he reached for the sky. Why did it turn out this way for David Hernandez and not the youngster with every advantage and opportunity?

Why have so many children of prominent and loving parents grown up in ideal circumstances only to reject it all for the streets of Atlanta, San Francisco, or New York? Good answers are simply not available. It apparently comes down to this: God chooses to use individuals in unique ways. Beyond that mysterious relationship, we must simply conclude that some kids seem born to make it and others are determined to fail. Someone reminded me recently that the same boiling water that softens the carrot also hardens the egg. Likewise, some individuals react positively to certain circumstances and others negatively. We don't know why.

Two things are clear to me from this understanding. First, parents have been far too quick to take the credit or blame for the way their children turn out. Those with bright young superstars stick out their chests and say, "Look what we accomplished." Those with twisted and irresponsible kids wonder, *Where did we go wrong?* Well, neither is entirely accurate. No one would deny that parents play an important role in the development and training of their children. But they are only part of the formula from which a young adult is assembled.

Second, behavioral scientists have been far too simplistic in their explanation of human behavior. We are more than the aggregate of our experiences. We are more than the quality of our nutrition. We are more than our genetic heritage. We are more than our biochemistry. And we are more than our parents' influence. God has created us as unique individuals, capable of independent and rational thought that is not attributable to any other source. That is what makes the task of parenting so challenging and rewarding. Just when you think you have your kids figured out, you had better brace yourself! Something new is coming your way.

Q: Does Scripture confirm that babies have temperaments or personalities before birth?

A: Yes, in several references we learn that God knows and relates to unborn children as individuals. He said to the prophet Jeremiah, "Before I formed you in the womb I knew you, and before you were born I consecrated you; I appointed you a prophet to the nations" (Jeremiah 1:5, RSV). The apostle Paul said we were also chosen before birth (see Ephesians 1:4). And in a remarkable account, we are told of the prenatal development of the twins Jacob and Esau. As predicted before their birth, one turned out to be rebellious and tough while the other was something of a mama's boy. They were fighting before they were born and continued in conflict through much of their lives (see Genesis 25:22-27). Then later, in one of the most mysterious and disturbing statements in the Bible, the Lord said, "Jacob have I loved, but Esau have I hated" (Romans 9:13, KJV). Apparently, God discerned a rebellious nature in Esau before he was born and knew that he would not be receptive to the divine Spirit.

These examples tell us that unborn children are unique individuals with whom God is already acquainted. They also confirm, for me at least, the wickedness of abortion, which destroys those embryonic little personalities.

Q: How can you say that precious little newborns come into the world inherently evil? I agree with the experts who say that babies are born good and they only learn to do wrong later.

A: Please understand that the issue here is not with the purity or innocence of babies. No one would question their preciousness as creations of God. The point of disagreement concerns the tendencies and inclinations they have inherited. People who believe in innate goodness would have us believe that human beings are naturally unselfish, honest, respectful, kind to others, self-controlled, obedient to authority, etc. Children, as you indicated, then subsequently learn to do wrong when they are exposed to a corrupt and misguided society. Bad *experiences* are responsible for bad behavior. To raise healthy kids, then, it is the task of parents to provide a loving environment and then stay out of the way. Natural goodness will flow from within.

This is the humanistic perspective on childish nature. Millions of people believe it to be true. Most psychologists have also accepted and taught this notion throughout the twentieth century. There is only one thing wrong with the concept. It is entirely inaccurate.

Q: How can you be so sure about the nature of children? What evidence do you have to support the belief that their tendency is to do wrong?

A: We'll start with what the "owner's manual" has to say about human nature. Only the Creator of children can tell us how He made them, and He has done that in Scripture. It teaches that we are born in sin, having inherited a disobedient nature from Adam. King David said, "In sin did my mother *conceive* me" (Psalm 51:5, KJV, italics added), meaning that this tendency to do wrong was transmitted genetically. Paul said this sinful nature has infected every person who ever lived. "For *all* have sinned, and come short of the glory of God" (Romans 3:23, KJV, italics added). Therefore, with or without bad associations, children are naturally inclined toward rebellion, selfishness, dishonesty, aggression, exploitation, and greed. They don't have to be taught these behaviors. They are natural expressions of their humanness.

Although this perspective is viewed with disdain by the secular world today, the evidence to support it is overwhelming. How else do we explain the pugnacious and perverse nature of every society on earth? Bloody warfare has been the centerpiece of world history for more than five thousand years. People of every race and creed around the globe have tried to rape, plunder, burn, blast, and kill each other century after century. Peace has been but a momentary pause when they have stopped to reload! Plato said more than 2,350 years ago: "Only dead men have seen an end to war."[19] He was right, and it will continue that way until the Prince of Peace comes.

Not only have nations warred against each other since the beginning of time, we also find a depressing incidence of murder, drug abuse, child molestation, prostitution, adultery, homosexuality, and dishonesty among individuals. How would we account for this pervasive evil in a world of people who are naturally inclined toward good? Have they really drifted into these antisocial and immoral behaviors despite their inborn tendencies? If so, surely *one* society in all the world would have been able to preserve the goodness with which children are born. Where is it? Does such a place exist? No, although admittedly some societies are more moral than others. Still, none reflect the harmony that might be expected from the natural goodness theorists. Why not? Because their basic premise is wrong.

Q: What, then, does this biblical understanding mean for parents? Are they to consider their babies guilty before they have done anything wrong?
A: Of course not. Children are not responsible for their sins until they reach an age of accountability—and that time frame is known only to God. On the other hand, parents should not be surprised when rebellious or mischievous behavior occurs. It *will* happen, probably by the eighteenth month or before. Anyone who has watched a toddler throw a temper tantrum when she doesn't get her way must be hard-pressed to explain how the phrase "innate goodness" became so popular! Did her mother or father model the tantrum for her, falling on the floor, slobbering, kicking, crying, and screaming? I would hope not. Either way, the kid needs no demonstration. Rebellion comes naturally to her entire generation—although in some individuals it is more pronounced than in others.

For this reason, parents can and must train, mold, correct, guide, punish, reward, instruct, warn, teach, and love their kids during the formative years. Their purpose is to shape that inner nature and keep it from tyrannizing the entire family. Ultimately, however, only Jesus Christ can cleanse it and make it wholly acceptable to the Master. This is what the Bible teaches about people, and this is what I firmly believe.

Q: If it is natural for a toddler to break all the rules, should he be disciplined for his defiance?
A: You are on to something important here. Many of the spankings and slaps given to toddlers can and should be avoided. Toddlers get in trouble

most frequently because of their natural desire to touch, bite, taste, smell, and break everything within their grasp. However, this exploratory behavior is not aggressive. It is a valuable means for learning and should not be discouraged. I have seen parents slap their two-year-olds throughout the day for simply investigating their world. This squelching of normal curiosity is not fair to the youngster. It seems foolish to leave an expensive trinket where it will tempt him and then scold him for taking the bait. If little fat fingers insist on handling the trinkets on the lower shelf, it is much wiser to distract the child with something else than to discipline him for his persistence. Toddlers cannot resist the offer of a new plaything. They are amazingly easy to interest in less fragile toys, and parents should keep a few alternatives available for use when needed.

When, then, should the toddler be subjected to mild discipline? When he openly defies his parents' spoken commands! If he runs the other way when called, purposely slams his milk glass onto the floor, dashes into the street while being told to stop, screams and throws a tantrum at bedtime, hits his friends—these are the forms of unacceptable behavior that should be discouraged. Even in these situations, however, all-out spankings are not often required to eliminate the behavior. A parent's firm rap to the fingers or command to sit in a chair for a few minutes will convey the same message just as convincingly. Spankings should be reserved for a child's moments of greatest antagonism, usually occurring after the third birthday.

The toddler years are critical to a child's future attitude toward authority. He should be taught to patiently obey without being expected to behave like a more mature child.

Without watering down anything I have said earlier, I should also point out that I am a firm believer in the judicious use of grace (and humor) in parent-child relationships. In a world in which children are often pushed to grow up too fast and too soon, their spirits can dry out like prunes beneath the constant gaze of critical eyes. It is refreshing to see parents temper their inclination for harshness with a measure of unmerited favor. There is always room for more loving forgiveness within our home. Likewise, there's nothing that rejuvenates the parched, delicate spirit of a child faster than when a lighthearted spirit pervades the home and regular laughter fills its halls. Heard any good jokes lately?

FOUR

Shaping the Will

THE YOUNG MOTHER of a defiant three-year-old girl once approached me in Kansas City to thank me for my books and tapes. She told me that a few months earlier her little daughter had become increasingly defiant and had managed to buffalo her frustrated mom and dad. They knew she was manipulating them but couldn't seem to regain control. Then one day they were in a bookstore and happened upon a copy of my first book, *Dare to Discipline* (now revised and called *The New Dare to Discipline*).[1] They bought a copy and learned that it is appropriate, from my perspective, to spank a child under certain well-defined circumstances. My recommendations made sense to these harassed parents, who promptly used that technique the next time their daughter gave them reason to do so. But the little girl was just bright enough to figure out where they had picked up the new idea. When the mother awoke the next morning, she found her copy of *Dare to Discipline* floating in the toilet! That darling little girl had done her best to send my book off to the sewer where it belonged. I suppose that is the strongest editorial comment I've received on any of my writings!

This incident with the toddler was not an isolated case. Another child selected my book from an entire shelf of possibilities and threw it into the fireplace. I could easily become paranoid about these hostilities. Dr. Benjamin Spock, the late pediatrician who wrote the widely acclaimed *Dr. Spock's Baby and Child Care,* was loved by millions of children who grew up under his influence.[2] But I have apparently been resented by two generations of kids who wanted to catch me in a blind alley on some cloudy night.

I continue to receive the most delightful mail from children and their parents about the subject of discipline. A college student approached me with a smile and handed me a poem written just for me. It read: "Roses are red, Violets are blue. When I was a kid, I got spanked 'cause of you." Sorry about that, sir!

A mother wrote to tell me that she took her daughter to the doctor for her routine childhood inoculations. The youngster came home that evening and told her father, "I just got my shots for mumps, measles, and rebellion." Don't you wish there was an injection for that type of behavior? I would have had my adolescents given a big dose at least once a week.

A little eight-year-old girl mailed me this note:

> *Dear Dobinson*
> *You are a mean and curle thing. You and your dumb sayings won't take you to Heaven.*
>
> > *Kristy P.*
>
> *P.S. Kids don't like wippens.*

It is obvious that children are aware of the contest of wills between generations, which can become something of a game. Lisa Whelchel, former child actress on the television sitcom *The Facts of Life,* described a funny encounter with her four-year-old boy, Tucker. She related the story in her excellent book, *Creative Correction.* Lisa and her husband were going out to dinner and left the children with a babysitter. As they were standing at the door, she said to her son, "I really want you to do your best to obey the babysitter tonight."

Tucker immediately replied, "Well, Mom, I just don't know if I can do that."

"Why not?" she asked.

With a straight face, he answered, "There's so much foolishness built up in my heart, I don't think there is any room for goodness and wisdom."

"Well," Lisa said, "maybe we need to step into the bathroom and drive that foolishness out."

With that, Tucker replied, "W-wait a minute. I feel the foolishness going away all by itself—the goodness is coming in right now!"[3]

Lisa's encounter with her son did not represent a serious challenge to her authority and should have been (and, in fact, was) responded to with a smile. But when a real donnybrook occurs between generations, it is extremely important for the parents to "win." Why? A child who behaves in ways that are disrespectful or harmful to himself or others often has a hidden motive. Whether he recognizes it or not, he is usually seeking to verify the existence and stability of the boundaries. This testing has much the same function as a police officer in years past who turned doorknobs at places of business after dark. Though he tried to open the doors, he hoped they were locked and secure. Likewise, a child who defies the leadership of his parents is reassured when they remain confident and firm under fire. It creates a sense of security for a kid who lives in a structured environment in which the rights of other people (and his own) are protected by well-defined limits.

With that said, let's hurry along now to the how-tos of shaping a child's will. I've boiled this complex topic down to six straightforward guidelines that I hope will be helpful, the first of which is most important and will be dealt with in greater detail.

First: Begin Teaching Respect for Authority While Children Are Very Young

The most urgent advice I can give to the parents of an assertive, independent child is to establish their positions as strong but loving leaders when Junior and Missy are in the preschool years. This is the first step toward helping them learn to control their powerful impulses. Alas, there is no time to lose. As we have seen, a naturally defiant youngster is in a high-risk category for antisocial behavior later in life. She is more likely to challenge her teachers in school and question the values she has been taught. Her temperament leads her to oppose anyone who tries to tell her what to do. Fortunately, this outcome is not inevitable, because the complexities of the human personality make it impossible to predict behavior with complete accuracy. But the probabilities lie in that direction. Thus, I will repeat my most urgent advice to parents: that they begin shaping the will of the particularly aggressive child very early in life. (Notice that I did not say to crush his will or to destroy it or to snuff it out, but to rein it in for his own good.) But how is that accomplished?

Well, first let me tell you how *not* to approach that objective. Harshness, gruffness, and sternness are not effective in shaping a child's will. Likewise, constant whacking and threatening and criticizing are destructive and counterproductive. A parent who is mean and angry most of the time is creating resentment that will be stored and come roaring into the relationship during adolescence or beyond. Therefore, every opportunity should be taken to keep the tenor of the home pleasant, fun, and accepting. At the same time, however, parents should display confident firmness in their demeanor. You, Mom and Dad, are the boss. You are in charge. If you believe it, the tougher child will accept it also. Unfortunately, many mothers today are tentative and insecure in approaching their young children. If you watch them with their little boys and girls in supermarkets or airports, you will see these frustrated and angry moms who are totally confused about how to handle a given misbehavior. Temper tantrums throw them for a loop, as though they never expected them. Actually, they have been coming on for some time.

A pediatrician friend told me about a telephone call he received from the anxious mother of a six-month-old baby.

"I think he has a fever," she said nervously.

"Well," the doctor replied, "did you take his temperature?"

"No," she said. "He won't let me insert the thermometer."

There is trouble ahead for this shaky mother. There is even more danger for her son in the days ahead. He will quickly sense her insecurity and step into the power vacuum she has created. From there, it will be a wild ride all the way through adolescence.

Here are some nuts-and-bolts suggestions for avoiding the trouble I have described. Once a child understands who is in charge, he can be held accountable for behaving in a respectful manner. That sounds easy, but it can be very difficult. In a moment of rebellion, a little child will consider his parents' wishes and defiantly choose to disobey. Like a military general before a battle, he will calculate the potential risk, marshal his forces, and attack the enemy with guns blazing. When that nose-to-nose confrontation occurs between generations, it is extremely important for the adult to display confidence and decisiveness. The child has made it clear that he's looking for a fight, and his parents would be wise not to disappoint him! Nothing is more destructive to parental leadership than for a mother or father to equivocate during that struggle. When parents consistently lose those battles, resorting to tears and screaming and other signs of frustration, some dramatic changes take place in the way they are seen by their children. Instead of being secure and confident leaders, they become spineless jellyfish who are unworthy of respect or allegiance.

Susanna Wesley, mother of eighteenth-century evangelists John and Charles Wesley, reportedly bore nineteen children. Toward the end of her life, John asked her to describe in writing her philosophy of mothering for him. Copies of her reply are still in existence today. As you will see from the excerpts that follow, her beliefs reflect a traditional understanding of child rearing. She wrote:

> In order to form the minds of children, the first thing to be done is to conquer the will, and bring them into an obedient temper. To inform the understanding is a work of time, and must with children proceed by slow degrees as they are able to bear it; but the subjecting of the will is a thing which must be done at once, and the sooner the better!
>
> For by neglecting timely correction, they will contract a stubbornness and obstinacy which is hardly ever after conquered, and never without using such severity as would be painful to me as to the children. In the esteem of the world, those who withhold timely correction would pass for kind and indulgent parents, whom I call cruel parents, who permit their children to get habits which they know must afterward be broken. Nay, some are so stupidly fond as in sport to teach their children to do things which in the after while, they must severely beat them for doing.
>
> Whenever a child is corrected, it must be conquered; and this will be no hard matter to do, if it be not grown headstrong by too much indulgence. And, if the will of a child is totally subdued, and if it be brought to revere and stand in awe of the parents, then a great many childish follies and inadvertencies may be passed by. Some should be overlooked and taken no notice of, and others mildly reproved. But no willful transgressions ought ever to be forgiven children without chastisement, more or less as the nature and circumstances of the offense shall require.
>
> I cannot dismiss this subject. As self-will is the root of all sin and misery, so whatever cherishes this in children insures

their after wretchedness and faithlessness. Whatever checks
and mortifies, promotes their future happiness and piety. This
is still more evident if we further consider that Christianity is
nothing less than doing the will of God, and not our own; that
the one grand impediment to our temporal and eternal happiness being this self-will. No indulgence of it can be trivial, no
denial unprofitable.[4]

Does that sound harsh by our modern standards? Perhaps. While I would
have balanced the approach with greater compassion and gentleness, I
believe that Mrs. Wesley's basic understanding was correct. If the strong-
willed child is allowed by indulgence to develop "habits" of defiance and
disrespect during his or her early childhood, those characteristics will not
only cause problems for the parents, but will ultimately handicap the child
whose rampaging will was never brought under self-control.

Does this mean that Mom or Dad should be snapping orders all day
long, disregarding the feelings and wishes of the child? Certainly not! I
would not want to be treated that way, and you wouldn't either. Most of
the time, you can talk things through and come to a mutual understanding.
Furthermore, there is nothing wrong with negotiating and compromising
when disagreements occur between generations. Six-year-old Lance may
voluntarily rest or nap in the afternoon so that he can watch a late evening
children's program on television. Mom may offer to drive her ten-year-old
daughter to soccer practice, provided she agrees to straighten and clean her
room. There are countless situations such as these during childhood when
a "no-win, no-lose" agreement can be reached without imposing constant
demands and threats on a youngster. These mutually agreed-upon conclusions will not undermine parental leadership and won't reinforce a spirit
of rebellion, even in a tough-minded child.

On the other hand, there is a time to speak in that tone of voice that
says, kindly but firmly, "Please do it now, because I said so." One can't
always negotiate with a child or give repetitive explanations and requests for
cooperation. Every command doesn't have to end with a question mark, as
in, "Would you like to go take your bath now?" Sometimes you simply have
to step in and be the boss. As we saw in the last chapter, it is this expression
of authority that many modern parental advisers resist tooth and nail. They
never want moms and dads to sound as though they are in charge. Some

even refer to that style of management as "power games." One writer of books for parents expressed his permissive philosophy this way:

> The stubborn persistence of the idea that parents must and should use authority in dealing with children has, in my opinion, prevented for centuries any significant change or improvement in the way children are raised by parents and treated by adults. Children resent those who have power over them. In short, children want to limit their behavior themselves, if it becomes apparent to them that their behavior must be limited or modified. Children, like adults, prefer to be their own authority over their behavior.[5]

I couldn't disagree more. God has installed parents as leaders for a finite period of time. When they are afraid or unwilling to fulfill that responsibility, the strong-willed child is positively driven to step to the front and begin running things. As we have seen, it is his passion to take charge anyway. If you as a mom or dad won't be the boss, I guarantee that your tough-as-nails kid will grab that role. That is the beginning of sorrows for both generations.

The New Testament, which the Scripture tells us is "God-breathed" (2 Timothy 3:16), speaks eloquently to this point. We read in 1 Timothy 3:4-5, "He [speaking of the father] must have proper authority in his own household, and be able to control and command the respect of his children" (Phillips). Colossians 3:20 expresses this divine principle to the younger generation: "Children, obey your parents in all things: for this is well pleasing unto the Lord" (KJV). I find no place in the Bible where our little ones are designated as codiscussants at a conference table, deciding what they will and will not accept from the older generation. Power games, indeed.

Why is parental authority so vigorously supported throughout the Bible? Is it simply catering to the whims of oppressive, power-hungry adults, as some would have us believe? No, the leadership of parents plays a significant role in the development of a child! By yielding to the loving authority (leadership) of his parents, a child learns to submit to other forms of authority that will confront him later in his life. Without respect for leadership, there is anarchy, chaos, and confusion for everyone concerned.

There is an even more important reason for the preservation of authority in the home. Children who are acquainted with it learn to yield to the benevolent leadership of God Himself. It is a fact that a child identifies his parents with God in the early days, whether the adults want that role or not. Specifically, most children see God the way they perceive their earthly fathers (and, to a lesser degree, their mothers). This fact was illustrated in our home when our son, Ryan, was just two years old. Since his babyhood, he had seen his sister, mother, and father say grace before eating our meals, because we always thank God for our food in that way. But because of his age, the little toddler had never been asked to lead the prayer. On one occasion when I was out of town, Shirley put the lunch on the table and spontaneously turned to Ryan, saying, "Would you like to pray for our food today?" Her request apparently startled him and he glanced around nervously, then clasped his little hands together and said, "I love you, Daddy. Amen."

When I returned home and heard about Ryan's prayer, it was immediately apparent that my son had actually confused me with God. And I'll confess, I wished he hadn't! I appreciated the thought, but I was uncomfortable with its implications. It was too big a job for an ordinary dad to handle. There were times when I'm sure I disappointed our children—times when I was too tired to be what they needed from me—times when my human frailties were all too apparent. The older they became, the greater was the gap between who I was and who they had thought I was—especially during the storms of adolescence. No, I didn't want to represent God to my son and daughter. But whether I liked it or not, they thought of me in those terms, and your younger children probably see you that way too!

In short, the Creator has given parents the awesome responsibility of representing Him to their children. As such, they should reflect two aspects of divine nature to the next generation. First, our heavenly Father is a God of unlimited love, and our children must become acquainted with His mercy and tenderness through our own love toward them. But make no mistake about it: our Lord is also the possessor of majestic authority! The universe is ordered by a sovereign God who requires obedience from His children and has warned that "the wages of sin is death" (Romans 6:23). To show our little ones love without authority is as serious a distortion of God's nature as to reveal an iron-fisted authority without love.

From this perspective, then, a child who has only "negotiated" with his parents and teachers during times of intense conflict has probably not learned to submit to the authority of the Almighty. If this youngster is allowed to behave disrespectfully to Mom and Dad, sassing them and disobeying their specific orders, then it is most unlikely that he will turn his face up to God about twenty years later and say humbly, "Here am I, Lord; send me!" To repeat, a child learns to yield to the authority of God by first learning to submit to (rather than bargain with) the leadership of his parents.

But what did the apostle Paul mean in his first letter to Timothy where he referred to parents having the "proper authority"? Was he giving them the right to browbeat their children, disregarding their feelings and instilling fear and anxiety in them? No. There is a wonderful balance taught by Paul in this letter and in Ephesians 6:4. It reads, "Fathers, do not exasperate your children; instead, bring them up in the training and instruction of the Lord."

We'll move more quickly now through the five other general guidelines for shaping the will of a child.

SECOND: DEFINE THE BOUNDARIES BEFORE THEY ARE ENFORCED

Preceding any disciplinary event is the necessity of establishing reasonable expectations and boundaries for the child. She should know what is and is not acceptable behavior before she is held responsible for it. This precondition will eliminate the sense of injustice that a youngster feels when she is punished or scolded for violating a vague or unidentified rule.

THIRD: DISTINGUISH BETWEEN WILLFUL DEFIANCE AND CHILDISH IRRESPONSIBILITY

Let's return briefly to the letter written by Susanna Wesley, who recommended that a mother or father overlook "childish follies and inadvertencies" but never ignore "willful transgressions." What did she mean? She was referring to the distinction between what I would call childish irresponsibility and "willful defiance." There is a world of difference between the two. Understanding the distinction will be useful in knowing how to interpret the meaning of a behavior and how to respond to it appropriately. Let me explain.

Suppose little David is acting silly in the living room and falls into a table, breaking several expensive china cups and other trinkets. Or suppose Ashley loses her bicycle or leaves her mother's coffeepot out in the rain. Perhaps four-year-old Brooke reaches for something on her brother's plate and catches his glass of milk with her elbow, baptizing the baby and making a frightful mess on the floor. As frustrating as these occurrences are, they represent acts of childish irresponsibility that have little meaning in the long-term scheme of things. As we all know, children will regularly spill things, lose things, break things, forget things, and mess up things. That's the way kids are made. These behaviors represent the mechanism by which children are protected from adult-level cares and burdens. When accidents happen, patience and tolerance are the order of the day. If the foolishness was particularly pronounced for the age and maturity of the individual, Mom or Dad might want to have the youngster help with the cleanup or even work to pay for the loss. Otherwise, I think the event should be ignored. It goes with the territory, as they say.

There is another category of behavior, however, that is strikingly different. It occurs when a child defies the authority of the parent in a blatant manner. She may shout "I will not!" or "You shut up!" or "You can't make me." It may happen when Junior grabs a handful of candy bars at the checkout and refuses to give them back, or when he throws a violent temper tantrum in order to get his way. These behaviors represent a willful, haughty spirit and a determination to disobey. Something very different is going on in those moments. You have drawn a line in the dirt, and the child has deliberately flopped his bony little toe across it. You're both asking, *Who is going to win? Who has the most courage? Who is in charge here?* If you do not conclusively answer these questions for your strong-willed children, your child will precipitate other battles designed to ask them again and again. That's why you must be prepared to respond immediately to this kind of stiff-necked rebellion. It is what Susanna Wesley meant when she wrote, "Some [misbehavior] should be overlooked and taken no notice of [referring to childish irresponsibility], and others mildly reproved. But no willful transgressions ought ever to be forgiven children without chastisement, more or less as the nature and circumstances of the offense shall require." Susanna arrived at this understanding 250 years before I came along. She learned it from the nineteen kids who called her Mama.

Brace yourself now, because I'm about to recommend something to you that will be controversial in some circles. You may not even agree with it, but hear me out. On those occasions when you find yourself and your strong-willed child in one of those classic battles of the will, it is not the time to discuss the virtues of obedience. You shouldn't send Jack or Jane to his or her room to pout. Time-out doesn't work very well and time-in is a total failure. Bribery is out of the question. Crying and begging for mercy are disastrous. Waiting until tired ol' Dad comes home to handle matters at the end of the day will be equally unproductive. None of these touchy-feely responses and delaying maneuvers are going to succeed. It all comes down to this: When you have been challenged, it is time for you to take charge—to defend your right to lead. When mothers and fathers fail to be the boss in a moment like that, they create for themselves and their families a potential lifetime of heartache. Or as Susanna Wesley said, "No indulgence of [willful defiance] can be trivial, no denial unprofitable." Therefore, I believe a mild and appropriate spanking is the discipline of choice for a hot-tempered child between twenty months and ten years of age. I will talk at greater length in chapter 8 about corporal punishment, its advantages, its limitations, and the dangers of its misuse.

FOURTH: REASSURE AND TEACH
AFTER THE CONFRONTATION IS OVER

After a time of conflict during which the parent has demonstrated his right to lead (particularly if it resulted in tears for the child), the youngster between two and seven (or older) will probably want to be loved and reassured. By all means, open your arms and let him come! Hold him close and tell him of your love. Rock him gently and let him know again why he was punished and how he can avoid the trouble next time. This is a teachable moment, when the objective of your discipline can be explained. Such a conversation is difficult or impossible to achieve when a rebellious, stiff-necked little child is clenching her fist and taking you on. But after a confrontation has occurred—especially if it involved tears—the child usually wants to hug you and get reassurance that you really care for her. By all means, open your arms and let her snuggle to your breast. And for the Christian family, it is extremely important to pray with the child at that time, admitting to God that we have all sinned and no one is perfect. Divine forgiveness is a marvelous experience, even for a very young child.

FIFTH: AVOID IMPOSSIBLE DEMANDS

Be absolutely sure that your child is capable of delivering what you require. Never punish him for wetting the bed involuntarily or for not becoming potty trained by one year of age or for doing poorly in school when he is incapable of academic success. These impossible demands put the child in an irresolvable conflict: there is no way out. That condition brings unnecessary risks to the human emotional apparatus. Besides that, it is simply unjust.

SIXTH: LET LOVE BE YOUR GUIDE!

A relationship that is characterized by genuine love and affection is likely to be a healthy one, even though some parental mistakes and errors are inevitable.

These six steps should, in my view, form the foundation for healthy parent-child relationships. There is one more ingredient that will round out the picture. We will read about it in the next chapter.

QUESTIONS & ANSWERS

Q: You said we need to interpret the intent of children so that we can know how to discipline properly. What if I'm not sure? What if my child behaves in ways that may or may not be willfully defiant? How can I tell the difference?

A: That question has been asked of me dozens of times. A mother will say, "I think Garrett was being disrespectful when I told him to take his bath, but I'm not sure what he was thinking."

There is a very straightforward solution to this parental dilemma: Use the next occasion for the purpose of clarifying. Say to your son, "Garrett, your answer to me just now sounded disrespectful. I'm not sure how you intended it. But just so we understand each other, don't talk to me like that again." If it occurs again, you'll know it was deliberate. Most confusion over how to discipline results from parents' failure to define the limits properly. If you're hazy on what is acceptable and unacceptable, then your child will be doubly confused.

Most children will accept the boundaries if they understand them and are sure you mean business when you set them up.

Q: If you had to choose between a very authoritarian style of parenting and one that is permissive and lax, which would you prefer? Which is healthier for kids?

A: Both extremes leave their characteristic scars on children, and I would be hard-pressed to say which is more damaging. At the oppressive end of the continuum, a child suffers the humiliation of total domination. The atmosphere is icy and rigid, and he lives in constant fear. He is unable to make his own decisions, and his personality is squelched beneath the hobnailed boot of parental authority. Lasting characteristics of dependency, deep-seated anger, and serious adolescent rebellion often result from this domination.

But the opposite extreme is also damaging to kids. In the absence of adult leadership, the child is her own master from earliest babyhood. She thinks the world revolves around her heady empire, and she often has utter contempt and disrespect for those closest to her. Anarchy and chaos reign in her home. Her mother is often the most frazzled and frustrated woman on the block. It would be worth the hardship and embarrassment she endures if her passivity produced healthy, secure children. It typically does not.

The healthiest approach to child rearing is found in the safety of the middle ground between disciplinary extremes. I attempted to illustrate that reasonable parenting style on the cover of my first book, *Dare to Discipline,* which included this little diagram:

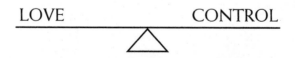

Children tend to thrive best in an environment where these two ingredients, love and control, are present in balanced proportions. When the scale tips in either direction, problems usually begin to develop at home.

Unfortunately, parenting styles in a culture tend to sweep back and forth like a pendulum from one extreme to the other.

Q: I could use some advice about a minor problem we're having. Tim, my six-year-old, loves to use silly names whenever he speaks to my husband and me. For example, this past week it's been "you big hot dog." Nearly every time he sees me now he says, "Hi, hot dog." Before that it was "dummy," then "moose" (after he studied M for moose in school). I know it's silly and it's not a huge problem, but it gets so annoying after such a long time. He's been doing this for a year now. How can we get him to talk to us with more respect, calling us Mom or Dad, instead of hot dog and moose? Thank you for any advice you can offer.

A: What we have here is a rather classic power game, much like those we have discussed before. And contrary to what you said, it is not so insignificant. Under other circumstances, it would be a minor matter for a child to call his parents a playful name. That is not the point here. Rather, strong-willed Tim is continuing to do something that he knows is irritating to you and your husband, yet you are unable to stop him. That is the issue. He has been using humor as a tactic of defiance for a full year. It is time for you to sit down and have a quiet little talk with young Timothy. Tell him that he is being disrespectful and that the next time he calls either you or his father a name of any kind, he will be punished. You must then be prepared to deliver on the promise, because he will continue to challenge you until it ceases to be fun. That's the way he is made. If that response never comes, his insults will probably become more pronounced, ending in adolescent nightmares. Appeasement for a strong-willed child is an invitation to warfare.

Never forget this fact: The classic strong-willed child craves power from the time he's a toddler and even earlier. Since Mom is the nearest adult who is holding the reins, he will hack away at her until she lets him drive his own buggy. I remember a mother telling me of a confrontation with her tough-minded four-year-old daughter. The child was demanding her own way and the mother was struggling to hold her own.

"Jenny," said the mother, "you are just going to have to do what I tell you to do. I am your boss. The Lord has given me the responsibility for leading you, and that's what I intend to do!"

Jenny thought that over for a minute and then asked, "How long does it have to be that way?"

Doesn't that illustrate the point beautifully? Already at four years of age, this child was anticipating a day of freedom when no one could tell her what to do. There was something deep within her spirit that longed for control. Watch for the same phenomenon in your child. If he's a toughie, it will show up soon.

Q: Isn't a mother manipulating the child by using rewards and punishment to get him to do what she wants?
A: No more than a factory supervisor manipulates his employees by docking their pay if they arrive late. No more than a police officer manipulates a speeding driver by giving him a traffic ticket. No more than an insurance company manipulates that same driver by increasing his premium. No more than the IRS manipulates a taxpayer who files his return one day late by charging a penalty for his tardiness. The word *manipulation* implies a sinister or selfish motive of the one in charge. I don't agree.

Q: You have described the nature of willfully defiant behavior and how parents should handle it. But does all unpleasant behavior result from rebellion and disobedience?
A: No. Defiance can be very different in origin from the "challenge" response I've been describing. A child's negativism may be caused by frustration, disappointment, fatigue, illness, or rejection and therefore must be interpreted as a warning signal to be heeded. Perhaps the toughest task in parenthood is to recognize the difference between these behavioral messages. A child's resistant behavior always contains a message to his parents, which they must decode before responding.

For example, a disobedient youngster may be saying, *I feel unloved now that I'm stuck with that screaming baby brother. Mom used to care for me; now nobody wants me. I hate everybody.* When this kind of message underlies the defiance, the parents should move quickly to pacify its cause. The art of good parenthood, then, revolves around the interpretation of behavior.

Q: I'm never completely certain how to react to the behavior of my children. Can you give some specific examples of misbehaviors that should be punished, as well as others that can be ignored or handled differently?
A: Let me list a few examples at various age levels, asking that you decide how you would handle each matter before reading my suggestions. (Most of these items represent actual situations posed to me by parents.)

Example: I get very upset because my two-year-old boy will not sit still and be quiet in church. He knows he's not supposed to be noisy, but he hits his toys on the pew and sometimes talks out loud. Should I spank him for being disruptive?

My reply: The mother who wrote this question revealed a rather poor understanding of toddlers. Most two-year-olds can no more fold their hands and sit quietly in church than they can swim the Atlantic Ocean. They squirm and churn and burn every second of their waking hours. No, this child should not be punished. He should be left in the nursery where he can shake the foundations without disturbing the worshippers.

Example: My four-year-old son came into the house and told me he had seen a lion in the backyard. He was not trying to be funny. He really tried to convince me that this lie was true and became quite upset when I didn't believe him. I want him to be an honest and truthful person. Should I have spanked him?

My reply: Definitely not. There is a very thin line between fantasy and reality in the mind of preschool children, and they often confuse the two. I remember, for example, the time I took my son to Disneyland when he was three years of age. He was absolutely terrified by the wolf who stalked around with the three pigs. Ryan took one look at those sharp, jagged teeth and screamed in terror. I have a priceless video of him scrambling for the safety of his mother's arms. After we returned home, I told Ryan there was a "very nice man" inside the wolf suit who wouldn't hurt anyone. My son was so relieved by that news that he needed to hear it repeatedly.

He would say, "Dad?"

"What, Ryan?"

"Tell me 'bout that nice man!"

You see, Ryan was not able to distinguish between the fantasy character and a genuine threat to his health and safety. I would guess that the lion story related in the question above was a product of the same kind of confusion. The child may well have believed that a lion was in the backyard. This mother would have been wise to play along with the game while making it perfectly clear that she didn't believe the story. She could have said, "Oh, my goodness! A lion in the backyard. I sure hope he is a friendly old cat. Now, Jonathan, please wash your hands and come eat lunch."

Example: John is in the second grade and is playing around in school. Last month his teacher sent home a note telling us of his misbehavior, and he threw it away. We discovered at open house the following week that he had lied to us and destroyed the note. What would you have done?

My reply: That was a deliberate act of disobedience. After investigating the facts, I probably would have given John a spanking for his misbehavior in school and for being untruthful to his parents. I would then talk to his teacher about why he was cavorting in school and consider why he was afraid to bring home the note.

FIVE

PROTECTING THE SPIRIT

I MUST OFFER a very important clarification and precaution at this point related to the task of shaping the will of strong-willed children. The reader might conclude from what I have written that I think of "little people" as the villains and their parents as the inevitable good guys. Of course that is not true. Children, including those who regularly challenge authority, are delightful little creatures who need buckets of love and understanding every day of their life. Furthermore, it is vitally important to establish a *balanced* environment for them, wherein discipline and occasional punishment are matched by patience and respect and affection. The "slap 'em across the mouth" approach to child management, even for a kid who is determined to break all the rules, is a disaster. It wounds not only the body but inflicts permanent damage on the spirit as well.

Our objective, then, is not simply to shape the will, but to do so without breaking the spirit. To understand this dual objective of parenting, we need to clarify the distinction between the will and the spirit. The will, as we have seen, represents one's deeply ingrained desire to have his or her way. The intensity of this passion for independence varies from person to person, but it exists to one degree or another in almost all human beings. It may not show up in very compliant individuals until the twenties, thirties, or even beyond, but the telltale signs are there, nonetheless, waiting to be expressed when the circumstances are right. The eating disorder anorexia, for example, is believed to be related to this muted self-will that eventually asserts itself over the issue of food. At least in this arena, the "good little girl," and relatively fewer "nice little boys," can gain a measure of control over his or her circumstances in adolescence or young adulthood, despite agonizing pleas and warnings of parents, doctors, and friends.

The self-will of a very independent child, by contrast, may be fully operational at birth. It is remarkable how early it can make its presence known. Studies of the neonatal period indicate that at two or three days of age, an infant is capable of manipulating parents to get what he wants and needs. In 1999, psychologist Amanda Woodward, a professor at the University of Chicago, released a study concluding that long before the child can talk, he or she is able to size up adults and learn how to interact with them to his or her advantage.[1] This finding would not be surprising to the parents of strong-willed infants who have walked the floor in the wee small hours, listening to their tiny baby making his wishes abundantly clear.

A year or two later, some toddlers can become so angry that they are capable of holding their breath until they lose consciousness. Anyone who has ever witnessed this full measure of rage has been shocked by its power. It can also be quite audacious. The mother of one headstrong three-year-old told me her daughter refused to obey a direct command because, as she put it, "You're just a mommy, you know!" Another toddler screamed every time her mother grabbed her hand to guide her through a parking lot. She would yell at the top of her lungs: "Let go! You're hurting me!" The embarrassed mother, who was just trying to ensure her child's safety, would then have to deal with the hostile looks of other shoppers who thought she was abusing her child.

Truly, willfulness is a fascinating component of the human personality. It is not fragile or wobbly. It can and must be molded, shaped, and brought under the authority of parental leadership. Haven't you read news stories describing suicidal adults who stood on ledges or bridges, threatening to jump? Some of them have defied the combined forces of the Army, the Navy, and the Marine Corps, which sought desperately to save their lives. Even though these people had been emotionally sandbagged by life, their determination to control their own destiny remained intact and functional. My point is that parents will not harm a child by taking steps to gain control of a child's rebellious nature, even though it sometimes involves confrontation, sternness, warnings, and, when appropriate, reasonable punishment. Only by accepting the inevitable challenges to parental authority and then by "winning" at those critical moments can parents teach a headstrong boy or girl civilized behavior. And only then will that child be given the ability to control his or her own impulses in the years to come.

Now that we've discussed the necessity of shaping the will during early childhood, let's consider the other parental obligation that must be given emphasis. Whereas the will is made of titanium and steel, the human spirit is a million times more delicate. It reflects the self-concept or the sense of worthiness that a child feels. It is the most fragile characteristic in human nature and is especially vulnerable to rejection, ridicule, and failure. It must be handled with great care.

How, then, are we to shape the will while preserving the spirit? It is accomplished by establishing reasonable boundaries in advance and then enforcing them with love, while avoiding any implications that a child is unwanted, unnecessary, foolish, ugly, dumb, burdensome, embarrassing, or a terrible mistake. Any accusation or reckless comment that assaults the worth of a child, such as "You are so stupid!" can do lifelong damage. Other damaging remarks include "Why can't you make decent grades in school like your sister?" "You have been a pain in the neck ever since the day you were born!" "I told your mother it was stupid to have another child," "There are times when I would like to put you up for adoption," and "How could anyone love a fat slob like you?" Would parents actually say such hurtful things to a child? Unfortunately, they can, and they do. We are all capable of hurling harsh words at a child or teenager when we are intensely angry or frustrated. Once such mean, cutting words have left our lips, even though we may be repentant a few hours later, they have a way of burning their way into a child's soul where they may remain alive and virulent for the next fifty years.

This topic is so vitally important that I made it a centerpiece of my book *Bringing Up Boys*. Let me quote from a portion of that discussion, which should be especially relevant for parents who are dealing with a sometimes irritating strong-willed child.

> [Words] are so easy to utter, often tumbling out without much reason or forethought. Those who hurl criticism or hostility at others may not even mean or believe what they have said. Their comments may reflect momentary jealousy, resentment, depression, fatigue, or revenge. Regardless of the intent, harsh words sting like killer bees. Almost all of us, including you and me, have lived through moments when a parent, a teacher, a friend, a colleague, a husband, or a wife said something that cut to the

quick. That hurt is now sealed forever in the memory bank. That is an amazing property of the spoken word. Even though a person forgets most of his or her day-by-day experiences, a particularly painful comment may be remembered for decades. By contrast, the individual who did the damage may have no memory of the encounter a few days later.

[Senator] Hillary Rodham Clinton told a story about her father, who never affirmed her as a child. When she was in high school, she brought home a straight-A report card. She showed it to her dad, hoping for a word of commendation. Instead, he said, "Well, you must be attending an easy school." Thirty-five years later the remark still burns in Mrs. Clinton's mind. His thoughtless response may have represented nothing more than a casual quip, but it created a point of pain that has endured to this day.[2]

If you doubt the power of words, remember what John the disciple wrote under divine inspiration. He said, "In the beginning was the Word, and the Word was with God, and the Word was God" (John 1:1). John was describing Jesus, the Son of God, who was identified personally with words. That makes the case about words as well as it will ever be demonstrated. Matthew, Mark, and Luke each record a related prophetic statement made by Jesus that confirms the eternal nature of His teachings. He said, "Heaven and earth will pass away, but my words will never pass away" (Matthew 24:35). We remember what He said to this hour, more than two thousand years later. Clearly, words matter.

There is additional wisdom about the impact of words written in the book of James. The passage reads:

When we put bits into the mouths of horses to make them obey us, we can turn the whole animal. Or take ships as an example. Although they are so large and are driven by strong winds, they are steered by a very small rudder wherever the pilot wants to go. Likewise the tongue is a small part of the body, but it makes great boasts. Consider what a great forest is set on fire by a small spark. The tongue also is a fire, a world of evil among the parts of the body. It corrupts the

*whole person, sets the whole course of his life on fire, and is itself set
on fire by hell.* (James 3:3-6)

Have you ever set yourself on fire with sparks spraying from
your tongue? More important, have you ever set a child's spirit
on fire with anger? All of us have made that costly mistake. We
knew we had blundered the moment the comment flew out of
our mouth, but it was too late. If we tried for a hundred years,
we couldn't take back a single remark. The first year Shirley and
I were married, she became very angry with me about something
that neither of us can recall. In the frustration of the moment she
said, "If this is marriage, I don't want any part of it." She didn't
mean it and regretted her words almost immediately. An hour later
we had reconciled and forgiven each other, but Shirley's statement
could not be taken back. We've laughed about it through the years
and the issue is inconsequential today. Still, there is nothing either
of us can do to erase the utterance of the moment.

Words are not only remembered for a lifetime, but if not
forgiven, they endure beyond the chilly waters of death. We read
in Matthew 12:36: "I tell you that men will have to give account
on the day of judgment for every careless word they have spoken."
Thank God, those of us who have a personal relationship with
Jesus Christ are promised that our sins—and our harsh words—
will be remembered against us no more and will be removed "as
far as the east is from the west" (Psalm 103:12). Apart from that
atonement, however, our words will follow us forever.

I didn't intend to preach a sermon here, because I am
not a minister or a theologian. But I find great inspiration for all
family relationships within the great wisdom of the Scriptures.
And so it is with the impact of what we say. The scary thing for
us parents is that we never know when the mental videotape
is running during our interactions with children and teens. A
comment that means little to us at the time may stick and be
repeated long after we are dead and gone. By contrast, the warm
and affirming things we say about our sons and daughters may
be a source of satisfaction for decades. Again, it is all in the
power of words.

Here's something else to remember. The circumstances that precipitate a hurtful comment for a child or teen are irrelevant to their impact. Let me explain. Even though a child pushes you to the limit, frustrating and angering you to the point of exasperation, you will nevertheless pay a price for overreacting. Let's suppose you lose your poise and shout, "I can't stand you! I wish you belonged to someone else." Or "I can't believe you failed another test. How could a son of mine be so stupid!" Even if every normal parent would also have been agitated in the same situation, your child will not focus on his misbehavior or failure in the future. He is likely to forget what he did to cause your outburst. But he will recall the day you said you didn't want him or that he was stupid. It isn't fair, but neither is life.

I know I'm stirring a measure of guilt into the mix with these comments. (My words are powerful too, aren't they?) My purpose, however, is not to hurt you but to make you mindful that everything you say has lasting meaning for a child. He may forgive you later for "setting the fire," but how much better it would have been to have stayed cool. You can learn to do that with prayer and practice.

It will also help to understand that we are most likely to say something hurtful when we are viscerally angry—when we are so perturbed that we aren't thinking rationally. The reason is because of the powerful biochemical reaction going on inside. The human body is equipped with an automatic defense system called the fight-or-flight mechanism, which prepares the entire organism for action. When we're upset or frightened, adrenaline is pumped into the bloodstream, setting off a series of physiological responses within the body. In a matter of seconds, the individual is transformed from a quiet condition to an "alarm reaction" state. The result is a red-faced father or mother who shouts things he or she had no intention of saying.

These biochemical changes are involuntary, operating quite apart from conscious choice. What is voluntary, however, is our reaction to them. We can learn to take a step back in a moment of excitation. We can choose to hold our tongue and remove ourselves from a provoking situation. As you have heard, it is wise to count to ten (or five hundred) before responding. It is extremely important to do this when we're dealing with children who anger us. We can control the impulse to lash out verbally or physically and avoid doing what we will certainly regret when the passion has cooled.

What should we do when we have lost control and said something that has deeply wounded a child? We should begin to repair the damage as quickly as possible. I have many fanatic golfing friends who have tried in vain to teach me their crazy game. They never give up even though it is a lost cause. One of them told me that I should immediately replace the divot after digging yet another hole with my club. He said that the quicker I could get that tuft of grass back in place, the faster its roots would reconnect. My friend was talking about golf, but I was thinking about people. When you have hurt someone, whether a child, a spouse, or a colleague, you must dress the wound before infection sets in. Apologize, if appropriate. Talk it out. Seek to reconcile. The longer the "divot" bakes in the sun, the smaller its chances for recovery will be. Isn't that a wonderful thought? Of course, the apostle Paul beat us to it. He wrote almost two thousand years ago, "Do not let the sun go down while you are still angry" (Ephesians 4:26). That Scripture has often been applied to husbands and wives, but I think it is just as valid with children.[3]

One more time: The goal in dealing with a difficult child is to shape the will without breaking the spirit. Hitting both targets is sometimes easier said than done. Perhaps it will help to share a letter from a mother who was having a terrible time with her son Jake. Her description of this child and her responses to him illustrate precisely how not to deal with a difficult boy or girl. (Note: The details of this letter have been changed slightly to conceal the identity of the writer.)

Dear Dr. Dobson:
More than anything else in this world, I want to have a happy fam-
ily. We have two girls, ages three and five, and a boy who is ten. They

don't get along at all. The boy and his father don't get along either. And I find myself screaming at the kids and sitting on my son to keep him from hitting and kicking his sisters.

His teacher of the past year thought he needed to learn better ways of getting along with his classmates. He had some problems on the playground and had a horrible time on the school bus. And he didn't seem to be able to walk from the bus stop to our house without getting in a fight or throwing rocks at somebody. So I usually pick him up and bring him home myself.

He is very bright but writes poorly and hates to do it. He is impulsive and quick-tempered (we all are now). He is tall and strong. Our pediatrician says he has "everything going for him." But Jake seldom finds anything constructive to do. He likes to watch television, play in the water, and dig in the dirt.

We are very upset about his diet but haven't been able to do anything about it. He drinks milk and eats Jell-O and crackers and toast. In the past he ate lots of hot dogs and bologna, but not much lately. He also craves chocolate and bubble gum. We have a grandma nearby who sees that he gets lots of it. She also feeds him baby food. We haven't been able to do anything about that, either.

Jake's teachers, the neighbor children, and his sisters complain about his swearing and name-calling. This is really an unfortunate situation because we're always thinking of him in a bad light. But hardly a day goes by when something isn't upset or broken. He's been breaking windows since he was a toddler. One day in June he came home early from school and found the house locked, so he threw a rock through his bedroom window, broke it, and crawled in. Another day recently he tried the glass cutter on our bedroom mirror. He spends a great deal of time at the grandma's who caters to him. We feel she is a bad influence, but so are we when we're constantly upset and screaming.

Anyhow, we have what seems to be a hopeless situation. He is growing bigger and stronger but not any wiser. So what do we do or where do we go?

My husband says he refuses to take Jake anywhere ever again until he matures and "acts like a civilized human being." He has threatened to put him in a foster home. I couldn't send him to a foster home. He needs people who know what to do with him. Please help us if you can.

Mrs. T.

P.S. Our children are adopted and there isn't much of anything left in our marriage.

This was a very sad plea for help, because the writer was undoubtedly sincere when she wrote, "more than anything else in this world, I want to have a happy family." From the tone of her letter, however, it was unlikely that she *ever* realized that greatest longing. In fact, that specific need for peaceful coexistence and harmony apparently led to many of her problems with Jake. She lacked the courage to do battle with him. It's possible that he suffered from ADHD (attention deficit/hyperactivity disorder), which I will discuss in an upcoming chapter. However, for the sake of our discussion here, let's look at the two very serious mistakes this mom made with her son.

First, Mr. and Mrs. T. failed to shape Jake's will, although he was begging for their intervention. It is an unsettling thing to be your own boss at ten years of age—unable to find even one adult who is strong enough to earn your respect. Why else would Jake have broken every rule and attacked every symbol of authority? He waged war on his teacher at school, but she was also baffled by his challenge. All she knew to do was call his trembling mother and report, "Jake needs to learn better ways of getting along with his classmates." (That was a kind way of putting it. I'm sure there were more caustic things the teacher could have said about this boy's classroom behavior!)

Jake was a brat on the school bus, he fought with his classmates on the way home, he broke windows and cut mirrors, he used the foulest language, and he tormented his sisters. He ate junk food and refused to complete his academic assignments or accept any form of responsibility. Can there be any doubt that Jake was screaming, "Look! I'm doing it all wrong! Doesn't anyone love me enough to care? Can't anyone help me? I hate the world and the world hates me!"

Mrs. T. and her husband were totally perplexed and frustrated. She responded by "screaming at the kids" and "sitting on [her] son" when he misbehaved. No one knew what to do with him. Even Grandma was a bad influence. Mom resorted to anger and high-pitched weeping and wailing.

There is *no* more ineffective approach to child management than volcanic displays of anger, as we will see in the following chapter.

In short, Mrs. T. and her husband had totally abdicated their responsibility to provide leadership for their family. Note how many times she said, in essence, *we are powerless to act*. These parents were distressed over Jake's poor diet but wrote that they "haven't been able to do anything about it." Jake's grandmother fed him junk food and bubble gum, but they weren't able to do anything about that either. Likewise, they couldn't stop him from swearing or tormenting his sisters or breaking windows or throwing rocks at his peers. One has to ask "Why not?" Why was the family ship so difficult to steer? Why did it end up dashed to pieces on the rocks? The problem was that the ship and the crew had no captain! They drifted aimlessly in the absence of a leader—a decision maker who could guide them to safe waters.

The T. family not only failed to shape Jake's rampaging will, they also assaulted his wounded spirit with every conflict. Not only did they scream and cry and wring their hands in despair, but they demeaned his sense of personal worth and dignity. Can't you hear his angry father shouting, "Why don't you grow up and act like a civilized human being? Well, I'll tell you something! I'm through with you, boy! I'll never take you anywhere again or even let anyone know that you are my son. As a matter of fact, I'm not sure you are going to *be* my son for very long. If you keep acting like a lawless thug we're going to throw you out of the family—we're going to put you into a foster home. Then we'll see how you like it!" And with each accusation, Jake's self-esteem moved down another notch. But did these personal assaults make him sweeter and more cooperative? Of course not! He just became meaner and more bitter and more convinced of his own worthlessness. You see, Jake's spirit had been crushed, but his will still raged at hurricane velocity. And sadly, he then turned his self-hatred on his peers and family.

If circumstances had permitted (in other words, if I had been married to someone else), it would have been my pleasure to have had Jake in our home for a period of time. I don't believe it was too late to save him, and I would have felt challenged by the opportunity to try. How would I have approached this defiant youngster? By giving him the following message as soon as his suitcase was unpacked: "Jake, there are several things I want to talk over with you, now that you're a member of the family. First, you'll soon learn how much we love you in this house. I'm glad you're here, and I hope these will be the happiest days of your life. And you should know that I care about your feelings and problems and concerns. We invited you here because we wanted you to come, and you will receive the same love and respect that is given to our own children. If you have something on your mind, you can come right out and say it. I won't get angry or make you regret expressing yourself. Neither my wife nor I will ever intentionally do anything to hurt you or treat you unkindly. You'll see that these are not just empty promises that you're hearing. This is the way people act when they care about each other, and we already care about you.

"But, Jake, there are some other things you need to understand. There are going to be some definite rules and acceptable ways of behaving in this home, and you are going to have to live within them, just as our other children do. I will have them written for you by tomorrow morning. You will carry your share of responsibilities and jobs, and your schoolwork will be given high priority each evening. And you need to understand, Jake, that my most important job as your guardian is to see that you behave in ways that are healthy to yourself and others. It may take you a week or two to adjust to this new situation, but you're going to make it and I'm going to be here to see that you do. And when you refuse to obey, I will punish you immediately. In fact, I'm going to be right on your neck until you figure out that you can't beat the system. I have many ways to make you miserable, and I'm prepared to use them when necessary. This will help you change some of the destructive ways you've been acting in recent years. But even when I must discipline you, know that I will love you as much as I do right now. Nothing will change that."

The first time Jake disobeyed what he knew to be my definite instructions, I would have reacted decisively. There would have been no screaming or derogatory accusations, although he would quickly discover that I meant what I said. The following morning we would have discussed the issue rationally, reassuring him of our continuing love, and then started over.

Even the most delinquent children typically respond well to this pairing of love and consistent discipline! And it is a prescription for use in your own home too. I strongly suggest that you give it a go.

QUESTIONS & ANSWERS

Q: My husband and I are divorced, so I have to handle all the discipline of the children myself. How does this change the recommendations you've made about discipline in the home?

A: Not at all. The principles of good discipline remain the same, regardless of the family setting. The procedures do become somewhat harder for one parent to implement since he or she has no additional support when the children become testy. Single mothers and fathers have to play both roles, which is not easily done. Nevertheless, children do not make allowances for difficult circumstances. As in any family, parents must earn their respect or they will not receive it.

Q: What do you think of the phrase "Children should be seen and not heard"?

A: That statement reveals a profound ignorance of children and their needs. I can't imagine how any loving adult could raise a vulnerable little boy or girl by that philosophy.

Q: Would you go so far as to apologize to a child if you felt you had been in the wrong?

A: I certainly would—and indeed, I have. A number of years ago I was burdened with pressing responsibilities that fatigued me and made me irritable. One particular evening I was especially grouchy and short-tempered with my ten-year-old daughter. I knew I was not being fair but was simply too tired to correct my manner. Through the course of the evening, I blamed Danae for things that were not her fault and upset her needlessly several times. After going to bed, I felt bad about the way I had behaved, and I decided to apologize the next morning. After a good night of sleep and a tasty breakfast, I felt much more optimistic about life. I approached my daughter before she left for school and said, "Danae, I'm sure you know that daddies are not perfect human beings. We get tired and irritable just like other people, and there are times when we are not proud of the way we behave. I know I wasn't fair with you last night. I was terribly grouchy, and I want you to forgive me."

Danae put her arms around me and shocked me down to my toes. She said, "I knew you were going to have to apologize, Daddy, and it's okay; I forgive you."

Can there be any doubt that children are often more aware of the struggles between generations than their busy, harassed parents are?

SIX

THE MOST
COMMON MISTAKE

IN OUR DISCUSSION of Jake and his family, I said that trying to control children by displays of anger and verbal outbursts is *the* most ineffective approach to management. It not only doesn't work, but it actually makes things worse. Researchers at the University of Washington, Dr. Susan Spieker and colleagues, found that parents who attempt to control their children by yelling and insulting them are likely to cause even more disruptive and defiant behavior.[1] It makes sense, doesn't it? If you yell at your kids, they will yell back at you—and more! Furthermore, there is an interactive effect. As the child becomes more rebellious, the parent becomes even angrier.

Unfortunately, when frustrated *most* adults fall into precisely that pattern of parenting. Educators often make the same mistake. I once heard a teacher say on national television, "I like being a professional educator, but I hate the daily task of teaching. My children are so unruly that I have to stay mad at them all the time just to control the classroom." How utterly demoralizing to be required to be mean and bad-tempered day in and day out to keep kids from going wild. Yet many teachers (and parents) know of no other way to make them obey. Believe me, it is exhausting and counterproductive! Let's look at why anger doesn't work.

Consider your *own* motivational system. Suppose you are driving home from work one afternoon, exceeding the speed limit by forty miles per hour. A police officer is standing on the corner, but there isn't much he can do in response. He has no car, no motorcycle, no badge, no gun, and no authority to write tickets. All he can do is scream insults at you and shake his fist as you pass. Would that cause you to slow down? Of course not! You might smile and wave as you hurry by. The officer's anger only emphasizes his impotence.

On the other hand, imagine yourself tearing through a school zone one morning on the way to the office. You suddenly look in the rearview mirror and see a black-and-white squad car bearing down on you from behind. Eight red lights are flashing and the siren is screaming. The officer uses his loudspeaker to tell you to pull over to the curb. When you have stopped, he opens his door and approaches your window. He is six foot nine, has a voice like the Lone Ranger's, and wears a big gun on his hip. His badge is gleaming in the light. He is carrying a little leather-bound book of citations that you have seen before—last month. The officer speaks politely but firmly, "Sir, I have you on radar traveling sixty-five miles per hour in a twenty-mile-per-hour zone. May I see your driver's license, please?" The officer doesn't scream, cry, or criticize you. He doesn't have to. You become putty behind the wheel. You fumble nervously to locate the small plastic card in your wallet (the one with the picture you hate). Your hands get sweaty and your mouth is dry as a bone. Your heart pounds like crazy in your throat. Why are you so breathless? It is because the course of *action* that the police officer is about to take is notoriously unpleasant. It will dramatically affect your future driving habits or, if you do not change, even cause you to do a lot of walking in the days ahead.

Six weeks later you go before a judge to learn your fate. He is wearing a black robe and sits high above the courtroom. Again, you are a nervous wreck. Not because the judge yells at you or calls you names—but because he has the power to make your day a little more unpleasant.

Neither the police officer nor the judge need to rely on anger to influence your behavior. They have far more effective methods of getting your attention. Their serenity and confidence are part of the aura of authority that creates respect. But what if they fail to understand that and begin to cry and complain? What if one of them says, "I don't know why you won't drive right. We've told you over and over that you can't break the law like this. You just continue to disobey no matter what we do." Then getting red-faced, he adds, "Well, I'll tell you this, young man, we're not going to take this anymore. Do you hear? Believe me, you're going to regret this . . . "

I'm sure you get the point. Anger does not influence behavior unless it implies that something irritating is about to happen. By contrast, *disciplinary action* does cause behavior to change. Not only does anger not work, I am convinced that it produces a destructive kind of disrespect in the minds of our children. They perceive that our frustration is caused by our inability to control the situation. We represent justice to them, yet we're on the verge of tears as we flail the air with our hands and shout empty threats and warnings.

I am not recommending that parents and teachers conceal their legitimate emotions from their children. I am not suggesting that we be like bland and unresponsive robots that hold everything inside. There are times when our boys and girls become insulting or disobedient to us, and revealing our displeasure is entirely appropriate. In fact, it *should* be expressed at a time like that, or else we will appear phony and wimpy. But it should never become a *tool* to get children to behave when we have run out of options and ideas. It is ineffective and can be damaging to the relationship between generations.

Let me give you another illustration that may be helpful. It will represent any one of 20 million homes on a typical evening. Henry is in the second grade and a constant whirlwind of activity. He has been wiggling and giggling since he got up that morning, but incredibly, he still has excess energy that needs to be burned. His mom is not in the same condition. She has been on her feet since staggering out of bed at 5:30 A.M. She fixed breakfast for the family, cleaned up the mess, got Dad off to work, sent Henry to school, and if she is employed, dropped off the younger kids at a day care center and rushed off to work. Or if she is a stay-at-home mom, she settled into a long day of trying to keep the preschoolers from killing each other. By late afternoon, she has put in nine hours of work without a rest. (Toddlers don't take breaks, unless they are nappers, so why should their mothers?)

Despite Mom's fatigue, she can hardly call it a day. Dad comes home from work and tries to help, but he is tired too. Mom still has at least six hours of work left to do, including grocery shopping, cooking dinner, giving baths to the little ones, changing their diapers, tucking them into bed, and helping Henry with his homework. I get depressed just thinking about such weary moms still working as the day draws to a close.

Henry is not so sympathetic, however, and arrives home from school in a decidedly mischievous mood. He can't find anything interesting to do, so he begins to irritate his uptight mother. He teases his little sister to the point of tears, pulls the cat's tail, and spills the dog's water. Mom is nagging by this time, but Henry acts like he doesn't notice. Then he goes to the toy closet and begins tossing out games and boxes of plastic toys and dumping out enough building blocks to construct a small city. Mom knows that someone is going to have to clean up all that mess, and she has a vague notion about who will get that assignment. The intensity of her voice is rising again. She orders him to the bathroom to wash his hands in preparation for dinner. Henry is gone for fifteen minutes. When he returns, his hands are still dirty. Mom's pulse is pounding through her arteries by this time and there is a definite migraine sensation above her left eye. Does this sound familiar?

Finally, Henry's bedtime arrives. But he does not *want* to go to bed, and he knows it will take his harassed mother at least thirty minutes to get him there. Henry does not do *anything* against his wishes unless his mother becomes very angry and blows up at him. Henry is sitting on the floor, playing with his games. Mom looks at her watch and says, "Henry, it's nearly eight o'clock [a thirty-minute exaggeration], so gather up your toys and go take your bath." Now Henry and Mom both know that she didn't mean for him to immediately take a bath. She merely wanted him to start thinking about taking his bath. She would have fainted dead away if he had responded to her empty command.

Approximately ten minutes later, Mom speaks again. "Now, Henry, it's getting later and you have school tomorrow; I want those toys picked up and then I want you in that tub!" She still does not expect Henry to obey, and he knows it. Her real message is, "We're getting closer, Hank." Henry shuffles around and stacks a box or two to demonstrate that he heard her. Then he settles down for a few more minutes of play. Six minutes pass and Mom issues another command, this time with more passion and threat in her voice, "Now listen, young man, I told you to get a move on, and I meant it!" To Henry, this means he must get his toys picked up and m-e-a-n-d-e-r toward the bathroom door. If his mother rapidly pursues him, then he must carry out the assignment posthaste. However, if Mom's mind wanders before she performs the last step of this ritual, or if the phone miraculously rings, Henry is free to enjoy a few minutes' reprieve.

You see, Henry and his mother are involved in a familiar one-act play. They both know the rules and the role being enacted by the opposite actor. The entire scene is preprogrammed, scripted, and computerized. It's a virtual replay of a scenario that occurs night after night. Whenever

Mom wants Henry to do something he dislikes, she progresses through graduated steps of phony anger, beginning with calmness and ending with a red flush and threats. Henry does not have to move until she reaches her flash point, which signals that she is ready to do something about it. How foolish this game is. Since Mom controls Henry with empty threats, she must stay half-irritated all the time. Her relationship with her children is contaminated, and she ends each day with a pulsing headache. She can never count on instant obedience, because it takes her at least twenty or thirty minutes to work up a believable degree of anger.

How much better it is to use action to achieve the desired behavior and avoid the emotional outburst. Hundreds of approaches will bring a desired response: some involve minor pain; others offer a reward to a less naughty child.

When a parent's calm request for obedience is ignored by a child, Mom or Dad should have some means of making their youngster want to cooperate. For those who can think of no such device, I will suggest one: There is a muscle lying snugly against the base of the neck. Anatomy books list it as the trapezius muscle, and when firmly squeezed, it sends little messengers to the brain saying, "This hurts: Avoid recurrence at all costs." The pain is only temporary; it can cause no damage the way I am suggesting its use. But it is an amazingly effective and practical recourse for parents when their youngster ignores a direct command to move.

Let's return to the bedtime scene with Henry and suggest how it could have been replayed more effectively. To begin, his mother should have forewarned him that he had fifteen more minutes to play. No one, child or adult, likes a sudden interruption of his activity. It then would have been wise to set the alarm clock or the stove buzzer. When the fifteen minutes passed and the buzzer sounded, Mom should have quietly told Henry to go take his bath. If he didn't move immediately, she could have taken Henry's face in her hands, looked him straight in the eye and said with conviction but not with frustration, "Do it NOW. Do you understand?" If the lad believes in his heart of hearts that she is prepared to punish him for delaying, no punishment will be necessary. If Henry learns that this procedure or some other unpleasantness is invariably visited upon him in such a moment, he will move before the consequences ensue. Authority, you see, is a subtle thing. It is conveyed mostly by confidence and determination, and sometimes a little bluster.

As for the use of punishment, I know that some readers could argue that the deliberate, premeditated application of minor pain to a small child is a harsh and unloving thing to do. To others, it will seem like pure barbarism. I obviously disagree. Given a choice between a harassed, screaming, threatening mother who blows up several times a day and a mom who has a reasonable, controlled response to disobedience, I would certainly recommend the latter. In the long run, the quieter home is better for Henry, too, because of the avoidance of strife between generations.

On the other hand, when a youngster discovers there is no threat behind the millions of words he hears, he stops listening to them. The only messages he responds to are those reaching a peak of emotion, which means much screaming and yelling. The child is pulling in the opposite direction, fraying Mom's nerves and straining the parent-child relationship. In the absence of action early in the conflict, the parent usually ends up punishing anyway. The consequences are also more likely to be severe, because by then the adult is irritated and out of control. And instead of the discipline being administered in a calm and judicious manner, the parent has become unnerved and frustrated, swinging wildly at the belligerent child. There is no reason for a fight to have occurred. The situation could have ended very differently if Mom had exhibited an attitude of confident authority.

Let's go back to Henry and his mother. Speaking softly, almost pleasantly, Mom says, "You know what happens when you don't mind me; now I don't see any reason why I should have to make you uncomfortable just to get your cooperation tonight, but if you insist, I'll play the game with you. When the buzzer sounds you let me know what the decision is."

The child then has the choice to make, and the advantages to him of obeying his mother's wishes are clear. She need not scream. She need not threaten to shorten his life. She need not become upset. She is in command. Of course, Mother will have to prove two or three times that she will apply the pain or other punishment if necessary. Occasionally throughout the coming months, Henry will check to see if she is still at the helm. That question is easily answered.

Understanding the interaction between Henry and his mother can be very helpful to parents who have become screamers and don't know why. Let's look at their relationship during that difficult evening as diagrammed in figure 3. Note that Henry's mother greets him at the front door after school, which represents a low point of irritation. From that time forward, however, her emotion builds and intensifies until it reaches a moment of explosion at the end of the day.

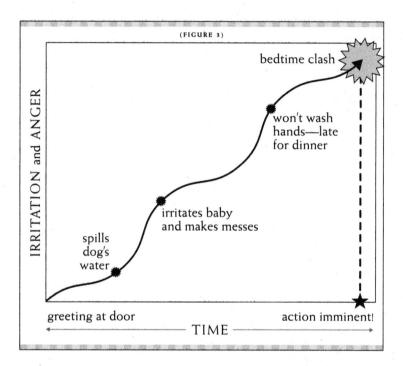

(FIGURE 3)

By her ultimate display of anger at bedtime, Mom makes it clear to Henry that she is through warning and is now ready to take definite action. You see, most parents (even those who are very permissive) have a point on the scale beyond which they will not be pushed; inevitable punishment looms immediately across that line. The amazing thing about children is that they know *precisely* where their parents typically draw the line. We adults reveal our particular points of action to them in at least six or eight subtle ways: Only at those moments do we use their middle names ("Jessica Emily Smith, get in that tub!"). Our speech becomes more staccato and abrupt ("Young! Lady! I! Told! You! . . . "). Our faces turn red (an important clue), we jump from our chair, and the child knows it is time to cooperate. It's all a game.

The other interesting thing about children is that, having identi- fied the circumstances that immediately precede disciplinary action, they will take their parents directly to that barrier and bump it repeatedly but will *seldom* go beyond it deliberately. Once or twice Henry will ignore his mother's emotional fireworks, just to see if she has the courage to deliver on her promise. When that question has been answered, he will do what she demands in the nick of time to avoid punishment.

Now this brings us to the punch line of this important discussion. I must admit that what I am about to write is difficult to express and may not be fully understood by my readers. It may, however, be of value to parents who want to stop fighting with their children.

I have said that parental anger often signals to a child that the parents have reached their action line. Therefore, children obey, albeit reluctantly, only when Mom and Dad get mad, indicating that they will now resort to punishment. On the other hand, the parents observe that the child's sur- render occurs simultaneously with their anger and inaccurately conclude that their emotional explosion is what forced the youngster to yield. Thus, their anger seems necessary for control in the future. They have grossly misunderstood the situation.

Returning one more time to the story of Henry, remember that his mother tells him repeatedly to take his bath. Only when she blows up does he get in the tub, leading her to believe that her anger produced his obedience. She is wrong! It was not her anger that sent Henry to the tub—it was the *action* he believed to be imminent. Her anger was nothing more than a tip-off that Mom was frustrated enough to spank his bottom. Henry *cares* about that!

I have written this entire chapter in order to convey this one message: You don't need *anger* to control children. You *do* need strategic action. Furthermore, you can apply the action anywhere on the time line that is convenient, and children will live contentedly within that boundary. In fact, the closer the action moves to the front of the conflict, the less punishment is required and the less often it is necessary. A squeeze of the trapezius muscle is not a sufficient deterrent at the end of a two-hour struggle, whereas it is more than adequate when the conflict is minimal. (Incidentally, I do not recommend that mothers weighing fewer than 120 pounds squeeze the shoulder muscles of their big teenagers. There are definite risks involved in that procedure. The general rule to follow is, if you can't reach it, don't squeeze it.)

The late Dr. Benjamin Spock, who wrote the perennial best seller,

Dr. Spock's Baby and Child Care, was severely criticized for his laissez-faire approach to child rearing.[2] He was blamed for weakening parental authority and producing an entire generation of disrespectful and unruly children. To the man on the street, Dr. Spock became a symbol of permissiveness and overindulgence in parent-child relationships. It was a bum rap. I had lunch with him one day after we had been guests on a national television show and found our views to be surprisingly similar on most things not political.

Perhaps in response to the criticism that he experienced, Dr. Spock published a clarifying article entitled "How Not to Bring Up a Bratty Child." In it he wrote, "Parental submissiveness doesn't avoid unpleasantness; it makes it inevitable." A child's defiance, he said, "makes the parent increasingly more resentful, until it finally explodes in a display of anger."[3] He continued, "The way to get a child to do what must be done, or stop doing what should not be done, is to be clear and definite each time. . . . Parental firmness also makes for a happier child."[4] Finally, right before his death at ninety-three years of age, the old pediatrician was quoted as saying, "It's fine for parents to respect their children, but they often forget to ask for respect back."[5]

Dr. Spock was absolutely right. If you don't take a stand with your child early, she is *compelled* by her nature to push you further. Terrible battles are inevitable, especially during the adolescent years. The hesitant and guilt-ridden parent who is most anxious to avoid confrontation often finds himself or herself screaming and threatening throughout the day, and ultimately thrashing the child. Indeed, physical abuse may be the end result. However, if Mom and Dad have the courage and conviction to provide firm leadership from the earliest days of childhood, administering it in a context of genuine love, both generations will enjoy an atmosphere of harmony and respect. That is precisely what I have been trying to teach for over thirty years!

Contained in this simple explanation is an understanding of children that some adults comprehend intuitively, and which others never quite grasp. The concept involves the delicate balance between love and control, recognizing that implementing a reasonable and consistent action line does not assault self-worth; instead, it represents a source of security for an immature child.

I have had many mothers say to me over the years: "I don't understand my kids. They will do exactly what their father demands, but they won't mind me at all." There may be several reasons for this differential. First, fathers can be much more intimidating than mothers just by their "presence." The fact is that dads are often much bigger physically and have a deeper voice that has a way of encouraging a child to respond more quickly to their discipline. Second, children often look to their father for approval, and when he expresses his disappointment to them, they take it more to heart. Finally, and most pertinent here, because mothers usually spend more time with their children, they often get worn down and stop following through with discipline. When that's the case, children are bright enough to notice that Dad draws his action line earlier than Mom—and they'll behave accordingly.

There's another factor: Children often understand these forces better than their parents, who are bogged down with adult responsibilities and worries. That is why so many kids are able to win the contest of wills; they devote their *primary* effort to the game, while we grown-ups play only when we must. One father overheard his five-year-old daughter, Laura, say to her little sister, who was doing something wrong, "Mmmmm, I'm going to tell Mommy on you. No! I'll tell Daddy. He's worse!" Laura had evaluated the disciplinary measures of her two parents and concluded that one was more effective than the other.

This same child was observed by her father to have become especially disobedient and defiant. She was irritating other family members and looking for ways to avoid minding her parents. Her dad decided not to confront her directly about this change in behavior, but to punish her consistently for every offense until she settled down. For three or four days, he let Laura get away with nothing. She was spanked, stood in the corner, and sent to her bedroom. At the conclusion of the fourth day, she was sitting on the bed with her father and younger sister. Without provocation, Laura pulled the hair of the toddler, who was looking at a book. Her dad promptly took action and disciplined her. Laura did not cry, but sat in silence for a moment or two, and then said, "Hurrummph! All of my tricks are not working!"

If you think back to your own childhood years, you may remember similar events in which the disciplinary techniques of adults were consciously analyzed and their weaknesses probed. When I was a child, I once spent the night with a rambunctious friend who seemed to know every move his parents were going to make. Earl was like a military general who had deciphered the enemy code, permitting him to outmaneuver his opponents at every turn. After we were tucked into our own twin beds that night, he gave me an astounding description of his father's temper.

Earl said, "When my dad gets angry, he uses some really bad words that will amaze you." (He listed three or four startling examples.) I replied, "I don't believe it!" Mr. Walker was a very tall, reserved, Christian man who seemed to have it all together. I just couldn't conceive of him saying the words Earl had quoted.

"Want me to prove it to you?" said Earl mischievously. "All we have to do is keep on laughing and talking instead of going to sleep. My dad will come and tell us to be quiet over and over, and he'll get madder and madder every time he has to settle us down. Then you'll hear the cuss words. Just wait and see."

I was a bit dubious about the plan, but I did want to see the dignified Mr. Walker at his profane best. So Earl and I kept his poor father running back and forth like a yo-yo for over an hour. And as predicted, he became more intense and hostile each time he returned to our bedroom. I was getting very nervous and would have called off the demonstration, but Earl had been through it all before. He kept telling me, "It won't be long now."

Finally, about midnight, it happened. Mr. Walker's patience expired. He came thundering down the hall toward our room, shaking the entire house as his feet pounded the floor. He burst through the bedroom door and leaped on Earl's bed, flailing away at the boy, who was safely buried beneath three or four layers of blankets. Then from his lips came a stream of words that had seldom reached my tender ears. I was shocked, but Earl was delighted.

Even when his father was whacking the covers with his hand and screaming profanities, Earl raised up and shouted to me, "Did ya hear 'im? Huh? Didn't I tell ya? I told ya he would say it!" It's a wonder that Mr. Walker didn't kill his son at that moment!

I lay awake that night thinking about the episode and made up my mind *never* to let a child manipulate me like that when I grew up. Don't you see how important disciplinary techniques are to a child's respect for his parents? When a forty-five–pound bundle of trouble can deliberately reduce his powerful mother and father to a trembling, snarling mass of frustration, then something changes in the relationship. Something precious is lost. The child develops an attitude of contempt that is certain to erupt during the stormy adolescent years to come. I sincerely wish every adult understood that simple characteristic of human nature.

I've met a few wily grown-ups who had a great ability to lead kids. One of them lived near us in Arcadia, California. He owned and operated Bud Lyndon's Swim School and had a remarkable comprehension of the principles of discipline. I enjoyed sitting poolside just to watch the man work. However, there are few child developmentalists who could explain why he was so successful with the little swimmers in his pool. He was not soft and delicate in his manner; in fact, he tended to be somewhat gruff. When the kids got out of line, he splashed water in their faces and said sternly, "Who told you to move? Stay where I put you until I ask you to swim!" He called the boys "men of tomorrow" and other pet names. His class was regimented, and every minute was utilized purposefully. But would you believe it, the children loved Bud Lyndon. Why? Because they knew he loved them. Within his gruff manner was a message of affection that might escape the adult observer. Mr. Lyndon never embarrassed a child intentionally, and he covered for the youngster who swam poorly. He delicately balanced his authority with a subtle affection that attracted children like the pied piper. Mr. Bud Lyndon understood the meaning of discipline with love.

When I was in ninth grade I had an athletic coach who affected me in the same way. He was the master of the moment, and no one *dared* challenge his authority. I would have fought wild lions before tackling Mr. Ayers. Yes, I feared him. We all did. But he never abused his power. He treated me courteously and respectfully at a time when I needed all the dignity I could get. Combined with his acceptance of the individual was an obvious self-confidence and ability to lead a pack of adolescent wolves who had devoured less capable teachers. And that's why my ninth-grade gym coach had a greater influence on me than any other person during my fifteenth year. Mr. Craig Ayers understood discipline with love.

Not all parents can be like Mr. Lyndon or Mr. Ayers, and I would not suggest that they try. Nor would it be wise for a parent at home to display the same gruffness that is appropriate on the athletic field or at the pool. Parents must fit their disciplinary approach to their own personality patterns and the responses that feel natural. However, the overriding principle remains the same for men and women, mothers and fathers, coaches and teachers, pediatricians and psychologists: It involves discipline with love, a reasonable introduction to responsibility and self-control, parental leadership with a minimum of anger, respect for the dignity and worth of the child, realistic boundaries that are enforced with confident firmness, and a judicious use of rewards and punishments to those who challenge and resist. It is a system that bears the approval of the Creator Himself.

QUESTIONS & ANSWERS

Q: It's easy for you to tell me not to get angry at my children, but there are times when they just make me furious. For example, I have a horrible time getting my ten-year-old daughter ready for school in the morning. She will get up when I insist, but she dawdles and plays as soon as I leave the room. I have to goad and push and warn her every few minutes or she will be late. So I get more and more angry and usually end up screaming insults at her. I know this is not the best way to handle her, but she makes me so mad! Tell me how I can get her moving without this emotion every day.

A: You are playing right into your daughter's hands by assuming the responsibility for getting her ready every morning. A ten-year-old should definitely be able to handle that task on her own, but your anger is not likely to bring about her independence. Let me offer a possible solution that has been helpful to others. It will focus on a child named Debbie.

Debbie's morning time problem related primarily to her compulsivity about her room. She would not leave for school unless her bed was made perfectly and every trinket was in its proper place. This was not something her mother taught her; Debbie was always very meticulous about her possessions. (I should add that her brother never had this problem.) Debbie could have easily finished those tasks on time if she was motivated to do so, but she was never in a particular hurry. So Mom began to fall into the same habit you described—warning, threatening, pushing, shoving, and ultimately becoming angry as the clock moved toward the deadline.

Debbie's mother and I discussed the problem and agreed that there had to be a better method of getting through the morning. I subsequently created a system that we called "checkpoints." It worked like this: Debbie was instructed to get out of bed before 6:30 each morning. It was her responsibility to set her alarm and get herself up. As soon as she got up, she immediately went to the kitchen, where a chart was taped to the refrigerator door. She then circled "yes" or "no" for the first checkpoint (getting up by 6:30) for that day. Even one minute late was considered a missed item. It couldn't have been more simple. She either did or did not get up by 6:30.

The second checkpoint occurred at 7:10. By that time, Debbie was required to have her room straightened to her own satisfaction, be dressed, have her teeth brushed and hair combed, and so forth, and be ready to practice the piano. Forty minutes was ample time for these tasks, which could actually be done in ten to fifteen minutes if she wanted to hurry. Thus, the only way she could miss the second checkpoint was to ignore it deliberately.

Now, what meaning did the checkpoints have? Did failure to meet them bring anger and wrath and gnashing of teeth? Of course not. The consequences were straightforward and fair. If Debbie missed one checkpoint, she was required to go to bed thirty minutes earlier than usual that evening. If she missed two, she hit her pillow an hour before her assigned hour. She was permitted to read during that time in bed, but she could not watch television or talk on the telephone. This procedure took all the morning pressure off of the mother and placed it on Debbie's shoulders, where it belonged. There were occasions when Mom would get up just in time to fix breakfast, only to find Debbie sitting soberly at the piano, clothed and ready for the day.

This system of discipline can serve as a model for parents whose children have similar behavioral problems. It was not oppressive; in fact, Debbie seemed to enjoy having a target to shoot for. The limits of acceptable performance were defined beyond question. The responsibility was clearly placed on the child. Consequences of noncompliance were fair and easily administered. And this system required no adult anger or foot stomping.

You can adapt this concept in order to resolve the thorny conflicts in *your* home too. The only limit lies in the creativity and imagination of the parent.

Q: Sometimes my husband and I disagree on our discipline and argue in front of our children about what is best. Do you think this is damaging?

A: Yes, I do. You and your husband should present a united front, especially when children are watching. If you disagree on an issue, it can be discussed later in private. Unless the two of you can come to a consensus, your children will begin to perceive that standards of right and wrong are arbitrary. They will also make end runs around the tougher parent to get the answer they want. There are even more serious consequences for boys and girls when parents are radically different in their approach.

Here's the point of danger: Some of the most hostile, aggressive teenagers I've seen come from family constellations where the parents have leaned in opposite directions in their discipline. Suppose the father is unloving and disinterested in the welfare of his kids. His approach is harsh and physical. He comes home tired and may knock them around if they get in his way. The mother is permissive by nature. She worries every day about the lack of love in the father-child relationships. Eventually she sets out to compensate for it. When Dad sends their son to bed without his dinner, Mom slips him milk and cookies. When he says no to a particular request, she finds a way to say yes. She lets the kids get away with murder because it is not in her spirit to confront them.

What happens under these circumstances is that the authority figures in the family contradict each other and cancel each other out. Consequently, the child is caught in the middle and often grows up hating both. It doesn't always work that way, but the probability for trouble is high. The middle ground between extremes of love and control must be sought if we are to produce healthy, responsible children.

Q: I see now that I've been doing many things wrong with my children. Can I undo the harm?

A: I doubt it is too late to do things right, although your ability to influence your children lessens with the passage of time. Fortunately we are permitted to make many mistakes with our kids. They are resilient, and they usually survive our errors in judgment. It's a good thing they do, because none of us can be a perfect parent. Besides, it's not the occasional mistakes that hurt a child—it is the consistent influence of destructive conditions throughout childhood that does the damage.

Q: My six-year-old has suddenly become mouthy and disrespectful at home. She told me to "buzz off" when I asked her to take out the trash, and she calls me names when she gets angry. I feel it is important to permit this emotional outlet, so I haven't tried to suppress it. Do you agree?

A: I'm afraid I don't. Your daughter is aware of her sudden defiance, and she's waiting to see how far you will let her go. If you don't discourage disrespectful behavior now, you can expect some wild experiences during the adolescent years to come.

With regard to your concern about emotional ventilation, you are right that your daughter needs to express her anger. She should be free to say almost anything to you provided it is said in a respectful manner. It is acceptable to say, "I think you love my brother more than me" or "You weren't fair with me, Mommy." There is a thin line between what is acceptable and unacceptable behavior at this point. The child's expression of strong frustration, even resentment and anger, should be encouraged if it exists. You certainly don't want her to bottle it inside. On the other hand, you should not permit your daughter to resort to name-calling and open rebellion. "Mom, you hurt my feelings in front of my friends" is an acceptable statement. "You stupid idiot, why didn't you shut up when my friends were here?!" is absolutely unacceptable.

If your daughter approaches you respectfully, as described in the first statement, it would be wise for you to sit down and try to understand the child's viewpoint. Be big enough to apologize if you have wronged her in some way. If you feel you are in the right, however, calmly explain why you acted as you did and tell your daughter how she can avoid a collision next time. It is possible to ventilate feelings without sacrificing parental respect, and the child should be taught how to do it. This communication tool will be very useful later in life, especially in marriage.

SEVEN

GEARING DISCIPLINE TO THE NEEDS OF CHILDREN

YVONNE, A MOTHER from San Antonio, wrote, "I was at the library with my twenty-month-old, Christy. I asked the librarian to help me locate *The Strong-Willed Child,* which was new at the time. As the librarian was filling out a form to request the book from a neighboring library, Christy threw herself on the floor in a tantrum because I wouldn't let her run between the shelves. The lady looked at me and asked, 'Shall we put *RUSH* on it?' "

While the broad principles I have provided to this point are widely applicable to children, each boy and girl is different, requiring his or her parents to interpret and apply them individually to the complex personality patterns evident in that particular youngster. Added to that challenge is the fact that the target is always moving. Developmental stages are in constant flux, so that Mom and Dad must be prepared to zig and zag year by year. An approach that is entirely appropriate and effective at age five may be obsolete by six or seven, creating a need for something entirely different. Then adolescence comes crashing onto the scene, and everything is thrown up for grabs. The best I can do to assist you in responding to this ever-changing pattern is to offer some guidelines for each age category and suggest that you use them to formulate your own techniques and understanding.

Let's begin at birth and weave our way through the childhood years. Please understand that this discussion is by no means exhaustive and merely suggests the general nature of disciplinary methods at specific periods.

BIRTH TO SEVEN MONTHS

No *direct* discipline is necessary for a child under seven months of age, regardless of the behavior or circumstance. Many parents do not agree and find themselves swatting a child of six months for wiggling while being diapered or for crying at midnight. This is a serious mistake. A baby is incapable of comprehending his offense or associating it with the resulting punishment. At this early age, infants need to be held, loved, touched, and soothed with the human voice. They should be fed when hungry and kept clean and dry and warm. It is probable that the foundation for emotional and physical health is laid during this first six-month period, which should be characterized by security, affection, and warmth.

On the other hand, it is possible to create a fussy, demanding baby by rushing to pick him up every time she utters a whimper or sigh. Infants are fully capable of learning to manipulate their parents through a process called reinforcement, whereby any behavior that produces a pleasant result will tend to recur. Thus, a healthy baby can keep her mother or father hopping around her nursery twelve hours a day (or night) by simply forcing air past her sandpaper larynx. To avoid this consequence, you need to strike a balance between giving your baby the attention she needs and establishing her as a tiny dictator. Don't be afraid to let her cry for a reasonable period of time (which is thought to be healthy for the lungs). It is necessary, though, to listen to the tone of her voice to determine if she's crying because of random discontent or genuine distress. Most parents learn to recognize this distinction very quickly.

In keeping with our theme, I need to say the obvious: Yes, Virginia, there *are* easy babies and difficult babies! Some seem determined to dismantle the homes into which they were born; they sleep cozily during the day and then howl in protest all night; they are often colicky and spit up the vilest stuff on their clothes (usually on the way to church); they control their internal plumbing until you hand them to friends, and then they let it blast. Instead of cuddling into the fold of the arms when being held, they stiffen rigidly in search of freedom. And parents who wonder shortly after birth, "Will this baby survive?" may find themselves leaning sock eyed over a vibrating crib at 3 A.M., asking, "Will *we* survive?"

Both generations usually recover before long, and this disruptive beginning becomes nothing but a dim memory for the parents. And from that demanding tyrant will grow a thinking, loving human being with an eternal soul and a special place in the heart of the Creator. To the exhausted and harassed parents, let me say, "Hang tough! You're doing *the* world's most important assignment."

EIGHT TO FOURTEEN MONTHS

Many children will begin to test the authority of their parents during the second seven-month period. The confrontations will be minor and infrequent before the first birthday, yet the beginnings of future struggles can be seen. Our daughter, Danae, for example, challenged Shirley for the first time when she was just nine months old. My wife was waxing the kitchen floor when Danae crawled to the edge of the linoleum. Shirley said, "No, Danae," gesturing to the child not to enter the kitchen. Since our daughter began talking very early, she clearly understood the meaning of the word *no*. Nevertheless, she crawled straight onto the sticky wax. Shirley picked her up and sat her down in the doorway, while saying *no* more firmly. Not to be discouraged, Danae scrambled back onto the newly mopped floor. My wife took her back, saying *no* even more firmly as she put her down. Seven times this process was repeated, until Danae finally yielded and crawled away in tears. As best as we can recall, that was the first direct collision of wills between my daughter and wife. Many more encounters were to follow.

How do parents discipline a one-year-old? Very carefully and gently! Children at this age are easy to distract and divert. Rather than jerking a china cup from their hands, show them a brightly colored alternative— and then be prepared to catch the cup when it falls. When unavoidable confrontations occur, as with Danae crawling onto the waxy floor, win them by firm persistence—not by punishment. Again, don't be afraid of the child's tears, which can become a potent weapon to avoid naptime or bedtime or a diaper change. Have the courage to lead the child without being harsh or mean or gruff.

Before leaving this dynamic time of life, I must share with you the findings of a ten-year study of children between the ages of eight and eighteen months. While this investigation, known as Harvard University's Preschool Project, was completed more than twenty-five years ago, its findings are still relevant for today. The researchers, led by Dr. Burton White, studied the young children intently during the ten-year period, hoping to discover how experiences in the early years of life contribute to the development of a healthy, intelligent human being. The conclusions from this exhaustive effort are summarized below, as reported originally in the *American Psychological Association Monitor:*[1]

- It is increasingly clear that the origins of human competence are to be found in a critical period of development between eight and eighteen months of age. The child's experiences during these brief months do more to influence future intellectual competence than any time before or after.

- The single most important environmental factor in the life of the child is the mother. According to Dr. White, "she is on the hook" and carries more influence on her child's experiences than any other person or circumstance.

- The amount of *live* language directed to a child (not to be confused with television, radio, or overheard conversations) is vital to her development of fundamental linguistic, intellectual, and social skills. The researchers concluded, "Providing a rich social life for a twelve- to fifteen-month-old child is the best thing you can do to guarantee a good mind."

- Those children who are given free access to living areas of their homes progress much faster than those whose movements are restricted.

- The nuclear family is the most important educational delivery system. If we are going to produce capable, healthy children, it will be by strengthening family units and by improving the interactions that occur within them.

- The best parents in the study were those who excelled at three key functions:
  1. They were superb designers and organizers of their children's environments.
  2. They permitted their children to interrupt them for brief thirty-

second episodes, during which personal consultation, comfort, information, and enthusiasm were exchanged.

3. They were "firm disciplinarians while simultaneously showing great affection for their children." (I couldn't have said it better myself.)

These findings speak eloquently about the issues that matter most in early childhood. I hear within them an affirmation and validation of the concepts to which I have devoted my professional life.

FIFTEEN TO TWENTY-FOUR MONTHS

It has been said that all human beings can be classified into two broad categories: those who would vote yes to the various propositions of life and those who would be inclined to vote no. I can tell you with confidence that each toddler around the world would definitely cast a negative vote! If there is one word that characterizes the period between fifteen and twenty-four months of age, it is *no!* No, they don't want to eat their cereal. No, they don't want to play with their building blocks. No, they don't want to take a bath. And you can be sure that, no, they don't want to go to bed, ever. It is easy to see why this period of life has been called "the first adolescence," because of the negativism, conflict, and defiance of the age.

Dr. T. Berry Brazelton authored a helpful book called *Toddlers and Parents* that included an insightful description of the "terrible twos."[2] The following quote is his classic description of a typical eighteen-month-old boy named Greg. Although I have never met this little fellow, I know him well . . . as you will when your child becomes a toddler.

When Greg began to be negative in the second year, his parents felt as if they had been hit by a sledge hammer. His good nature seemed submerged under a load of negatives. When his parents asked anything of him, his mouth took on a grim set, his eyes narrowed, and, facing them squarely with his penetrating look, he replied simply, "no!" When offered ice cream, which he loved, he preceded his acceptance with a "no." While he rushed out to get his snowsuit to go outside, he said "no" to going out.

His parents' habit of watching Greg for cues now began to turn sour. He seemed to be fighting with them all of the time.

When he was asked to perform a familiar chore, his response was, "I can't." When his mother tried to stop him from emptying his clothes drawer, his response was, "I have to." He pushed hard on every familiar imposed limit, and never seemed satisfied until his parent collapsed in defeat. He would turn on the television set when his mother left the room. When she returned, she turned it off, scolded Greg mildly, and left again. He turned it on. She came rushing back to reason with him, to ask him why he'd disobeyed her. He replied, "I have to." The intensity of her insistence that he leave it alone increased. He looked steadily back at her. She returned to the kitchen. He turned it on. She was waiting behind the door, swirled in to slap his hands firmly. He sighed deeply and said, "I have to." She sat down beside him, begging him to listen to her to avoid real punishment. Again he presented a dour mask with knitted brows to her, listening but not listening. She rose wearily, he walked over to the machine to turn it on. As she came right back, tears in her eyes, to spank him, she said, "Greg, why do you want me to spank you? I hate it!" To which he replied, "I have to." As she crumpled in the chair, weeping softly with him across her lap, Greg reached up to touch her wet face.

After this clash, Mrs. Lang was exhausted. Greg sensed this and began to try to be helpful. He ran to the kitchen to fetch her mop and her dustpan, which he dragged in to her as she sat in her chair. This reversal made her smile and she gathered him up in a hug.

Greg caught her change in mood and danced off gaily to a corner, where he slid behind a chair, saying "hi and see." As he pushed the chair out, he tipped over a lamp which went crashing to the floor. His mother's reaction was, "No, Greg!" He curled up on the floor, his hands over his ears, eyes tightly closed, as if he were trying to shut out all the havoc he had wrought.

As soon as he was put into his high chair, he began to whine. She was so surprised that she stopped preparation of his food, and took him to change him. This did not settle the issue, and when she brought him to his chair again, he began to squirm and twist. She let him down to play until his lunch was ready. He lay on the floor, alternately whining and screeching. So unusual was this that she . . . felt his forehead for fever. . . . Finally, she returned to fixing his lunch. Without an audience, Greg subsided.

When she placed him in his chair again, his shrill whines began anew. She placed his plate in front of him with cubes of food to spear with his fork. He tossed the implement overboard, and began to push his plate away, refusing the food. Mrs. Lang was nonplussed, decided he didn't feel well, and offered him his favorite ice cream. Again, he sat helpless, refusing to feed himself. When she offered him some, he submissively allowed himself to be fed a few spoonfuls. Then he knocked the spoon out of her hand and pushed the ice cream away. Mrs. Lang was sure that he was ill.

Mrs. Lang extracted Greg from his embattled position, and placed him on the floor to play while she ate lunch. This, of course, wasn't what he wanted either. He continued to tease her, asking for food off her plate, which he devoured greedily. His eagerness disproved her theory of illness. When she ignored him and continued to eat, his efforts redoubled. He climbed under the sink to find the bleach bottle which he brought to her on command. He fell forward onto the floor and cried loudly as if he'd hurt himself. He began to grunt as if he were having a bowel movement and to pull on his pants. This was almost a sure way of drawing his mother away from her own activity, for she'd started trying to "catch" him and put him on the toilet. This was one of his signals for attention, and she rushed him to the toilet. He smiled smugly at her, but refused to perform. Mrs. Lang felt as if she were suddenly embattled on all fronts—none of which she could win.

When she turned to her own chores, Greg produced the bowel movement he'd been predicting.[3]

This, my friends, was not a description of a typical toddler. Greg was a classic strong-willed child. He was having fun at the expense of his mama, and he almost took the measure of her. I'll talk in a moment about how such a child should be handled.

The picture painted by Dr. Brazelton sounds pretty bleak, and admittedly, there are times when a two-year-old can dismantle the peace and tranquility of a home. (Our son, Ryan, loved to blow bubbles in the dog's water dish—a game that horrified us.) However, with all of its struggles, there is no more delightful time in life than this period of dynamic blossoming and unfolding. New words are being learned daily, and the cute verbal expressions of that age will be remembered for a half century. It is a time of excitement over fairy tales and make-believe and furry puppy dogs. And most important, it is a precious time of loving and warmth that will scurry by all too quickly. There are millions of older parents with grown children today who would give all they possess to relive those bubbly days with their toddlers.

Let me make a few recommendations about discipline that will, I hope, be helpful when a toddler is on the warpath. I must hasten to say, however, that the negativism of this turbulent period is both normal and healthy, and *nothing* will make an eighteen-month-old act like a five-year-old. Time is the only real "cure."

Now, let's talk about Greg. His kind of misbehavior is what Mrs. Susanna Wesley was referring to when she wrote, "In order to form the minds of children, the first thing to be done is to conquer the will, and bring them into an obedient temper. To inform the understanding is a work of time, and must with children proceed by slow degrees as they are able to bear it; but the subjecting of the will is a thing which must be done at once, and the sooner the better!" I'm not sure Mrs. Lang accomplished that purpose.

When times of confrontation occur with a strong-willed toddler such as Greg, mild slaps on the bottom or the hand can begin between fifteen and eighteen months of age. They should be relatively infrequent and must be reserved for the kind of defiance he displayed over the television set. He understood what was expected of him but he refused to comply. This behavior is what I have been referring to as willful defiance. Greg was clearly taunting his mother and testing the limits of her endurance. Mrs. Lang mishandled the situation. I'm not being critical of her. I fully understand her frustration and am sure that most mothers would have responded similarly. Nevertheless, she needed to win that battle decisively in order to avoid endless recurrences down the road, but she failed to get that done.

Look again at the mistakes this mother made. When Greg turned the television set on after she had pointedly turned it off, Mrs. Lang "scolded Greg mildly." He did it again and she "came rushing back to reason with him." Then she asked him why he disobeyed her. He said "I have to" and turned the television on again. Finally, Mom "swirled in to slap his hands firmly." Slapping Greg's hands was the right thing to do, but it came far too late. She should have done that after he had been warned once and then disobeyed again. Mrs. Lang's other measures were not only ineffective, but they made things worse. It is a total waste of time to "reason" with a toddler in a moment of defiance, and certainly, one does not whine and ask him "why?" You will never get a satisfactory answer to that question. If Greg had had a few more years on him and told the truth, he would have said, "Because I'm trying to drive you nuts, that's why." Mrs. Lang wound up begging her strong-willed boy to listen and obey, and then cried when he forced her to punish him. Those were all the wrong things to have done.

I have concentrated on this story because it is applicable to millions of parents who have been led to believe that mild punishment is somehow harmful to children, and that even if it is applied, it should be a last resort after scolding, whining, begging, crying, explaining repeatedly, and trying to reason. These responses to blatant misbehavior undermine authority and put the parent on the same level with the child. What heady stuff it is for a two-year-old to take on a powerful adult and reduce her to tears.

Mrs. Lang should have come back into the room after the television set went on the second time and sat down with a word of advice for her little boy. She should have put her hands on either side of his head, looked him straight in the eyes, and said firmly, "Listen to me, Greg. Mommy does not want you to touch the television set again. Do you hear me? DON'T TOUCH IT AGAIN. Do you understand?" What she would have been doing in that moment was drawing the boundary lines vividly in Greg's mind. Then if he went back to the set for round three, she should have been standing nearby. The hand-slapping response should have occurred right then. It would not have been necessary to explain or reason. It would have been enough that his mother had given him an order. For most children, tears would have occurred and quenched the rebellious mood Greg was in. In most cases, that would have ended the matter. If he was especially tough, Greg might have tested his mother again. Without screaming or crying or begging, she would have needed simply to outlast him, no matter how long it took. Remember that Dr. Brazelton said Greg never seemed satisfied until his mother collapsed in defeat. That is why Mom should never have let that happen. This toddler should have come out of this encounter with the shocking belief that *Mom means business. I don't like what happened to me. I'd better do what she says.*

This response by the mother *must* be done without abusing the child physically or emotionally. I am convinced from my many years of working with parents that a frustrated woman like Mrs. Lang is less likely to do something unthinkable if she is empowered to handle the challenge early—before it becomes a donnybrook—rather than wait until she is too frazzled to control herself.

Let me caution parents not to punish toddlers for behavior that is natural and necessary to learning and development. Exploration of their environment, for example, is of great importance to intellectual stimulation. You and I will look at a crystal trinket and obtain whatever information we seek from that visual inspection. Toddlers, however, will expose it to all their senses. They will pick it up, taste it, smell it, wave it in the air, pound it on the wall, throw it across the room, and listen to the pretty sound it makes when shattering. By that process, they learn a bit about gravity, rough versus smooth surfaces, the brittle nature of glass, and some startling things about their parent's anger. (This is not what Greg was doing. He was not exploring. He was disobeying.)

Am I suggesting that kids, strong-willed or otherwise, be allowed to destroy a home and all of its contents? No, but neither is it right to expect curious toddlers to keep their fat little fingers to themselves. Parents should remove those items that are fragile or particularly dangerous and then strew their children's path with fascinating objects of all types. Permit them to explore everything that is not breakable. Do not ever punish them for touching something, regardless of its value, that they *did not know was off-limits.* With respect to dangerous items, such as electric plugs and stoves, as well as a few untouchable objects such as the TV controls, it is possible and necessary to teach and enforce the command "Don't touch!" After making it clear what is expected, a slap on the hand will usually discourage repeat episodes.

Entire books have been written about disciplining young children. I wrote a couple of them. I have only touched on the subject here to give a flavor of the proper approach to management of toddlers—even a confirmed revolutionary like Greg.

Two to Three Years of Age

Perhaps the most frustrating aspect of raising children between two and three is their tendency to spill things, destroy things, eat horrible things, fall off things, flush things, kill things, and get into things. They also have a knack for doing embarrassing things, like sneezing on the man seated near them at McDonald's. During the toddler years, any unexplained silence of more than thirty seconds can throw an adult into a sudden state of panic. What mother has not had the thrill of opening the bedroom door, only to find Hurricane Hannah covered with lipstick from the top of her head to the carpet on which she stands? Beside her is a red handprint she has placed in the center of the carpet. Throughout the room is the aroma of Chanel No. 5, with which she has anointed a younger sibling. Wouldn't it be interesting to hold a national convention sometime, bringing together all the mothers who have experienced similar traumas?

When my daughter was two years of age, she was fascinated the first time she watched me shave in the morning. She stood captivated as I put the shaving cream on my face and began using the razor. That should have been my first clue that something was up. The following morning, Shirley came into the bathroom to find our dog, Siggie, sitting in his favorite spot on the furry lid of the toilet seat. Danae had covered his head with lather and was systematically shaving the hair from his shiny skull! Shirley screamed, "Danae!" which sent Siggie and his barber scurrying for safety. It was a hilarious sight to see the little wiener dog standing in the bedroom with nicks and bald spots on his head.

When Ryan was the same age, he had an incredible ability to make messes. He could turn something over and spill it faster than any kid I've ever seen, especially at mealtime. (Once while eating a peanut-butter sandwich, he thrust his hand through the bottom side. When his fingers emerged at the top they were covered with peanut butter, and Ryan didn't recognize them. The poor lad clamped down severely on his index finger.) Because of this destructive inclination, Ryan heard the word *mess* repeatedly from Shirley and me. It became one of the most important words in his vocabulary. One evening while taking a shower I left the door ajar and got some water on the floor. As you might expect, Ryan came thumping around the corner and stepped in it. He looked up at me and said in the gruffest voice he could manage, "Whuss all this mess in hyere?"

You *must* keep a sense of humor during the twos and threes in order to preserve your own sanity. But you must also proceed with the task of instilling obedience and respect for authority. Thus, most of the comments written in the preceding section also apply to the child between twenty-two and thirty-six months of age. Although the older toddler is much different physically and emotionally than he was at eighteen months, the tendency to test and challenge parental authority is still very much in evidence. In fact, when young toddlers consistently win the early confrontations and conflicts, they become even more difficult to handle in the second and third years. Then a lifelong disrespect for authority often begins to settle into their young minds. Therefore, I cannot overemphasize the importance of instilling two distinct messages within your child before she is forty-eight months of age:

- "I love you more than you can possibly understand. You are precious to me and I thank God every day He let me raise you!"
- "Because I love you, I must teach you to obey me. That is the only way I can take care of you and protect you from things that might hurt you. Let's read what the Bible tells us: 'Children, obey your parents in the Lord, for this is right' " (Ephesians 6:1).

The broad principle, which appears throughout this book, bears repeating. Healthy parenting can be boiled down to those two essential ingredients: love and control. They must operate in a system of checks and balances. Any concentration on love to the exclusion of control usually breeds disrespect and contempt. Conversely, an authoritarian and oppressive home atmosphere is deeply resented by the child who feels unloved or even hated. The objective for the toddler years is to strike a balance between mercy and justice, affection and authority, love and control.

Specifically, how does one discipline a naughty two- or three-year-old child? One possible approach is to require her to sit in a chair and think about what she has done. This is the concept often referred to as a time-out. Most children of this age are bursting with energy and absolutely hate to spend ten dull minutes with their wiggly posteriors glued to a chair. To some individuals, this form of punishment can be even more effective than a spanking and is remembered longer.

Parents to whom I have recommended using time-outs have often asked, "But what if they won't stay in the chair?" The same question is asked with reference to the child's tendency to pop out of bed after being tucked in at night. These are examples of the direct confrontation I have been describing. Parents who cannot require a toddler to stay on a chair for a few minutes or in bed at the end of the day are not yet in command of the child. There is no better time than now to change the relationship.

I would suggest that the youngster be placed in bed and given a little speech, such as, "Brandon, this time Mommy means business. Are you listening to me? Do *not* get out of this bed. Do you understand me?" Then when his feet touch the floor, give him one swat on the legs or backside with a small paddle or belt. (I'll explain later why a neutral object is better, in my opinion, than using the hand.) Put the paddle on the dresser where the child can see it, and promise him one more stroke if he gets up again. Walk confidently out of the room without further comment. If he rebounds again, fulfill your promise and offer the same warning if he doesn't stay in bed. Repeat the episode until the child acknowledges that you are boss. Then hug him, tell him how you love him, and remind him how important it is for him to get rest so that he won't be sick, etc.

Your purpose in this painful exercise (painful for both parties) is not only to keep the child in bed but to confirm your leadership in his mind. It is my opinion that too many parents lack the courage to win these confrontations and are kept off balance and on the defensive ever after. Remember: You are the benevolent boss. Act like it.

FOUR TO EIGHT YEARS

By the time a child reaches four years of age, the focus of discipline should not only be on his or her behavior, but also on the *attitudes* motivating it. The task of shaping this expression of the personality can be relatively simple or incredibly difficult, depending on the basic temperament of a particular child. Some youngsters are naturally warm and loving and trusting, while others sincerely believe the world is out to get them. Some enjoy giving and sharing, while their siblings may be selfish and demanding. Some smile throughout the day while others complain about everything from toothpaste to broccoli.

Furthermore, these attitudinal patterns are not consistent from one time to the next. They tend to alternate cyclically between rebellion and obedience. In other words, a time of intense conflict and defiance (if properly handled) gives way to a period of love and cooperation. Then when

Mom and Dad relax and congratulate themselves for doing a super job of parenting, their little chameleon changes colors again.

Some might ask, "So what? Why should we be concerned about the attitudes of a boy or girl?" Indeed, there are many child-rearing specialists who suggest ignoring negative attitudes, including those that are unmistakably defiant in tone. Here is an example of what some of them say:

> This [recommendation that parents ignore disobedience] works best with annoying, but not harmful, behavior like bad language or tantrums. Effective ignoring involves not talking or looking at the child or using any body language that indicates attention.[4]

Another advocate of this naive approach was Dr. Luther Woodward, whose recommendations are paraphrased in a book that is now thankfully out of print, *Your Child from Two to Five*.[5] This was Dr. Woodward's ill-considered advice:

> What do you do when your preschooler calls you a "big stinker" or threatens to flush you down the toilet? Do you scold, punish . . . or sensibly take it in your stride?[6]

Dr. Woodward recommended a positive policy of understanding as the best and fastest way to help a child outgrow this verbal violence. He wrote, "When parents fully realize that all little tots feel angry and destructive at times, they are better able to minimize these outbursts. Once the preschooler gets rid of his hostility, the desire to destroy is gone and instinctive feelings of love and affection have a chance to sprout and grow. Once the child is six or seven, parents can rightly let the child know that he is expected to be outgrowing sassing his parents."[7]

Dr. Woodward then warned his readers that the permissive advice he was offering would not be popular with onlookers. He wrote: "But this policy takes a broad perspective and a lot of composure, especially when friends and relatives voice disapproval and warn you that you are bringing up a brat."[8]

In this case, your friends and relatives would probably be right. This suggestion (published during the permissive 1950s and typical of other writings from that era) is based on the erroneous notion that children will develop sweet and loving attitudes if adults will permit and encourage their emotional outbursts and their sassiness during childhood. It didn't work for Dr. Woodward's generation, and it won't be successful with your children. The child who has been calling his mother a big stinker (or worse) for six or seven years is unlikely to yield to parental leadership during the storms of adolescence. By then, the opportunity to shape the will of a strong-willed child is long gone, after which rebellious behavior will be a virtual certainty.

I expressed my divergent views on this subject in *The New Dare to Discipline* as follows:

> I believe that if it is desirable for children to be kind, apprecia-
> tive, and pleasant, those qualities should be taught—not hoped
> for. If we want to see honesty, truthfulness, and unselfishness in
> our offspring, then these characteristics should be the conscious
> objectives of our early instructional process. If it is important to
> produce respectful, responsible young citizens, then we should
> set out to mold them accordingly. The point is obvious: *Heredity
> does not equip a child with proper attitudes; children will learn what
> they are taught.* We cannot expect the coveted behavior to appear
> magically if we have not done our early homework.[9]

I fear that many parents today are failing to teach attitudes in their children that will lead to successful and responsible lives.

But how does one shape the attitudes of children? Most parents find it easier to deal with outright disobedience than with unpleasant characteristics of temperament or personality. Let me restate two age-old suggestions, and then I'll offer a system that can be used with the especially disagreeable child.

There is no substitute for parental modeling of the attitudes we wish to teach. Someone wrote, "The footsteps a child follows are most likely to be the ones his parents thought they covered up." It is true. Our children are watching us carefully, and they instinctively imitate our behavior. Therefore, we can hardly expect them to be kind and giving if we are consistently grouchy and selfish. We will be unable to teach appreciativeness if we never say please or thank you at home or abroad. We will not produce honest children if we teach them to lie over the phone to someone trying to collect payment from us by saying, "Dad's not home." In these matters, our boys and girls quickly discern the gap between what we say and what we do. And of the two choices, they usually identify with our behavior and ignore our empty proclamations.

Most of the favorable attitudes that should be taught are actually extrapolations of the Judeo-Christian ethic, including honesty, respect, kindness, love, human dignity, obedience, responsibility, reverence, and so forth. And how are these time-honored principles conveyed to the next generation? The answer was provided by Moses in the words he wrote more than three thousand years ago in the book of Deuteronomy: "These commandments that I give you today are to be upon your hearts. Impress them on your children. Talk about them when you sit at home and when you walk along the road, when you lie down and when you get up. Tie them as symbols on your hands and bind them on your foreheads. Write them on the doorframes of your houses and on your gates" (Deuteronomy 6:6-9).

In other words, we can't instill these attitudes during a brief, two-minute bedtime prayer or during formal training sessions. We must *live* them from morning to night. They should be reinforced during our casual conversation, being punctuated with illustrations, demonstrations, compliments, and chastisement. Finally, let me suggest an approach for use with the strong-willed or negative child (age six or older) for whom other forms of instruction have been ineffective. I am referring specifically to the sour, complaining child who is making himself and the rest of his family miserable. The problem in disciplining such a child is the need to define the changes that are desired and then reinforce the improvements when they occur. Attitudes are abstractions that a six- or eight-year-old may not fully understand, and we need a system that will clarify the target in his mind.

Toward this end, I have developed an attitude chart (see illustration on the following page) that translates these subtle mannerisms into concrete, mathematical terms. Please note: The system that follows is *not* appropriate for the child who merely has a bad day or displays temporary unpleasantness associated with illness, fatigue, or environmental circumstances. Rather, it is a remedial tool to help change persistently negative and disrespectful attitudes by making the child conscious of her problem.

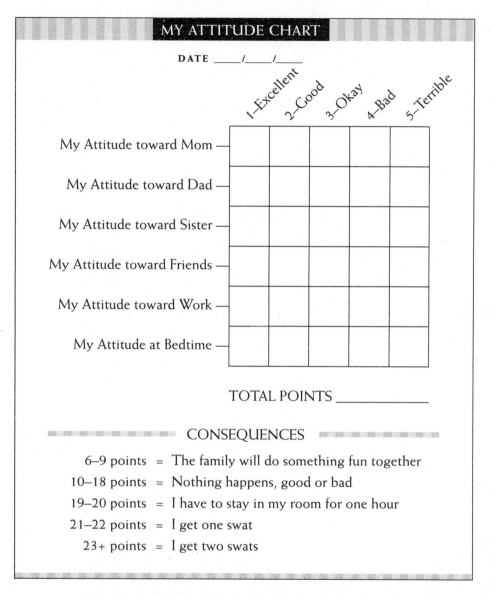

MY ATTITUDE CHART

DATE _____/_____/_____

	1–Excellent	2–Good	3–Okay	4–Bad	5–Terrible
My Attitude toward Mom —					
My Attitude toward Dad —					
My Attitude toward Sister —					
My Attitude toward Friends —					
My Attitude toward Work —					
My Attitude at Bedtime —					

TOTAL POINTS _____

CONSEQUENCES

6–9 points = The family will do something fun together

10–18 points = Nothing happens, good or bad

19–20 points = I have to stay in my room for one hour

21–22 points = I get one swat

23+ points = I get two swats

The attitude chart should be prepared and then reproduced, since a separate sheet will be needed each day. Place an *X* in the appropriate square for each category, and then add the total points "earned" by bedtime. Although this nightly evaluation process has the appearance of being objective to the child, it is obvious that the parents can influence the outcome by considering it in advance (it's called cheating). Mom and Dad may want Michael or Rebecca to receive eighteen points on the first night, barely missing the punishment but realizing he or she must stretch the following day. I must emphasize, however, that the system will fail miserably if a naughty child does not receive the punishment she deserves or if she hustles to improve but does not receive the family fun she was promised. This approach is nothing more than a method of applying reward and punishment to attitudes in a way that children can understand and remember.

For the child who does not fully comprehend the concept of numbers, it might be helpful to plot the daily totals on a cumulative graph, such as the one provided below.

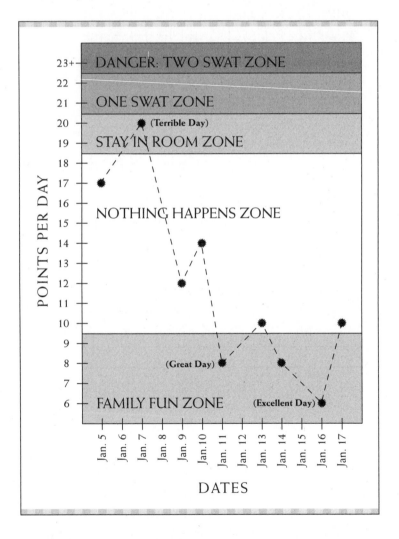

I don't expect everyone to appreciate this system or to apply it at home. In fact, parents of compliant, happy children will be puzzled as to why it would ever be needed. However, mothers and fathers of sullen, ill-tempered children will comprehend more quickly. Take it or leave it, as the situation warrants.

NINE TO TWELVE YEARS

Ideally, the foundation has been laid during the first nine years that will then permit a general loosening of the lines of authority. Every year that passes should bring fewer rules, less direct discipline, and more independence for the child. This does not mean that a ten-year-old is suddenly emancipated; it does mean that she is permitted to make more decisions about her daily living than when she was six. It also means that she should be carrying more responsibility each year of her life.

Physical punishment should be relatively infrequent during this period immediately prior to adolescence. Studies show that corporal punishment loses its effectiveness after the age of ten and should be discontinued. However, as is the case with all human beings, there are exceptions to the rules. Some strong-willed children absolutely demand to be spanked, and their wishes should be granted. However, compliant youngsters should have experienced their last round of corporal punishment by the end of their first decade (or even four years earlier). Some never need it at all.

The overall objective during this final preadolescent period is to teach the child that his actions have inevitable consequences. One of the most serious casualties in a permissive society is the failure to connect those two factors: behavior and consequences. Too often, a three-year-old child screams insults at her mother, but Mom stands blinking her eyes in confusion or simply ignores the behavior. A first-grader launches an attack on his teacher, but the school makes allowances for his age or is fearful of a lawsuit and takes no action. A ten-year-old is caught stealing candy in a store but is released with a reprimand. A fifteen-year-old sneaks the keys to the family car, but his father bails him out when he is arrested. A seventeen-year-old drives like a maniac, and her parents pay the higher insurance premiums after she wraps the family car around a telephone pole. You see, all through childhood some loving parents seem determined to intervene between behavior and consequences, breaking the connection and preventing the valuable learning that could have occurred.

Thus, it is possible for a young man or woman to enter adult life not really knowing that life can be harsh—that every move directly affects the

330 THE NEW STRONG-WILLED CHILD

future and that irresponsible behavior eventually produces sorrow and pain. One of the saddest sights is the adult who did not learn that behaviors have inevitable consequences and makes mistake after mistake that could easily have been avoided. Such a person applies for his first job and arrives late for work three times during the first week; then, when he is fired in a flurry of hot words, he becomes bitter and frustrated. It was the first time in his life that Mom and Dad couldn't come running to rescue him from unpleasant circumstances. Or an individual gets married and has children but bounces from job to job trying to "find himself" while his family struggles financially. (Unfortunately, many parents still try to bail out their grown children even when they are in their twenties, and sometimes even their thirties.) What is the result? This overprotection produces emotional cripples who often develop lasting characteristics of dependency and a kind of perpetual adolescence.

How does one connect behavior with consequences? Parents must be willing to let children experience a reasonable amount of pain when they behave irresponsibly. When Craig misses the school bus through his own dawdling, let him walk a mile or two and enter school in midmorning (unless safety factors prohibit this). If Caitlin carelessly loses her lunch money, let her skip a meal. Obviously, it is possible to carry this principle too far, being harsh and inflexible with an immature child. But the best approach is to expect boys and girls to carry the responsibility that is appropriate for their age and occasionally to taste the bitter fruit that irresponsibility bears.

Let me offer an illustration that may be read to an eleven- or twelve-year-old child. The following story was published a few days after an eclipse of the sun had occurred:

Tipton, Ind. (UPI)—Ann Turner, 15, is living proof of the danger of trying to watch a solar eclipse with the naked eye. Now she is blind.

On March 7, despite the warnings she had read, Ann "took a quick look through the window" at her home at the solar eclipse in progress.

"For some reason, I just kept staring out of the window," she told Pat Cline, a reporter for the *Tipton Daily Tribune*. "I was fascinated by what was taking place in the sky.

"There was no pain or feeling of discomfort as I watched. I stood there perhaps four or five minutes when Mom caught me and made me turn away from the window."

Ann said she "saw spots before my eyes but I didn't think much about it." Shortly afterward, she walked downtown and suddenly realized when she looked at a traffic signal that she could not read signs.

Frightened, Ann turned around and headed home. As she neared the porch, she said, she found she was "walking in darkness."

She was too scared to tell her family until the next day, although she "had an intuition or suspicion that something terrible was happening."

"I cried and cried," she said. "I didn't want to be blind. God knows I didn't want to live in darkness the rest of my life.

"I kept hoping the nightmare would end and I could see again but the darkness kept getting worse. I was scared. I had disobeyed my parents and the other warnings. I could not go back and change things. It was too late."

When Mr. and Mrs. Coy Turner learned what had happened, they took Ann to specialists. But the doctors shook their heads and said they could not help Ann regain her sight. They said she is 90 percent blind and can make out only faint lines of large objects on the periphery of what used to be her normal sight field.

With the help of a tutor, Ann is going ahead with her education. She is learning to adjust to the world of darkness.[10]

After reading this dramatic story to your boy or girl, it might be wise to say, "This terrible thing happened to Ann because she didn't believe what she was told by her parents and other adults. She trusted her own judgment instead. And the reason I read this to you is to help you understand that you might soon be in a situation that is similar to Ann's. As you go into your teen years, you will have many opportunities to do some things that we have told you are harmful. For example, someone may try to convince you to take illegal drugs that seem harmless at the time but end up resulting in all sorts of health problems later on. Someone else, perhaps even a teacher, may tell you that it is okay for you to experiment sexually with someone as long as you do it 'safely,' and you may end up with a disease that will ravage your body and cause numerous problems for you and the person you eventually marry. Just like Ann, you may not realize the consequences until it is too late. That is why it will be so important for you to *believe* the warnings that you've been taught rather than to trust your own judgment. Many young people make mistakes during the teenage years that will affect the rest of their life, and I want to help you avoid those problems. But the truth of the matter is, only you can set your course and choose your pathway. You can accept what your eyes tell you, like Ann did, or you can believe what your mother and I have said, and more important, what we read in God's Word. I have confidence that you will make the right decisions, and it's going to be fun watching you grow up."

There is so much that should be said about this late childhood era, but the limitations of time and space force me to move on. In conclusion, the period between ten and eleven years of age often represents the final time of closeness and unpretentious love between parent and child until the child reaches young adulthood. Enjoy it to the maximum, for believe me, there are more tumultuous days coming! (I have chosen to reserve the discussion of adolescent discipline for a separate chapter because of the significance of the topic.)

I'll end with a final illustration. I was once accompanied on a speaking trip by my wife, Shirley, requiring us to leave Danae and Ryan with their grandparents for a full week. Shirley's parents are dear people and loved our children very much. However, two bouncing, jumping, giggling little rascals can wear down the nerves of *any* adult, especially ones trying to enjoy their golden years. When we returned home from the trip I asked my father-in-law how the children behaved and whether or not they caused him any problems. He replied in his North Dakota accent, "Oh no! Dere good kids. But the important thing is, you jus' got to keep 'em out in da open."

That was probably the best disciplinary advice ever offered. Many behavioral problems can be prevented by simply avoiding the circumstances that create them. And especially for boys and girls growing up in congested cities, perhaps what we need most is to get 'em "out in da open." It's not a bad idea.

QUESTIONS & ANSWERS

Q: My five-year-old is developing a problem with lying, and I don't know how to handle it. What can I do to get him to tell the truth?
A: Lying is a problem every parent must deal with. All children distort the truth from time to time, and some become inveterate liars. Responding appropriately is a task that requires an understanding of child development

and the characteristics of a particular individual. I'll offer some general advice that will have to be modified to fit specific cases.

First, understand that a young child may or may not fully comprehend the difference between lies and the truth. There is a very thin line between fantasy and reality in the mind of a preschool boy or girl. So before you react in a heavy-handed manner, be sure you know what he understands and what his intent is.

For those children who are clearly lying to avoid unpleasant consequences or to gain an advantage of some sort, parents need to use that circumstance as a teachable moment. The greatest emphasis should be given to telling the truth in all situations. It is a virtue that should be taught—not just when a lie has occurred, but at other times as well. In your devotions with the children, read Proverbs 6:16-19 together: "There are six things the LORD hates, seven that are detestable to him: haughty eyes, a lying tongue, hands that shed innocent blood, a heart that devises wicked schemes, feet that are quick to rush into evil, a false witness who pours out lies and a man who stirs up dissension among brothers."

These are powerful verses around which to structure devotional periods with children. Explain who Solomon was, why his teachings are so important to us, and how Scripture helps us. It is like a flashlight on a dark night, guiding our footsteps and keeping us on the right path. It will even protect us while we are asleep, if we will bind it on our heart forever. Memorize Proverbs 6:16-19 together so it can be referred to in other contexts. Use it as a springboard to discussions of virtues and behavior that will please God. Each verse can be applied to everyday situations so that a child can begin to feel accountable for what he does and says.

Returning to the specific issue of lying, point out to the child that in a list of seven things the Lord hates most, two of them deal with dishonesty. Telling the truth is something God cares about, and therefore it should matter to us. This will explain why you are going to insist that your son or daughter learn to tell the truth even when it hurts to do so. Your goal is to lay a foundation that will help you underscore a commitment to honesty in the future.

The next time your child tells a blatant lie, you can return to this discussion and to the Scripture on which it was based. At some point, when you feel the maturity level of the youngster makes it appropriate, you should begin to insist that the truth be told and to impose mild punishment if it isn't. Gradually, over a period of years, you should be able to teach the virtue of truthfulness to your son or daughter.

Of course, you can undermine everything you're trying to establish if you are dishonest in front of your kids. Believe me, they will note it and behave likewise. If Daddy can twist the truth, he'll have little authority in preventing his kids from doing the same.

Q: I like your idea of balancing love with discipline, but I'm not sure I can do it. My parents were extremely rigid with us, and I'm determined not to make that mistake with my kids. But I don't want to be a pushover, either. Can you give me some help in finding the middle ground between extremes?

A: Maybe it would clarify the overall goal of your discipline to state it in the negative. It is not to produce perfect kids. Even if you implement a flawless system of discipline at home, which no one in history has done, your children will still be children. At times they will be silly, lazy, selfish, and, yes, disrespectful. Such is the nature of the human species. We as adults have the same weaknesses. Furthermore, when it comes to kids, that's the way they are wired. Boys and girls are like clocks; you have to let them run. My point is that the purpose of parental discipline is not to produce obedient little robots who can sit with their hands folded in the parlor thinking patriotic and noble thoughts! Even if we could pull that off, it wouldn't be wise to try.

The objective, as I see it, is to take the raw material our babies arrive with on this earth and gradually mold it, shaping them into mature, responsible, God-fearing adults. It is a twenty-year process that involves progress, setbacks, successes, and failures. When the child turns thirteen, you'll swear for a time that he's missed everything you thought you had taught—manners, kindness, grace, and style. But then maturity begins to take over, and the little green shoots from former plantings start to emerge. It is one of the richest experiences in life to watch that blossoming at the latter end of childhood.

Q: Do you think there is a relationship between permissive parenting and teen violence, especially at home?

A: Without question. Teen violence, at home and in public, has many causes, but permissive parenting is one of them. Many years ago, I came across an article on this subject and put it in my files. Though it is now old, it still answers the question you have posed. It is quoted below, in part:

> Two scientists at the Institute of Psychiatry and Human Behavior at the University of Maryland Medical School have identified what they call *a new syndrome of family violence: parent battering.*
>
> The term includes both physical assault and serious threats of physical harm by children and young people.
>
> Although the scientists do not know for sure, they suspect that the syndrome is not uncommon.
>
> It seems to occur, they find, in families of all classes in which "one or both parents have abdicated the executive position" and no one, except possibly the battering child, is in charge.
>
> An almost universal element in the families is that they deny the seriousness of the child's aggressive behavior.
>
> For instance, a father who was almost killed when his son pushed him downstairs insisted that the boy had no problems with his temper.
>
> Dr. Henry T. Harbin and Dr. Dennis Madden found that one of the most remarkable features of the cases they studied was the parents' tolerant response to the attack.
>
> In one case, a youth of eighteen stabbed his mother, missing her heart by an inch, yet she was quite willing to let her son continue living at home.
>
> Instead of asserting parental authority in the face of threats or attack, parents frequently gave in to their children's demands.
>
> Even if their lives were in danger, they did not always call the police, and when questioned later they often lied to protect their children—and their self-image as effective parents.
>
> Confronting the aberrant behavior of the child implies an admission of failure, the researchers said.
>
> Another reason for denial was "to maintain an illusion, a myth of family harmony," to avoid thinking the unthinkable that the family was disintegrating.

"For parents to admit that their offspring have actually tried to kill them arouses massive anxiety and depression," the researchers believe.

When parents were asked who they would like to be in charge of a hypothetical family, few said that mothers or fathers should make the rules and some said that everyone in the family should be equal.

If battering children who were undergoing treatment at the violence clinic wanted to stop therapy or drop out of school, parents often answered, "Whatever you want to do."

Dr. Harbin said that, ideally, both parents should take a firm hand, but in any case, "someone needs to be in charge."[11]

Q: Isn't it our goal to produce children with self-discipline and self-reliance? If so, how does your approach to external discipline imposed by parents get translated into internal control?

A: Many authorities suggest that parents take a passive approach to their children for the reason implied by your question: They want their kids to discipline themselves. But since young people lack the maturity to generate self-control, they stumble through childhood without experiencing either internal or external discipline. Thus, they enter adult life having never completed an unpleasant assignment or accepted an order they disliked or yielded to the leadership of their elders. Can we expect such a person to exercise self-discipline in young adulthood? I think not. That individual doesn't even know the meaning of the word.

My belief is that parents should introduce their children to discipline and self-control by any reasonable means available, including the use of external influences, when they are young. By being required to behave responsibly, children gain valuable experience in controlling their impulses and resources. Year by year, responsibility is gradually transferred from the shoulders of the parents directly to the children. Eventually, they will act on what they learned in their earlier years—on their own initiative.

To illustrate, children should be required to keep their room relatively neat when they are young. Then somewhere during the midteens, their own self-discipline should take over and provide the motivation to continue the task. If it does not, the parents should close the door and let them live in a dump, if that is their choice.

In short, self-discipline does not come automatically to those who have never experienced it. Self-control must be learned, and it must be taught.

EIGHT

Corporal Punishment & the Strong-Willed Child

Behind in His Reading

Junior bit the meter man,
Junior kicked the cook.
Junior's antisocial now
(According to the book).

Junior smashed the clock and lamp,
Junior hacked the tree.
(Destructive trends are treated
In chapters 2 and 3.)

Junior threw his milk at Mom,
Junior screamed for more.
(Notes of self-assertiveness
Are found in chapter 4.)

Junior tossed his shoes and socks
Out into the rain.
(Negation, that, and normal—
Disregard the stain).

Junior got in Grandpop's room,
Tore up his fishing line.
That's to gain attention
(See page 89).

Grandpop seized a slipper and
Yanked Junior 'cross his knee.
(Grandpop hasn't read a book
Since 1923).[1]

Dear ol' Grandpop. He may have been a little old-fashioned in his ideas, but he certainly knew how to handle Junior. So did most members of his generation. Moms and dads long before 1923 would never have put up with rebellious behavior from strong-willed children. Nor would they have been permitted to defy their elders or harass other members of the family. Drug usage and early sexual behavior would have brought the roof down on the kids who tried them. Unfortunately, in their zeal to make children behave properly, Victorian parents had a tendency to be *too* tough, *too* intimidating, and *too* punitive. Many of them were downright oppressive to vulnerable little kids who were doing nothing more than being childish.

I wish I could say that we in the twenty-first century are more enlightened and less likely to harm our children than our forebears, but it is not true. Growing up is a dangerous venture for millions of little people around the world who are suffering untold miseries at the hands of those who should be protecting and nurturing them.

No subject distresses me more than the tragedy of child abuse, which is depressingly common today. It is probable that a youngster living within a mile or two of your house is experiencing physical or emotional abuse in one form or another. It occurs in both poor and affluent homes, although the incidence is higher in inner-city neighborhoods. There and elsewhere, parents who are addicted to alcohol and illegal drugs are most likely to hurt or neglect kids.

During my years as a professor of pediatrics at a medical school, there was a steady stream of boys and girls who had been burned, bruised, and broken who were brought into our emergency hospital. Their little minds were warped by the awful circumstances of their lives. The incidence of abuse is even greater today. One of the common traumas seen in children's hospitals everywhere occurs when angry parents jerk boys and girls up by their arms, dislocating shoulders or elbows.

Diseased children sometimes suffer terribly, of course, but most of them experience some measure of emotional support to help them cope with their circumstances. For many of those boys and girls who have been beaten by a relative, however, there is no one to care, no one who understands. There is no one to whom he or she can go to express their longings and fears. They cannot escape. They cannot explain why they are hated. And many of them are too young to even call for help.

One such tragedy involved a six-year-old girl named Elisa Izquierdo, who was found dead in a lower Manhattan housing project in 1995.[2] Rescue workers discovered deep-red blotches, either welts or cigarette burns, over her entire body. There were enormous bruises near her kidney, on her face, and around her temples. Her genitals had been damaged severely, and the bone in her right pinkie finger jutted through the skin. Michael Brown, one of the fire fighters who tried to revive Elisa, said, "In my twenty-two years of service . . . this is the worst case of child abuse I have ever seen."[3] Elisa's mother, a crack-cocaine addict, admitted to making the little girl sleep in her own urine and feces and to hitting Elisa so hard that she flew headfirst into a concrete wall, permanently crippling her. In addition, she slid snakes down her daughter's throat to "exorcise" demons, held her upside down and used her curly hair as a mop, and used a hairbrush to damage the helpless little girl's genitals.[4]

In another case, a father killed his three-year-old son in order to win back his girlfriend. The man taped a garbage bag over the boy's head and sealed his mouth with duct tape. The father said the boy was crying when he left him, but he went ahead and drove away anyway.[5]

Obviously, these are extreme cases of physical abuse that horrify us all. But emotional neglect and rejection can also leave deep scars and wounds on the mind and body of children, sometimes resulting in physical symptoms decades later. In 1997, researchers at Harvard University, Drs. Linda Russek and Gary Schwartz, released a study revealing that children who perceive a lack of parental warmth and closeness early in life faced health problems later in life.[6] The forty-year study found that 91 percent of college men who reported a lack of closeness with their mothers had a greater risk of developing coronary heart disease, duodenal ulcers, high blood pressure, or alcoholism.[7] By contrast, the study found that only

45 percent of those surveyed who felt that they did have a close relationship with their mothers had suffered from one of these ailments.[8] Russek and Schwartz found a similar association between lack of closeness with a father and later health problems. They concluded:

> The effects of feelings of warmth and closeness appear to be addictive. . . . Since parents are usually the meaningful source of social support in early life, the perception of parental love and caring may have important biological and psychological health and illness implications throughout life.[9]

Other studies have also demonstrated a link between family stress and a number of physical problems. For example, an investigation reported in *Archives of Disease in Childhood* linked stress with slow growth in children.[10] The researchers found that "a total of 31.1 percent of children who had experienced family conflict were of short stature compared with 20.2 percent of those who had not."[11] They hypothesized that "stress reduces the release of growth hormones and increases the secretion of stress hormones (glucocorticoids), which can then damage the [brain] hippocampus" and interfere with the brain's learning and memory functions.[12]

These and other studies offer strong evidence that the foundation laid during childhood can affect a person throughout his or her adult life.

Given the delicate relationship between parents and their children and the rising incidence of physical and emotional assaults on boys and girls, the last thing I want to do is to provide a rationalization or justification for anything that could hurt them. Let me say it once more: I don't believe in harsh, oppressive, demeaning discipline, even when it is well-intentioned. Such destructive parenting is antithetical to everything I believe and stand for. At the risk of sounding self-serving, let me say that among the honors and awards I have received through the years, the one I value most is a bronze statue of a small boy and girl. The arm of one of the children is outstretched as though reaching for the loving hand of an adult. The inscription on the base of the statue, given by an organization dedicated to the prevention of child abuse, designated me as "The Children's Friend" in that year.

Considering this lifelong commitment to the welfare of children, why would I recommend corporal punishment as a management tool? It is a very good question, especially in view of the many articles and editorials appearing in the media these days that resoundingly condemn its use. Convincing the public that corporal punishment is universally harmful has become an unrelenting crusade within certain elements of the liberal media. I believe their efforts have been terribly misguided.

I would be quick to acknowledge that corporal punishment *can* be harmful when used wrongly. It *is* possible . . . even easy . . . to create an aggressive child who has observed violent episodes at home. If he is routinely beaten by parents, or if he witnesses physical violence between angry adults, the child will not fail to notice how the game is played. Thus, corporal punishment that is not administered according to very carefully thought-out guidelines has the potential to become dangerous. Parenthood does not give the right to slap and intimidate a child because Dad had a bad day or Mom is in a lousy mood. It is this kind of unjust discipline that causes some well-meaning authorities to reject corporal punishment altogether.

Just because a useful technique can be used wrongly, however, is no reason to reject it altogether. Many children desperately need this resolution to their disobedience. In those situations when the child fully understands what he is being asked to do or not to do but refuses to yield to adult leadership, an appropriate spanking is the shortest and most effective route to an attitude adjustment. When he lowers his head, clenches his fists, and makes it clear he is going for broke, justice must speak swiftly and eloquently. This response does not create aggression in children, but it does help them control their impulses and live in harmony with various forms of benevolent authority throughout life.

There is another reason I believe the proper use of corporal punishment is in the best interest of children. Strong-willed boys and girls can be terribly irritating to their parents, as we all know. Most of them have figured out how to press all the right (or wrong) buttons to make their moms and dads absolutely furious. One father said that nothing in his adult experience could make him more angry than the rebellious behavior of his ten-year-old son, day after day. Given that kind of volatile interaction, I am convinced that a determined, hard-nosed kid in the hands of an immature or emotionally unstable parent is a recipe for disaster. The likelihood of physical damage to that youngster is enormous, and it becomes even greater if the parents have been stripped of the ability to control challenging behavior before it gets out of hand.

When permissive advice-givers convince moms and dads that they can, and must, manage their children by talking and reasoning during nose-to-nose confrontations, the parents get more and more frustrated as the misbehavior intensifies. Eventually, too many of them blow up, and when they do, anything can happen. I am convinced that child abuse often emerges from that scenario in one way or another. How much better, and safer, it is for moms and dads to administer a judicious and carefully measured spanking to a child (or even a well-timed swat or two), before she and her parents are both out of control. It is even more advantageous for a savvy strong-willed child to know that spanking is an option, leading him to back off before he goes too far. By depriving parents of this possibility, the well-meaning counselors and psychologists inadvertently set up tough-minded kids for disaster at home.

The recommendations that I offer in this book, therefore, are intended not only to help moms and dads raise their children properly. I also seek to protect children from harm. Firm discipline, when administered with love, helps provide that protection.

Here's an example of corporal punishment administered correctly and with the desired result. It was relayed to me by a father, William Jarnagin, a certified public accountant, who wrote me the following letter. It speaks volumes about the proper approach to parent-child relationships:

Dear Dr. Dobson:

This is a note of thanks for your work in strengthening the American family. My wife and I have recently read four of your books and we have profited very much from them.

Please permit me to relate a recent experience with our six-year-old son, David. Last Friday night, my wife, Becky, told him to pick up some orange peelings he had left on the carpet, which he knows is a "no-no." He failed to respond, and as a result received one slap on his behind, whereupon he began an obviously defiant temper tantrum.

Since I had observed the whole episode, I then called for my paddle and applied it appropriately, saw to it that he picked up and properly disposed of the orange peelings, and sent him straight to bed, since it was already past his bedtime. After a few minutes, when his emotions had had a chance to settle down, I went to his room and explained that God had instructed all parents who truly love their children to properly discipline them, etc., and that we truly love him and therefore would not permit such defiant behavior.

The next morning, after I had gone to work, David presented his mother with the following letter, together with a little stack of ten pennies:

> From David and Deborah
> To Mom and Dad
> Ross Dr. 3d house
> Sellmer, Tennasse
> 39718
> Dear Mom and Dad
> here is 10 Cints for
> Pattelling me when I
> really neded and that
> gos for Deborah to I
> love you
> Love yur son David
> and yur Doter Deborah

Oh, incidentally, Deborah is our one-year-old daughter whose adoption should be final sometime in June.

Keep up your good work and may God bless you.

Sincerely,

William H. Jarnagin

Mr. William Jarnagin understands the appropriate response of a father to a child's defiance. It is neither harsh nor insulting nor dangerous nor whimsical. Rather, it represents the firm but loving discipline that is required for the best interest of the child. How fortunate is the boy or girl whose father and mother still comprehend that timeless concept.

If you have read my earlier books offering child-rearing advice, including *The New Dare to Discipline,* you may be aware that I have addressed this subject of corporal punishment extensively for many years.[13] Rather than repeating those other recommendations and explanations, I would like to devote the rest of this chapter to a very thorough article written by two noted physicians, Den A. Trumbull, M.D., and S. DuBose Ravenel, M.D.

It was actually intended for physicians and was published in Focus on the Family's *Physician* magazine.[14] This informative review, provided below, summarizes current research and answers eight often-heard arguments against corporal punishment.

TO SPANK OR NOT TO SPANK

A look at an age-old question that baffles many physicians

—

BY DEN A. TRUMBULL, M.D., AND S. DUBOSE RAVENEL, M.D.

Primary-care physicians advise parents on many child-rearing issues. On the list of the most difficult is the issue of disciplinary spanking. Despite years of traditional acceptance, professional societies, including the American Academy of Pediatrics (AAP), have recently suggested that spanking can be harmful to children. In a surprising move recently, however, the AAP released a special report that suggests spanking may not be harmful to a child's health. In a supplement to the October 1996 *Pediatrics*, the cochairpersons, Drs. Stanford Friedman and Kenneth Schonberg of the Albert Einstein College of Medicine, summarized the findings of an AAP-sponsored conference last year that was devoted to reviewing the research on spanking. "Given a relatively 'healthy' family life in a supportive environment, spanking in and of itself is not detrimental to a child or predictive of later problems," they report.

The AAP's findings recognize what many physicians have believed for years and what John Lyons of the Northwestern University School of Medicine found in his research review: Studies demonstrate beneficial, not detrimental, effects of spanking. These findings, however, do not change the fact that opposition to parents spanking their children has been growing in elite circles of society over the past 15 years. No doubt much of this opposition springs from a sincere concern for the well-being of children. Child abuse is a reality, and stories of such abuse are horrifying. But while loving and effective discipline is not harsh and abusive, neither should it be weak and ineffectual. Indeed, disciplinary spanking can fall within the boundaries of loving discipline and need not be labeled abusive.

Or so most Americans seem to think. According to a recent Voter/ Consumer Research poll commissioned by the Family Research Council, 76 percent of the more than 1,000 Americans surveyed said that spanking was an effective form of discipline in their home when they were children. These results are made more impressive by the fact that nearly half of those who answered otherwise grew up in homes in which they were never spanked. Taken together, more than four out of five Americans who as children were spanked by their parents say that it was effective discipline.

Some critics claim that spanking a child is abusive and contributes to adult dysfunction. These allegations arise from studies that fail to distinguish appropriate spanking from other forms of punishment.

Abusive forms of physical punishment such as kicking, punching, and beating are commonly grouped with mild spanking. Furthermore, the studies usually include, and even emphasize, corporal punishment of adolescents rather than focusing on preschool children, where spanking is more appropriate and effective. This blurring of distinctions between spanking and physical abuse, and between children of different ages, gives critics the illusion of having data condemning all disciplinary spanking.

There are several arguments commonly leveled against disciplinary spanking. Ironically, most of these arguments can be used against other forms of discipline. Any form of discipline (time-out, restriction, etc.), when used inappropriately and in anger, can distort a child's perception of justice and harm his emotional development. In light of this, let us examine some of the unfounded arguments promoted by spanking opponents.

ARGUMENT 1: Many psychological studies show that spanking is an improper form of discipline.

COUNTERPOINT: Researchers John Lyons, Rachel Anderson, and David Larson, M.D., of the National Institute of Healthcare Research in 1993 conducted a systematic review of the research literature on corporal punishment. They found that 83 percent of the 132 identified articles published in clinical and psychosocial journals were opinion-driven editorials, reviews, or commentaries devoid of new empirical findings. Moreover, most of the empirical studies were methodologically flawed by grouping the impact of abuse with spanking. The best studies demonstrated beneficial, not detrimental, effects of spanking in certain situations. Building upon this review, Dr. Robert E. Larzelere published an exhaustive review of the corporal punishment literature in the October 1996 supplement to *Pediatrics*. He also found insufficient data to condemn the use of spanking by parents.

ARGUMENT 2: Physical punishment establishes the moral righteousness of hitting other persons who do something that is wrong.

COUNTERPOINT: The "spanking teaches hitting" belief has gained in popularity over the past decade but is not supported by objective evidence. A distinction must be made between abusive hitting and nonabusive spanking. A child's ability to discriminate hitting from disciplinary spanking depends largely upon the parent's attitude toward spanking and the parent's procedure for spanking. There is no evidence in the medical literature that a mild spank to the buttocks of a disobedient child by a loving parent teaches the child aggressive behavior.

The critical issue is how spanking (or, in fact, any punishment) is used, more so than whether it is used. Physical abuse by an angry, uncontrolled parent will leave lasting emotional wounds and cultivate bitterness in a child. The balanced, prudent use of disciplinary spanking, however, is a deterrent to aggressive behavior with some children. Researchers at the Center for Family Research at Iowa State University studied 332 families to examine both the impact of corporal punishment and the quality of parental involvement on three adolescent outcomes—aggressiveness, delinquency, and psychological well-being. The researchers found a strong association between the quality of parenting and each of these three outcomes. Corporal punishment, however, was not adversely related to any of these outcomes. This study proves that quality of parenting is the chief determinant of favorable or unfavorable outcomes.

According to a study by Dan Olweus reported in *Developmental Psychology* in 1980, childhood aggressiveness is actually more closely linked to maternal permissiveness and negative criticism than to even abusive physical discipline.

It is unrealistic to expect that children would never hit others if their parents would only exclude spanking from their disciplinary options. Most toddlers (long before they are ever spanked) naturally attempt to hit others when conflict or frustration arises. The continuation of this behavior is largely determined by how the parent or caregiver responds. If correctly disciplined, the hitting will become less frequent. If ignored or ineffectively disciplined, the hitting will likely persist and even escalate. Thus, instead of contributing to greater violence, spanking can be a useful component in an overall plan to effectively teach a child to stop aggressive hitting.

ARGUMENT 3: Since parents often refrain from hitting until their anger or frustration reaches a certain point, the child learns that anger and frustration justify the use of physical force.

COUNTERPOINT: A 1995 study published in *Pediatrics* indicates that most parents who spank do not spank on impulse but purposefully spank their children with a belief in its effectiveness. Furthermore, the study revealed no significant correlation between the frequency of spanking and the anger reported by mothers. Actually, the mothers who reported being angry were not the same parents who spanked.

Reactive, impulsive hitting after losing control due to anger is unquestionably the wrong way for a parent to use corporal punishment. Eliminating all physical punishment in the home, however, would not remedy such explosive scenarios. It could even increase the problem.

When effective spanking is removed from a parent's disciplinary repertoire, he or she is left with nagging, begging, belittling, and yelling as soon as the primary disciplinary measures, such as time-out and logical consequences, have failed. By contrast, if proper spanking is proactively used in conjunction with other disciplinary measures, better control of the particularly defiant child can be achieved and moments of exasperation are less likely to occur.

ARGUMENT 4: Physical punishment is harmful to a child.

COUNTERPOINT: Any disciplinary measure—physical, verbal or emotional—can harm a child when carried to an extreme. Excessive scolding and berating of a child by a parent is emotionally harmful. Excessive use of isolation (time-out) for unreasonable periods of time can humiliate a child and ruin the measure's effectiveness.

Obviously, excessive or indiscriminate physical punishment is harmful and abusive. An appropriately administered spanking of a forewarned, disobedient child, however, is not harmful when administered in a loving, controlled manner.

Without the prudent use of spanking for the defiant child, a parent risks being inconsistent and rationalizing the child's behavior. This inconsistent manner of parenting is confusing and harmful to the child and is damaging to the parentchild relationship. There is insufficient evidence that proper disciplinary spanking is harmful to the child.

DISCIPLINE: Training that corrects, molds or perfects moral character.

Discipline (regardless of the method) is effective only when it involves

- truth brought forth in love;
- confession by the guilty party;
- forgiveness by the parent who is responsible for the discipline;
- resolution for the original problem; and
- assurance of continuity of love.

ARGUMENT 5: Spanking teaches a child that "might makes right," that power and strength are most important, and that the bigger can force their will upon the smaller.

COUNTERPOINT: Parental power is commonly exerted in routine child rearing, and spanking is only one example. Other situations where power and restraint are exercised by the average parent include:

- the young child who insists on running from his parent in a busy mall or parking lot
- the toddler who refuses to sit in his car seat
- the young patient who refuses to hold still as a vaccination is administered or as a laceration is repaired

Control over the child is necessary at times to ensure safety, health, and proper behavior. Classic child-rearing studies have shown that some degree of power assertion and control is essential for optimal child rearing. When power is exerted in the context of love and for the child's benefit, the child will not perceive it as bullying or demeaning.

ARGUMENT 6: Spanking is an ineffective solution to misbehavior.
COUNTERPOINT: Though the specific use of appropriate spanking has rarely been studied, there is evidence of its short-term and long-term effectiveness. When combined with reasoning, the use of negative consequences (including spanking) has been shown to decrease the recurrence of misbehavior with preschool children.

In clinical field trials where parental spanking has been studied, it has consistently been found to reduce the subsequent frequency of noncompliance with time-out. Spanking as an enforcement of time-out is a component of several well-researched parent-training programs and popular parenting texts.

Dr. Diana Baumrind of the Institute of Human Development at the University of California–Berkeley conducted a decade-long study of families with children three to nine years old. Baumrind found that parents employing a balanced disciplinary style of firm control (including spanking) and positive encouragement experienced the most favorable outcome in their children. Parents taking extreme approaches to discipline (authoritarian types using excessive punishment with less encouragement or permissive types using little punishment and no spanking) were less successful.

Baumrind concluded that evidence from this study "did not indicate that negative reinforcement or corporal punishment per se were harmful or ineffective procedures, but rather the total patterns of parental control determined the effects on the child of these procedures."

This approach of balanced, authoritative parenting employing the occasional use of spanking is advocated by several child-rearing experts. In the hands of loving parents, a spanking to the buttocks of a defiant toddler in appropriate settings is a powerful motivator to correct behavior and an effective deterrent to disobedience.

ARGUMENT 7: Spanking leads a parent to use harmful forms of corporal punishment that lead to physical child abuse.
COUNTERPOINT: The abuse potential when loving parents use appropriate disciplinary spanking is very low. Since parents have a natural affection for their children, they are more prone to underuse spanking than overuse it. Both empirical data and professional opinion oppose any causal relationship between spanking and child abuse.

Surveys indicate that 70 percent to 90 percent of parents of preschoolers use spanking, yet the incidence of physical child abuse in America is about 5 percent. Statistically, the two practices are far apart. Furthermore, according to the National Committee to Prevent Child Abuse, over the past decade reports of child abuse have steadily risen while approval for parental spanking has steadily declined.

Teaching parents appropriate spanking may actually reduce child abuse, according to Dr. Robert E. Larzelere in his review article on corporal punishment published in 1994 in *Debating Children's Lives*. Parents who are ill-equipped to control their child's behavior, or those who take a more permissive approach (refusing to use spanking), may be more prone to explosive attacks on their child, according to research.

Parental child abuse is an interactive process involving parental competence, parental and child temperaments, and situational demands. Abusive parents are more angry, depressed, and impulsive, and emphasize punishment as the predominant means of discipline. Abused children are more aggressive and less compliant than children from nonabusive families. There is less interaction between family members in abusive families, and an abusive mother displays more negative than positive behavior. The etiology of abusive parenting is multifactorial and cannot be simply explained by a parent's use of spanking.

In a reply to spanking opposition in a 1995 issue of *Pediatrics*, Drs. Lawrence S. Wissow and Debra Roter of the Johns Hopkins University's pediatrics department acknowledge that a definitive link between spanking and child abuse has yet to be established.

Finally, the Swedish experiment to reduce child abuse by banning spanking seems to be failing. In 1980, one year after this ban was adopted, the rate of child beatings was twice that of the United States. According to a 1995 report from the government organization Statistics Sweden, police reports of child abuse by family members rose fourfold from 1984 to 1994, while reports of teen violence increased nearly sixfold.

Most experts agree that spanking and child abuse are not on the same continuum but are very different entities. With parenting, it is the "user" and how a measure is used much more than the measure used that determine the outcome of the disciplinary effort. Clearly, spanking can be safely used in the discipline of young children with an excellent outcome. The proper use of spanking may actually reduce a parent's risk of abusing the child.

ARGUMENT 8: Spanking is never necessary.

COUNTERPOINT: All children need a combination of encouragement and correction as they are reared to become socially responsible individuals. In order for correction to deter disobedient behavior, the consequence imposed upon the child must outweigh the pleasure of the disobedient act. For very compliant children, milder forms of correction will suffice, and spanking may never be necessary. For more defiant children who refuse to comply with or be persuaded by milder consequences such as time-out, spanking is useful, effective, and appropriate.

Summary
Disciplinary spanking should be evaluated from a factual, objective perspective. It must be distinguished from abusive, harmful forms of corporal punishment. Appropriate disciplinary spanking can play an important role in optimal child development and has been found in prospective studies to be a part of the parenting style associated with the best outcomes. There is no convincing evidence that mild spanking is harmful. Indeed, spanking is supported by history, research and a majority of primary care physicians.[15]

Many thanks to Drs. Trumbull and Ravenel for allowing us to reprint this enlightening article. Both men are board-certified pediatricians in private practice and members of the Section on Developmental and Behavior Pediatrics of the American Academy of Pediatrics.

I'll conclude by sharing a related "Parent's Guide," also written by Dr. Trumbull. It offers nine specific guidelines on the use of disciplinary spanking.

PARENT'S GUIDE
Guidelines to Disciplinary Spanking

If your child is unruly, and you're at your wit's end, take a break and consider these guidelines before you spank your child.

1. Spanking should be used selectively for clear, deliberate misbehavior, particularly that which arises from a child's persistent defiance of a parent's instruction. It should be used only when the child receives at least as much encouragement and praise for good behavior as correction for problem behavior.
2. Milder forms of discipline, such as verbal correction, time-out and logical consequences, should be used initially, followed by spanking

when noncompliance persists. Spanking has shown to be an effective method of enforcing time-out with the child who refuses to comply.

3. Only a parent (or in exceptional situations, someone else who has an intimate relationship of authority with the child) should administer a spanking.

4. Spanking should not be administered on impulse or when a parent is out of control. A spanking should always be motivated by love for the purpose of teaching and correcting, never for revenge.

5. Spanking is inappropriate before 15 months of age and is usually not necessary until after 18 months. It should be less necessary after 6 years, and rarely, if ever, used after 10 years of age.

6. After 10 months of age, one slap to the hand of a stubborn crawler or toddler may be necessary to stop serious misbehavior when distraction and removal have failed. This is particularly the case when the forbidden object is immovable and dangerous, such as a hot oven door or an electrical outlet.

7. Spanking should always be a planned action, not a reaction, by the parent and should follow a deliberate procedure.

- The child should be forewarned of the spanking for designated problem behaviors.
- Spanking should always be administered in private (bedroom or restroom) to avoid public humiliation or embarrassment.
- One or two spanks should be administered to the buttocks. This is followed by embracing the child and calmly reviewing the offense and the desired behavior in an effort to reestablish a warm relationship.

8. Spanking should leave only transient redness of the skin and should never cause physical injury.

9. If properly administered spankings are ineffective, other appropriate disciplinary responses should be tried, or the parent should seek professional help. A parent should never increase the intensity of spankings.[16]

Questions & Answers

Q: I have to fight with my nine-year-old daughter to get her to do *anything* she doesn't want to do. It's so unpleasant that I've about decided not to take her on. Why should I try to force her to work and help around the house? What's the downside of my just going with the flow and letting her off the hook?

A: It is typical for nine-year-olds to not want to work, of course, but they still need to. If you permit a pattern of irresponsibility to prevail in your child's formative years, she may fall behind in her developmental timetable leading toward the full responsibilities of adult living. As a ten-year-old, she won't be able to do anything unpleasant since she has never been required to stay with a task until it is completed. She won't know how to give to anyone else because she's thought only of herself. She'll find it hard to make decisions or control her own impulses. A few years from now, she will steamroll into adolescence and then adulthood completely unprepared for the freedom and obligations she will find there. Your daughter will have had precious little training for those pressing responsibilities of maturity.

Obviously, I've painted a worst-case scenario with regard to your daughter. You still have plenty of opportunity to help her avoid such an outcome. I just hope your desire for harmony doesn't lead you to do what will be harmful to her in later years.

Q: We have an adopted girl who came to us when she was four years old. She is very difficult to handle and does pretty much what she pleases. For us to make her obey would be very unpleasant for her, and frankly we don't feel we have the right to do that. She has been through a lot in her short life. Besides, we're not her real parents. Do you think she'll be okay if we just give her a lot of love and attention?

A: I'm afraid what you have is a formula for serious problems with this girl later on. The danger is in seeing yourselves as substitute or stand-in parents who don't have the right to lead her. That is a mistake. Since you have legally adopted this child, you *are* her "real" parents, and your failure to see yourselves that way may be setting up the defiant behavior you mentioned. It is a common error made by parents of older adopted children. They pity their youngsters too much to confront them. They feel that life has already been too hard on them, and they must not make things worse by discipline and occasional punishment. As a result, they are tentative and permissive with a child who is crying out for leadership.

Transplanted children have the same need for guidance and discipline as those remaining with their biological parents. One of the surest ways to make them feel insecure is to treat them like they are different, unusual, or brittle. If the parents view such a child as an unfortunate waif to be shielded, he will tend to see himself that way too.

Parents of sick and disabled children often make this same mistake. They find discipline harder to implement because of the tenderness they feel for the child. Thus, a boy or girl with a heart condition or a terminal illness can become a little terror, simply because the usual behavioral boundaries are not established and defended. It must be remembered that the need to be led and governed is almost universal in childhood, and it isn't lessened by other problems and difficulties in life. In some cases, the desire for boundaries is actually increased by other troubles, for it is through loving control that parents build security and a sense of personal worth in a child.

Returning to the question, I advise you to love that little girl like crazy—and hold her to the same standards of behavior that you would your own flesh and blood. Remember, you *are* her parents!

Q: There is a child living near us who is not being harmed physically, but her parents are destroying her emotionally. You can't believe the screams and accusations that come from their house. So far, Child Protective Services has not intervened to rescue the little girl. Isn't it illegal to berate a child like this?
A: It is illegal in most states to abuse a child emotionally, but bad parenting can be difficult to define. Unfortunately, it is not illegal to raise a boy or girl without love unless neglect can be documented. It is usually not illegal to humiliate a child either. These forms of rejection may be even more harmful than some forms of physical abuse, but they are tougher to prove and are often not prosecutable. When emotional abuse occurs, as with the girl who lives near you, there may be no way to rescue her from this tragic situation. Nevertheless, I would report the incident to Child Protective Services and hope for intervention.

Q: What advice would you give parents who recognize a tendency within themselves to abuse their kids? Maybe they're afraid they'll get carried away when spanking a disobedient child. Do you think they should avoid corporal punishment as a form of discipline?

A: That's exactly what I think. Anyone who has ever abused a child— or has ever felt herself losing control during a spanking—should not put herself in such a situation. Anyone who has a violent temper that at times becomes unmanageable should not use that approach. Anyone who secretly enjoys the administration of corporal punishment should not be the one to implement it. And grandparents ("Grandpop" from the poem in chapter 8 included) probably should not spank their grandkids, unless the parents have given them permission to do so.

Q: Do you think you should spank a child for every act of disobedience or defiance?
A: Certainly not. Corporal punishment should be a rather infrequent occurrence. There is an appropriate time for a child to sit in a chair to think about his misbehavior, or he might be deprived of a privilege, sent to his room for a time-out, or made to work when he had planned to play. In other words, you should vary your response to misbehavior, always trying to stay one step ahead of the child. Your goal is to continually react in a way that benefits the child and is in accordance with his "crime." In this regard, there is no substitute for wisdom and tact in the parenting role.

Q: On what part of the body would you administer a spanking?
A: It should be confined to the buttocks area, where permanent damage is very unlikely. I don't believe you should slap a child on the face or jerk him around by the arm. If you spank a child only on the behind, you will be less likely to inflict any physical injury on him.

Q: How long do you think a child should be allowed to cry after being punished or spanked? Is there a limit?
A: Yes, I believe there should be a limit. As long as the tears represent a genuine release of emotion, they should be permitted to fall. But crying can quickly change from inner sobbing to an expression of protest aimed at punishing the enemy. Real crying usually lasts two minutes or less but may continue for five. After that point, the child is merely complaining, and the change can be recognized in the tone and intensity of his voice. I would require him to stop the protest crying, usually by offering him a little more of whatever caused the original tears. In younger children, crying can easily be stopped by getting them interested in something else.

Q: There is some controversy over whether a parent should spank with his or her hand or with some other object, such as a belt or a paddle. What do you recommend?

A: I recommend a neutral object of some type. For those who disagree on this point, I'd encourage them to do what seems right. It is not a critical issue to me. The reason I suggest a switch (a small, flexible twig from a tree) or paddle is because the hand should be seen as an object of love—to hold, hug, pat, and caress. If you're used to suddenly disciplining with the hand, your child may not know when she's about to be swatted and can develop a pattern of flinching when you make an unexpected move. This is not a problem if you take the time to use a neutral object.

My mother always used a small switch, which could not do any permanent damage. But it stung enough to send a very clear message. One day when I had pushed her to the limit, she actually sent me to the backyard to cut my own instrument of punishment. I brought back a tiny little twig about seven inches long. She could not have generated anything more than a tickle with it. Mom never sent me on that fool's errand again.

Q: Is there an age when spankings can begin?

A: There is no excuse for spanking babies or children younger than fifteen to eighteen months of age. Shaking an infant can cause brain damage and even death! But midway through the second year (eighteen months), boys and girls become capable of understanding what you're telling them to do or not do. They can then very gently be held responsible for how they behave. Suppose a strong-willed child is reaching for an electric socket or something that will hurt him. You say, "No!" but he just looks at you and continues reaching toward it. You can see the mischievous smile on his face as he thinks, *I'm going to do it anyway!* I'd encourage you to speak firmly so that he knows he is pushing the limit. If he persists, slap his fingers just enough to sting. A small amount of pain goes a long way at that age and begins to introduce to the child the reality of the physical world and the importance of listening to what you say.

Through the next eighteen months, gradually establish yourself as a benevolent boss: mean what you say and say what you mean. Contrary to what you may have read in popular literature, this firm but loving approach to child rearing will *not* harm a toddler or make him violent. On the contrary, it is most likely to produce a healthy, confident child.

Q: I have spanked my children for their disobedience, and it didn't seem to help. Does this approach fail with some children?
A: Children are so tremendously variable that it is sometimes hard to believe that they are all members of the same human family. Some kids can be crushed with nothing more than a stern look; others seem to require strong and even painful disciplinary measures to make a vivid impression. This difference usually results from the degree to which a child needs adult approval and acceptance. The primary parental task is to see things as the child perceives them, thereby tailoring the discipline to the child's unique needs. Accordingly, it is appropriate to punish a boy or girl when he or she knows it is deserved.

In a direct answer to your question, disciplinary measures usually fail because of fundamental errors in their application. It is possible for twice the amount of punishment to yield half the results. I have made a study of situations in which parents have told me that their children disregard punishment and continue to misbehave. There are four basic reasons for this lack of success:

1. The most common error is whimsical discipline. When the rules change every day and when punishment for misbehavior is capricious and inconsistent, the effort to change behavior is undermined. There is no inevitable consequence to be anticipated. This entices children to see if they can beat the system. In society at large, it also encourages criminal behavior among those who believe they will not face the bar of justice.

2. Sometimes a child is more strong-willed than his parent—and they both know it. He just might be tough enough to realize that a confrontation with his mom or dad is really a struggle of wills. If he can withstand the pressure and not buckle during a major battle, he can eliminate that form of punishment as a tool in the parent's repertoire. Does he think through this process on a conscious level? Usually not, but he understands it intuitively. He realizes that a spanking *must not* be allowed to succeed. Thus, he stiffens his little neck and guts it out. He may even refuse to cry and may say, "That didn't hurt." The parent concludes in exasperation, "Spanking doesn't work for my child."

3. The spanking may be too gentle. If it doesn't hurt, it doesn't

motivate a child to avoid the consequence next time. A slap with the hand on the bottom of a diapered two-year-old is not a deterrent to anything. Be sure the child gets the message—while being careful not to go too far.

4. For a few children, spankings are simply not effective. A child who has attention deficit/hyperactivity disorder (ADHD), for example, may be even more wild and unmanageable after corporal punishment. Also, a child who has been abused may identify loving discipline with past abuse. Finally, the very sensitive child might need a different approach. Let me emphasize once more that children are unique. The only way to raise them correctly is to understand each boy or girl as an individual and design parenting techniques to fit the needs and characteristics of that particular child.

Q: Do you think corporal punishment eventually will be outlawed?
A: I don't doubt that an effort will be made to end it. In fact, an attempt to outlaw corporal punishment was made in California in 1982, until the politicians were told by parents to back off.[17] The tragedy of child abuse has made it difficult for people to understand the difference between viciousness to kids and constructive, positive forms of punishment. Also, there are many "children's-rights advocates" in the Western world who will not rest until they have obtained the legal right to tell parents how to raise their children. In Sweden, corporal punishment and other forms of discipline are already prohibited by law.[18] Canadian courts have flirted with the same decision but ruled otherwise.[19] The American media has worked to convince the public that all spanking is tantamount to child abuse and therefore should be outlawed. If corporal punishment is banned, it will be a sad day for families, and especially for children!

NINE

BITTER BROTHERS & SURLY SISTERS

I F PARENTS WERE asked to indicate the most irritating feature of child rearing, I'm convinced that sibling rivalry would win hands down. It has the capacity of driving otherwise sane and self-controlled adults a little crazy. Children are not content just to hate each other in private. They attack one another like miniature warriors, mobilizing their troops and probing for a weakness in the defensive line. They argue, hit, kick, scream, grab, taunt, tattle, and sabotage the opposing forces. I knew one child who deeply resented being sick with a cold while his older sibling was healthy, so he secretly blew his nose on the mouthpiece of his brother's clarinet! The big losers from such combat, of course, are the harassed parents who must listen to the noise of the battlefield and then try to patch up the wounded.

Sibling rivalry is not new, of course. It was responsible for the first murder on record (when Cain killed Abel) and has been present in virtually every home with more than one child from that time to this. The underlying source of this conflict is old-fashioned jealousy and competition between children. An excellent illustration of this irritating situation was written by Willard and Marguerite Beecher in their book *Parents on the Run*. They wrote:

> It was once believed that if parents would explain to a child that he was having a little brother or sister, he would not resent it. He was told that his parents had enjoyed him so much that they wanted to increase their happiness. This was supposed to avoid jealous competition and rivalry. It did not work. Why should it? Needless to say, if a man tells his wife he has loved

361

her so much that he now plans to bring another wife into the home to "increase his happiness," she would not be immune to jealousy. On the contrary, the fight would just begin—in exactly the same fashion as it does with children.[1]

We can learn some valuable lessons about siblings and how they interact with one another from an elementary principle of physics: A hotter object nearby will gradually raise the temperature of a cooler one. Do you get the picture? A rebellious child usually makes the compliant youngster harder to handle. That is especially true if the strong-willed child is older. It is not unusual for parents to realize that their fun-loving, go-along-to-get-along boy or girl is starting to pick up the aggressive attitudes and behavior of the tougher brother or sister. In fact, every member of a family is influenced by a particularly difficult youngster, usually for the worse.

There is another factor that can be irritating and frustrating to moms and dads. Strong-willed and compliant kids often resent each other deeply. The tougher individuals dislike their prissy siblings who do everything right and are punished far less often. The easy children, on the other hand, get sick and tired of seeing the rebellious sib take on Mom or Dad and often come out the winner. The compliant children are also expected by them to "just take it" at times, because parents are weary of fighting with (and losing to) the rebellious youngster. The old adage that "the squeaky wheel gets the grease" applies here. Strong-willed kids tend to get away with more because they simply never give up and their parents become exasperated just trying to hang in there.

I described this interactive effect in my book *Parenting Isn't for Cowards,* especially as it relates to the health and well-being of the compliant child in the world of a strong-willed sibling. The compliant child "often has difficulties holding his own with his siblings, [and he] is more likely to internalize his anger and look for ways to reroute it."[2]

This represents a serious (but very quiet) threat to the well-being of the compliant child. My greatest concern for him is the ease with which he can be underestimated, ignored, exploited, or shortchanged at home. Haven't you seen two-child families where one youngster was a stick of dynamite who blew up regularly and the other was an all-star sweetheart? Under those circumstances it is not unusual for parents to take their cooperative sibling for granted. If there is an unpleasant job to be done, he will be expected to do it. Mom and Dad just don't have the energy to fight with the tiger.

If one child is to be chosen for a pleasant experience, it will probably go to the brattier of the two. He would scream bloody murder if excluded. When circumstances require one child to sacrifice or do without, you know who will be elected. Parents who favor the strong-willed child in this way are aware that they are being unfair, but their sense of justice has yielded to the pressures of practicality. They are simply too depleted and frustrated to risk irritating the tougher kid.

The consequences of such inequity should be obvious. Even though the compliant child goes along with the program and does not complain, he may accumulate a volume of resentment through the years. Isn't that what seems to have occurred to the brother of the Prodigal Son, as described by Jesus in Luke 15:11-32? He was the hardworking, responsible, compliant member of the family. Apparently, his kid brother was irresponsible, flighty, and very strong-willed. If we may be permitted to extrapolate a bit from the biblical account, it seems likely that there was little love lost between these brothers, even before the prodigal's impulsive departure.

The disciplined elder brother resented the spoiled brat who got everything he asked for. Nevertheless, the older brother kept his thoughts to himself. He would not want to upset his father, whom he respected enormously. Then came that incredible day when little brother demanded his entire inheritance in one lump sum. The compliant son overheard the conversation and gasped in shock. *What audacity!* he thought. Then, to his amazement he heard his father grant the playboy's request. He could hear the clink of numerous gold coins being counted. The elder brother was furious. We can only assume that the departure of this sibling meant Big Bud would have to handle double chores and work longer hours in the fields. It wasn't fair that the load should fall on him. Nevertheless, he said nothing. Compliant people are inclined to hold their feelings inside, but they are capable of harboring great resentment.

The years passed slowly as the elder brother labored to maintain the farm. The father had grown older by then, placing a heavier strain on this firstborn son. Every day he labored from dawn to dusk in the hot sun. Occasionally, he thought about his brother living it up in the far country, and he was briefly tempted. But, no. He would do what was right. Pleasing his father was the most important thing in his life.

Then, as we remember, the strong-willed goof-off ran out of money and became exceedingly hungry. He thought of his mom's cooking and the warmth of his father's fire. He clutched his rags around him and began the long journey home. When he was yet afar off, his father ran to meet him—embracing him and placing the royal robes around his shoulders. The fatted calf was killed and a great feast planned. That did it. The compliant brother could take no more. The Prodigal Son had secured through his folly what the elder brother could not gain through his discipline: the approval and affection of his father. His spirit was wounded!

Whether my interpretation of this parable is faithful to the meaning of the Scripture will be left to the theologians. Of this I am certain, however: Strong-willed and compliant siblings have played out this drama since the days of Cain and Abel, and the responsible brother or sister often feels like the loser. He holds his feelings inside and then pays a price for storing them. He is more susceptible as an adult to ulcers, hypertension, colitis, migraine headaches, and a wide range of other psychosomatic illnesses. Furthermore, his sense of utter powerlessness can drive his anger underground. It may emerge in less obvious quests for control.

It is not necessary or healthy to allow children to destroy each other and make life miserable for the adults around them. Sibling rivalry is difficult to cure, but it certainly can be treated. Toward that end, let me offer three suggestions that should be helpful in achieving at least a state of armed neutrality at home.

1. Don't inflame the natural jealousy of children

Sibling rivalry is a virtual inevitability, especially between strong-willed kids, but at least Mom and Dad should seek to avoid the situations that make it worse. One of these red flags is comparing children unfavorably with each other, since they are always looking for a competitive edge. The question in a child's mind is not, "How am I doing?" it is, "How am I doing compared with Mike [or Blake or Sarah]?" The issue is not how fast a child can run, but who crosses the finish line first. A boy does not care how tall he is; he is vitally interested in who is tallest. Children systematically measure themselves against their peers on everything from skateboarding ability to who has the most friends. Both sexes are especially sensitive to any failure that occurs and is talked about openly within their own family. Accordingly, parents who want a little peace at home should guard against comparative comments that routinely favor one child over another. To violate this principle is to set up even greater rivalry between them.

Perhaps an illustration will help make the case. When I was about ten years old, I loved to play with a couple of dogs that belonged to two families in the neighborhood. One was a pug bulldog mix with a very bad attitude and a low dog IQ. His one big trick was that he was crazy about chasing and retrieving tennis balls. The other dog was a sweet, passive Scottie named Baby. He didn't have any tricks at all, except to bark from morning to night. One day as I was tossing the ball for the bulldog, it occurred to me that it might be interesting to throw it in the direction of Baby. That turned out to be a very dumb idea. The ball rolled under the Scottie with the grouch in hot pursuit. The bulldog went straight for Baby's throat and hung on. It was an awful scene. Neighbors came running from everywhere as the Scottie screamed in terror. It took ten minutes and a garden hose for the adults to pry loose the bulldog's grip. By then Baby was almost dead. He spent two weeks in the animal hospital, and I spent two weeks in the doghouse. I was hated by the entire town.

I have thought about that experience many times and have since recognized its application to most human relationships. Indeed, it is just as simple to precipitate a fight between people as it is between dogs. All that is necessary is to toss a ball, symbolically, in the direction of one of the rivals and then step back and watch the brawl. It can be done by repeating negative comments made by one about the other or by baiting the first in the presence of the second. It can be accomplished in business by assigning similar territory to two managers. They will tear each other to pieces in the places where their responsibilities overlap. Alas, it happens every day.

This principle is especially applicable to siblings. It is remarkably easy to make them mortal enemies. All a parent must do is toss a ball in the wrong direction. The natural antagonism and competitiveness of kids will do the rest.

Children and teens are particularly uptight about the matter of physical attractiveness and body characteristics. It is highly inflammatory to commend one child at the expense of the other. Suppose, for example, that Rachel is permitted to hear this casual remark about her sister: "Becky sure is going to be a gorgeous girl." The very fact that Rachel was not mentioned will probably establish the two girls as rivals. If there is a significant difference in beauty between the two, you can be sure that Rachel has already concluded, *Yeah, I'm the ugly one.* When her fears are then confirmed by her peers, resentment and jealousy are generated.

Beauty is the most significant factor in the self-esteem of children and teenagers. Anything that parents utter on this subject within the hearing of children should be screened carefully. It has the power to make siblings hate one another.

Intelligence is another hot button for children. It is not uncommon to hear parents say in front of their children, "I think Alissa is actually brighter than Mark." Bang! Here comes another battle. Adults sometimes find it difficult to comprehend how powerful that kind of comparison can be in a child's mind. Even when the comments are unplanned and spoken offhandedly, they convey how a child is seen within the family. We are all vulnerable to the power of that bit of information.

Children (especially teens) are also extremely competitive with regard to physical attributes and athletic abilities. Those who are slower, weaker, and less coordinated than their brothers or sisters are rarely able to accept "second best" with grace and dignity. Consider, for example, the following note given to me by the mother of two boys. It was written by her nine-year-old son to his eight-year-old brother the evening after the younger child had beaten him in a race.

> *Dear Jim:*
> *I am the greatest and your the badest. And I can beat everybody in a race and you can't beat anybody in a race. I'm the smartest and your the dumbest. I'm the best sport player and your the badest sport player. And your also a hog. I can beat anybody up. And that's the truth. And that's the end of this story.*
>
> > *Yours truly,*
> > *Richard*

This note is humorous to me because Richard's motive was so poorly disguised. He had been badly stung by his humiliation on the field of honor, so he came home and raised the battle flags. He probably spent the next eight weeks looking for opportunities to fire torpedoes into Jim's soft underbelly. Such is the nature of humankind.

Here is another example: One of my assistants at Focus on the Family has an older brother who was a child prodigy at music. The elder sibling was playing Mozart sonatas on the piano at age six, while his younger brother and sister were lucky to plunk out "Chopsticks." At recital after recital, they would hear acclamation for their brother's abilities and then the offhand remark, "Oh, you did okay too."

After seven years of pleading and begging, the younger brother finally convinced his mother that he would never rival his brother at the piano and that he needed to find his own identity by playing the saxophone. A few weeks later, he brought home his saxophone and started to practice. Of course, since he was just learning the notes, he was not quite ready to solo with a band. His older brother, with whom he had always had a good relationship (and does to this day), came over, picked up the saxophone, and at the drop of a hat, played like someone who had been practicing for fifteen years. The younger brother, totally humiliated, started a knock-down-drag-out fight. Eventually, the younger brother became quite good at the saxophone—and developed a healthy identity of his own. But a less confident child might have pulled into a shell of resentment and refused to try anything perceived as risky. So much of human behavior turns on these rather straightforward principles.

Am I suggesting, then, that parents eliminate all aspects of individuality within family life or that healthy competition should be discouraged? Of course not. Competition drives us to reach for the best that is within. I am saying, however, that in matters of beauty, brains, athletic ability, and anything else valued in the family or neighborhood, children should know that in their parents' eyes, they are respected and have equal worth with their siblings. Praise and criticism *at home* should be distributed as evenly as possible, although some children will inevitably be more successful in the outside world. Finally, we should remember that children do not build fortresses around strengths—they construct them to protect weakness. Thus, when a child begins to brag and boast and attack her siblings, she is revealing the threats she feels at that point. Our sensitivity to those signals will help minimize the potential for jealousy within our children.

2. Establish a workable system of justice at home

Sibling rivalry is also at its worst when there are inadequate or inconsistently applied rules that govern the interaction between kids—when the "lawbreakers" do not get caught, or, if apprehended, are set free without standing trial. It is important to understand that laws in a society are established and enforced for the purpose of protecting people from each other. Likewise, a family is a minisociety with the same requirements for property rights and physical protection.

For purposes of illustration, suppose that I live in a community where there is no established law. Police officers do not exist and there are no courts to whom disagreements can be appealed. Under those circumstances, my neighbor and I can abuse each other with impunity. He can take my lawn mower and throw rocks through my windows, while I steal the peaches from his favorite tree and dump my leaves over his fence. This kind of mutual antagonism has a way of escalating day by day, becoming ever more violent with the passage of time. When permitted to run its natural course, as in early American history, the end result can be feudal hatred and murder.

Individual families are similar to societies in their need for law and order. In the absence of justice, "neighboring" siblings begin to assault one another. The older child is bigger and tougher, which allows her to oppress her younger brothers and sisters. But the junior member of the family is not without weapons of his own. He can strike back by breaking the toys and prized possessions of the older sibling and interfering when friends are visiting. Mutual hatred then erupts like an angry volcano, spewing its destructive contents on everyone in its path.

Too often, however, children who appeal to their parents for intervention are left to fight it out among themselves. Mom or Dad may not have sufficient disciplinary control to enforce their judgments. In other families, they are so exasperated with constant bickering among siblings that they refuse to get involved. In still others, they require an older child to live with an admitted injustice "because your sister is smaller than you." Thus, they tie the older child's hands and render him utterly defenseless against the mischief of his younger sibling. And in the many families today in which both parents work, the children may be busily disassembling each other at home with no supervision whatsoever.

I will say it again: One of the most important responsibilities of parents is to establish an equitable system of justice and a balance of power at home. There should be reasonable rules that are enforced fairly for each member of the family. For purposes of illustration, let me list the beginnings of a set of "laws" on which to build a protective shield around each child. They can never be implemented perfectly, but this is a place to start:

- A child is *never* allowed to make fun of the other in a destructive way. Period! This must be an inflexible rule with no exceptions.
- Each child's room is his or her private territory. There must be locks on both doors, and permission to enter is a revocable privilege. (Families with more than one child in each bedroom can allocate available livin-g space for each youngster.)
- As much as possible, the older child is not permitted to tease the younger child.
- The younger child is forbidden from harassing the older child.
- The children are not required to play with each other when they prefer to be alone or with other friends.
- Parents mediate any genuine conflict as quickly as possible, being careful to show impartiality and extreme fairness.

As with any system of justice, this plan requires (1) respect for leadership of the parents, (2) willingness of the parents to mediate, (3) reasonable consistency over time, and (4) occasional enforcement or punishment. When this approach is accomplished with love, the emotional tone of the home can be changed from one of hatred to (at least) tolerance.

3. Recognize that the hidden "target" of sibling rivalry is you

The third general principle is a matter of understanding how kids think. Their conflict often becomes a way of manipulating parents. Quarreling and fighting provide an opportunity for both children to capture adult attention. It has been written, "Some children had rather be wanted for murder than not wanted at all." Toward this end, a pair of obnoxious kids can tacitly agree to bug their parents until they get a response—even if it is an angry reaction.

One father told me about the time his son and his nephew began to argue and then beat each other with their fists. Both fathers were nearby and decided to let the fight run its natural course. During the first lull in the action, one of the boys glanced sideways toward the passive men and said, "Isn't anybody going to stop us before we get hurt?!" The fight, you see, was something neither boy wanted. Their violent combat was directly related to the presence of the two adults and would have taken a different form if the boys had been alone. Children will "hook" their parents' attention and intervention in this way.

Believe it or not, this form of sibling rivalry is easiest to control. The parents must simply render the behavior unprofitable to each participant. I would recommend that you review the problem (for example, a morning full of bickering) with the children and then say, "Now, listen carefully. If the two of you want to pick on each other and make yourselves miserable, then be my guests [assuming there is a fairly equal balance of power between them]. Go outside and argue until you're exhausted. But it's not going to occur under my feet anymore. It's over! And you know that I mean business when I make that kind of statement. Do we understand each other?"

Having made the boundaries clear, I would act decisively the instant either child returned to his bickering in my presence. If the children had separate bedrooms, I would confine one child to each room for at least thirty minutes of complete boredom without radio, computer, or television. Or I would assign one to clean the garage and the other to mow the lawn. Or I would make them both take an unscheduled nap. My purpose would be to make them believe me the next time I asked for peace and tranquility.

It is simply not necessary to permit children to destroy the joy of living. And what is most surprising, children are the happiest when their parents enforce reasonable limits with love and dignity. But there is nothing simple when it comes to raising children. Obviously, it is no job for cowards.

QUESTIONS & ANSWERS

Q: We are planning our family very carefully and want to space the children properly. Is there an ideal age span that will bring greater harmony between them?
A: Children who are two years apart and of the same sex are more likely to be competitive with one another. On the other hand, they are also more likely to enjoy mutual companionship. If your babies are four or more years apart, there will be less camaraderie between them, but you'll at least have

only one child in college at a time. My evasive reply to your question reflects my personal bias: There are many more important reasons for planning a baby at a particular time than the age of those already born. Of greater significance are the health of the mother, the parents' desire for another child, financial considerations, and the stability of the marriage. The relative age of the siblings is not one of the major determiners, in my opinion.

Q: My older child is a great student and earns straight As year after year. Her younger sister, now in the sixth grade, is completely bored in school and won't even try. The frustrating thing is that the younger girl is probably brighter than her older sister. Why would she refuse to apply her abilities like this?

A: There could be many reasons for your younger daughter's academic disinterest, but let me suggest the most probable explanation. Children will often refuse to compete when they think they are likely to place second instead of first. Therefore, a younger child may avoid challenging an older sibling in her area of greatest strength. If Son Number One is a great athlete, then Son Number Two may be more interested in collecting butterflies. If Daughter Number One is an accomplished pianist, then Daughter Number Two may scorn music and take up tennis. This is the exact scenario that I described in the story about my assistant and his older brother. The younger sibling did not have the desire (or the ability) to compete against his older sibling at the piano and desperately wanted to do something else in which he would not be compared unfavorably.

This rule does not always hold true, of course, depending on the child's fear of failure and the way he estimates his chances of competing successfully. If his confidence is high, he may blatantly wade into the territory owned by his big brother, determined to do even better. However, the more typical response is to seek a new area of compensation that is not yet dominated by a family superstar.

If this explanation fits the behavior of your younger daughter, then it would be wise to accept something less than perfection from her school performance. Siblings need not fit the same mold—nor can we force them to do so.

Q: I am a single parent with two strong-willed young boys who are just tearing each other apart. I think I could deal with their sibling rivalry

if only I had some encouragement and practical help in dealing with everyday life. The pressure of working, cooking dinner, and doing the job of two parents leaves me sapped and unable to deal with their constant bickering. What encouragement can you offer to those of us who are single parents? Each day seems more difficult than the one before it. Can you help plead our case to those who don't understand what we're facing?

A: According to the *Statistical Abstract of the United States,* there are now over 12 million single-parent homes in the United States.[3] In my view, single parents have the toughest job in the universe! Hercules himself would tremble at the range of responsibilities people like you must handle every day. It's difficult enough for two parents with a solid marriage and stable finances to satisfy the demands of parenting. For a single mother or father to do that task excellently over a period of years is evidence of heroism.

The greatest problem faced by single parents, especially a young mother like yourself, is the overwhelming amount of work to be done. Earning a living, fixing meals, caring for kids, helping with homework, cleaning the house, paying bills, repairing the car, handling insurance, doing the banking, preparing the income tax returns, shopping, etc., can require twelve hours or more a day. She must continue that schedule seven days a week all year long, sometimes with no support from family or anyone else. It's enough to exhaust the strongest and healthiest woman. Then where does she find time and energy to meet her own social and emotional needs—and how does she develop the friendships on which that part of her life depends? Single parenting is no easier for fathers, who may find themselves trying to comb their daughter's hair and explain menstruation to their preteen girls.

There is only one answer to the pressures single parents face. It is for the rest of us to give these moms and dads a helping hand. They need highly practical assistance, including the friendship of two-parent families who will take their children on occasion to free up some time. Single moms need the help of young men who will play catch with their fatherless boys and take them to the school soccer game. They need men who will fix the brakes on the minivan and patch the leaky roof. On the other hand, single dads need someone who can help them nurture their children, and if they have a daughter, teach her how to be a lady.

Single parents need prayer partners who will hold them accountable in their walk with the Lord and bear their burdens with them. They need an extended family of believers to care for them, lift them up, and remind them of their priorities. Perhaps most important, single parents need to know that the Lord is mindful of their circumstances.

Clearly, I believe it is the responsibility of those of us in the church to assist you with your parenting responsibilities. This requirement is implicit in Jesus' commandment that we love and support the needy in all walks of life. He said, "I tell you the truth, whatever you did for one of the least of these brothers of mine, you did for me" (Matthew 25:40). That puts things in perspective. Our efforts on behalf of a fatherless or motherless child are seen by Jesus Christ as a direct service to Himself!

This biblical assignment is even more explicitly stated in James 1:27: "Religion that God our Father accepts as pure and faultless is this: to look after orphans and widows in their distress."

Thankfully, churches today are becoming more sensitive to the needs of single parents. More congregations are offering programs and ministries geared to the unique concerns of those with particular needs. I'd advise all single parents to find such a church or fellowship group and make themselves at home there. Christian fellowship and support can be the key to survival.

THE STRONG-WILLED ADOLESCENT

(Is There Any Other Kind?)

ALAS, WE ARRIVE now at the door of adolescence, that dynamic time of life that comes in with a pimple and goes out with a beard—or to put it another way, it comes in with a bicycle and ends with a car. It's an exciting time of life, but to be honest, I wouldn't want to stumble through it again. I doubt if you would either. We adults remember all too clearly the fears and jeers and tears of our tumultuous youth. Perhaps that is why many parents begin to tremble and quake when their children approach the adolescent years, especially if one or more of them have been the fireball of the family.

One of the curious aspects of the teen experience today, which wasn't true thirty years ago, is its largely homogenized nature around the world. For example, adults who have traveled internationally may have recognized a certain kind of graffiti spray painted on buildings, bridges, and trains wherever they go. It looks about the same in Sydney, Chicago, London, Moscow, or Berlin. Somehow kids around the world know how to duplicate those scrawled block letters that mark gang territories. Teens in far-flung places are busily imitating each other in almost every other regard too. They are determined to look alike, dress alike, and "be" alike wherever they are found. Kids even have their own international language of sorts that adapts to the ever-changing jargon of the moment.

What is the common bond that links young people together? It is the worldwide pop culture, which knows no geographical boundaries. MTV, the most watched television cable network in the world, is the primary vehicle driving this conformity. Its wretched twenty-four–hour programming is seen now in more than 377 million households every day, mostly by impressionable teens or young adults.[1] The corporate conglomerate makes billions of dollars marketing pop culture—and rebellion—to a generation. Its executives are not only keenly aware of the influence they are having around the world—that is precisely what they are striving for. One of their corporate ads pictures the back of a teenager's head with MTV shaved in his hair. The copy reads, "MTV is not a channel. It's a cultural force. People don't watch it, they love it. MTV has affected the way an entire generation thinks, talks, dresses, and buys."[2] The amazing thing about this ad is that MTV not only admits they are trying to manipulate the young and immature; they spend big bucks bragging about it.

MTV is not the only degrading cultural force that is operating on the international scene. The American entertainment industry also shapes the worldwide community negatively through its distribution of movies, television, videos, and the Internet. This is why the kids in Kenya and Fiji and Santiago and Budapest tend to pant after the same Hollywood starlets, dance with the same rock musicians, and model themselves, unfortunately, after the same immoral antiheroes such as Madonna and Britney Spears and Eminem. It is why tattooing, body piercing, strange multicolored hairstyles, and scantily clad girls have a similar look wherever one goes.

One of the most disgusting and disturbing examples of debauchery within the pop culture was seen at Super Bowl XXXVIII, held in February 2004. It included a halftime show that was pure filth, complete with crotch-grabbing antics, explicit sexual and violent lyrics, bumping and grinding movements, and girls who looked like prostitutes wearing garter belts and little else. The show, if it can be called that, featured pop singers Janet Jackson and Justin Timberlake. At the concluding moment of the performance, Timberlake pulled off the top of her outfit, revealing a bare breast. Millions of people around the world, many of them wide-eyed children and impressionable teens, were watching this disgraceful performance.[3] The program was produced and sponsored by—who else?—MTV and its coconspirators at CBS and the NFL. With this program these money-grubbing executives contributed once more to the degenerate morals of a generation of young people in every country on earth. No wonder decent people in other nations hate the United States and consider it a wicked influence for their children. At least with regard to Hollywood and the pop culture industry, they are absolutely right!

Even more disturbing is that MTV airs this kind of immorality day after day on cable television, though most parents are too busy doing their own thing to notice.

What this means is that the job of raising kids, especially those seething with rebellion, has become much more difficult. A hundred years ago, when fourteen-year-old Billy Bob Brown, the strong-willed son of Farmer Brown, began to get snippy around the house, his dad could take him out to the back forty acres and "get his mind straight." There they were, just the two of them, working through their conflict. And usually, Billy Bob quickly figured out that he had better shape up—or else. Now, teen pop culture imposes on parent-child relationships a vast and enormously influential network of ideas, enticements, sexuality, profanity, support, and, mostly, an articulation of anger that compounds the difficulties of growing up.

According to environmentalist and author Bill McKibben, "If you had set out to create a culture purposefully damaging to children, you couldn't do better than America at the end of the twentieth century [and well into the next]."[4] Columnist, author, and radio talk-show host Michael Medved put it this way: "There has been a shift from a supportive culture . . . to a deliberately assaultive culture."[5] Western culture is increasingly radical, sexual, and revolutionary. It is determined to take your kids to hell, and your greatest wisdom and experience will be required to stop it.

A good place to begin is by monitoring your child's access to the mass media. According to a recent survey, children ages two through eighteen spend on average five hours and twenty-nine minutes every day watching television, listening to music, or playing computer and video games. That total increases for children over eight, who spend nearly forty hours a week engaged in some sort of media-related activity. The survey also found that 53 percent of children have a television in their bedroom, which includes 32 percent of two- to seven-year-olds and 65 percent of eight- to eighteen-year-olds. Seventy percent of all children have a radio in their room, and 16 percent have a computer.[6]

What an ominous description this report provides of American children (and those around the world) in the twenty-first century! It is all related to the frantic pace of living. We adults are too exhausted and harried to care for those we love most. We hardly know what they are doing at home, much less when they are away. What a shame! Yankelovich Partners, Inc., said the image of families gathered around a single TV set in the family room is fading. Instead, many kids are off by themselves, where they can choose anything that they want to see. Ann Clurman, a partner at Yankelovich, said, "Almost everything children are seeing is essentially going into their minds in some sort of uncensored or unfiltered way."[7]

I strongly urge you to get those devices, whether they are television sets, computers, or DVDs *out of the bedroom*. Locate them in the family room, where they can be monitored and where the amount of time spent on them is regulated. How can you do less for your children? It is also our responsibility to watch various forms of entertainment *with* our boys and girls when they are young. Otherwise, our kids are sitting ducks for the con men of our time who want to control their hearts and minds.

I wrote in greater detail about these and other adolescent dangers in my book *Bringing Up Boys*. Those who are looking for greater help at this point can consult that source. For now, here is a summary of that discussion:

> Well, dear parents, I know that what I have shared in this chapter has been upsetting. It is no wonder that many of you feel caught in the backwash of a postmodern culture whose only god is self-gratification and whose only value is radical individualism. Nevertheless, you do need to know the truth and what you can do to protect those you love. . . . Here are some things to consider:
>
> First, let's give priority to our children. In days gone by, the culture acted to shield them from harmful images and exploitation. Now it's open season for even the youngest among us. Let's put the welfare of our boys [and girls] ahead of our own convenience and teach them the difference between right and wrong. They need to hear that God is the author of their rights and liberties. Let's teach them that He loves them and holds them to a high level of moral accountability.
>
> Second, let's do everything in our power to reverse the blight of violence and lust that has become so pervasive across this land. Let's demand that the entertainment moguls stop producing moral pollutants. Let's recapture from the courts that system of self-rule that traditionally allowed Americans to debate their deepest differences openly and reach workable

solutions together. Radical individualism is destroying us! Postmodernism is a cancer that rots the soul of humanity. The creed that proclaims, "If it feels good, do it!" has filled too many hospitals with drug-overdosed teenagers, too many prison cells with fatherless youth, too many caskets with slain young people, and caused too many tears for bewildered parents.

Finally, let's vow together today to set for our children the highest standards of ethics and morality and to protect them, as much as possible, from evil and death. Our families can't be perfect, but they *can* be better—much better.[8]

With that, I'll offer some other ideas and suggestions that relate to all adolescents, including those who are harder to handle.

1. Give teenagers the gifts they hunger for most—respect and dignity!

As we all know, the period of early adolescence is typically a painful time of life, marked by rapid physical and emotional changes. This characteristic difficulty was expressed by a seventh-grade boy who had been asked to recite Patrick Henry's historic speech at a special program commemorating the birth of the United States. But when the young man stood nervously before an audience of parents, he became confused and blurted out: "Give me puberty or give me death!" His statement is not as ridiculous as it sounds. Many teens sincerely believe they must choose between these dubious alternatives.

The thirteenth and fourteenth years commonly are the most difficult twenty-four months in life. A preadolescent child of ten or twelve suddenly awakens to a brand-new world around him, as though his eyes were opening for the first time. That world is populated by agemates who scare him out of his wits. His greatest anxiety, even exceeding the fear of death, which is remote and unthinkable, is the possibility of rejection or humiliation in the eyes of his peers. This ominous threat will lurk in the background for years, motivating kids to do things that make absolutely no sense to the adults who watch. It is impossible to comprehend the adolescent mind without understanding this terror of the peer group.

Related to this social vulnerability are the doubt and feelings of inferiority that reach an all-time high at this age. An adolescent's worth as a human being hangs precariously on peer-group acceptance, which is notoriously fickle. Thus, relatively minor evidences of rejection or ridicule are of major significance to those who already see themselves as fools and failures. It is difficult to overestimate the impact of having no one to sit with on the school-sponsored field trip, not being invited to an important event, being laughed at by the "in" group, waking up in the morning to find seven shiny new pimples on your oily forehead, or being humiliated by the boy or girl you thought had liked you. Some adolescents consistently face these kinds of social catastrophes throughout their teen years. It makes some of the most strong-willed among them downright mean at home.

Dr. Urie Bronfenbrenner, now retired from Cornell University, identified early adolescence as the most destructive period of life. Bronfenbrenner recalls being asked during a U.S. Senate hearing to indicate the most critical years in a child's development. He knew the senators expected him to emphasize the importance of preschool experience, reflecting the popular notion that all significant learning takes place during the first six years of life. However, Bronfenbrenner said he had never been able to validate that assumption. He agreed that the preschool years are vital, but so is every other phase of childhood. In fact, he told the Senate committee that the middle school years are probably the most critical to the development of a child's mental health. It is during this period of self-doubt that the personality is often assaulted and damaged beyond repair. Consequently, said Bronfenbrenner, it is not unusual for students to enter junior high school as happy, healthy children—and then emerge two years later as broken, discouraged teenagers.[9]

I couldn't agree more emphatically. Both physical and emotional dangers lurk everywhere at this time. I'll never forget a vulnerable girl named Diane who was a student when I was in high school. She attended modern-dance classes and was asked to perform during an all-school assembly program. Diane was in the ninth grade and had not yet begun to develop sexually. As she spun around the stage that day, the unthinkable happened! The top of her strapless blouse suddenly let go (it had nothing to grip) and dropped to her waist. The student body gasped and then roared with laughter. It was terrible! Diane stood clutching frantically at her bare body for a split second and then fled from the stage in tears. She never fully recovered from the tragedy during her high school years. And you can bet that her "friends" made sure she didn't.

Middle school students are typically brutal to each other, attacking and slashing a weak victim in much the same way a pack of wolves kills and devours a deformed caribou. They act this way because they are afraid of being bullied themselves, according to Dorothy Espelage, the author of a study of 558 students at a Midwestern middle school. "Kids don't have the skills to stop [bullying]," Espelage said. "They also fear that if they try, attention will turn to them. They also have a sense that it's all in fun—but to the victims, it's not funny." Espelage and her colleagues found that 80 percent of the students in their study said they had engaged in physical aggression, social ridicule, teasing, name-calling, and threats within the last thirty days.[10]

Another study, done by researchers at the University of Georgia and the University of Minnesota, found that bullying peaks when youngsters make the move from elementary to middle school. Their findings suggest that teasing and threatening are just part of the search for status. "Once the dominance is established and their place with their new friends is secure, the aggression subsides," the study's authors wrote.[11]

I have witnessed firsthand the brutality of the young. When I was in my twenties, I had the privilege of teaching in a public middle school. For two years, I taught science and math to 225 rambunctious troops each day, although I learned much more from them than they did from me. There on the firing line, my concepts of discipline and child development began to solidify. The workable, practical solutions were validated, while the lofty theories dreamed up by academics exploded like so much TNT when tested on the battlefield each day.

One of the most important lessons I learned in those years was the linkage between self-worth (or self-hatred) and rebellious behavior. I observed very quickly during my teaching career that I could impose all manner of discipline and classroom rules for my students, provided I treated each young person with genuine dignity and respect. I earned my students' friendship before and after school, during lunch, and through classroom encounters. I was tough, especially when challenged, but never discourteous, mean, or insulting. I defended the underdog and tenaciously tried to build each child's confidence and self-respect. However, I never compromised my standards of deportment. Students entered my class-room without talking each day. They did not behave disrespectfully, curse, or stab one another with ballpoint pens. I was clearly the captain of the ship, and I sailed it with military zeal.

The result of this combination of kindness and firm discipline stands as one of the most pleasant memories of my professional life. I loved my students and had every reason to believe that I was loved in return. I actually missed them on weekends (a fact my wife never quite understood). At the end of the final year when I was packing my books and saying good-bye, twenty-five or thirty teary-eyed kids hung around my gloomy room for several hours and finally stood sobbing in the parking lot as I drove away. And, yes, this twenty-six-year-old teacher also shed a few tears of his own that day. It is no wonder that one of my favorite movies, released in 1996, is *Mr. Holland's Opus,* which portrays a teacher who embodies the characteristics I have described. (Please forgive this self-congratulatory paragraph. I haven't bothered to tell you about my failures, which are far less interesting.)

If you can communicate kindness to your oppressed and harassed teenagers, even to those who are sullen and difficult, then many of the usual disciplinary problems of adolescence can be circumvented. That is, after all, the best way to deal with people of any age.

Let's look now at the second suggestion, which can be, in effect, a means of implementing the first.

2. The key to the puzzle

There is often an irrationality associated with adolescence that can be terribly frustrating to parents. It is difficult at that time to reason your way out of conflict. Let me offer an illustration that may explain the problem.

In graduate school I was told a story about a medical student who was required as part of his training to spend a few weeks working in a psychiatric hospital. Unfortunately, he was given little orientation to the nature of mental illness, and he mistakenly thought he could reason his patients back to a world of reality. One schizophrenic inmate was of particular interest to him, because the man believed himself to be dead.

"Yeah, it's true," the patient would tell anyone who asked. "I'm dead. Been dead for years."

The intern couldn't resist trying to talk the schizophrenic out of his delusion. He sat down with the patient and said, "I understand you think you're dead. Is that right?"

"Sure is," replied the man. "I'm deader than a doornail."

The intern continued, "Well, answer me this: Do dead people bleed?"

"No, of course not," replied the schizophrenic, sounding perfectly sane.

The intern then took the patient's hand in his own and stuck a needle into the fleshy part of his thumb. As the blood oozed from the puncture, the schizophrenic gasped and exclaimed, "Well, what do you know! Dead people do bleed!"

There may be times when you may find yourself holding similar conversations with your uncomprehending adolescent. These moments will likely occur while you are trying to explain why he must be home by a certain hour, why she should keep her room straight, why he can't have the car on Friday night, or why it doesn't really matter that she wasn't invited to the cool party given by the most popular kid in the senior class. These issues defy reason, and teens are more likely to respond instead to the dynamic emotional, social, and chemical forces that propel them. I can also assure you, from the survey of thirty-five thousand parents mentioned earlier, that the strong-willed child is especially susceptible to these internal and sometimes irrational forces. Whatever testiness was there in the past twelve years is most likely to get worse before it gets better.

Let me quote from a *US News & World Report* article that helps articulate this phenomenon:

> One day, your child [if naturally compliant] is a beautiful, charming 12-year-old, a kid who pops out of bed full of good cheer, clears the table without being asked, and brings home good grades from school. The next day, your child bursts into tears when you ask for the salt and listens to electronic music at maximum volume for hours on end. Chores? Forget it. Homework? There's little time, after talking to friends on the phone for five hours every night. Mornings? Your bluebird of happiness is flown, replaced by a groaning lump that can scarcely be roused out of bed. Welcome to adolescence.[12]

What is going on here? Why the sudden volatility and irrationality? The answer is straightforward. It's the mischievous hormones that have begun to surge! They are the key to understanding nearly everything that doesn't add up in the teen years. The emotional characteristics of a suddenly rebellious teenager, or the worsening of them, are rather like premenstrual syndrome (PMS) or severe menopause in women. Obviously, dramatic changes are going on inside! If the upheaval was caused entirely by environmental factors, its onset in puberty would not be so predictable. The emotional changes I have described arrive right on schedule, timed to coincide precisely with the onset of physical maturation. Both changes, I contend, are driven by a common hormonal assault. Human chemistry apparently goes haywire for a few years, affecting mind as much as body.

Does this understanding make it easier for parents to tolerate and cope with the reverberations of puberty? Probably not, but it should. For several years, a teenager may not interpret his world accurately. His social judgment is impaired. His fear of danger is muted, and his view of responsibility is warped. Therefore, it is a good idea not to despair when it looks as though everything you have tried to teach your kid seems to have been forgotten—or never learned. He is going through a metamorphosis that has turned everything upside down. But stick around. He'll regain his equilibrium in due time and your relationship will stabilize—providing *you're* not the one who is insane by that point.

And now a word of advice for parents of a strong-willed girl whose personality becomes downright nasty every month. I strongly recommend that you encourage your daughter to plot the particulars of her menstrual cycle on a graph. Talk to her about PMS and how it influences behavior, self-esteem, and moods. Ask her to record when her period begins and ends each month, as well as how she feels before, during, and after her cycle. (Don't bring up the subject until she is in midcycle.) I think you and she will see that the emotional blowups that tear the family apart are predictable and recurring. Premenstrual tension during adolescence can produce a flurry of tornadoes every twenty-eight days. If you know they are coming, you can retreat to the storm cellar when the wind begins to blow. Unfortunately, many parents never seem to notice the regularity and predictability of depression, agitation, and conflict with their daughter. Watch the calendar. It will tell you so much about your girl.

Emotional balance in teenage boys is not as cyclical as it is in girls, but boys' behavior is equally influenced by hormones. Everything from sexual passion to aggressiveness is motivated by the new chemicals that surge through their veins.

Having made the case for hormonal influences, now let me add that nothing is as simple as it sounds.

Recent studies reveal that hormones are not the only culprits in the mix. Immaturity is also caused by incomplete brain development during early adolescence. These findings were summarized in the same *US News & World Report* article I quoted from earlier. Here is what was written:

> And just as a teenager is all legs one day and all nose and ears the next, different regions of the brain are developing on different timetables. For instance, one of the last parts to mature is in charge of making sound judgments and calming unruly emotions. And the emotional centers in the teenage brain have already been revving up, probably under the influence of sex hormones. This imbalance may explain why your intelligent 16-year-old doesn't think twice about getting into a car driven by a friend who is drunk, or why your formerly equable 13-year-old can be hugging you one minute and then flying off the handle the next.[13]

Researchers have also discovered that a teenager's brain goes through an experience called pruning, in which the brain purges itself of neurons and synapses it no longer finds useful. These neurons and synapses are developed between the ages of nine and ten and then are eliminated as the brain decides which to retain. Thus, until the prefrontal cortex of the brain has gone through this pruning process, most young teenagers do not have all of their brainpower at their disposal, especially the power to make good judgments. This can also result in teenagers having difficulty managing multiple tasks.[14]

Isn't that interesting? These findings should be helpful when the kid you brought into the world in love, and for whom you would give your very life, accuses you of being Attila the Hun and hisses like a snake when told no. This negativism isn't entirely your fault. And this individual, when grown, will look back and talk with you about how cantankerous she was during this time.

Remember the mother named Joy, who appeared with a panel on a Focus on the Family radio broadcast and told us how her impossibly rebellious, strong-willed daughter wrote an emotional letter from college, apologizing and saying her mother was her best friend? That is not an unusual outcome. I will say more about this optimistic prognosis in the final chapter.

The bottom line is that the adolescent years represent a transition period that will soon pass. Don't be too discouraged when the storms are raging. Keep your confidence when under fire, and do the best you can to work your way through these conflicts. And by all means stay in touch with your kids, even when you and they are having trouble understanding each other. Remember that your formerly pleasant and happy child, who seemingly degenerated overnight into a sour and critical anarchist, may also be worried about what is happening to her. She may be confused by the resentment and anger that have become so much a part of her personality. She clearly needs the patient reassurance of loving parents who can explain the normality of this agitation and help her ventilate the inner tension. It's a job for Superparent!

3. Pry open the door of communication

But how can you talk to someone who won't talk—someone whose language consists of seven phrases: I dunno. I don't care. Leave me alone. I need money. Can I have the car? My friends think you're unfair. And, I didn't do it. Prying open the door of communication with an angry adolescent can require more tact and skill than any other parenting assignment. Often, mothers and fathers act like adolescents, shouting and screaming and engaging in endless battles that leave them exhausted but without strategic advantage. There has to be a better way of communicating than shouting at one another. Let me propose an alternative.

For purposes of illustration, suppose that Brian is now fourteen years old and has entered a period of remarkable defiance. He is breaking rules right and left and seems to hate the entire family. He becomes angry when his parents discipline him, of course, but even during tranquil times he seems to resent them for merely being there. Last Friday night he arrived home an hour beyond his curfew but refused to explain where he was or why he was late. What course of action would be best for his parents to take?

Let's assume that you are Brian's father. I would recommend that you invite him out to breakfast on a Saturday morning, leaving the rest of the family at home. It would be best if this event occurred during a relatively tranquil time, certainly not in the midst of a hassle or intergenerational battle. Admit that you have some important matters to discuss with him that can't be communicated adequately at home, but don't tip your hand before Saturday morning.

Then at the appropriate moment during breakfast, convey the following messages (or an adaptation thereof):

A. Brian, I wanted to talk to you this morning because of the changes that are taking place in you and in our home. We both know that the past few weeks have not been very pleasant. You have been angry most of the time and have become disobedient and rude. And your mother and I haven't done so well either. We've become irritable, and we've said things that we've regretted later. This is not what God wants of us as parents or of you as our son. There has to be a better way of solving our problems. That's why we're here.

B. As a place to begin, Brian, I want you to understand what is happening. You have gone into a new period of life known as adolescence. This is the final phase of childhood, and it is often a very stormy and difficult few years. Nearly everyone goes through these rough times during their early teens, and you are right on schedule. Many of the problems you face today were predictable from the day you were born, simply because growing up has never been an easy thing to do. There are even greater pressures on kids today than when we were young. I've said that to let you know this: We love you as much as we ever did, even though the past few months have been difficult in our home.

C. What is actually taking place, you see, is that you have had a taste of freedom. You are tired of being told what to do. Within certain limits, that is healthy evidence that you are growing up and becoming your own man. However, you want to be your own boss and make your own decisions without interference from anyone. Brian, you will get what you want in a very short time. You are fourteen now, and you'll soon be fifteen and seventeen and nineteen. You will be grown before we know it, and your mom and I will no longer have any responsibility for you. The day is coming when you will marry whomever you wish, go to whatever school you choose, and select the profession or job that suits you. Your mother and I will not seek to make those decisions for you. We will respect your adulthood. Furthermore, Brian, the closer you get to that day, the more freedom we plan to give you. You have more privileges now than you had last year, and that trend will continue. We will soon set you free, and you will be accountable only to God and yourself.

D. But, Brian, you must understand this message: You are not grown yet. During the past few weeks, you have wanted your mother and me to leave you alone—to let you stay out half the night if you choose, to fail in school, to carry no responsibility at home. And you have blown up whenever we have denied even your most extreme demands. The truth of the matter is, you have wanted us to grant you a twenty-year-old's freedom during your fourteenth year, although you still expect to have your shirts ironed and your meals fixed and your bills paid. You have wanted the best of both worlds with none of the responsibilities or limitations of either. It doesn't work that way. So what are we to do? The easiest thing would be for us to let you have your way. There would be no hassles and no conflict and no more frustration. Many parents of fourteen-year-olds have done just that. But we must not yield to this temptation. You are not ready for complete independence, and we would be showing hatred (instead of love) for you if we surrendered at this time. We would regret our mistake for the rest of our life, and you would soon blame us too. And as you know, you have two younger sisters who are watching you very closely, who must be protected from the things you are teaching them.

E. Besides, Brian, God has given us a responsibility as parents to do what is right for you, and He is holding us accountable for the way we do that job. I want to read you an important passage from the Bible that describes a father named Eli, a priest in the temple, who did not discipline and correct his two unruly teenage sons. [Read the dramatic story from 1 Samuel 2:12-17, 22-25, 27-34; 3:11-14; 4:1-4 and 10-22.] It is very clear that God was angry with Eli for permitting his sons to be disrespectful and disobedient. Not only did He allow the sons to be killed in battle, but He also punished their father for not accepting his parental responsibilities.

This assignment to parents can be found throughout the Bible: Mothers and fathers are expected to train their children and discipline them when required. What I'm saying is that God will not hold us blameless if we let you behave in ways that are harmful to yourself and others. The Bible also tells parents not to overcorrect and demoralize their children. We're going to try harder to conform to that Scripture too.

F. That brings us to the question of where we go from this moment. I want to make a pledge to you, here and now: Your mother and I intend to be more sensitive to your needs and feelings than we've been in the past. We're not perfect, as you well know, and it is possible that you will feel we have been unfair at one time or another. If that occurs, you can express your views and we will listen to you. We want to keep the door of communication wide open between us. When you seek a new privilege, I'm going to ask myself this question, "Is there any way I can grant this request without harming Brian or other people?" If I can permit what you want in good conscience, I will do so. I will compromise and bend as far as my best judgment will let me.

G. But hear this, Brian. There will be some matters that cannot be compromised. There will be occasions when I will have to say no. And when those times come, you can expect me to stand like the Rock of Gibraltar. No amount of violence and temper tantrums and door slamming will change a thing. In fact, if you choose to fight me in those remaining areas, then I promise that you will lose big-time. Admittedly, you're too big and grown up to spank, but I can still make you uncomfortable. And that will be my goal. Believe me, Brian, I'll lie awake nights figuring out how to make you miserable. I have the courage and the determination to do my job during these last few years you are at home, and I intend to use all of my resources for this purpose, if necessary. So it's up to you. We can have a peaceful time of cooperation at home, or we can spend this last part of your childhood in unpleasantness and struggle. Either way, you will arrive home when you are told, you will carry your share of responsibility in the family, and you will continue to respect your mother and me.

H. Finally, Brian, let me emphasize the message I gave you in the beginning. We love you more than you can imagine, and we're going to remain friends during this difficult time. There is so much pain in the world today. Life involves disappointment and loss and rejection and aging and sickness and ultimately death. You haven't felt much of that discomfort yet, but you'll taste it soon enough. So with all that heartache outside our door, let's not bring more of it on ourselves. We need each other. We need you, and believe it or not, you still need us occasionally. We're going to be praying for you every day and asking the Lord to lead and guide you. I know He will answer that prayer. And that, I suppose, is what I wanted to convey to you this morning. Let's make it better from now on.

Do you have things that need to be said to me?

The content of this message should be modified to fit individual circumstances and the needs of particular adolescents. And the response from the teenager will vary tremendously from person to person. An open boy or girl may reveal deep feelings at such a moment of communication, permitting a priceless time of catharsis and ventilation. On the other hand, a stubborn, defiant, proud adolescent may sit immobile with head downward. But even if your teenager remains stoic or hostile, at least the cards have been laid on the table and parental intentions have been explained.

4. Keep them moving

And now a word of practical advice for the parents of very strong-willed adolescents. They simply must not be allowed to get bored. Giving them large quantities of unstructured time is asking for trouble. The hormones that surge through their youthful bodies, especially testosterone in boys, will often lead them in the direction of danger or trouble. That's why unsupervised time after school, when parents are at work, can lead to harmful behavior. This is hardly new advice. The old adage warns, "An idle mind is the devil's workshop." True enough. My advice is to get these energetic, mischievous teenagers occupied in constructive activities (without overdoing it). See that they get into a good youth program (a Bible-believing church would be the best place to start, from my perspective) and/or become involved in athletic pursuits, music, hobbies, animal care, part-time jobs, or an academic interest such as electronics or agriculture. Obviously, implementing this suggestion is not as urgent for the parents of compliant kids, but the idea is still relevant. By whatever means, you must find a way to keep their gangly legs churning.

One way to help accomplish that is to direct your teenagers to positive messages that are relevant to their lives. I strongly recommend, for example, the online teen resources *Breakaway* (for boys) and *Brio* (for girls), which attempt to address teen issues in a language adolescents can understand. For information about these resources, go to www.breakaway .com or www.briomag.com.

Not only should adolescents be busy doing constructive things, but they desperately need personal connectedness to their family. Every available study draws this conclusion. When parents are involved intimately with their kids during the teen years and when their relationship leads to an active family life, rebellious and destructive behavior is less likely to occur. Drs. Blake Bowden and Jennie Zeisz studied 527 teenagers at Cincinnati Children's Hospital to learn what family and lifestyle characteristics were related to mental health and adjustment. Their findings were significant.

Adolescents whose parents ate dinner with them five times a week or more were the least likely to be on drugs, depressed, or in trouble with the law. They were more likely to be doing well in school and surrounded by a supportive circle of friends. By contrast, the more poorly adjusted teens ate with their parents only three evenings a week or less. What Bowden's study shows is that children do far better in school and in life when they spend time with their parents, and specifically when they get together almost every day for conversation and interaction.[15]

This is one of *the* most effective tools for helping your teen through the dangerous years of adolescence. And, yes, it works with strong-willed children, too.

5. Use incentives and privileges to advantage

As I pointed out previously, one of the most common mistakes parents of rebellious kids make is allowing themselves to be drawn into endless verbal battles that leave them exhausted but without strategic advantage. Don't subject your daughter to perpetual threats and finger-wagging accusations and insulting indictments. And most important, don't nag her endlessly. Adolescents hate to be nagged by Mommy and Daddy! When that occurs, they typically protect themselves by appearing deaf. Thus, the quickest way to terminate all communication between generations is to follow a young person around the house, repeating the same monotonous messages of disapproval with the regularity of a cuckoo clock.

What, then, is the proper response to slovenliness, disobedience, defiance, and irresponsibility? That question takes us back to the threat, implied to Brian, that his father would make him miserable if he did not cooperate. Don't let the news leak out, but the tools available to implement that promise are relatively weak. Since it is unwise (and unproductive) to spank a teenager, parents can only manipulate environmental circumstances when discipline is required. They have the keys to the family automobile (unless the teen has her own car, taking away a prize bargaining chip) and can allow their teenager to use it. They may grant permission to go to the beach or to the mountains or to a friend's house or to a party. They control the family purse and can choose to share it or loan it or dole it or close it. They can ground their adolescent or deny use of the telephone, MP3 player, or television for a while.

Now, obviously, these are not very influential motivators and are at times totally inadequate for the situation. After we have appealed to reason, cooperation, and family loyalty, all that remain are relatively ineffective methods of punishment. We can only link our kids' behavior with desirable and undesirable consequences and hope the connection will be enough to elicit their cooperation.

If that sounds pretty weak, let me admit what I am implying: A willful, angry sixteen-year-old boy or girl *can* win a confrontation with his or her parents today if worst comes to worst. The law has totally shifted in teenagers' favor. For example, they can have sex, conceive a child, and, in many states, abort a child without their parents' knowledge. Drugs and alcohol are easy to obtain. Very few adult privileges and vices can be denied a teenager who has a passion for independence and the will to fight. Under some circumstances in certain states, a sixteen-year-old can be legally emancipated and freed from all parental supervision. Sometimes in cases of extreme rebellion, your reaction in a crisis has to be based on bluster and intimidation. It isn't enough, but you run with what is available to you.

As I said earlier, the culture is not on your side. Every spark of adolescent discontent is fanned into a smoldering flame. The grab for the buying power of children and teens has become intense, and marketers are after them almost from the time they leave the womb. Often, teenagers are given money by guilt-ridden parents who neglect them as they pursue their careers. In fact, in 1998, teenagers spent a record $141 billion—an average of $4,548 each![16] In addition, many teens have free rein in shopping malls, charge cards in hand. One teenage girl, when asked if her parents trusted her with a credit card, laughed out loud and said, "I max out my gas card every month. My parents pay for it," adding that she was not sure of her credit limit. She went on to say that she spent several hundred dollars a month on gas, cigarettes, and food and only stopped when her card was rejected. "I know I can't handle my own credit card. I can't even handle my checking account," she concluded.[17]

Our culture assaults teens with every antisocial message imaginable and appeals to their weaknesses and lack of adult judgment. Parents must step into the gap. If parents are absent during this crucial time, the results can be disastrous. We need look no further than the example of Eric Harris and Dylan Klebold, the two young men involved in the Columbine High School tragedy in 1999. Left alone for hours by their parents, they turned to the Internet and violent video games, eventually carrying out their aggression in a murderous spree in the halls of their school. When teens are isolated from their parents, they are more vulnerable to serious emotional problems, including suicide.[18] I think the need for parental involvement is best expressed by Patricia Hersch, author of *A Tribe Apart: A Journey into the Heart of American Adolescence,* who said, "Every kid I talked to at length eventually came around to saying without my asking that they had wished they had more adults in their lives, especially their parents."[19]

So what is the answer? That takes us back to the importance of laying a foundation of respect for parental authority during the early years of a child's development. Without that foundation—without a touch of awe in a child's perception of his mother or father—the balance of power and control is definitely shifted toward the younger combatant.

As Patricia Hersch stated, and despite what the perception may be, teenagers desperately want to be connected to their parents during the tumultuous years of adolescence. In 1999, the National Longitudinal Study on Adolescent Health found that teenagers who feel more connected and comfortable with their parents, teachers, and other adults are less likely to commit violence, use illegal drugs, or become sexually active.[20]

Another national survey of teens done by the Horatio Alger Foundation found that a majority of adolescents felt that the decline of the family, along with "sagging moral and social values," was one of the biggest problems they face. In fact, they rated family to be more important to personal success than making a contribution to society. Jennifer Park, who helped prepare the report on the survey, said, "Family is very important. This is something that is really constant throughout the whole generation."[21]

Let me share an experience from my own life that I included in my book *Bringing Up Boys.* When I was sixteen years old, I began to play some games that my mother viewed with alarm. I had not yet crossed the line into all-out rebellion, but I was definitely leaning in that direction. My father was a minister who traveled constantly during that time, and Mom was in charge. One night, we had an argument over a dance I wanted to go to, and she objected. I openly defied her that night. I said, in effect, that I was going and if she didn't like it, that was just too bad. Mom became very quiet, and I turned in a huff to go into my bedroom. I paused in the hall when I heard her pick up the phone and call my dad, who was out of town. She simply said, "I need you." What happened in the next few days shocked me down to my toes. My dad canceled his four-year speaking schedule and put our house up for sale. Then he accepted a pastoral assignment seven hundred miles south. The next thing I knew, I was on a train heading for Texas and a new home in the Rio Grande Valley. That permitted my dad to be at home with me for my last two years of high school. During these years we hunted and fished together and bonded for a lifetime. There in a fresh environment, I made new friends and worked my way through the conflict that was brewing with my mom. I didn't fully understand until later the price my parents paid to do what was best for me. It was a very costly move for them, personally and professionally, but they loved me enough to sacrifice at a critically important time. In essence, they saved me. I was moving in the wrong direction, and they pulled me back from the cliff. I will always appreciate these good people for what they did.

There is more to the story, of course. It was difficult making new friends in a strange high school at the beginning of my junior year. I was lonely and felt out of place in a town that failed to acknowledge my arrival. My mother sensed this feeling of friendlessness and, in her characteristic way, was hurting with me. One day, after we had been in the community for about two weeks, she took me by the hand and pressed a piece of paper into the palm. She looked in my eyes and said, "This is for you. Don't tell anybody. Just take it and use it for anything you want. It isn't much, but I want you to get something that looks good to you."

I unfolded the paper, which turned out to be a twenty-dollar bill.

It was money that my mother and father didn't have, considering the cost of the move and my dad's small salary. But no matter, I stood at the top of their priorities during these stormy days. We all know that money won't buy friends, and twenty dollars (even then) did not change my life significantly. Nevertheless, my mother used that method of saying to me: "I feel what you feel; I know it's difficult right now, but I'm your friend and I want to help." All troubled teens should be so fortunate as to have parents who are pulling for them and praying for them and feeling for them, even when they are at their most unlovable.

I have been suggesting that parents be willing to take whatever corrective action is required during the adolescent years, but to do it without nagging, moaning, groaning, and growling. Let love be your guide! Even though it often doesn't seem like it, your teen desperately wants to be loved and to feel connected to you. Anger does not motivate teenagers. That is why the parent or teacher who can find the delicate balance between love and firm discipline is the one who ends up winning the heart of teenagers. The adult who screams and threatens but does not love is only going to fuel teenage rebellion.

There is hope. Laurence Steinberg, a psychology professor at Temple University, observed: "Parents are caught by surprise [by adolescence]. They discover that the tricks they've used in raising their kids effectively during childhood stopped working." However, he advised parents that if they stick it out, things will improve. "I have a 14-year-old son," Steinberg said, "and when we moved out of the transition phase into middle adolescence, we saw a dramatic change. All of a sudden, he's our best friend again."[22]

This brings us to another important understanding of adolescence and the strong-willed kids who live there.

6. Hold on with an open hand

Another serious mistake made by parents of older teenagers (sixteen to nineteen years of age) is refusing to grant them the independence and maturity they require. Our inclination as loving guardians is to hold our kids too tightly, despite their attempts to squirm free. We try to make all their decisions, keep them snugly beneath our wings, and prevent even the possibility of failure. And in so doing, we force our young adults into one of two destructive patterns: Either they passively accept our overprotection and remain dependent "children" into adult life or they rise up in great wrath to reject our bondage and interference. They lose on both counts. On the one hand they become emotional cripples who are incapable of independent thought, and on the other they grow into angry, guilt-ridden adults who have severed ties with the family they need. Indeed, parents who refuse to grant appropriate independence to their older adolescents are courting disaster not only for their children but also for themselves.

Let me state it more strongly: I believe American parents are not very good at letting go of their grown children. This observation was power- fully illustrated in a book written years ago, *What Really Happened to the Class of '65?* [23] The book's narrative begins in the midsixties when *Time* magazine selected the senior class of Palisades High School in southern California as the focus for its cover story on "Today's Teenager." The editors had clearly chosen the cream of the crop for their report. These graduating young men and women lived in one of the wealthiest school districts in America, with an average income in 1965 of $42,000 per family (which would perhaps exceed $400,000 today). Listed among the members of their class were the children of many famous people, including James Arness, Henry Miller, Karl Malden, Betty Hutton, Sterling Hayden, and Irving Wallace.[24] These students were part of the most beautiful, healthiest, best educated, and most affluent generation in history, and they knew it. Little wonder that *Time* perceived them to be standing "on the fringe of a golden era" as they left high school and headed for college.[25] Their future sparkled like the California sunrise on a summer day.

But that was in 1965. Ten years later, two members of that class, Michael Medved and David Wallechinsky, became interested in investigat- ing what really *did* happen to the optimistic young graduates of Palisades High School. Had they achieved the anticipated promise of glory and accomplishment? It was a fascinating (although profane and vulgar) commentary on a generation of overindulged kids, not only from Pacific Palisades, but from all across the United States. It focused on the major stereotypes populating American secondary schools, including the gor- geous cheerleader, the cool quarterback, the intellectual, the goof-off, the nerd, the dreamboat, the flirt, the underachiever, and the wild girl (who reportedly made love to 425 boys before losing count). One by one, their private lives and personal histories were revealed.[26]

As it turned out, the class of 1965, far from entering a "golden era," was plagued by personal tragedy and emotional unrest. In fact, the students who graduated from American high schools in that year may be the most unstable and lost generation of young men and women ever produced in our country. A few weeks after they received their diplomas, our cities began to burn during the long, hot summer of racial strife. That signaled the start of the chaos to come. They entered college at a time when drug abuse was not only prevalent but almost universal for students and teachers alike. Intellectual pursuits were the first casualty in this narcotic climate. The Vietnam War soon heated campus passions to an incendiary level, generating anger and disdain for the government, the president, the military, both political parties, and, indeed, the American way of life. That hostility gave rise to bombings, riots, and the burning of "establishment" edifices.

This generation of college students had already witnessed the brutal assassination of their idol, John F. Kennedy, when they were barely sixteen years old. Then at a critical point in their season of passion, they lost two more beloved heroes, Robert Kennedy and Martin Luther King Jr. Those murders were followed by the street wars that punctuated the 1968 Democratic Convention and the killing of students at Kent State University. These violent convulsions reached their overt culmination in the wake of President Nixon's military foray into Cambodia, which virtually closed down American campuses. As our population ages, fewer and fewer people lived through and remember those tumultuous days. Nevertheless, they represented a knife edge in Western culture, separating what came before with what we have known since.

Accompanying the social upheaval of that era was a sudden disintegration of moral and ethical principles, such as has never occurred in the history of humankind. All at once, there were no definite values. There were no standards. No absolutes. No rules. No traditional beliefs on which to lean. Nor could anyone over thirty even be trusted. And some bright-eyed theologians chose that moment of confusion to announce the death of God. It was a distressing time to be young—to be groping aimlessly in search of personal identity and a place in the sun. That was the social setting for the students who entered college or went into the workforce during the late 1960s.

The class of '65 caught that cultural revolution right between the eyes, and their personal lives thereafter have reflected the changes of the times. In case after case, they tasted the sordid and seamy offerings of a valueless society. They became hooked on heroin, LSD, barbiturates, and alcohol. They experienced broken marriages and sexual extravaganzas and experimental lifestyles. They produced unwanted children who hadn't the slightest chance of being raised properly. By 1978, the year I wrote the first edition of *The Strong-Willed Child*, 11 percent of the Palisades class had served time in jail, and one individual (the school's most popular "dreamboat") had committed suicide. At least eighteen members of the class had been hospitalized for psychiatric treatment. A former teacher at Palisades High School characterized the decade from 1965 to 1975 as "the saddest years of the century."[27] I certainly agree.

My reason for describing this depressing era in such detail is to point out the mistakes made during that period. Unfortunately, the conditions that produced it are still evident today! The errors lumbered into by those parents were not only powered by disruptive social forces, they were also caused by parental failure to allow the class of 1965 to grow up. Although the older generation exercised very little influence over their sons and daughters after graduation, they nevertheless failed to emancipate them. An amazingly consistent pattern is evident throughout the book, with moms and dads bailing their kid out of jail, paying their bills, making it unnecessary for them to work, and encouraging them to live at home again. They offered volumes of unsolicited advice to accompany their undeserved and unappreciated material gifts. The result was disastrous.

Let me personalize the issues before us. How can you avoid making similar mistakes with your child, and especially with your strong-willed son or daughter? It is a very important question, because the more rebellious and frustrating your kid is, the more likely you are to give too much, tolerate too much, advise too much, and rescue too much. These blunders come down to a common thread—one that results from hanging on too tightly when you should be letting go. In so doing, you run the risk of making emotional cripples out of your recently minted adults. This is what the parents in Palisades did in the late sixties. But you can do better.

Here's how not to fall into the same pattern: Begin preparing a child for their ultimate release during the toddler years, before a relationship of dependence is established. Unfortunately, the natural inclination of parents is to do the opposite. As Domeena Renshaw wrote:

It may be messier for the child to feed himself; more untidy for him to dress himself; less clean when he attempts to bathe himself; less perfect for him to comb his hair; but unless his mother learns to sit on her hands and allow the child to cry and to try, she will overdo for the child, and independence will be delayed.[28]

This process of granting appropriate independence must continue throughout the elementary school years. Parents should permit their kids to go to summer camp even though it might be safer to keep them at home. They should allow them to spend the night with their friend when invited. The kids should make their own bed, take care of their animals, and do their homework. In short, the parental purpose should be to grant increasing freedom and responsibility year by year, so that when the child gets beyond adult control, he or she will no longer need it.

When this assignment is handled properly, a high school senior should be largely emancipated, even though he still lives with his parents. If I may share another personal example, this was the case during my last year at home. When I was seventeen years of age, my parents tested my independence by going on a two-week trip and leaving me behind. They loaned me the family car, and gave me permission to invite my (male) friends to spend the fourteen nights at our home. I remember being surprised by this move and the obvious risks they were taking. I could have thrown fourteen wild parties, wrecked the car and destroyed our house. Frankly, I wondered if they were wise to give me that much latitude. I did behave responsibly (although our house suffered the effects of some typical adolescent horseplay). After I was grown and married, I asked my mother why she took those risks—why she left me unsupervised for two weeks. She smiled and replied, "Because I knew in approximately one year you would be leaving for college, where you would have complete freedom with no one to tell you how to behave. And I wanted to expose you to that independence while you were still under my influence." Her intuitive wisdom was apparent once more. She was preparing me for the ultimate release, which often causes an overprotected young person to behave foolishly the moment she escapes the heavy hand of authority.

Our objective as parents, then, is to do nothing for boys and girls that they can profit from doing for themselves. I admit the difficulty of implementing this policy. Our deep love for our children makes us tremendously vulnerable to their needs. Life inevitably brings pain and sorrow to little people, and we hurt when they hurt. When others ridicule them or laugh at them, when they feel lonely and rejected, when they fail at something important, when they cry in the midnight hours, when physical harm threatens their existence—these are the trials that seem unbearable to those of us who watch from the sidelines. We want to rise like a mighty shield to protect them from life's sting—to hold them snugly within the safety of our embrace. Yet there are times when we must let them struggle. Children can't grow without taking risks. Toddlers can't walk initially without falling down. Students can't learn without facing some hardships. And ultimately, an adolescent can't enter young adulthood until we release him from our protective custody. But as I have indicated, parents in the Western world find it difficult to let their offspring face and conquer the routine challenges of everyday living. This was typical for members of the class of 1965, whose parents prevented them from solving their problems by always doing the job for them. These same parents also failed to provide a moral and spiritual foundation for them.

Let me offer three guidelines for our parenting efforts during the final era of childhood. The first is simply: *Hold on with an open hand.* This implies that we still care about the outcome during early adulthood, but we must not clutch our children too tightly. Our grip must be relaxed. We should pray for them, love them, and even offer advice to them when it is sought. But the responsibility to make personal decisions must be borne by the next generation, and they must also accept the consequences of those choices.

Another phrase expressing a similar concept is *Hold them close and let them go.* This seven-word suggestion could almost represent the theme of my book. Parents should be deeply involved in the lives of their young children, providing love, protection, and authority. But when those children reach their late teens and early twenties, the cage door must be opened to the world outside. That is the most frightening time of parenthood, particularly for Christian mothers and fathers who care so deeply about the spiritual welfare of their family. How difficult it is to await an answer to the question, "Did I train them properly?" The tendency is to retain control in an attempt to avoid hearing the wrong reply to that all-important question. Nevertheless, our sons and daughters are more likely to make proper choices when they do not have to rebel against our meddling interference to gain their independence.

The third guideline could easily have been one of King Solomon's proverbs, although it does not appear in the Bible. It states, *If you love something, set it free. If it comes back to you, then it's yours. If it doesn't return, then it never was yours in the first place.* This little aphorism contains great wisdom. It reminds me of a day a number of years ago when a wild coyote pup trotted in front of our house in southern California. He had strayed into our residential area from the nearby mountains. I managed to chase him into our backyard, where I trapped him in a corner. After fifteen or twenty minutes, I succeeded in placing a collar and leash around his neck. He fought the noose with all his strength, jumping, diving, gnawing, and straining at the tether. Finally, in exhaustion, he submitted to his servitude. He was my captive, to the delight of the neighborhood children. I kept the little rascal for an entire day and considered trying to make a pet of him. However, I contacted an authority on coyotes, who told me the chances were very slim that I could tame his wild streak. Obviously, I could have kept him chained or caged, but he would never really have belonged to me. I asked a game warden to return the lop-eared creature to his native territory in the canyons above Los Angeles. You see, his friendship meant nothing to me unless I could set him free and retain him by his own choice.

My point is that love demands freedom. This is true not only of relationships between animals and humans, but also in all interpersonal interactions. For example, the quickest way to destroy romantic love between a husband and wife is for one partner to clamp a steel cage around the other. I've seen hundreds of women trying unsuccessfully to demand love and fidelity from their husband. It doesn't work. Think back to your dating experiences before marriage. Do you recall that any romantic relationship was doomed the moment one partner began to worry about losing the other, phoning six or eight times a day and hiding behind trees to see who was competing for the lover's attention? That hand-wringing performance will devastate a perfectly good love relationship in a matter of days. To repeat: *Love demands freedom.*

Why else did God give us the choice of either serving Him or rejecting His companionship? Why did He give Adam and Eve the option of eating forbidden fruit in the Garden of Eden, instead of forcing their obedience? Why didn't He just make men and women slaves who were programmed to worship at His feet? The answers are found in the meaning of love. God gave us a free choice because there is no significance to love that knows no alternative. It is only when we come to Him because we hungrily seek His fellowship and communion that the relationship has any validity. Isn't this the meaning of Proverbs 8:17: "I love them that love me; and those that seek me early shall find me" (KJV)? That is the love that only freedom can produce. It cannot be demanded or coerced or required or programmed against our will. It can only be the product of a free choice, a concept that is honored even by the Almighty.

The application of this perspective to older adolescents and those in their early twenties should be obvious. There comes a point where our record as parents is in the books, our training has been completed, and the moment of release has arrived. As I did with the young coyote, we must unsnap the leash and remove the collar. If our child runs, he runs. If she marries the wrong person, she marries the wrong person. If he takes drugs, he takes drugs. If our children go to the wrong school, reject their faith, refuse to work, or squander their resources on liquor and prostitutes, then they must be permitted to make these destructive choices. But it is not our task to pay the bills, ameliorate the consequences, or support their folly.

Adolescence is not an easy time of life for either generation. In fact, it can be downright terrifying. But the key to surviving this emotional experience is to lay the proper foundation and then face this time with courage. Even the rebellion of the teen years can be a healthy factor. This conflict contributes to the process by which an individual changes from a dependent child to a mature adult, taking his place as a coequal with his parents. Without that friction, the relationship could continue to be an unhealthy mommy-daddy-child triad late into adult life, with serious implications for future marital harmony. If the strain between generations was not part of the divine plan of human development, it would not be so universally prevalent, even in homes where love and authority have been maintained in proper balance. And remember that billions of other parents have trod the same journey from childhood to adolescence and beyond. Most of them survived it. And you will too!

7. *Above all else, introduce your kids to Jesus Christ and then ground them thoroughly in the principles of your faith. This is job #1.*
This word of advice is relevant to Christian parents of both strong-willed

and compliant children. Everything of value depends on one primary responsibility—that of providing your kids with an unshakable faith in Jesus Christ. How can anything else compare in significance to this goal of keeping the family circle unbroken in the life to come? What an incredible objective to work toward!

If the salvation of our children is really that vital to us, then our spiritual training should begin before children can even comprehend what it is all about. They should grow up seeing their parents on their knees before God, talking to Him. They will learn quickly at that age and will never forget what they've seen and heard. Even if they reject their faith later, the seeds planted during that time will be with them for the rest of their lives. This is why we are instructed to "bring them up in the nurture and admonition of the Lord" (Ephesians 6:4, KJV).

Again, I was fortunate to have had parents who understood this principle. After I was grown they told me that I attempted to pray before I learned to talk. I watched them talk to God and tried to imitate the sounds I had heard. At three years of age, I made a conscious decision to become a Christian. You may think it impossible at such an age, but it happened. I remember the occasion clearly today. I was attending a Sunday evening church service and was sitting near the back with my mother. My father was the pastor, and he invited those who wished to do so to come pray at the altar. Fifteen or twenty people went forward, and I joined them spontaneously. I recall crying and asking Jesus to forgive my sins. I know that sounds strange, but that's the way it occurred. It is overwhelming for me to think about that event today. Imagine the King of the universe, Creator of all heaven and earth, caring about an insignificant kid barely out of toddlerhood! It may not make sense, but I know He met me at that altar.

Not every child will respond that early or dramatically, of course, nor should he. Some are more sensitive to spiritual matters than others, and they must be allowed to progress at their own pace. But in no sense should we as parents be casual or neutral about our children's training. Their world should sparkle with references to Jesus and to our faith. That is the meaning of Deuteronomy 6:6-9: "These commandments that I give you today are to be upon your hearts. Impress them on your children. Talk about them when you sit at home and when you walk along the road, when you lie down and when you get up. Tie them as symbols on your hands and bind them on your foreheads. Write them on the doorframes of your houses and on your gates."

I believe this commandment from the Lord is one of the most crucial passages for parents in the entire Bible. It instructs us to surround our children with godly teaching. References to spiritual things are not to be reserved just for Sunday morning or even for a bedtime prayer. They should permeate our conversation and the fabric of our lives. Why? Because our children are watching our every move during those early years. They want to know what is most important to us. If we hope to instill within them a faith that will last for a lifetime, then they must see and feel our passion for God.

As a corollary to that principle, I must remind you that children miss nothing in sizing up their parents. If you are only half convinced of your beliefs, they will quickly discern that fact. Any ethical weak spot—any indecision on your part—will be incorporated and then magnified in your sons and daughters. Like it or not, we are on the hook. Their faith or their faithlessness is usually a reflection of our own. As I've said, our children will eventually make their own choices and set the course of their life, but those decisions will be influenced by the foundation we have laid.

That brings me to another extremely important point, even though it is controversial. I firmly believe in acquainting children with God's judgment and wrath while they are young. Nowhere in the Bible are we instructed to skip over the unpleasant Scriptures in our teaching. The wages of sin is death, and children have a right to understand that fact.

I remember my mother reading the story of Samson to me when I was about nine years old. After this mighty warrior fell into sin, you will recall, the Philistines put out his eyes and held him as a common slave. Some time later, Samson repented before God, and he was forgiven. He was even given back his awesome strength. But my mother pointed out that he never regained his eyesight, nor did he ever live in freedom again. He and his enemies died together as the temple collapsed upon them.

"There are terrible consequences to sin," she told me solemnly. "Even if you repent and are forgiven, you will still suffer for breaking the laws of God. They are there to protect you. If you defy them, you will pay the price for your disobedience."

Then she talked to me about gravity, one of God's physical laws. "If you jump from a ten-story building, you can be certain that you will crash when you hit the ground. It is inevitable. You must also know that God's moral laws are just as real as His physical laws. You can't break them without crashing sooner or later."

Finally, she taught me about heaven and hell and the great Judgment Day when those who have been covered by the blood of Jesus will be separated eternally from those who have not. It made a profound impression on me.

Many parents would not agree with my mother's decision to acquaint me with the nature of sin and its consequences. They have said to me, "Oh, I wouldn't want to paint such a negative picture for my kids. I want them to think of God as a loving Father, not as a wrathful judge who punishes us." In so doing, they withhold a portion of the truth from their children. He is both a God of love and a God of judgment. There are 116 places in the Bible where we are told to "fear the Lord." By what authority do we eliminate these references in describing who God is to our children?

I am thankful that my parents and my church had the courage to acquaint me with the warning notes in Scripture. This awareness of sin and its consequences has kept me moral at times when I could have fallen into sexual sin. Biblical faith was a governor—a checkpoint beyond which I was unwilling to go. By that time I was not afraid of my parents. I could have fooled them. But I could not get away from the all-seeing eye of the Lord. I knew I would stand accountable before Him someday, and that fact gave me the extra motivation to make responsible decisions.

I can't overstate the importance of teaching divine accountability, especially to your strong-willed children. Since their tendency is to test the limits and break the rules, they will need this internal standard to guide their behavior. Not all will listen to it, but some will. But while doing that, be careful to balance the themes of love and justice as you teach your children about God. To tip the scales in either direction is to distort the truth and create confusion in a realm where understanding is of utmost significance.

QUESTIONS & ANSWERS

Q: Which year is most challenging when raising a strong-willed child?

A: Based on our survey of thirty-five thousand parents, the most rebellious year of childhood is eighteen. That is because a boy or girl in late adolescence feels he or she is "grown" and therefore resents anything that even resembles parental leadership or authority. It makes no difference that the young person is still living under Mom and Dad's roof and eating at their table. Teens have an intense desire to say, "Get off my back!" The second most challenging year is sixteen, and the third is fourteen. These findings vary from one individual to another, but those three years typically produce the most conflict and resentment. Then, if the young adult moves out, things get much better quickly.

Q: Generally speaking, what kind of discipline do you recommend for a teenager who is habitually miserable to live with?

A: That takes us back to what I wrote about using action to get action, rather than using anger to get action. The action approach offers one of the few tools available to very heady teenagers. Any time you can get them to do what is necessary without becoming furious, you are ahead of the game. Let me provide a few examples of how this might be accomplished.

1. I've been told that years ago in Russia, teenagers convicted of using drugs were denied their driver's license for years. Here in the United States, Michigan lawmakers recently passed a law prohibiting students from getting their license if they were caught calling in a prank bomb threat.[29] Both tactics have proved effective.

2. When my daughter was a teenager, she used to slip into my bathroom and confiscate my razor, my shaving cream, my toothpaste, or my comb. Of course, she never brought them back. Then after she had gone to school, I would discover that something was missing. There I was with wet hair or "fuzzy" teeth, trying

to locate the confiscated item in her bathroom. It was not a big deal, but it was irritating at the time. Can you identify?

I asked Danae a dozen times not to do this, but to no avail. Thus, the phantom (that would be me) struck without warning one cold morning. I hid everything she needed to put on her "face" and then left for the office. My wife told me she had never heard such wails and moans as were uttered that day. Our daughter plunged desperately through bathroom drawers looking for her toothbrush, comb, and hair dryer. My problem never resurfaced.

3. A family living in a house with a small hot-water tank was continually frustrated by their teenager's endless showers. Everyone who followed him had to take a cold bath. Screaming at him did no good. Once he was locked behind the bathroom door, he stayed in the steamy stall until the last drop of warm water had been drained. Solution? In midstream, Dad stopped the flow of hot water by turning a valve at the tank. Cold water suddenly poured from the nozzle. Junior popped out of the shower in seconds.

4. A single mother couldn't get her daughter out of bed in the morning until she announced a new policy: The hot water would be shut off promptly at 6:30 A.M. The girl could either get up on time or bathe in ice water. Another mother had trouble getting her eight-year-old out of bed each morning. She then began pouring bowls of frozen marbles under the covers with him each morning. The marbles ran to the center of the bed, precisely where his body lay. The sleepy boy arose quite quickly.

5. Instead of standing in the parking lot and screaming at students who drive too fast, school officials now put huge bumps in the road that jar the teeth of those who ignore them. They do the job quite nicely.

6. You as the parent have the car that a teenager needs, the money that he covets, and the authority to grant or withhold privileges. If push comes to shove, these chips can be exchanged for commitments to live responsibly, share the workload at home, and stay off little brother's back. This bargaining process works for younger kids too. I like the one-to-one trade-off for television

viewing time. It permits a child to watch one minute of television for every minute spent reading.

The possibilities are endless.

Q: My sixteen-year-old daughter is driving me crazy. She is disrespectful, noisy, and selfish. Her room looks like a pigpen, and she won't work any harder in school than absolutely necessary to get by. Everything I taught her, from manners to faith, seems to have sailed through her ears. What in the world should my husband and I do now?

A: I'm going to offer you some patented advice that may not make sense or seem responsive to the problem you've described. But stay with me. The most important thing you can do for your daughter is to just get her through it. The concept is a bit obscure, so let me make an effort to explain it.

Imagine your daughter is riding in a small canoe called *Puberty* on the Adolescent River. She soon comes to a turbulent stretch of white water that rocks her little boat violently. There is a very real danger that she will capsize and drown. Even if she survives today's rapids, it seems inevitable that she will be caught in swirling currents downstream and plunge over the falls. That is the apprehension harbored by millions of parents with kids bouncing along on the wild river. It's the falls that worry them most.

Actually, the typical journey down the river is much safer than believed. Instead of the water becoming more violent downstream, it eventually transitions from frightening rapids to tranquility once more. What I'm saying is that I believe your daughter is going to be okay even though she is now splashing and thrashing and gasping for air. Her little boat is more buoyant than you might think. Yes, a few individuals do go over the falls, usually because of drug abuse or another addictive behavior. But even some of those kids climb back in the canoe and paddle on down the river. Most will regain their equilibrium in a few years. In fact, the greatest danger of sinking a boat could come from parents!

The philosophy we applied with our teenagers (and you might try with yours) can be called "loosen and tighten." By this I mean we tried to loosen our grip on everything that had no lasting significance and tighten down on everything that did. We said yes whenever we possibly could to give support to the occasional no. And most important, we tried never to get too far away from our kids emotionally.

It is simply not prudent to write off a son or daughter, no matter how foolish, irritating, selfish, or insane a child may seem to be. You need to be there, not only while his or her canoe is bouncing precariously, but also after the river runs smooth again. You have the remainder of your life to reconstruct the relationship that is now in jeopardy. Don't let anger fester for too long. Make the first move toward reconciliation. And, finally, be respectful, even when punishment or restrictions are necessary.

Then wait for the placid water in the early twenties.

Q: Give me a straightforward answer to the question: How can I best survive the tumultuous years of my three strong-willed teenagers?
A: I have long recommended that parents whose kids are in the middle of a tumultuous adolescent experience must maintain a "reserve army." Let me explain: A good military general will never commit all his troops to combat at the same time. He maintains a reserve force that can relieve the exhausted soldiers when they falter on the front lines. I wish parents of adolescents would implement the same strategy. Instead, they commit every ounce of their energy and every second of their time to the business of living, holding nothing in reserve for the challenge of the century. It is a classic mistake that can be disastrous for parents of strong-willed adolescents.

The problem begins with a basic misunderstanding during the preschool years. I hear mothers say, "I don't plan to work until the kids are in kindergarten. Then I'll get a job." They appear to believe that the heavy demands on them will end magically when they get their youngest in school. In reality, the teen years will generate as much pressure on them as the preschool era did. An adolescent turns a house upside down . . . literally and figuratively. Not only is the typical rebellion of those years an extremely stressful experience, but the chauffeuring, supervising, cooking, and cleaning required to support an adolescent can be exhausting. Someone within the family must reserve the energy to cope with those new challenges. Mom is usually the candidate of choice. Remember, too, that menopause and a man's midlife crisis are scheduled to coincide with adolescence, which makes a wicked soup! It is a wise mother who doesn't exhaust herself at a time when so much is going on at home.

I know it is easier to talk about maintaining a lighter schedule than it is to secure one. It is also impractical to recommend that all mothers not seek formal employment during this era. Millions of women have to work for economic reasons, including the rising number of single parents in our world. Others choose to pursue busy careers. That is a decision to be made by a woman and her husband, and I would not presume to tell them what to do.

But decisions have inevitable consequences. In this case, there are biophysical forces at work that simply must be reckoned with. If, for example, 80 percent of a woman's available energy in a given day is expended in getting dressed, driving to work, doing her job for eight or ten hours, and stopping by the grocery store on the way home—then there is only 20 percent left for everything else. Maintaining the family, cooking meals, cleaning the kitchen, relating to her husband, and engaging in all other personal activities must be powered by that diminishing resource. It is no wonder that her batteries are spent by the end of the day. Weekends should be restful, but they usually are not. Thus, she plods through the years on her way to burnout.

This is my point: A woman in this situation has thrown all her troops into frontline combat. She has no reserve to call on. In that weakened condition, the routine stresses of raising an adolescent can be overwhelming. Let me say it again. Raising boisterous teenagers is an exciting and rewarding, but also frustrating, experience. Teens' radical highs and lows affect our mood. The noise, the messes, the complaints, the arguments, the sibling rivalry, the missed curfews, the paced floors, the wrecked cars, the failed tests, the jilted lovers, the wrong friends, the busy telephone, the pizza on the carpet, the ripped new shirt, the rebellion, the slammed doors, the mean words, the tears—it's enough to drive a rested mother crazy. But what about a career woman who already gave at the office, then came home to this chaos? Any unexpected crisis or even a minor irritant can set off a torrent of emotion. There is no reserve on which to draw. In short, the parents of adolescents should save some energy with which to cope with aggravation!

Whether or not you are able to accept and implement any of this advice is your business. It is mine to offer, and this is my best shot. To help you get through the turbulence of adolescence, you should:

1. Keep the schedule simple.
2. Get plenty of rest.
3. Eat nutritious meals.
4. Stay on your knees.

When fatigue leads adults to act like hot-tempered teenagers, anything can happen at home.

Q: My son is now sixteen years old. We wish that we had instilled in him earlier many of the principles that you have talked about. He throws his clothes around the house, refuses to help with routine tasks, and generally makes life miserable for everyone else. Is there any hope for shaping his will at this rather late age?
A: If any approach will succeed in charging his sluggish batteries or motivating him to live within the rules, it will probably involve an incentive-and-disincentive program of some variety. The following three steps might be helpful in initiating such a system:

1. Decide what is important to the youngster for use as a motivator. Two hours with the family car on date night is worth the world to a sixteen-year-old who has just gotten his or her license. (This could be the most expensive incentive in history if the young driver is a bit shaky behind the wheel.) An allowance is another easily available source of inspiration. Teenagers have a great need for cold cash today. A routine date with Helen Highschool might cost twenty dollars or more—in some cases far more. Yet another incentive may involve a fashionable article of clothing that would not ordinarily be within your teen's budget. Offering him or her a means of obtaining such luxuries is a happy alternative to the whining, crying, begging, complaining, and pestering that might occur otherwise. Mom says, "Sure, you can have the ski sweater, but you'll have to earn it." Once an acceptable motivator is agreed upon, the second step can be implemented.
2. Formalize the agreement. A contract is an excellent means of settling on a common goal. Once an agreement has been written, it is signed by the parent and the teen. The contract may include a point system that enables your teenager to meet the goal in a

reasonable time period. If you can't agree on the point values, you could allow for binding arbitration from an outside party. Let's examine a sample agreement in which Marshall wants an iPod, but his birthday is ten months away and he's flat broke. The cost of the player is approximately $150. His father agrees to buy the device if Marshall earns ten thousand points over the next six to ten weeks doing various tasks. Many of these opportunities are outlined in advance, but the list can be lengthened as other possibilities become apparent:

a. For making bed and straightening room each
   morning . . . . 50 points
b. For each hour of studying . . . . 150 points
c. For each hour of housecleaning or yard work . . 300 points
d. For being on time to breakfast and dinner . . . . . . 40 points
e. For babysitting siblings (without conflict)
   . . . . 150 points per hour
f. For washing the car each week . . . . 250 points
g. For arising by 8:00 A.M. Saturday morning . . . . 100 points

While the principles are almost universally effective, the method will vary. With a little imagination, you can create a list of chores and point values that works in your family. It's important to note that points can be gained for cooperation and lost for resistance. Disagreeable and unreasonable behavior can be penalized fifty points or more. (However, penalties must be imposed fairly and rarely or the entire system will crumble.) Also, bonus points can be awarded for behavior that is particularly commendable.

3. Finally, establish a method to provide immediate rewards. Remember that prompt reinforcement achieves the best results. This is necessary to sustain teens' interest as they move toward the ultimate goal. A thermometer-type chart can be constructed, with the point scale listed down the side. At the top is the ten-thousand-points mark, beside a picture of an iPod or other prize. Each evening, the daily points are totaled and the red portion of the thermometer is extended upward. Steady, short-term progress might earn Marshall a bonus of some sort—perhaps a CD

of his favorite musician or a special privilege. If he changes his mind about what he wishes to buy, the points can be diverted to another purchase. For example, five thousand points is 50 percent of ten thousand and would be worth $75 toward another purchase. However, do not give your child the reward if he does not earn it. That would eliminate future uses of reinforcement. Likewise, do not deny or postpone the goal once it is earned.

The system described above is not set in concrete. It should be adapted to the age and maturity of the adolescent. One youngster would be insulted by an approach that would thrill another. Use your imagination and work out the details with your son or daughter. This suggestion won't work with every teenager, but some will find it exciting. Lots of luck to you.

ELEVEN

DEALING WITH THE ADHD CHILD

W E COME NOW to a subject of great relevance to the parents of strong-willed children who also happen to have a condition known as attention deficit/hyperactivity disorder, or ADHD. Any physical problem that increases the level of activity and reduces self-control in a youngster is almost certain to create management problems. It is worse when that boy or girl is also inclined to resist parental authority. The conjunction of those characteristics is likely to make life difficult, and in some cases highly stressful for his mother, his father, his siblings, and his teacher.

This connection between hyperactivity and defiance has been documented clinically. Dr. Bill Maier, psychologist in residence at Focus on the Family, indicated that between 40 and 60 percent of kids with ADHD may have a condition known as Oppositional Defiant Disorder, or ODD, which manifests itself with a pattern of persistent arguing with adults; losing one's temper frequently; refusing to follow orders; deliberately annoying others; and showing recurrent anger, resentfulness, spitefulness, and vindictiveness.[1] ODD and ADHD is a volatile cocktail, to be sure.

Given this understanding, ADHD is a condition that we should consider carefully in our discussion of the strong-willed child. Thankfully, much definitive research has already been done. Many books on the subject of ADHD have been published in recent years; they've been written by researchers and clinicians who have spent their professional life working with and on behalf of affected children. Therefore, it is unnecessary for me to go into great detail here when other sources are so readily available. Instead, I will provide an overview of ADHD and address some of the disciplinary issues that are typically encountered with a tough-minded, hyperactive boy or girl.

First, let me speak to the controversy surrounding ADHD. Talk-show hosts, lay columnists, and many parents have strong opinions about this disorder, and some of the most vocal among them are simply wrong. The uninformed culture would tell us today that ADHD is a fad diagnosis without scientific support and that the problem would go away if parents simply knew how to discipline their kids better. It is not true. Certainly, many parents do need to learn better ways of managing their children, but that is another issue. ADHD is a physical and emotional disorder that has not been dreamed up by aggressive health professionals who claim to see it popping up everywhere. It may be overdiagnosed because there are no simple lab tests to confirm the condition; nevertheless, no evidence exists to indicate that parents and their doctors are routinely "drugging" kids unnecessarily or that a large number of teachers want to medicate students because they don't have the skills to control them in the classroom. While some abuses may occur, those generalizations are unfair and inaccurate.

I can tell you from personal experience that when a boy or girl does have the disorder and when it is pronounced, it certainly doesn't have to be concocted by somebody. I have seen ADHD kids—even preschoolers— who were all afterburner and no rudder. They could not hold still for more than a few seconds and seemed to be frantically driven from within. I remember one little two-year-old girl whose parents brought her to see me at Children's Hospital. This toddler was virtually climbing on my head and shoulders within moments of entering my office. There was fatigue and frustration on the faces of her parents, who were worn out from chasing their little dynamo from morning to night. Try telling exhausted moms and dads like this couple that their child's condition was imaginary. You'll quickly learn how strongly they feel about your mistaken hypothesis.

With that, I'll provide a primer for parents who suspect that their strong-willed child has ADHD. First, we'll review a comprehensive cover story published about this subject in *Time* (1994), which is still accurate today.*

Fifteen years ago, no one had ever heard of attention deficit/hyperactivity disorder. Today it is the most common behavioral disorder in American children, the subject of thousands of studies and symposiums and no small degree of controversy. Experts on ADHD say it afflicts as many as 3.5 million youngsters, or up to 5 percent of those under 18. It is two or three times as

---

likely to be diagnosed in boys as in girls. The disorder has replaced what used to be popularly called "hyperactivity," and it includes a broader collection of symptoms. ADHD has three main hallmarks: extreme distractibility, an almost reckless impulsiveness, and in some but not all cases, a knee-jiggling, toe-tapping hyperactivity that makes sitting still all but impossible.

For children with ADHD, a ticking clock or sounds and sights caught through a window can drown out a teacher's voice, although an intriguing project can absorb them for hours. Such children act before thinking; they blurt out answers in class. They enrage peers with an inability to wait their turn or play by the rules. These are the kids no one wants at a birthday party.

For kids who are hyperactive, the pattern is unmistakable, says Dr. Bruce Roseman, a pediatric neurologist with several offices in the New York City area, who has ADHD himself. "You say to the mother, 'What kind of personality did the child have as a baby? Was he active, alert? Was he colicky?' She'll say, 'He wouldn't stop—waaah, waaah, waaah!' You ask, 'When did he start to walk?' One mother said to me, 'Walk? My son didn't walk. He got his pilot's license at one year of age. His feet haven't touched the ground since.' You ask, 'Mrs. Smith, how about the terrible twos?' She'll start to cry, 'You mean the terrible twos, threes, fours, the awful fives, the horrendous sixes, the awful eights, the divorced nines, the I-want-to-die tens!'"

There is no question that ADHD can disrupt lives. Kids with the disorder frequently have few friends. Their parents may be ostracized by neighbors and relatives, who blame them for failing to control the child. "I've gotten criticism of my parenting skills from strangers," says the mother of a hyperactive boy in New Jersey. "When you're out in public, you're always on guard. Whenever I'd hear a child cry, I'd turn to see if it was because of Jeremy."

School can be a shattering experience for such kids. Frequently reprimanded and tuned out, they lose any sense of self-worth and fall ever further behind in their work. More than a quarter are held back a grade; about a third fail to graduate from high school. ADHD kids are also prone to accidents, says neurologist Roseman. "These are the kids I'm going to see in the emergency room this summer. They rode their bicycle right into the street and didn't look. They jumped off the deck and forgot it was high."

But the psychological injuries are often greater. By ages five to seven, says Dr. Russell Barkley, author of *Taking Charge of ADHD*, half to two-thirds are hostile and defiant. By ages 10 to 12, they run the risk of developing what psychologists call "conduct disorder"—lying, stealing, running away from home and ultimately getting into trouble with the law. As adults, says Barkley, 25 percent to 30 percent will experience substance-abuse problems, mostly with depressants like marijuana and alcohol. One study of hyperactive boys found that 40 percent had been arrested at least once by age 18—and these were kids who had been treated with stimulant medication; among those who had been treated with the drug plus other measures, the rate was 20 percent—still very high.

It is an article of faith among ADHD researchers that the right interventions can prevent such dreadful outcomes. "If you can have an impact with these kids, you can change whether they go to jail or to Harvard Law School," says psychologist Judith Swanson at the University of California Irvine. . . .

Whether ADHD is a brain disorder or simply a personality type, the degree to which it is a handicap depends not only on the severity of the traits but also on one's environment. The right school, job or home situation can make all the difference. The lessons of ADHD are truisms. All kids do not learn in the same way. Nor are all adults suitable for the same line of work. Unfortunately, American society seems to have evolved into a one-size-fits-all system. Schools can resemble factories: put the kids on the assembly line, plug in the right components and send 'em out the door. Everyone is supposed to go to college; there is virtually no other route to success. In other times and in other places, there have been alternatives: apprenticeships, settling a new land, starting a business out of the garage, going to sea. In a conformist society, it becomes necessary to medicate some people to make them fit in.

Surely an epidemic of attention deficit/hyperactivity disorder is a warning to us all. Children need individual supervision. Many of them need more structure than the average helter-skelter household provides. They need a more consistent approach to discipline and schools that tailor teaching to their individual learning styles. Adults too could use a society that's more flexible in its expectations, more accommodating to differences. Most of all, we all need to slow down. And pay attention.[2]

This article provides us with a basic understanding of ADHD in graphic terms. Sounds pretty scary, doesn't it? However, before concluding that the disorder will condemn your child to a life of misery and failure, I have much more positive news for you. An excellent book, entitled *Why A.D.H.D. Doesn't Mean Disaster*, published in 2004, was written by three of my professional colleagues.[3] They are Dr. Walt Larimore, vice president of medical outreach at Focus on the Family; Mrs. Diane Passno, one of Focus on the Family's executive vice presidents; and Dr. Dennis Swanberg, a minister, speaker, and beloved humorist. Dr. Swanberg and his son both have pronounced ADHD. Diane has a brilliant daughter, Danielle, who graduated from Dartmouth with a degree in engineering. She was high school valedictorian and homecoming queen, a state-champion athlete, and an all-around great kid. And, yes, she has ADHD too.

These authors are well-qualified to tell us how to live successfully with the disorder and to explain why it can actually be an asset. It will provide encouragement to every parent of a rip-snortin', rootin'-tootin', go-get-'em kid who is affected by ADHD.

The following quotation sets the tone for the book. It was written by Paul Elliott, M.D., who said:

> In my opinion, the ADD brain structure is not truly an abnormality. In fact, I believe a very good case can be made that it is not only normal, though in the minority, but may well be a superior brain structure. However, the talents of the person with ADD brain structure are not those rewarded by our society in its current stage of development. In other words, the problems of the person with ADD are caused as much by the way we have our society, educational system, and the business methods organized as by other factors more directly related to the ADD itself.[4]

Mrs. Passno laid out her thesis:

> Many parents need a new perspective about their kids who have been diagnosed with attention deficit/hyperactivity disorder. ADHD is a buzzword for our generation of parents and kids. The last thing in the world a parent wants to learn is that their beloved little bundle of joy has a prognosis that might limit his opportunities, particularly when he's just starting out. The stereotype ADHD has given to these kids is simply awful. And most parents lack either the understanding or the confidence to challenge the conventional thinking.
>
> Stereotyping kids is deceptive and dangerous. It can do unseen damage to a child's understanding of who he is and what he is able to accomplish in life. As early as kindergarten, what most kids do when they are told they are destined to fail is they begin to live up to the expectation. They become classic underachievers.
>
> [We] have a goldfish that will probably outlive everyone in our family. This twenty-nine–cent prize had been in a bowl

on the kitchen sink for the past six years, swimming around and around in a tight little circle. One day, I moved Sgt. Pepper to a huge tank, six times the size of his old domain. For the first several days, he continued to swim in the same tight little circles the size of his old bowl. He didn't understand that his world had expanded. In the same way, a child who becomes "that ADHD kid who drives everyone nuts" may never understand what he can accomplish with his unique set of gifts. And if he is never given permission to be anything different, most likely, he never will.[5]

Dennis Swanberg, who holds an earned Ph.D., weighed in on the subject, sharing his perspective as a person who has learned to cope very successfully with his own and his son's ADHD. He wrote:

This book has been a particular passion of mine for years. It has been my privilege, first in the pulpit, and later as a public speaker with my own television program, to overcome the barriers ADHD poses and find the benefits. None of these successes were even on my radar screen when I was young and struggled simply to get through another day at school. But if I can make it, anyone can. I hope to encourage those of you who are having similar difficulties with raising a kid like I was.

Even so, our main purpose for writing this book is to encourage you and help you consider that attention deficit/hyperactivity disorder can be a *dividend* rather than a disorder or mental disability. It can be turned into a blessing rather than a curse, an asset rather than a handicap. Sure, there will always be challenges and frustrations associated with something out of the ordinary like ADHD. But by the time you finish this book, we hope and pray that no matter whether you have ADHD yourself, or are the parent of an ADHD child, you will see your future from a hopeful new perspective.[6]

I think you get the flavor of the book and why I hope those of you who have an affected child will read it. It is filled with many success stories about kids and parents who overcame ADHD.

We'll devote the balance of this chapter to a question-and-answer format. I'll share the podium with my friend, Dr. Walt Larimore.

Questions & Answers

Q: I know that I can't diagnose my own son, but it would be helpful if you would list the kinds of behavior to look for in him. What are the typical characteristics of someone with ADHD?

A: Dobson: Psychiatrists Edward M. Hallowell and John J. Ratey are authors of an excellent book entitled *Driven to Distraction*.[7] In it they list twenty symptoms that are often seen in a person with ADHD. These are among the criteria used by doctors to make the diagnosis:

1. A sense of underachievement, of not meeting one's goals (regardless of how much one has accomplished)
2. Difficulty getting organized
3. Chronic procrastination or trouble getting started
4. Many projects going simultaneously; trouble with follow-through
5. Tendency to say what comes to mind without necessarily considering the timing or appropriateness of the remark
6. An ongoing search for high stimulation
7. A tendency to be easily bored
8. Easy distractibility, trouble focusing attention, tendency to tune out or drift away in the middle of a page or a conversation, often coupled with an ability to focus at times
9. Often creative, intuitive, highly intelligent
10. Trouble going through established channels, following proper procedure
11. Impatient; low tolerance for frustration
12. Impulsive, either verbally or in action, as in impulsive spending of money, changing plans, enacting new schemes or career plans, and the like

13. Tendency to worry needlessly, endlessly; tendency to scan the horizon looking for something to worry about alternating with inattention to or disregard for actual dangers
14. Sense of impending doom, insecurity, alternating with high risk-taking
15. Depression, especially when disengaged from a project
16. Restlessness
17. Tendency toward addictive behavior
18. Chronic problems with self-esteem
19. Inaccurate self-observation
20. Family history of ADD, manic-depressive illness, depression, substance abuse, or other disorders of impulse control or mood

Q: Does ADHD go away as children grow up? If not, what are the implications for the adult years?

A: Dobson: We used to believe the problem typically disappeared with the onset of puberty. That's what I was taught in graduate school. Now it is known that ADHD is a lifelong condition for about two-thirds of those affected, influencing behavior from the cradle to the grave. The symptoms may lessen in time for some, but not for the majority. Some ADHD adults learn to be less disorganized and impulsive as they get older. They channel their energy into sports activities or professions in which they function very well. Others have trouble settling on a career or holding a job. Follow-through remains a problem as they flit from one task to another. They are particularly unsuited for desk jobs, such as accounting positions or other assignments that demand attention to detail, long hours of sitting, and the ability to juggle many balls at once.

Another characteristic of ADHD in adolescence and adulthood is the thirst for high-risk activity. Even as children, they are accident-prone, and their parents get well acquainted with the local emergency room personnel. As they get older, rock climbing, bungee jumping, car racing, motorcycle riding, white-water rafting, and related activities are among their favorite pursuits. Adults with ADHD are sometimes called "adrenaline junkies" because they are hooked on the high produced by the high octane adrenaline rush associated with dangerous behavior. Others are more susceptible to drug use, alcoholism, and other addictive behaviors.

One study revealed that approximately 40 percent will have been arrested by eighteen years of age.[8]

Some of those who have ADHD are at higher risk for marital conflict too. It can be very irritating to a compulsive, highly ordered husband or wife to be married to a "messie"—someone whose life is chaotic and who forgets to pay the bills, fix the car, or keep records for income-tax reports. Such a couple may need professional counseling to help them learn to work together and capitalize on each other's strengths.

Q: How common is ADHD?
A: Larimore: Here is what we know about the incidence of the disorder. The *Journal of the American Medical Association (JAMA)* stated that ADHD "is among the most common neurodevelopmental disorders in children."[9] The *British Medical Journal* estimated that approximately 7 percent of school-age children have ADHD—and that boys are affected three times as often as girls.[10] A 1995 Virginia study showed that 8 percent to 10 percent of young school children were taking medication for ADHD.[11] Boys are twice as likely to have ADHD and a learning disability. Rates of diagnosis of ADHD are twice as high in Caucasian children as in Latinos and African-Americans.[12]

Q: Are the brains of people with ADHD different?
A: Larimore: Although the cause of ADHD is unknown, the theories abound. Some believe it is associated with subtle differences in brain structure. Brain scans reveal a number of subtle changes in the brain of those diagnosed with ADHD. In fact, one of the former names for ADHD was "minimal brain disorder."

Others say it's related to neural pathways, neurotransmitters, or brain chemistry—particularly abnormalities in the brain chemical dopamine. Still other researchers believe ADHD is related to the brain's blood supply or electrical system. Recent research has raised the question of whether frequent exposure in early childhood to rapid electronic stimuli (such as television and computers) might contribute to this problem.

Richard DeGrandpre, Ph.D., in his book *Ritalin Nation: Rapid-Fire Culture and the Transformation of Human Consciousness* theorizes about what he called a "sensory addiction phenomenon."[13] Dr. DeGrandpre believes that early exposure to electronic sensory bombardment, especially at a time when the brain is just forming connections and synapses, may result in biological or neurological effects, including, but not limited to, ADHD.

DeGrandpre believes that these effects can be exaggerated in the absence of parental structure. He points out that people in Western nations live in an incredibly stimulating world; there are constant stimuli experienced by even a very young child. I don't know that we can really get rid of it all, but we can encourage parents to provide a structured environment so children can learn to deal with and perhaps limit these stimuli.

One source of information that may support DeGrandpre's theory is the experience of the Amish, who typically forgo modern conveniences such as computers and television. Among these children who are protected from this stimulation, ADHD appears to be very uncommon. Researchers have reported that out of two hundred Amish children followed prospectively and compared with the non-Amish population, symptoms of ADHD were unusual.[14]

Q: What about prescription stimulant medications?

A: Larimore: Many parents call or write us at Focus on the Family to ask about using prescription medications for ADHD. They've heard the controversies and they are worried that starting a child on medication might be a bad decision. On the other hand, many worry that not prescribing it may also be harmful. They ask, "What should we do?"

Without doubt, the use of prescription drugs for both children and adults can be very successful as a short-term treatment of ADHD. There is a virtual mountain of evidence supporting the safety and effectiveness of using medications, although none of these studies extended for more than two years. According to these studies, 70 percent to 95 percent of ADHD patients benefit from appropriate medication.[15] These medications seem to reduce disruptive behavior dramatically, improve school performance, and even raise IQ test scores. The medications seem to be equally effective for both boys and girls.

The most commonly prescribed drugs are Ritalin, Concerta, Strattera, Dexedrine, and Adderall. In most instances, these substances have a remarkably positive effect—at least for the short term.[16]

Q: There are so many options. Which is best?

A: Larimore: The treatment for ADHD should be individualized and tailored for each child and each family. So, while there is no "best" course of treatment, there are a number of excellent options. Learning more about them can assist you in working with your child's physician in choosing among these alternatives.

One problem with some of the older ADHD medications was that their effects didn't last more than a few hours at most. This meant that extra doses would have to be given at school or later in the afternoon once the child was home. Worse yet, when the short-acting medications wore off, a rebound effect sometimes occurred, during which the child's symptoms and behaviors actually worsened! This not only created difficulty for the school, it also caused embarrassment for the child and led to noncompliance.

Other side effects of the stimulant medications included anxiety, nervousness, palpitations (irregular heartbeat), sweating, and insomnia (difficulty going to sleep). More rare side effects included irritability, mood swings, depression, withdrawal, hallucinations, and loss of spontaneity. The friends of one of my young patients told her, "Carla, please don't take your medication before you come to our party. You'll be no fun!"

But I have good news. Newer medications are now available to solve this problem for many patients. Every medication has undesirable side effects and should be administered only when indicated and appropriate. Ritalin, for example, has a number of potential side effects. It can reduce the appetite and cause insomnia in some patients. Nevertheless, for the vast majority of ADHD patients, newer prescription treatments are remarkably effective and safe.

Let me offer one caution, however. The main danger of drug abuse from stimulants is from your child's friends or classmates who do not have ADHD and want to use the stimulant to get high. In one study, 16 percent of ADHD children had been approached to sell, give, or trade their medication.[17] As shocking as those numbers are, the problem of Ritalin abuse seems to be worsening.

So to protect your ADHD child's friends, be sure to carefully supervise their use of stimulants.

Q: My six-year-old son is not only hyperactive, but he wets the bed as well. Can you offer advice for dealing with that recurring problem?
A: Dobson: Your child probably suffers from enuresis, which usually

426   THE NEW STRONG-WILLED CHILD

occurs in children who are developmentally immature. It is more common in children with ADHD. Each child has his own timetable of maturation, and some are in no great hurry. However, enuresis can cause both emotional and social distress for the older child. Thus, it is wise that this problem be conquered during the early childhood years, if possible.

There have been some promising developments in recent years. In April 1999, Japanese researchers produced an electronic alarm that is effective in stopping kids from bed-wetting. The machine, which was devised by a urologist and a telephone maker, measures a child's brain waves and monitors the bladder. When a child has to urinate, the alarm goes off and tells the child it is time to go to the toilet.[18]

An alarm works well with children because bed-wetting often occurs during very deep sleep, making it difficult for them to learn nighttime control on their own. Their mind does not respond to the signal or reflex action that ordinarily awakens light sleepers. The alarm is loud enough to awaken most deep sleepers and get them to the bathroom.

Consult your family physician or a urologist for the best course of treatment for your child. There is a range of options now available for you, including a drug called Desmopressin, which helps regulate urine production.

Q: I am not sure if my son has ADHD, but he is hyperactive and drives everyone crazy. He simply does not fit in with his peers. He always seems to be left out when other kids play, and he has trouble making friends. He just won't, or can't, carry on a sustained conversation with other children and usually winds up acting silly and driving them away. Does this sound like ADHD? Do you have any advice on how we can make him fit in better with the group?
A: Dobson: There are many disorders that could account for the characteristics you describe. ADHD is only one of them. Another is Asperger syndrome, which is a neurological problem related to autism. Yet another is called Rett syndrome. And still another is called Tourette syndrome. In some cases, there is no defined diagnosis. In other cases, the unique personality of a particular child without an abnormality may simply irritate other children and bring on rejection and ridicule.

We now know that an individual's success in life, along with his personal happiness, depends greatly on his emotional intelligence—his ability to function well in a group and develop strong relationships. Psychologist Willard Hartup of the University of Minnesota said, "Children who are generally disliked, who are aggressive and disruptive, who are unable to sustain close relationships with other children and who cannot establish a place for themselves in the peer culture, are seriously at risk in the years ahead." Intervention for these youngsters is obviously needed and can be very beneficial.[19]

Once more, let me emphasize that it is extremely important for parents to recognize the complexity of children and seek professional help when needed. Assistance for a child with specialized needs is available in most cities today, but you as a parent have to find it. University child-development centers might be a good place to begin your search.

Q: Is ADHD inherited?

A: Larimore: There is increasing evidence from medical studies that genetic factors play a role in ADHD. Jacquelyn Gillis and her team, then at the University of Colorado, reported in 1992 that the risk of ADHD in a child whose identical twin has the disorder is between eleven and eighteen times greater than that of a nontwin sibling of a child with ADHD. She showed that between 55 percent and 92 percent of the identical twins of children with ADHD eventually develop the condition.[20]

A large study in Norway of 526 identical twins (who inherit exactly the same genes) and 389 fraternal twins (who are no more alike genetically than siblings born years apart) found that these children had nearly an 80 percent chance of inheriting ADHD. They concluded that up to 80 percent of the differences in attention, hyperactivity, and impulsivity between people with ADHD and those without the disorder can be explained by genetic factors.[21]

What does this mean for your family? Simply that if one or both of the parents have ADHD, their child is more likely to have ADHD as well. If that is the case, dealing with an affected child may remind Mom or Dad of some painful memories from their own childhood or teenage years. This can make it even more difficult to deal with the child. Furthermore, the unaffected siblings may be more likely to have children of their own with ADHD. These are just a few of the reasons why many therapists recommend counseling for the entire family.

Q: What are some of the ways that ADHD affects the family?

A: ADHD is not a problem that affects only the affected individual. The time and effort required to deal with ADHD can significantly disrupt the entire family.

In most families, the mother has the greatest emotional, relational, and spiritual risk in caring for an ADHD child. Although these kids can be intensely loving, they can also turn on their moms in a second. They can be verbally or emotionally abusive to their parents, which can wound parents deeply. They can be wonderful one day and horrible the next—or they can change from hour to hour.

Moms of ADHD kids need to quickly give up the delusion that their homes will be immaculate or that every meal will be a joyous family affair. ADHD parents have to learn that they are not perfect and that they may need help. Not only can they be rejected and hurt by their child, these parents may have to face the rejection, hostility, or animosity of children, other adults, or neighbors.

The ADHD child is often physically aggressive and must be taught to convert physical aggression into verbal expression (a skill some adults need to learn!). He or she may be verbally abusive. Once again, learning how to teach your child to redirect this harmful behavior into constructive behavior is essential. Parents of ADHD kids quickly learn that they cannot force or coerce their kids to be like "normal" kids—many of them will never adhere to that ideal. They are wired differently, and their parents need to learn a wide variety of parenting skills to cope with, teach, train, and creatively discipline these unique kids.

Let's not forget the siblings. They also have to live with the ADHD child—who can make life miserable for his unaffected brothers and sisters. Medical studies are beginning to show that siblings can also be at risk for emotional problems. These siblings can be chronically victimized by the ADHD child, who may bully them; verbally or physically abuse them; and be intense, demanding, and obnoxious.

Further, if siblings do not receive the attention and time that they need and deserve—because of the time and effort diverted to the ADHD child—they may feel alienated, rejected, or unloved. These feelings can lead to a range of behavioral problems, especially in adolescence. Therefore, many ADHD care providers recommend that siblings be part of the family counseling. The good news is that the skills these siblings gain will be helpful to them for life.

Q: What about homeschooling for ADHD youngsters?
A: Larimore: For many kids with learning difficulties, homeschooling can be an educational alternative—especially for the parents who are dedicated to doing this and are willing to do what is required. I have talked to many doctors of ADHD patients who relate encouraging examples of kids who have done much better when they've entered a homeschool environment.

Q: We have a five-year-old son who has been diagnosed with ADHD. He is really difficult to handle, and I have no idea how to manage him. I know he has a neurological problem, so I don't feel right about making him obey like we do our other children. It is a big problem for us. What do you suggest?
A: Dobson: I understand your dilemma, but I urge you to discipline your son. Every youngster needs the security of defined limits, and the ADHD boy or girl is no exception. Such a child should be held responsible for his or her behavior, although the approach may be a little different. For example, most children can be required to sit on a chair for disciplinary reasons, whereas some very hyperactive children would not be able to remain there. Similarly, corporal punishment is sometimes ineffective with a highly excitable little bundle of electricity. As with every aspect of parenthood, disciplinary measures for the ADHD child must be suited to his or her unique characteristics and needs.

Q: How, then, should I discipline my ADHD child?
A: Dobson: Let me offer some guidelines for how to train and guide your youngster. The following eighteen suggestions were included in an excellent book by Dr. Domeena Renshaw, *The Hyperactive Child.*[22] Regrettably, her book is now out of print, but her advice is still valid.

1. Be consistent in rules and discipline.
2. Keep your own voice quiet and slow. Anger is normal. Anger can be controlled. Anger does not mean you do not love a child.
3. Try hard to keep your emotions cool by bracing for expected

turmoil. Recognize and respond to any positive behavior, however small. If you search for good things, you will find a few.

4. Avoid a ceaselessly negative approach: "Stop"—"Don't"—"No."

5. Separate behavior, which you may not like, from the child's person, whom you like, e.g., "I like you. I don't like your tracking mud through the house."

6. Have a very clear routine for this child. Construct a timetable for waking, eating, playing, watching TV, studying, doing chores, and going to bed. Follow it flexibly when he disrupts it. Slowly your structure will reassure him until he develops his own.

7. Demonstrate new or difficult tasks using action accompanied by short, clear, quiet explanations. Repeat the demonstration until learned. This uses audiovisual-sensory perceptions to reinforce the learning. The memory traces of a hyperactive child take longer to form. Be patient and repeat.

8. Designate a separate room or a part of a room that is his own special area. Avoid brilliant colors or complex patterns in decor. Simplicity, solid colors, minimal clutter, and a worktable facing a blank wall away from distractions assist concentration. A hyperactive child cannot filter out overstimulation himself yet.

9. Do one thing at a time: Give him one toy from a closed box; clear the table of everything else when he's coloring; turn off the radio/TV when he is doing homework. Multiple stimuli prevent him from concentrating on his primary task.

10. Give him responsibility, which is essential for growth. The task should be within his capacity, although the assignment may need much supervision. Acceptance and recognition of his efforts (even when imperfect) should not be forgotten.

11. Read his pre-explosive warning signals. Quietly intervene to avoid explosions by distracting him or discussing the conflict calmly. Removal from the battle zone to the sanctuary of his room for a few minutes is useful.

12. Restrict playmates to one or at most two at one time, because he is so excitable. Your home is most suitable so you can provide structure and supervision. Explain your rules to the playmate and briefly tell the other parent your reasons.

13. Do not pity, tease, be frightened by, or overindulge this child.

He has a special condition of the nervous system that is manageable.

14. Know the name and dose of his medication. Give it regularly. Watch and remember the effects to report back to your physician.

15. Openly discuss with your physician any fears you have about the use of medications.

16. Lock up all medications to avoid accidental misuse.

17. Always supervise the taking of medication, even if it is routine over a long period of years. Responsibility remains with the parents! One day's supply at a time can be put in a regular place and checked routinely as he becomes older and more self-reliant.

18. Share your successful "helps" with his teacher. The outlined ways to help your hyperactive child are as important to him as diet and insulin are to a diabetic child.

Q: What else would you recommend to parents?

A: Larimore: Learn as much as you can about the disorder. Successful management of ADHD involves a range of options, and you need to become acquainted with them. They begin with the diagnosis.

People living with ADHD are usually greatly relieved to learn that they have an identifiable, treatable condition. They are gratified (as are their parents) to learn that they've done nothing wrong. This condition is not caused; people are born with it. It's part of their design and makeup. Best of all, God can and does use ADHD in His particular plan for their life.

One organization that may be able to help is CHADD (Children and Adults with Attention-Deficit/Hyperactivity Disorder). It has an exceptional amount of evidence-based and trustworthy information available and can identify some parent support groups. However, let me share a caution here. Parent support groups, if not carefully organized, can turn into "gripe-and-whine" sessions. That is not helpful and is sometimes discouraging. All of us need someone to gripe to on occasion, no doubt, but there should be some direction to the group. Someone needs to say, "Okay, now that we've heard everyone's complaints, what can we do about them?" I've known parents who came home from such a group and reacted negatively to their child because of what they talked about at the support group. That's not helpful for the parent or the child.

Second, commit to giving your child unconditional love. The most important treatment for children with ADHD is abundant affection and affirmation. They are frequently accused of not trying, of being lazy, of not being a good kid. Teachers get angry at them. Some classmates get upset with them because they often don't do well in school, and they begin to treat them disrespectfully. My heart goes out to these youngsters.

Let's face it, these ADHD kids don't always make us feel or look good. Love, to me, is being committed to doing what this individual kid needs, regardless of the circumstances. These children often have greater needs than those who are not affected.

Many times they feel like they are second-class individuals. I've had kids in my practice tell me, "There's something wrong with me." I've had ADHD children actually say, "God made a mistake when He put me together. That's why I'm here."

Part of loving these special kids is to help them discover the great giftedness that God has given them—to show them that God didn't make a mistake when He made them.

Children simply do not all have to fit the same mold, even in school. For many of these youngsters, parents may need to de-emphasize academics. Simply put, for many ADHD kids, there are things that are more important than academics, such as being loved and accepted by family and friends just the way that God made them. Your child needs to understand that God has a place for her and has given her a special gift, and that she does have specialized abilities. She needs to know that you are going to work with her to discover and develop those special gifts and skills, and that you can't wait to see what God's going to do with her. This may be far more important to your ADHD child than getting too excited over the fact that she is not doing quite as well in the classroom as others.

Loving these kids unconditionally does *not* mean expecting them to do less than their best—the best that *they* can do. It does mean directing and encouraging them to overcome challenges and achieve those things that they are uniquely gifted in doing.

The important point to make to your child is that a diagnosis of ADHD is not a handicap. He is in the same boat as some famous people, who, if not officially diagnosed with the disorder, had symptoms and behaviors remarkably akin to those with ADHD: Albert Einstein, Tom Cruise, Henry Winkler (the Fonz!), John Lennon, Winston Churchill, Henry Ford,

Stephen Hawking, Alexander Graham Bell, Presidents Woodrow Wilson, John F. Kennedy, and Dwight D. Eisenhower, Generals George Patton and William Westmoreland . . . and the list goes on. What a remarkable group of which to be a part!

TWELVE

A Final Word
of Encouragement

IT'S TIME NOW to put a ribbon on this pleasant foray into the life of strong-willed children and those who have the responsibility of raising them. I'll close by sharing a few thoughts that come straight from my heart.

Many wonderful emotions accompany the exhilarating privilege of bringing a baby into the world and then watching that little tyke begin to grow and learn and develop. How well I remember our son and daughter taking their first step, saying their first word, riding their first tricycle, praying their first prayer, and progressing rapidly through the many other exciting milestones of childhood. The first day of kindergarten was a highly emotional morning for me, when I placed our precious little girl on the steps of the bus, moved back to take her picture, and watched as she and the other children rode slowly down the street. Then I wiped away a tear as I walked back to the house. Our baby was growing up.

There would be many other joyful and bittersweet experiences along the way, as Shirley and I gradually realized the breathtaking brevity of the parenting years. Even when our kids were in elementary school, we were already starting to dread the day when our parenting responsibilities would be over. Predictably, in what seemed like a moment of time, a cold wind of change blew through our home, leaving an empty nest that took some getting used to.

Yes, being a mom or dad is one of the most marvelous experiences in living, and I feel compassion for infertile couples who have been denied the privilege of procreation. But men and women who are granted that precious gift know that a measure of pain and sorrow comes with it. Kids

435

often struggle with a variety of learning problems, physical disabilities, accidents, diseases, and/or social difficulties. Then come the tumultuous years of adolescence when, for some teens more than others, every day can be a challenge. All of these stress points are exacerbated when a child has a willful temperament and a tendency to fuss and argue and disobey. Parents raising such a youngster sometimes feel as though they live every day on a battlefield.

It is on behalf of those frustrated, discouraged, and confused parents that I have written this book. I have wanted, especially, to put an arm around moms and dads who feel like an utter failure in this most important responsibility in life. They (perhaps *you*) wanted to be a perfect parent, doing that job with greater success than any other. Instead, it now looks as though every good intention has been misinterpreted, resented, and resisted. Is that where you are today?

At times do you find yourself thinking, *I love this kid more than anything in the world, but I don't really like him or her very much? We can't get along for more than ten minutes without clashing over relatively insignificant matters. Why does this child make me so angry, when what I want most is harmony and love? Why is our relationship so unsatisfying and disturbing? What did I do to mess up something that began with such promise and hope? Not only have I failed my child, I have failed God, too.*

Let's talk about those feelings for a moment, which are common at one time or another within almost all caring moms and dads. Parenthood can be a very guilt-inducing proposition. Babies come into our life when we are young and immature, and there are no instruction manuals to guide our first halting steps. There is no manufacturing tag on a newborn's wrist that says, "Some assembly required." So we take these tiny human beings home with us, not yet knowing who they are, and then proceed to bumble along as best we can. As a consequence, many of the day-by-day decisions we make on their behalf are the result of sheer guesswork, as we hope against hope that we are doing the right thing. Our own inadequacies also get in the way. We become tired and frustrated and selfish, which sometimes affects our judgment. In those moments, we react without thinking and realize the next morning that we handled things all wrong.

In short, children are so maddeningly complex that it is impossible to raise them without making many blunders and mistakes. After about twenty years of on-the-job training, we begin to figure out what parenting is all about. By then it is time to let go and pretend we don't care anymore.

Added to these difficulties are our own personal problems, which can include marital conflict or divorce, physical illness, financial pressures, and the other cares of living. Our unmet needs, such as those experienced by single parents, also can lead us into behavior that will later seem terribly foolish. Do I sound as though I'm whining here? I hope not. I'm simply attempting to articulate the discomfort that occurs for parents of strong-willed children when they begin to feel that they have botched the assignment. (The parents of compliant children may not fully understand this emotional reaction, although there is usually enough stress in child rearing to affect everybody.)

Despite these discouraging moments, it is my firm conviction that bearing and raising children is worth everything it costs us. Along with the difficulties come the greatest joys and rewards life has to offer. How could that be true? How can the very thing that brings us anxiety and frustration be the source of such happiness and fulfillment? There is an obvious contradiction here that bears consideration.

Christian writer C. S. Lewis tried to express the palpable pain that he experienced when he lost his wife to cancer. He would not have been so devastated by her passing, he said, if he had not allowed himself to love her with all his heart. In the movie *Shadowlands,* based on this period of Lewis's life, he wondered if it would have been better never to have loved at all and avoided the risk of losing the woman he adored. It would certainly have been safer to live in a fortress, protecting himself from disappointment and grief by remaining emotionally detached and uncaring. Lewis considered these responses to sorrow and concluded that, in the end, love is worth the risk. This is the way he penned it:

> To love at all is to be vulnerable. Love anything and your heart will certainly be wrung and possibly broken. If you want to make sure of keeping it intact, you must give your heart to no one, not even to an animal. Wrap it carefully around with hobbies and little luxuries . . . lock it up safe in the casket or coffin of your selfishness. But in that casket—safe, dark, motionless, airless—it will change. It will not be broken; it will

become unbreakable, impenetrable, irredeemable. . . . The only place outside heaven where you can be perfectly safe from all the dangers of love is hell![1]

Then Lewis concluded: "We love to know that we are not alone."

Doesn't this insight speak eloquently of the pain associated with parenthood? It certainly does to me. This is what bearing and raising children comes down to. Loving those we have borne *is* a risky business, but one that also brings great joy and happiness. Even though there are often trials and tears associated with the challenge, it is a noble journey. We as parents are given the privilege of taking the raw materials that comprise a brand-new human being and then molding him or her day-by-day into a mature, disciplined, productive, and God-fearing adult who will someday live in eternity. Doing that job right, despite its setbacks and disappointments, is one of the greatest achievements in living.

I want to offer hope to those moms and dads today who are demoralized at this stage of the journey. First, you must recognize that strong-willed children are *not* a liability, and you should never let yourself feel victimized or cheated by having borne one of them. DO NOT compare your child with the "perfect" children of your relatives or friends. They will have their share of problems too in time. Admittedly, a tough-minded kid is tougher to raise and at times may push you right to the edge. But that wonderful assertiveness and determination will be an asset when your child is grown. That irritating temperament was a gift from God, and He makes no mistakes.

You should also recognize that these kids often possess a certain strength of character that will help them grab the opportunities that come their way. When they make up their minds to reach for something, they are likely to stay with it until the goal is achieved. They are also less susceptible to peer pressure, maybe not during early adolescence, but as maturity begins to set in. What I said before bears repeating. Though they typically argue and fight and complain throughout their years at home, the majority will turn around when they reach young adulthood and do what their parents most desire. Better days are around the corner.

However, the realization of that potential appears to depend on the provision of a structured early home environment led by loving, fair-minded mothers and fathers who are clearly tougher and wiser than their children. Those who are reasonably effective in shaping the will without breaking the spirit are going to appreciate the person their child eventually becomes.

That is what we found when we surveyed thirty-five thousand parents. More than 85 percent of adult strong-willed children who rebelled significantly during their teenage years came back to what they had been taught—entirely or at least somewhat. Only 15 percent were so headstrong that they rejected their family's core values in their midtwenties. These findings tell us that you, too, are probably doing a better job with your kids than you think. Future years will confirm that the guilt that haunted your thoughts and invaded your dreams was unjustified and self-imposed.

In short, the youngster who sometimes exasperates you today probably has little green buds growing all over his tree, even if all you see now are the barren twigs of winter. It will take time for him or her to flower, of course, but springtime is on its way. Trust me on this one.

It is always encouraging for me to hear from parents who have lived through the stresses of parenting and discovered that the principles of good parenting are valid. They work because they came from the Creator of children. One mother of a very strong-willed child sent me a letter some years ago after concluding, much too early, that my advice *didn't* work and that I must not have understood hardnosed youngsters like her own. This is what she wrote:

Dear Dr. Dobson:

After purchasing your book, The Strong-Willed Child, *I must tell you I was disappointed. The beginning was encouraging, but then the rest was devoted to general child-rearing techniques. I thought the entire book would be written about the strong-willed child. Are you sure you know what one is? Nearly every child is strong-willed, but not every child is "strong-willed!"*

Our third (and last) daughter is "strong-willed!" She is twenty-one months old now, and there have been times when I thought she must be abnormal. If she had been my firstborn child there would have been no more in this family. She had colic day and night for six months, then we just quit calling it that. She was simply unhappy all the time. She began walking at eight months and she became a merciless bully with her sisters. She pulled hair, bit, hit, pinched, and pushed with all her might. She yanked out a handful of her sister's long black hair.

This mother went on to describe the characteristics of her tyrannical daughter, which I have heard thousands of times. She then closed, advising me to give greater emphasis to the importance of corporal punishment for this kind of youngster.

I wrote her a cordial letter in reply and told her I understood the frustration. I attempted to encourage her and offer hope for the future. Five years later, she wrote me again:

Dear Dr. Dobson,

This letter is long overdue, but thank you! Thank you for a caring reply to what was probably not a very nice letter from a discouraged mom. Thank you for your positive remarks, the first I had had in a long time.

Perhaps you would be interested in an update on our Sally Ann. Back when I wrote to you, she was probably a perfect "10" when it came to strong-willedness. "Difficult" hardly scratches the surface of descriptive words for her babyhood. As Christian parents, we tried every scriptural method we could find for dealing with her. I had decided she was abnormal. Something so innocent as offering her morning juice (which she loved) in the wrong glass threw her into thirty minutes of tantrums—and this was before she could really talk! Family dinners were a nightmare.

Before she turned two, Sally Ann would regularly brutalize her older sisters, ages four, eight, and twelve, even bringing the twelve-year-old to tears many times. A spanking from me did not deter her in the least. Finally, in prayer one day the Lord plainly showed me that her sisters must be allowed to retaliate—something I was strictly against (and still am!). However, in this case, all I can say is that it worked. I carefully and clearly told my three girls (with little Sally Ann in my lap) what they were to do the next time they were attacked by their littlest sister: they were to give her a good smack on the top of her chubby little leg, next to her diaper. Sally got the point: within two days the attacks ceased.

Disciplining our youngest was never easy, but with God's help, we persevered. When she had to be spanked, we could expect up to an hour of tantrums. It would have been so easy to give in and ignore the misbehavior, but I am convinced that, without it, our Sally would have become at best a holy terror, and at worst, mentally ill. Tell your listeners that discipline does pay off, when administered according to the Word of God.

Sally today is a precious seven-year-old and a joy to her family. She is still rather strong-willed, but it is well within normal limits now! She is very bright and has a gentle, creative, and sympathetic nature unusual in one so young. I know the Lord has great plans for her. She has already asked Jesus into her life and knows how to call upon Him when she has a need (like fear from a nightmare, etc.).

In conclusion, though I still don't think you went far enough in your book, loving discipline certainly is the key. With perseverance!

Thank you and may God's continued blessing be upon you and your household and your ministry, through Jesus Christ our Lord.

In His love,
Mrs. W. W.

Once again, I wrote to this mother and concluded with these words:

Thank you too, Mrs. W., for your original letter and for this update. It was a special treat to hear from you again. You're obviously on the right track with Sally Ann. Hang in there during the adolescent challenges that still lie before you.

James Dobson

If Mrs. W. reads this revised edition of The New Strong-Willed Child, I want her to know that I had her in mind when I set out to rewrite it. I'd like to ask her if I got it closer to the target this second time around. She sounds like a mom I would like to meet.

Let's review the important concepts I have put forward one more time, focusing especially on the principles calculated to produce a positive outcome in the years to come.

1. You should not blame yourself for the temperament with which your child was born. She is simply a tough kid to handle, and your task is to match her stride for stride.
2. Your strong-willed child is in greater danger because of his inclination to test the limits and scale the walls. Your utmost diligence and wisdom will be required to deal with him. You simply have to be tougher than he is, but do it without being angry and oppressive.
3. If you fail to understand his lust for power and independence, you can exhaust your resources and bog down in guilt. It will benefit no one.
4. For parents who have just begun, take charge of your baby now, hold tightly to the reins of authority, and quickly begin building into her an attitude of respect and obedience. You will need every ounce of awe you can muster in coming years. Once you have established your right to lead, begin to let go of the reins systematically, year by year.
5. Don't panic, even during the storms of adolescence. They never last forever. The sun will shine again, producing, perhaps, a beautiful rainbow over your spirit. *You're going to get through this.*
6. Don't let your child stray too far from you emotionally. Stay in touch. Don't write him off, even when your every impulse is to do just that. He needs you now more than ever before.
7. Give that kid time to find herself, even if she appears not to be searching.
8. Most importantly, I urge you to hold your children before the Lord in fervent prayer day by day by day. Begin every morning with a prayer for wisdom and guidance. I am convinced that there is no other true source of confidence in parenting. There is not enough knowledge in the books, mine or anyone else's, to counteract the evil that surrounds our kids today. We must bathe them in fervent prayer when we are in our prayer closet, saying words similar to these:

"Lord, You know my inadequacies. You know my weaknesses, not only in parenting, but in every area of my life. I'm doing the best I can to raise my kids properly, but it may not be good enough. As You provided the fish and the loaves to feed the five thousand hungry people, now take my meager effort and use it to bless my family. Make up for the things I do wrong. Satisfy the needs that I have not met. Compensate for my blunders and mistakes. Wrap Your great arms around my children, and draw them close to You. And be there when they stand at the great crossroads between right and wrong. All I can give them is my best, and I will continue to do that. I submit them to You now and rededicate myself to the task You have placed before me. The outcome rests securely in Your hands."

I've found that God is faithful, as a loving Father, to hear and answer that cry of the heart. Turn to Him for solace when you've reached the end of your rope. He will be there to comfort you and work within the soul of your beloved child.

Well, we began this discussion twelve chapters ago with the story of our dog, Siggie, and his revolutionary tendencies. Let's end with an update. Siggie is long gone now, but we still miss him. It's hard to explain how a worthless old hound could be so loved by his family, although I'm sure other dog lovers will understand our sentiment. We were somewhat prepared for Siggie's demise, after being told by the vet that he had developed a progressive heart leak, but the moment of crisis came without warning.

I was brushing my teeth early one morning when I heard Siggie's sharp cry. He could scream like a baby, and my wife rushed to his assistance.

"Jim, come quickly!" she said. "Siggie is having a heart attack!" I rushed into the family room, toothbrush still in hand. Siggie was lying just outside his bed, and he appeared to be in great pain. He was hunched down on his paws; his eyes unfocused and glassy. I bent down and petted him gently and agreed that he was probably dying. I was not sure what to do for a dog in the midst of a heart attack, since paramedics are somewhat sensitive about offering their services to animals. I certainly wasn't going to give him CPR. I picked up Siggie and laid him carefully on his bed, and he rolled on one side and remained completely motionless. His feet were rigidly held together, and it did, indeed, look as though the end had come.

I returned to my study to telephone the veterinarian, but Shirley called me again. She had taken a closer look at the immobile dog and discovered the nature of his problem. (Are you ready for this?) There are little claws or toenails on the sides of a dog's legs, and Siggie had somehow managed to get them hooked! That is why he couldn't move, and why he yelped when he tried to walk. There is not another dog anywhere in the world that could have handcuffed (pawcuffed?) himself, but with Siggie anything was possible. Shirley unhooked his toenails, and the senile old dog celebrated by running around like a puppy again.

When I am an old man thinking back on the joys of parenting—the Christmas seasons and the camping trips and the high-pitched voices of two bubbly children in our home—I will also remember a stubborn little dachshund named Sigmund Freud and his mild-mannered canine successor, Mindy, who made such important contributions to our family throughout those happy days. One of them was stubborn as a mule; the other just wanted to do everything right. But we loved them both, and so it was with our children. One of them was strong-willed and the other compliant (but sneaky at times). They are grown now, and both of them turned out to be great human beings who love their parents (especially me) and are deeply committed to Jesus Christ. It doesn't get any better than that.

"I have no greater joy than to hear that my children are walking in the truth."
(3 JOHN 1:4)

ENDNOTES

CHAPTER 1
1. Jon Meacham, *Franklin and Winston: An Intimate Portrait of an Epic Friendship* (New York: Random House, 2003), 15.

CHAPTER 2
1. Henry Wadsworth Longfellow, "There Was a Little Girl," *Random Memories* (Boston: Houghton Mifflin, 1922), 15.

CHAPTER 3
1. John Caldwell Holt, *Escape from Childhood: The Needs and Rights of Children* (New York: Penguin Books, 1974).

2. Jim Stingley, "Advocating Children's Liberation," *Los Angeles Times* (July 28, 1974).

3. Raymond Corsini and Genevieve Painter, "A Marvelous New Way to Make Your Child Behave," *Family Circle* (April 1975): 26.

4. Oklahoma State Department of Health Web page, "Positive Discipline," http://www.health.state.ok.us/program/mchecd/posdisc.html.

5. L. S. Kabada, "Discipline Debate: Parents, Parenting Experts Divided over Dealing with Children's Behavior," *Chicago Tribune* (June 27, 1999): CN 7.

6. Stella Chess and Alexander Thomas, *Know Your Child: An Authoritative Guide for Today's Parents* (New York: Basic Books, 1987).

7. Ibid.

8. Ibid.

9. Ibid.

10. Ibid.

11. Ibid.

12. Ibid.

13. T. J. Bouchard, L. L. Heston, E. D. Eckert, M. Keyes, and S. Resnick, "The Minnesota Study of Twins Reared Apart: Project Description and Sample Results in the Developmental Domain" (1981).

14. Ibid.

15. M. McGue and D. T. Lykken, "Genetic Influence on Risk of Divorce," *Psychological Science* 3 (1992): 368–373.

16. Ibid.

17. James C. Dobson, Internal Study of 35,000 Parents. First published in *Parenting Isn't for Cowards* (Dallas: Word Publishing, 1987).

18. Dobson, *Parenting Isn't for Cowards.*

19. As quoted in General Douglas MacArthur's farewell speech, West Point (May 12, 1962).

CHAPTER 4

1. James C. Dobson, *The New Dare to Discipline* (Carol Stream, IL: Tyndale House Publishers, 1996).

2. B. Spock and S. J. Parker, *Dr. Spock's Baby and Child Care* (New York: Pocket Books, 1998).

3. Lisa Whelchel, *Creative Correction* (Carol Stream, IL: Tyndale House Publishers, 2000).

4. Susanna Wesley, "The Journal of John Wesley: The Mother of the Wesleys," http://www.ccel.org/w/wesley/journal/htm/vi.iv.xx.htm.

5. Thomas Gordon, *Parenting Effectiveness Training: The Proven Program for Raising Responsible Children* (New York: Three Rivers Press, 2000).

CHAPTER 5

1. Ronald Kotulak, "Babies Learn to Reason Earlier than Thought, Researcher Finds," *Chicago Tribune* (January 7, 1999): N4.

2. Martha Sherrill, "Mrs. Clinton's Two Weeks out of Time: The Vigil for Her Father, Taking a Toll Both Public and Private," *The Washington Post* (April 3, 1993): C1.

3. James C. Dobson, *Bringing Up Boys* (Carol Stream, IL: Tyndale House Publishers, 2001).

CHAPTER 6

1. "Parents May Worsen Terrible Twos," *Fort Worth Star Telegram* (April 7, 1999): 5.

2. Spock and Parker, *Baby and Child Care.*

3. Benjamin Spock, "How Not to Bring Up a Bratty Child," *Redbook* (February 1974): 29–31.

4. Ibid.

5. Ibid.

CHAPTER 7

1. *American Psychological Association Monitor* 7, no. 4 (1976).

2. T. Berry Brazelton, *Toddlers and Parents: A Declaration of Independence* (New York: Delacorte Press, 1974), 101–110.

3. Ibid.

4. Oklahoma State Department of Health Web page, "Positive Discipline."

5. Luther Woodward, *Your Child from Two to Five*, ed. Morton Edwards (New York: Permabooks, 1955), 95–96.

6. Ibid.

7. Ibid.

8. Ibid.

9. Dobson, *The New Dare to Discipline*.

10. Reprinted by permission of United Press International.

11. H. T. Harbin and D. J. Madden, "Battered Parents: A New Syndrome," *American Journal of Psychiatry* 136 (1979): 1288–1291.

CHAPTER 8

1. Author Unknown. The poem "Behind in His Reading" was sent to me by Freda Carver, a former librarian at Focus on the Family.

2. Patrice O'Shaughnessy with Michael S. C. Claffey, Russ Buettner, Robert Gearty, Anemona Hartocollis, and Barbara Ross, "Child's Doomed Life," *New York Daily News* (November 26, 1995): 5.

3. Ibid.

4. Ibid.

5. Ibid.

6. L. G. Russek and G. E. Schwartz, "Perceptions of Parental Caring Predict Health Status in Midlife: A 35-Year Follow-Up of the Harvard Mastery of Stress Study," *Psychosomatic Medicine* 59, no. 2 (1997): 144–149.

7. Ibid.

8. Ibid.

9. Ibid.

10. Scott M. Montgomery, Mel J. Bartley, and Richard G. Wilkinson, "Family Conflict and Slow Growth," *Archives of Disease in Childhood* 77 (1997): 326–330.

11. Ibid.

12. Ibid.

13. Dobson, *The New Dare to Discipline.*

14. Den A. Trumbull and S. Dubose Ravenel, "To Spank or Not to Spank," *Physician.*

15. Ibid.

16. Ibid.

17. Internal memo (January 28, 1982). Phone conversation with California Assemblyman John Vasconcellos, citing recommendations contained in the report from the Commission on Crime Control and Violence.

18. Ben Sherwood, "Even Spanking Is Outlawed: Once-Stern Sweden Leads Way in Children's Rights," *Los Angeles Times* (August 11, 1985): A2.

19. Kathleen Engman, "Corporal Punishment v. Child Abuse: Society Struggles to Define 'Reasonable Force,' " *The Ottawa Citizen* (December 30, 1996): C8.

CHAPTER 9

1. Marguerite and Willard Beecher, *Parents on the Run: A Commonsense Book for Today's Parents* (New York: Crown Publishers, Inc., 1955), 6–8.

2. Dobson, *Parenting Isn't for Cowards.*

3. U.S. Census Bureau, "Census 2000 Summary," http://factfinder.census.gov/servlet/QTTable?_bm=y&-geo_id=01000US&-qr_name=DEC_2000_SF1_U_QTP10&-ds_name=DEC_2000_SF1_U&-_lang=en&-_sse=on.

CHAPTER 10

1. Nielsen Report, 2000.

2. MTV Media Kit (1993).

3. *Associated Press* (February 2, 2004): "Nielsen estimates that 143.6 million people watched at least part of the game."

4. D. Donahue, "Struggling to Raise Good Kids in Toxic Times: Is Innocence Evaporating in an Open-Door Society?" *USA Today* (October 1, 1998): D1.

5. Ibid.

6. Ellen Edwards, "Plugged-In Generation: More than Ever, Kids Are at Home with Media," *Washington Post* (November 18, 1999): A1.

7. David Bauder, "Survey: It May Not Be Punishment to Send Children to Their Rooms," *Associated Press* (June 26, 1997).

8. Dobson, *Bringing Up Boys*.

9. Urie Bronfenbrenner, "The Social Ecology of Human Development," *Brain and Intelligence: The Ecology of Child Development*, ed. Fredrick Richardson (Hyattsville, Md.: National Educational Press, 1973).

10. K. Bosworth, D. L. Espelage, and T. R. Simon, "Factors Associated with Bullying Behavior in Middle School Students," *Educational Research* 41, no. 2 (1999): 137–153.

11. Maria Bartini and Anthony Pellegrini, "Dominance in Early Adolescent Boys: Affiliative and Aggressive Dimensions and Possible Functions," *Merrill-Palmer Quarterly* (2001).

12. Shannon Brownlee, Roberta Hotinski, Bellamy Pailthorp, Erin Ragan, and Kathleen Wong, "Inside the Teen Brain," *US News & World Report* (August 9, 1999): 44.

13. Ibid.

14. Ibid.

15. B. S. Bowden and J. M. Zeisz, "Supper's On! Adolescent Adjustment and Frequency of Family Mealtimes," paper presented at 105th annual meeting of the American Psychological Association, Chicago (1997).

16. Daisy Yu, "A Consumer Underclass: Scorned Teens," *Los Angeles Times* (March 18, 2001): B13.

17. Ibid.

18. James Brooke, "Terror in Littleton: The Overview: 2 Students in Colorado School Said to Gun Down As Many As 23 and Kill Themselves in a Siege," *The New York Times* (April 21, 1999): A6.

19. Patricia Hersch, *A Tribe Apart: A Journey into the Heart of American Adolescence* (New York: Ballantine Books, 1999).

20. M. D. Resnick, P. S. Bearman, R. W. Blum, K. E. Bauman, K. M. Harris, J. Jones, J. Tabor, T. Beuhring, R. Sieving, M. Shew, M. Ireland, L. H. Bearinger, and J. R. Udry, "Protecting Adolescents from Harm: Finding from the National Longitudinal Study on Adolescent Health," *Journal of the American Medical Association* 278; "New Analyses of National Data Reveal Risk, Protective Factors for Youth Violence and Other Risks, Leading Researchers Report at Capitol Hill Briefing," PR Newswire (June 3, 1999).

21. Andrea Billups, "The State of Our Nation's Youth: Most Teenagers Rate Parents Number 1: Poll Shows Fear of Violence, Worry over Decline of Families," *The Washington Times* (August 11, 1999): A6.

22. Barbara Kantrowitz and Pat Wingert with Anne Underwood, "How Well Do You Know Your Kid?" *Newsweek* (May 10, 1999): 36.

23. Michael Medved and David Wallechinsky, *What Really Happened to the Class of '65?* (New York: Random House, Inc., 1976).

24. Ibid.

25. Ibid.

26. Ibid.

27. Ibid.

28. Domeena C. Renshaw, *The Hyperactive Child* (Chicago: Nelson-Hall Publishers, 1974).

29. Deborah Davis Locker, "Bomb Threats Shake Hartland District: Schools Boost Security, Add Cameras after Six Warning Notes Are Left," *The Detroit News* (November 5, 2002): C5.

CHAPTER 11

1. Dennis Swanberg, Diane Passno, and Walt Larimore, *Why A.D.H.D. Doesn't Mean Disaster* (Carol Stream, IL: Tyndale House Publishers, 2004); Russell A. Barkley, "Attention Deficit Hyperactivity Disorder," online lecture, University of Massachusetts Medical Center, Worcester, Mass.

2. Claudia Wallis, "Life in Overdrive: Doctors Say Huge Numbers of Kids and Adults Have Attention Deficit Disorder: Is It for Real?" *Time* (July 18, 1994): 42.

3. Swanberg, Passno, and Larimore, *Why A.D.H.D. Doesn't Mean Disaster.*

4. Ibid.

5. Ibid.

6. Ibid.

7. Edward Hallowell and John Ratey, *Driven to Distraction: Recognizing and Coping with Attention Deficit Disorder from Childhood through Adulthood* (New York: Simon & Schuster, 1995), 73–76.

8. Wallis, "Life in Overdrive," 42.

9. L. Goldman, M. Genel, R. Bezman, and P. Slanetz, "Diagnosis and Treatment of Attention-Deficit/Hyperactivity Disorder in Children and Adolescents," *Journal of the American Medical Association* (April 1998): 1100–1107.

10. J. P. Guevara and M. T. Stein, "Evidence Based Management of Attention Deficit Hyperactivity Disorder," *British Medical Journal* (November 2001): 1232–1235.

11. G. B. LeFever, K. V. Dawson, and A. L. Morrow, "The Extent of Drug Therapy for Attention Deficit-Hyperactivity Disorder among Children in Public Schools," *American Journal of Public Health* (September 1999): 1359–1364.

12. Centers for Disease Control and Prevention report (May 2002), http://www .cdc.gov/nchs/releases/02news/attendefic.htm.

13. R. J. DeGrandpre, *Ritalin Nation: Rapid-Fire Culture and the Transformation of Human Consciousness* (New York: W. W. Norton & Company, 2000).

14. D. Papolos and J. Papolos, *The Bipolar Child* (New York: Broadway Books, 1999), chapter 6.

15. S. Pliszka, "The Use of Psychostimulants in the Pediatric Patient," *Pediatric Clinics of North America* (October 1998): 1087, citing J. Elia, B. G. Borcherding, J. L. Rapoport, and C. S. Keysor, "Methylphenidate and Dextroamphetamine Treatments of Hyperactivity: Are There True Nonresponders?" *Psychiatry Research* (February 1991): 141–155.

16. "Medication for Children with Attentional Disorders." American Academy of Pediatrics Committee on Children with Disabilities and Committee on Drugs, *Pediatrics* (August 1996): 301–304.

17. C. J. Musser, P. A. Ahmann, F. W. Theyer, P. Mundt, S. K. Broste, and N. Mueller-Rizner, "Stimulant Use and the Potential for Abuse in Wisconsin As Reported by School Administrators and Longitudinally Followed Children," *Journal of Developmental Behavior Pediatrics* (June 1998): 187–192.

18. Mari Yamaguchi, "Japan Develops Gadget to Alert Bed-Wetting Children," *Associated Press* (April 20, 1999).

19. Willard Hartup, http://www.personal.psu.edu/faculty/j/g/jgp4/research/ clippings/rroom.htm.

20. J. J. Gillis, J. W. Gilger, B. F. Pennington, and J. C. DeFries, "Attention Deficit Disorder in Reading Disabled Twins: Evidence for a Genetic Etiology," *Journal of Abnormal Child Psychology* (June 1992): 303–315.

21. H. Gjone, J. Stevenson, and J. M. Sundet, "Genetic Influence on Parent-Reported Attention-Related Problems in a Norwegian General Population Twin Sample," *Journal of the American Academy of Child and Adolescent Psychiatry* (May 1996): 588–596.

22. Renshaw, *The Hyperactive Child,* 118–120.

CHAPTER 12

1. C. S. Lewis, *The Four Loves* (New York: Harvest Books, 1971).

BOOK Three

PARENTING
ISN'T FOR
COWARDS

THIS BOOK IS AFFECTIONATELY DEDICATED TO THE MOTHERS OF THE WORLD, *especially the one to whom I am married, who have dedicated themselves to the care and training of the next generation. They have been maligned, goaded, blamed, and ridiculed in recent years, but most have stood their ground. Quietly and confidently they have continued to love and nourish their children and prepare them for a life of service to God and to mankind. There is no more important assignment on the face of the earth, and I hope this book will make their task a bit less difficult.*

CONTENTS

Parenting Isn't for Cowards

ONE

THE CHALLENGE

HAVE YOU NOTICED? Being a good parent seems to have become more difficult in recent years. It never has been all that easy, of course. For one thing, babies come into the world with no instructions and you pretty much have to assemble them on your own. They are also maddeningly complex, and there are no guaranteed formulas that work in every instance. The techniques that succeed magnificently with one child can fail bewilderingly with another.

Many parents do not understand this frustrating aspect of child-rearing because they have never experienced it. Through no great achievement of their own, they managed to produce a house full of "easy" children. My wife and I are acquainted with a family like that. They were blessed with three of the most perfect children you are likely to find. All three made straight A's in school, kept their rooms perpetually clean, were musically talented, ate with one hand in their laps, were first-team athletes, spoke politely and correctly to adults, and even had teeth that didn't need straightening! It was almost disgusting to see how well they turned out.

Predictably, our friends awarded themselves complete credit for the successes of their children. They were also inclined, at the drop of a hat, to tell you how to raise yours. Overconfidence oozed from their fingertips.

But then an interesting thing happened. The Lord, who must have a sense of humor, gift-wrapped a little tornado and sent it as a surprise package on the mother's fortieth birthday. That family has been stumbling backward ever since. Their little caboose, who is now six years old, is as tough as nails and twice as sharp. He loves to fight with his parents and already knows considerably more than they. Just ask him. He'll tell you.

The funny thing about his parents is that they quit giving child-rearing advice shortly after his birth. Their job suddenly got tougher!

When I think of these parents today, I'm reminded of a photograph in my files of an elegantly dressed woman who is holding a cup of coffee. Her little finger is cocked ever so daintily to the side and her face reveals utter self-assurance. Unfortunately, this woman does not yet know that her slip has collapsed around her feet. The caption reads, "Confidence is what you have before you understand the situation." Indeed!

More than one tough-minded youngster has sandblasted the confidence of his parents. That's how he gets his kicks. If you have raised only compliant children who smiled regularly and then hustled off to do your bidding, then beware. You may not yet understand the situation. And the Lord could send *you* a surprise package too. Of this fact I'm certain: If you produce enough babies, you will discover sooner or later that there is nothing simple about human beings...of *any* age.

From the mail I receive from parents it is clear to me that many are struggling with their responsibilities at home. To learn why, I asked one thousand mothers and fathers to describe the frustrations they were experiencing in child-rearing. Their answers were fascinating. Some talked of sticky telephones, wet toilet seats, and knotted shoestrings. Others told the most delightful stories.

I'll never forget the mother who had been cooped up with her toddler for several weeks. In a desperate effort to get out of the house, she decided to take her son to a Muppet movie...his first. As soon as they arrived in the theater, the mother discovered a minor technical problem. The child didn't weigh enough to keep the spring seat down. There was nothing left to do but hold this churning, squirming two-year-old on her lap throughout the movie.

It was a mistake. Sometime during the next two hours, they lost control of a large Pepsi and a king-sized box of buttered popcorn! That gooey mixture flowed over the child onto the mother's lap and down her legs. She decided to sit it out since the movie was almost over. What she didn't know, unfortunately, was that she and her son were being systematically cemented together. When the movie was over, they stood up and the mother's wraparound skirt came unraveled. It stuck to the bottom of the toddler and followed him up the aisle! She stood there clutching her slip and thanking the Lord she had taken time to put one on!

Can't you see this mother desperately begging the child to drag her skirt back within reach? Parenthood can certainly be humiliating at times. It also seems specifically designed to irritate us. Tell me why it is that a toddler never throws up in the bathroom? Never! To do so would violate some great unwritten law in the universe. It is even more difficult to understand why he will gag violently at the sight of a perfectly wonderful breakfast of oatmeal, eggs, bacon, and orange juice...and then go out and drink the dog's water. I have no idea what makes him do that. I only know that it drives his mother crazy!

Obviously, the parents who participated in our "Frustrations of Parenthood" poll did not just share their humorous experiences. They also provided some surprising and distressing answers. Rather than criticizing their children, as one might have expected, the most common response focused on their own inadequacies as mothers and fathers! Specific answers revealed the great self-doubt so prevalent among parents today:

- "not knowing how to cope with children's problems"
- "not being able to make the kids feel secure and loved"
- "I've lost confidence in my ability to parent."
- "I've failed my children."
- "I'm not the example I should be."
- "seeing my own bad habits and character traits in my children"
- "inability to relate to my children"
- "dealing with guilt when it seems that I have failed my sons"
- "inability to cope"
- "It's too late to go back and do it right."
- "I'm overwhelmed by the responsibility of it all."

Isn't it incredible to observe just how tentative we have become about this task of raising children? Parenting is hardly a new technology. Since Adam and Eve graced the Garden, seventy-seven billion people have lived on this earth, yet we're still nervous about bringing up the baby. It is a sign of the times.

I'm quite certain that parents in past decades spent less energy worrying about their children. They had other things on their minds. I remember talking to my dad about this subject a few years before his death. Our children were young at the time and I was feeling the heavy responsibility of raising them properly.

I turned to my father and asked, "Do you remember worrying about me when I was a kid? Did you think about all the things that could go wrong as I came through the adolescent years? How did you feel about these pressures associated with being a father?"

Dad was rather embarrassed by the line of questioning. He smiled sheepishly and said, "Honestly, Bo," (his pet name for me) "I never really gave that a thought."

How do we explain his lack of concern? Was it because he didn't love me or because he was an uninvolved parent? No. He prayed for me until the day he died. And as I have said on many occasions, he was a wonderful father to me. Instead, his answer reflected the time in which I grew up. People worried about the depression that was just ending, and the war with Germany, and later the cold war with Russia. They did not invest much effort in hand-wringing over their children...at least not until a major problem developed. Trouble was not anticipated.

And why not? Because it was easier to raise kids in that era. I attended high school during the "Happy Days" of the 1950s, and I never saw or even heard of anyone taking an illegal drug. It happened, I suppose, but it was certainly no threat to me. Some of the other students liked to get drunk, but alcohol was not a big deal in my social environment. Others played around with sex, but the girls who did were considered "loose" and were not respected. Virginity was still in style for males *and* females. Occasionally a girl came up pregnant, but she was packed off in a hurry and I never knew where she went. Homosexuals were very weird and unusual people. I heard there were a few around but I didn't know them personally. Most of my friends respected their parents, went to church on Sunday, studied hard enough to get by, and lived a fairly clean life. There were exceptions, of course, but this was the norm. It's no wonder my parents were concentrating on other anxieties.

It is also no wonder that parents are more concerned in the present era. Their children are walking through the Valley of the Shadow! Drugs, sex, alcohol, rebellion, and deviant lifestyles are everywhere. Those dangers have never been so evident to me as they are today.

I'm writing this book in the heart of London, where my family has joined me for a couple of months. This wonderful and historic city is also the home of some of the most pitiful young people I've ever seen. Rockers and punkers and druggies are on the streets in search of something. Who knows what? Girls with green and orange hair walk by with strange-looking boyfriends. At least I think they're boys. They wear earrings and have blue Mohawk haircuts that stick four inches in the air. While gazing at that sight, a clang! clang! clang! sound is heard from the rear. The Hare Krishnas are coming. They dance by with their shaved heads and monk-like robes. Gays parade arm in arm and prostitutes advertise their services. I stand there thinking, *What in heaven's name have we allowed to happen to our kids?*

The same phenomenon is occurring in the United States and Canada. It is sometimes overwhelming to see what has happened to a value system that served us so well. When my daughter was eighteen, I attended a program put on by the music department at her high school. Sitting in front of me was one of Danae's girlfriends. At intermission we chatted about her plans, and she told me she would soon enroll at the University of California, Berkeley. She had just returned from a visit to the school and mentioned casually that something had bothered her about the dormitory in which she would reside. She had learned that the men and women lived side by side, and they also shared the same bathrooms. What concerned this pretty young lady was that there was no curtain on the shower stall!

This is the world in which our children are growing up. Obviously, conservative communities still exist where traditional values are honored. Millions of kids still want to do what is right. But dangerous enticements are there, too, and parents know it. Some live in fear that the dragon of adolescence will consume their sons and daughters before they have even started out in life. That anxiety can take the pleasure out of raising children.

There is, however, another reason for the crisis of confidence that many parents are experiencing today. Mothers, especially, have been placed in an impossible bind. They have been blamed for everything that can conceivably go wrong with children. Even when their love and commitment are incalculable, the experts accuse them of making grievous errors in toilet training, disciplining, feeding, medicating, and educating their youngsters. They are either overpossessive or undernourishing. One psychiatrist even wrote an entire book on the dangers of religious training of all types. Thus, no matter how diligently "Mom" approaches her parenting responsibilities, she seems destined to be accused of twisting and warping her children.

Not only have mothers been blamed by the experts for things beyond their control, but they have also been quite willing to criticize themselves. Consider again the list of statements cited from our poll of parents. Eighty percent of the respondents were women, and their most frequent comment was, "I'm a failure as a mother!" What nonsense! Women have been *taught* to blame themselves in this way, and it is time to set the record straight.

I don't believe that the task of procreation was intended to be so burdensome. Of course it is demanding. But modern parents have saddled themselves with unnecessary guilt, fear, and self-doubt. That is not the divine plan. Throughout the Scriptures, it is quite clear that the raising of children was viewed as a wonderful blessing from God—a welcome, joyful experience. And today, it remains one of the greatest privileges in living to bring a baby into the world...a vulnerable little human being who looks to us for all his needs. What a wonderful opportunity it is to teach these little ones to love God with all their hearts and to serve their fellow man throughout their lives. There is no higher calling than that!

The book you are reading, then, is intended as a celebration of parenthood. We've had enough of groveling and self-condemnation. What we need now is a double dose of confidence in our ability to raise our children properly. We also need to consider the specific frustrations that prevent us from enjoying our kids while they are young. Toward this end, the chapters that follow will deal with the contest of wills between generations, with the perils of adolescence, with parental burnout and its causes, and with the other stress points that irritate and depress us. There is a more satisfying way to raise children, as I believe the reader will see. And there is no better time than now to apply it. Our sons and daughters will be grown so quickly, and these days at home together will be nothing but a distant memory. Let's make the most of every moment.

TWO

THE TOUGH & THE GENTLE

I N THE DAYS of the wild and woolly West, a lone cowboy went riding through a valley and came unexpectedly upon an Indian lying motionless on the road. His right ear was pressed to the ground, and he was muttering soberly to himself. "Ummm," he said. "Stagecoach! Three people inside. Two men, one woman. Four horses. Three dapple gray, one black. Stagecoach moving west. Ummmmm." The cowboy was amazed and said, "That's incredible, pardner! You can tell all that just by listening to the ground?" The Indian replied, "Ummmmmm. No! Stagecoach run over me thirty minutes ago!"

When I first heard that story I was reminded of the mothers, bless them all, who are raising one or more rambunctious preschoolers simultaneously. If you are one of them, haven't you had moments like that Indian when you found yourself lying flat on the floor and muttering to yourself, "Mmmmm. Three kids. Dirty hands. Wet diapers. Mud on feet. Tearing through the house. Making me crazy! Help!"?

If you've been in this posture lately, then take heart. You are not alone. Millions of parents, past and present, can identify with the particular stresses you are experiencing right now. A child between eighteen and thirty-six months of age is a sheer delight, but he can also be utterly maddening. He is inquisitive, short-tempered, demanding, cuddly, innocent, and dangerous at the same time. I find it fascinating to watch him run through his day, seeking opportunities to crush things, flush things, kill things, spill things, fall off things, eat horrible things—and think up ways to rattle his mother. Someone said it best: The Lord made Adam from the dust of the earth, but when the first toddler came along, He added *electricity!*

Adolescents are interesting too, and we'll discuss them at length in later chapters. But toddlers are a breed apart. Bill Cosby said he could conquer the world if he could somehow manage to mobilize about two hundred aggressive two-year-olds. It wouldn't surprise me. His army should definitely include an energetic lad named Frankie who belongs, more or less, to some friends of ours.

Little Frankie is a classic toddler. One day recently he pulled a chair over to the front window and carefully placed it inside the drapes. He was standing there staring out at the world when his mother came looking for him. She spied his little white legs protruding beneath the drapes and quietly slipped in behind him. Then she heard him speaking to himself in very somber terms. He was saying, "I've *got* to get out of here!"

I could fill a book with wonderful pronouncements from the mouths of preschool children. They are among the most delightful little people on the face of the earth. But returning to our thesis, they (and all children) bring a special kind of stress into the lives of their parents. Humorist Erma Bombeck said in one of her books that she was frustrated by her children from the moment they were born. She remembered *how* she got three kids, but she couldn't recall *why*. She decided maybe they were a 4-H project that got out of hand.

For some parents, the overwhelming responsibility associated with child-rearing is not so funny. As indicated in the preceding chapter, there appears to be a growing number of husbands and wives today who are not coping well with parenthood. They've reached the end of the rope and it is frazzled. The letters they send to me are replete with self-condemnation, guilt, and anger. Many seem to have experienced a kind of physical exhaustion that leaves them confused and depressed.

High on the list of irritants which keeps them off balance and agitated is the tendency of some children to test, challenge, resist, and blatantly defy authority. These rebellious youngsters can create more stress in a single afternoon than their mothers can handle in a week. I wrote about them in an earlier book entitled *The Strong-Willed Child*, but they continue to fascinate me. For years I have watched them operate and wondered what makes them tick. I have interviewed adults who had been rebellious teenagers, and asked them what they were thinking during their season of anger. Even they do not fully understand themselves. I have resolved to investigate further.

On behalf of those readers who have never encountered him, let me describe the tough-minded child. At birth he looks deceptively like his more compliant sibling. He weighs seven pounds and is totally dependent on those who care for him. Indeed, he would not survive for more than a day or two without their attention. Ineffectual little arms and legs dangle aimlessly in four directions, appearing to be God's afterthoughts. What a picture of vulnerability and innocence he is!

Isn't it amazing, given this beginning, what happens in twenty short months? Junior then weighs twenty-five pounds and he's itching for action. Would you believe this kid who couldn't even hold his own bottle less than two years ago now has the gall to look his two-hundred-pound father straight in the eye and tell him where to get off? What audacity! Obviously, there is something deep within his soul that longs for control. He will work at achieving it for the rest of his life.

In the early 1970s I had the privilege of living near one of these little spitfires. He was thirty-six months old at the time and had already bewildered and overwhelmed his mother. The contest of wills was over. He had won it. His sassy talk was legendary in the neighborhood, not only to his mother but to anyone who got in his way. Then one day my wife saw him ride his tricycle down the driveway and into the street, which panicked his mother. We lived on a curve, and the cars came around that bend at high speed. Mom rushed out of the house and caught up with her son as he pedaled down the street. She took hold of his handlebars to redirect him, and he came unglued.

"Get your dirty hands off my tricycle!" he screamed. His eyes were squinted in fury. As Shirley watched in disbelief, this woman did as she was told. The life of her child was in danger, and yet this mother did not have the courage to confront him. He continued to ride down the street, and she could only stand and watch.

How could it be that a tiny little boy at three years of age was able to buffalo his thirty-year-old mother in this way? Well, it was clear to any observer that she had no idea how to manage him. But also, he was simply tougher than she—and they both knew it. This mild-mannered woman had produced an iron-willed kid who was giving her fits, and you can be sure that her physical and emotional resources were continually drained by his antics.

Contrast this independent youngster with his easygoing counterpart at the other end of the continuum. The compliant child approaches people from an entirely different direction. He wants to please them because he needs their approval. A word of displeasure or even the slightest frown from his parents can be disturbing to him. He is a lover, not a fighter.

A few years ago I talked with the mother of one of these easygoing kids. She was concerned about the difficulties her son was having in nursery school. He was regularly being bullied by more aggressive children, but it was not within him to defend himself. Thus, every afternoon when his mother came to get him, he had been whacked and harassed by these other boys. Even the girls were joining in the fun.

"You must defend yourself!" his mother said again and again. "Those other children will keep hitting you until you make them stop!"

Each day she urged her little lover to be more assertive, but it contradicted his nature to do so. Finally, his frustration became so great that he began trying to follow his mother's advice. As they were on the way to school one morning he said, "Mom! If those kids pick on me again today...I'm...I'm...I'm going to beat them up! Slightly."

How does one beat up an opponent *slightly?* I don't know, but it made perfect sense to this compliant child. He didn't want to use any more force than was absolutely necessary to survive. Why? Because he had a peace-loving nature. His parents didn't teach it to him. It simply *was.*

As most mothers know, this kind of compliant child and his strong-willed sibling are so distinct that they could almost be from different planets. One cuddles to your embrace and the other kicks you in the navel. One is a natural sweetheart and the other goes through life like hot lava. One follows orders and the other gives them. Quite obviously, they are marching to a different set of drums.

I must make it clear that the compliant child is not necessarily wimpy or spineless. That fact is very important to our understanding of his nature and how he differs from his strong-willed sibling. The distinction between them is *not* a matter of confidence, willingness to take a risk, sparkling personality, or other desirable characteristics. Rather, the issue under consideration is focused on the strength of the will—the inclination of some children to resist authority and determine their own course, as compared with those who are willing to be led. It is my supposition that these temperaments are prepackaged before birth and do not have to be cultivated or encouraged. They will make themselves known soon enough.

Not everyone concurs. Many psychologists and psychiatrists of the past would have disagreed violently with this understanding. Sigmund Freud, the father of psychoanalysis, and J. B. Watson, the creator of behaviorism, believed that newborns come into the world as "blank slates" on which the environment would later write. For them, a baby had no inborn characteristics of personality that distinguished him from other infants. Everything he would become, both good and evil, would result from the experiences to be provided by the world around him. He could make no independent decisions because he had no real freedom of choice...no ability to consider his circumstances and act rationally on them. Watson even rejected the existence of a mind, viewing the brain as a simple switchboard that responded automatically to external stimuli. Hence, his system of thinking has been called, "Psychology out of its mind."

Watson bragged during the 1920s that he could train any infant "to become any type of specialist I might select...doctor, lawyer, artist, merchant-chief and, yes, even beggarman and thief." He thought children were simply "raw material" for parents "to fashion in ways to suit themselves."

In short, this belief that all behavior is caused is called *determinism*, and it will have significance for us in later discussions. I first heard the concept when I was in graduate school. I didn't accept it then, and I certainly don't believe it now. As a Christian psychologist, I have always filtered man-made theories through the screen of Scripture, and in this instance, determinism hangs up in the wire. If it were true, we would be unable to worship and serve God as a voluntary expression of our love. We would be mere puppets on a string, responding to the stimuli around us.

It is becoming clear today just how far off-base these classical psychologists have been in their interpretation of human behavior. There is no doubt, as they said, that the environment is enormously influential in molding and shaping our personalities, but they failed to recognize our ability to think, to choose, and to respond according to our own temperaments. We are rational human beings who can override our experience and external influences. Furthermore, at birth, except for identical twins, no two of us are alike. And how foolish it was to have thought otherwise. If God makes every grain of sand and every snowflake like no other on earth, how simplistic it was to have believed He mass-produced little human robots. We are, after all, made in *His* image.

A blob of tissue? A blank slate? A mass of protoplasm? Hardly! Individual differences in temperament can be discerned at birth or shortly thereafter. In one remarkable scriptural reference we even see references to a strong-willed temperament before the child was born. Genesis 16:11–12 reports a striking conversation between an angel of the Lord and Abraham's pregnant servant girl, Hagar. He said, "You are now with child and you will have a son. You shall name him Ishmael, for the LORD has heard of your misery. He will be a wild donkey of a man; his hand will be against everyone and everyone's hand against him, and he will live in hostility toward all his brothers."

Does that sound like anyone you know? I've met a few wild donkeys in my time, to be sure. In another example from the book of Genesis, we are told of the prenatal development of the twins, Jacob and Esau. One was rebellious and tough while the other was something of a mama's boy. They were also enemies before they were born and continued in conflict through much of their lives (see Genesis 25:22–27). Then later, in one of the most mysterious and disturbing chapters in the Bible, the Lord said, "Jacob have I loved, but Esau have I hated" (Romans 9:13, KJV). Apparently, God discerned a rebellious nature in Esau before he was born and knew that he would not be receptive to the divine Spirit.[1]

Behavioral scientists are now observing and documenting the subtle understandings that have been evident in the Scriptures for thousands of years. One of the most ambitious of these efforts to study the temperaments of babies has been in progress for more than three decades. It is known as the New York Longitudinal Study. The findings from this investigation, led by psychiatrists Stella Chess and Alexander Thomas, are reported in their excellent book for parents entitled, *Know Your Child*. I recommend it enthusiastically to anyone interested in child development.

To my delight, Chess and Thomas found that babies not only differ significantly from one another at the moment of birth, but those differences tend to be rather persistent throughout childhood. Even more interestingly, they observed three broad categories or patterns of temperaments into which the majority of children can be classified. The first they called "the difficult child," who is characterized by negative reactions to people, intense mood swings, irregular sleep and feeding schedules, frequent periods of crying, and violent tantrums when frustrated.

Does that sound familiar?

The second pattern is called "the easy child," who manifests a positive approach to people, quiet adaptability to new situations, regular sleep and feeding schedules, and a willingness to accept the rules of the game. The authors concluded, "Such a youngster is usually a joy to her parents, pediatrician, and teachers." Amen.

The third category was given the title "Slow-to-warm-up" or "shy." These youngsters respond negatively to new situations and they adapt slowly. However, they are less intense than difficult children and they tend to have regular sleeping and feeding schedules. When they are upset or frustrated, they typically withdraw from the situation and react mildly, rather than exploding with anger and rebellion.

Not every child fits into these categories, of course, but approximately 65 percent do. Chess and Thomas also emphasize that babies are fully human at birth, being able immediately to relate to their parents and begin learning from their environments. I doubt if that news will come as a surprise to most parents, who never believed in the "blank slate" theory, anyway. Ask the mother who has raised a houseful of children. She will tell you that each of her kids had a different personality...a different "feel"...the first time she held the little one in her arms. She is right.

It should not be difficult to understand why these findings from longitudinal research have been exciting to me. They confirm my own observations, not only about the wonderful complexity of human beings, but also about the categories of temperament identified by Chess and Thomas. Nevertheless, basic questions remain to be answered.

What do we really know about these strong-willed and compliant children? (We'll leave our consideration of the shy child to a future book.) How persistent are their personality traits as they grow older? What are the teen years like for each? How do their parents feel about raising them? Does the strong-willed child have an advantage over the compliant child socially or academically or in achievement during early adulthood? These questions have never been answered, to my knowledge, since we have only recently admitted that temperamental differences exist. It was this dearth of information that led me to initiate a large-scale inquiry of my own into the subject.

Initially, a questionnaire was developed for use with parents (see appendix). By completing this research instrument, parents provided extensive information regarding their own temperaments and those of their children. Specifically, they were asked to evaluate each member of the family on a five-point scale as follows: (1) very compliant; (2) rather compliant; (3) average; (4) rather strong-willed; (5) very strong-willed. No effort was made to define these categories because my interest was only in those children at the extremes, (categories [1] and [5]). The other records were ignored, except for the provision of demographic information.

I then asked detailed questions about the children and how their parents felt about raising them. More than thirty-five thousand families participated in the study and the data were analyzed at the University of Southern California Computer Center. I was assisted in the analysis by my good friend, Malcolm Williamson, Ph.D., whose specialties are measurement and statistics. We generated a mountain of computerized information that could fill five books this size, but we will just hit the highlights here. Let me say that this has been a fascinating journey into human nature, and I wish to express appreciation to the families who shared their experiences with me. I believe the information I have learned through this effort is available nowhere else in the world.

We'll discuss those findings in the next two chapters.

THREE

WHAT 35,000 PARENTS SAID ABOUT THEIR CHILDREN

ALL RIGHT, CLASS. I'm ready to distribute your midterm examination. We will soon see how well you understand the differences between very strong-willed and very compliant children. Close your books, please, and clear your desks of everything but pencils. Do not copy from your neighbor. We will discuss the correct answers after you have turned in your completed examination. Any questions? Good. Oh, by the way—if you fail this test you will be required to baby-sit with nine strong-willed toddlers for the next six weeks! You may begin.

MULTIPLE CHOICE

1. **It would be interesting to know when a baby is due whether he is likely to be difficult or easy to raise. Based on our data, we can take an educated guess. What do you think the ratio is between very strong-willed and very compliant children?**
   - (1) There are about twice as many very compliant children.
   - (2) There are almost three times as many very strong-willed children.
   - (3) There is about the same number of both.
   - (4) There are about twice as many strong-willed children.

2. **Is it tougher to raise boys or girls? The answer may depend in part on the temperaments of each. When we consider only strong-willed children, what is the ratio of males to females?**
   - (1) Males outnumber females by about 5 percentage points.
   - (2) Females outnumber males by about 9 percentage points.
   - (3) Males outnumber females by about 31 percentage points.
   - (4) There is no difference between the sexes.

3. **Let's consider only easy-to-raise children now. What is the ratio of males to females among these compliant children?**
   - (1) Males outnumber females by about 10 percentage points.
   - (2) Females outnumber males by about 6 percentage points.
   - (3) Males outnumber females by about 19 percentage points.
   - (4) There is no difference between the sexes.

4. **Select the accurate statement below:**
   - (1) Firstborn children are more likely to be very strong-willed.
   - (2) Secondborn children are more likely to be very strong-willed.
   - (3) Thirdborn children are more likely to be very strong-willed.
   - (4) There is no strong tendency for temperament to be related to birth order.

5. **Select the accurate statement below: (Answers relate to when the temperament is identified.)**
   - (1) Less than 10 percent of very strong-willed children are recognizable at birth to 3 months.
   - (2) About a third of very strong-willed children are recognizable at birth to 3 months.
   - (3) The vast majority of very strong-willed children are recognizable at birth to 3 months.
   - (4) Only a few very strong-willed children are recognizable until toddlerhood, when 98 percent "show up."

6. **Is the temperament of the child inherited from the parents?**
   - (1) The data suggest that it is.
   - (2) The data suggest that it is not.

7. **What happens to the rebellious nature of very strong-willed children as they move through the years?**
    (1) Very few rebel until midadolescence, when a peak of 30 percent occurs.
    (2) After a peak of 20 percent rebel in toddlerhood, very little rebellion occurs until early adolescence.
    (3) Approximately 40 percent rebel in toddlerhood, and the percentages rise in every age category through adolescence, reaching a peak of 74 percent in the teen years.
    (4) Rebellion remains hidden, more or less, until early adolescence when an "explosion" occurs, reaching a peak of 63 percent at fifteen years of age.

8. **This next item refers to one of the most important findings from our study. It asks the question, what can be expected from compliant children—those easy, happy, cooperative kids—as they go through adolescence and young adulthood? Do they rebel? If so, how commonly? First, please indicate the percentage of these kids whom you think go into severe rebellion in either adolescence or young adulthood.**
    (1) 3 percent
    (2) 26 percent
    (3) 52 percent
    (4) 76 percent
    (5) 89 percent

9. **What percent of very compliant children eventually go into mild rebellion in either adolescence or young adulthood?**
    (1) 14 percent
    (2) 33 percent
    (3) 41 percent
    (4) 79 percent
    (5) 91 percent

10. **Which individual has an edge in academic achievement during the teen years?**
    (1) The very strong-willed child.
    (2) The very compliant child.
    (3) Neither; there is no significant difference between them.

11. **Which individual typically makes the best social adjustment in adolescence?**
    (1) The very strong-willed child.
    (2) The very compliant child.
    (3) Neither; there is no significant difference between them.

12. **One of the characteristics of the compliant child during the early years is the ease with which his parents can mold and shape him. He is very responsive to their leadership. Given that flexibility, how does he respond to peer pressure? Or, asked another way, which child (strong-willed or compliant) is more likely to be "peer dependent" during adolescence?**
    (1) The very strong-willed child.
    (2) The very compliant child.
    (3) Neither; there is no significant difference between them.

13. **Which individual is more likely to have the higher self-esteem in adolescence?**
    (1) The very strong-willed child.
    (2) The very compliant child.
    (3) Neither; there is no significant difference between them.

14. **Parents were asked to indicate how their grown sons and daughters had achieved in adult pursuits. Which group do you think succeeded best?**
    (1) The very strong-willed.
    (2) The very compliant.
    (3) There was no significant difference between them.

Well, that's the end of our little quiz. I hope you won't feel too bad if you flunked it. Honestly, I'm not sure I could have passed it before seeing the findings from our study. Apparently, there is broad misunderstanding among parents of these special children with unusually tough or easy attitudes toward authority. Indeed, I administered this quiz to many groups of young parents before writing my book. They didn't do so hot, either. In fact, it was typical for them to get from 4 to 6 items correct. One man answered 12 of the 14 items accurately, and he was given the "Superdad of the Year" award. When asked how he knew so much about very strong-willed and very compliant kids, he replied, "I raised one of each!"

Now, I'll repeat a simplified version of each question from the test, give the correct answer, and then provide additional information about the issue at hand.

Question 1: What is the ratio of very strong-willed to very compliant children?

Answer: (4) There are about twice as many very strong-willed children (7,899 very strong-willed vs. 4,340 very compliant).

Actually, the true ratio of very strong-willed to very compliant children is more like 3 to 1 than 2 to 1. Why? Because many of the 4,340 children in the very compliant category were infants who had not yet been recognized as strong-willed. Their parents reported them to be compliant, but a surprise is coming their way. When those children under thirty months are eliminated from our analysis, 74 percent of the children being studied were very strong-willed and 24 percent very compliant.

Question 2: What is the ratio of males to females within the category of very strong-willed children?

Answer: (1) Males outnumber females by about 5 percentage points...52.5 to 47.5.

Question 3: What is the ratio of males to females within the category of very compliant children?

Answer: (2) Females outnumber males by about 6 percentage points...53 to 47.

Question 4: Select the accurate statement below (regarding birth order and temperament).
Answer: (4) There is no strong tendency for temperament to be related to birth order.

There is a slight trend toward compliance for firstborn children and strong-willed for secondborn. However, our assumption is that these characteristics are *inborn*, and should not be highly influenced by an environmental factor such as birth order. That is what we found.

Question 5: Select the accurate statement below (regarding the age when the strong-willed child is recognized).
Answer: (2) About a third (36 percent) of very strong-willed children are recognized at birth.

By one year of age, 66 percent are identified, and 92 percent by age three. Compliant children tend to be recognized earlier: 43 percent between birth and three months, 74 percent by one year, and 93 percent by the third birthday.

Question 6: Is the temperament of the child inherited from the parents?
Answer: (1) *Yes.* The data suggest that it is.

Though there are many exceptions, there does seem to be a tendency for the temperaments of the parents to be reproduced in their children. Perhaps the environment has influenced our findings here, but I think genetics played the dominant role. There does seem to be an inherited component, even though it sometimes fails to materialize. It is not uncommon, for example, to produce three or four easy-to-raise children followed by a pistol.

Question 7: What happens to the rebellious nature of very strong-willed children as they move through the years?
Answer: (3) Approximately 40 percent rebel in toddlerhood, and the percentages rise in every age category through adolescence, reaching a peak of 74 percent in the teen years.

The data clearly reveal that the percentage of very strong-willed children who rebel begins high in toddlerhood and never lets up until adulthood. There is no lull of any significance between toddlerhood and adolescence. This is important information, even though somewhat unpleasant, for parents who want to predict the patterns of behavior from their tough-minded kids.

I hope this information will not be discouraging to parents of strong-willed children. It is true that a significant percentage will be in rebellion at any one time (from 40 to 74 percent), while the percentage who cooperate ranges from 23 percent to a low of 11 percent in adolescence. The data also shows, however, a rapid decline of rebellion in young adulthood; it drops precipitously from 74 to 36 percent. In fact, slightly more strong-willed children cooperate than rebel in the age twenty-to-twenty-four category. The battles are still in progress for about a third of the individuals, but most of the fire is spent. They'll soon join the human race again. I'll share other good news in a moment.

Now we come to a most surprising discovery from the study. It came in answer to questions 8 and 9.

Question 8: What percentage of very compliant children eventually go into severe rebellion in either adolescence or young adulthood?
Answer: (1) Only 3 percent!

Question 9: What percentage of very compliant children eventually go into *mild* rebellion in either adolescence or young adulthood?
Answer: (1) Only 14 percent!

Contrary to popular belief, the very compliant child rarely goes through severe rebellion. Only a small percentage (14 percent) defy their parents even in an insignificant manner. Of the 14 percent who did test the limits of authority, it was a brief passageway during adolescence. The figure drops to 8 percent in young adulthood.

It is amazing that the vast majority of these compliant children (91 percent) do not become difficult during the terrible twos, and they remain cooperative up to the time of the adolescent valley. Even during the teen years, only 17 percent go into rebellion (that figure includes mild and severe rebellion).

Finally, we need to look at this same issue from another angle to learn (1) how stable is the tendency to rebel across time, and (2) at what age does the highest percentage of rebellion occur? To get at these issues we asked parents to evaluate their very strong-willed children and very compliant children in various time frames from toddlerhood to adulthood. We were interested in the individuals going through severe defiance at each of those age points.

According to our figures, *severe* rebellion is relatively rare before thirteen years of age, even for the very strong-willed child. It then spikes to 26 percent during adolescence before expending its energy in early adulthood. By contrast, 97 percent of compliant children do not experience severe rebellion at all.

Question 10: Which individual is more likely to have an edge in academic achievement?
Answer: (2) The very compliant child.

More than three times as many very strong-willed teenagers made D's and F's during the last two years of high school as did compliant teenagers (19 percent versus 5 percent). Conversely, twice as many compliant adolescents made A's (45 percent versus 25 percent). Of all very compliant teenagers, 79 percent were A and B students, compared with 53 percent of very strong-willed kids. The same pattern was also evident in grades six, nine, and to a lesser degree, in college.

Question 11: Which individual typically makes the best social adjustment in adolescence?
Answer: (2) The very compliant child.

Again, there is a remarkable difference between these two categories of children, favoring the compliant child by a wide margin. During adolescence, 35 percent of the compliant children were said to have "no social problems," compared with only 15 percent of the strong-willed. Likewise, 5 percent of the compliant had "many social problems" compared with 16 percent of the strong-willed. Only 2 percent of the compliant were "generally disliked," but 9 percent of the strong-willed were given this designation. A similar pattern was seen for younger children, as well.

It would appear that the youngster who is challenging the authority of his parents and starting little insurrections at home is also more likely to behave offensively with his peers. We should point out, however, that the majority of strong-willed children do not have great social problems.

Question 12: Which individual is more likely to be "peer dependent" in adolescence...that is, which is more easily influenced by group opinion and peer pressure?
Answer: (1) The very strong-willed child.

The compliant teenagers turned out to be considerably less peer dependent than the strong-willed. I had assumed that these kids who had been so easy for their parents to mold and influence would also be more vulnerable to pressure from their peer group. After all, one of their unique characteristics is the desire to please other people. Why wouldn't that sensitivity extend to friends and associates? I even made a statement to that effect in my first film series, "Focus on the Family," during which I stated:

> I am not speaking derogatorily of the strong-willed child. I don't think it's "bad kid versus good kid." I think the defiant child has greater potential for character development and for accomplishment and leadership. Yes, it is more difficult to raise him.
>
> But maybe the same characteristics that cause a toddler to stamp his foot and say no to you will cause him, thirteen years later, to say no to the peer group when they offer him drugs. We need to shape his will and give him the ability to shape his own impulses.

I was wrong. But no one is perfect. There was an enormous difference in the degree of peer dependency between the two groups of adolescents. Some 58 percent of the strong-willed teenagers were judged by their parents to have been greatly influenced by agemates. This compares with only 24 percent of the compliant adolescents. Since peer dependency is one of the demons behind drug abuse, alcoholism, and sexual promiscuity, this characteristic of strong-willed teenagers is of serious concern to us.

Question 13: Which individual is more likely to have the higher self-esteem in adolescence?
Answer: (2) The very compliant child.

It is difficult to overestimate the importance of this finding in favor of the compliant child. He is *much* more likely to feel good about himself than his strong-willed sibling. Only 19 percent of the teenagers in this category either disliked themselves (17 percent) or felt extreme self-hatred (2 percent). Of the very strong-willed teenagers, however, 43 percent either disliked themselves (35 percent) or experienced extreme self-hatred (8 percent). The differences were also evident at the positive end of the scale, although they were not quite so dramatic. A picture is emerging of the compliant child being more at peace with himself, as well as being at peace with his parents.

Why do strong-willed children have a greater tendency to doubt their own worth in this way? It is difficult to say, except to affirm that they are more unsettled in every aspect of their lives. We do know that lower self-esteem is related to the excessive peer dependency, academic difficulties, social problems, and even the rebellion we have seen. Acceptance of one's intrinsic worth is the core of the personality. When it collapses, everything else begins to quiver.

Question 14: Finally, parents were asked to indicate how their grown sons and daughters had achieved in their adult pursuits. Which group do you think succeeded best, the strong-willed or the compliant?
Answer: (2) The very compliant.

Again, the pattern held...69 percent of compliant children, then as young adults, were considered to be successful or highly successful by their parents. Only 56 percent of the strong-willed were given this accolade. When one looks at the frequency of failure in the same context, the compliant come out winners once more: 11 percent versus 22 percent.

Most of the parents with whom I have shared these findings have been surprised by the outcome. They expected strong-willed individuals to emerge on top in this category. Their aggressiveness should have produced a faster start, or so the common wisdom goes. On closer examination, however, the compliant young man or woman succeeds in early business pursuits because he plays by the rules. He finds out what the boss wants and promptly gives it to him. It would also appear that he is going through less personal turmoil in this post-adolescent era. He is thereby freer to get on with the business of living.

These findings would not surprise Bill Haughton, a successful real estate broker and former Marine living in Dallas, Texas. He was in the industrial distribution business for thirty years, starting as the first employee and eventually selling the company in 1980 when there were 450 employees in 40 locations. Bill and I have become good friends, and I once asked him how he had selected new employees. His answer was surprising. He said the first thing he wanted to know about any young man who applied for a job was the nature of his relationship with his father. If it was stormy, he would not hire him.

Bill explained his reasoning: "If a boy learned to accept authority under his dad, the chances were good that he would later accept the leadership of his employers. But if he was a rebel, he was more likely to cause difficulties in my business."

I then asked Bill how he screened women. Again, his perspective was unique, even if controversial. He said, "Women are more difficult to assess in the beginning. You don't really know them until they are on the job. Unfortunately, they can be meaner than men. When I realize I have hired an office malcontent, someone who is always working to get to the head of the pecking order, then I know I have erred. She will create continual morale problems. She must go or my shop will be chaotic!"

Bill Haughton's philosophy of employee hiring represents a practical application of the findings confirmed in our study. It explains, perhaps, why the strong-willed man or woman typically gets off to a slower start in business than the more compliant individual. Bosses and supervisors want employees who will follow instructions and avoid hassles with coworkers. Incidentally, in another study of people who were fired from their places of employment, fewer than 20 percent lost their jobs for the lack of technical knowledge and skill. More than 80 percent were released because of their inability to get along with *people*. That is their Achilles heel, despite their aptitude for a particular kind of work. Thus, the easygoing young man or woman has a distinct advantage in early positions of employment. That is precisely what we found.

But let me speculate about how this picture might change with the passage of time. Since our study was limited to those individuals twenty-four years of age and younger, I have wondered what happens to those who are forty and older. It is my supposition that strong-willed individuals will eventually emerge as the entrepreneurs and leaders. Their desire for independence and their aggressive temperaments might cause them to outproduce their compliant counterparts in the long run.

My good friend, Dr. Malcolm Williamson, whom I referred to earlier, has assessed the personality traits of thousands of adults in the workforce. His research shows clearly that corporation presidents are characteristically dominant (strong-willed), aggressive, self-confident, fast-paced, and highly independent. Conversely, he finds a high percentage of vice presidents and middle management executives are "servants." They carry out company policy very well. They tend to be loyal, dedicated perfectionists who do not want to be wrong. And yes, they tend to be compliant.

I believe our study would have confirmed these findings if we had extended the time frame for two more decades. Perhaps we will do so someday.

CONCLUSION

Now that I have thoroughly depressed the parents of very strong-willed children, let me make two summarizing comments and offer a few encouraging thoughts.

First, there was another finding from our study which should provide hope to every mother and father on the battlefield today. It concerns the return to parental values by these most difficult individuals when they reach adulthood. We learned that 53 percent of even the most strong-willed and rebellious children eventually return to the values of their parents, outright. When that figure is combined with those who are "somewhat" accepting of parental perspectives, it means 85 percent of these hardheaded, independent individuals will eventually lean toward their parents' point of view by the time adolescence is over. Only 15 percent are so headstrong that they reject everything their family stood for, and I'll wager that there were other problems and sources of pain in most of those cases.

What this means, in effect, is that these tough-minded kids will fuss and fight and complain throughout their years at home, but the majority will turn around as young adults and do what their parents most desired. Remember, also, that there was a category of individuals whom we described as "rather strong-willed," who have not been considered in any of these analyses. It is virtually certain that the percentage of these less antagonistic kids who accept parental values is higher than those represented above. It is also reassuring to know, in this context, that even the *most* defiant individuals who go through awful rebellion in adolescence are likely to come back to parental values...partially if not entirely. Furthermore, if we could evaluate these individuals at thirty-five instead of twenty-four years of age, even fewer would still be in rebellion against parental values.

Second, I urge you as parents of strong-willed children not to feel "cheated" or depressed by the assignment of raising such individuals. All human beings arrive with a generous assortment of flaws, including the very compliant child. Yes, it is more difficult to raise an independent little fellow, but you can do it! You can, through prayer and supplication before the Lord, bring him to that period of harmony in early adulthood that makes the effort worthwhile. I also believe that you can increase the odds of transmitting your values to these individuals by following some time-honored principles which we will discuss. So hang in there! Nothing of any real value in life comes easy anyway, except the free gift of salvation from Jesus Christ.

Let's look now, in chapter 4, at the ways parents react to defiant and compliant children. You might find your own reflection somewhere in the discussion that follows.

FOUR

What 35,000
Parents Said About
Themselves

Y OU WILL RECALL from the first chapter that many parents told us they were *intensely* frustrated by their child-rearing responsibilities. More than 30 percent responding to our survey said, in effect, "I am a failure as a parent!" and "I simply can't cope with my kids." But who are these mothers and fathers who have felt such despair at home? I believe we now have revealing answers to that and other important questions.

The thirty-five thousand parents who participated in our study not only gave us valuable information about their strong-willed and compliant children (reported in chapter 3), but they also described their own feelings and attitudes about raising them. Their responses were surprising in many contexts. Let's look at a few of the more relevant findings, some of which were alarming.

One of the items on the questionnaire (see appendix) asked parents to rate the amount of stress that was created by their children's temperaments. Then we divided the sample to compare the responses of parents of very compliant children versus those of the very strong-willed.

The results were dramatic. We found that 95 percent of parents raising very compliant children felt good about the job they were doing, compared with only 11 percent of the parents of strong-willed children. On the negative side, 1 percent of the parents of compliant children rated the assignment generally difficult or unpleasant, compared with 72 percent of those raising strong-willed kids. Obviously, we have identified the bulk of frustrated parents from this one item on our questionnaire.

A second item was intended to explore further the reactions of parents to children with easy or difficult personalities. We asked for this information: "Generally speaking, select the sentence that best describes how you feel about raising your very strong-willed or very compliant children." The four alternative statements were:

1. "It has been a struggle that has often left me depressed, guilt-ridden, and exhausted."
2. "It has been difficult but exciting and rewarding too."
3. "It has been a very positive experience."

Parents of strong-willed children were then given this fourth choice:

4. "He/she was difficult in the early years, but the adolescent years were less stormy and difficult."

Parents of compliant children were then given this fourth choice:

4. "He/she was a joy in the early years, but adolescence was extremely stressful for both generations."

Having obtained responses from 4,801 parents, we divided the sample into eight subgroups in an attempt to identify the parents in greatest distress. We were looking at both strong-willed and compliant mothers and fathers as they interacted with their very strong-willed and very compliant children.

Even a cursory examination of these responses makes it clear that strong-willed children are a source of great frustration not only to their mothers, which we expected, but also to their fathers. Lynn Caine, writing in her book *What Did I Do Wrong?*, said this about men: "Fathers...seemed not to share either the guilt or the blame.... They did not feel hated or inadequate or responsible for them. *That* was for women to feel.... I have seldom met a guilty father.... Perhaps our guilt is a condition of womankind, a weakness of the sex, the natural softness of the nurturer."[1]

According to our findings, Mrs. Caine is wrong. Fathers *do* struggle when their children rebel. Strong-willed children not only affect mothers and fathers equally, but they create about the same degree of stress for strong-willed and compliant parents. Very strong-willed mothers, for example, reported the same level of positive interaction (6 percent) as very strong-willed fathers with their very strong-willed children. The lowest positive rating (4 percent) occurred for very compliant fathers raising very strong-willed children. In short, every adult who works with these rambunctious youngsters is affected by the tension they create! We will come back to this point in a moment.

Let's turn our attention now from how parents *feel* to how they *discipline*. Some equally dramatic findings turned up at this point. Our primary interest was in the handling of very strong-willed versus very compliant children. We asked those completing the questionnaire to indicate which parent related best to the children at various age levels.

From this analysis and several dozen others, it was apparent that mothers of strong-willed children are especially vulnerable to their rebellious kids. As indicated earlier, fathers also struggle and feel guilty in reference to them. Nevertheless, men appear willing to accept an increasing share of the child-rearing responsibility with the passage of time. Mothers begin in complete charge of their young children, handling 78 percent of their strong-willed toddlers. From there, they slide downhill in every age category through adolescence. Fathers actually related to the greater percentage of individuals between thirteen and twenty years of age by a few percentage points. A rebound then occurs in young adulthood, favoring mothers again. We are assuming that this transfer of parenting responsibilities from women to men occurs because mothers dislike confrontation and are less comfortable than fathers with the power games played by these tougher sons and daughters.

Of greater significance in this context is the percentage of children to whom *neither* parent related very well. It begins at about 5 percent for the earliest years and rises gradually until age thirteen. A peak of 24 percent of cases in the adolescent years spells trouble! One-fourth of these tough-minded youngsters do not get along well with *either* mother or father, and 14 percent are still charting their own course in young adulthood. Like their parents, these are the teens who desperately need outside influence of the right type.

When responses to the question, "Who handles the child best?" were plotted by sex, it was noted that fathers carry an even greater responsibility for strong-willed sons than they do with their daughters. Surprisingly, however, girls were just as rebellious as boys during adolescence.

Let's compare responses, now, from parents of very compliant children. The pattern is dramatically different. Mothers are rated highest in the birth-to-age-two category (nearly 90 percent of cases) and even at their low point, under 60 percent for compliant kids ages thirteen to twenty, they still outrank fathers.

It does not require a statistician to draw meaning from these data. Clearly, mothers love compliant children. Fathers are fond of them, too, but Mom is in the driver's seat throughout childhood. Only a small percentage of compliant children feel alienated from both parents (a maximum of 5 percent during adolescence).

Upon seeing these figures for the first time, a struggling mother of a strong-willed tribe said to me wearily, "Where do I get some of those compliant kids?!" I don't know, but the chances are great that *her* parents would also have wanted that information.

From the outset of this study I was especially interested in the relationship between mothers and their daughters. Many psychologists have described a so-called "thing" which seemingly occurs between females in the same house. Whether it is a phenomenon of "two women in the kitchen" or a natural competitiveness for the attention of the husband/father, there does seem to be some validity to it. It is not unusual for a mother to say during this period, "I don't like either my son *or* my daughter right now." Evidences of such difficulties were found in our study. For example, only 36 percent of mothers related best to their strong-willed daughters during adolescence. Conflict was evident in the remaining two-thirds of the cases. Other examples of that antagonism were also unearthed in our study.

Another interesting factor was noted regarding mothers' and fathers' discipline. Parents were asked to rate themselves as permissive, rather easy, average, rather strict, or rigid/severe. We then cross-tabulated that rating against children's social success at various ages. They were categorized as having no problems, generally liked, average, generally disliked, and having many problems. This is what we found: For the children with many problems, their parents tended to be either permissive with them or they were rigid/severe. The pattern held through many analyses and at virtually each age category from childhood to adulthood. The conclusion is that when children are beset by major social problems, their parents react in extreme ways—either by throwing up their hands and refusing to discipline them at all, or by becoming so rigid and severe as to oppress them. This analysis and several others made it clear that the kind of discipline a parent applies is a function of the child's well-being and of his temperament. When he is unusually difficult or beset by numerous problems, parenting effectiveness sometimes suffers accordingly.

Summary

As indicated earlier, I could fill many books with the massive amount of information generated from this study of thirty-five thousand parents. Admittedly, this was a *retrospective* investigation instead of a more scientific *longitudinal* effort. Nevertheless, the findings speak for themselves. The gap between strong-willed and compliant children is indeed a chasm, and those differences in temperament and behavior have a dramatic effect on those who are raising them.

Perhaps it is now evident why I am especially concerned about parents raising very strong-willed children. I believe many of these mothers and fathers are near the breaking point today. Their sense of guilt is overwhelming, and yet they have typically carried their pain in silence. I would expect the incidences of child abuse, child abandonment, parental alcoholism, and other evidences of family disintegration to be inordinately high in this category. And of course, it is not a category or a group at all. I'm talking about real *people*—living, breathing mothers and fathers who are going down for the count.

If you are one of those struggling parents who has wept in the midnight hours, the balance of this book is for you. While we will also address the special problems encountered by compliant children, the greater urgency must be on the rebellious individual and his family. There is hope for him and for you, his parents.

FIVE

WITH LOVE
TO PARENTS
WHO HURT

S OME TIME AGO, I attended a wedding ceremony held in a beautiful garden setting. After the minister instructed the groom to kiss his
bride, approximately 150 colorful, helium-filled balloons were released
into the blue California sky. It was a pleasant sight that reminded me of
a similar moment during the 1984 Olympics in Los Angeles. Within a
few seconds, the balloons were scattered across the heavens—some rising
hundreds of feet overhead and others cruising toward the horizon. The
distribution was curious. They all began from a common launching pad,
were filled with approximately the same amount of helium, and ascended
into the same conditions of sun and wind. Nevertheless, within a matter
of several minutes they were separated by a mile or more. A few balloons
struggled to clear the upper branches of trees, while the show-offs became
mere pinpoints of color on their journey to the sky. How interesting, I
thought—and how symbolic of children.

We have already agreed that babies do not begin life's journey from
a common launching pad. They also vary in their ability to fly. Let's face
it. Some carry more helium than others. But even if they were identical at
birth, they would not remain equivalent for long. Environmental influences
would carry them in infinite directions within the span of a few days. From
that point forward, they only drift farther apart. Some kids seem to catch all
the right breezes. They soar effortlessly to the heights. Their parents beam
with pride for having created superior balloons. Others wobble danger-
ously close to the trees. Their frantic folks run along underneath, huffing
and puffing to keep them airborne. It is an exhausting experience.

I want to offer a word of encouragement at this point to the parents of every low-flying kid in the world today. There's usually one or more in each family. They're not all strong-willed and rebellious, of course. Some are physically handicapped. Others have learning disabilities or peculiar personalities or serious illnesses. Some have other characteristics that bring ridicule from their peers. What is it that worries you about your different child? Is he overweight or underweight or very short or tall or clumsy or lazy? Or is he so terribly selfish and unpleasant that he has alienated everyone he's met except (or including) you? Is the story of your family written somewhere within the flight plan of your "special balloon"?

May I gently put my arm around you through the pages of this book? I understand your pain and your fears. Your hopes rise and fall with the altitude of this different youngster. You awaken in the wee hours of the morning, worrying and praying for his survival. You have nightmares that his balloon will go into a frantic loop-the-loop and then plunge in a power dive to the earth. You would give your life to prevent this catastrophe, but that wouldn't help. You're all he has.

If you've launched only high-flying sons and daughters, then you won't comprehend the sentiment of these words. You may even think them foolish. It is very difficult to understand the depression and apprehension that can accompany the rearing of such a child unless you've been through it. It is also embarrassing. Why? Because of the crazy notion that parents are responsible for everything their child becomes. They are praised or blamed for his successes and failures—all of them. If he is gorgeous, brilliant, artistic, athletic, scholarly, and polite, his folks get an A+ for having made him that way. But if he is ordinary, uncoordinated, indolent, homely, unpleasant, and dull, they fail the course. Mom and Dad are particularly accountable for their child's misbehavior, even years after he is beyond their control or influence. I hear from parents almost every day who share stories similar to this one:

> Dear Dr. Dobson:
> We have four children including a boy and girl in college. They are doing beautifully and have become everything parents dream of. We also have a twelve-year-old boy whose brain was damaged at birth. He's a beautiful child who works extremely hard to keep his head above water. Finally, we have a thirteen-year-old boy who has been strong-willed from "day one," as you often say.

*We've been Christians for seven years, and we've done every-
thing possible to help this child—from prayer, to moving this past
year, to putting him in a Christian school, to weekly family counseling sessions.*

*Tonight we had to sit with our son in front of the pastor, the
minister of education, and members of the Christian school board to
request that he not be kicked out of school with only six weeks left.
The verdict: He's out! The comment was made by the minister of
education to this effect, "What kind of parents are you not to have
more control over your son?"*

*We are desperate! Everything we can think of has been tried
with this child. We love him dearly but I sure see why parents abuse
their children. I'm an X-ray technician and I see too many brain-
damaged children from abuse. Maybe at this moment that is what
keeps me from beating him. But why do these school administrators
put more guilt on us when people like you try so hard to help us
handle it? We have enough guilt already, knowing that we are failures
at parenting.*

Please help. We are desperate!

God bless you,
Elaine

If we talked to the school board and the minister of education, we
might hear a different story about these parents and their rebellious son.
Perhaps they did cause his defiant behavior, but I doubt it. When we look
at their other children, we see they are doing fine. No, I think the parents are victims of the cruel misunderstanding of which we have spoken.
They and other contemporary parents have been taught that children are
born neutral and good. If the children go wrong, it is because someone
wreaks havoc upon them. All behavior is caused, say the experts. The child
chooses nothing. He merely responds to his experiences.

As indicated earlier, this theory is called *determinism*, and if it is valid,
then the responsibility for every lie, every school failure, every act of defiance eventually circles around to his family—especially to his mother.
This is why she has been blamed for all the problems and even the silly
imperfections that beset her children. Is it any wonder that one thousand

mothers and fathers who responded to our "frustrations of parenthood poll" gave as their most common answer, "I am a failure as a parent"?

I remember boarding a commercial airliner a few years ago on a trip from Los Angeles to Toronto. No sooner had I become comfortable than a mother sat down two seats from me and promptly placed her three-year-old son between us. *Oh boy!* I thought. *I get to spend five hours strapped next to this little live wire.* I expected him to drive his mother and me crazy by the time we landed. If my son, Ryan, had been strapped in a chair at that age and given nothing to do, he would have dismantled the entire tail section of the plane by the time it landed. My father once said about Ryan, "If you allow that kid to become bored, you *deserve* what he will do to you."

To my surprise, the toddler next to me sat pleasantly for five long hours. He sang little songs. He played with the ashtray. For an hour or two he slept. But mostly, he engaged himself in thought. I kept expecting him to claw the air, but it never happened. His mother was not surprised. She acted as though all three-year-olds were able to sit for half a day with nothing interesting to do.

Contrast that uneventful episode with another flight I took a few months later. I boarded a plane, found my seat, and glanced to my left. Seated across from me this time was a well-dressed woman and a *very* ambitious two-year-old girl. Correction! The mother was seated but her daughter was most definitely not. This little girl had no intention of sitting down—or slowing down. It was also obvious that the mother did not have control of the child, and indeed, Superman himself might have had difficulty harnessing her. The toddler shouted "No!" every few seconds as her mother tried to rein her in. If Mom persisted she would scream at the top of her lungs while kicking and lunging to escape. I looked at my watch and thought, *What is this poor woman going to do when she is required to buckle that kid in her seat?*

I could see that the mother was accustomed to losing these major confrontations with her daughter. Obviously, the child was used to winning. That arrangement might have achieved a tentative peace at home or in a restaurant, but this was different. They were faced with a situation on the plane where the mother *couldn't* give in. To have allowed the child to roam during takeoff would have been dangerous and impermissible under FAA regulations. Mom *had* to win—perhaps for the first time ever.

In a few minutes, the flight attendant came by and urged the mother to buckle the child down. Easy for her to say! I will never forget what occurred in the next few minutes. The two-year-old threw a tantrum that must have set some kind of international record for violence and expended energy. She was kicking, sobbing, screaming, and writhing for freedom! Twice she tore loose from her mom's arms and scurried toward the aisle. The mortified woman was literally begging her child to settle down and cooperate. Everyone in our section of the plane was embarrassed for the humiliated mother. Those of us within ten feet were also virtually deaf by that point.

Finally, the plane taxied down the runway and took off with the mother hanging onto this thrashing toddler with all her strength. Once we were airborne, she was able at last to release the little fireball. When the crisis was over, the mother covered her face with both hands and wept. I felt her pain too.

Why didn't I help her? Because my advice would have offended the mother. The child desperately needed the security of strong parental leadership at that moment, but the woman had no idea how to provide it. A few sharp slaps on the legs would probably have taken some of the fire out of her. The affair could have ended with a sleeping child curled in her mother's loving arms. Instead, it set the stage for even more violent and costly confrontations in the years ahead.

It is interesting to speculate on how the mothers on these two airplanes probably felt about themselves and their very different toddlers. I would guess that the woman with the passive little boy was significantly overconfident. Raising kids for her was duck soup. "You tell 'em what to do and expect 'em to do it!" she could have said. Some mothers in her comfortable situation hold unconcealed disdain for parents of rebellious children. They just can't understand why others find child-rearing so difficult.

The mother of the second toddler, on the other hand, was almost certainly experiencing a great crisis of confidence. I could see it in her eyes. She wondered how she had managed to make such a mess of parenting in two short years! Somehow, she had taken a precious newborn baby and twisted her into a monster. But how did it happen? What did she do to cause such outrageous behavior? She may ask those questions for the rest of her life.

I wish she had known that at least part of the problem resided in the temperament of the child. It was her nature to grab for power, and the mother was making a serious mistake by granting it to her.

This is my point: Parents today are much too willing to blame themselves for everything their children (or adolescents) do. Only in this century have they been so inclined. If a kid went bad one hundred years ago, he was a bad kid. Now it's the fault of his parents. Admittedly, many mothers and fathers *do* warp and twist their children during the vulnerable years. I am not pleading their cases. Believe me, I know that our society today is peppered with terrible parents who don't care about their kids. Some are addicted to alcohol, gambling, pedophilia, pornography, or just plain selfishness. This book is not written to soothe their guilt. But there are others who care passionately about their sons and daughters, and they do the best they can to raise them properly. Nevertheless, when their kids entangle themselves in sin and heartache, guess who feels reponsible for it? Behavior is caused, isn't it? The blame inevitably makes a sweeping U-turn and lodges itself in the hearts of the parents.

I am particularly concerned about the mother and father who give the highest priority to the task of parenthood. Their firstborn child is conceived in love and born in great joy. They will neither talk nor think of much else for the next three years. The first smile; the first word; the first birthday; the first step. Every milestone is a cause for celebration. They buy him a tricycle and they teach him to fly a kite. And they patch up the bird with the broken wing. Only the best will do for this inheritor of the family name. They buy him Child-Craft books and teach him to sing. They show him how to pray. It is a labor of love that knows no limits.

Before they know it, their precious little lad is ready for kindergarten. How time flies! They buy him new clothes and cut his hair and get him a Snoopy lunch pail. "Hurry, now," says his mom on the first day of school. "Let's don't be late." She walks with him across the street and waits for the big yellow bus that stops on the corner. It arrives presently and the door opens. She places the child on the first step and then moves backward to take his picture. The door closes and the bus rumbles slowly down the street. Mom watches as long as it is in sight, and then she turns toward her house. She cries quietly as she crosses the street. Her baby is growing up.

The years pass so quickly but it is a happy time. The boy learns to ride a bicycle and soon he's heavily into bugs and snakes and spiders. He gives Little League a try and Dad attends every game. You'd think it was the World Series! There is nothing this father would not do for his son. The boy loves his mom and dad, too, although he has a mind of his own. He has always been somewhat assertive and independent. His cousins think he is a brat. Some of the church folks think he is spoiled. His parents think he's just immature. All three are right.

The tenth, eleventh, and twelfth years are marked by increasing tension in the house, but major blowups have not yet occurred. Then, suddenly, the roof falls in. The boy turns thirteen and a dramatic change settles over him. Overnight, almost, he has become distant and edgy. He explodes whenever he is frustrated, which seems to happen every few days. He also resents his parents for the first time. He shrinks back when they touch him, and he objects to the pet names they have always used. He hates his mom's cooking and complains about the way she irons his shirts. It is a very tough year.

At fourteen, he spends long hours in his room with his door closed. Because life has become intolerable at home he talks vaguely about running away. His parents are utterly bewildered. What did they do? How have they changed? They feel no different, yet this son whom they love so much has targeted them as his enemies. Why? They are hurt and confused.

When he is fifteen, Mom is cleaning his room one day and finds some weird-looking cigarettes behind a bookend. "Could it be? Would he really? Oh no! Not our son!" Then they discover a bottle of little red pills in the bottom drawer of his dresser. "Where is he getting the money?"

Every day is a struggle now for his mother and father. He will not yield to their leadership. This young man, whom they have cherished, seems bent on destroying himself before he is grown. He comes home at all hours of the night reeking of alcohol and smoke. If they demand to know where he's been, he blows up. "Get off my back!" he screams. They are worried sick.

Dad talks to the juvenile authorities on the phone. "I just can't control him," he says. "Sorry," the officer replies, "there's nothing we can do until he commits a serious crime. Even then we can be of little help. There are so many.... "

At sixteen, the boy buys himself a car. Now he is really emancipated. His folks rarely see him. He fails four classes as a sophomore and quits school as a junior. From there to his nineteenth year, he is involved in three automobile accidents, gets seven tickets for speeding, and finally, is arrested for driving under the influence. He spends a night in the tank for that one, which nearly kills his mother. Dad's car insurance policy is summarily cancelled.

Now, at twenty, he's living with a girl who is not his wife. She had an abortion last year and is pregnant again. They fight continually over money. He's never held a job for more than three months and they're living on food stamps and State assistance. A friend tells his parents that their son is snorting cocaine now.

Most painful of all to his mother and father is his rejection of their faith. He says he hates their religion and never accepted a word of it. "You can believe what you want," he sneers, "but don't try to sell it to me." Long-term, unrelenting depression settles over their home like a thick black cloud.

Does this frightening scenario actually occur in solid, secure, loving Christian homes? Yes, occasionally it does. And when it happens to *you* and your family, it might as well be a worldwide plague. I feel great tenderness toward parents who have been there. One of them, a mother of three grown daughters, wrote to me recently. This is what she said:

Dear Dr. Dobson:

Your radio interview with Dr. John White was so helpful. I had already read his book, Parents in Pain, *but it ministered to me again. [Incidentally, I recommend this book highly to my readers.]*

We have three daughters, ages twenty, twenty-three, and twenty-four, raised as well as we could do it. I read Kesler and I read Trobisch. I did the best I could to be a good example and to follow Christian standards. I spent hours trying to show them that each one was valued and loved immensely. I tried to give them room to be individuals, and we both enjoyed watching them develop into adults. In our zeal we never even bought a TV set!!!

Results: We have two daughters who couldn't have turned out better and one who couldn't have turned out worse. Our oldest daughter is a college graduate, has a productive job, is loving her Christian walk and is a joy to have around.

Daughter #3 caused us untold grief and worry and finally at age eighteen ran off with a twenty-nine-year-old thrice-married ex-convict (who was still married to wife #3). For three weeks I sat at the kitchen table all day in shock.

I didn't know that anyone could endure that much pain and still live. At first I thought I would commit suicide. Then I thought I would go around forever with FAILURE branded on my forehead. My husband and I had long discussions about whether we should drop out of the church and not attempt to minister to others because of our failure. It shook our marriage to the roots. We felt like twenty-six years went down the drain. It was so embarrassing to see people who knew what had happened. It was worse to run into people who didn't know, because they might ask how our girls were. I would cut people absolutely dead so they wouldn't have a chance to ask.

I complained to God for "letting it happen." For many weeks I considered giving up the Christian walk, but on the other hand I could hardly wait for church and the Bible study because of the help I knew was there. Finally I did come to the point where I had to admit to God that I had to stick with Him because only He had the words of eternal life, but I could hardly pray for months because my heart was like a rock.

Now, almost exactly two years have passed. We finally know where she is, and only this week she has decided that she would even write us a letter.

There is a special group of parents at church who have formed an unspoken brotherhood because their children have broken their hearts, and other parents with all good kids lightly compare notes while the rest of us sit silently with aching hearts.

I tell you, Dr. Dobson, that it would be easier to bury the children than it would be to see them using their bodies for such shameful purposes—those bodies that we've lovingly washed, bandaged, dressed, stuffed good food and vitamins into, kept out of the lake, and off of the roads—using their lives to advance the cause of Satan. I sincerely hope that you never hear your kid say, "I hate you. You've ruined my life, and I never want to see you again," and walk out coolly.

I want to tell you something else about the effect this has had on our family that we didn't expect. Our oldest daughter says: "I will never have any children." Parents spend years doing their best for the *children, and suddenly at age fourteen the parents become despised enemies. I refuse to put up with that for myself.*

I could go on for several more paragraphs, but I think you get the idea, as much as you could, not having gone through it yourself.

God bless you. Keep up the good work.

Sincerely,
Mary Alice

This mother was right. I have never experienced the kind of pain she has described, for which I'm grateful. But I believe I understand it. I have witnessed the same trauma in hundreds of families. It is one of the most devastating experiences in living. Most of the parents I have known who are dealing with adolescent or postadolescent rebellion respond precisely as Mary Alice did. They blame themselves. Note that she felt as though the word "failure" had been branded across her forehead. She was so humiliated she contemplated suicide. She and her husband thought of dropping out of church because they considered themselves no longer worthy as Christians. These are the words of guilt-ridden parents who have believed the great lie. In their minds, they had destroyed their own precious daughter. They were convinced that even God could not forgive so great a sin.

Guilt is one of the most painful emotions in human experience. Sometimes it is valid and represents the displeasure of God Himself. When that is the case, it can be forgiven and forgotten. On other occasions, it is entirely of our own creation. Mary Alice and her husband appear to be victims of this self-imposed condemnation, as are thousands of other parents. As with the writer of the earlier letter, this mother and her husband had raised three girls by the same philosophy and technique. If they were such horrid parents, why did two daughters turn out so well? I believe the vast differences between these three young women is traceable more to their own temperaments and choices than to the successes and failures of their parents. Nevertheless, Mary Alice felt totally responsible for the mess her youngest daughter was in. It wasn't fair. But that's the way mothers are made.

This tendency to assume the responsibility for everything our teenagers and grown children do is not only a product of psychological mumbo-jumbo (determinism) but it reflects our own vulnerabilities as parents. We know we are flawed. We know how often we fail. Even under the best of circumstances, we are forced time after time to guess at what is right for our children. Errors in judgment occur. Then our own selfishness surfaces and we do and say things that can never be undone. All these shortcomings are then magnified tenfold when a son or daughter goes bad.

Finally, the inclination toward self-condemnation also reflects the way Christians have been taught to believe. Though I am not a theologian, it is apparent to me that a serious misunderstanding of several key passages has occurred. The error has produced false condemnation for circumstances that exceed parental control or influence.

Consider, for example, the pastor who wrote me in anguish after his twenty-one-year-old son impregnated his girlfriend on a Christian college campus. The minister was devastated. He felt as guilty, as though he had personally been caught in an adulterous affair. This anguished man, who was a successful and popular pastor, wrote a letter of confession to his church and resigned as their leader. He cited Titus 1:6 as evidence of his unworthiness to continue in the ministry.

The verse he quoted is a portion of the apostle Paul's statement of qualifications for church leadership. Paul said a bishop must be "the husband of but one wife, a man whose children believe and are not open to the charge of being wild and disobedient." You may draw your own conclusions from this Scripture, but I believe it refers to much younger children than the pastor's son. This young man was twenty-one years of age and had gone away to college. He was no longer a child!

Remember, also, that males and females were considered grown much earlier in Paul's day. They often married between fourteen to sixteen years of age. Thus, when Paul referred to a man having his children in proper subjection, I believe he was talking about *children*. He intended to disqualify men who had chaotic families and those who were unable to discipline or manage their young sons and daughters. That is a far cry from holding a man responsible for the rebellious behavior of his grown offspring, or in this instance, for a single sinful event. They are beyond his control.

The pastor who wrote to me might take solace from reading again the book of Genesis. It would appear that God Himself would not qualify for church leadership according to the pastor's interpretation of Titus 1:6, because His wayward "children," Adam and Eve, fell into sin. Obviously, in my view, something is wrong with this interpretation of the Scriptures.

Ezekiel 18 is also helpful to us in assessing blame for the sinful behavior of grown children. God's way of looking at that situation is abundantly clear:

> The word of the LORD came to me: "What do you people mean by quoting this proverb about the land of Israel: 'The fathers eat sour grapes, and the children's teeth are set on edge'?
>
> "As surely as I live, declares the Sovereign LORD, you will no longer quote this proverb in Israel. For every living soul belongs to me, the father as well as the son—both alike belong to me. The soul who sins is the one who will die." (Ezekiel 18:1–4)

Then in verse 20 he concludes: "The son will not share the guilt of the father, nor will the father share the guilt of the son. The righteousness of the righteous man will be credited to him, and the wickedness of the wicked will be charged against him."

These words from the Lord should end the controversy once and for all. Each adult is responsible for his own behavior, and that of no one else.

So where does this leave us as Christian parents? Are we without spiritual resources with which to support our sons and daughters? Absolutely not! We are given the powerful weapon of intercessory prayer which must never be underestimated. The Scriptures teach that we can pray effectively for one another and that such a petition "availeth much" (James 5:16, KJV). God's answer to our request will not remove the freedom of choice from our children, but He will grant them clarity and understanding in charting their own course. They will be given every opportunity to make the right decisions regarding matters of eternal significance. I also believe the Lord will place key individuals in the paths of the ones for whom we pray—people of influence who can nudge them in the right direction.

Shirley and I prayed this prayer for our son and daughter throughout their developmental years: "Be there, Father, in the moment of decision when two paths present themselves to our children. Especially during that time when they are beyond our direct influence, send others who will help them do what is righteous and just."

I believe God honors and answers that kind of intercessory prayer. I learned that from my grandmother, who seemed to live in the presence of God. She had prayed for her six children throughout their formative years, but her youngest son (my father) was a particularly headstrong young man. For seven years following his high school graduation, he had left the church and rejected its teachings. Then, as it happened, an evangelist came to town and a great spiritual awakening swept their local church. But my father would have no part of it and refused even to attend.

One evening as the rest of the family was preparing to go to church, my father (who was visiting his parents' home) slipped away and hid on the side porch. He could hear his brothers chatting as they boarded the car. Then one of them, Willis, said suddenly, "Hey, where's Jim? Isn't he going tonight?"

Someone else said, "No, Willis. He said he isn't ever going to church again."

My father heard his brother get out of the car and begin searching for him all over the house. Willis had experienced a personal relationship with Jesus Christ when he was nine years old, and he loved the Lord passionately. He had held tightly to his faith throughout adolescence when his brothers (including my father) mocked him unmercifully. They had called him "Preacher Boy," "Sissy," and "Goody-Goody." It only made him more determined to do what was right.

My dad remained silent as Willis hurried through the house calling his name. Finally, he found his brother sitting silently in the swing on the side porch.

"Jim," he said, "aren't you going with us to the service tonight?"

My dad said, "No, Willis. I'm through with all of that. I don't plan to ever go back again."

Willis said nothing. But as my father sat looking at the floor, he saw big tears splashing on his brother's shoes. My father was deeply moved that Willis would love him that much, after the abuse he had taken for his Christian stand.

I'll go just because it means that much to him, my dad said to himself.

Because of the delay my father had caused, the family was late arriving at the church that night. The only seats left were on the second row from the front. They streamed down the aisle and were seated. A song evangelist was singing and the words began to speak to my dad's heart. Just that quickly, he yielded. After seven years of rebellion and sin, it was over. He was forgiven. He was clean.

The evangelist at that time was a man named Bona Fleming, who was unusually anointed of God. When the singer concluded, Reverend Fleming walked across the platform and put his foot on the altar rail. He leaned forward and pointed his finger directly at my dad.

"You! Young man! Right there! Stand up!"

My father rose to his feet.

"Now, I want you to tell all these people what God did for you while the singer was singing!"

My dad gave his first testimony, through his tears, of the forgiveness and salvation he had just received. Willis was crying too. So was my grandmother. She had prayed for him unceasingly for more than seven years.

To the day of his death at sixty-six years of age, my father never wavered from that decision. His only passion was to serve the God with whom he had fallen in love during a simple hymn. But where would he have been if Willis had not gone to look for him? How different life would have been for him...and for me. God answered the prayers of my grandmother by putting a key person at the critical crossroads.

He will do as much for your children, too, if you keep them in your prayers. But until that moment comes, pray for them in *confidence*—not in regret. The past is the past. You can't undo your mistakes. You could no more be a perfect parent than you could be a perfect human being. Let your guilt do the work God intended and then file it away forever. I'll bet Solomon would agree with that advice.

SIX

SUGGESTIONS FOR PARENTS OF YOUNG CHILDREN

THE BEST WAY to deal with parental guilt, of course, is to prevent it from occurring in the first place. We've taken a step in that direction by exposing false guilt resulting from circumstances beyond our control. But we must not go too far in that direction. Parents are accountable before God to meet their responsibilities to their children, and He is vitally concerned about their welfare. Jesus said that anyone who would hurt the faith of a little child would be better off sinking in the sea with a millstone attached to his neck. That warning is relevant to us as mothers and fathers. Our failure to love and discipline our children often inflicts upon them a weak and damaged faith. There is no greater tragedy in life!

We also want to do our best for our kids because we love them dearly. In that spirit, then, let me offer a few suggestions to parents of babies and children who have not yet reached their thirteenth birthdays.

1. Go with the Flow
I took my son Ryan and one of his friends on a ski trip when they were about twelve years of age. As we rode the gondola to the top of the mountain, I decided to snap the boys' picture with the beautiful scenery visible behind them. While I focused the shot, Ryan began clowning and waving at the camera. Ricky, on the other hand, sat glumly and quietly beside him.

"Come on, Rick!" said Ryan. "Loosen up! Smile for the camera!"

Ricky never changed his expression but simply said dryly, "I'm not that kind of person."

He was right. Ricky is reserved and dignified while Ryan is spontaneous and flamboyant. It's the way they are constructed. In a thousand years of practice Ricky could not be like Ryan, and Ryan would come unstitched if he had to be as controlled as Ricky. It was interesting to see how the boys recognized and accepted their differences in basic temperaments.

A surprising degree of diversity can occur even between children born to the same parents. For example, there were five boys in my father's family. The oldest two were twins who developed into great athletes. One went on to coach football at Byrd High School in Shreveport, Louisiana. The next eldest was Willis, who wore thick glasses and could neither catch nor throw a ball. He earned a Ph.D. in Shakespearean literature at the University of Texas and then taught college English for forty-five years.

The next in line was a gifted businessman who saved part of every dollar he ever earned. He was president of two Coca-Cola bottling plants when he died.

Finally, there was my dad—a sensitive artist by desire and a minister by the calling of God. With the exception of the twins, these brothers could not have been more unique if they had come from four different families. My father didn't even look like his brothers, being six feet four inches tall while the others were five feet nine or less. Obviously, God had taken a common genetic pool and fashioned five unique and distinct individuals from it.

Some of my readers might be wondering if we are absolutely sure that my grandfather was really the sire of this crew, but there's no doubt about that. I am reminded, however, of a man who lay dying and called his wife to his bedside. He then turned to her and said, "Mildred, I've always wanted to ask you about the youngest of our twelve children. He just doesn't look like me, and I've waited all these years to confront you. Is he really mine?"

"Yes, George, he's yours," said Mildred, "but the other eleven aren't."

That's a terrible joke, but it illustrates the diversity of offspring that can come from two fertile parents. It also raises an important question: What happens when you as a mother or father don't like the particular temperament with which your child is equipped? That is a common source of agitation among parents. Though they may never even admit their negative feelings to each other, they struggle with the fact one child is a profound disappointment to them. He is an embarrassment in public and an irritant at home. It may be his extreme shyness that galls them, or his extrovertish personality—or maybe his giddiness. Perhaps it is an athletic father with an uncoordinated son, or an overweight mother who desperately wanted, but didn't get, a thin daughter. For whatever reason, they had hoped to see the signs of greatness emerging in this child; instead, he turns out to be an intolerable misfit in the family. What then, my friends? What happens if *you* are the mother or father who dislikes one or more of your offspring?

Let's acknowledge that some children are easier to love than others. Haven't you heard it said about a particular boy or girl, "That is the sweetest kid I've ever known. I could just hug him to pieces"? We've all seen children like that who naturally attract us to them. But there are other children, millions of them, who lack that natural charm. They push people away from them, including their own families, without even understanding why.

When bonding fails to occur between parents and a particular child, both generations stand to suffer. The mother, especially, is likely to experience great feelings of guilt for her lack of affection for this individual. She recognizes his emotional needs and knows it is her responsibility to meet them, but something inside makes it difficult to respond. Instead, she reacts negatively toward this son or daughter. Ordinary childish behavior that would have been ignored in one of her other kids may bring flashes of anger toward this "problem" individual. Then she experiences more guilt for hurting someone so innocent and vulnerable. It is an emotional pit into which many parents have tumbled.

Such rejection is even more destructive from the child's point of view. Even if he can't explain it, he can feel the wall that separates him from his parents. He is especially sensitive to any preference or bias in favor of his siblings. By comparing himself with them, he gets a clearer picture of his standing in the family. If he concludes he is unloved and hated in that inner circle, his pain may manifest itself in unrestrained rebellion during the adolescent years. I've seen it happen a thousand times.

A guest on our Focus on the Family radio broadcast, who I'll call Susan, described her own experiences as a rejected child. Her father had returned from World War II in 1945 to discover that his wife had given birth to a baby girl who wasn't his. Susan was that infant. As the living symbol of his wife's infidelity, she was hated by her father. When she was nine years old, she found a loaded 38-caliber pistol hidden in a drawer.

She was showing it to a friend when her mother burst into the room. The woman grabbed the gun from Susan and said, "I hid this pistol so your dad wouldn't shoot you with it. He hates your guts and one of these days he will kill you."

For the next five years, Susan was subjected to the most terrible rejection at home. Then when she was fourteen, her mother said with intensity, "I just have to be really honest with you, Susan. You've been a problem in our marriage since the day you were born, and your dad hates you. He will never change. The best thing for you to do is to leave." Susan packed a bag and headed for California.

A person of lesser character would have been shattered by such mistreatment at home. Susan, however, managed to land on her feet. She was introduced to Jesus Christ while still a teenager, and she has devoted her life to helping others cope with their own pressures and fears.

Susan's story illustrates the intense hatred that parents can harbor for one or more of their children. When it occurs during the formative years, the despised son or daughter usually becomes twisted and crippled for the rest of his or her life. But we have been describing a more subtle and less deliberate form of rejection. It occurs in response to what might be called a parent's "private disappointment." It is not as overt as the hatred inflicted on Susan, but its pain can be almost as devastating.

Let me offer a few suggestions that may help. First, I believe it is possible in many cases to override one's emotions by an ironclad determination of the will. Feelings often follow behavior. If you make up your mind to love and care for each of your children equally, you might be surprised to find that the barriers isolating that "special" boy or girl are crumbling. What I'm saying is that human emotions are flighty and fickle. You *must* rule them with the rational mind. Do not permit yourself to be repelled from that youngster who needs and depends on you for his very sustenance. The stakes are too high!

Second, be especially wary of the game called "comparison." It's a killer! I'm convinced that most parents indulge regularly in this practice of comparing their kids with everyone else's. They want to know who is brightest, tallest, prettiest, healthiest, most mature, most athletic, and most obedient. It is fun to play as long as they win. Sooner or later, however, they're bound to lose. Their son's or daughter's greatest weakness will glow in the light of another child's strengths. It is an unsettling experience.

Our concern, of course, is for the parents whose child compares unfavorably with every other child around him. Perhaps he is mentally slow or physically handicapped or emotionally unbalanced. His parents hammer themselves with his shortcomings every day of his life. They strain to make him become what he is not...what he can never be. Little things gnaw at their insides. The children's program at church, for example, features the bright cutie who wows the congregation. *Just once*, they think, *would it hurt to choose our daughter? Would it violate some unwritten law of the universe to feature the least remarkable child in the starring role?* They think these thoughts, but they say nothing. No one would understand.

Have you played the comparison game? Have you thought to yourself, *If only Laurie was more like April, who is so soft and feminine. Laurie is so... so brash, you know? There are times when I just wish she could be—different?*

Don't do it, parents. I've lived long enough to know that circumstances may not be as they seem. April may turn out to be the problem child in the long run. Laurie may be the jewel. Either way, the worth of these kids is not dependent on the characteristics that separate them. None of us is perfect, and there is room in this world for every individual into whom an eternal soul has been breathed. My advice is to take the child God sends to you and "go with the flow." You and he will be much more contented for it!

I know this is difficult advice to follow. Parents of the shy child, for example, often ask me how they can pull him out of his shell and make him outgoing with strangers. At home he says the most profound things and shares his observations on the universe. But in public, his tongue becomes wedged to the side of his cheek. His neck curves downward and he appears deaf.

"Billy," says his exasperated father, "can't you say hello to Pastor Wilson? Billy? Billy! Has the cat got your tongue?"

The cat does *not* have Billy's tongue. It is merely stuck to his jaw, to the embarrassment of his father.

Why is Billy so introverted? Is it because he has been hurt or rejected in the past? Perhaps. But it is more likely that he was born that way, and no amount of goading by his parents will make him outgoing, flamboyant, or confident. It is a function of his temperament. Thus, I am again recommending that his parents go with the flow—accepting Billy the way God made him.

On behalf of the parent who has the greatest difficulty accepting a child the way he is, it might be helpful to ventilate those feelings with a husband, wife, or close friend. Then determine to love this unlovable boy or girl come what may. You *can* do it! There are qualities in your special youngster that may not have been seen before. Find them. Cultivate them. And then give God time to make something beautiful in his little life!

2. Grab the Reins of Authority Early

I cannot overemphasize the importance of "taking charge" of a strong-willed child during the early years of his life. This is not accomplished by being harsh, gruff, or stern. Instead, the relationship is produced by confident and steady leadership. You are the boss. You are in charge. If you believe it, the child will accept it also.

Unfortunately, many mothers are tentative and insecure in approaching their young children today. A pediatrician friend told me about a telephone call he received from the anxious mother of a six-month-old baby.

"I think he has a fever," she said nervously.

"Well," the doctor replied, "did you take his temperature?"

"No," she said, "he won't let me insert the thermometer."

I genuinely hope this woman's baby does not turn out to be a gutsy toddler bent on world dominion. He'll blow his shaky mother right out of the saddle. Like the little girl on the airplane, he will sense her insecurity and step into the power vacuum she has created.

Susannah Wesley, mother of eighteenth-century evangelists John and Charles Wesley, reportedly raised seventeen vigorous and healthy children. Toward the end of her life, John asked her to express her philosophy of mothering to him in writing. Copies of her reply are still in existence today. As you will see from the excerpts that follow, her beliefs reflect the traditional understanding of child-rearing:

> In order to form the minds of children, the first thing to be done is to conquer the will, and bring them into an obedient temper. To inform the understanding is a work of time, and must with children proceed by slow degrees as they are able to bear it; *but the subjecting of the will is a thing which must be done at once, and the sooner the better!*
>
> For by neglecting timely correction, *they will contract a*

stubbornness and obstinancy which is hardly ever after conquered, and never without using such severity as would be painful to me as to the children. In the esteem of the world, those who withhold timely correction would pass for kind and indulgent parents, whom I call cruel parents, who permit their children to get habits which they know must afterward be broken. Nay, some are so stupidly fond as in sport to teach their children to do things which in the after while, they must severely beat them for doing.

Whenever a child is corrected, it must be conquered; and this will be no hard matter to do, if it be not grown headstrong by too much indulgence. And, if the will of a child is totally subdued, and if it be brought to revere and stand in awe of the parents, then a great many childish follies and inadvertencies may be passed by. Some should be overlooked and taken no notice of, and others mildly reproved. *But no willful transgressions ought ever to be forgiven children, without chastisement, more or less as the nature and circumstances of the offense shall require.*

I cannot dismiss this subject. *As self-will is the root of all sin and misery, so whatever cherishes this in children insures their after [sic] wretchedness and faithlessness, whatever checks and mortifies, promotes their future happiness and piety.* This is still more evident if we further consider that Christianity is nothing less than doing the will of God, and not our own; that the one grand impediment to our temporal and eternal happiness being this self-will. No indulgence of it can be trivial, no denial unprofitable.

Does that sound harsh by twenty-first-century standards? Perhaps. I might use different words to guard against parental oppression and overbearance. Nevertheless, in my view, Mrs. Welsey's basic understanding is correct. If the strong-willed child is allowed by indulgence to develop "habits" of defiance and disrespect during his early childhood, those characteristics will haunt him for the next twenty years. Note also that Mrs. Wesley recommended overlooking "childish follies and inadvertencies," but never to ignore "willful transgressions." What did she mean?

I attempted to distinguish between these categories of behavior in my earlier book, *Dare to Discipline*. It is interesting to see the congruity between my perspective and that of Mrs. Wesley, in spite of the two hundred-plus years separating our times. Perhaps we drew our understandings from the same source...? This is what I wrote years ago:

> The issue of respect can be a useful tool in knowing when to punish and how excited one should get about a given behavior. First, the parent should decide whether an undesirable behavior represents a direct challenge of his authority—to his position as the father or mother. Punishment should depend on that evaluation. For example, suppose little Walter is acting silly in the living room and he falls into a table, breaking many expensive china cups and other trinkets. Or suppose he loses his bicycle or leaves Dad's best saw out in the rain. These are acts of childish irresponsibility and should be handled as such. Perhaps the parent should have the child work to pay for the losses—depending on the age and maturity of the child, of course. However, these examples do not constitute direct challenges to authority.

Thus far, I was dealing with what Mrs. Wesley called "follies and inadvertencies." Then we turned a corner.

> They do not emanate from willful, haughty disobedience. In my opinion, spankings should be reserved for the moment a child (age ten or less) expresses a defiant "I will not!" or "You shut up!" When a youngster tries this kind of stiff-necked rebellion, you had better take it out of him, and pain is a marvelous purifier. When nose to nose confrontation occurs between you and your child, it is not the time to have a discussion about the virtues of obedience. It is not the occasion to send him in his room to pout. It is not appropriate to wait until poor, tired old dad comes plodding in from work, just in time to handle the conflicts of the day. You have drawn a line in the dirt, and the child has deliberately flopped his big hairy toe across it. Who is going to win? Who has the most courage? Who is in charge

here? If you do not answer these questions conclusively for the child, he will precipitate other battles designed to ask them again and again. It is the ultimate paradox of childhood that a youngster wants to be controlled, but he insists that his parents earn the right to control him.[1]

The tougher the temperament of the child, the more critical it is to "shape his will" early in life. However, I must hasten to repeat the familiar disclaimers that have accompanied all my other writings on this subject. I am not recommending harshness and rigidity in child-rearing techniques! I don't believe in parental oppression, and indeed, our own children were not raised in such an atmosphere. Furthermore, I want to make it clear that corporal punishment is not to be imposed on babies.

Parents should not even shake their infants in anger. As a child's head is being jerked back and forth his brain can strike the inside of the skull, causing concussions and even death. Frustrated and exhausted parents will sometimes do this to a colicky baby or one who has other irritating characteristics. It is tragic and it is against the law. If you fear you will inflict this or some other kind of violence on your child or if you have already hurt him, please call a local hotline (or 1-800-422-4453); you should seek immediate professional assistance. You owe it to your little one to get help before it is too late.

No. The philosophy I am recommending is not born of harshness. It is conceived in love. Corporal punishment is reserved specifically for moments of willful, deliberate, on-purpose defiance by a child who is old enough to understand what he is doing. These challenges to authority will begin at approximately fifteen months of age and should be met with loving firmness. A thump on the fingers or a single stinging slap on the upper legs will be sufficient to say, "You must listen when I tell you no." By your persistence you will establish yourself as the leader to whom the child owes obedience. At the same time, however, you must seek numerous and continual ways of telling this youngster how much you adore him. That formula of love and discipline has been tested and validated over many centuries of time, and it will work for you.

But why have we stressed the necessity of bringing a strong-willed child into subjection during the younger years? Can't it be accomplished later if necessary? Yes, it can, but as Susannah Wesley said, the cost becomes much higher even at four or five years of age. Why is that true?

Perhaps we can explain the process this way: Have you ever wondered why young children can learn to speak perfect Russian, Chinese, Spanish, Hebrew, or any other language to which they are exposed? No trace of an accent will be manifested. But twenty or more years later, most individuals will only be able to approximate the sounds made by natives of the particular region. Researchers now know why this is true. It is explained by a process known as "phoneme contraction" (or "sound dropout"). The larynx of a young child assumes a shape necessary to make the sounds he is learning to use at the time. It then solidifies or hardens in those positions, making it impossible or very difficult to make other sounds later in life. Thus, there is a brief window of opportunity when anything is possible, linguistically. It will soon be history.

A child's attitude toward parental authority is also like that. He passes through a brief window of opportunity during late infancy and toddlerhood when respect and "awe" can be instilled. But that pliability will not last long. If his early reach for power is successful, he will not willingly give it up—ever.

Before we leave this topic of early discipline, let me issue a warning about a common mistake made by parents of more than one child. Psychologist Bruce Baldwin calls it "sibling drift." By that he refers to the tendency of parents to require more of first- or secondborn children. They must earn or fight for everything they get. But as subsequent children come along, the parents begin to wear down. They are preoccupied elsewhere. We obtained definite evidence of this sibling drift from our survey of parents. With the arrival of each new child, the discipline of parents tended to loosen. More than 40 percent of compliant mothers, for example, were rather strict with their first-born children. But for a fourth child, the percentage of rather strict compliant mothers dropped to less than 20 percent. The pattern was not quite so pronounced among strong-willed parents, but it occurred nevertheless.

Without seeing these findings, Dr. Baldwin wrote, "The net effect is less stringent parental discipline and consequently diminished self-discipline in younger children. As a parent, you must exert constant energy to counter this trend so younger children grow up as responsible adults too."[2] We obviously agree.

3. Raising the Compliant Child

Early discipline is not nearly so critical for the easygoing youngster. Even extremely permissive parents sometimes do no lasting harm to these happy and contented kids, because they are not looking for a fight. They are so good, in fact, that their parents are often blinded to a different set of problems which can develop right under their noses. Specifically, there are three pitfalls that must be avoided by parents of very compliant children. All of them tend to creep up from behind.

1. It is very easy to cultivate a long-term dependency relationship with the compliant individual. The bond between generations is so satisfying to the mother, especially, and so secure for the child, that neither is willing to give it up. Yet it must change in time. God did not intend for adults and their parents to have the same relationship as they did when the kids were small. Growth and maturity demand that children wriggle free from their parents' clutches and establish independent lives of their own. The compliant child has a more difficult time disengaging from the security of his nest because there has been no conflict there. By contrast, the strong-willed child is often desperate to get free. This process by which late adolescents and grown "children" are granted their independence is so important that I've devoted an entire chapter (11) to that topic.
2. The compliant child often has difficulties holding his own with his siblings.
3. The compliant child is more likely to internalize his anger and look for ways to reroute it.

These last two items deserve additional explanation because they represent a serious (but very quiet) threat to the well-being of the compliant child. My greatest concern for him is the ease with which he can be underestimated, ignored, exploited, or shortchanged at home. Haven't you seen two-child families where one youngster was a stick of dynamite who blew up regularly, and the other was an All-Star sweetheart? Under those circumstances it is not unusual for parents to take their cooperative sibling for granted. If there is an unpleasant job to be done, he will be expected to do it. Mom and Dad just don't have the energy to fight with the tiger.

If one child is to be chosen for a pleasant experience, it will probably go to the brattier of the two. He would scream bloody murder if excluded. When circumstances require one child to sacrifice or do without, you know who will be elected. Parents who favor the strong-willed child in this way are aware that they are being unfair, but their sense of justice has yielded to the pressures of practicality. They are simply too depleted and frustrated to risk irritating the tougher kid.

The consequences of such inequity should be obvious. Even though the compliant child goes along with the program and does not complain, he may accumulate a volume of resentment through the years. Isn't that what seems to have occurred to the brother of the Prodigal Son? He was the hardworking, responsible, *compliant* member of the family. Apparently, his kid brother was irresponsible, flighty, and very strong-willed. If we may be permitted to extrapolate a bit from the biblical account in Luke 15:11–32, it seems likely that there was little love lost between these sons, even before the prodigal's impulsive departure.

Disciplined elder brothers usually resent the spoiled brat who gets everything he asks for. Nevertheless, the older brother kept his thoughts to himself. He did not want to upset his father, whom he respected enormously. Then came that incredible day when little brother demanded his entire inheritance in one lump sum. The compliant son overheard the conversation and gasped in shock. *What audacity!* he thought. Then, to his amazement he heard his father grant the playboy's request. He could hear the clink of numerous gold coins being counted. Elder brother was furious. We could only assume that the departure of this sibling meant he would have to handle double chores and work longer hours in the fields. It wasn't fair that the load should fall on him. Nevertheless, he said nothing. Compliant people are inclined to hold their feelings inside.

The years passed slowly as the elder brother labored to maintain the farm. The father had grown older by then, placing a heaver strain on this firstborn son. Every day he labored from dawn to dusk in the hot sun. Occasionally, he thought about his brother living it up in the far country, and he was briefly tempted. But no. He would do what was right. Pleasing his father was the most important thing in his life.

Then, as we remember, the strong-willed goof-off ran out of money and became exceedingly hungry. He thought of his mom's cooking and the warmth of his father's fire. He clutched his rags around him and began the long journey home. When he was yet afar off, his father ran to meet him—embracing him and placing the royal robes around his shoulders. The fatted calf was killed and a great feast planned. That did it. The compliant brother could take no more. The prodigal son had secured through his folly what the elder brother could not gain through his discipline; the approval and affection of his father. His spirit was wounded!

Whether my interpretation of this parable is or is not true to the Scriptures will be left to the theologians to decide. Of this I am certain, however: Strong-willed and compliant siblings have played out this drama since the days of Cain and Abel, and the responsible kid often feels like the loser. He holds his feelings inside and then pays a price for storing them. He is more susceptible as an adult to ulcers, hypertension, colitis, migraine headaches, and a wide range of other illnesses. Furthermore, his sense of utter powerlessness can drive his anger underground. It may emerge in less obvious quests for control.

That introduces the significance of food as an instrument of power, which we will discuss presently. It also calls to mind the twin eating disorders of anorexia and bulimia. The anorectic individual can literally starve herself to death if not treated. She either reduces her intake of food radically or else she eats a normal meal and then promptly vomits. Sometimes she exercises compulsively while ingesting only 200 to 400 calories per day. Before long a 130-pound woman may weigh less than 80 pounds, and yet she may still believe herself to be overweight. The bulimic person follows the opposite pattern. She gorges uncontrollably and then "purges" herself by vomiting or using laxatives. Bulimia is called a "closet" disease because it often occurs in secret. It has been estimated that 20 to 30 percent of all American women of college age engage in bulimic activity! Diana, the late princess of Wales, admitted to struggling with this disorder.

Both anorexia and bulimia are thought to be minimally related to food itself. Instead, they represent a desire for *control*. The typical anorectic patient is a female in late adolescence or early adulthood. She is usually a compliant individual who was always "a good little girl." She did not play power games to any great extent. She conformed to her parents' expectations, although resenting them quietly at times. She withheld her anger and frustration at being powerless throughout the developmental years. Her father, and perhaps her mother, were strong individuals who took her submission for granted. Then one day, her need for control was manifested in a serious eating disorder. There, at least, was one area where she could be the boss.

Treatment for anorectic and bulimic individuals is a lengthy therapeutic process, and must remain the subject for another day. However, prevention of this and other common difficulties among formerly compliant children is definitely of concern to us here. I would offer these rather obvious recommendations to the parents of compliant children—especially the female of the species.

1. Treat them with respect, even when it is not demanded at gunpoint.
2. Keep them talking. Urge them to express their feelings and frustrations. Show them how to ventilate.
3. Give them their fair share in comparison to other children in the family and help them hold their own with more aggressive siblings. Remember that fences make good neighbors!
4. Grant them power commensurate with their ages. Within reason, they should make their own choices regarding clothing, hair styles, food preferences, selections of courses in school, etc. It would be quicker and more efficient to impose these decisions on the compliant individual. Resist the temptation!
5. Hold them close and then let them go. Do not continue to "parent" them after the task should be completed.
6. Keep an eye on your daughter's weight after thirteen years of age. Seek prompt help from specialists if signs of trouble develop.

There's nothing simple about raising kids, is there? Even in the case of the "easiest" children, being a parent requires all the intelligence, tact, wisdom, and cunning we can muster. Obviously, it is no job for cowards.

4. Keep Your Sense of Humor

Laughter is the key to survival during the special stresses of the child-rearing years. If you can see the delightful side of your assignment, you can also deal with the difficult. Almost every day I hear from mothers who would agree. They use the ballast of humor to keep their boats in an upright position. They also share wonderful stories with me.

One of my favorites came from the mother of two small children. This is what she wrote.

Dear Dr. Dobson:

A few months ago, I was making several phone calls in the family room where my three-year-old daughter, Adrianne, and my five-month-old son, Nathan, were playing quietly. Nathan loves Adrianne, who has been learning how to mother him gently since the time of his birth.

I suddenly realized that the children were no longer in view. Panic-stricken, I quickly hung up the phone and went looking for the pieces. Down the hall and around the corner, I found the children playing cheerfully in Adrianne's bedroom.

Relieved and upset, I shouted, "Adrianne, you know you are not allowed to carry Nathan! He is too little and you could hurt him if he fell!"

Startled, she answered, "I didn't, Mommy."

Knowing he couldn't crawl, I suspiciously demanded, "Well, then, how did he get all the way into your room?"

Confident of my approval for her obedience, she said with a smile, "I rolled him!"

He is still alive and they are still best friends.

Can't you imagine how this kid felt during his journey down the hall? I'll bet the walls and ceiling are still spinning past his eyes! He didn't complain, however, so I assume he enjoyed the experience.

Another parent told me that her three-year-old daughter had recently learned that Jesus will come to live in the hearts of those who invite Him. That is a very difficult concept for a young child to assimilate, and this little girl didn't quite grasp it. Shortly thereafter she and her mother were riding in the car, and the three-year-old suddenly came over and put her ear to her mother's chest.

"What are you doing?" asked the mother.

"I'm listening to Jesus in your heart," replied the child. The woman permitted the little girl to listen for a few seconds, and then she asked, "Well. What did you hear?"

The child replied, "Sounds like He's making coffee to me."

Who else but a toddler would come up with such a unique and delightful observation? If you live or work around kids, you need only listen. They will punctuate your world with mirth. They will also keep you off balance much of the time. I learned that fact several years before I became a father. As part of my professional training at the University of Southern California, I was required to teach elementary school for two years. Those were among the most informative years of my life, as I quickly learned what kids are like. It was also an initiation by fire.

Some days were more difficult than others, like the morning a kid named Thomas suddenly became ill. He lost his breakfast (thirty-seven scrambled eggs) with no warning to his fellow students or to me. I can still recall a room full of panic-stricken sixth-graders climbing over chairs and desks to escape Thomas's volcanic eruptions. They stood around the walls of the room, holding their throats and going "eeeeuuuuyuckk!" One of them was more vocal in his disgust than the others, prompting a fellow student to say, "I wouldn't talk, Norbert. You did it last year!"

It was quite a morning for a new teacher. The lunch bell saved me, and having lost my appetite, I went outside to supervise students on the playground. Since I had not grown up in California, I was interested in an apparatus called tetherball. As I stood there watching two boys competing violently with each other, a cute little sixth-grade girl named Doris came and stood beside me. Presently she asked, "Would you like to play?"

"Sure," I said. It was a mistake.

Doris was twelve years old and she was a tetherball freak! I was twenty-five years old and I couldn't get the hang of the game. The tether would change the trajectory of the ball and I kept swinging wildly at the air. My students gathered around, and I became very self-conscious about my performance. There I was, six feet two inches tall and a self-proclaimed jock, yet I was getting clobbered by this little girl. Then it happened.

Doris decided to go for broke. She spiked the ball with all her might and drove it straight up my nose. I never even saw it coming. The whole world began spinning and my nose was vibrating like a tuning fork. I really thought I was going to die. My eyes were streaming tears and my ears were humming like a beehive. Yet, what could I do? Twenty kids had seen Doris ring my bell, and I couldn't let them know how badly I was hurt. So I went on playing even though I couldn't see the ball. It's a wonder Doris didn't whack me again.

Thank goodness for the afternoon bell. I took my pulsating nose back to the classroom and resolved to accept no more challenges from seventy-five-pound girls. They're dangerous.

5. The Establishment of Faith

Finally, may I urge you as parents of young children, whether compliant or strong-willed, to provide for them an unshakable faith in Jesus Christ. This is your *most* important function as mothers and fathers. How can anything else compare in significance to the goal of keeping the family circle unbroken in the life to come? What an incredible objective to work toward!

If the salvation of our children is really that vital to us, then our spiritual training should begin before children can even comprehend what it is all about. They should grow up seeing their parents on their knees before God, talking to Him. They will learn quickly at that age and will never forget what they've seen and heard. Even if they reject their faith later, the remnant of it will be with them for the rest of their lives. This is why we are instructed to "...bring them up in the nurture and admonition of the Lord" (Ephesians 6:4, KJV).

Again, I was fortunate to have had parents who understood this principle. After I was grown they told me that I attempted to pray before I learned to talk. I watched them talk to God and then attempted to imitate the sounds I had heard. Two years later, at three years of age, I made a conscious decision to become a Christian. You may think it impossible at such an age, but it happened. I remember the occasion clearly today. I was attending a Sunday evening church service and was sitting near the back with my mother. My father was the pastor, and he invited those who wished to do so to come pray at the altar. Fifteen or twenty people went forward, and I joined them spontaneously. I recall crying and asking Jesus to forgive my sins. I know that sounds strange, but that's the way it occurred. It is overwhelming for me to think about that event today. Imagine the King of the universe, Creator of all heaven and earth, caring about an insignificant kid barely out of toddlerhood! It makes no sense, but I know it happened.

Not every child will respond that early or dramatically, of course, nor should they. Some are more sensitive to spiritual matters than others, and they must be allowed to progress at their own pace. But in no sense should we as their parents be casual or neutral about their training. Their world should sparkle with references to Jesus and to our faith. That is the meaning of Deuteronomy 6:6–9, "These commandments that I give you today are to be upon your hearts. Impress them on your children. Talk about them when you sit at home and when you walk along the road, when you lie down and when you get up. Tie them as symbols on your hands and bind them on your foreheads. Write them on the doorframes of your houses and on your gates."

I believe this commandment from the Lord is one of the most crucial verses for parents in the entire Bible. It instructs us to surround our children with godly teaching. References to spiritual things are not to be reserved just for Sunday morning or even for a bedtime prayer. They should permeate our conversation and the fabric of our lives. Why? Because our children are watching our every move during those early years. They want to know what is most important to us. If we hope to instill within them a faith that will last for a lifetime, then they must see and feel our passion for God.

As a corollary to that principle, I must remind you that children miss nothing in sizing up their parents. If you are only half-convinced of your beliefs, they will quickly discern that fact. Any ethical weak spot—any indecision on your part—will be incorporated and then magnified in your sons and daughters. Like it or not, we are on the hook. Their faith or their faithlessness will be a reflection of our own. As I've said, our children will eventually make their own choices and set the course of their lives, but those decisions will be influenced by the foundations we have laid. Someone said, "The footsteps a boy follows are the ones his father thought he covered up." It is true.

That brings me to another extremely important point, even though it is controversial. I firmly believe in acquainting children with God's judgment and wrath while they are young. Nowhere in the Bible are we instructed to skip over the unpleasant Scriptures in our teaching. The wages of sin is death, and children have a right to understand that fact.

I remember my mother reading the story of Samson to me when I was about nine years old. After this mighty warrior fell into sin, you will recall, the Philistines put out his eyes and held him as a common slave. Some time later, Samson repented before God and he was forgiven. He was even given back his awesome strength. But my mother pointed out that he never regained his eyesight nor did he ever live in freedom again. He and his enemies died together as the temple collapsed upon them.

"There are terrible consequences to sin," she told me solemnly. "Even if you repent and are forgiven, you will still suffer for breaking the laws of God. They are there to protect you. If you defy them, you will pay the price for your disobedience."

Then she talked to me about gravity, one of God's physical laws. "If you jump from a ten-story building, you can be certain that you will crash when you hit the ground. It is inevitable. You must also know that God's *moral* laws are just as real as His physical laws. You can't break them without crashing sooner or later."

Finally, she taught me about heaven and hell and the great Judgment Day when those who have been covered by the blood of Jesus will be separated eternally from those who have not. It made a profound impression on me.

Many parents would not agree with my mother's decision to acquaint me with the nature of sin and its consequences. They have said to me, "Oh, I wouldn't want to paint such a negative picture for my kids. I want them to think of God as a loving Father, not as a wrathful judge who punishes us." In so doing, they withhold a portion of the truth from their children. He is both a God of love and a God of judgment. There are 116 places in the Bible where we are told to "fear the Lord." By what authority do we eliminate these references in describing who God is to our children?

I am thankful that my parents and my church had the courage to acquaint me with the "warning note" in Scripture. It was this awareness of sin and its consequences that kept me moral at times when I could have fallen into sexual sin. Biblical faith was a governor—a checkpoint beyond which I was unwilling to go. By that time I was not afraid of my parents. I could have fooled them. But I could not get away from the all-seeing eye of the Lord. I knew I would stand accountable before Him someday, and that fact gave me the extra motivation to make responsible decisions.

I can't overstate the importance of teaching divine accountability to your strong-willed children, especially. Since their tendency is to test the limits and break the rules, they will need this internal standard to guide their behavior. Not all will listen to it, but some will. But while doing that, be careful to *balance* the themes of love and justice as you teach your children about God. To tip the scales in either direction is to distort the truth and create confusion in a realm where understanding is of utmost significance.

SEVEN

POWER GAMES

IN OUR EFFORTS to understand the strong-willed child, we must ask ourselves why he or she is so fond of conflict. If given the opportunity to choose between war and peace, most of us would prefer tranquility. Yet the tough-minded kid goes through life like a runaway lawn mower. He'll chew up anything that gets in his way. The taller the grass, the better he survives and thrives. What makes him like that? What drives him to challenge his mother and defy his father? They are not his enemies. Why would he resist their loving leadership from the earliest days of childhood? Why does he seem to enjoy irritating his siblings and goading his neighbors? Why does he throw erasers when his teachers turn their backs, and why won't he do his homework? Indeed, why can't he be like his compliant brothers and sisters?

These are interesting questions that I have pondered for years. Now I believe I'm beginning to understand some of the motivating forces that drive the strong-willed kid to attack his world. Deep within his or her spirit is a raw desire for *power*. We can define power in this context as control—control of others, control of our circumstances and, especially, control of ourselves. The strong-willed child is not the only one who seeks power, of course. He differs from the rest of the human family only in degree, not in kind. We all want to be the boss, and that desire is evident in very young children. Remember the toddler who rode his tricycle into the street and shouted angrily at his mother? The real issue between them was a matter of power and who would hold it. We see the same struggle when an adolescent slams doors and flees in his car, or when a husband and wife fight over finances, or when an elderly woman refuses to move to a nursing home. The common thread is the desire to run our own lives—and that of everyone else if given the chance. We vary in intensity of this impulse, as we will see, but it seems to motivate all of us to one degree or another.

The desire for control appears to have its roots in the very early hours after birth. Studies of newborns indicate that they typically "reach" for the adults around them on the first or second day of life. By that I mean they behave in ways designed to entice their guardians to meet their needs. Some will perfect the technique in the years that follow.

Even mature adults who ought to know better are usually involved in power games with other people. It happens whenever human interests collide, but it is especially prevalent in families. Husbands, wives, children, siblings, in-laws, and parents all have reason to manipulate each other. It is fascinating to sit back and watch them push, pull, and twist. In fact, I've identified sixteen techniques that are used to obtain power in another person's life. Perhaps you will think of additional approaches as you read the list that follows:

1. *Emotional Blackmail*: "Do what I want or I'll get very angry and go all to pieces."
2. *The Guilt Trip*: "How could you do this to me after I've done so much for you?"
3. *Divine Revelation*: "God told me you should do what I want."
4. *The Foreclosure*: "Do what I want or I won't pay the bills."
5. *The Bribe*: "Do what I want and I'll make it worth your time."
6. *By Might and by Power*: "Shut up and do what I tell you!"
7. *The Humiliation*: "Do what I want or I'll embarrass you at home and abroad."
8. *The Eternal Illness*: "Don't upset me. Can't you see I'm sick?"
9. *Help from Beyond the Grave*: "Your dear father (or mother) would have agreed with me."
10. *The Adulterous Threat*: "Do what I want or I'll find someone who will."
11. *The In-law Ploy*: "Do what I want and I'll be nice to your sweet mother."
12. *The Seduction*: "I'll make you an offer you can't afford to refuse," or as Mae West said to Cary Grant, "Why doncha come up and see me some time?" She also said she used to be Snow White but she drifted.

Special approaches used by adolescents:

13. *Teenage Terror*: "Leave me alone or I'll pull a stupid adolescent stunt" (suicide, drugs, booze, wrecking the car, or hitchhiking to San Francisco).
14. *The Flunkout*: "Let me do what I want or I'll get myself booted out of Woodrow Wilson Junior High School."
15. *Fertile Follies*: "Do what I want or I'll present you with a baby!" (This threat short-circuits every nerve in a parent's body.)
16. *The Tranquilizer*: "Do what I want and I won't further complicate your stressful life."

Manipulation! It's a game any number can play, right in the privacy of your own home. The objective is to obtain power over the other players, as we have seen. It will come as no surprise to parents, I'm sure, that children can be quite gifted at power games. That is why it is important for mothers and fathers to consider this characteristic as they attempt to interpret childish behavior. Another level of motivation lies below the surface issues that seemingly cause conflicts between generations. For example, when a three-year-old runs away in a supermarket, or when a nine-year-old refuses to straighten his room, or when a twelve-year-old continues to bully his little brother, or when a sixteen-year-old smokes cigarettes or drinks liquor, they are making individual statements about power. Their rebellious behavior usually represents more than a desire to do what is forbidden. Rather, it is an expression of independence and self-assertion. It is also a rejection of adult authority, and therein lies the significance for us.

Power games begin in earnest when children are between twelve and fifteen months of age. Some get started even earlier. If you've ever watched a very young child continue to reach for an electric plug or television knob while his mother shouts "No!" you've seen an early power game in progress. It is probably not a conscious process at this stage, but later it will be. I'm convinced that a strong-willed child of three or older is inclined to challenge his mom and dad whenever he believes he can win. He will carefully choose the weapons and select the turf on which the contest will be staged. I've called these arenas "the battlefields of childhood." Let's look at some of the Gettysburgs, Stalingrads, or Waterloos that have gone down in family history.

BEDTIME

One of the earliest contests begins at eighteen months and one day of age, give or take a few hours. At precisely that time, a toddler who has gone to bed without complaining since he was born will suddenly say, "I'm not getting back in that crib again for as long as I live." That is the opening salvo in what may be a five-year battle. It happens so quickly and unexpectedly that parents may be fooled by it. They will check for teething problems, a low-grade fever, or some other discomfort. "Why *now*?" they ask. I don't know. It just suddenly occurs to toddlers that they don't want to go to bed anymore, and they will fight it tooth and nail.

Although the tactics change a bit, bedtime will continue to be a battlefield for years to come. Any creative six-year-old can delay going to bed for at least forty-five minutes by an energetic and well-conceived system of stalling devices. By the time his mother gets his pajamas on, brings him six glasses of water, takes him to the bathroom twice, helps him say his prayers, and then scolds him for wandering out of his bedroom a time or two, she is thoroughly exhausted. It happens night after night.

A college friend of mine named Jim found himself going through this bedtime exercise every evening with his five-year-old son, Paulie. Jim recognized the tactics as a game and decided he didn't want to play anymore. He sat down with his son that evening and said, "Now, Paulie, things are going to be different tonight. I'm going to get you dressed for bed; you can have a drink of water and then we'll pray together. When that is done I'm walking out the door and I don't intend to come back. Don't call me again. I don't want to hear a peep from you until morning. Do you understand?"

Paulie said, "Yes, Daddy."

When the chores were completed, final hugs were exchanged and the lights were turned out. Jim told his son good night and left the room. Sweet silence prevailed in the house. But not for long. In about five minutes, Paulie called his father and asked for another drink of water.

"No way, Paulie," said his dad. "Don't you remember what I said? Now go to sleep."

After several minutes, Paulie appealed again for a glass of water. Jim was more irritated this time. He spoke sharply and advised his son to forget it. But the boy would not be put off. He waited for a few minutes and then reopened the case. Every time Paulie called his dad, Jim became more irritated. Finally, he said, "If you ask for water one more time, I'm going to come in there and spank you!"

That quieted the boy for about five minutes and then he said, "Daddy, when you come in here to spank me would you bring me a glass of water please?"

The kid got the water. He did not get the spanking.

One of the ways of enticing children (perhaps age four to eight) to go to bed is by the use of fantasy. For example, I told my son and daughter about "Mrs. White's Party" when they were little. Mrs. White was an imaginary lady who threw the most fantastic celebrations in the middle of the night. She ran an amusement park that made Disneyland boring by comparison. Whatever was of interest to the children was worked into her repertoire—dogs, cats, sweets of all varieties, water slides, cartoons, thrilling rides, and anything else that excited Danae's and Ryan's imaginations. Of course, the *only* way they could go to Mrs. White's Party was to be asleep. No one who was awake would ever get an invitation. It was fun to watch our son and daughter jump into bed and concentrate to go to sleep. Though it never happened, I wish I could have generated such interest that they would have actually dreamed about Mrs. White. Usually, the matter was forgotten the next morning.

By hook or crook, fantasy or reality, you must win the great bedtime battle. The health of your child (and maybe your own) is at stake.

FOOD

The dinner table is another major battlefield of childhood, but it should be avoided. I have strongly advised parents not to get suckered into this arena. It is an ambush. A general always wants to engage the other army in a place where he can win, and mealtime is a lost cause. A mother who puts four green beans on a fork and resolves to sit there until the child eats them is in a powerless position. The child can outlast her. And because meals come around three times a day, he will eventually prevail.

Instead of begging, pleading, bribing, and threatening a child, I recommend that good foods be placed before him cheerfully. If he chooses not to eat, then smile and send him on his way. He'll be back. When he returns, take the same food out of the refrigerator, heat it and set it before him again. Sooner or later, he will get hungry enough to eat. Do not permit snacking or substituting sweets for nutritious foods. But also do not fear the physical effects of hunger. A child will not starve in the presence of good things to eat. There is a gnawing feeling inside that changes one's attitude from "Yuck!" to "Yum!" usually within a few hours.

We have already talked about anorexia and bulimia, eating disorders related to parental power. Obviously, food can be the focal point of great struggles between generations.

SCHOOLWORK

Perhaps there is *no* greater source of conflict between generations today than schoolwork, and especially that portion assigned to be done at home. This is another battlefield where all the advantages fall to the youngster. Only he knows for sure what was assigned and how the work is supposed to be done. The difficult child will capitalize on this information gap between home and school, claiming that "I got it all done in school," or "I have nothing to do tonight." He reminds me of the kid who brought home four F's and a C on his report card. When his dad asked what he thought the problem was, he said, "I guess I've been concentrating too hard on one subject."

Parents should know that *most* students go through an academic valley sometime between the sixth and ninth grades in school. Some will quit working altogether during this time. Others will merely decrease their output. Very few will remain completely unaffected. The reason is the massive assault made on adolescent senses by the growing-up process. Self-confidence is shaken to its foundation. Happy hormones crank into action and sex takes over center stage. Who can think about school with all that going on? Or better yet, who wants to? As parents, you should watch for this diversion and not be dismayed when it comes. We'll discuss the underachiever later in this book.

VACATIONS AND SPECIAL DAYS

Tell me why it is that children are the most obnoxious and irritating on vacations and during other times when we are specifically trying to please them? By all that is fair and just, you would expect them to think, *Boy! Mom and Dad are really doing something nice for us. They are taking us on this expensive vacation when they could have spent the money on themselves. And Dad would probably have preferred to go fishing (that's true) or something else he wanted to do. But they care about us and have included us in their plans. Wow!*

I'm going to be as nice and cooperative as possible. I'll try to get along with my sister and I won't make any unusual demands. What a fun trip this will be!

Do kids think that way? Fat chance! There is no such thing as inter-generational gratitude.

Before the family has even left town, the troops are fighting over who gets to sit by the window and which one will hold the dog. Little Sister yells, "I'm telling!" every few minutes. Tensions are also building in the front seat. By the time they get to Phoenix, Dad is ready to blow his cork. It was tough enough for him to complete his office work and pack the car. But this bickering is about to drive him crazy. For four hundred miles, he has endured arguments, taunts, jabs, pinches, tears, tattling, and unscheduled bathroom breaks. Now he's starting to lose control. Twice he swings wildly at writhing bodies in the backseat. He misses and hurts his shoulder. He's driving faster by this time but he's quit talking. The only clues to what he's feeling are his bloodshot eyes and the occasional twitch in his left cheek. Happy vacation, Pop. You have thirteen days to go.

I once received a letter from a mother who had just returned from a stressful vacation similar to the one I described. For days, their two sons had whined and complained, insulting and fighting with each other. They kicked the back of their father's seat for hours at a time. Finally, his fuse burned down to the dry powder. He pulled the car over to the side of the road and jerked the boys outside. Judgment Day had arrived. After spanking them both, he shoved them back into the car and warned them to keep their mouths shut. "If I hear a peep from either of you for thirty minutes," he warned, "I'll give you some more of what you just had!" The boys got the message. They remained mute for thirty minutes, after which the older lad said, "Is it all right to talk now?"

The father said sternly, "Yes. What do you want to say?"

"Well," continued the boy, "when you spanked us back there my shoe fell off. We left it in the road."

It was the only good pair of shoes the kid owned. This time Mom went berserk and flailed at the backseat like a crazy lady. So ended another great day of family togetherness.

Is this the way parents should deal with a period of irritation from their children? Of course not, but let's face it. Parents are people. They have their vulnerabilities and flash points too. The children should have been separated or perhaps offered spankings much earlier in the journey. It is when parents are desperately trying to avoid punishment that their level of irritation reaches a dangerous level. By then, anything can happen. That is why I have contended that those who oppose corporal punishment on the grounds that it leads to child abuse are wrong. By stripping parents of the ability to handle frustrating behavior at an early stage, they actually increase the possibility that harm will be done to children as tempers rise.

Before we leave the matter of family vacations, let's deal with why it is that children seem to become more obnoxious on those special days. There are two good reasons for it. First, adults and children alike tend to get on each other's nerves when they are cooped up together for extended periods of time. But also, a difficult child apparently feels compelled to reexamine the boundaries whenever he thinks they may have moved. This was certainly true of our children. On days when we planned trips to Disneyland, ski trips, or other holidays, we could count on them to become testy. It was as though they were obligated to ask, "Since this is a special day, what are the rules now?" We would sometimes have to punish or scold them during times when we were specifically trying to build relationships. Your strong-willed kids may do the same. Perhaps that's why Erma Bombeck said, "The family that plays together gets on one another's nerves."

Other battlefields of early childhood include clothing and hair styles, doing the dishes and household chores, demands for candy and treats in supermarkets, getting up in time to catch the school bus, taking regular baths, talking sassy to mom, and keeping the child's room clean. (One mother told me her ten-year-old's bedroom was such a mess that she would have to get a tetanus shot to walk through it.) The number of these routine skirmishes between parents and children is virtually endless. A child can use almost any pretext to launch a new crusade—or had you already noticed?

To repeat our thesis, these trouble spots between generations are not simply matters of differing opinion. If the conflicts amounted to no more than that, then negotiation and compromise would resolve them very quickly. Instead, they represent staging areas where the authority of the parent can be challenged and undermined. The question being asked is not so much, "Can I have my way?" as it is, "Who's in charge here?" (Remember, now, that I'm describing the motivation of very strong-willed children. The compliant child is more subtle in his maneuvers for power.)

With the passage of time, the battles do tend to become more intense.

What began as relatively minor struggles over bedtime or homework can develop into the most terrible conflicts. Some teenagers put their parents through hell on earth. Deep, searing wounds are inflicted that may never fully heal. For now, however, I want to conclude this discussion by explaining the great significance of power and its ramifications for parents. Everything said to this point is merely prologue to the message in paragraphs that follow. Please give special emphasis to this remaining section as you read.

The sense of power that is so attractive to children and to the rest of humanity is actually a very dangerous thing. Men have deceived, exploited, and killed to get it. Those who have achieved it have often been destroyed in its grasp. Lord Acton said, "Power corrupts, and absolute power corrupts absolutely." History has proved him right.

The most bloodthirsty men who ever lived were driven by an insatiable lust for power. In his effort to dominate the world, Adolph Hitler set off a conflagration that claimed fifty million lives. Joseph Stalin is said to have murdered twenty to thirty million people during his reign of terror. On one occasion, Stalin reportedly sent his secret police to the little town where he was raised with orders to kill the teachers who had instructed him as a child. Imagine the brutality! Apparently, he wanted to leave no witnesses to his mediocre beginnings. This is where the lust for power leads when it is unbridled.

Our concern, however, is not limited to the behavior of dictators and despots. Power has a negative effect wherever it comes to rest. I've known many famous physicians and surgeons, for example, who exercised vast authority in the medical community. Patients worshiped them; nurses feared them; colleagues respected them; and friends envied them. They seemed to have it all. But how did this adulation affect their personalities? Did they grow more humble and self-effacing as their ego needs were met? Hardly! They tended to become more infantile in their demands, or they became tyrannical and sought to crush anyone who got in their way.

Notorious physicians are not the only ones who have trouble handling power. The same is true of successful actors, musicians, ministers, lawyers, and military generals in times of war. Study the historical profiles of great military generals like George Patton or Douglas MacArthur. Most were proud and arrogant men. A story is told about the haughty British general, Bernard Montgomery, who was giving a speech near the end of his life. He said, "You will remember when God said to Moses there in the wilderness—and I think rightly so—" Who but a commander of armies would dare critique the words of the Lord Himself?

United States presidents have also been known to take themselves too seriously, and Lyndon Johnson was among the worst. During his years in the White House, he was a power monger, terrorizing his aides for their minor mistakes and oversights. I'm told, for example, that he became furious when they forgot to restock the presidential airplane with root beer, his favorite soft drink. "No rut beer!?" he would scream in his Texas drawl. "Whaddaya mean no rut beer?!" He couldn't believe anyone would have the audacity to ignore his whims in this way.

It is interesting that five United States presidents in the twentieth century won landslide electoral victories and achieved the power to which they were entitled. Predictably, perhaps, all five experienced their greatest crises shortly thereafter. Harding and the Teapot Dome Scandal; Roosevelt and the Supreme Court debacle; Johnson and the Vietnam war; Nixon and the Watergate affair; and Reagan and the Iran-Contra connection. Time after time, history illuminates the destructive nature of raw power. Proverbs 27:21 states, "Man is tested by the praise he receives."

Chuck Colson lived through the Watergate debacle that brought down President Richard Nixon. As a senior member of the White House staff during an era when presidential influence was maximal, Colson knew how to use power. He was also quite willing to abuse it. He worked just a few feet from the Oval Office and his orders carried the authority of the president himself. By simply making a phone call, he could send a detachment of troops anywhere in the world. He could have the presidential helicopter land on the White House lawn within minutes to take him where he wished to go. He conferred with the Soviets and with our allies on matters of monumental importance. Yes, Chuck Colson experienced the meaning of political power in all its glory, and his fall from that lofty perch was one of the most dramatic descents in American history.

After his conviction in the Watergate scandal, Colson was sentenced to serve two years in the federal penitentiary at Maxwell Prison Camp in Florida. Upon arrival, this proud governmental leader was systematically shorn of his dignity. He was stripped, searched, and dusted for lice. He was placed in an eight-foot cell with a stinking open toilet. A guard came by every two hours and shined a flashlight in his eyes. Colson, who had conferred with prime ministers, emperors, and princes, now lived and worked with rapists, murderers, thieves, and child molesters. He was utterly powerless for some seven months.

How impressive it is that Chuck Colson chose not to reconstruct his power base when he was released from prison. He could have gone back to his law practice in New York, with its six-figure income, a yacht, and the other trappings of opulence. Instead, he founded Prison Fellowship Ministries to assist the down-and-outers of the world. Why would a man deny himself in that way?

Because he found a "higher power" in a personal relationship with Jesus Christ. It totally revolutionized his life. I admire this man greatly and am honored to call him my friend.

If you talk to Chuck Colson today, he will warn you of the dangers of power. He should know. He was nearly destroyed by it. He will also tell you how he manipulated naive Christians when he was in the White House. He dazzled them with presidential power and molded them to his political purposes. Finally, he will remind you that Jesus came without power and consistently resisted His disciples' desire for it. Jesus taught them, "He who is least among you all—he is the greatest" (Luke 9:48).

Perhaps you have foreseen how this discussion of presidential politics and professional pride is related to the discipline of children, but let me lay it out. If power can be destructive to mature adults who think they know how to handle it, imagine what it will do to a mere child. Think again of the three-year-old boy on the tricycle, described in the second chapter. He had already achieved virtual independence from his mother. There he was, fresh out of *babyhood,* yet he had become his own boss. That's pretty heady stuff for a kid who's only three feet high. How would he choose to use all that power? Well, for starters he insisted on riding his tricycle down a busy boulevard. He is fortunate that his first taste of freedom didn't put him under the wheels of a four-thousand-pound automobile. There will be other risks in future years, of course.

One of the characteristics of those who acquire power very early is a prevailing attitude of disrespect for authority. It extends to teachers, ministers, policemen, judges, and even to God Himself. Such an individual has never yielded to parental leadership at home. Why should he submit himself to anyone else? For a rebellious teenager it is only a short step from there to drug abuse, sexual experimentation, running away, and so on. The early acquisition of power has claimed countless young victims by this very process.

What do we recommend then? Should parents retain every vestige of power for as long as possible? No! Even with its risks, self-determination is a basic human right, and we must grant it systematically to our children. To withhold that liberty too long is to incite wars of revolution. My good friend, Jay Kesler, observed that Mother England made that specific mistake with her children in the American colonies. They grew to become rebellious "teenagers" who demanded their freedom. Still she refused to release them, and unnecessary bloodshed ensued. Fortunately, England learned a valuable lesson from that painful experience. Some 171 years later, she granted a peaceful and orderly transfer of power to another tempestuous offspring named India. Revolution was averted.

This, then, is our goal as parents: We must not transfer power too early, even if our children take us daily to the battlefield. Mothers who make that mistake are some of the most frustrated people on the face of the earth. On the other hand, we must not retain parental power too long, either. Control will be torn from our grasp if we refuse to surrender it voluntarily. The granting of self-determination should be matched stride for stride with the arrival of maturity, culminating with complete release during early adulthood.

Sounds easy, doesn't it? We all know better. I consider this orderly transfer of power to be one of the most delicate and difficult responsibilities in the entire realm of parenthood. We'll talk more about the "how to" in subsequent chapters.

EIGHT

TOO POOPED
TO PARENT

W E WANT TO deal now with the problem of parental exhaustion and its effect on mothers and fathers of young children. Chronic fatigue has become an everyday occurrence for the majority of parents in North America, and its implications are difficult to overestimate. Without question, the best book I have read on this subject is entitled *Parent Burnout*, by Dr. Joseph Procaccini and Mark Kiefaber.[1] The authors describe how parents manage to squander their resources and ultimately fail in the task they care about most: raising healthy and responsible children. If you have staggered under the pressures of parenthood, I hope you will buy and read that book. In the meantime, let me provide a broad outline of its central message and add a few thoughts of my own.

Not surprisingly, perhaps, the most likely candidates for early exhaustion are the parents who are radically committed to their children. After all, if there is no "fire" there can be no burnout. These zealous and dedicated mothers and fathers are determined to provide every advantage and opportunity for the next generation from the earliest days of infancy. That is where their hearts lie. That is what they care about most. Their devotion leads them to make what they consider to be small sacrifices on behalf of the children. They often discontinue all recreational, romantic, and restful activities that would take them away from home. Even long-term friends with whom they used to associate are now given lame excuses or are ignored altogether.

COMPULSIVE PARENTING

Everything focuses on the children. They are often unwilling to leave the kids with a baby-sitter for more than a few moments. Not even Mother Teresa would qualify as guardian for an evening. They would simply never forgive themselves if something went wrong while they were frivolously indulging in fun or entertainment. Imagine how they would feel if the announcer said over the public address system, "May I have your attention? Would Mr. or Mrs. James Johnson come to a house telephone, please? Your baby-sitter needs to know where the fire extinguisher is." No way! It's not worth it. They choose to stay home.

Sometimes this exclusivity with the baby even extends to grandparents, who are enormously insulted by the situation. They have accumulated twenty-five years of parenting experience and yet they are not trusted with the grandkids for a single evening. White-hot anger flows between generations and may be remembered for the rest of their lives. Nevertheless, the parents dig in and isolate themselves further.

In other cases, grandparents are simply not available to help shoulder the load. They may live a thousand miles away and come to visit only once or twice a year. But let's be honest. Other grandmas don't want to be bothered. They're busily chasing careers of their own. The following poem, shared with me by Florence Turnridge, delightfully makes that case.

WHERE HAVE ALL THE GRANDMAS GONE?

> In the dim and distant past,
> > When life's tempo wasn't fast,
> Grandma used to rock and knit,
> > Crochet, tat and baby-sit.
> When the kids were in a jam,
> > They could always call on "Gram."
> In that day of gracious living,
> > Grandma was the gal for giving.
>
> BUT today she's in the gym,
> > Exercising to keep slim,
> She's off touring with the bunch,
> > Or taking clients out to lunch.

Going north to ski or curl,
All her days are in a whirl.
Nothing seems to stop or block her,
Now that Grandma's off her rocker!!!

Author Unknown[2]

If she's not careful, Grandma will also burn herself out and be back in her rocker again. Either way, she may not be able to offer the support to her children that grandparents provided in centuries past. The extended family is gone, leaving a young mother isolated and alone. She may pass two or four or even ten years without a significant break from the tasks of child-rearing. She feels it is a minor sacrifice to make for so great a purpose. And yet, her perspective on life is distorted. The routine events of her world are interpreted in terms of this one dimensional value system. Anything that might have the remotest negative influence on her kids becomes deeply disturbing to her, leading to overreaction and conflict. Insignificant childhood squabbles in the neighborhood, for example, or idle comments from church members can bring surprisingly heated responses. And Lord help the teacher or Sunday school worker who fails to deliver!

Compulsive parenting can also be destructive to a marriage, especially when only one parent is so inclined. If it is the mother, she may give herself totally to the children and have nothing left for her husband. He believes she has gone a little wacky with this mothering thing, and may even resent the kids for taking her away from him. She, in turn, despises his selfishness and becomes sole defender and caregiver for their children. A wedge is thereby driven between them that may someday destroy the family.

SUPERPARENTING

Please understand that I am not critical of the motives behind what might be called "superparenting." Children *are* worth our very best efforts to raise them properly, and I have spent twenty years urging parents to give them their due. Nevertheless, even a noble and necessary task can be taken to such extremes that it becomes harmful to both the giver and the receiver. In the child's case, there is a direct link between superparenting and overprotection, an egocentric perspective on life, and in some cases, a prolonged dependency relationship with parents. In the adult context, obsessive child-rearing can lead inexorably to the condition known as parental burnout.

Procaccini and Kiefaber have provided an insightful explanation of how burnout occurs in the compulsive parent, or for that matter, in anyone who fails to take care of himself. Their concept is based on five key premises, as follows: (1) human energy is a precious resource that makes possible everything we wish to do; (2) energy is a *finite* quantity—there is a limited supply available to each of us; (3) *whenever the expenditure of energy exceeds the supply, burnout begins;* (4) parents who hope to accomplish the goals they have set for themselves and their children must not squander their vital resources foolishly; and (5) wasteful drains on that supply should be identified and eliminated, and priority given to rebuilding the reserve.

From this explanation it is understandable why burnout is an occupational hazard for parents who reserve nothing for themselves. It should also be clear why superparenting is a natural trap for those of us who share the Christian faith. Deeply ingrained within us is a philosophy that lends itself to compulsive child-rearing. The family ranks near the top of our value system, and our way of life focuses on self-sacrifice and commitment to others. Does it not seem reasonable, therefore, that we would pour every resource into this awesome task? That is our God-given assignment, isn't it?

Well, of course, it is, but I would point out that the apostle Paul advocates moderation in *all* things (Philippians 4:5). Remember, too, that Jesus took time to rest and care for His body. On one occasion, He got in a boat and rowed away from the multitudes of sick and needy people on the shore. He could have remained there and healed thousands more, but He had apparently reached the limits of His strength. Parents *must* learn to monitor their own bodies, too, and conserve their energy for the long haul. That is, after all, in the very best interest of their children.

Lest we be misunderstood, extremely dedicated mothers and fathers are not the only parents who are inclined to overextend their resources. The routine experiences of living in today's stressful environment are sufficient in themselves to wear us out. Urgent demands are made simultaneously by our jobs, our churches, our children's schools, our friends, and our civic responsibilities. The great movement of women into the labor force has left millions of mothers on the brink of nervous collapse as they attempt to combine full-time employment with full-time responsibilities at home. In her book, *Having It All*, Helen Gurley Brown advised women that it is possible to achieve multiple competing goals. She is wrong, except in rare cases. Something has to give. Again, when the demand for energy exceeds the supply, *for whatever reason*, burnout is inevitable. And children are almost always the losers in the competition for that limited resource.

But what is it like to experience parental burnout? According to Procaccini and Kiefaber, it occurs in five progressive stages, each more stressful than the ones before. The first can be called the "Gung-Ho" stage, which has been described in preceding paragraphs. It may actually begin with the discovery of pregnancy and continue for several years. Very subtly, then, parents can move from the first to the second stage of burnout, which is characterized by persistent doubts. They know something is definitely wrong at this point, but may fail to realize how rapidly they are losing altitude. They are frequently irritated by the children and find themselves screaming on occasions. Quite often they feel drained and fatigued. A full range of psychosomatic symptoms may come and go, including back and neck aches, upset stomach, ulcers and colitis, hypertension, headaches, diarrhea, and constipation. Still, the individual may wonder, *Why do I feel this way?* Some time ago I received a classic letter from a father in the second stage of parental burnout. This is what he wrote (emphasis mine):

> *The reason I'm writing is that the Lord has blessed us so much, and I should be full of joy. But I have been depressed for about ten months now.*
>
> *I don't know whether to turn to a pastor, a physician, a psychologist, a nutritionist, or a chiropractor.*
>
> *Last September the Lord blessed us with a beautiful baby boy. He is just wonderful. He is cute and smart and strong. We just can't help but love him. But he has been very demanding. The thing that made it hardest for me was last semester Margie was taking classes three nights a week to finish her B.A. degree, and I took care of little Danny. He cried and sobbed the whole time we were together. He would eventually go to sleep if I would hold him, but then I was*

afraid to put him down for fear he would wake up. I was used to being able to pay my bills, work out the budget, read, file mail, answer letters, type lists, etc., in the evening, but all this had to be postponed until Margie was here.

It was a real depressing time for me. I just couldn't handle all that crying. It was worse because Margie was breast-feeding him. I got very tired and started having a great deal of trouble getting up in the morning to go to work. I started getting sick very easily.

I have not been able to cope with these things. I really should be at work at 8:00, but I haven't been there before 9:00 or 9:30 in months. It seems like I'm always fighting the flu. I love our baby a lot and I wouldn't trade him for anything in the world. But I don't understand why I'm so depressed. Sure, Margie gets tired because we can't seem to get Danny to bed before 11 or 12 midnight and he wakes up twice per night to be fed. But she's not depressed. All this getting awakened at night really gets to me, and I don't even have to get up to feed him.

Another thing that has been a constant struggle is leaving Danny in the nursery at church. He isn't content to be away from us very long so they end up having to track Margie down almost every Sunday. We hardly ever get to be together. This has been going on for eleven months now.

There are a couple of other things that probably contribute to my depression. They are (1) responsibilities at work; we're short-handed and I'm trying to do too much; (2) spending too many weekends with yard work or trying to fix up our fixer-upper house; and (3) our finances, which are very limited. Sixty-four percent of our income goes to pay for our house and there's not much left over. We don't want Margie to go to work, so we are on a meticulous budget. It's down to the bare essentials, now. I get so tired of that.

We have all the things we would ever dream of at our age (twenty-seven). Our own neat little house in a good neighborhood, a job I consider a ministry. We have a fine healthy boy, each other, and not least of all, our life in Christ.

I have no reason to be depressed and tired all the time. I come home from work so exhausted that I don't even want Danny near me. He hangs on to Margie, and she can't even fix dinner if I don't get him out of her hair. I just don't know how she stands it.

She must have a higher tolerance as far as not getting anything done is concerned.

If you have any insights as to what I should do, please let me know. Thanks and God bless you.

Jack

This twenty-seven-year-old father is well on the way toward burning out. The surprising thing is that Jack is bewildered by it. When one looks at his impossible schedule, it is no wonder that his mind and body are rebelling. After handling an extremely demanding job, he comes home to a fussy baby, a wife in night school, and mountains of bills and paperwork to do. On weekends he is rebuilding his run-down house! Finally, Jack made it clear that he and his wife have no time alone together, no fun in their lives, no social life, no regular exercise, and no escape from the baby. No wonder!

In addition to his other pressures, Jack can't even get an uninterrupted night's sleep. He climbs into bed about midnight, but is awakened at least twice before morning. That is probably the key to his depression. Some individuals are extremely vulnerable to loss of sleep, and this man appears to be one of them. I am another. Our son, Ryan, did not sleep through the night once in his first four months, and I thought I was going to die. Do you remember what that was like with your newborns? There is no sound on earth quite like the piercing screech of an infant in the wee small hours of the morning. (Incidentally, people who say they "sleep like a baby" probably never had one.)

It may be impossible for this family to make immediate and sweeping changes in their lifestyle, but that's what is necessary to avoid greater problems. Margie is coping for the moment, but she will eventually crack too. I would recommend for starters that they postpone reconstructing their house, spending that money instead on childcare and weekend trips to the mountains or beach. They both desperately need at least one day a week away from the baby. Breast-feeding is a problem, but there are solutions to it. Will the child scream when they leave? Yes. Will that hurt him? Not nearly as much as having parents who are too worn out to care for him.

TRANSITION

What will happen if this couple does not find some source of relief? Well, fortunately, their baby will not always be so demanding. But toddlerhood lies ahead and new babies are always a possibility. If they continue to give out without taking in, they will slide from the second stage of burnout into the third. According to Procaccini and Kiefaber, this is the most critical phase. They called it the *transition stage* because decisions are usually made during this period that will determine the well-being of the family for years to come. They will either recognize the downward path they are on and make changes to reverse it, or else they will continue their plunge toward chaos.

What is felt during this third stage is indescribable fatigue, self-condemnation, great anger, and resentment. For the first time, a couple in this situation openly blames the kids for their discontent. One of the reasons they were so excited about parenthood was their idealistic expectation of what children are like. They honestly did not know that little boys and girls can be, and usually are, demanding, self-centered, sloppy, lazy, and rebellious. It wasn't supposed to be this way! In fact, they expected the kids to meet *their* needs for love and appreciation. Instead it is give! give! give! take! take! take! Depression and tears are daily visitors.

PULLING AWAY

The human mind will not tolerate that level of agitation for very long. It will seek to protect itself from further pain. As indicated earlier, this transition phase usually leads either to beneficial changes or to a destructive self-defense. The latter occurs in stage four, which the authors call pulling away. The individual withdraws from the family and becomes "unavailable" to the children. The mother may not even hear them, even though they tug at her skirt and beg for her attention. She may slip into alcoholism or drug or tranquilizer abuse to dull her senses further. If forced to deal with the minor accidents and irritants of childhood, such as spilled milk or glue on the carpet, she may overreact violently and punish wildly. Fantasies of "slinging the brat against the wall" or "bashing him good" may recur in this angry and guilt-ridden parent. Obviously, child abuse is only an inch away. It occurs thousands of times daily in most Western countries.

If asked to explain what she is feeling, a mother in the fourth stage of burnout will say something like this, "I just can't deal with the kids right now." I counseled a woman in this situation who told me, referring to her children, "They hang around my ankles and beg for this or that, but I'll tell you, I kick 'em off. I'm not going to let 'em destroy my life!" She was a living, breathing stick of dynamite waiting to be ignited. People who reach this stage not only pull away from their children, but they tend to become isolated from their spouses and other family members too. Thus, being physically and psychologically exhausted, guilt-ridden to the core, drenched in self-hatred and disappointed with life, these parents descend into the fifth stage of burnout.

THE FINAL PHASE

The final phase is called *chronic disenchantment* by Procaccini and Kiefaber. It is characterized by confusion and apathy. The individual at this stage has lost all meaning and purpose in living. Identity is blurred. Weeks may pass with nothing of significance being remembered. Sexual desire is gone and the marriage is seriously troubled. Recurring thoughts may focus on suicide, "cracking up," or running away. Clearly, this individual is desperately in need of counseling and a radical shift in lifestyle. If nothing changes, neither generation will ever be quite the same again.

And it is all so unnecessary!

Now let's take a closer look at the typical home today. Most of my readers will never reach the latter stages of burnout described above. Life is hard, but it isn't that hard. Some of you, however, will spend your parenting years in a state of general fatigue and stress, perhaps characterized by stage two. You'll crowd your days with junk...with unnecessary responsibilities and commitments that provide no lasting benefits. Precious energy resources will be squandered on that which only seems important at the moment. Consequently, your parenting years will pass in a blur of irritation and frustration. How can you know if this is happening even now? Well, continual screaming, nagging, threatening, punishing, criticizing, and scolding of children is a pretty sure tip-off. There must be a better way to raise our sons and daughters.

One of the most common mistakes of young families is to duplicate the error of the young father who wrote to me. Jack and Margie attempted to accomplish too much too soon. I flinch when a newly married couple tells me they intend during their first two years together to go to school, have a baby, work full time, fix up a house, moonlight for extra money, and teach Sunday school class.

It is a hare-brained plan. The human body will not tolerate that kind of pressure. And when one's body is finally exhausted, an interesting thing happens to the emotions. They also malfunction.

You see, the mind, body, and spirit are very close neighbors and one usually catches the ills of the other. You'll recall that Jack did not understand his depression. He had every reason to be happy. He was miserable. Why? Because his depleted physical condition greatly affected his mental apparatus. And if the truth were known, his spiritual life probably wasn't all that inspiring either. The three departments of our intellectual apparatus are tightly linked and they tend to move up and down as a unit. (Remember how Elijah became depressed and wanted to die immediately after his exhausting confrontation with the prophets of Baal?) This is why it is so important for us to maintain and support the triad: mind, body, and spirit. If one breaks down, the entire engine begins to sputter.

In summary, I join the authors of *Parent Burnout* in urging you to use your physical resources carefully and wisely in the years ahead. Raising children is not unlike a long-distance race in which the contestants must learn to pace themselves. If you blast out of the blocks as though you were running a sprint, you will inevitably tire out. You'll gasp and stumble as the road winds endlessly before you. Then when you come to heartbreak hill, better known as adolescence, there will be no reserve with which to finish the course. Parenting, you see, is a marathon, and we have to adopt a pace that we can maintain for two or even three decades. That is the secret of winning.

A balanced life makes that possible!

NINE

SUGGESTIONS FOR PARENTS OF ADOLESCENTS

ADOLESCENCE IS A fascinating and crazy time of life. It reminds me in some ways of the very early space probes that blasted off from Cape Canaveral in Florida. I remember my excitement when Colonel John Glenn and the other astronauts embarked on their perilous journeys into space. It was a thrilling time to be an American.

People who lived through those years will recall that a period of maximum danger occurred as each spacecraft was reentering the earth's atmosphere. The flier inside was entirely dependent on the heat shield on the bottom of the capsule to protect him from temperatures in excess of one thousand degrees Fahrenheit. If the craft descended at the wrong angle, the astronaut would be burned to cinders. At that precise moment of anxiety, negative ions would accumulate around the capsule and prevent all communication with the earth for approximately seven minutes. The world waited breathlessly for news of the astronaut's safety. Presently, the reassuring voice of Chris Craft would break in to say, "This is Mission Control. We have made contact with Friendship Seven. Everything is A-OK. Splashdown is imminent." Cheers and prayers went up in restaurants, banks, airports, and millions of homes across the country. Even Walter Cronkite seemed relieved.

The analogy to adolescence is not so difficult to recognize. After the training and preparation of childhood are over, a pubescent youngster marches out to the launching pad. His parents watch apprehensively as he

547

climbs aboard a capsule called adolescence and waits for his rockets to fire. His father and mother wish they could go with him, but there is room for just one person in the spacecraft. Besides, nobody invited them. Without warning, the mighty rocket engines begin to roar and the "umbilical cord" falls away. "Liftoff! We have liftoff!" screams the boy's father.

Junior, who was a baby only yesterday, is on his way to the edge of the universe. A few weeks later, his parents go through the scariest experience of their lives: They suddenly lose all contact with the capsule. "Negative ions" have interfered with communication at a time when they most want to be assured of their son's safety. Why won't he talk to them?

This period of silence does not last a few minutes, as it did with Colonel Glenn and friends. It may continue for years. The same kid who used to talk a mile a minute and ask a million questions has now reduced his vocabulary to nine monosyllabic phrases. They are "I dunno," "Maybe," "I forget," "Huh?" "No!" "Nope," "Yeah," "Who—me?" and "He did it." Otherwise, only "static" comes through the receivers—groans, grunts, growls, and gripes. What an apprehensive time it is for those who wait on the ground!

Years later when Mission Control believes the spacecraft to have been lost, a few scratchy signals are picked up unexpectedly from a distant transmitter. The parents are jubilant as they hover near their radio. Was that *really* his voice? It is deeper and more mature than they remembered. There it is again. This time the intent is unmistakable. Their spacey son has made a deliberate effort to correspond with them! He was fourteen years old when he blasted into space and now he is nearly twenty. Could it be that the negative environment has been swept away and communication is again possible? Yes. For most families, that is precisely what happens. After years of quiet anxiety, parents learn to their great relief that everything is A-OK onboard the spacecraft. The "splashdown" occurring during the early twenties can then be a wonderful time of life for both generations.

Isn't there some way to avoid this blackout period and the other stresses associated with the adolescent voyage? Not with some teenagers, perhaps the majority. It happens in the most loving and intelligent of families. Why? Because of two powerful forces that overtake and possess boys and girls in the early pubescent years. Let's talk about them.

The *first* and most important is hormonal in nature. I believe parents and even behavioral scientists have underestimated the impact of the biochemical changes occurring in puberty. We can see the effect of these hormones on the physical body, but something equally dynamic is occurring in the brain. How else can we explain why a happy, contented, cooperative twelve-year-old *suddenly* becomes a sullen, angry, depressed thirteen-year-old? Some authorities would contend that social pressure alone accounts for this transformation. I simply don't believe that.

The emotional characteristics of a suddenly rebellious teenager are rather like the symptoms of premenstrual syndrome or severe menopause in women, or perhaps a tumultuous midlife crisis in men. Obviously, dramatic changes are going on inside! Furthermore, if the upheaval were caused entirely by environmental factors, its onset would not be so predictable in puberty. The emotional changes I have described arrive right on schedule, timed to coincide precisely with the arrival of physical maturation. Both characteristics, I contend, are driven by a common hormonal assault. Human chemistry apparently goes haywire for a few years, affecting mind as much as body.

If that explanation is accurate, then what implications does it have for parents of early adolescents? First, understanding this glandular upheaval makes it easier to tolerate and cope with the emotional reverberations that are occurring. For several years, some kids are not entirely rational! Just as a severely menopausal woman may accuse her innocent and bewildered husband of infidelity, a hormonally depressed teenager may not interpret his world accurately, either. His social judgment is impaired. Therefore, don't despair when it looks like everything you have tried to teach your kid seems to have been forgotten. He is going through a metamorphosis that has turned everything upside down. But stick around. He'll get his legs under him again!

I strongly recommend that parents of strong-willed and rebellious females quietly plot the particulars of her menstrual cycle. Not only should you record when her period begins and ends each month, but also make a comment or two each day about her mood. I think you will see that the emotional blowups that tear the family apart are cyclical in nature. Premenstrual tension at that age can produce a flurry of tornadoes every twenty-eight days. If you know they are coming, you can retreat to the storm cellar when the wind begins to blow. You can also use this record to teach your girls about premenstrual syndrome and how to cope with it. Unfortunately, many parents never seem to notice the regularity and predictability of severe conflict with their daughters. Again, I recommend that you watch the calendar. It will tell you so much about your girls.

Emotional balance in teenage boys is not so cyclical, but their behavior is equally influenced by hormones. Everything from sexual passion to aggressiveness is motivated by the new chemicals that surge through their veins.

I indicated that there were two great forces which combine to create havoc during adolescence, the first having an hormonal origin. The other is social in nature. It is common knowledge that a twelve- or thirteen-year-old child suddenly awakens to a brand-new world around him, as though his eyes were opening for the first time. That world is populated by agemates who scare him out of his wits. His greatest anxiety, far exceeding the fear of death, is the possibility of rejection or humiliation in the eyes of his peers. This ultimate danger will lurk in the background for years, motivating him to do things that make absolutely no sense to the adults who watch. It is impossible to comprehend the adolescent mind without understanding this terror of the peer group.

I'll never forget a vulnerable girl named Lisa who was a student when I was in high school. She attended modern-dance classes and was asked to perform during an all-school assembly program. Lisa was in the ninth grade and had not begun to develop sexually. As she spun around the stage that day, the unthinkable happened! The top to her strapless blouse suddenly let go (it had nothing to grip) and dropped to her waist. The student body gasped and then roared with laughter. It was terrible! Lisa stood clutching frantically at her bare body for a moment and then fled from the stage in tears. She never fully recovered from the tragedy. And you can bet that her "friends" made sure she remembered it for the rest of her life.

Such a situation would also humiliate an adult, of course, but it was worse for a teenager like Lisa. An embarrassment of that magnitude could even take away the desire to live; and indeed, thousands of adolescents are killing themselves every year. We must ask ourselves, why? How do we explain this paralyzing social fear at an age when other kinds of dangers are accepted in stride? Teenagers are known to be risk-takers. They drive their cars like maniacs, and their record for bravery in combat ranks among the best. Why, then, can an eighteen-year-old be taught to attack an enemy gun emplacement or run through a minefield, and yet he panics in the quiet company of his peers? Whence cometh this great vulnerability?

I believe the answer is to be found, again, in the nature of *power* and how it influences behavior. Adolescent society is based on the exercise of raw force. That is the heart and soul of its value system. It comes in various forms, of course. For girls, there is no greater social dominance than physical beauty. A truly gorgeous young woman is so powerful that even the boys are often terrified of her. She rules in a high school setting like a queen on her throne, and in fact, she is usually elected to some honor with references to royalty in its name (Homecoming Queen, All-school Queen, Sweetheart's Queen, Football Queen). The way she uses this status to intimidate her subjects is in itself a fascinating study in adolescent behavior.

Boys derive power from physical attractiveness too, but also from athletic accomplishment in certain prescribed sports, from owning beautiful cars, and from learning to be cool under pressure. It is also a function of sheer physical strength.

Do you remember what the world of adolescence was like for you? Do you recall the power games that were played—the highly competitive and hostile environment into which you walked every day? Can you still feel the apprehension you experienced when a popular (powerful) student called you a creep or a jerk, or he put his big hand in your face and pushed you out of the way? He wore a football jersey which reminded you that the entire team would eat you alive if you should be so foolish as to fight back. Does the memory of the junior-senior prom still come to mind occasionally, when you were either turned down by the girl you loved or were not asked by the boy of your dreams? Have you ever had the campus heroes make fun of the one flaw you most wanted to hide, and then threaten to mangle you on the way home from school?

Perhaps you never went through these stressful encounters. Maybe you were one of the powerful elite who oppressed the rest of us. But your son or daughter could be on the other end of the continuum. A few years ago I talked to a mother whose seventh-grade daughter was getting butchered at school each day. She said the girl awakened an hour before she had to get up each morning and lay there thinking about how she could get through her day without being humiliated.

Typically, power games are more physical for adolescent males than females. The bullies literally force their wills on those who are weaker. That is what I remember most clearly from my own high school years. I had a number of fights during that era just to preserve my turf. There was one dude, however, whom I had no intention of tackling. His name was Killer McKeechern and he was the terror of the town. It was generally believed that Killer would destroy anyone who crossed him. That theory was never tested, to my knowledge. No one dared. At least, not until I blundered along.

When I was fifteen years old and an impulsive sophomore, I nearly ended a long and happy manhood before it had a chance to get started. As I recall, a blizzard had blown through our state the night before, and a group of us gathered in front of the school to throw snowballs at passing cars. (Does that tell you something about our collective maturity at the time?) Just before the afternoon bell rang, I looked up the street and saw McKeechern chugging along in his "chopped" 1934 Chevy. It was a junk heap with a cardboard "window" on the driver's side. McKeechern had cut a three-by-three inch flap in the cardboard, which he lifted when turning left. You could see his evil eyes peering out just before he went around corners. When the flap was down, however, he was oblivious to things on the left side of the car. As luck would have it, that's where I was stand-ing with a huge snowball in my hand—thinking very funny and terribly unwise thoughts.

If I could just go back to that day and counsel myself, I would say, "Don't do it, Jim! You could lose your sweet life right here. McKeechern will tear your tongue out if you hit him with that snowball. Just put it down and go quietly to your afternoon class. Please, son! If *you* lose, I lose!" Unfortunately, no such advice wafted to my ears that day and I didn't have the sense to realize my danger. I heaved the snowball into the upper atmosphere with all my might. It came down just as McKeechern drove by and, unbelievably, went through the flap in his cardboard window. The mis-sile obviously hit him squarely in the face, because his Chevy wobbled all over the road. It bounced over the curb and came to a stop just short of the Administration Building. Killer exploded from the front seat, ready to rip someone to shreds (me!). I'll never forget the sight. There was snow all over his face and little jets of steam were curling from his head. My whole life passed in front of my eyes as I faded into the crowd. *So young!* I thought.

The only thing that saved me on this snowy day was McKeechern's inability to identify me. No one told him I had thrown the snowball, and believe me, I didn't volunteer. I escaped unscathed, although that brush with destiny must have damaged me emotionally. I still have recurring nightmares about the event thirty-five years later. In my dreams, the chimes ring and I go to open the front door. There stands McKeechern with a shotgun. And he still has snow on his face. (If you read this story, Killer, I do hope we can be friends. We were only kids, you know? Right, Killer? Huh? Right! Howsa car?)

Why have I reminded you of the world of adolescent power? Because your teenagers are knee deep in it right now. That is why they are nervous wrecks on the first day of school, or before the team plays its initial game, or any other time when their power base is on the line. The raw nerve, you see, is not really dominance, but self-esteem. One's sense of worth is dependent on peer acceptance at that age, and that is why the group holds such enormous influence over the individual. If he is mocked, disrespected, ridiculed, and excluded—in other words, if he is stripped of power—his delicate ego is torn to shreds. As we have said, that is a fate worse than death itself. Social panic is the by-product of that system.

Now, what about your sons and daughters? Have you wondered why they come home from school in such a terrible mood? Have you asked them why they are so jumpy and irritable through the evening? They cannot describe their feelings to you, but they may have engaged in a form of combat all day. Even if they haven't had to fight with their fists, it is likely that they are embroiled in a highly competitive, openly hostile environment where emotional danger lurks on every side. Am I overstating the case? Yes, for the kid who is coping well. But for the powerless young man and woman, I haven't begun to tell their stories.

To help parents cope with these special stresses of the adolescent years, let me offer five suggestions that have been beneficial to others, as follows:

1. Boredom Is Dangerous to Energetic Teenagers. Keep Them Moving.

The strong-willed adolescent simply must not be given large quantities of unstructured time. He will find destructive ways to use such moments. My advice is to get him involved in the very best church youth program you can find. If your local congregation has only four bored members in its junior high department and seven sleepy high schoolers, I would consider changing churches. I know that advice could be disruptive to the entire family and I'm sure most pastors would disagree, but you must save that volatile kid. Obviously, such radical action is not as necessary for the more compliant individual or for one who has other wholesome outlets for his energy. But if you're sitting on a keg of dynamite, you have to find ways to keep the powder dry! Not only can this be done through church activities, but also by involvement with athletics, music, horses or other animals, and part-time jobs. You must keep that strong-willed kid's scrawny legs churning!

2. Don't Rock the Boat.

In my second film series, entitled *Turn Your Heart Toward Home,* I offered this advice to parents of teenagers: "Get 'em through it." That may not sound like such a stunning idea, but I believe it has merit for most families— especially those with one or more tough-minded kids. The concept is a bit obscure, so I will resort to a couple of pictures to illustrate my point.

When parents of strong-willed children look ahead to the adolescent river, they often perceive it to be like this one.

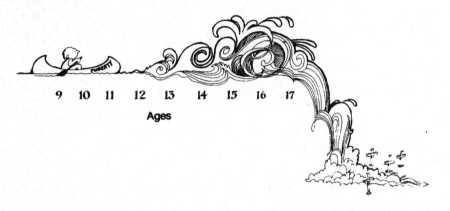

In other words, they expect the early encounter with rapids to give way to swirling currents and life-threatening turbulence. If that doesn't turn over their teenagers' boat, they seem destined to drown farther downstream when they plunge over the falls.

Fortunately, the typical journey is much safer than anticipated. Most often it flows like the picture below.

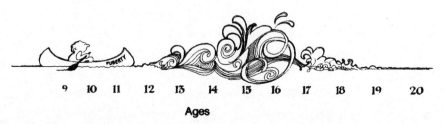

What I'm saying is that the river usually descends not into the falls but into smooth water once more. Even though your teenager may be splashing and thrashing and gasping for air, it is not likely that his boat will capsize. It is more buoyant than you might think. Yes, a few individuals do go over the falls, usually because of drug abuse. Even some of them climb back in the canoe and paddle on down the river. In fact, the greatest danger of sinking the boat could come from...*you!*

This warning is addressed particularly to idealistic and perfectionistic parents who are determined to make their adolescents—*all* of them—perform and achieve and measure up to the highest standard. A perfectionist, by the way, is a person who takes great pains with what he does and then gives them to everyone else. In so doing, he rocks a boat that is already threatened by the rapids. Perhaps another child could handle the additional turbulence, but our concern is for the unsteady kid—the one who lacks common sense for a while and may even lean toward irrational behavior. Don't unsettle his boat any more than you must!

I'm reminded of a waitress who recognized me when I came into the restaurant where she worked. She was not busy that day and wanted to talk about her twelve-year-old daughter. As a single mother, she had gone through severe struggles with the girl, whom she identified as being *very* strong-willed.

"We have fought tooth and nail for this entire year," she said. "It has been awful! We argue nearly every night, and most of our fights are over the same issue."

I asked her what had caused the conflict, and she replied, "My daughter is still a little girl but she wants to shave her legs. I feel she's too young to be doing that and she becomes so angry that she won't even talk to me. This has been the worst year of our lives together."

I looked at the waitress and exclaimed, "Lady, buy your daughter a razor!"

That twelve-year-old girl was paddling into a time of life that would rock her canoe good and hard. As a single parent, Mom would soon be trying to keep this rebellious kid from getting into drugs, alcohol, sex and pregnancy, early marriage, school failure, and the possibility of running away. Truly, there would be many ravenous alligators in her river within a year or two. In that setting, it seemed unwise to make a big deal over what was essentially a nonissue. While I agreed with the mother that adolescence should not be rushed into prematurely, there were higher goals than maintaining a proper developmental timetable.

I have seen other parents fight similar battles over nonessentials such as the purchase of a first bra for a flat-chested preadolescent girl. For goodness sake! If she wants it that badly, she probably needs it for social reasons. Run, don't walk, to the nearest department store and buy her a bra. The objective, as Charles and Andy Stanley wrote, is to *keep your kids on your team.* Don't throw away your friendship over behavior that has no great moral significance. There will be plenty of real issues that require you to stand like a rock. Save your big guns for those crucial confrontations.

Let me make it very clear, again, that this advice is not relevant to every teenager. The compliant kid who is doing wonderfully in school, has great friends, is disciplined in his conduct and loves his parents is not nearly so delicate. Perhaps his parents can urge him to reach even higher standards in his achievements and lifestyle. My concern, however, is for that youngster who *could* go over the falls. He is intensely angry at home and is being influenced by a carload of crummy friends. Be very careful with him. Pick and choose what is worth fighting for, and settle for something less than perfection on issues that don't really matter. *Just get him through it!*

What does this mean in practical terms? It may indicate a willingness to let his room look like a junkyard for a while. Does that surprise you? I don't like lazy, sloppy, undisciplined kids any more than you do, but given the possibilities for chaos that this angry boy or girl might precipitate, spit-shined rooms may not be all that important.

You might also compromise somewhat regarding the music you let him hear. I'm *not* condoning hard rock and heavy metal, which is saturated with explicit and illicit sex and violence today. But neither can you ask this gogo teenager to listen to your "elevator music." Perhaps a compromise can be reached. Unfortunately, the popular music of the day is the rallying cry for rebellious teenagers. If you try to deny it altogether to a strong-willed kid, you just might flip his canoe upside down. You have to ask yourself this question, "Is it worth risking everything of value to enforce a particular standard upon this son or daughter?" If the issue *is* important enough to defend at all costs, then brace yourself and make your stand. But think through those intractable matters in advance and plan your defense of them thoroughly.

The philosophy we applied with our teenagers (and you might try with yours) can be called "loosen and tighten." By this I mean we tried to loosen our grip on everything that had no lasting significance, and tighten down on everything that did. We said yes whenever we possibly could, to give support to the occasional no. And most importantly, we tried never to get too far away from our kids emotionally.

It is simply not prudent to write off a son or daughter, no matter how foolish, irritating, selfish, or insane a child may seem to be. You need to be there, not only while their canoe is bouncing precariously, but after the river runs smooth again. You have the remainder of your life to reconstruct the relationship that is now in jeopardy. Don't let anger fester for too long. Make the first move toward reconciliation. And try hard not to hassle your kids. They *hate* to be nagged. If you follow them around with one complaint after another, they are almost forced to protect themselves by appearing deaf. And finally, continue to treat them with respect, even when punishment or restrictions are necessary. Occasionally, you may even need to say, "I'm sorry!"

My father found it very difficult to say those words. I remember working with him in the backyard when I was fifteen years of age, on a day when he was particularly irritable for some reason. I probably deserved his indignation, but I thought he was being unfair. He crabbed at me for everything I did, even when I hustled. Finally, he yelled at me for something petty and that did it. He capsized my canoe. I threw down the rake and quit. Defiantly I walked across our property and down the street while my dad demanded that I come back. It was one of the few times I ever took him on like that! I meandered around town for a while, wondering what would happen to me when I finally went home. Then I strolled over to my cousin's house on the other side of town. After several hours there, I admitted to his father that I had had a bad fight with my dad and he didn't know where I was. My uncle persuaded me to call home and assure my parents that I was safe. With knees quaking, I phoned my dad.

"Stay there," he said. "I'm coming over."

To say that I was apprehensive for the next few minutes would be an understatement. In a short time Dad arrived and asked to see me alone.

"Bo," he began. "I didn't treat you right this afternoon. I was riding your back for no good reason and I want you to know I'm sorry. Your mom and I want you to come on home now."

He made a friend for life.

3. Maintain a Reserve Army.

A good military general will never commit all his troops to combat at the same time. He maintains a reserve force that can relieve the exhausted soldiers when they falter on the front lines. I wish parents of adolescents would implement the same strategy. Instead, they commit every ounce of their energy and every second of their time to the business of living, holding nothing in reserve for the challenge of the century. It is a classic mistake which can be disastrous for parents of strong-willed adolescents. Let me explain.

The problem begins with a basic misunderstanding during the preschool years. I hear mothers say, "I don't plan to work until the kids are in kindergarten. Then I'll get a job." They appear to believe that the heavy demands on them will end magically when they get their youngest in school. In reality, the teen years will generate as much pressure on them as did the preschool era. An adolescent turns a house upside down... literally and figuratively. Not only is the typical rebellion of those years an extremely stressful experience, but the chauffeuring, supervising, cooking, and cleaning required to support an adolescent can be exhausting. *Someone* within the family must reserve the energy to cope with those new challenges. Mom is the candidate of choice. Remember, too, that menopause and a man's midlife crisis are scheduled to coincide with adolescence, which makes a wicked soup! It is a wise mother who doesn't exhaust herself at a time when so much is going on at home.

I know it is easier to talk about maintaining a lighter schedule than it is to secure one. It is also impractical to recommend that mothers not seek formal employment during this era. Millions of women have to work for economic reasons, including the rising number of single parents in our world. Others choose to pursue busy careers. That is a decision to be made by a woman and her husband, and I would not presume to tell them what to do.

But decisions have inevitable consequences. In this case, there are biophysical forces at work which simply must be reckoned with. If, for example, 80 percent of a woman's available energy in a given day is expended in getting dressed, driving to work, doing her job for eight or ten hours, and stopping by the grocery store on the way home—then there is only 20 percent left for everything else. Maintenance of the family, cooking meals, cleaning the kitchen, relating to her husband, and all other personal activities must be powered by that diminishing resource. It is no wonder that her batteries are spent by the end of the day. Weekends should be restful, but they are usually not. Thus, she plods through the years on her way to burnout.

This is my point: A woman in this situation has thrown all her troops into front-line combat. As we saw in the previous chapter on burnout, she is already exhausted but there is no reserve on which to call. In that weakened condition, the routine stresses of raising an adolescent can be overwhelming. Let me say it again. Raising boisterous teenagers is an exciting and rewarding but also a frustrating experience. Their radical highs and lows affect our moods. The noise, the messes, the complaints, the arguments, the sibling rivalry, the missed curfews, the paced floors, the wrecked car, the failed test, the jilted lover, the wrong friends, the busy telephone, the pizza on the carpet, the ripped new blouse, the rebellion, the slammed doors, the mean words, the tears—it's enough to drive a *rested* mother crazy. But what about our career woman who already "gave at the office," then came home to this chaos? Any unexpected crisis or even a minor irritant can set off a torrent of emotion. There is no reserve on which to draw. In short, the parents of adolescents should save some energy with which to cope with aggravation!

Whether or not you are able to accept and implement my advice is your business. It is mine to offer it, and this is my best shot: To help you get through the turbulence of adolescence, you should:

1. Keep the schedule simple.
2. Get plenty of rest.
3. Eat nutritious meals.
4. Stay on your knees.

When fatigue leads adults to act like hot-tempered teenagers, anything can happen at home.

4. The Desperate Need for Fathers.

It is stating the obvious, I suppose, to say that fathers of rebellious teenagers are desperately needed at home during those years. In their absence, mothers are left to handle disciplinary problems alone. This is occurring in millions of families headed by single mothers today, and I know how tough their task has become. Not only are they doing a job that should have been shouldered by two; they must also deal with behavioral problems that fathers are more ideally suited to handle. It is generally understood that a man's larger size, deeper voice, and masculine demeanor make it easier for him to deal with defiance in the younger generation. Likewise, I believe the exercise of authority is a mantle ascribed to him by the Creator.

Not only are fathers needed to provide leadership and discipline during the adolescent years, but they can be highly influential on their sons during this period of instability. (We will discuss fathers and daughters presently.) Someone has said, "Link a boy to the right man and he seldom goes wrong." I believe that is true. If a dad and his son can develop hobbies together or other common interests, the rebellious years can pass in relative tranquility. What they experience may be remembered for a lifetime.

I recall a song, written by Dan Fogelberg, that told about a man who shared his love of music with his elderly father. It is called "Leader of the Band," and its message touches something deep within me. This is the way it should be:

An only child
Alone and wild
A cabinet maker's son
His hands were meant
For different work
And his heart was known to none—
He left his home
And went his lone
And solitary way
And he gave to me
A gift I know I never can repay.

A quiet man of music
Denied a simpler fate
He tried to be a soldier once
But his music wouldn't wait

He earned his love through discipline
A thundering, velvet hand
His gentle means of sculpting souls
Took me years to understand.

The leader of the band is tired
And his eyes are growing old
But his blood runs through my instrument
And his song is in my soul—

My life has been a poor attempt
To imitate the man
I'm just a living legacy
To the leader of the band.

My brothers' lives were different
For they heard another call
One went to Chicago
And the other to St. Paul
And I'm in Colorado
When I'm not in some hotel
Living out this life I've chose
And come to know so well.

I thank you for the music
And your stories of the road
I thank you for the freedom
When it came my time to go—
I thank you for the kindness
And the times when you got tough
And, papa, I don't think I
Said "I love you" near enough—

The leader of the band is tired
And his eyes are growing old
But his blood runs through my instrument
And his song is in my soul—
My life has been a poor attempt
To imitate the man
I'm just a living legacy
To the leader of the band.
I am the living legacy to
The leader of the band.[1]

Can't you see this man going to visit his aged father today, with a lifetime of love passing between them? That must have been what God had in mind when he gave dads to boys. Let me address the reader directly: What common ground are you cultivating with *your* impressionable son? Some fathers build or repair cars with them; some construct small models or make things in a wood shop. My dad and I hunted and fished together. There is no way to describe what those days meant to me as we entered the woods in the early hours of the morning. How could I get angry at this man who took time to be with me? We had wonderful talks while coming home from a day of laughter and fun in the country.

I've tried to maintain that kind of contact with my son, Ryan. We've rebuilt a Model A Ford together. We've also hunted rabbits, quail, pheasant, and larger game since he turned twelve. As it was with my father, Ryan and I have had some meaningful conversations while out in the fields together. For example, we got up one morning and situated ourselves in a deer blind before the break of day. About twenty yards away from us was a feeder which operated on a timer. At 7:00 A.M. it automatically dropped kernels of corn into a pan below.

Ryan and I huddled together in this blind, talking softly about whatever came to mind. Then through the fog, we saw a beautiful doe emerge silently into the clearing. She took nearly thirty minutes to get to the feeder near where we were hiding. We had no intention of shooting her, but it was fun to watch this beautiful animal from close range. She was extremely wary, sniffing the air and listening for the sounds of danger. Finally, she inched her way to the feeder, still looking around skittishly as though sensing our presence. Then she ate a quick breakfast and fled.

I whispered to Ryan, "There is something valuable to be learned from what we have just seen. Whenever you come upon a free supply of high quality corn, unexpectedly provided right there in the middle of the forest, be careful! The people who put it there are probably sitting nearby in a blind, just waiting to take a shot at you. Keep your eyes and ears open!"

Ryan may not always remember that advice, but I will. It isn't often a father says something that he considers profound to his teenage son. One thing is certain: This interchange and the other ideas we shared on that day would not have occurred at home. Opportunities for that kind of communication have to be created. And it's worth working to achieve.

Before we leave the subject of fathers interacting with their sons,

I want to reflect briefly on a *mother's* contribution to that relationship. Women can help the generations bond together or they can drive a wedge between them. This concept was expressed beautifully in a book entitled *Fathers and Sons* by Lewis Yablonsky. The author observed that mothers are the *primary* interpreters of fathers' personality, character, and integrity to their sons. In other words, the way boys see their fathers is largely a product of the things their mothers have said and the way she feels. In Yablonsky's case, his mother destroyed the respect he might have had for his father. This is what he wrote:

> I vividly recall sitting at the dinner table with my two brothers and father and mother and cringing at my mother's attacks on my father. "Look at him," she would say in Yiddish. "His shoulders are bent down, he's a failure. He doesn't have the courage to get a better job or make more money. He's a beaten man." He would keep his eyes pointed toward his plate and never answer her. She never extolled his virtues or persistence or the fact that he worked so hard. Instead she constantly focused on the negative and created an image to his three sons of a man without fight, crushed by a world over which he had no control.
>
> His not fighting back against her constant criticism had the effect of confirming its validity to her sons. And my mother's treatment and the picture of my father did not convey to me that marriage was a happy state of being, or that women were basically people. I was not especially motivated to assume the role of husband and father myself from my observations of my whipped father.
>
> My overall research clearly supports that the mother is the basic filter and has enormous significance in the father-son relationship.[2]

Though Yablonsky did not say so, it is also true that fathers can do great damage to the conception their children may have of their mother. Very early on I found that when I was irritated with Shirley for some reason, my attitude was instantly picked up by our son and daughter. They seemed to feel, "If Dad can argue with Mom, then we can too." It became clear to me just how important it was for me to express my love and admiration for Shirley. However, I could *never* do that job of building respect for my wife as well as she did for me! She made me a king in my own home. If our son and daughter believed half of what she told them about me, I would have been a fortunate man. The close relationship I enjoy with Danae and Ryan today is largely a product of Shirley's great love for me and the way she "interpreted" me to our kids. I will always be grateful to her for doing that!

FATHERS AND DAUGHTERS

Let's talk now about fathers and daughters. Most psychologists believe, and I am one of them, that all future romantic relationships to occur in a girl's life will be influenced positively or negatively by the way she perceives and interacts with her dad. If he is an alcoholic and a bum, she will spend her life trying to replace him in her heart. If he is warm and nurturing, she will look for a lover to equal him. If he thinks she is beautiful, worthy, and feminine, she will be inclined to see herself that way. But if he rejects her as unattractive and uninteresting, she is likely to carry self-esteem problems into her adult years.

I have also observed that a woman's willingness to accept the loving leadership of her husband is significantly influenced by the way she perceived the authority of her father. If he was overbearing, uncaring, or capricious during her developmental years, she may attempt to grab the reins of leadership from her future husband. But if dad blended love and discipline in a way that conveyed strength, she will be more willing to yield to the confident leadership of her husband.

None of these tendencies or trends is absolute, of course. Individual differences can always produce exceptions and contradictions. But this statement will be hard to refute: A good father will leave his imprint on his daughter for the rest of her life.

Many fathers are also called upon to perform another vitally important role during the adolescent years. It occurs when tension begins to develop between mothers and teenage girls. That conflict is very common among the ladies of the house, and as you recall, it showed up in the findings from our study of temperaments. Several years may pass when they don't even *like* each other very much.

In that setting, fathers are desperately needed as peacemakers and mediators. I have found that teenagers who are greatly irritated with one parent will sometimes seek to preserve their relationship with the other. It's like a country at war in search of supportive allies. If fathers are chosen in that triangle, they can use the opportunity to settle their daughters and "interpret" their mothers in a more favorable light. They may also be able to help their wives ventilate their anger and understand their role in perpetuating the conflict. Without this masculine influence, routine skirmishes can turn into World War III.

In conclusion, I have this recurring message for today's fathers—especially to those who have teenagers at home: Don't let these years get away from you. Your contributions to your kids could rank as your greatest accomplishments in life—or your most oppressive failures. If you're not yet convinced of your importance at home, read the article that follows. If it doesn't touch your heart you may not have one.

DAD COMING HOME WAS THE REAL TREAT
by Howard Mann

When I was a little boy I never left the house without kissing my parents goodbye.

I liked kissing my mother because her cheek felt mushy and warm, and because she smelled of peppermints. I liked kissing my father because he felt rough and whiskery and smelled of cigars and witch hazel.

About the time I was 10 years old, I came to the conclusion that I was now too big to kiss my father. A mother, OK. But with a father, a big boy should shake hands—man to man, you see.

He didn't seem to notice the difference or to mind it. Anyway, he never said anything about it. But then he never said much about anything, except his business.

In retrospect, I guess it was also my way of getting even with him. Up until then, I had always felt I was something special to him. Every day, he would come home from that mysterious world of his with a wondrous treat, just for me. It might be a miniature baseball bat, engraved with Babe Ruth's signature. It might be a real honeycomb with waffle-like squares soaked in honey. Or it might be exotic rahat, the delectable, jellied Turkish candies, buried in powdered sugar and crowded into a little wooden crate.

How I looked forward to his coming home each night! The door flung open and there he stood. I would run to him, hug him while he lifted me high in his arms.

I reached my peak the day of my seventh birthday. I woke up before anyone else in the family and tiptoed into the dining room. There, on the heavy mahogany table, was a small, square wristwatch with a brown leather strap, stretched out full length in a black velvet box. Could it really be for me? I picked it up and held it to my ear. It ticked! Not a toy watch from the 5-and-10, but a real watch like grown-ups wore. I ran into his bedroom, woke up Father and covered him with kisses. Could any boy possibly be as happy as me?

Later, it began to change. At first, I wasn't aware it was happening. I supposed I was too busy with school and play and having to make new friends all the time. (We moved every two years, always seeking a lower rent.)

The flow of treats dried up. No more bats or honeycombs. My father gradually disappeared from my life. He would come home late, long after I had gone to sleep. And he would come home with his hands empty. I missed him very much, but I was afraid to say anything. I hoped that he would come back to me as strangely as he had left. Anyhow, big boys weren't supposed to long for their fathers.

Years after he died, my mother talked about how the Depression had "taken the life out of him." It had crushed his dream of being a "big man." He no longer had money for treats. He no longer had time for me.

I am sorry now. I look at his picture and his crinkly hazel eyes and wish that he were here today. I would tell him what is happening with me now and talk about things that he might like to hear—politics, foreign events and how business is doing. And I would put my arms around his neck and say, "Pop, you don't have to bring me anything—just come home early." And I would kiss him.[3]

5. Handling the Very Toughest Cases.

Go back with me now to the story I told about my dad's apology during our brief disagreement in the backyard. He took all the blame for that confrontation and in essence, "ate humble pie." I must make it clear that it is not always wise to assume this posture. In fact, I believe most parents of very difficult teenagers go too far in that direction. There is a time for parents to get off their knees and *quit* apologizing. They have sought to avoid conflict by groveling and appeasing their strong-willed adolescents, and in so doing, they have made what turns out to be a tragic mistake. Please remember this fact: To a power-hungry tyrant of any age, appeasement only inflames his lust for more power. Behavioral research has now demonstrated this relationship between insecure, permissive parents and violent, delinquent teenagers.

Dr. Henry Harbin and Dr. Denis Madden observed a significant increase in the number of vicious attacks on parents by their unruly children. Working at the University of Maryland's Medical School, these psychiatrists also studied the circumstances surrounding this form of family violence. Surprisingly, they found that "parent battering" usually occurs when "one or both parents have abdicated the executive position" and when no one is in charge. No one, that is, except possibly the violent child.

Harbin and Madden also observed that "an almost universal element" in the parent-battering cases was the parents' unwillingness to admit the seriousness of the situation. They did not call the police, even when their lives were in danger; they lied to protect the children and they continued to give in to their demands. Parental authority had collapsed.

One father was almost killed when his angry son pushed him down a flight of stairs. He insisted that the boy did not have a bad temper. Another woman was stabbed by her son, missing her heart by an inch. Nevertheless, she continued letting him live at home.

Drs. Harbin and Madden concluded that appeasement and permissiveness are related to youthful violence, and that both parents should lead with firmness. "Someone needs to be in charge," they said.[4]

Obviously, I agree wholeheartedly with these psychiatrists. Having been appointed by President Ronald Reagan to serve on the National Advisory Commission to the Office of Juvenile Justice and Delinquency Prevention, I am very familiar with the pattern of youthful violence. I've seen cold-blooded killers who were no more than thirteen years of age. Many of them came from homes where authority was weak or nonexistent. It is a formula for cranking out very tough criminals at an early age.

That brings us to the most difficult question with which parents are ever confronted: What can be done in those cases when parental leadership collapses altogether? What resources are available to mothers and fathers when an adolescent continually breaks the law, intimidates or attacks his family, and does precisely what he wishes? If appeasement makes matters worse, as we have seen, what other approaches can we suggest?

Though it would be glib to imply that there are simple answers to such awesome questions, I believe one organization was on the right track. It was called TOUGHLOVE, founded by Phyllis and David York. TOUGHLOVE was dedicated to helping out-of-control parents regain the upper hand in their own homes. Their basic philosophy was one of confrontation that is designed to bring a belligerent teenager to his senses.

The TOUGHLOVE concept began during the early 1980s, after counselors Phyllis and David York had run into serious problems with their eighteen-year-old daughter. She broke every rule and eventually held up a cocaine dealer in Lansdale, Pennsylvania. She was soon arrested at gunpoint in the Yorks' home. That got their attention.

From this painful experience, the Yorks began to formulate the TOUGHLOVE principles. They are simple enough: Forgiveness and understanding are laudable responses to defiance, but they do not work with the most difficult cases. As David York said, "I started out being this nice therapist. 'Let me listen, let me be this daddy to you guys.' And what really needs to happen is to grab these kids and say, 'You really can't do that. You've got to follow the rules here, and if you don't we're going to call the police and have you locked up!'"

Instead of groveling and whining, parents of rebellious teens are encouraged to stand firm and take appropriate action. This may include taking away the family car, restricting use of the telephone, and refusing to intervene when the teen is in jail. It may also involve locking a drug user out of his home. A note on the front door informs him that he will be welcome there only if he enrolls in a drug-rehab program. A teen who comes home hours after his curfew may find a note instructing him to spend the night with another family that is willing to take him in.

Time magazine, 8 June 1981, quoted TOUGHLOVE mothers as follows, "It's just old-fashioned discipline, where the parents run the home and there is cooperation among the family members." Another said she turned in her son, Jeff, seventeen, to the police after he confessed to robbing a nearby home to support his drug habit. "Police enrolled him in a rehabilitation program," said *Time*, "and now he is back home, working and attending Narcotics and Alcoholics Anonymous."

Many similar examples are cited in the Yorks' book *Toughlove*. But as might be expected, most parents lack the confidence and understanding needed to implement the principles on their own. They need the support of other parents who are going through the same trauma. That's why the TOUGHLOVE organization was founded. It put harassed parents in touch with one another. Then if a teenager was sent to prison, for example, his distressed mother and father could ask other members of their local TOUGHLOVE group to visit him first, or to accompany them to the prison. It was an idea whose time had come.

The article in *Time* magazine concluded with this statement:

TOUGHLOVE brings parents together to buck up one another at meetings and to follow the progress of problem youngsters. If a runaway is picked up in another state or a youngster is arrested, members in the group are ready to go to the scene. Says Ted Wachtel, president of the Community Service Foundation in Sellersville, Pa., which sponsors the TOUGHLOVE movement: "If a child winds up in prison, it is sometimes too much of an emotional experience for the parents to go at first, so other members of the group make the visits."

TOUGHLOVE does not work all the time, but so far it has been an effective way of uniting parents to square off against the youngsters' own powerful peer group that endorses drug taking and rebelliousness. One tactic of TOUGHLOVE is to make a list of a youngster's closest friends, then go out and meet the parents of the friends and try to make an alliance. The message: Don't feel guilty; don't get into shouting matches with youngsters; don't be a victim; get over disillusionment. Says the TOUGHLOVE self-help manual for parents: "We really were not prepared for such a rapidly changing culture full of distractions like dope, violence, and a peer group that means more to our children than a home and family." In TOUGHLOVE's view, the time has come for parents to stand up against a hostile culture.[5]

What was the public response to the TOUGHLOVE concept? There were twenty-five groups in 1981. Many more groups formed across the United States and in Australia, Canada, New Zealand, and South Africa. It became an international movement.

Did I recommend them personally? Yes, with two reservations: (1) TOUGHLOVE was not a Christian organization, although I never knew them to contradict our basic beliefs. I wish a similar national program existed that emphasized prayer and Scripture, but I know of none. In the meantime, TOUGHLOVE got the job done. (2) Any franchised program like this will be no better than the people who operate it on a local level. You could get a lemon, so to speak. I will say this, however: I have heard very little criticism of the TOUGHLOVE program in all these years. Hundreds of grateful parents wrote to me after the Yorks were guests on our Focus on the Family radio broadcast. One woman told our program director, "TOUGHLOVE literally saved my life. I would not have survived without it."

Whether or not you are in need of the radical support provided by TOUGHLOVE, I invite you to read an interesting article written about it by columnist Ann Landers. This article was also published in 1981, the year TOUGHLOVE burst on the scene, and was originally incorporated in *Family Circle* magazine, November 3 of that year. Note the similarity in philosophy to what we have been discussing throughout this book. Obviously, I do not agree with Landers's criticism of the Bible, and I will deal with her misinterpretation of Proverbs 22:6 in the upcoming question-and-answer chapter.

Here's the way Ann Landers saw it:

I never thought I'd live to see the day when I'd actually argue with the Bible...especially since I've frequently quoted the very passage I no longer feel applies "Train up a child in the way he should go...and...he will not depart from it," meaning that if you carefully train your child, he or she will turn out well. Yet, unfortunately, the last 15 years have produced a great deal of evidence disproving this biblical directive. My desk is groaning from the weight of letters that sound a lot like this one.

> Dear Ann Landers:
>
> We took our children to church, we didn't send them. We never had sitters. If we couldn't get his mother or mine to stay, the children came with us or we didn't go. We invested so much love and time and energy in our sons and daughters, yet they became involved with truancy, drugs, shoplifting, a pregnancy—every kind of trouble you might expect from street kids. What went wrong?

Being a firm believer that the twigs grew in the direction they were bent, I didn't know how to respond to these anguished, guilt-ridden parents. Their letters describing years of tender loving care didn't square with what was happening to their children. Many carefully nurtured twigs seemed to be growing in bizarre and unpredictable directions. I had to rethink my answers and come up with something better.

A few years ago I printed a letter that said volumes. It was from a high school student who came across her mother's diary; the letter contained an entry the mother had written:

> All adolescent kids have diaries these days. Well, I think it's time for mothers to have diaries, too. We ought to keep a daily chronicle reporting the heart-aches of parents who did the best they could with their mixed-up sons and daughters. Only the kids suffer, do they? Only their feelings are hurt? Well, move over, children, your parents are having a very hard time trying to bring you up to be self-reliant, decent citizens. It seems like the cards are stacked against us. The more we give, the less we get back.

What's gone wrong? Obviously something has. I don't pretend to know all the answers, but after reading thousands of letters from teenagers in trouble, teachers who see them almost every day, guidance counselors who listen to them, and parents who are wringing their hands in despair, I have concluded that peer pressure is a far more dominant factor in shaping teenage behavior than parental influence.

The experts with whom I checked (juvenile authorities, drug-abuse and mental-health counselors, some psychologists, a few psychiatrists) supported my notion. I'm not suggesting that parental training and role models mean nothing. What I am saying is that in our present-day culture what a teenager's peers think of him carries more weight than what his parents say.

The need to be accepted, the fear of being outside the charmed circle, the desire to be "in" is vitally important to adolescents today. And, all too often that means keg parties, getting drunk, smoking dope, popping uppers and downers, snorting cocaine, using angel dust and acid, and having sex.

Moreover, a generation that has grown up with its eyeballs hooked onto a TV screen is constantly searching for ways to combat boredom and anesthetize themselves against the pain of growing up. Teenagers (and adults, as well) have discovered that alcohol and drugs can put troubles on the back burner and make you feel "different."

According to a report put out in 1980 by the Department of Health, Education and Welfare (now called Department of Health and Human Services), one out of 10 high school students regularly uses pot. This means these kids smoke at least one or two joints every day. I happen to believe that this figure is too low. High school teachers have written to tell me that on Monday mornings, at least one-third of the juniors and seniors walk into classrooms stoned. An even more frightening fact is that some of these students drive themselves to school, which helps explain why auto accidents are today's leading cause of death among teenagers. And emergency room attendants tell us that approximately 65 percent of all fatal teenage accidents are alcohol or drug-related.

How can parents combat outside influences that run counter to everything they have tried to teach their children? What advice do I have for them? Plenty. And I've already had responses telling me it works. The following letter opened my eyes and sent me in a completely new direction. It came from Bucks County, Pennsylvania.

> Dear Ann:
>
> Please print this for parents with unreachable, mixed-up, always-in-trouble teenagers. I know where they are coming from. My husband and I have been there and there's no hell like it.
>
> We, too, were desperate and without hope. Our son was a bum, in debt, stealing from us, on drugs, breaking up the furniture, cursing and hitting us. We were beside ourselves with anxiety and fear. We tried everything to please him, and nothing worked. The nicer we were, the worse he got.
>
> Finally we called the police. They gave us the phone number of an organization called

TOUGHLOVE. From that day on we became members of a community network of parents who are successfully coping with their kids' hostile, antisocial behavior.

Before we came to TOUGHLOVE, we were ashamed and felt weak and guilty because we couldn't stand up to our son. We thought that no other parents in the community had failed as miserably as we had. Then we met other members of TOUGHLOVE and discovered that we were no longer helpless. We had the support of other parents, the police, the schools, the courts, and rehabilitation facilities.

We didn't have to throw our son out of the house, nor did we have to continue to take his abuse. We laid down a whole new set of rules and gave him a choice. He could live by our rules or get out. He chose to stay.

I'm enclosing a pamphlet that tells you more about TOUGHLOVE. Please, Ann, share it with your readers. It's the greatest thing that happened to us and we want to spread the word. Thanks for your help.

Forever Grateful

I read the pamphlet and it made a lot of sense. It explained a program designed to help parents who feel heartsick and helpless about their teenagers. The program asks parents to choose which road they want to take. Will it be confrontation, firm guidelines and mutual respect—or excuses (as usual), denial, gutlessness, continued indulgence and bribery? It encourages parents to meet the crisis head on, take a stand and demand cooperation.

Actually, the permissive method of child-rearing surfaced in the '40s, blossomed in the '50s and gained total respectability in the '60s. Psychiatrists and psychologists told us that if we spoke softly to our children; held, rocked and cuddled them; let them stop soiling their diapers and panties when they decided it was time to stop; allowed them to get the anger out of their systems, being careful never to say, "No, you can't do that" unless they started to burn down the house, they would develop healthy egos and grow up to be well-adjusted young men and women, self-assured, highly motivated and a joy to us.

We beat down our natural instincts, slavishly adhered to the teachings of these "experts" and developed dark circles and high blood pressure while our kids talked back to us, spit on us, hit us, broke their toys and threw themselves in the aisles of supermarkets (or department stores) until they got their way. These same kids turned out to be selfish, spoiled, hostile, disrespectful, lazy, and unmotivated. They had no respect for us, their teachers, or the law.

To add insult to injury, some psychiatrists charged up to $100 an hour to tell us, "There are no bad children...only bad parents."

The sad truth of the matter is that for too many years parents have been bamboozled by "experts," and have sopped up half-baked theories in "how-to" books instead of using the brains God gave them and reacting to their natural instincts when their kids pushed them too far in an attempt to test limits.

I'll never forget a letter I received from a 19-year-old just three years ago. She had no friends and couldn't hold a job because she was always shooting her mouth off, telling acquaintances, colleagues and bosses exactly what she thought of them. "I was brought up that way..." she declared. "I was allowed to say anything to anybody. My parents raised me that way and now I am all messed up and it's their fault. Any suggestions, Ann?"

I replied, "Yes...accept responsibility and quit blaming your parents for your mean mouth and foul moods. If you don't like the way you are—go to work on yourself and become something different. Enough of this 'You damaged me. Now take care of me' nonsense. It's a cop-out. Guilt laid on parents by you kids is so thick you can cut it with a knife—and all it does is perpetuate financial and emotional dependence and create a climate of hostility and ultimate failure."

So what can parents do with kids who have them backed against the wall? They can make a 180-degree turn and go the TOUGHLOVE route. Heaven knows reasoning, pleading, crying, threatening, and bribing hasn't worked. It's time to try something else, and I believe self-help groups like TOUGHLOVE are the most effective approach to problemsolving.

People who have shared the same problems and triumphed over them give one another tremendous strength. They say, "I did it; you can do it too. I'll help show you how."

Parents today encounter the following problems all too often. You are confused when your teenager comes home in varying states of intoxication or completely stoned—yet denies he's had alcohol or dope even though you've found drug paraphernalia in his room. You're heartsick and don't know what to do because your child is failing in school. Your 15-year-old takes things that belong to others. Your sophomore student lives in a filthy room and refuses to do any chores in the house. Your star-athlete son gets into trouble with the law. Your daughter stays out past curfew.

So mothers and fathers ask themselves why they're such rotten parents and say, "I'd like to kill that kid for putting us through this"...or, "A lot of our friends have the same trouble, they just don't talk about it." Or, "It's all our fault, so now we have to take care of them."

Bullfeathers!!!!!!!!!

You need TOUGHLOVE if you feel helpless and unable to cope with your teenagers' behavior or if you feel victimized by them, disappointed in yourself as a parent, guilty because you think you have done a rotten job and are frightened by the potential for violence in yourself and your children. These feelings are experienced by the affluent, the disadvantaged, middle income families, the uneducated, intellectual, single, divorced, married, permissive, repressive, black and white. Anybody.

Remember, you have the right to a night's sleep without worrying where your kid is—or being awakened by a phone call from the police or a hospital or a drunk teenager who's stranded somewhere. It's time you started taking care of yourself and letting your teenager be responsible for his or her actions. That's where the concepts of TOUGHLOVE come in.

You must find the courage to withdraw your money, influence, affection, anger, guilt and pleas that he or she learn to shape up. You must begin to make real demands entailing severe consequences. You must make it clear that you will not live in a house with people who mistreat you and do not respect the rules you have laid down. You do not need your teenager's approval. You're the boss. The sooner your youngster understands this, the better.

Of course, after years of accepting blame and guilt laid on by some psychiatrists, it's not easy to make this turn-about alone. You'll need help. Telephone the parents of your kids' friends. Tell them, "I'm worried about my children's behavior. Will you come to a meeting at my house tonight?" They'll probably say, "Thank heaven you called. I have been worried sick about mine too."

Call your neighbors even if they don't have children. You'll need allies in this battle and they can help. Call an understanding clergyman and sympathetic schoolteachers. Call those you know who work with delinquent children. They know the ropes.

Once you start a support group, other parents will want to join. Your local school may become interested. They're just as eager as you are to learn how to deal with difficult kids. Never in the history of our country has there been so much trouble disciplining children. Last year there were over 70,000 assaults on teachers in our public schools. When principals and teachers learn that parents are banding together to demand that their kids be respectful, law-abiding citizens, they'll want to be part of this effort.

Of course, it's unrealistic to expect unruly, anti-social children to change overnight. Some will become extremely hostile and resentful when they discover they are no longer in control. This is where the support of friends and neighbors comes in.

When Johnny does not come home at midnight, which was the curfew you laid down, lock the door and bolt it. Tack a note on the outside saying, "It's past midnight. You are not welcome here. Go to the Pattersons or the Smiths or some other neighbors."

Arrange with these people to take your kid when he breaks the house rules. Agree to take their kids when they do the same. Often teenagers will talk more easily with their friends' parents than with their own. This can be an excellent beginning. Then negotiate with the Pattersons or Smiths about the terms under which Johnny will be allowed to return home.

Not all kids are in trouble. We see many children who are law-abiding, generous, kind and a pleasure to have around. They're not spaced out on drugs; they're not running away from home and they're not driving their parents crazy. Chances are that these children were not raised by books. They were raised according to clearly defined guidelines. If they went beyond these guidelines, the consequences were sure and swift.

If you have a kid in trouble whom you've always catered to, don't feel guilty. Most of the child-rearing teachings of the past two years encouraged parents to treat children as equals and let them learn by doing their own thing.

Remember, too, as I said earlier—peer pressure means more to most children than what their parents say. There are countless factors over which parents have no control.

The economics of the country, for example, the postWorld War II money boom, with TV showing us all those wonderful things we simply couldn't live without...all have created a wildly acquisitive society.

And let's not forget Vietnam—the biggest mistake this country ever made. The richly deserved disgrace of losing to a small country 10,000 miles away not only infuriated a whole generation of young people, but made them anti-American and provided them with an excuse to look like bums. It also helped them get heavily involved with drugs.

But that belongs to history and now we must look to the future. We must get back to the basics and love our children enough to stop protecting them against their destructive, self-defeating behavior. Because in the end, if we allow them to destroy themselves, they will destroy us, too.[6]

TEN

QUESTIONS & ANSWERS

OUR DISCUSSION TO this point has dealt with some heavy and troublesome issues. Other topics have been complex and difficult to explain. To help gather up the loose ends and clarify the areas we've touched superficially, we will devote this chapter to a question-and-answer format. We will hopscotch through the preceding discussions to anticipate the questions that would have been asked if I were talking directly to parents instead of writing to them.

Let's proceed, now, with the first question, which relates to the Scripture misunderstood by Ann Landers.

Q. You have said that the children of godly parents sometimes go into severe rebellion and never return to the faith they were taught. I have seen that happen to some wonderful families that loved the Lord and were committed to the church. Still, it appears contradictory to Scripture. How do you interpret Proverbs 22:6, which says, "Train up a child in the way he should go, and when he is old, he will not depart from it"? Doesn't that verse mean, as it implies, that the children of wise and dedicated Christian parents will never be lost? Doesn't it promise that all wayward offspring will return, sooner or later, to the fold?

A. I wish Solomon's message to us could be interpreted that confidently. I know the common understanding of the passage is to accept it as a divine guarantee, but it was not expressed in that context. Psychiatrist John White, writing in his excellent book, *Parents in Pain*, has helped me understand that the Proverbs were never intended to be absolute *promises* from God. Instead, they are *probabilities* of things which are likely to occur. Solomon, who wrote the Proverbs, was the wisest man on the earth at that time. His purpose was to convey his divinely inspired observations on the way human nature and God's universe work. A given set of circumstances can be expected to produce certain consequences. Several of these observations, including Proverbs 22:6, have been lifted out of that context and made to stand alone as promises from God. If we insist on that interpretation, then we must explain why so many other Proverbs do not inevitably prove accurate. For example:

> *Lazy hands make a man poor, but diligent hands bring wealth* (10:4). (Have you ever met a diligent...but poor...Christian? I have.)
>
> *The blessing of the* LORD *brings wealth, and he adds no trouble to it* (10:22).
>
> *The fear of the* LORD *adds length to life, but the years of the wicked are cut short* (10:27). (I have watched some beautiful children die with a Christian testimony on their lips.)
>
> *No harm befalls the righteous, but the wicked have their fill of trouble* (12:21).
>
> *Plans fail for lack of counsel, but with many advisers they succeed* (15:22).
>
> *Gray hair is a crown of splendor; it is attained by a righteous life* (16:31).
>
> *The lot is cast into the lap, but its every decision is from the* LORD (16:33).
>
> *A tyrannical ruler lacks judgment, but he who hates ill-gotten gain will enjoy a long life* (28:16).

We can all think of exceptions to the statements above. To repeat, they appear to represent likelihoods rather than absolutes with God's personal guarantee attached. This interpretation of Proverbs is somewhat controversial among laymen, but less so among biblical scholars. For example, the *Bible Knowledge Commentary*, prepared by the faculty of the Dallas Theological Seminary, accepts the understanding I have suggested. This commentary is recognized for its intense commitment to the literal interpretation of God's Word, yet this is what the theologians wrote:

Some parents, however, have sought to follow this directive but without this result. Their children have strayed from the godly training the parents gave them. This illustrates the nature of a "proverb." A proverb is a literary device whereby a general truth is brought to bear on a specific situation. Many of the proverbs are not absolute guarantees for they express truths that are necessarily conditioned by prevailing circumstances. For example, verses 3–4, 9, 11, 16, and 29 do not express promises that are always binding. Though the proverbs are generally and usually true, occasional exceptions may be noted. This may be because of the self-will or deliberate disobedience of an individual who chooses to go his own way—the way of folly instead of the way of wisdom. For that he is held responsible. It is generally true, however, that most children who are brought up in Christian homes, under the influence of godly parents who teach and live God's standards, follow that training.[1]

Obviously, the humanistic concept of determinism has found its way even into the interpretation of Scripture. Those who believe Proverbs 22:6 offers a guarantee of salvation for the next generation have assumed, in essence, that a child can be programmed so thoroughly as to *determine* his course. The assignment for them is to bring him up "in the way that he should go." But think about that for a moment. Didn't the great Creator handle Adam and Eve with infinite wisdom and love? He made no mistakes in "fathering" them. They were also harbored in a perfect environment with none of the pressures we face. They had no in-law problems, no monetary needs, no frustrating employers, no television, no pornography, no alcohol or drugs, no peer pressure, and no sorrow. They had *no excuses!* Nevertheless, they ignored the explicit warning from God and stumbled into sin. If it were ever possible to avoid the ensnarement of evil, it would have occurred in that sinless world. But it didn't. God in His love gave Adam and Eve a choice between good and evil and they abused it. Will He now withhold that same freedom from your children? No. Ultimately, they will decide for themselves. That time of decision is a breathtaking moment for parents, when everything they have taught appears to be on the line. But it must come for us all.

Q. You obviously feel very strongly about this misinterpretation of Scripture. What are its implications?

A. I am most concerned for dedicated and sincere Christian parents whose grown sons and daughters have rebelled against God and their own families. These mothers and fathers did the best they could to raise their children properly, but they lost them anyway. That situation produces enormous guilt in itself, quite apart from scriptural understandings. Then they read in the book of Proverbs that God has promised—absolutely guaranteed—the spiritual welfare of children whose parents trained them up properly. What are they to conclude, then, in light of continued rebellion and sin in the next generation? The message is inescapable! It must be their fault. They have damned their own kids by failing to keep their half of the bargain. They have sent their beloved children to hell by their parenting failures. This thought is so terrible for a sensitive believer that it could actually undermine his sanity.

I simply do not believe God intended for the *total* responsibility for sin in the next generation to fall on the backs of vulnerable parents. When we look at the entire Bible, we find no support for that extreme position. Cain's murder of Abel was not blamed on his parents. Joseph was a godly man and his brothers were rascals, yet their father and mother (Jacob and Rachel) were not held accountable for the differences between them. The saintly Samuel raised rebellious children, yet he was not charged with their sin. And in the New Testament, the father of the Prodigal Son was never accused of raising his adventuresome son improperly. The boy was apparently old enough to make his own headstrong decision, and his father did not stand in his way. This good man never repented of any wrongdoing— nor did he need to.

It is not my desire to let parents off the hook when they have been slovenly or uncommitted during their child-rearing years. There is at least one biblical example of God's wrath falling on a father who failed to discipline and train his sons. That incident is described in 1 Samuel 2:22–36, where Eli, the priest, permitted his sons to desecrate the temple. All three were sentenced to death by the Lord. Obviously, He takes our parenting tasks seriously and expects us to do likewise. But He does not intend for us to grovel in guilt for circumstances beyond our control!

Q. Referring to the point you made about young married couples who overcommit themselves, you warned against trying to do too much too soon. I don't want to make that mistake, yet I do hope to get married and go on to graduate school. Would you be more specific about the advice you would offer to people like me?

A. It seems only yesterday that I was faced with some similar questions in my own life. I was a third-year student in college, hoping to earn a Ph.D., get married, have children, buy a home, and earn a living in the next few years. Because I was young, I thought there were no limits to what I could accomplish. But then my aunt, Lela London, heard a Christian psychologist named Clyde Narramore speak one day, and he offered to spend an afternoon with any promising student who wanted to enter the field of mental health. "We need Christians in this work," he said, "and I'll help those who are interested." I called Dr. Narramore a few days later and he graciously agreed to see me. This busy man gave me two hours of his time in the living room of his home. I still remember his words thirty years later. Among other things, he warned me not to get married too quickly if I wanted to get through school and become a practicing psychologist.

He said, "A baby will come along before you know it and you will find yourself under heavy financial pressure. That will make you want to quit. You'll sit up nights caring for a sick child and then spend maybe $300 in routine medical bills. Your wife will be frustrated and you will be tempted to abandon your dreams. Don't put yourself in that straitjacket."

I accepted Dr. Narramore's advice and waited until I was twenty-four years old and had almost finished my master's degree before Shirley and I were married. We then delayed our first child for five more years until I had completed the coursework for my doctorate. It was a wise choice, although today I am listed in the *Guinness Book of Records* as "Oldest Living Father of a Teenager." Life is a trade-off, as they say.

Though Dr. Narramore did not say so, I assure you that marital problems are almost inevitable when couples overcommit themselves during the early years. The bonding that should occur in the first decade requires time together—time that cannot be given if it is absorbed elsewhere. My advice to you is to hold onto your dreams, but take a little longer to fulfill them. Success will wait, but a happy family will not. To achieve the former and lose the latter would be an empty victory, at best.

Let me toss in this afterthought. I read an article in the *Los Angeles*

Times about a man named J. R. Buffington. His goal in life was to produce lemons of record-breaking size from the tree in his backyard. He came up with a formula to do just that. He fertilized the tree with ashes from the fireplace, some rabbit-goat manure, a few rusty nails, and plenty of water. That spring, the scrawny little tree gave birth to two gigantic lemons, one weighing over five pounds. But every other lemon on the tree was shriveled and misshapen. Mr. Buffington is still working on his formula.

Isn't that the way it is in life? Great investments in a particular endeavor tend to rob others of their potential. I'd rather have a tree covered with juicy lemons than a record-breaking but freakish crop, wouldn't you? *Balance* is the word. It is the key to successful living...and parenting.

Keep trying, Mr. Buffington. Have you thought about using licorice?

Q. My three-year-old son can be counted on to behave like a brat whenever we are in the mall or in a restaurant. He seems to know I will not punish him there in front of other people. How should I handle this tactic?

A. They tell me that a raccoon can usually kill a dog if he gets him in a lake or river. He will simply pull the hound underwater until he drowns. Most other animals would also prefer to do battle on the turf of their own choosing. It works that way with young children too. If they're going to pick a fight with Mom or Dad, they'd rather stage it in a public place, such as a supermarket or in the church foyer. They are smart enough to know that they are "safer" in front of other people. They will grab candy or speak in disrespectful ways which would never be attempted at home. Again, the most successful military generals are those who surprise the enemy in a terrain advantageous to their troops. Public facilities represent the "high ground" for a rambunctious preschooler.

You may be one of the parents who has fallen into this trap. Rather than having to discipline in public, you have inadvertently created "sanctuaries" where the old rules are not enforced. It is a certainty that your strong-willed son or daughter will behave offensively and disrespectfully in those neutral zones. There is something within the child that almost forces him to "test the limits" in situations where the resolve of adults is in question. Therefore, I recommend that you issue a stern warning *before* you enter those public arenas, making it clear that the same rules will apply. Then if he misbehaves, simply take him back to the car or around the corner and do what you would have done at home. His public behavior will improve dramatically.

Q. I could use some advice about a minor problem we're having. Tim, my six-year-old, greatly loves to use silly names whenever he speaks to my husband and me. For example, this past week it's been "you big hot dog." Nearly every time he sees me now he says, "Hi, hot dog." Before that it was "dummy," then "moose" (after he studied M for moose in school).

I know it's silly and it's not a huge problem, but it gets so annoying after such a long time. He's been doing this for a year now. How can we get him to talk to us with more respect, calling us Mom or Dad, instead of hot dog and moose?

Thank you for any advice you can offer.

A. What we have here is a rather classic power game, much like those we have discussed before. And contrary to what you said, it is not so insignificant. Under other circumstances, it would be a minor matter for a child to call his parents a playful name. That is not the point here. Rather, strong-willed Tim is continuing to do something that he knows is irritating to you and your husband, yet you are unable to stop him. That is the issue. He has been using humor as a tactic of defiance for a full year. It is time for you to sit down and have a quiet little talk with young Timothy. Tell him that he is being disrespectful and that the next time he calls either you or his father a name of any kind, he will be punished. You must then be prepared to deliver on the promise, because he will continue to challenge you until it ceases to be fun. That's the way he is made. If that response never comes, his insults will probably become more pronounced, ending in adolescent nightmares. Appeasement for a strong-willed child is an invitation to warfare.

Never forget this fact: The classic strong-willed child craves power from his toddler years and even earlier. Since Mom is the nearest adult who is holding the reins, he will hack away at her until she lets him drive his own buggy. I remember a mother telling me of a confrontation with her tough-minded four-year-old daughter. The child was demanding her own way and the mother was struggling to hold her own.

"Jenny," said the mother, "you are just going to have to do what I tell you to do. I am your boss. The Lord has given me the responsibility for leading you, and that's what I intend to do!"

Jenny thought that over for a minute and then asked, "How long does it have to be that way?"

Doesn't that illustrate the point beautifully? Already at four years of age, this child was anticipating a day of *freedom* when no one could tell her what to do. There was something deep within her spirit that longed for control. Watch for the same phenomenon in your child. If he's a toughie, it will show up soon.

Q. You have explained the dangers of power to both children and adults. But there's no great virtue in being completely powerless either, is there? What does it do to a person to be without influence or credibility in today's society?

A. You've asked an insightful question. There is reason to be concerned about those who have been stripped of all social power in this day. The elderly, the handicapped, the poverty-stricken, the homeless, the sick, and the dying are often among that number.

My father was given a glimpse of their plight toward the end of his life. I'll never forget visiting him in the hospital for the final time after his massive heart attack. I flew in from Cincinnati that night and rushed to his bedside. I sat with him through the late hours and talked about his circumstances. He was in a contemplative mood. Dad told me that the medical staff had given him good care, but they somehow managed to convey disrespect for him. He was not angry and he didn't ask me to intercede on his behalf. That was not his point. He had simply made an observation that troubled him. He said the young doctors and nurses responded to him as though he were an old man. He was only sixty-six years of age then and was still engaged full time as a college professor. He had been a very energetic man until the pruning knife of time did its dastardly work. Now, life was rapidly winding down and he seemed to know it.

Then he said, "I have seen during these past few days what it is like to experience the absolute powerlessness of old age—where you are totally dependent on someone who does not value you as a person. I understand for the first time the disrespect that accompanies advanced age in this country. It is a frightening thing."

Millions of older people know precisely what my dad was trying to express. Being powerless is difficult even when accompanied by love and acceptance. Dependency is terrifying when surrounded by disrespect. I believe this is why Jesus came to help the down-and-outers—the wounded, lame, and sick. He touched the leper who had not been approached in years. And He told His disciples, "It is not the healthy who need a doctor, but the sick" (Mark 2:17). He admonished us all, "I tell you the truth, whatever you did for one of the least of these brothers of mine, you did for me" (Matthew 25:40). What incredible compassion He had for those who hurt—for the powerless people of the world. I wish I could point them all to Him. He is a friend who will stick closer than a brother.

Q. The greatest power struggle in our home is schoolwork, which you mentioned, and especially homework. Our fifth grader simply will not do it! When we force him to study, he sits and stares, doodles, gets up for water, and just kills time. Furthermore, we never know for sure what his assignments are. What would you recommend?

A. Let me offer a short discourse on school achievement, based on years of interaction with parents. I served as a teacher and I've worked as a high school counselor. Believe me, I know the agitation that mothers and fathers feel when their kids will not use the abilities God has given them. This is the situation with which they are faced: The kind of self-discipline necessary to succeed in school appears to be distributed among children on a continuum from one extreme to the other. Students at the positive end of the scale (Type I, I'll call them) are by nature rather organized individuals who care about details. They take the educational process very seriously and assume full responsibility for assignments given. They also worry about grades, or at least, they recognize their importance. To do poorly on a test would depress them for several days. They also like the challenge offered in the classroom. Parents of these children do not have to monitor their progress to keep them working. It is their way of life...and it is consistent with their temperament.

At the other end of the continuum are the boys and girls who do not fit in well with the structure of the classroom (Type II). If their Type I siblings emerge from school cum laude, these kids graduate "Thank You, Laude!" They are sloppy, disorganized, and flighty. They have a natural aversion to work and love to play. They can't wait for success and they hurry on without it. Like bacteria that gradually become immune to antibiotics, the classic underachievers become impervious to adult pressure. They withstand a storm of parental protest every few weeks and then, when no one is looking, they slip back into apathy. They don't even hear the assignments being given in school and seem not to be embarrassed when they fail to complete them. And, you can be sure, they drive their parents to distraction.

There are several important understandings about Type I and II kids that may help parents deal with their differences. First, these characteristics are not highly correlated with intelligence. By that I mean there are bright children who are at the flighty end of the scale, and there are slow-learning individuals who are highly motivated. The primary difference between them is a matter of temperament and maturity, rather than IQ.

Second, Type II kids are not inferior to Type I. Yes, it would be wonderful if every student used the talent he possessed to best advantage. But each child is a unique individual. All don't have to fit the same mold. I know education is important today, and we want our children to go as far as they can, academically. But let's keep our goals in proper perspective. It is possible that the low achiever will outperform the academic superstar in the long run. There are countless examples of that occurring in the real world (Einstein, Edison, Roosevelt). Don't write off that disorganized, apparently lazy kid as a lifelong loser. He may surprise you.

Third, you will *never* turn a Type II youngster into a Type I scholar by nagging, pushing, threatening, and punishing. It isn't in him. If you try to squeeze him into something he's not, you will only produce aggravation for yourself and anger from the child. That effort can fill a house with conflict. I have concluded that it is simply not worth the price it extracts.

On the other hand, I certainly do not recommend that children be allowed to float through life, avoiding responsibility and wasting their opportunities. My approach to the underachiever can be summarized in these suggestions: (1) He lacks the discipline to structure his life. Help him generate it. Systematize his study hours. Look over his homework to see that it is neat and complete, et cetera. (2) Maintain as close contact with the school as possible. The more you and your child's teacher communicate, the better. Only then can you provide the needed structure. (3) Avoid anger in the relationship. It does not help. Those parents who become most frustrated and irritated usually believe their child's irresponsibility is a deliberate thing. Usually it is not. Approach the problem as one of temperament rather than acts of defiance. (4) Having done what you can to help, accept what comes in return. Go with the flow and begin looking for other areas of success for your child. Let me say it once more: Not every individual can be squeezed into the same mold. There is room in this world for the creative "souls" who long to breathe free. I'll bet some of you as parents approached life from the same direction.

Q. How do you feel about homework being given by schools? Do you think it is a good idea? If so, how much and how often?
A. Having written several books on discipline and being on the record as an advocate of parental authority, my answer may surprise you: I believe homework can be destructive and counterproductive if it is not handled very carefully. I am especially concerned about large quantities of homework that are given routinely during elementary school. Little kids are asked to sit for six or more hours a day doing formal classwork. Then they take that tiring bus ride home and guess what? They're placed at a desk and told to do more assignments. For a wiry, hyperactive child or even for a fun-loving youngster, that is asking too much. Learning for them becomes an enormous bore, instead of the exciting panorama that it should be.

I remember a mother coming to see me because her son was struggling in school. "He has about five hours of homework per night," she said. "How can I make him *want* to do it?"

"Are you kidding?" I told his mother. "*I* wouldn't do that much homework!"

Upon investigation, I found that the private school which he attended vigorously denied giving him that many assignments. Or rather, they didn't give the *other* students that much work. They did expect the slower boys and girls to complete the assignments they didn't get done in the classroom each day plus finish the homework. For the plodders like this youngster, that meant up to five hours of work nightly. There was no escape from books throughout their entire day. What a mistake!

Excessive homework during the elementary school years also has the potential of interfering with family life. In our home, we were trying to do many things with the limited time we had together. I wanted our kids to participate in church activities, have some family time, and still be able to kick back and waste an hour or two. Children need opportunities for unstructured play—swinging on the swings and throwing rocks and playing with basketballs. Yet by the time that homework was done, darkness had fallen and dinnertime had arrived. Then baths were taken and off they went to bed. Something didn't feel right about that kind of pace. That's why I negotiated with our children's teachers, agreeing that they would complete no more than one hour per night of supervised homework. It was enough!

Homework also generates a considerable amount of stress for parents. Their kids either won't do the assignments or they get tired and whine about it. Tensions build and angry words fly. I'm also convinced that child abuse occurs right at that point for some children. When Shirley was teaching the second grade, one little girl came to school with both eyes black and swollen. She said her father had beaten her because she couldn't learn her spelling words. That is illegal now, but it wasn't then. The poor youngster will remember those beatings for a lifetime and will always think of herself as "stupid."

Then there are the parents who do the assignments *for* their kids just to get them over the hump. Have you ever been guilty of that illegality? Shame on you! More specifically, have you ever worked for two weeks on a fifth-grade geography project for your nonacademic eleven-year-old—and then learned later that you got a C on it?! That's the ultimate humiliation.

In short, I believe homework in elementary school should be extremely limited. It is appropriate for learning multiplication tables, spelling words, and test review. It is also helpful in training kids to remember assignments, bring books home, and complete them as required. But to load them down night after night with monotonous bookwork is to invite educational burnout.

In junior high classes, perhaps an hour of homework per night should be the maximum. In high school, those students who are preparing for college may handle more work. Even then, however, the load should be reasonable. Education is a vitally important part of our children's lives, but it is only *one* part. Balance between these competing objectives is the key word.

Q. May I go back to the story of the undisciplined toddler on the airplane? You described her as being unruly and unwilling to be buckled in her seat. How would you have handled that situation?
A. Well, I think I mentioned that a few sharp slaps on the legs would have

curtailed her temper tantrum and given control back to the mother. On the other hand, the crisis need never have developed. The mother should have anticipated that situation and brought some sugarless mints and a few interesting toys or playthings. That would have been so easy to do. Instead, mom and daughter were like two freight trains coming together on the same track. A violent collision was inevitable. I just happened to be there to witness the crash.

Q. You've made a big deal over the issue of newborns and whether or not they come into the world with complex temperaments or as "blank slates." When all is said and done, what difference does it make? Children are children, and we take them as we find them. Why does it matter whether they began with "something" or with "nothing"?

A. It is easy to see how you could assume that this issue is of academic interest only, with no practical application. Nothing could be further from the truth. These contrasting ways of perceiving children have far-reaching implications and will influence parenting techniques throughout the developmental years. Let me explain.

The "blank slate" theory holds that children are born neutral but with a penchant for "good." Their natural tendency is to love, give, work, cooperate, and learn. The failure of the individual to behave in these positive ways does not result from any internal flaw, but rather from a corrupt and misguided society. Bad *experiences* are responsible for bad behavior. Therefore, it is the task of parents to provide a loving environment and then stay out of the way. Natural goodness will flow from it. As long as major mistakes are avoided, there will be no negative stimuli to distort or warp the developing individual. Rebellion and disobedience do not emanate from love. Thus, parental discipline is of lesser significance because there is no inner nature to be confronted.

This is the humanistic perspective on childish nature. Millions of Americans and Canadians, the majority no doubt, believe it to be true. Most psychologists have also accepted and taught it throughout the twentieth century. There is only one thing wrong with the concept: It is entirely inaccurate.

It is impossible to understand human nature without consulting the "Owners Manual." Only the Creator of children can tell us how He made them, and He has done that in Scripture. It teaches that we are born in sin, having inherited a disobedient nature from Adam. King David said, "In sin did my mother *conceive* me" (Psalm 51:5, KJV), meaning that this tendency to do wrong was transmitted genetically. It has infected every person who ever lived. "For *all* have sinned, and come short of the glory of God" (Romans 3:23, KJV). Therefore, with or without bad experiences, a child is naturally inclined toward rebellion, selfishness, dishonesty, aggression, exploitation, and greed. He does not have to be taught these behaviors. They are inevitable expressions of his humanness.

Although this perspective on man is mocked in the secular world today, abundant evidence attests to its accuracy. How else do we explain the pugnacious and perverse nature of every society on earth? Bloody warfare has been the centerpiece of world history for more than 5,000 years. People of every race and creed around the globe have tried to rape, plunder, burn, blast, and kill each other century after century. Peace was merely a momentary pause when they stopped to reload! Plato said more than 2,350 years ago, "Only dead men have seen an end to war." He was right, at least until the Prince of Peace comes.

Furthermore, in the midst of these warring nations we find a depressing incidence of murder, drug abuse, child molestation, prostitution, adultery, homosexuality, and dishonesty. How do we explain this pervasive evil in a world of people who are naturally inclined toward good? Have they really drifted into these antisocial behaviors despite their inborn tendencies? If so, surely *one* society in all the world has been able to preserve the goodness with which children are born. Where is it? Does such a place exist? No, even though some societies are more moral than others, none reflects the harmony which might be expected from the "blank slate" theorists. Why not? Because the premise is wrong.

What, then, does this biblical understanding mean for parents? Are they to look on their babies as guilty before they have done wrong? Of course not. Children are not responsible for their sins until they reach an age of accountability—and that time frame is known best to God. On the other hand, parents would be wise to anticipate and deal with rebellious behavior when it occurs. And it *will* occur, probably by the eighteenth month or before. Anyone who has watched a toddler throw a violent temper tantrum when he doesn't get his way must be hard-pressed to explain how that particular "blank slate" got so mixed up! Did his mother or father model the tantrum for him, falling on the floor, slobbering, kicking, crying, and screaming? I would hope not. Either way, the kid needs no demonstration. Rebellion comes naturally to him.

Parents can, and must, train, shape, mold, correct, guide, punish, reward, instruct, warn, teach, and love their kids during the formative years. Their purpose is to control that inner nature and keep it from tyrannizing the entire family. Ultimately, however, only Jesus Christ can cleanse it and make it "wholly acceptable" to the Master.

You know what? I believe I've preached a sermon. And I'm not even a minister.

Q. Generally speaking, what kind of discipline do you use with a teenager who is habitually miserable to live with?
A. In addition to what I've already written on this subject, let me offer this thought: The general rule is to use action—not anger—to reach an understanding. Anytime you can get teenagers to do what is necessary without becoming furious at them, you are ahead of the game. Let me provide a few examples of how this might be accomplished.

(1) In Russia, I'm told that teenagers who are convicted of using drugs are denied driver's licenses for years. It is a very effective approach.

(2) When my daughter was a teenager, she used to slip into my bathroom and steal my razor, my shaving cream, my toothpaste, or my comb. Of course, she never brought them back. Then after she had gone to school, I would discover the utensils missing. There I was with wet hair or "fuzzy" teeth, trying to locate the confiscated item in *her* bathroom. It was no big deal, but it was irritating at the time. Can you identify?

I asked Danae a dozen times not to do this, but to no avail. Thus, the phantom struck without warning one cold morning. I hid everything she needed to put on her "face," and then left for the office. My wife told me she had never heard such wails and moans as were uttered that day. Our daughter plunged desperately through bathroom drawers looking for her toothbrush, comb, and hair dryer. The problem has never resurfaced.

(3) A family living in a house with a small hot-water tank was continually frustrated by their teenager's endless showers. Screaming at him did no good. Once he was locked behind the bathroom door, he stayed in the steamy stall until the last drop of warm water had been drained. Solution? In midstream, Dad stopped the flow of hot water by turning a

valve at the tank. Cold water suddenly poured from the nozzle. Junior popped out of the shower in seconds.

(4) A single mother couldn't get her daughter out of bed in the morning until she announced a new policy: The hot water would be shut off promptly at 6:30 A.M. The girl could either get up on time or bathe in ice water. Another mother had trouble getting her eight-year-old out of bed each morning. She then began pouring bowls of frozen marbles under the covers with him each morning. He arose quite quickly.

(5) Instead of standing in the parking lot and screaming at students who drive too fast, school officials now put huge bumps in the road that jar the teeth of those who ignore them. It does the job quite nicely.

(6) You as the parent have the car that a teenager needs, the money that he covets, and the authority to grant or withhold privileges. If push comes to shove, these chips can be exchanged for commitments to live responsibly, share the workload at home, and stay off little brother's back. This bargaining process works for younger kids too. I like the "one to one" trade-off for television viewing time. It permits a child to watch one minute of television for every minute spent reading. The possibilities are endless.

Q. Would you ever, under any circumstances, have permitted a son or daughter to bring a roomie of the opposite sex into your home to live?
A. No. It would have been dishonoring to God and a violation of the moral principles on which Shirley and I have staked our lives. I was willing to bend for my kids, but never that far.

Q. Are there times when good, loving parents don't like their own kids very much?
A. Yes, just as there are times in a good marriage when husbands and wives don't like each other for a while. What you should do in both situations is hang tough. Look for ways to make the relationship better, but never give up your commitment to one another. That is especially true during the teen years, when the person we see will be *very* different in a few years. Wait patiently for him to grow up. You'll be glad you did.

NOTE: The following item was originally published in my earlier book, *Straight Talk to Men*, but it is also being included here because of its relevancy to the topic. Someone needs to read this message! Is it you?

Q. My wife and I are new Christians, and we now realize that we raised our kids by the wrong principles. They're grown now, but we continue to worry about the past and we feel great regret for our failures as parents. Is there anything we can do at this late date?

A. Let me deal, first, with the awful guilt you are obviously carrying. There's hardly a parent alive who does not have some regrets and painful memories of failures as a mother or a father. Children are infinitely complex as I've indicated, and we cannot be perfect parents any more than we can be perfect human beings. The pressures of living are stressful and we get tired and irritated; we are influenced by our physical bodies and our emotions, which sometimes prevent us from saying the right things and being the model we should be. We don't always handle our children as unemotionally as we wish we had, and it's very common to look back a year or two later and see how wrong we were in the way we approached a problem.

All of us experience these failures! That's why each of us should get alone with the Creator of parents and children and say: "Lord, You know my inadequacies. You know my weaknesses, not only in parenting, but in every area of my life. I did the best I could, but it wasn't good enough. As You broke the fishes and the loaves to feed the five thousand, now take my meager effort and use it to bless my family. Make up for the things I did wrong. Satisfy the needs that I have not satisfied. Wrap Your great arms around my children, and draw them close to You. And be there when they stand at the great crossroads between right and wrong. All I can give is my best, and I've done that. Therefore, I submit to You my children and myself and the job I did as a parent. The outcome now belongs to You."

I know God will honor that prayer, even for parents whose job is finished. The Lord does not want you to suffer from guilt over events you can no longer influence. The past is the past. Let it die, never to be resurrected. Give the situation to God, once and for all time. I think you'll be surprised to learn that you're no longer alone! "Forgetting what is behind and straining toward what is ahead, I press on toward the goal to win the prize for which God has called me heavenward in Christ Jesus" (Philippians 3:13–14).

For the benefit of the discouraged mother of a strong-willed toddler who feels like she's about to lose her mind, I am herewith providing a portion of two letters sent to me a few years ago. The first was written by an exasperated mother who felt she did not get the help she needed in my book *The Strong-Willed Child*. The second letter came from the same woman, five years later. The first letter, written October 14, 1978:

Dear Dr. Dobson,

After purchasing your new book I must tell you I was disappointed. The beginning was encouraging, but then the rest was devoted to general child-rearing techniques. I thought the entire book was written about the strong-willed child. Are you sure you know what one is? Nearly every child is strong-willed, but not every child is strong-willed!

Our third (and last) daughter is strong-willed! She is twenty-one months old now, and there have been times when I thought she must be abnormal. If she had been my firstborn child there would have been no more in this family. She had colic day and night for six months, then we just quit calling it that. She was simply unhappy all the time. She began walking at eight months and she became a merciless bully with her sisters. She pulled hair, bit, hit, pinched, and pushed with all her might. She yanked out a handful of her sister's long black hair.

NOTE: This mother went on to describe the characteristics of her tyrannical daughter which I have heard thousands of times. She then closed, advising me to give greater emphasis to the importance of corporal punishment for this kind of youngster. I wrote her a cordial letter in reply and told her I understood her frustration. Five years later, she wrote to me again, as follows:

February 2, 1983

Dear Dr. Dobson,

This letter is long overdue, but, thank you! Thank you for a caring reply to what was probably not a very nice letter from a discouraged mom. Thank you for your positive remarks, the first I had had in a long time.

Perhaps you would be interested in an update on our Sally Ann. Back when I wrote to you, she was probably a perfect "10" when it came to strong-willedness. Difficult *hardly scratches the surface of descriptive words for her babyhood. As Christian parents, we tried every scriptural method we could find for dealing with her. I had decided she was abnormal. Something so innocent as offering her her morning juice (which she loved) in the wrong glass threw her into thirty minutes of tantrums—and this was before she could really talk!*

Family dinners were a nightmare. Before she turned two, Sally Ann would regularly brutalize her older sisters, ages four, eight, and twelve, even having the twelve-year-old in tears many times. A spanking from me did not deter her in the least. Finally, in prayer one day the Lord plainly showed me that her sisters must be allowed to retaliate, something I was strictly against (and still am!). However, in this case, all I can say is that it worked. I carefully and clearly told my four girls (little Sally Ann in my lap) what they were to do the next time they were attacked by their littlest sister: They were to give her a good smack on the top of her chubby little leg, next to her diaper. Sally got the point: Within two days the attacks ceased.

Disciplining our youngest was never easy, but with God's help, we persevered. When she had to be spanked, we could expect up to an hour of tantrums. It would have been so easy to give in and ignore the misbehavior, but I am convinced that, without it, our Sally would have become at best a holy terror, and at worst, mentally ill. Tell your listeners that discipline does pay off, when administered according to the Word of God.

Sally today is a precious six-year-old and a joy to her family. She is still rather strong-willed, but it is well within normal limits now! She is very bright and has a gentle, creative, and sympathetic nature unusual in one so young. I know the Lord has great plans for her. She has already asked Jesus into her life and knows how to call upon Him when she has a need (like fear from a nightmare, et cetera).

In conclusion, though I still don't think you went far enough in your book, loving discipline certainly is the key. With perseverance!

Thank you, and may God's continued blessing be upon you and your household and your ministry, through Jesus Christ our Lord.

In His love,
Mrs. W. W.

FINAL NOTE: Thank you, too, Mrs. W. It was a special treat to hear from you again. You're on the right track with Sally Ann. Discipline with love was God's idea. Oh, and by the way, this book was written for you. Did I get it said this time?

—*James Dobson*

ELEVEN

RELEASING YOUR GROWN CHILD

W E COME NOW to the final task assigned to mothers and fathers... that of releasing grown children and launching them into the world of adulthood. It is also one of the most difficult. Several years ago, we explored this topic by conducting another informal poll of the Focus on the Family radio listeners. I asked them to react to this question: "What are the greatest problems you face in dealing with your parents or in-laws, and how will you relate differently to your grown children than your parents have to you?" An avalanche of mail flooded my offices in the next few days, eventually totaling more than twenty-six hundred detailed replies.

We read every letter and catalogued the responses according to broad themes. As is customary in such inquiries, the results surprised our entire staff. We fully expected in-law complaints to represent the most common category of concerns. Instead, it ranked fifth in frequency, representing only 10 percent of the letters we received. The fourth most commonly mentioned problem, at 11 percent, related to sickness, dependency, senility, and other medical problems in the older generation. In third place, at 19 percent, was general concern for the spiritual welfare of un-Christian parents. The second most common reply, representing 21 percent, expressed irritation and frustration at parents who didn't care about their children or grandchildren. They never came to visit, wouldn't baby-sit, and seemed to follow a "me-first" philosophy.

That brings us to the top of the hit parade of problems between adults and their parents. May I have the envelope please? (Drum roll in background.) And the winner is, the inability or unwillingness of parents to release their grown children and permit them to live their own lives. An incredible 44 percent of the letters received made reference to this failure of older adults to let go. It was as though some of the writers had been waiting for years for that precise question to be asked. Here are a few of their comments:

1. "Mother felt my leaving home was an insult to her. She couldn't let go, couldn't realize I needed to become an independent person, couldn't understand that I no longer needed her physical help, although I did need her as a person. Quite unintentionally she retarded my growing up by thirty-five years."

2. "One of the greatest problems is to have my parents see me as an adult, not as a child who doesn't know the best way to do things. As a child, I played a specific role in my family. Now as an adult, I wish to change my role, but they will not allow it."

3. "Our parents never seemed able to grasp the reality of the fact that we had grown from dependent children, to capable, responsible adults. They did not recognize or appreciate our abilities, responsibilities, or contributions to the outside world."

4. "I am fifty-four years old but when I visit my mother I am still not allowed to do certain things such as peel carrots, etc., because I do not do them correctly. Our relationship is still child-parent. I am still regularly corrected, criticized, put down, and constantly reminded of what terrible things I did fifty years ago. Now we are not talking about major criminal acts, just normal childish disobedience during the preschool years. I was the youngest of five and the only daughter and I still hear, 'I would rather have raised another four boys than one daughter.' Pray for me, please. I need Jesus to help me forgive and forget."

We received literally hundreds of letters expressing this general concern. The writers wanted desperately to be free, to be granted adult status, and especially, to be respected by their parents. At the same time, they were saying to them, "I still love you. I still need you. I still want you as my friend. But I no longer need you as the authority in my life."

I remember going through a similar era in my own life. My parents handled me wisely in those years, and it was rare to have them stumble into common parental mistakes. However, we had been a very close-knit family, and it was difficult for my mother to shift gears when I graduated from high school. During that summer, I traveled fifteen hundred miles from home and entered a college in California. I will never forget the exhilarating feeling of freedom that swept over me that fall. It was not that I wanted to do anything evil or previously forbidden. It was simply that I felt accountable for my own life and did not have to explain my actions to my parents. It was like a fresh, cool breeze on a spring morning. Young adults who have not been properly trained for that moment sometimes go berserk in the absence of authority, but I did not. I did, however, quickly become addicted to that freedom and was not inclined to give it up.

The following December, my parents and I met for Christmas vacation at the home of some relatives. Suddenly, I found myself in conflict with my mom. She was responding as she had six months earlier when I was still in high school. By then, I had journeyed far down the path toward adulthood. She was asking me what time I would be coming in at night, and urging me to drive the car safely, and watching what I ate. No offense was intended, mind you. My mother had just failed to notice that I had changed and she needed to get with the new program, herself.

Finally, there was a brief flurry of words between us and I left the house in a huff. A friend picked me up and I talked about my feelings as we rode in the car. "Darn it, Bill!" I said. "I don't *need* a mother anymore!"

Then a wave of guilt swept over me, as though I had said, "I don't love my mother anymore." I meant no such thing. What I was feeling was the desire to be friends with my parents instead of accepting a line of authority from them. My wish was granted by my mom and dad very quickly thereafter.

Most parents in our society do not take the hint so easily. I'm convinced that mothers and fathers in North America are among the very best in the world. We care passionately about our kids and would do anything to meet their needs. But we are among the worst when it comes to letting go of our grown sons and daughters. In fact those two characteristics are linked. The same commitment that leads us to do so well when the children are small (dedication, love, concern, involvement), also causes us to hold on too tightly when they are growing up. I will admit to my own difficulties in this area. I understood the importance of turning loose before our kids were born. I wrote extensively on the subject when they were still young. I prepared a film series in which all the right principles were expressed. But when it came time to open my hand and let the birds fly, I struggled mightily!

Why? Well, fear played a role in my reluctance. We lived for many years in Los Angeles, where weird things are done by strange people every day of the year. For example, our daughter was held at gunpoint on the campus of the University of Southern California late one night. Her assailant admonished Danae not to move or make a noise. She figured her chances of survival were better by defying him right then than by cooperating. She fled. The man did not shoot at her, thank God. Who knows what he had in mind for her?

A few days later, my son was walking his bicycle across a busy road near our home when a man in a sports car came around the curve at high speed. Skid marks later showed he was traveling in excess of eighty miles per hour. Ryan saw that he was going to be hit, and he jumped over the handlebars and attempted to crawl to safety. The car was fishtailing wildly and careening toward our son. It came to a stop just inches from his head, and then the driver sped off without getting out. Perhaps he was on PCP or cocaine. Thousands of addicts live in Los Angeles, and innocent people are victimized by them every day.

Such near misses make me want to gather my children around me and never let them experience risk again. Of course, that is impossible and would be unwise even if they submitted to it. Life itself is a risk, and parents must let their kids face reasonable jeopardy on their own. Nevertheless, when Danae or Ryan leave in the car after a visit, I'm still tempted to say, "Be sure to keep the shiny side up and the rubber side down!"

What are *your* reasons for restricting the freedom of your grown or nearly grown children? In some cases, if we're honest, we need them too much to let them go. They have become an extension of ourselves, and our egos are inextricably linked to theirs. Therefore, we not only seek to hold them to us, but we manipulate them to maintain our control. As described in chapter 7, we use guilt, bribery, threats, intimidation, fear, and anger to restrict their freedom. And sadly, when we win at this game, we *and* our offspring are destined to lose.

Many of the letters we received in response to our poll were written by young adults who had not yet broken free. Some stories they told were almost hard to believe in a culture which legally emancipates its children at such a young age. Consider this excerpt from a young lady with very possessive parents:

> I'm twenty-three and the eldest of three children. My parents are still overprotective. They won't let go. I have a career and a very stable job, but they will not allow me to move out on my own. They still try to discipline me with a spanking using a belt and hold me to a 10:00 P.M. curfew. Even if it is a church activity, I must be home by 10:00 P.M. If it's out of town or impossible for me to be home by that time, I'm not allowed to go. I have high Christian moral standards and they trust me, but they are just overprotective.

Can you imagine these parents spanking this twenty-three-year-old woman for her minor infractions and disobediences? Though I do not know the girl or her parents, it would appear that they have a classic dependency problem occurring commonly with a very compliant child. No self-respecting strong-willed individual would tolerate such dominance and disrespect. A compliant girl might, while harboring deep resentment all the while.

In a sense, this twenty-three-year-old is equally responsible for her lack of freedom. She has permitted her parents to treat her like a child. First Corinthians 13:11 says, "When I was a child, I talked like a child, I thought like a child, I reasoned like a child. When I became a man, I put childish ways behind me." What could be more childish than for a woman in her twenties to yield to a physical thrashing for arriving home after 10:00 P.M.? Of course, I believe young adults should continue to listen to the accumulated wisdom of their parents and to treat them with respect. However, the relationship must change when adolescence is over. And if the parents will not or cannot make that transformation, the son or daughter is justified in respectfully insisting that it happen. For the very compliant child, that tearing loose is extremely difficult to accomplish!

Parents who refuse to let go often force their sons or daughters to choose between two bad alternatives. The first is to accept their domination and manipulation. That is precisely what the twenty-three-year-old girl had done. Instinctively, she knew her parents were wrong, but she lacked the courage to tell them so. Thus, she remained under their authoritative umbrella for a couple of years too long. She was like an unborn baby in the tenth or eleventh month of pregnancy. Granted, the womb was safe and warm, but she could grow no more until she got past the pain and indignities of childbirth. She was overdue for "delivery" into the opportunities and responsibilities of adulthood.

To repeat our now familiar theme, it is the very compliant child who often yields to the tyranny of intimidation. Some remain closeted there for forty years or more. Even if they marry, their parents will not grant emancipation without a struggle, setting the stage for lifelong in-law problems.

The other alternative is to respond like a mountainous volcano which blows its top. Hot lava descends on everything in its path. Great anger and resentment characterize the parent-child relationship for years, leaving scars and wounds on both generations. The strong-willed individual typically chooses this response to parental domination. He isn't about to let anyone hem him in, but in the process of breaking free, he loses the support and fellowship of the family he needs.

The legendary Beatles rock group often sang about drug usage and revolution, among other antiestablishment themes. But occasionally, their music was devastatingly incisive. One of their best renditions was recorded in 1967. It went to the heart of this matter of breaking free. The lyrics described a young woman whose parents had held on too long, forcing her to steal away in the early morning hours. Perhaps you will feel the pain of her confused parents as you read the words to "She's Leaving Home."

> *Wednesday morning at five o'clock as the day begins*
> *Silently closing her bedroom door*
> *Leaving the note that she hoped would say more*
> *She goes downstairs to the kitchen clutching*
>   *her handkerchief*
> *Quietly turning the backdoor key*
> *Stepping outside, she is free.*
> *She (We gave her most of our lives)*
> *Is leaving (Sacrificed most of our lives)*
> *Home (We gave her everything money could buy).*
> *She's leaving home after living alone*
>   *for so many years. Bye-Bye.*

Father snores as his wife gets into her dressing gown
Picks up the letter that's lying there
Standing alone at the top of the stairs
She breaks down and cries to her husband,
"Daddy, our baby's gone!"
Why would she treat us so thoughtlessly?
How could she do this to me?
She (We never thought of ourselves)
Is leaving (Never a thought for ourselves)
Home (We struggled hard all our lives to get by).
She's leaving home after living alone
*   for so many years. Bye-Bye.*

Friday morning at nine o'clock she is far away
Waiting to keep the appointment she made
Meeting a man from the motor trade
She (What did we do that was wrong?)
Is having (We didn't know it was wrong)
Fun (Fun is the one thing that money can't buy).
Something inside that was always denied
*   for so many years. Bye-Bye.*
She's leaving home. Bye-Bye.[1]

There must be a better way to launch a postadolescent son or daughter, and of course there is. It is the responsibility of parents to release the grip and set the fledgling adult free to make it on his own. But alas, independence sometimes fails not because parents have withheld it, but because immature sons and daughters refuse to accept it. They have no intention of growing up. Why should they? The nest is too comfortable at home. Food is prepared, temperature is regulated, clothes are laundered, and all bills are paid. There is no incentive to face the cold world of reality, and they are determined not to budge. Some even refuse to work. They keep hours like hamsters, staying up (and out) all night and then sleeping half the day. They sit around the house listening to electronic music and waiting for a dish to rattle in the kitchen. Three months worth of dirty underwear and who knows what else are stuffed under the bed. Life is a lark, albeit a boring one. Even when they do move away for a time, they inevitably run out of money and come dragging home at mealtime. Their parents remind me of a man with a new boomerang. He would have made it fine except he went crazy trying to throw the old one away.

I received a letter from the mother of one of these perpetual free-loaders a few years ago. Let me share what she asked and how I replied:

Q. We have a twenty-one-year-old who is still living at home. He does not want to come under our authority, and he breaks all the rules we have set up as minimum standards of behavior. He plays his stereo so loudly that it drives me crazy, and he comes in every night after 1 A.M. I know he needs his freedom, but I worry about our younger children who are trying to get away with the same things their big brother does. How would you balance the rights and privileges of this young adult with our needs as a family?

A. It is very difficult for a strong-willed twenty-one-year-old to continue living at home, and it will become even more unsettling with every year that passes. The demand for independence and freedom in such cases is almost always in conflict with the parents' expectations and wishes. Your son's unwillingness to respect your reasonable requests is a surefire indication that he needs to face life on his own. Also, the bad modeling he is providing for your younger siblings is a serious matter. I think it is time to help him pack. At the very least, he should be made to understand that his continued residency at home is conditional. Either live with the rules—or live with the YMCA.

I know it's difficult to dislodge a homebound son or daughter. They are like furry puppies who hang around the back door waiting for a warm saucer of milk. How can you yell "Shoo!" at someone so lost and needy? But to let them stay year after year, especially if they are pursuing no career goals or if they are disrespectful at home, is to cultivate irresponsibility and dependency. That is not love, even though it may feel like it.

We are agreed, then, that independence and freedom must be granted to those who have passed through the far side of adolescence. But how is that accomplished? The Amish have a unique approach to it. Their children are kept under the absolute authority of their parents through-out childhood. Very strict discipline and harsh standards of behavior are imposed from infancy. When they turn sixteen years of age, however, they enter a period called "Rumspringa." Suddenly, all restrictions are lifted.

They are free to drink, smoke, date, marry, or behave in ways that horrify their parents. Some do just that. But most don't. They are even granted the right to leave the Amish community if they choose. But if they stay, it must be in accordance with the rules of convention. The majority accept the heritage of their forefathers, not because they must, but because they wish to.

Although I admire the Amish and many of their approaches to child-rearing, I believe the Rumspringa concept is too precipitous. To take a child overnight from total domination to absolute freedom is an invitation to anarchy. Perhaps it works in the controlled environment of Amish country, but it is usually disastrous for the rest of us. I've seen families emulate this "instant adulthood" idea, lifting parental governance overnight. The result has been similar to what occurred in African colonies when European leadership was suddenly withdrawn. Bloody revolutions were often fought in the heady spirit of freedom.

It is better, I believe, to begin releasing your children during the preschool years, granting independence that is consistent with their age and maturity. When a child can tie his shoes, let him—yes, require him—to do it. When he can choose his own clothes within reason, let him make his own selection. When he can walk safely to school, allow him the privilege. Each year, more *responsibility* and *freedom* (they are companions) are given to the child so that the final release in early adulthood is merely the final relaxation of authority. That is the theory, at least. Pulling it off is sometimes quite difficult.

However you go about transferring the reins of authority—the rudiments of power—to your children, the task should be completed by twenty and no later than twenty-two years of age. To hold on longer is to invite revolution.

TWELVE

A FINAL THOUGHT

P ERHAPS WE CAN summarize our discussion of parenthood and its tougher dimensions by answering a question posed to me recently by a puzzled mother. It went something like this:

> Tell me why it is that some kids with every advantage and opportunity seem to turn out bad, while others raised in terrible homes become pillars in the community? I know one young man, for example, who grew up in squalid circumstances, yet he is such a fine person today. How did his parents manage to raise such a responsible son when they didn't even seem to care?

Curious cases of this type are not so uncommon around us and they validate the theme of this book. As we have seen, environmental influences in themselves will not account for the behavior we observe in our fellowman. There is something else there—something from within—that also operates to make us who we are. Some behavior is caused and some plainly isn't.

For example, I had dinner with two parents who have unofficially "adopted" a thirteen-year-old boy. This youngster followed their son home one afternoon, and then asked if he could spend the night. As it turned out, he stayed with them for almost a week without so much as a phone call coming from his mother. It was later learned that she works sixteen hours a day and has no interest in her son. Her alcoholic husband divorced her several years ago and left town without a trace. The boy had been abused, unloved, and ignored through much of his life.

Given this background, what kind of kid do you think he is today—a druggie? A foul-mouthed delinquent? A lazy, insolent bum? No. He is polite to adults; he is a hard worker; he makes good grades in school and he enjoys helping around the house. This boy is like a lost puppy who desperately wants a good home. He has begged the family to adopt him officially so he could have a real father and a loving mother. His own mom couldn't care less.

How is it that this teenager could be so well-disciplined and polished despite his lack of training? I don't know. It is simply within him. He reminds me of my wonderful friend, David Hernandez. David and his parents came to America illegally from Mexico more than forty years ago and nearly starved to death before they found work. They eventually survived by helping to harvest the potato crop throughout the state of California. During this era, David lived under trees or in the open fields. His father made a stove out of an oil drum half-filled with dirt. The open campfire was their home.

David never had a roof over his head until his parents finally moved into an abandoned chicken coop. His mother covered the boarded walls with cheap wallpaper and David thought they were living in luxury. Then one day, the city of San Jose condemned the area and David's "house" was torn down. He couldn't understand why the community would destroy so fine a place.

Given this beginning, how can we explain the man that Dave Hernandez became? He graduated near the top of his class in high school and was granted a scholarship to college. Again, he earned high marks and four years later entered Loma Linda University School of Medicine. Once more, he scored in the top 10 percent of his class and continued in a residency in obstetrics and gynecology. Eventually, he served as a professor of OB/GYN at both Loma Linda University and the University of Southern California Medical Schools. Then at the peak of his career, his life began to unravel.

I'll never forget the day Dr. Hernandez called me on the telephone. He had just been released from hospital care following a battery of laboratory tests. The diagnosis? Sclerosing cholangitis, a liver disorder that is invariably fatal. We lost this fine husband, father, and friend six years later at the age of forty-three. I loved him like a brother and I still miss him today.

Again, I ask, how could such discipline and genius come from these infertile circumstances? Who would have thought that this deprived Mexican boy sitting out there in the dirt would someday become one of the most loved and respected surgeons of his era? Where did the motivation originate? From what bubbling spring did his ambition and thirst for knowledge flow? He had no books, took no educational trips, knew no scholars. Yet he reached for the sky. Why did it happen to David Hernandez and not the youngster with every advantage and opportunity? Why have so many children of prominent and loving parents grown up in ideal circumstances, only to reject it all for the streets of San Francisco or New York? Good answers are simply not available. It apparently comes down to this: God chooses to use some individuals in unique ways. Beyond that mysterious relationship, we must simply conclude that some kids seem born to make it and others are determined to fail. Someone reminded me recently that the same boiling water that softens the carrot also hardens the egg. Likewise, some individuals react positively to certain circumstances and others negatively. We don't know why.

One thing is clear to me: Behavioral scientists have been far too simplistic in their explanation of human behavior. We are more than the aggregate of our experiences. We are more than the quality of our nutrition. We are more than our genetic heritage. We are more than our biochemistry. And certainly, we are more than our parents' influence. God has created us as unique individuals, capable of independent and rational thought that is not attributable to *any* source. That is what makes the task of parenting so challenging and rewarding. Just when you think you have your kids figured out, you had better brace yourself! Something new is coming your way.

I've spent more than half my life studying children, yet my own kids continue to surprise and fascinate me. I remember calling home some years ago from a city in Georgia where I had traveled for a speaking engagement. Danae, who was then thirteen years of age, picked up the phone and we had a warm father-daughter chat. Then she said, "Oh, by the way, Dad, I'm going to be running in a track meet next Saturday."

"Really?" I said. "What distance have you chosen?"

"The 880," she replied.

I gasped. "Danae, that is a very grueling race. Do you know how far 880 yards is?"

"Yes," she said. "It's a half-mile."

"Have you ever run that far before?" I asked.

She said that she hadn't, even in practice. I continued to probe for information and learned that nine schools would be competing in the meet, which was only three days away. My daughter intended to compete against a field of other runners who presumably had been training for weeks. I was concerned.

"Danae," I said, "you've made a big mistake. You're about to embarrass yourself and I want you to think it over. You should go to your coach and ask to run a shorter race. At that speed 880 yards will kill you!"

"No, Dad," she said with determination. "No one else signed up for the 880, and I want to run it."

"Okay," I replied, "but you're doing it against my better judgment."

I thought about that beloved kid the rest of the week and wondered what humiliation was in store for her. I called again on Saturday afternoon.

"Guess what, Dad!" Danae said cheerfully. "I won the race today!" She had indeed finished in first place, several yards ahead of her nearest competitor. The following year, also without training, she won the same race by fifty yards and set a school record that may still be standing.

Wow! I said to myself. *The kid has talent. She'll be a great runner someday.* Wrong again. She ran and won two races in the ninth grade, came in second in the next, and then lost interest in track. End of story.

So much for fatherly wisdom in all its glory.

Obviously, I am deeply respectful of the human personality and the stunning complexity of even our youngest members. In a sense, this entire book has been a testimony to them and to those of you as parents who are dedicated to their care. I admire each of you greatly and I hope we have been of assistance in fulfilling your awesome responsibility. Now in these concluding paragraphs, I would like to express two or three final thoughts directly to the mothers and fathers of very rebellious kids. I am especially concerned about you.

First, I know your task is difficult and there are times when you feel like throwing in the towel. But you must remain steady. Someday, you will look back on this difficult period of conflict and be thankful that you stayed on course—that you continued to do what was right for those children whom God loaned to you for a season. This era will pass so quickly, and the present stresses will seem insignificant and remote. What will matter to you then will be the loving relationships you built with your family, even when other parents ran away or buried themselves in work. You will also have the knowledge of a job well done in the eyes of the Creator Himself.

Therefore, I hope you will resist the temptation to feel cheated or deprived because of the difficult temperament of your son or daughter. You are certainly not alone. In an earlier survey of 3,000 parents, we found that 85 percent of families had at least one strong-willed child. So, you are not an exception or the butt of some cruel cosmic joke. This is parenthood. This is human nature. Most of us who have raised two or more kids have gone through some of the same stresses you are experiencing. We survived, and you will too. You can handle the assignment.

Let me review the concepts we have considered in our meandering discussion of children:

1. You are not to blame for the temperament with which your child was born. He is simply a tough kid to handle and your task is to rise to the challenge.
2. He is in greater danger because of his inclination to test the limits and scale the walls. Your utmost diligence and wisdom will be required to deal with him.
3. If you fail to understand his lust for power and independence, you can exhaust your resources and bog down in guilt. It will benefit no one.
4. If it is not already too late, by all means, take charge of your babies. Hold tightly to the reins of authority in the early days, and build an attitude of respect during your brief window of opportunity. You will need every ounce of "awe" you can get during the years to come. Once you have established your right to lead, begin to let go systematically, year by year.
5. Don't panic, even during the storms of adolescence. Better times are ahead. A radical turnaround usually occurs in the early twenties.
6. Stay on your child's team, even when it appears to be a losing team. You'll have the rest of your life to enjoy mutual fellowship if you don't overreact to frustration now.
7. Give him time to find himself, even if he appears not to be searching.

8. Most importantly, I urge you to hold your children before the Lord in fervent prayer throughout their years at home. I am convinced that there is no other source of confidence and wisdom in parenting. There is not enough knowledge in the books, mine or anyone else's, to counteract the evil that surrounds our kids today. Our teenagers are confronted by drugs, alcohol, sex, and foul language wherever they turn. And, of course, the peer pressure on them is enormous. We must bathe them in prayer every day of their lives. The God who made your children *will* hear your petitions. He has promised to do so. After all, He loves them more than you do.

Finally, I have a word of encouragement prepared especially for those of you who are depressed today. It is a message written by a loving mother named Joan Mills, who must be a very special lady. She expressed her feelings about her children in an article that initially appeared in a 1981 issue of *Reader's Digest.* It is called "Season of the Empty Nest," and I believe you will be touched by the warmth of these words.

Remember when the children built blanket tents to sleep in? And then scrambled by moonlight to their own beds, where they'd be safe from bears? And how proud and eager they were to be starting kindergarten? But only up to the minute they got there? And the time they packed cardboard suitcases in such a huff? "You won't see us again!" they hollered. Then they turned back at the end of the yard because they'd forgotten to go to the bathroom. It's the same thing when they're twenty or twenty-two, starting to make their own way in the grown-up world. Bravado, pangs, false starts, and pratfalls. They're half in, half out. "Good-bye, good-bye! Don't worry, Mom!" They're back the first weekend to borrow the paint roller and a fuse and a broom. Prowling the attic, they seize the quilt the dog ate and the terrible old sofa cushions that smell like dead mice. "Just what I need!" they cheer, loading the car.

"Good-bye, good-bye!" implying forever. But they show up without notice at suppertimes, sighing soulfully to see the familiar laden plates. They go away again, further secured by four bags of groceries, the electric frying pan, and a cookbook.

They call home collect, but not as often as parents need to hear. And their news makes fast-graying hair stand on end: "...so he forgot to set the brake, and he says my car rolled three blocks backward down the hill before it was totaled!" "...simple case of last hired, first fired, no big deal. I sold the stereo, and..."

"Mom! Everybody in the city has them! There's this roach stuff you put under the sink. It's..."

I gripped the phone with both hands in those days, wishing I could bribe my children back with everything they'd ever wanted—drum lessons, a junk-food charge account, anything. I struggled with an unbecoming urge to tell them once more about hot breakfasts and crossing streets and dry socks on wet days.

"I'm so impressed by how you cope!" I said instead.

The children scatter, and parents draw together, remembering sweet-shaped infants heavy in their arms, patched jeans, chicken pox, the night the accident happened, the rituals of Christmases and proms. With wistful pride and a feeling for the comic, they watch over their progeny from an effortfully kept distance. It is the season of the empty nest.

Slowly, slowly, there are changes. Something wonderful seems to hover then, faintly heard, glimpsed in illumined moments. Visiting the children, the parents are almost sure of it.

A son spreads a towel on the table and efficiently irons a perfect crease into his best pants. (*Ironing board,* his mother thinks, adding to a mental shopping list.) "I'm taking you to a French restaurant for dinner," the young man announces. "I've made reservations."

"Am I properly dressed?" his mother asks, suddenly shy. He walks her through city streets within the aura of his assurance. His arm lies lightly around her shoulders.

Or a daughter offers her honored guest the only two chairs she has and settles into a harem heap of floor pillows. She has raised plants from cuttings, framed a wall full of prints herself, spent three weekends refinishing the little dresser that glows in a square of sun.

Her parents regard her with astonished love. The room has been enchanted by her touch. "Everything's charming," they tell her honestly. "It's a real home."

Now? Is it *now?* Yes. The something wonderful descends. The generations smile at one another, as if exchanging congratulations. The children are no longer children. The parents are awed to discover adults.

It *is* wonderful, in ways my imagination had not begun to dream of. How could I have guessed—how could they?—that of my three, the shy one would pluck a dazzling array of competencies out of the air and turn up, chatting with total poise, on TV shows? That the one who turned his adolescence into World War III would find his role in arduous, sensitive human service? Or that the unbookish, antic one, torment of his teachers, would evolve into a scholar, tolerating a student's poverty and writing into the night?

I hadn't suspected that my own young adults would be so ebulliently funny one minute, and so tellingly introspective the next: so openhearted and unguarded. Or that growing up would inspire them to buy life insurance and three-piece suits and lend money to the siblings they'd once robbed of lollipops. Or that walking into their houses, I'd hear Mozart on the tape player and find books laid out for me to borrow.

Once, long ago, I waited nine months at a time to see who they would be, babes newly formed and wondrous. "Oh, *look!*" I said, and fell in love. Now my children are wondrously new to me in a different way. I am in love again.

My daughter and I freely share the complex world of our inner selves, and all the other worlds we know. Touched, I notice how her rhythms and gestures are reminding of her grandmother's or mine. We are linked by unconscious mysteries and benignly watched by ghosts. I turn my head to gaze at her. She meets my look and smiles.

A son flies the width of the country for his one vacation in a whole long year. He follows me around the kitchen, tasting from the pots, handing down the dishes.

We brown in the sun. Read books in silent synchrony.

He jogs. I tend the flowers. We walk at the unfurled edge of great waves. We talk and talk, and later play cribbage past midnight. I'm utterly happy.

"But it's your vacation!" I remind him. "What shall we do that's special?"

"This," he says. "Exactly this."

When my children first ventured out and away, I felt they were in flight to outer space, following a curve of light and time to such unknowns that my heart would surely go faint with trying to follow. I thought this would be the end of parenting. Not what it is—the best part; the final, firmest bonding; the goal and the reward.[1]

QUESTIONNAIRE
FOR PARENTS ABOUT THEIR CHILDREN WHOM THEY BELIEVE TO BE STRONG-WILLED OR COMPLIANT

I. **The items in this section ask general questions about you as a parent.**

  A. Individual completing this survey:

    Mother ❏   Father ❏   Both parents together ❏

  B. Mother (if you are the father answering for the mother, please circle the number you think she would have circled).

As a child, I was:

Very Strong-Willed	Strong-Willed	Neither	Compliant	Very Compliant
1	2	3	4	5

  C. Father (if you are the mother answering for the father, please circle the number you think he would have circled):

As a child, I was:

Very Strong-Willed	Strong-Willed	Neither	Compliant	Very Compliant
1	2	3	4	5

II. Even though this questionnaire deals only with your oldest strong-willed or compliant child (if any), it is important to know how you evaluate the temperament of all your children. Please rate them on the scale below.

	First-Born	Second-Born	Third-Born	Fourth-Born	Fifth-Born	Sixth-Born	Seventh-Born
Sex M/F	___	___	___	___	___	___	___
Current Age	___	___	___	___	___	___	___

Please circle one characteristic below:

Children	Very Compliant	Cooper-ative	Average	Uncooper-ative	Very Strong-Willed
Firstborn	1	2	3	4	5
Secondborn	1	2	3	4	5
Thirdborn	1	2	3	4	5
Fourthborn	1	2	3	4	5
Fifthborn	1	2	3	4	5
Sixthborn	1	2	3	4	5
Seventhborn	1	2	3	4	5

III. The items in this section ask questions about your child(ren) whom you consider to be either strong-willed or compliant. It is possible that you had more than one child in each category. If so, please answer the questions for the oldest strong-willed child and/or the oldest compliant child. If you only had a child in one of the two categories, please ignore the other. If you had children who were neither strong-willed nor compliant, please place an X _____ here and return the questionnaire to us uncompleted.

	Strong-Willed Child	Compliant Child
A. Sex:	M ☐ F ☐	M ☐ F ☐
B. Current age:	_____	_____
C. Order of birth (lst, 2nd,...):	_____	_____

D. Age at which the temperament was first recognized:

	Strong-Willed Child	Compliant Child
	M ☐ F ☐	M ☐ F ☐
Birth to 3 months:	_____	_____
3 to 6 months:	_____	_____
6 to 12 months:	_____	_____
1 to 3 years:	_____	_____
3 to 6 years:	_____	_____

E. Discipline of father (if you are the mother answering for the father, circle the number you think he would have circled):

Strong-Willed Child

Permissive	Rather Easy	Average	Rather Strict	Rigid and severe
1	2	3	4	5

Compliant Child

Permissive	Rather Easy	Average	Rather Strict	Rigid and severe
1	2	3	4	5

F. Discipline of mother (if you are the father answering for the mother, circle the number you think she would have circled):

Strong-Willed Child

Permissive	Rather Easy	Average	Rather Strict	Rigid and severe
1	2	3	4	5

Compliant Child

Permissive	Rather Easy	Average	Rather Strict	Rigid and severe
1	2	3	4	5

G. The amount of stress created for the parents by the child's temperament: (Note: "1" indicates that the child was a joy to raise and caused virtually no disharmony or agitation for the parents; "2" means the child was generally pleasant and easy to raise; "3" means average, "4" means the child was generally difficult to raise; "5" means the child was unpleasant and caused great disharmony and agitation in the home.)

Strong-Willed Child

Total Joy	Generally Pleasant	Average	Difficult	Unpleasant
1	2	3	4	5

Compliant Child

Total Joy	Generally Pleasant	Average	Difficult	Unpleasant
1	2	3	4	5

H. Which parent related to and handled the child best at each
   age level?

Strong-Willed Child

Age	Mother	Father	Only One Parent Present	Neither Parent Did Well
0–2	1	2	3	4
2–4	1	2	3	4
4–6	1	2	3	4
6–13	1	2	3	4
13–20	1	2	3	4
20 to present	1	2	3	4

Compliant Child

Age	Mother	Father	Only One Parent Present	Neither Parent Did Well
0–2	1	2	3	4
2–4	1	2	3	4
4–6	1	2	3	4
6–13	1	2	3	4
13–20	1	2	3	4
20 to present	1	2	3	4

I. Degree of rebellion against adult authority and values at each
age level:

Strong-Willed Child

Age	Complete Acceptance	Rather Cooperative	Average Response	Rather Defiant	Total Rejection
0–2	1	2	3	4	5
2–4	1	2	3	4	5
4–6	1	2	3	4	5
6–13	1	2	3	4	5
13–20	1	2	3	4	5
20 to present	1	2	3	4	5

Compliant Child

Age	Complete Acceptance	Rather Cooperative	Average Response	Rather Defiant	Total Rejection
0–2	1	2	3	4	5
2–4	1	2	3	4	5
4–6	1	2	3	4	5
6–13	1	2	3	4	5
13–20	1	2	3	4	5
20 to present	1	2	3	4	5

J. Describe the temperament of your child at *each* age level up to the present time (or to age 24, if applicable):

Strong-Willed Child

Age	Very Compliant	Coopera-tive	Average	Very Uncoopera-tive	Defiant
1–2	1	2	3	4	5
3–4	1	2	3	4	5
5–6	1	2	3	4	5
7–8	1	2	3	4	5
9–10	1	2	3	4	5
11–12	1	2	3	4	5
13–14	1	2	3	4	5
15–16	1	2	3	4	5
17–18	1	2	3	4	5
19–20	1	2	3	4	5
21–22	1	2	3	4	5
23–24	1	2	3	4	5

Compliant Child

Age	Very Compliant	Coopera-tive	Average	Very Uncoopera-tive	Defiant
1–2	1	2	3	4	5
3–4	1	2	3	4	5
5–6	1	2	3	4	5
7–8	1	2	3	4	5
9–10	1	2	3	4	5
11–12	1	2	3	4	5
13–14	1	2	3	4	5
15–16	1	2	3	4	5
17–18	1	2	3	4	5
19–20	1	2	3	4	5
21–22	1	2	3	4	5
23–24	1	2	3	4	5

K. Has your grown child (age 20 or older) accepted your values and established a good working relationship with you as his parents?

Strong-Willed Child

Yes	No	Somewhat	N/A
1	2	3	4

Compliant Child

Yes	No	Somewhat	N/A
1	2	3	4

L. Social adjustment at each age level:

Strong-Willed Child

Age	No Social Problems	Generally Liked	Average Response	Generally Disliked	Many Social Problems
4–6	1	2	3	4	5
6–13	1	2	3	4	5
13–20	1	2	3	4	5
20 to present	1	2	3	4	5

Compliant Child

Age	No Social Problems	Generally Liked	Average Response	Generally Disliked	Many Social Problems
4–6	1	2	3	4	5
6–13	1	2	3	4	5
13–20	1	2	3	4	5
20 to present	1	2	3	4	5

M. Influence of friends at each age level:

Strong-Willed Child

Age	No Influence by Peers	Little Influence by Peers	Average Response	Major Influence by Peers	Extremely Vulnerable to Peers
4–6	1	2	3	4	5
6–13	1	2	3	4	5
13–20	1	2	3	4	5
20 to present	1	2	3	4	5

Compliant Child

Age	No Influence by Peers	Little Influence by Peers	Average Response	Major Influence by Peers	Extremely Vulnerable to Peers
4–6	1	2	3	4	5
6–13	1	2	3	4	5
13–20	1	2	3	4	5
20 to present	1	2	3	4	5

N. Self-Concept:

Strong-Willed Child

Age	Excellent Self-Image	Generally Accepted Himself	Average Response	Generally Disliked Himself	Extreme Self-Hatred
4–6	1	2	3	4	5
6–13	1	2	3	4	5
13–20	1	2	3	4	5
20 to present	1	2	3	4	5

Compliant Child

Age	Excellent Self-Image	Generally Accepted Himself	Average Response	Generally Disliked Himself	Extreme Self-Hatred
4–6	1	2	3	4	5
6–13	1	2	3	4	5
13–20	1	2	3	4	5
20 to present	1	2	3	4	5

O. School achievement, generally, at each age level:
  (Note: Scale the same as common grading scale in school: "A" outstanding; "C" average; "F" fail.)

	Strong-Willed Child	Compliant Child
Preschool	A B C D F	A B C D F
Grades 1–6	A B C D F	A B C D F
Grades 7–9	A B C D F	A B C D F
Grades 10–12	A B C D F	A B C D F
College	A B C D F	A B C D F
Post College	A B C D F	A B C D F

P. For your child who is now grown, how well has he or she achieved in life?

Strong-Willed Child

Highly Successful	Rather Successful	Average	Rather Unsuccessful	Very Unsuccessful
1	2	3	4	5

Compliant Child

Highly Successful	Rather Successful	Average	Rather Unsuccessful	Very Unsuccessful
1	2	3	4	5

Q. Speaking generally, circle the number of the sentence that best describes how you feel about raising your strong-willed child:

1. It has been a struggle that has often left me depressed, guilt-ridden, and exhausted.
2. It has been difficult but exciting and rewarding too.
3. It has been a very positive experience.
4. He/she was difficult in the early years, but the adolescent years were less stormy and difficult.

R. Speaking generally, select the sentence that best describes how you feel about raising your compliant child:

1. It has been a struggle that has often left me depressed, guilt-ridden, and exhausted.
2. It has been difficult but exciting and rewarding too.
3. It has been a very positive experience.
4. He/she was a joy in the early years, but adolescence was extremely stressful for both generations.

Thank you so much for your help in conducting this informal research project.

CHAPTER 1

1. I recognize that this is deep water theologically speaking. Jacob was not rejected by God, and yet he, like Esau, was sinful and disobedient. Who among us can explain God's greater judgment on one than the other? In reference to the analogy between Jacob and Esau and the temperaments of children, I want to make it clear that the strong-willed child is no more evil or ungodly than his compliant sibling. His inclination toward disobedience may be greater, but I am certainly not casting them in terms of "good" versus "bad." They are simply different, and one is more difficult to handle than the other.

CHAPTER 4

1. Lynn Caine, *What Did I Do Wrong? Mothers, Children, Guilt* (New York: Arbor House, 1985), 136.

CHAPTER 6

1. Dr. James Dobson, *Dare to Discipline* (Carol Stream, Ill: Tyndale House, 1970), 27–28.
2. Bruce A. Baldwin, "Growing Up Responsible. (Part 2), Parental Problems with Discipline Procedures," *Piedmont Airline* (December 1985): 11.

CHAPTER 8

1. Joseph Procaccini and Mark W. Kiefaber, *Parent Burnout,* New York: Doubleday & Company, Inc., 1987.
2. F. Turnridge, reprinted with permission, 1987.

CHAPTER 9

1. "Leader of the Band" by Dan Fogelberg. © 1981 APRIL MUSIC, INC., and HICKORY GROVE MUSIC. All rights controlled and administered by APRIL MUSIC, INC. All rights reserved. International copyright secured. Used by permission.
2. Lewis Yablonsky, *Fathers and Sons* (New York: Simon and Schuster, Fireside Books, 1984), 134.
3. *Los Angeles Times*, 16 June 1985. Used with permission of the author, Harold Mann, Van Nuys, California.

4. "'Giving In' Often Seen When Kids Hit Parents," *Omaha World Herald*, 6 July 1979.
5. *Time*, 8 June 1981.
6. Ann Landers, *Family Circle*, 3 November 1981. Reprint.

CHAPTER 10

1. John Walvoord and Roy Zuck, eds., *Bible Knowledge Commentary, Old Testament* (Wheaton, Ill.: Victor Books, 1985), 953.

CHAPTER 11

1. "She's Leaving Home" by John Lennon and Paul McCartney. © 1967 NORTHERN SONGS LIMITED. All rights in the USA, CANADA, MEXICO, and the PHILIPPINES controlled and administered by BLACKWOOD MUSIC, INC., under license from ATV music (MACLEN). All rights reserved. International copyright secured. Used by permission.

CHAPTER 12

1. Reprinted by permission from the January 1981 *Reader's Digest*. Copyright © 1980 by THE READER'S DIGEST ASSOCIATION, INC.

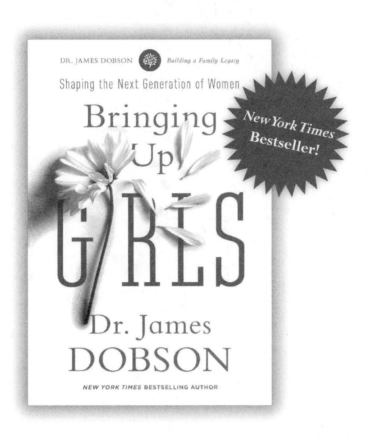

Bringing Up Boys by parenting expert and bestselling author Dr. James Dobson was, and continues to be, a runaway hit, selling over 2 million copies to date. Now Dr. Dobson presents his highly anticipated companion book: *Bringing Up Girls*. Based on extensive research, and handled with Dr. Dobson's trademark down-to-earth approach, the *New York Times* bestseller *Bringing Up Girls* will equip parents like you to raise your daughters to become healthy, confident, and successful women who overcome challenges specific to girls and women today and who ultimately excel in life.

978-1-4143-9132-8 (softcover)
978-1-4143-0127-3 (hardcover)
978-1-4143-3650-3 (7 audio CDs read by Dr. James Dobson)

DR. JAMES DOBSON · *Building a Family Legacy*

Shaping the Next Generation of Men

Bringing Up BOYS

Dr. James DOBSON

NEW YORK TIMES BESTSELLING AUTHOR

Finally, some sensible advice and caring encouragement on raising boys—from the nation's most trusted parenting authority, Dr. James Dobson. With so much confusion about the role of men in our society, it's no wonder so many parents and teachers are at a loss about how to bring up boys. Our culture has vilified masculinity, and as a result, boys are suffering. Parents, teachers, and others involved in shaping the character of boys have many questions. In *Bringing Up Boys*, Dr. James Dobson tackles these questions and offers advice and encouragement based on a firm foundation of biblical principles. *Bringing Up Boys* is a must-read book for anyone involved in the challenge of turning boys into good men.

978-1-4143-9133-5 (softcover)
978-0-8423-5266-6 (hardcover)
978-0-8423-2297-3 (audio CD; 6 discs)

CP0048

Tune in to
Dr. James Dobson's Family Talk.

To learn more about
Dr. James Dobson's Family Talk
or to find a station in your area,
visit www.drjamesdobson.org
or call (877) 732-6825.

Online Discussion *guide*

TAKE *your* TYNDALE READING
EXPERIENCE *to the* NEXT LEVEL

A FREE discussion guide for this book
is available at bookclubhub.net, perfect
for sparking conversations in your book
group or for digging deeper into the text
on your own.

www.bookclubhub.net

*You'll also find free discussion guides for
other Tyndale books, e-newsletters, e-mail
devotionals, virtual book tours, and more!*